Rob. Morris.

FREEMASONRY

IN THE

HOLY LAND

OR

HANDMARKS OF HIRAM'S BUILDERS:

EMRRACING

NOTES MADE DURING A SERIES OF MASONIC RESEARCHES,
IN 1868, IN ASIA MINOR, SYRIA, PALESTINE, EGYPT
AND EUROPE, AND THE RESULTS OF MUCH
CORRESPONDENCE WITH FREEMASONS
IN THOSE COUNTRIES.

BY

ROBERT MORRIS, LL.D.,

MASONIC WRITER AND LECTURER.

"Thus saith the LORD, Stand ye in the ways and see, and *ask for the old paths* where is the good way, and walk therein."—JEREMIAH 6:16.

"Forasmuch as many have taken in hand to set forth a declaration of those things which are most surely believed among us, it seemed good to me also to write that thou mightest know *the certainty* of those things wherein thou hast been instructed."—LUKE 1:1-2.

STONE GUILD PUBLISHING
PLANO, TEXAS
HTTP://WWW.STONEGUILDPUBLISHING.COM/

2009

SGP

Originally Published By:
KNIGHT & LEONARD, PRINTERS
1879

This Edition Copyright © 2008
Stone Guild Publishing, Inc.
Plano, Texas
http://www.stoneguildpublishing.com/

First Paperback Edition 2009

ISBN-13 978-1-60532-055-7
ISBN-10 1-60532-055-2

10 9 8 7 6 5 4 3 2

TO

HIS EXCELLENCY MOHAMMED RASCHID

PASHA-GENERAL OF SYRIA

HONORED SIR AND BROTHER:

IN my first interview with the zealous band of Freemasons, lovingly at labor in their *foyer maçonnique* at Smyrna, it was reported to me that the Governor-General of Syria and Palestine, the brave, wise, and learned MOHAMMED RASCHID, is one who delights to wear the Masonic apron, having shared joyfully in the mystic confidences of their fraternal group. And the brethren at Smyrna rejoiced to speak of the intelligence, urbanity, and Masonic skill of their renowned brother at Damascus, and favored me with letters of credence and introduction.

Early upon my arrival in Damascus, therefore, I hastened to pay my respects to your Excellency, and to present you the greetings of a half-million American Masons, who are working (in more than six thousand lodges) the same principles of Divine truth, justice, and fraternity in which you, yourself, were inducted in your Masonic initiation at Smyrna. At the same time I laid before your Excellency the peculiar mission upon which I had embarked, and solicited your valued approval and patronage.

I have now to acknowledge the very hearty manner in which your Excellency responded to my request; you afforded me the wisest counsel, and extended to me such aid as none can give as effectually as yourself.

Finally, when the plan of the present volume was matured, and I solicited, by letter, the honor of dedicating it to him to whom I am so much indebted, your Excellency granted me the favor, with an urbanity which is in keeping with all I had previously known and enjoyed of your character.

Since my return home, I have spoken in more than six hundred lodges, and reported to them the results of my Oriental study and labor. Everywhere I have made grateful mention of our distinguished Brother, the Vali of Syria; of his bravery in war, his wisdom in council, the respect and love of his people, and particularly his kindness to the American brother who had journeyed so far in pursuit of Masonic light. Should you, at any period, honor our country with a visit, your Excellency will find that this story of your kindness to the strange brother has come here before you; that the lineaments of your countenance are well known to us, and that a welcome awaits you, such as but few visitors have ever received from the Masonic fraternity. Would that your Excellency might so favor us! Would that the mother-land of Freemasonry might send such a representative to this great asylum of freedom, where the principles of the ancient Order have unrestricted sway, and every man feels that in his birth he is the equal of every other!

May it please your Excellency: Our earthly lot differs most widely. Your name is spread afar as one to whom God has entrusted the government of a people. Our forms of faith are diverse. In language, customs, modes of thought, we are cast in different moulds; but in Masonic UNITY we are one, and one in Masonic FAITH. As our hopes, and aims, and labors are one, we, trusting in one God, and doing, each of us, what we believe to be His expressed will, do humbly expect a common reward when we have passed that common lot which none can escape. To the Divine power, therefore, I tenderly commend your Excellency, both for this world and for that which is to come.

TO H. E. MOHAMMED RASCHID

This book, *Freemasonry in the Holy Land,* is, by permission, most respectfully and most fraternally

DEDICATED

PREFACE.

————

I OFFER this book to the Masonic public, in redemption of my pledges to the generous friends who furnished me the means both my expedition of 1868, and for publishing the book itself. That I have been more than three years getting it up, speaks, I think, for the thorough manner of its preparation.

Agreeably to the original promise, "the book is adapted to the plainest reader; one that the owner will take home and read in his domestic circle, and afterwards lend to his neighbors to read; equally a *reference-book* to the student, and a *hand-book* to the traveler; large enough to embrace so great a subject, yet no effort has been spared to compress the information. The *Common Gavel* has been used remorselessly in striking off excrescences. Written in the spirit of the Holy Writings, French and German infidelity has not made sufficient inroads into American Masonry, that less than nineteen-twentieths will welcome additional light upon the divine authenticity of the Bible, and such light I have attempted freely to diffuse through this volume.

Let every subscriber, after reading the book, bear me testimony that I have *kept the faith* with him.

I have avoided the mysterious and romantic style so common amongst writers upon Palestine, and have cultivated the colloquial. One would think, to read standard accounts of the trees and birds in the Holy Land, that they are different from birds and trees in other countries. Not so. Making allowance for difference in climate, nature is the same everywhere, and so I have used every-day words in describing them. I have embodied as much practical information as possible; comparing things Oriental with things Occidental; things in the experience of patriarchs and prophets with things in the experience of an American observer. And yet I have endeavored to preserve the gravity and dignity due to a theme around which cluster all our hopes in life, in death, and in the world to come.

In the abundance of my preparations, and the acreage of my readings-up for this book, I have not infrequently mingled others' thoughts with my own, and have entered them here often without special credit. In defense of this I can only say that such is the general usage of writers. If the reader, then, finds passages the property of other persons, he is at liberty to say so; I will not deny it; but, with the historian Rollin, I confess "that I do not scruple, nor am ashamed, to borrow that I may adorn and enrich my own history." My own credit, if any, shall consist in the skill with which I bind the beads of the chain together. In the thousands of notes and memorandums I have taken, it would be strange, indeed, if I could preserve the ear-marks of each.

In this book I have desired to popularize the study of the Scriptures, by removing some of the difficulties which the unlearned have found in reading them; by smoothing the way to obscure passages, so as to enable all to peruse the Sacred Book understandingly, and better to enjoy sermons and commentaries. Had the hundreds of thousands who make up the membership of our lodges this practical knowledge, how easy the teacher's task, in the coming generation, to diffuse the store of useful knowledge there is for mankind in this world!

If any object to the allusions and comparisons to American matters, so freely introduced through these pages, let me confess, old and

cosmopolitan as I am, that *patriæ fumus igne alieno luculentior*—
the very *smoke* of my own native land seems brighter to me than
the *fire* of any other. I trust, however, I have not exhibited this
sentiment anywhere offensively.

As the narrative of Arculf's Pilgrimage to Palestine, in the
eighth century, led to that passion for pilgrimage which has not
yet died out, but has made the nineteenth the most illustrious
century of all so I earnestly hope the publication of this book, the
first of its class, will inspire many a zealous tourist to visit those
countries *on Masonic errands,* and many a penman in his closet to
enlarge the literature of which I now make the commencement.
To show that the *web* and *woof* of Masonic tradition are true is, by
an easy transition, to prove the *figures of the pattern* real and
genuine.

In writing Arabic words I have endeavored, in general, to give
such English letters as will express them to the *ear* rather than
the *eye* For instance: instead of *harem* I write *hareem,* &c. Yet
this rule is but imperfectly carried out, after all; for were I to
adopt it rigidly *Sultan* would be *Sooltarn; Koran, Korarn; Hassan,
Hassarn,* &c If the reader would learn the exact sound of Arabic
words (a thing I never did), he must get an Arabic dictionary (and
then he can't do it!)

As so large a proportion of American Masons are professing
Christians—the demonstration at Baltimore, Maryland,
September, 1871 proving that our wisest and best members in
very large numbers rejoice to bear the symbolical emblem of the
MAN OF GOLGOTHA—I have not hesitated frequently "to name
the name of Jesus" in this volume, although no one has so often
and publicly demonstrated that Freemasonry was ten centuries
old when the Star of Bethlehem arose. Nor can our Jewish
brethren, many of whom have received a welcome into the
American lodges, complain that I neglected the interests

of their long-persecuted but now emerging society while I was in
the East. At the same time I have fully expressed my admiration
for much of the character and many of the precepts of Mohammed,
as embodied in the Koran. Avoiding the doctrinal points, and read
in the spirit of fraternal love, as illustrated in the lectures of
Freemasonry, that remarkable book, the Koran, might justly be
taken as a comment upon the much older, far wiser, and most
remarkable book ever written, THE OLD TESTAMENT of the
Hebrew dispensation. To those who are accustomed, without the
slightest examination, to denounce the Koran (as well as its
author), I will simply say, with Isaiah (8:20), "To the law and to
the testimony; if it speak not according to this word, it is because
there is no light in it." An unprejudiced mind will admit, not only
that the Koran contains far more quotations from and references
to the Bible, but is absolutely imbued more with the spirit of the
inspired word than a dozen of the best "Saints' Books" found on
the counter of any Catholic bookstore in New York. "To the
testimony!"

In affixing the names of my Masonic countrymen freely to
places renowned in history, I acknowledge, *ubique patriam
reminisci,* that I remembered my native country in all places, and
have attempted thus to join the West to the East by a new and
more affecting tie. The Masons who raised nine thousand dollars
and upwards to send me to Palestine, and enough, three years
afterwards, to publish this volume, have earned the right to
Masonic homes among the homes of the first Masons, and the
allotment I have made may be yet very much more largely
extended. Even though the idea is one strictly in the region of
romance, I shall be greatly mistaken if it does not lead to larger
explorations, freer offerings, and greater exertions in this
direction on the part of generations yet to come.

To Professor A. L. Rawson, of New York, so well known as "The

Oriental Artist," who has given his pencil exclusively, for a number of years, to Biblical illustration, I am indebted, not only for the maps and engravings in my volume, but for many practical and useful suggestions in the preparation of the work itself. Himself a thorough explorer in Eastern fields, he is giving his mature and experienced judgment to such works as Beecher's, Deems's, Crosby's, and other first-class writers on Biblical themes; his own excellent "Hand-Book of Bible Knowledge" meanwhile comparing favorably with the best of them.

Finally, if any one with dyspeptic tendencies feels to object to the attempt at humor that may possibly be detected in some of these pages, I bare my back to the lash. I *did* laugh while going, without guard or guide, through the once inspiring but now depressing lands of the tribes—laughed often and freely, and, even at the end of four years, my cachinations are renewed when I think of certain experiences connected with my journey. The ghost of old laughs thus haunting me so long and persistently, and giving its spirit to my ink, the reader is at liberty, without further dispensation, to laugh too.

THE LAND OF MILK AND HONEY.

"A good land and a large . . . a land flowing with milk and honey."
(Deut. 6:3, 11: 9, etc.)

O land of wondrous story, old Canaan bright and fair,
Thou type of home celestial, where the saints and angels are!
In heartfelt admiration we address thy hills divine,
And gather consolation on the fields of Palestine.

In all our lamentations, in the hour of deepest ill,
When sorrow wraps the spirit as the storm-clouds wrap the hill,
Some name comes up before us from thy bright immortal band,
As the shadow of a great rock falls upon a weary land.

The dew of *Hermon* falling yet, revives the golden days;
Sweet *Sharon* lends her roses still, to win the poet's lays;
In every vale the lily bends, while o'er them wing the birds
Whose cheerful notes so marvellously recall the Savior's words.

From *Bethlehem* awake the songs of Rachel and of Ruth,
From *Mizpah's* mountain-fastness mournful notes of filial truth;
Magdala gives narration of the Penitent thrice-blest,
And *Bethany* of sister-hosts who loved the gentle Guest.

Would we retrace the pilgrimage of Jesus Christ our Lord,
Behold his footsteps everywhere, on rocky knoll and sward;
From Bethlehem to Golgotha, his cradle and his tomb,
He sanctified old Canaan and accepted it his home.

He prayed upon thy mountain-side, he rested in thy grove,
He walked upon thy Galilee, when winds with billows strove:
Thy land was full of happy homes, that loving hearts did own,
E'en foxes and the birds of air—but Jesus Christ had none.

Thou land of milk and honey, land of corn and oil and wine,
How longs my hungry spirit to enjoy thy food divine!
I hunger and I thirst afar, the Jordan rolls between,
I faintly see thy paradise all clothed in living green.

My day of life declineth, and my sun is sinking low;
I near the banks of Jordan, through whose waters I must go:
Oh, let me wake beyond the stream, in land celestial blest,
To be forever with the Lord in Canaan's promised rest.

DIVISION FIRST—FACING THE EAST.

Whatsoever thy hand findeth to do, do it with thy might; for there is no work, nor device, nor knowledge, nor wisdom, *in the grave,* whither thou goest.—*Eccles.* 9:10.

Examine the condition of the Masonic institution, in the land of its nativity.

Observe those unaltered customs of the Orientals, whose types are preserved in the rituals of our lodges.

Inspect the traditional sites of Tyre, Gebal, Lebanon, Joppa, Succoth, Jerusalem, etc.

Collect relics of ancient days and specimens of the natural productions of the land.—*Numbers,* 8:21

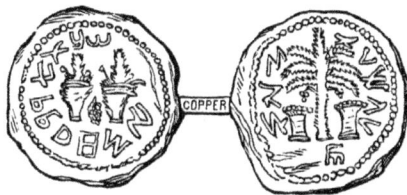

COIN OF JERUSALEM: SHEKEL.

CHAPTER I.

CONCEPTION AND PREPARATIONS.

VERY one who has undertaken to instruct Freemasons, must many times have yearned *to visit Palestine*, the mother-land of ancient affiliations, — the Orient, —the home of Abraham and David, —of Solomon and Zerubbabel, —of Jesus and Mohammed, —the School of the Sacred Writings. So many references to that country are contained in the Masonic rituals, it is a marvel that no one of us had made explorations there prior to 1868.

In common with my fellows in Masonic work, I had keenly experienced the Crusader's impulse *"to precipitate myself* upon the Syrian shore;" and often cast about me for the means to gratify the yearning. In the autumn of 1854, I came so near accomplishing this wish, that, by the favor of a loan of $1000 from the Grand Lodge of Kentucky, joined to the liberality of other friends, I reached New York, having my face earnestly "set towards Jerusalem." But here an unlucky accident frustrated my hopes, and turned me back to the Occident. Fire, which has so often proved my foe, consumed the Judson house, in which I was a lodger, and by destroying my papers and clothing, etc., so disarranged the scheme, that I could not carry it out successfully at the time.

Yet, for all that, though advancing years and the *res angustœ in domi*, the hard realities of life, interposed with a purpose almost inexorable, I never once resigned my determination to go to Palestine, but always in my Masonic descriptions spoke of "those traditional localities which someday I am resolved to visit." In the meantime, I continue the practice, established long before, of reading whatever publications promised to shed light upon the Lands of the East; and in church, Sunday-school, and elsewhere, lectured on the subject with a minuteness of detail that comelled me to study the theme in its various historical and scientific associations. This, in fact, served to *educate me* against the time when it might please the G.A.O.T.U. to grant me a furlough for

Oriental tour. In purchases of books for my Masonic collections, I gave prominence to those upon Oriental matters, as my old library, now in the keeping of the Grand Lodge of New York, will show. In brief, I sought to emulate the spirit of old Thomas à Kempis in his saying, *homo fervidus et diligens ad omnia paratur*—the earnest and diligent man is prepared for all things—and in the meantime found comfort in the promise of Virgil:

> *Forsan et hæc olim meminisse juvabit ;*
> *Durate et vosmet rebus servate secundis ;*

It may possibly be joyful some day to recall these trials; bear up against them, therefore, and be ready for better times when they come.

In 1867, circumstances proved somewhat encouraging to the fulfillment of my purpose. The opening of various lines of steamships from Europe to the Syrian coast was a favorable incident. The enlarged privileges granted by the Turkish government to foreigners sojourning in the Holy Land enabled a person in 1868 to explore twentyfold more than he could have done in 1858, and fortyfold more than in 1848. The publication of scores and hundreds of book of travel in Palestine obviates the necessity of a man's wasting time in merely *playing the tourist*, and justifies me in beginning, the moment of arrival, the work of *exploration*. The invaluable aids afforded the Bible student by such publications as Robinson's, Barclay's, Thompson's, etc., are so much more than mere books of travel, that the reader may in effect transport himself, by their assistance, to the Land of the Bible, being enabled to see with their eyes and hear with their ears whatever is needed to illuminate the sacred pages. In my domestic circle, the growing up of the younger members of my family, and the marriage of the elder, rendered father's presence at home less a matter of necessity that heretofore.

One thing more: my labors in the various departments of Masonic history, rituals, poetry, etc., seemed measurably *terminated*. Having no money-capital of my own for purposes of publication, and the field of Masonic literature affording little profit to authorship, I felt that in the issuance of *seventy-four* Masonic publications I had given sufficient evidence of my devotion to the old institution, and might justly claim exemption from further labors and losses in that direction, and enter upon a new field. Finally, a reasonably vigorous constitution, never impaired by excessive living or intemperance, some knowledge of the Scriptures in their original and translated forms, a large course of reading in matters relating to Oriental countries, a circle of Masonic friends reaching round the globe, and a *strong will* to execute whatever I undertook—these formed the encouragements that bore me out, at the age of fifty, to begin the service of Masonic exploration of the Holy Land, conceived so many years ago, of which the present volume is the record.

But how a Masonic exploration? What has the Masonic institution to do with the Holy Land? These are no questions for Freemasons to ask; but as my work will fall into the hands of, and perhaps be read by, those who are not of the "mystic tie," the query may properly be answered here. I respond, then, that the Holy Scriptures are the instruction books of the Lodge; and that a perfect knowledge of the Holy *Land* is needful to a perfect knowledge of the Holy *Scriptures.*

In 1867, then, I set upon the following plan to secure the necessary funds for my enterprise; I made up a list of Holy Land specimens, such as the fraternity were most likely to value—such as *I* should most value,—in the way of Biblical and Masonic illustrations, a catalogue embracing specimens of the woods, waters, earths, coins, fossils, etc., from Palestine, and proposed to supply them, at a specified rate, to those who would advance me money for the pilgrimage. The following extracts from my published proposals belong to the history of this enterprise:

"Those contributors who advance *ten dollars,* each shall be supplied with one hundred and fifty objects from the Holy Land, including specimens of the ancient building-stone of Jerusalem, Joppa, and Tyre; shells from the Sea of Galilee and Joppa; agates from the Arabian deserts; ancient coins; rock-salt from Usdum; an herbarium of ten plants; the traditional corn, wine, and oil of Masonry; earth from the clay-grounds near Succoth, etc., etc."

Contributors of *five dollars, three dollars,* and *two dollars,* respectively, were promised smaller cabinets composed of similar objects; those of *one dollar,* the Journal of the Expedition. A map of the Holy Land, arranged for Masonic purposes, was also a portion of the premiums promised.

Having decided upon the plan of appeal, I visited one hundred and thirty lodges in Indiana, Iowa, Kentucky, Illinois, West Virginia, Nebraska, and New York, and addressed the fraternity. I began by occupying an hour or two with recitations of Masonic poems, such as the Level and the Square, the Letter G., the Holy Bible, Our Vows, the Drunkard's Grave, the Five Points of Fellowship, the Emblems of the Craft, etc., and then laid before them my propositions for a Masonic mission to the Holy Land. In general, the offer was favorably responded to. The season, unfortunately, was one of extreme closeness in the money market, and portions of the country visited were suffering from scanty harvests. Some of my hearers probably deemed my proposals Quixotic; many others contributed the lowest amount asked for, viz., *one dollar;* yet nearly four hundred of them gave me *ten dollars each,* trusting, as they said, *to my pluck* to accomplish the end proposed, or willing to show their respect for an old and industrious laborer, who came before them with an appeal so reasonable and practical.

The whole number of contributors was 3,782; the aggregate of contributions was $9,631. Out of this, according to my proposals, provision was made for two years' support of my family; my own expenses, and those of my agent, Mr. G. W. Bartlett, while collecting the money; the expenses of the Oriental tour, for myself and Mr. Thomson; freights upon shipments of specimens; printing six issues of the Holy Land Journal for 3,782 contributors; printing catalogues, etc.; and preparing, labeling, packing, and forwarding nearly 70,000 specimens. It can readily be seen that the amount advanced me was short of my needs; the deficit, in fact, exceeded $1,200, and this I was compelled to make up out of the proceeds of lectures on my return home.

It is in evidence of the practicability of the plan upon which this money was collected, that a noted traveler is now (1872) before the public with proposals, borrowed from my program, to furnish objects of natural history on South America "to those who will advance him the necessary outfit for the journey to that country." By way of encouragement, I commend to him the adage of Periander of Corinth, one of "the Seven Wise Men" of antiquity; *industriæ nil impossibile,* anything can be accomplished by an *industrious* man!

In my addresses to the Lodges I proposed—

1. To explore that remarkable plain—once the center of intellectual light and the school of the seven liberal arts and sciences, also of commerce, religion, and letters—the *Plain of Phœnicia.*

2. To visit the secluded recesses, high among the Lebanons, where the remaining groves of cedar are found.

3. To search for those caves and bays at the base of Lebanon where the "flotes" of timber were made up for shipment to Joppa.

4. To sail down the coast to Joppa, in the track of Hiram's mariners.

5. To examine the ancient port of Joppa with systematic care.

6. To follow diligently upon the tracks of the Syrian architects, journeying from Joppa to Jerusalem; and to seek for the highway by which they penetrated the precipitous cliffs and bore upward their ponderous burdens.

7. To make thorough inspection of everything relating to Solomonic times, in and about Jerusalem.

8. To visit the plain of Jordan, especially the clay-ground between Succoth and Zarthan, where the brazen pillars and other holy vessels appertaining to the Temple were cast.

9. To explore the places named in Masonic lectures, such as Jerusalem, Bethlehem, Sodom, Jericho, Bethel, Hattin, Damascus, Bethany, Joppa, Tyre, Gebal, Lebanon, and others.

10. To make full collections of objects illustrating Masonic traditions and Biblical customs, these to be distributed generously to contributors on my return, upon plans previously arranged.

The following cuts of my Masonic flag are appropriate here:

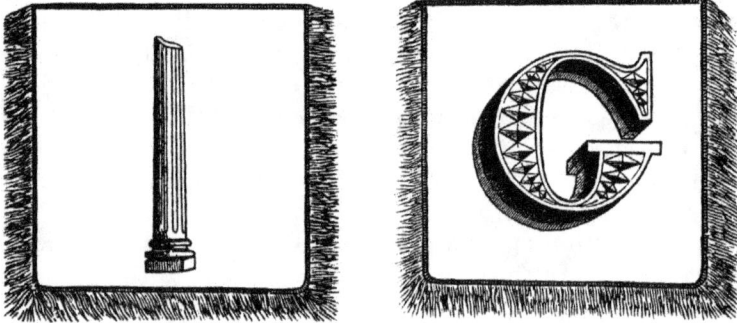

The idea of this was suggested by the flag used in Dr. Kane's Arctic Explorations of 1853. His banner, *the square and compass,* still extant in the archives of Kane Lodge, No. 454, New York City, was displayed at his masthead while passing down New York Bay, and, at the extreme northern termination of his journey, it was set up in the snow-drifts.

This little flag of mine accompanied me through all my wanderings.* The breeze that sighs across the granite reefs of Tyre blew out its silken folds, showing upon one side the initial-symbol of him

---

* The emblem of *The Broken Column* is my "Mark-Master's Mark," adopted at my exaltation in Lexington Chapter, No. 17, Lexington, Mississippi, in 1848.

whose *name* was adored equally in Phœnician and Jewish Lodges; on the other, the architect-symbol of him whose noble end dignifies the purpose and the work of every Mason's Lodge. Fastened upon the boughs of one of Lebanon's grandest cedars, it suggested a mysterious meaning to the sturdy limbs and evergreen foliage of the tree. Waved before the entrance of a rock-hewn tomb at Gebal, it seemed to call around me the spirits of those who, three thousand years ago, well understood its symbolical lessons. Fluttered in the gale that lifts the waters over the rocky ledge at Joppa, it recalled the days when the great fleets of Tyre came, "like doves to the windows," deep-laden, into this harbor, the square and compass on their foresails. Fluttered over the walls of Jerusalem, and in the deep quarry that underlies the city, it spoke in prophetic tones of the good time coming, when the Mason-craft shall yet build up Jerusalem, and the GOD we worship be worshipped there and everywhere.

The course pursued by the various Masonic journals in regard to this enterprise was almost uniformly generous in the extreme. Their columns were freely thrown open to my propositions; their editorial pens shaped words of encouragement and good counsel. It will not be deemed invidious if I mention by name the *Evergreen* (Dubuque, Iowa); the *Masonic Review* (Cincinnati, O.); the *Voice of Masonry* (Chicago, Illinois); the *National Freemason* (New York); the *Masonic Monthly* (Boston, Mass.); the *Dispatch* (New York), and the *Freemason's Monthly Magazine* (London, England), as taking the lead in brotherly encouragement and approval. Even Brother Findel, the German Masonic historian, whose theory of a *modern origin* of Freemasonry "does not recognize the importance of light from the East," still gave me "the brotherly word," and pledged me a cordial greeting in his own country. How truly has Sallust said: *idem velle et idem nolle ea demum firma amicitia est;* to possess the same likes and dislikes is, in point of fact, the foundation of lasting friendship. No words of mine can express my sense of all this kindness, and the friends of the Masonic Holy Land Mission of 1868 should bear in mind, what my own experience warned me of at the time, that an active opposition from either of those influential organs of Masonic sentiment might greatly have retarded the entire scheme.

No official expression was asked for from Grand Lodges, or other Masonic organizations; but it is proper to say that among the most generous supporters of my explorations were the Grand Masters of Iowa (Reuben Mickle); Nebraska (O. H. Irish); Minnesota (C. W

Nash); New York (S. H. Johnson); Canada (Wm. M. Wilson), and a large number of present and past Grand Lodge officers, of the first eminence, who forwarded me good words and material aid.

An assistant being deemed desirable, D. W. Thomson, of Illinois, formerly Grand Lecturer of that State, and a singularly zealous advocate of Ancient Craft Masonry, was accepted in that capacity. In the matter of collecting specimens, his services were of great utility; while his traveling experience, industry, and uniform good-nature and honesty rendered him an agreeable companion upon the journey.

Prior to my departure for New York, the following lines were composed and extensively disseminated, as a farewell, by correspondence and through the press:

MIZPEH.

They took stones and made a heap. And Laban said: This heap is a witness between me and thee. Therefore was the name of it called *Mizpeh:* for he said, The Lord watch between me and thee, when we are absent one from another.—*Genesis* 31:46.

> MIZPEH! well named the patriarchal stone,
>   Once fondly reared in Gilead's mountain-pass;
> Doubtless the EYE ALL-SEEING *did* look down
>   Upon that token of fraternal grace:
> And doubtless HE who reconciled those men,
> Between them *watched,* until they met again.
>
> So, looking eastward o'er the angry sea,—
>   The wintry blast, inhospitably stern,—
> Counting the scanty moments left to me
>   Till I go hence,—and haply *not* return,—
> I would, oh! Brethren, rear a MIZPEH too,
> Beseeching GOD to watch 'twixt me and you.
>
> It was HIS providence that made us one,
>   Who otherwise "perpetual strangers" were:
> HE joined our hands in amity alone,
>   And caused our hearts each other's woes to bear:
> HE kindled in our souls fraternal fire,—
> Befitting children of a common SIRE.
>
> In mutual *labors* we have spent our life;
>   In mutual *joys* sported at labor's close;
> With mutual *strength* warred against human strife;
>   And soothed with mutual *charity* its woes:
> So, sharing mutually what GOD hath given,
> With common *faith* we seek a kindred *Heaven.*

Bring stones, bring stones, and build the heap with me!
    Rear up a MIZPEH, though with many tears:—
Before I trust me to yon stormy sea,
    Hither with memories of many years!
Come round me, mystic Laborers, once more,
With loving gifts, upon this wintry shore.

Bring *Prayer:* the WATCHER in the heavens will heed;
    Bring *Types* significant of deathless hope:
Bring *Words* in whispers only to be said:
    Bring *Hand-grasps* strong to lift the helpless up:
Bring all those *Reminiscences* of light
That have inspired us many a wintry night.

Lay them on Mizpeh! and the names revered
    Of those who've vanished from our mystic Band:
Are we not taught that, with the faithful dead,
    In Lodge Celestial, we shall surely stand?
Oh, crown the pile with names of good and blest,
Whose memories linger, though they be at rest

Finished: and so I hope whatever betide,
    Though wandering far toward Oriental sun,
He who watched kindly on that mountain-side
    Will watch *between us* till the work is done:
LORD GOD ALMIGHTY! whence all blessings are.
Behold our MIZPEH and regard our prayer!

Be my defender while in foreign lands;
    Ward off the shafts of calumny accurst;
My labors vindicate, while MIZPEH stands,
    And hold my family in sacred trust;
Should I no more behold them, fond and dear,
I leave them, Brethren, to Masonic care.

Finally, if in haste, or careless mood,
    Forgetting pledge sealed in WORD DIVINE,
I've wounded any of the Brotherhood,
    Impute it not, this parting hour, a sin:
Forgive: lo! HE by whom all creatures live
Grants us forgiveness, even as *we* forgive!

One of the journals alluded to (the *National Freemason*) said of these lines: "The sentiments are touching and appropriate, and strictly in accordance with the conciliatory character of their author. However much some of the Brotherhood may have differed with Brother Morris in regard to his plan for Uniformity of Work, none who know him but will accord to him a pure and disinterested *purpose.* The confidential friend of such men as William B. Hubbard, Philip C. Tucker, Charles Scott, Salem Town, Henry Wingate, and other choice spirits of the generation that is fast dropping into the grave; the man who has published seventy-four different volumes of a Masonic character; the admitted good fellow, 'genial, witty, and wise,' of Masonic circles, everywhere, and withal the man who, at the age of fifty, has yet to find anything *in his pocket* to compensate him for labors given to the best interests of Freemasonry,—he cannot leave our shores for a long and laborious tour into Oriental countries without bearing with him, the 'God bless the old enthusiast! May his return be blessed!'"

So far as baggage, books, and introductions are concerned, I found it unnecessary to encumber myself inconveniently. Two suits of clothes and half a dozen books were quite sufficient. As to reading, a man going to Palestine must go carrying his reading *in his head;* he will get but little time to accumulate it there. Thomson's *Land and Book;* Osborne's *Past and Present of Palestine,* and a few others, amply sufficed me for reading on the journey. So far as clothing is concerned, the tailors in Beirut will make you up suits quite as good and one half cheaper than New York tradesmen. I had written a few leading Brethren, B. B. French, J. W. B. McLeod Moore, and others, soliciting letters of general introduction, and the request was cordially granted; but I never found occasion to use them. Cosmopolitan Consistory, New York City, kindly presented me an elegant diploma of the thirty-second degree. My own diploma as a Master Mason and member of Fortitude Lodge, No. 47, LaGrange, Kentucky, was, however, the only document I ever found occasion to use. Even my passport, which I had taken the precaution to procure from Washington, with some trouble and expense, was of not the slightest service to me, although I would recommend every traveler to take one.

After these preliminaries, it suffices to say that I took passage from New York, Sunday morning, February 2, 1868, having something in common with those of whom the poet long ago sang—

> Bound for holy Palestine,
> Nimbly we brushed the level brine.

All in azure steel arrayed:
O'er the waves our banners played,
And made the dancing billows glow;
High upon the trophied prow
Many a warrior-minstrel swung
His sounding harp, and boldly sung.—T. Wharton.

COIN OF BAR-CHOBAS.

CHAPTER II.

ELABORATE this chapter for the benefit of that large class of readers to whom "the ocean wave" is a romance, and who peruse the smaller incidents of travel with a relish. The critic may sneer at my title, "Crossing the Atlantic," ill-naturedly affirming that a thousand voyagers have already described the occurrences of ocean-life, and that nothing new can be said upon the subject. Very likely; yet to many of those who will peruse these "Hand-marks," the pennings of other Eastern travelers are as though they were never written. I have discovered, since my return, that nothing in a traveler's recollection is too trivial to interest those who *do not travel*, and that the most interesting facts in the tourist's journal are those which personally he may deem too trifling for publication. Hence I make this chapter of daily life upon the sea.

It was on the second day of February, 1868, and, of all the days in the year, a bright, cloudless "Lord's day," that I mounted the steps of the steamship "France," Captain Grace, to witness the casting-off of lines and her departure from Pier No. 47, North River, New York. The ferruginous mass moved reluctantly from her bed, seemingly regretful of the necessity of leaving the cozy seat on which she had reposed for two weeks. If, as the feminine pronoun implies, our ship has the tastes of a *woman,* she may well prefer her quiet berth, and the praises of the admiring crowds who have been so loud in their approval of her fine bust, figure-head, and form, to the icy waves of ocean, and the cold criticisms of sea monsters who await her coming yonder, during a winter-voyage of twelve days.

The moment of departure is a solemn one to me; the act of severing the last tie that binds me to my native land makes me sad. I cannot join in the parting words exchanged between ship and shore, but withdraw myself to a solitary place and consider, in a spirit of prayerful inquiry the questions, Shall I again tread those streets? Am I really justified in making this pilgrimage; or is it mere romance that is taking me, at my years, upon so long a journey? And may I expect the blessing of the GRAND MASTER upon an enterprise so much out of the accustomed routine of my profession? In that hour of self-examination, I solemnly declare it, I stood self-vindicated and supported by the feeling that something more than mere curiosity had moved me to the work I had undertaken, and that I could rely upon the same HAND which had untiringly led me up and down through an itinerancy of fifty years.

For myself, I can honestly aver that I look to nothing but hard labor, economical fare, and diligent study, during the months before me. In my traveling bags I have a judicious selection of works upon Oriental themes, with an ample supply of *paper* to fix my own observations. Members of the Masonic fraternity and others have forwarded me letters and credentials in generous supply. The moral and material encouragement of nearly four thousand friends is the basis of my mission, and I feel that the Godspeed of a half million more is wafted on the breezes behind me. And so in that mood, in a solitary corner of the busy ship, my thoughts review the situation.

In going down the bay I occupied the hours in writing parting letters to the members of my family, the wife of twenty-seven years, and the seven children who call me father; also to a number of devoted friends whose words and deeds clung to me in parting moments with a tenacity that nothing can loosen; and so I swung out upon that ocean which in Bible times no sailor dared even cross, but which now is underlaid by telegraphic wires, connecting my home at La Grange with the City of Jerusalem itself.

Out of three steamers announced to sail from New York across the Atlantic, February 1st, I chose this of the "National Line" of Liverpool boats. For one hundred dollars, American currency, a first-class passage was given, while the same accommodations in the "Cunard" line would cost one hundred and sixty-five dollars. Both are *English* lines, as all the American steamships were driven from the sea during the civil war. There is also a German line which stops at Havre, France, going, and at Southampton, England, coming. It was on this line that I returned in July, but I cannot recommend it to the reader.

The *France* is a fine new vessel, this being her fourth voyage. Her tonnage is 2,428 tons. In length she is 405 feet; in breadth of beam, 42 feet; in depth, from the upper deck to the keel, 30 feet. Like all the vessels of this line, she is a *screw*-propeller, that is, her instrument of propulsion is a *screw* set up at the stern, which, in the most mysterious manner and "in solemn silence," moves these five thousand tons of boat, and freight, and passengers, at the rate of ten miles an hour. As I could never *see* the screw, nor the machinery that moved it, I was fain to compare the whole apparatus to the silent, mysterious power that keeps in motion a well-disciplined Lodge of Masons. The analogy would be perfect were it not that a steamship is of the feminine gender, while a Masonic Lodge is usually the reverse!*

The steering apparatus of the *France* is, British-fashion, at the *stern,* placed in a small, cramped-up crypt, which holds a half-dozen sailors, who turn the spokes of the wheel in the same inartistic style that the Phoenicians practiced in the days of Sesostris. When an order is sent from the bow to the stern, it takes as many messengers to pass it from one to the other as for a general of division to move Company C of the 53d Regiment into line of battle, or as the W. M. requires to get his will and pleasure known to the Lodge, But it would never do for an Englishman to adopt a Yankee invention, and so steering-lines to their steamers and check-ropes to their railroad trains are postponed until after the millennium.

Our fine steamer is built of rolled iron plates, thirty inches wide and one inch thick, riveted together in the manner of steam-boilers, stanch and tight. There is not the least danger of these seams *ripping;* indeed, if the sewing-machine man who calls quarterly at my house to sell me a machine, will only invent such a *lock-stitch* as this, his fortune is made. We have three masts, and when the wind is fair, as it was the greater part of my voyage, the sails afford considerable assistance in propulsion. A reasonable supply of longboats, and life-boats, and jolly-boats are stowed along the sides of the vessel, suggesting that ocean-life is uncertain, and it is best to provide in fair weather for foul. The speed of the vessel may be seen from the following table of distances run for the first eight days, computed every day at HIGH XII:

---

* In all our Masonic communications on board the *France* we were never unmindful of the fact that *a lady* was present, even the good woman *France* herself, and we governed ourselves accordingly!

Monday, February		3, 260	miles.
Tuesday,	"	4, 260	"
Wednesday,	"	5, 268	"
Thursday,	"	6, 259	"
Friday,	"	7, 265	"
Saturday,	"	8, 272	"
Sunday,	"	9, 272	"
Monday,	"	10, 271	"

The remarkable uniformity of these daily footings-up will strike the reader; steamship travel, under a settled condition of weather, being almost as regular as life upon the rail.

Our ship is officered by a captain and four mates, or ship's officers, as they are termed; the latter being hearty, well-educated men, kept in training for promotion in due time: for as no man can be Master who has not served in training as Warden, so no man can be captain who has not served as mate. All the working charges of the ship are apportioned among these four, according to fixed rules of naval service. Besides these, there is a purser, who acts as quartermaster of the ship; a surgeon, six engineers, and assistants in abundance. The whole crew, from captain to chambermaid, numbers 104. Of course everything is intensely *British,* officers, crew, slush-buckets, &c., even down· to the acceptable sirloins of beef served daily to the passengers. The only thing on board that I can name *American* is the *coal,* and if the captain's expressed (and profane) opinion may be relied upon, even that were better *British* too. Every passenger on board, except three, talks about "going home" whenever Great Britain is named. Money is reckoned in "tuppences," and I had not been a week aboard before I could compute a considerable sum in £., s., and d., a thing which, it is said, none but a born Briton ever could do before me! That mythic animal, the British unicorn, is marked on all the ship's linen and furniture; in fact, Commodore Wilkes himself could not mistake the nationality of *this* steamer. Captain Grace is a rough-featured, rough-mannered sailor of thirty, taciturn and gruff, and most ridiculously misnamed; but, it is claimed, a *thorough sailor.* At all hours, by day and night, he is on the alert, and wet-nurses the ship, in nursery language, like a mother hovering over her babe. His pay is £600 per annum, a short $3,000. The only time I ever spoke to him was one Sunday morning, when I asked him if he would conduct the service of prayers, as is customary on ocean steamers. He declined in a single word, an extremely short one, and then the conversation flagged.

Nowhere will this portion of the grand Psalm 107 read with such vividness, as when you are lying, of a quiet Sunday hour, in your state-room at sea:

They that go down to the sea in ships, that do business in the great waters;
These see the works of the Lord and his wonders in the deep.
For he commanded and raised the stormy wind, which lifted up the waves thereof.
They mount up to the heaven; they go down to the depths; their soul is melted because of trouble.
They reel to and fro, and stagger like a drunken man, and are at their wit's end.
Then they cry to the Lord in their trouble, and he brought them out of their distresses.
He made the storm a calm, so that the waves thereof are still.
Then are they glad because they are quiet; so he brought them to their desired haven.

After this description of a first-class Atlantic steamer in the year of grace 1868, the following picture of a Phœnician vessel of B. C. 1000 will afford a forcible contrast. In one of my chapters I will describe the size, construction, and capacity of this old Tyrian barque, such as those invincible mariners sailed in, when they gathered up the treasures of the Roman world, passing through the Straits of Gibraltar, turning *to the right* as far as Scotland and the Baltic Sea, and *to the left* as far as the African coast trended southwards, and bringing from all quarters the gold, the tin, the copper, the marble, the ivory, the spices needed in the erection, adornment, and worship of Solomon's Temple.

The size and tonnage of one of these Phœnician vessels would scarcely compare now with a Lake Erie sloop. But hearts of oak controlled them, and coasting all the way round the northern shores of the Mediterranean they came out into the ocean between their own "Pillars of Hercules," and following the sinuous lines of Portugal, Spain, and France, struck finally into the mouth of the broad Channel, and reached the place of their destination. The importance of *tin* in hardening the copper, of which their cutting tools and war-like implements were made, justified all these pains, risks, and the twelve months' journeys necessary to procure it.

The particular matter, upon which my pen was engaged, through the four weeks' journey from New York to Beirut, was that of making an alphabetical agenda of places to be visited, and things to be done at each place. This, written out in a blank-book, was made so full, by the time I reached Palestine, as to afford me all the assistance that a company of guides could have rendered. Under the head of "Tyre," for instance, I had more than one hundred distinct facts and suggestions in alphabetical form, by which, when I visited that city, my researches were very greatly expedited.

Of cabin, or first-class passengers, we have twenty-four, with room for nearly one hundred; of steerage, or second-class passengers, there are sixty-four. The latter pay only twenty-five dollars each, for which they receive good, wholesome victuals, and the services of the ship's surgeon. To us of the cabin every possible convenience is, of course, afforded. An experienced surgeon is one of the regular officers of the ship, and his skill is ever at our command. Chambermaids are in attendance upon the ladies, and state-room stewards upon the gentlemen, all without extra charge. Three regular meals per diem are spread, besides a luncheon, which in itself is a meal.* Let me recall the eating arrangements: Breakfast is announced at 8 A. M., a substantial British meal, accompanied by the best of tea and tolerable coffee. Luncheon is at High XII, presenting soups, cold meats in large variety, bread, cheese, and pickles. Dinner appears at 4 P. M., Supper at 7½, the latter being made up of coffee, toast, bread, and cheese. Besides these, a passenger who, for any reason, fails to report himself at the regular hours, can be accommodated through the steward with a special supply of provisions, at any hour. The bar (fluid, not forensic) is stocked with wines, ales, and spirits, of a character rarely matched on the American side of the

---

* On the Bill of Fare of Feb. 5, *prairie chickens* appeared among the items of dinner.

"great drink," and these are charged to passengers who order them, at moderate prices. With such arrangements for table comforts, a man must be harder to please than I am if he can discover grounds of complaint.

Does the reader inquire whether I was seasick? *I was.* I never go upon water without being seasick. Even a slight swell on Lake Erie has sent me to the dead-level, incontinently. Was I not obliged to go ashore, on that little Cleveland fishing excursion which Peter Thatcher provided for me in 1863, and there, amidst the sneers of men and the laughter of women, settle my accounts in the most disgraceful manner? Yes; and in a sea voyage, therefore, I always make my calculations to give up the first few days to the tergiversations of my stomach. This reconciles me in some degree to the motion of the vessel, and, by the assistance of four or five spells of vomiting per diem, I come, in the course of time, to a mariner's *status.* As to *remedies,* all that a seasick person wants is something to assist him through his unpleasant paroxysms. Brandy and other spirits make a good toddy to stay his stomach after nausea, but will not prevent it. Citrate of magnesia may be recommended as a good thing to neutralize the acidity produced in the earlier stages of seasickness, and I advise you to provide yourself with some bottles of it; also some Brandreth pills; a flask of pure cordial gin; a quart-bottle of strong coffee, ready made; a few lemons, with white sugar, and some good sour apples. Dress warm; wear thick overshoes; walk a good deal in the fresh air; be regular in your habits; be sociable; rise with the seagull, and go to bed with the cook. When seasickness passes off, then follows an appetite, accompanied with elasticity of spirits and digestion, such as go with my best reminiscences of childhood.

The worst sufferers from the *mal de mer,* as the French call it, are those who cannot vomit, or who vomit with great difficulty and pain. Some of this class have scarcely a moment's ease during the voyage. Nausea, want of appetite, indigestion, and costiveness, produce low sprits, ill-temper, and a very hatred of existence. Such a one is reported to have said that the first day he went to sea he was afraid he should die; the third day he was afraid he should not! Ladies suffer more from seasickness than gentlemen. Pale, staggering, and wobegone, the gay and rosy damsels of our company were so transmogrified by the ungallant sea-god, that their best friends could scarcely recognize them. That class of persons who boast that they are *never seasick* (and there are always some bores of the sort), suffer, upon the whole, quite as much as the rest. For if they are never *seasick,* they are never *seawell,* but mope around during the voyage, the dullest of the company.

There is a piece of advice that I will offer you here: Do not suppose that anybody else cares a straw who you are, or where you are going. Travelers, like Freemasons, meet upon the level and part upon the square; and no one is valued a bawbee, except as he possesses powers of pleasing, *for the hour.* Fine manners, dignity, genteel breeding and the like will pine in the corner, while a cheerful readiness of song and anecdote brings its possessor into social prominence, enabling him both to receive and impart pleasure during the tedium of the way.

The time of ocean travelers is variously and generally *u*selessly employed. Industrious persons play checkers and cards; the rest walk the deck, eat, smoke, and sleep. How about myself? I give *so many* hours a day to the study of *Thomson* ("Land and Book;") *Barclay* ("City of the Great King"); *Osborne* ("Palestine, Past and Present"); the *Holy Writings* and other tomes bearing upon Oriental matters; *so many* to the composition of letters and memoranda; *so many* to *checkers* (my favorite vanity); and *so many* to refreshment and sleep. Everything on board conduces to regularity. The ship's bell at 12½ strikes *one,* at 1 strikes *two,* at 1½ strikes *three,* at 2 strikes *four,* at 2½ strikes *five,* at 3 strikes *six,* at 3½ strikes *seven,* at 4 strikes *eight,* which being the extent of its striking powers, a second series begins at 4½ and extends to 8. Each of these periods of four hours is termed a watch—of which there are six in the twenty-four. One of these intervals I am told is termed the Dog watch; but, although I listened attentively for *canine* indications, I could never detect them, and do not believe there was a dog on board. The traveler, when rendered sleepless by nausea and *ennui,* marks these solemn chimes of the ship's bell with feelings that he cannot analyze, but can never forget. How often they recalled to me the lines I have sung in so many a lodge-room and by so many a grave:

> Solemn strikes the funeral chime,
> Notes of our departing time;
> While we journey here below,
> Through a pilgrimage of wo.

I venture to say that the *genus loci,* the spirit that inhabits my old state-room (No. 13) on board the ship *France,* will testify to

having heard me sing it three score times and ten, as I lay there
and mused upon the lessons of the ship's bell.

There was almost nothing visible to the eye during our voyage.
Not a vessel, not an iceberg, not a whale. One traveler, indeed,
declares he saw a whale; but it is finally conceded that he only
saw the *spout*. Not a fragment of a wreck appeared in sight; in
fact, nothing at all but a large following of sea-gulls that took up
with us at Sandy Hook, nor left us a moment until we sighted the
Irish coast. How or when they rest, if indeed they ever *do* rest
upon these long flights of twelve days, is a mystery more than
Masonic. The sailors believe that when night comes on, the gulls
settle down upon the water to ride and sleep. But this can
scarcely be, for keen-eyed and strong-winged as they are, they
could not see and overtake the ship again after twelve hours' sail.
Their motive in pursuing us so closely is strictly mercenary, viz.,
to gather the fragments from the steward's pantry, which are
being constantly thrown into the water. These the sea-birds seize
with great expertness. Cast anything overboard, a pill-box, a
cracker, a piece of soap, or even a bit of a Masonic Monitor, and
fifty pairs of eyes detect it; fifty pairs of iron-gray wings "go in" for
it; then one strong fowl rises from the sea with it in his bill—all
with a velocity that makes you giddy to observe. Among the
various theories concerning the origin of sea-gulls, I will venture
my own, viz., that they are the *ghosts of newspaper reporters,*
condemned, for a season, to follow in the wake of outward-bound
vessels, as an expiation for the innumerable lies they told during
their earthly career!

A cheerful mind will derive amusement from almost any
combination of circumstances; and I gathered a fund of it in
watching our family of twenty-four passengers at their meals,
during a three-day' storm that came down on us about the
middle of the trip. The reader shall have his share of the fun.
Imagine everything fastened to the floor, tables, chair, etc., and
the ladies and gentlemen fastened as tightly to their seats as
human muscle can do it. The ship is swaying from side to side
like a five-second pendulum. Now she keels over to starboard to
an angle of forty-five degrees. Soup-plate in the right hand, a
convulsive grip upon the table with the left. *Raise
perpendiculars;* the hot soup slops over upon your hand. Away
goes the ship on the other side, forty-five degrees to larboard.
Lay levels; the soup spurts up your sleeve, in spite of all you can
do. Bang goes the ship again to starboard. *Try horizontals;* now

soup, plate and all are swashed into your bosom with a freedom, fervency, and zeal rarely equaled and never surpassed. And so for an hour the dinner is a running accompaniment of china, glasses, cutlery, and spoons, laughable to witness.

At 2 P.M. on the 13th of February, 1868, "we of the mystic level," as poor Burns used to call the Masonic fraternity, stole quietly away from the crowd to the Purser's room, and there, having previously tested each other, by ancient and approved methods, we opened a moot lodge upon the First Degree, "for Special Purposes." The names of our temporary dignitaries were these:

1. *Robert Morris,* late Grand Master of Masons in Kentucky, *as W. M.*

2. *David W. Thomson,* late Grand Lecturer of Illinois, *as S. W.*

3. *George Catchpole,* Senior Warden of Rose Lodge No. 590, Rose, Wayne Co., New York, *as J. W.*

4. *William Thomas,* of St. John's Lodge, New Brunswick (first officer of the Steamship France), *as Treasurer.*

5. *George Campbell,* of British Oak Lodge No. 831, Stratford, England (fourth officer of the Steamship France), *as Secretary.*

6. *W. G. Barrett,* of Piatt Lodge No. 194, New York City (Purser of the Steamship France), *as S. D.*

7. *James Wilson,* of Mariners' Lodge, Liverpool, England (Chief-Engineer of the Steamship France), *as J. D.*

8. *Thomas Hughes,* of Amity Lodge No. 323, of New York City (Chief Steward of the Steamship France), *as 1st Master of Cer.*

9. *William Carroll,* of Varick Lodge No. 31, Jersey City, N. J. (Chief Baker of the Steamship France), *as 2d Master of Cer.*

10. *William Dempster,* of Commonwealth Lodge No. 409, Brooklyn, N. Y., *as Tyler.*

This *symposium* was, in all respects, a notable one, and proceedings of a particularly pleasant character were had. Remarks were volunteered concerning the practical nature of a fraternity that, uniting the best elements of all societies, avoids the offensive peculiarities of any. The poem entitled The Checkered Pavement was recited by Mr. Thomson as the sequel to an address delivered by him in good style. My own share in the proceedings was made up of the following lines, composed the evening before, upon first beholding *Skellig Revolving Light* on the coast of Ireland:

THE SKELLIG LIGHT.

When hastening eastward o'er the waste,
By ocean-breakers rudely chased,
    Our eager eye seeks for the smile
    That marks the dangerous Skellig Isle,
We joy to catch the flashing ray
That guides, unerringly, our way.

What though in momentary gloom
Night may resume her sable plume,—
    What though the clouds may settle down,
    And threaten ocean's stormiest frown,—
Lo! flashing far across the main,
The Skellig Light beams out again!

So, wandering on life's stormy sea,
Oh, Craftsmen, by God's grace, may we
    The tempest-tost and weary find,
    In gloomiest hour, in saddest mind,
Our Skellig Light, from heavenly sun,
To draw us safely, smoothly on.

Should He withdraw His smiling face,
'Tis but to try our faithfulness:
    Should He our pilgrimage enshroud,
    He stands behind the threatening cloud:
And though He smite us with a blow,
It is His gentle chastening too!

Craftsmen, draw nigh and learn with me
These lessons from Freemasonry!
    Each implement in mystic hand
    Bids us this precept understand:
They who would serve the Master's state,
Must work in Faith, in Patience wait!

We sighted the Irish coast at 3 P.M., Wednesday, February 12,—and while I am writing this paragraph I see that on the Irish Grand Lodge Registry, 1872, are 327 lodges,—landed passengers at Queenstown the next morning;* were sailing up the Irish Channel all day

---

* This was in the middle of a Fenian scare, and every one of them, as I learned afterwards, was arrested, rigorously examined, and detained for twenty-four hours, under the apprehension that they had come to invade the land.

Thursday, and finally reached the docks of Liverpool by daylight of Friday, the 14th, after a pleasant voyage of twelve days, grateful to God, who had brought me thus far not only in safety, but with a degree of contentment and satisfaction that I had not anticipated. I shall ever remember the period of my passage from New York to Liverpool as *halcyonii dies,* days of peaceful enjoyment.

COIN OF TRYPHON.

3

CHAPTER III.

CROSSING ENGLAND AND THE CONTINENT.

LANDED at Liverpool Friday morning, February 14, 1868, and proceeded to London, so as to arrive at 5 P.M. of the same day. Of course I could observe little or nothing of Liverpool during a morning's stay. An edifice designated as "Masonic Hall," stands, however, not far from the railway station, and naturally enough I saw that. I regretted the necessity of passing a city so noted for its attention to Masonic interests as Liverpool; but the Marseilles steamer for Beirut was advertised for Tuesday, February 18, and the failure to secure a passage in her would entail the loss of ten days' time. Every hour's delay would abridge my stay in Palestine by so much.

Travelers' tales had led me to expect a severe examination of baggage in Liverpool; but I found John Bull much more complaisant than I had hoped for. The *modus operandi* of Custom-House search was simple enough. The six traveling bags containing the effects of myself and assistant lying in a corner by themselves, a burly-looking officer came up and asked:

"Have you any tobacco?"

"A little for my own use," responded my friend, "only enough for my own use." The package being exhibited (two pounds of tobacco), the officer continued, with this *non sequitur:* "Then I suppose you can give me a shilling to drink your health?"

At this unexpected suggestion—*obstupui, tacitus sustinuique pedem*—I stood astonished, and silently kept my feet. Recovering, however, in a moment, I passed the coin of the realm known by that denomination into his itching palm—without thinking of the violation of my vows as a Good Templar—and so covered the cost of the proposed imbibition. He may possibly have intended his remark as a joke, but it did not turn out so. This was my only examination. Not one of the five traveling-bags was opened, although capacious enough to contain cigars to supply even the Prince of Wales for a year. No other questions were asked, and I confess to have departed from Liverpool with most agreeable impressions.

The journey through England, in an express train making forty-five miles an hour, affords but scanty opportunities for observation. The railway fare, first-class, Liverpool to London, 210 miles, foots up about $9. Compare this with the Erie Railway, New York to Elmira, 270 miles, $8. The motion of cars on the Erie is smooth as oil; the English cars run like tin pans on wheel-barrows. The reason is they have only four wheels to a car while the Erie has twelve. I do much of my reading and writing while traveling in American cars, but you can do no writing here; and reading and talking are performed under difficulties.

The swiftness and safety of railway-travel in Great Britain, however, are proverbial. Accidents almost never occur. The carriages are awkwardly separated into small closets, transversely cut off from the main structure, each containing room for six passengers, three facing the front, three the rear. Into these little rooms you are locked by the conductor (styled the *guard*), and have no means of exit except through his key. Sleeping-cars, water-closets, fountains of drinking-water, and means of warming the vehicles, were alike unknown to *railway* travelers in England and Europe in the year of grace 1868. The weather seemed to me warm for the season; there was so little appearance of snow and ice that the plowmen were busy in hundreds of fields near the roadside.

Swiftly as we were drawn across this "right little, tight little" island of England, I gave thought to the subject alluded to in the last chapter—the voyages of the Phœnicians to these islands in the most ancient days.

Even before the Trojan war (B. C. 1184), and of course two centuries before Solomon's day, the sailors of Tyre came to the Isles of Tin (*Cassiterides*), lying between England and Ireland, to barter Oriental products for this metal, and to the Baltic for amber. The copper found abundantly in Asia Minor and Cyprus was alloyed at Tyre with tin, and so *bronze* was made, the proper material for arms, medals, statues, &c. All manner of tools were made of this alloy, bronze; the plowshare of the farmer, the pick of the miner, the hammer and compass of the architect, the burin of the engraver, arrowheads, lanceheads and javelins, swords, bucklers, helmets, cuirasses, &c. If tin is the *Pythias,* copper is the *Damon* of this compound.

Seeing so large a portion of the island covered by noblemen's parks reminds a man of his Horace: *jam pauca aratro juger a regiœ, moles relinquent*—the palaces of the great suffer scanty acreage to the plowman; and it does really puzzle the observer to see where the farms or the farmers are. Castles are distinct enough, and in numbers, but farm-houses, few and far between.

Arriving in London 5 P. M., I drove to Anderton's Hotel, No. 162 Fleet-street, a house which I had seen advertised, under a Masonic emblem, in a publication on board ship. It is an old establishment, and the rooms are dark and misty, but kept scrupulously clean. The waiters are attentive, and the "eating department" all that can be desired. The upper story of this hotel has long been used for Masonic meetings. Observing quite a pile of *Wardens' stations* lumbering up the stairs, it was explained that the lodge-rooms up-stairs are undergoing a course of cleansing and restoration, and the furniture removed for the purpose. At this hotel, I first remarked that on this side of the Atlantic *a traveler's name is not asked for*. His entity is simply that of *the number of his bedroom,* and his bills are made out accordingly. I have no idea that "the gentlemanly clerk" of Anderton's Hotel knows my name even to this day.

I need not say that I felt it to be a real deprivation to pass through London without calling upon the Masonic brethren there; but on my return I hoped to take more time, and give at least a sketch of Free Masonry as it exists in London, as well as in the three Grand Lodges of England, Scotland, and Ireland.

Saturday was spent in active pursuits. I visited St. Paul's Cathedral, to the top of which I climbed, only to look out through a fog so dense that the secretary of my lodge might write with it. It reminded me for all the world of ——— ———'s oration before the Grand Lodge of ———. Disgusted with the fog, I descended, making a vow that I would never go *up there* again. And I never have. In the *Whispering Gallery* I tried a Masonic communication with a friend, and found it went through intact. Visited the tomb of the honored builder of the cathedral, Christopher Wren, and read its appropriate epitaph, "Circumspice," &c., &c., so ridiculously applied on the seal of the State of Michigan.

Thence by the Thames River to Westminster; inspected the Parliament buildings, which I find already crumbling to dust as rapidly as the Court-House in Louisville, Kentucky; then spent a glorious two hours in Westminster Abbey.

The rest of the day was occupied in making preparations for departure, and at 8.30 P.M. I took the Southeastern Railway, at Cannon-street station, for Dover, which was reached at 10.30 P.M.

A visitor to Jerusalem is shown a spot, beneath the lantern in the Greek Chapel of the Holy Sepulcher, styled the geographical center of the earth. In a circle of pavement stands a short marble column to designate so remarkable a *punctum!* Traditions of various kinds cluster around the spot, one, particularly, that from here was taken the clay of which Adam was made! In the same light I view London, *the center of Ancient York Masonry.* From hence, in 1733, was sent the holy spark to our Western fields that has kindled into so goodly a blaze, one American lodge swelling (in 139 years) to nearly 9,000, and the four original lodges of London increasing, through England, Scotland, Ireland, the European nations, and the colonies in all quarters of the earth, to 4,000. Even the lodges of Mark Masters here (lodges whose rituals are based upon a mere *allusion* in the degree of fellow-craft) number in 1872 about 100, governed by a Mark Grand Lodge of England, whose officers are the princes of the land. This, then, is the true *Masonic Center* of the world; from this dust was our Masonic Adam molded!

The Grand Lodge of England is composed substantially of the same officers as our own, adding a few not usually nominated on our side of the water, such as Grand Superintendent of Works, Grand Director of Ceremonies, Grand Organist, &c. But what is peculiar to this country, and plainly grows out of the autocratic character of Freemasonry in monarchical countries, is the fact that all or nearly all the officers of the Grand Lodge are appointed by the Grand Master. This is particularly the case with the Grand Secretary, who, in England, is simply clerk of the Grand Lodge, wielding and assuming none of the despotic powers often so offensively assumed and wielded in the American Grand Lodges by that functionary.

Apropos of this absolute subordination of the Grand Secretary to the Grand Master, this anecdote is related of the Grand Lodge of England in 1868: Complaints had been made against the Grand Secretary for his want of communicativeness and courtesy to those who call upon him, &c., &c. This was producing considerable ill feeling in the Grand Lodge; and as the Earl of Zetland, the Grand Master, declined to interfere, or perhaps was unable to apply a remedy, and as there was no way to reach the Grand Secretary *except by displacing the Grand Master,* a distinguished London brother arose in open Grand Lodge, and *nominated himself* for Grand Master, expressly stating that the reason for this unprecedented and apparently immodest act was that a Grand Secretary ought to be appointed who would attend to the business of the office and pay a decent respect to the feelings of his brethren! Of course the nomination failed; indeed, it was not even seconded; yet it may, for all that, have some of the intended effect.

In addressing the Grand Master of England, Masonic etiquette demands that all communications shall pass through the hands of the Deputy Grand Master, the Grand Registrar, or the Grand Secretary; otherwise they will scarcely have attention. It is not likely, in point of fact, that such men as the Duke of Sussex, the Earl of Zetland, the Duke of Leinster, and noblemen of those high grades, give other consideration to the details of the Masonic institution than to preside at the ordinary and extraordinary communications of Grand Lodges, and the festivals that constitute the *sequelæ* of those occasions. No questions upon Masonic Law are submitted to the Grand Master. No *vexata questiones* of usage, of lodge altercations, of irregularities in Masonic proceedings, and the like, are pushed into his lordship's pocket to disturb the smooth digestion of his dinner. All these matters have a common direction here, that of the *Board of General Purposes,* as it is styled, a sort of *imperium in imperio,* happily unknown in the United States. This Board, I am told, so thoroughly digests the greater part of the business submitted to its charge, that it is *never heard of again.*

Neither does the Grand Master of England ever deliver formal addresses to his Grand Lodge. By this, it will be seen how easy is his berth, compared with that of an American Grand Master, who is often crowded with correspondence, sometimes tyrannized over by his own Grand Secretary, and scarcely ever allowed his little bill of "stationery and postage-money" for his trouble. It is social position alone that qualifies a gentleman here for the high office of Grand Master. The most exalted nobleman who will accept it has it, of right. Quoting from an article from the pen of my old coadjutor, Bro. E. D. Cooke, "The election of Grand Master in this country is not due to any knowledge a man may possess of the institution, or any ability on his part to perform the duties of that exalted position, but simply to the social position he may occupy." All this, it cannot be denied, sounds queerly to those who are accustomed to view the Masonic fraternity as a band of men who "meet upon the level and who part upon the square."

Americans visiting Europe are scarcely ever able to tell us anything of Freemasonry in that country, when they come home, even though they may themselves be members of the craft. This used to strike me strangely. On being questioned, they would reply that they could not find out the time of lodge-meetings; or that nobody could tell them where the lodge-room was. These replies are based upon ignorance of the peculiarities of the Order in England. Most Lodges here *have no halls;* but few of them have even a room of their own. They meet for the greater part in the upper rooms of taverns rented by the season. Their Masonic furniture and paraphernalia, which are extremely scanty, are brought out of chests and wardrobes and arranged for the single occasion. The meeting being over, these sacred objects are again concealed from public sight, and the room restored to travelers' uses. Of course, then, when you inquire of your landlord, your banker, or your general correspondent, "where is the lodge-hall?" he confesses his ignorance, and, if himself a non-Mason, most likely volunteers the opinion that there is no Freemason's Lodge in the place! Again, nearly all travelers from our own country to Europe go abroad *in the summer.* But at that season the Masonic Lodges *do not meet* at all. From about the middle of June to October there is no life in European Masonry whatever. No wonder then that our countrymen come back to us as ignorant upon peculiarities of the Order in foreign countries as they left. The remedies are twofold: *First,* to provide one's self with a Masonic Register of the foreign Lodges; *Second,* to go abroad *in the fall or winter,* when Freemasonry in all the Masonic countries of Europe is active.

Crossing the channel between Dover and Calais in a ferry-boat, compared with which the one that connects Snooksborough with Pumpkinville, on the Tennessee river, is a gorgeous palace, I left Calais at 1.30 A. M., Sunday, February 16, and reached the capital of France in six hours. Just as I hand this page to the printer (February 1, 1872), I notice that "the project of a steam-ferry across the Straits of Dover is approved by a commission of the French Assembly," and the editor of one of the New York papers commenting upon the fact justly says, had the estuary of the Delaware been as broad as the English Channel at Dover, it would long ago have been bridged by magnificent ferry-boats such as ply between New York and Jersey City. Yet the great cities of London and Paris have not hitherto been able to devise any better means of crossing their narrow sea than cock-boats, which make every one sick who sets foot on them. There is a prospect now, we are happy to see, of an improvement.

Owing to the detention of a piece of baggage by some blundering official, I was detained in Paris till 8 P. M. The system of forwarding baggage on the English and Continental railways is exactly what it was in our country in 1850; a century behind 1868. Anything like a "through baggage system" of duplicate checks has not passed through the wool of railway theorists in Europe, though, as far as Freemasonry is concerned, these Parisians have literature enough, seventeen Masonic periodicals being published here, and thirty-nine in Germany.

I spent Sunday in Paris by visiting Père la Chaise Cemetery, where the graves of Marshal Massena, Arago, Abélard and Heloise, and a host of others demand consideration. Thence to Notre-Dame Cathedral, of which I knew so much in youthful days from reading "The Hunchback" of Victor Hugo. Thence to the garden of the Tuileries and places adjacent. The Place de la Concorde is the most splendid collection of objects grand and sublime that I ever witnessed

At 8 P. M. left Paris for Marseilles; reached it at noon on Monday, after a delightful journey through the heart of France. But as the cars have no heating apparatus, the servants brought in a cylinder of hot water every hundred miles or so, and put it *under my feet,* giving me a vivid apprehension of a blow-up every minute. Called at the office of the great steamship line, *Messageries Impériales* (the Imperial Express Co.), and took second-class ticket to Beirut. At Marseilles visited *The Sailors' Club,* a philanthropic institution, on the model of our Young Men's Christian Associations. Also visited the American Consul to have passport *viséed;* but he assured me that this was unnecessary, unless I was going to Rome.

On Tuesday, February 18, at 5½ P. M., I sailed from Marseilles in the French steamer L'Amérique (*The America*). The harbor is a marvel of natural and artificial strength. The amount of shipping seen in it is very great, the iron steamers alone being a host. Only two meals a day are served on these boats, viz.: breakfast at 10 A. M., dinner at 5 P. M. But they give me a good cup of coffee and a crust of bread at rising, and I survive.

THE SHORES OF THE MEDITERRANEAN.

ABRAHAM'S OAK AT HEBRON.

STREET SCENES AT JERUSALEM.　SEE PAGES 402, ETC.

CHAPTER IV.

I passed too rapidly through Liverpool, London, Paris, and Marseilles, as I have said, spending but a day in each. It was a temptation hardly to be resisted to devote at least a month to revive old friendships, and form new ones among the Masons of those cities. But I had a higher work before me Moneys had been entrusted to me, a sacred deposit, to be expended *in Syrian Explorations,* so I listened not to the voice of the tempter, but turning my face sternly to *The Orient* I passed on.

I left Marseilles February 18th, on the French steamship *L'Amérique* (America), bound for Beirut, *via* Palermo, Messina, Syra, Smyrna, Rhodes, Mersina, Alexandrette, Latakia, and Tripoli, and due at Beirut March 3d. On *L'Amérique,* only one Masonic *passenger* was at first visible, Capt. E. H. Currey, of the brig *C. F. Eaton,* of New York, his membership being in Halifax, Nova Scotia, and one *officer,* Brother Le Maitre, first officer of the steamer *L'Amérique.* He is a resident of Marseilles, and particularly well informed in the details of French Masonry. Before we reached Smyrna another Mason, a fellow-passenger, came on board.

Passing southeastwardly, the Straits of Gibraltar, guarded by the Pillars of Hercules, were far on my right hand and of course invisible. These pillars, named respectively *Calpe* and *Abylo,* stood, in the days when giants might be imagined, the twin, prodigious monoliths similar in purpose to the artificial pyramids.

They must have struck the gaze of the astonished and awed discoverers navigating this silent Mediterranean as the colossal pillars on which burned the double lights of Baal. So to the Phœnician sailors who first descried and then stemmed boldly through these peaked and majestic straits,—so to those men of Tyre, whose devices were the fire-white horns of the globed Ashtaroth, appeared these monster rocks, pillar-portals, fire-topped as the last world-beacon closing in that classic sea.— *Jennings' Rosicrucians.*

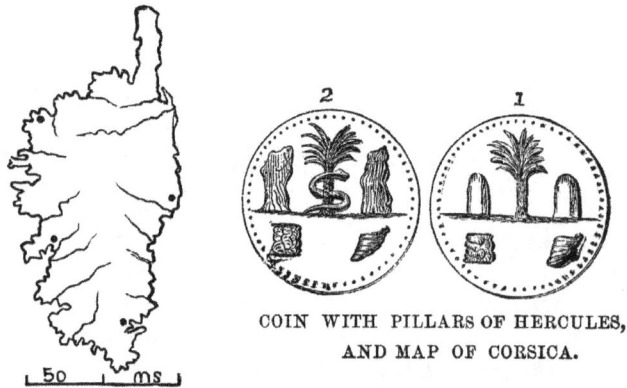

COIN WITH PILLARS OF HERCULES,
AND MAP OF CORSICA.

Passing the island of Corsica, I gave some hours of contemplation to that great man, our Masonic brother, born on this mountainous isle, *Napoleon Bonaparte.* It is about a century since his boyish eyes looked forth from those snowy crags over the beautiful and memorable sea before me. We need not endorse all his actions to acknowledge him as a brother. A Masonic fraternity was founded at Paris in 1816, by the adherents of the then exiled Napoleon. Its ritual comprised three degrees: 1. Knight; 2. Commander; 3. Grand Elect. The third degree was divided into three classes: 1. Secret Judge; 2. Perfect Initiate; 3. Knight of the Oaken Crown, all having reference to Napoleon. Bertrand, then a voluntary exile with his imperial master at St. Helena, was chosen Grand Master, the single aim of the whole being the restoration of Napoleon.—*Macoy's Masonic Cyclopedia.* (How perfect the parallel between this and the various Scotch and chapitral rites established to advance the restoration of the Pretender to the English crown.)

Among the medals struck during the brilliant career of Napoleon, there are several that commemorate his Masonic affiliation; one, dated December 31, 1807, has for motto, *Nova lux oculis effulsit et ingens*—new and great light bursts upon our vision. On the *obverse* is a cabinet of Masonic emblems, below a star with five radiating cusps, and the words Lodge Ecossaise Napoléon (Scottish Napoleon Lodge). On the *reverse* we have in French the words Silence, Friendship, Beneficence, with the square and compass grouped in an oak crown, and the words (in French) Orient of Leghorn, 1807.

In memory of this wonderful man whose patronage of the Masonic fraternity gave it an impetus in France and Europe which it never has lost, I begin at Corsica, marked "A" on the map, to locate the names of American Masons, and write here ten eminent in military as well as Masonic fame, viz.:—General Hancock, General Herron, General McClellan, General Hurlbut, General Washburn, General Butler, General Manson, General Woodruff, General Zollicoffer, General Anderson. [The announcement of the death of this excellent man reaches me while, in 1871, I am conning over this chapter.]

An excellent book upon Corsica is that of Hon. S. S. Cox, published in 1870, called, *A Search for Winter Sunbeams*. Before this, the island had been *terra incognita,* an unknown country. But Mr. Cox shows that it is the connecting link between the two continents, in the center of the basin of the Western Mediterranean. Its mountains are midway between the Atlas range and the Alps, and unite the fruitful vigor of the former with the rugged grandeur of the latter, and the vegetable growth of each. Like the Holy Land, this broken region produces everything, from the lemon, orange, and date, to the pine, ilex, and oak.

Between Italy and Sicily I first struck the track, figuratively speaking, of the great Christian itinerant and martyr, St. Paul, of whom I shall have more to say in this work. Here I began to realize that I was entering upon Scriptural scenes and events. To the left, yonder, almost in sight, was Rome, then and now, for many hundred years, closed to Freemasonry,* the scene of Paul's martyrdom, the place from which his most wonderful epistles were dated. Nearer was the Island of Caprera, on which the Grand Master of Italian Masons, Garibaldi, was then a political prisoner. He might have been in his doorway looking out upon our steamer as we passed. On the right, as I sailed, lay in the distance Malta, the scene of chivalric exploits, the place of Paul's shipwreck. Before me were the straits, on the right and left of which stood those ancient terrors, Scylla and Charybdis.

Sailing near Crotona, on the eastern coast of Italy, I recalled the name and labors of Pythagoras, commemorated in the *Freemason's Monitor* in these words: "Our ancient friend and brother, the great *Pythagoras,* who, in his travels through Asia, Africa, and Europe, was initiated into several orders of priesthood and raised to

---

* Since this page was written the Grand Lodge of Italy has been transferred to Rome, the Pope having lost all political power, and only remaining in Rome on sufferance. Verily the whirligig of time makes wondrous changes!

the sublime degree of a Master Mason." Here, at Crotona, his celebrated school of philosophy was established, about B.C. 539, in which the sciences enumerated in the Fellow-Crafts Lecture were inculcated, viz., grammar, rhetoric, logic, arithmetic, geometry, music, and astronomy. From Pythagoras (often erroneously accented on the penult) many of our Masonic lodges are named, as for instance *Crotona* Lodge No. 339, Ky.; and any number of *Pythagoras* lodges.

Masonic honors are paid to Pythagoras as the reputed discoverer of the forty-seventh problem of Euclid, thus acknowledged in the *Monitor:* "This wise philosopher enriched his mind abundantly in a general knowledge of things, and more especially in Geometry or Masonry; on this subject he drew out many problems and theorems, and among the most distinguished he erected this, which, in the joy of his heart, he called *Eureka,* in the Grecian language signifying *I have found it!* and upon the discovery of which he is said to have sacrificed a hecatomb. It teaches Masons to be general lovers of the arts and sciences." In the degree of *Eureka Hiatus,* however, this discovery is attributed to an aged brother, *Huramen,* who lived four hundred years earlier. Damon and Pythias, whose friendship was modeled after that of David and Jonathan, were pupils of the Pythagorean school, and lived about B.C. 387. Out of their story some ingenious Americans have recently modeled a "secret order," surnamed *Knights of Pythias.*

In memory of this wonderful man, who perhaps did more to shape the philosophy and *cultus* of the ancient world than any other, not inspired author, I have located here, at Crotona, marked "B" upon the map, the names of ten Masonic authors of modern times whose labors run parallel with those of the sublime Pythagoras, viz., George W. Chase, James B. Taylor, Giles F. Yates, Wilkins Tannehill, George Gray, J.W.S. Mitchell, A.T.C. Pearson, G.W. Steinbrenner, William S. Rockwell, and Sidney Hayden.

Passing the island of Paros, I reflected upon that famous fabric "which was supported by fourteen hundred and fifty-three columns and two thousand nine hundred and six pilasters, all hewn from the finest *Parian* marble." If this calculation is correct, the traffic between Joppa, the seaport of Jerusalem, and the quarries upon this island of Paros, must have been very extensive. With the small vessels employed in Phœnician commerce, it was a stupendous labor to convey such, and so many, columns and pilasters over the seas. I had no opportunity to see the quarries. The island itself is about thirty miles in length. The following outline cut will give an idea of it.

In memory of a place perpetuated in Masonic tradition, marked "C" upon the map, I locate the names of ten such "shafts of Parian marble" as King Solomon would have approved, viz., John Sheville, Jerome B. Borden, George W. Fleming, W. J. Millard, James Cruikshank, Elisha D. Cooke, James L. Enos, George D. Norris, Stillman Blanchard, and James Crooks.

MAP OF PAROS.

It was a trial to my feelings to skirt thus rapidly the coasts of Greece; debarred for want of time from visiting scenes with which my studies have familiarized me from boyhood. Toward the Acropolis, at Athens, I directed a longing gaze. The pilot guided me in pointing my finger toward it. He says that, like the hill on which Solomon's Temple stood, it is most accessible from the *northwest* Robinson says that on the oblong area of its leveled surface were collected the noblest monuments of Grecian taste. It was the very sanctuary of the arts, the glory and the religion of ancient Athens. Here stood the sixth of the seven ancient wonders of the world, the ivory and gold statue of Jupiter Olympus, erected by Phidias, B.C. 440, which measured thirty-nine feet in height.

To commemorate this ancient wonder, traditionally associated with Ancient Operative Masonry, at Athens, marked "D" on the map, I locate the names of ten Masonic characters as beautifully proportioned in their *moral* members as the statue of Jupiter was in the *physical,* viz., Daniel Sickels, J. L. Gould, George Babcock, John Robin McDaniel, Frank Darrow, Robert N. Brown, William Hacker, J. J. Rubottom, I. N. Stackhouse, and William S. Combs.

In conversation with our Greek pilot, when I told him that Solon, B.C. 600, laid it down, as the first essential condition of happiness, that a man should live in a *well-ordered country,* he shrugged his shoulders Greek fashion, and replied: "Lucky for Solon he does not live here now!"

At Syra we had taken in as a passenger Bro. R. Westfield, a member of Homer Lodge No. 806, at Smyrna. As we were to lie some forty-eight hours in Smyrna, I was fortunate in securing, through Bro. Westfield, an introduction to Bro. Franchia, Worshipful Master of Homer Lodge No. 806, and through him to a large number of Masons. A meeting was promptly called at 8.30 P.M. of February 25th, where I found about twoscore of the brethren, and enjoyed an entertainment as novel to me as it was delightful. I am sure I can never forget it. To understand my description the reader is informed that Smyrna is a city made up, in its foreign elements, of representatives of all civilized nations. It has in 1872 at least seven lodges and two Royal Arch Chapters, together with a Consistory S. P. R. S. 32°. The names of the various Masonic bodies, so far as I can gather them, are these:

1. *St. John's Royal Arch Chapter U. D.*—The dispensation for this chapter was granted by the G. G. High-Priest of the G. G. Royal Arch Chapter of the United States, May 6th, 1863. The period for the return of the dispensation (September, 1865) having been permitted, inadvertently, to elapse without the performance of that necessary duty, the labors of the chapter temporarily ceased; but movements were making to secure a new dispensation at once, and a warrant in September following. The elements incorporated in this chapter are of the very best. They work the American rituals pure and simple, and have good apartments fitted up expressly for Royal Arch use.*

2. *A Chapter* (name unknown to me).—Working Rosicrucian Masonry, under authority of the Italian Grand Orient. Of this, in my brief stay, I could not secure reliable reports. It had lately been set to work.

3. *Homer Lodge No. 806.*—Warranted in 1860. This has forty-five or fifty members, and is now the oldest working lodge in Smyrna. It is deservedly ranked as one of the best lodges on the English Register, outside the mother-country. The rituals are the English standards; furniture and equipments of the lodge the same.

4. *St. George Lodge No. 1,015.*—Authorized in 1866 by the Grand Lodge of England. This lodge has about sixty-five members.

---

* It is pleasant to add that, owing to representations I made to the proper author ides, they renewed the dispensation of this chapter in 1868, and the companions are now (in 1872) briskly at work. The chapter is reported, in the proceedings of the General Grand Royal Arch Chapter, September, 1871, as "St. John's, Smyrna, Turkey, May, 1863. September 18, 1868."

SMYRNA, FROM THE SEA.

PALMYRA: TADMOR.

HYDE CLARKE,
Formerly resident at Smyrna.

The rituals are in the Greek language, but, as I understand, translated literally from the English. The Greek population of Smyrna is very large and respectable.

5. *Decran Lodge No.* 1,014.—Warranted by the Grand Lodge of England in 1864. This lodge has about sixty members. The rituals are the same as those of St. George, but the membership is Armenian—a class here embracing many of the wealthiest people of the city.

6. *Stella Ionia Lodge No.* —.—Warranted by the Grand Lodge of Italy in 1864. This lodge has about seventy-five members. The rituals are Italian. I was unable to get much information concerning this lodge.

7. *Eleusinian Lodge No.* 987.—This was intended as a summer lodge at Ephesus, but its officers and members resided in Smyrna.

8. *Sion's Lodge.*—This was organized at the close of the year 1870, of Jewish brethren.

9. *St. John's Lodge No.* 952.—Working under English authority.

All these Smyrna lodges hold their meetings in the same room; a commodious, well-ventilated apartment, with handsome cornices, abundant ante-chambers, etc., etc. The arrangements of an English lodge will doubtless be novel to many of my readers. There is no Altar, but a pedestal directly in front of the Worshipful Master serves the purpose of one. The emblems usually delineated on the Master's carpet, such as the Ashlars, Globes, Tokens of Service, and the like, are presented here in the form of tangible objects grouped around and in front of the Master's station, and form very attractive images to the eye; more so, indeed, than merely painted emblems The stations of the officers are substantially the same as ours.

The form of notification sent out by the Worshipful Master was this: "An Emergency General Meeting of Masons will be held today, Tuesday, the 25th of February, at 8½ P.M., which all members are requested punctually to attend. The business of the evening will be to receive two American Masonic Brethren." Some of the names minuted for the Tyler's use on this Summons are: Thomas Janson, Secretary; F. Stano, F. W. Spiegelthal, W. Shotton, A. F. Raboly, James Rees, G. Perrin, T. Papworth, S. Papps, E. Parodis, J. O'Connor, N. Nubarian, G. Mollhausen, Louis Meyer, Arthur Lawson, Dr. Kossonis, Issigonis, St. Joly, Fres. Joly, Ed. Joly, Jo. Hadgi, C. R. Hefter, T. Hatton, L. Haco, E. Georganspula, J. Ganon, G. Fyfe, J. Fraser, Th. Franghia, F. Franghia, A. Fontrier, St. Dirutzuyan, J

Manusso Dani, Paul Clement, C. P. Charlton, Manoli Cassimati, P Batty, Jacob Berchten, J. Bottomly, R. Barnard, James Albon. The variety of languages represented in this nomenclature will forcibly strike the reader.

This "Emergency Lodge" was opened on the degree of Entered Apprentice at 8.30 P.M., it being then 1.44 P.M. at La Grange, Kentucky—difference in time, six hours thirty-six minutes. It was pleasant to observe that as each brother prepared himself "to serve" his Divine Master in the opening and work of the lodge, he "girded himself" (as intimated in Luke 16:8) with his apron, the badge of innocence, and quietly entered "the sacred retreat of friendship," the S. S. of Him who fashioned our hearts alike. (Ps. 33:15.)

A committee of six, two bearing large swords of state and wands, waited upon me in the reception-room and escorted me in. A Salute of Honor was given (the "Private Grand Honors" as we call the Salute), and I was inducted into the Oriental chair, and welcomed in an eloquent manner by Brother Carrére. My reply, which occupied about thirty minutes, was translated into French by Brother C. G. Carrére, LL.D., a barrister of high eminence here. The gracefulness and ease of his rendering cannot be surpassed. His manner is polished, yet dignified and commanding.

I began by solemnly saluting the assembly in the name of the speaker; of the Craft Universal; and of T. G. A. O. T. U., at whose right hand are eternal pleasures. (Ps. 16:11.) I told them how numerous is the great Fraternity in the United States, and of what classes of citizens it is composed. I assured them that we Americans are in general an inquiring people, and having been taught in our Masonic traditions that Freemasonry originated in Palestine, some four thousand of them had united in making me in some sort a representative for the purpose of initiating a series of investigations into the sacred land, and its ruins, scattered so abundantly and so mournfully there. I told them that I was then upon my journey to the Holy Land. I recalled to their memory one greatly beloved in Smyrna, who, I regretted to find, had returned to England after doing a good work for Freemasonry in the Levant, viz., Bro. Hyde Clark; and I assured them that my mission had his valued approbation. In a later chapter of this book I will give his portrait. I informed them that, by promise to my constituents at home, the results of my researches and a full account of my travels would be published for general perusal, and that copies should be placed in their hands. I told them that in my literary labors I had composed a number of poems, a few of which I would proceed to recite.

Then I gave them *The Level and Square; Our Vows; One Hour with You;* and *The Gavel Song;* all of which seemed to give them pleasure.

Responses were made by Bro. Carrére, Bro. Staab, and others in English, and one at considerable length in Greek by Bro. Dr. S. Karacoussis, a Greek physician of eminence here. This was interpreted to me by Bro. Carrére. The learned doctor takes the same view of the Oriental origin and antiquity of Freemasonry that we do. His theory of Masonic patriotism and benevolence is very lofty and grand. He encouraged me greatly in my Eastern researches, as indeed did they all. An invitation was tendered to me to spend some time here next summer, which I accepted, and we arranged for a Masonic Picnic to be held June 24th, 1868, at ancient Ephesus, about twenty-five miles south of Smyrna. This plan, however, failed, owing to my adopting a different route on my return home in June.

A call was then made upon me to close the lodge strictly upon the American system, which I did. Then we adjourned to refreshments, from which I managed to withdraw so as to be on board the steamer by midnight. As I had spent the day mostly in visiting bazaars, climbing to the great castle in the rear of the city, and perambulating it in all directions, it may readily be imagined that I was in a condition demanding repose.

As one evidence of the national variety that made up this meeting, I mention the names of Bro. Landon, an *American;* Westfield, a *German;* Franghia, Cassimarti, Dirutzuyan, Fontrier, Georganspula, Staab, Karacoussis, Hadji, Issigonis, Nubarian, Raboly, Stepham, Jedeschi, Jimoni, Thukides, and Venezeans, of the *Greek, French, Armenian,* and *English.* The only American brother resident here, whose acquaintance I formed, was Brother Landon, originally from Boston, Worshipful Master of the Lodge at Ephesus; more than forty years a Mason, and in whom the sacred fire was burning unimpaired. His death in 1870 left a wide hiatus in that Masonic and social circle.

I cannot leave the subject of my visit to Smyrna without recalling the truly Masonic earnestness manifested by all. The Oriental usage of meeting and parting *with a kiss* of peace (Romans 16:16), while it seems strange in others, appears strangely *appropriate* among these Levant Masons. When I mentioned casually, in the reception-room, that the first money which, as a little boy, I ever possessed, I gave, in 1826, to the cause of suffering Greece, the Greek brethren present almost smothered me with kisses. And when I said *farewell* to the party who accompanied me to the ship on the 26th, the same salutations were exchanged. I confess that I never before felt the universality of Freemasonry as now, and never estimated so highly its mighty powers for good.

One ceremony they perform in these Smyrna lodges I may relate without a violation of confidence. Whenever in my remarks to the Lodge I used the name of Deity, all my auditors arose and stood before that "shadowed image" to which the sweet bard of Scottish Freemasonry refers, as

> "That hieroglyphic bright
> Which none but Craftsmen ever saw."

As every reader can learn what he wants to know by looking for "Smyrna" in the Cyclopedia, I occupy but short space with a description. This city, styled the ornament of Asia (*agalma tees Asias*), was celebrated by the ancients as one of the fairest and noblest cities of Ionia. It was founded, probably, by a woman of the same name, an Amazon, of the Cumæans, about B.C. 1015, the period when King David was "preparing with all his might, for the house of his God, gold, silver, brass, iron, wood, onyx-stones and all manner of precious stones and marble stones in abundance." (1 Chr. 29:2.) Although *ten times* destroyed by fierce throes of nature and fiercer men, Smyrna has *ten times* risen from her ruins, and is still the largest commercial city of Asia Minor, promising even to eclipse Constantinople. Herodotus, B.C. 444, says, "it has the finest sky and climate in the world, and a soil extremely productive." Great names are associated with Smyrna. *Pythagoras* was born about B.C. 570 at Samos, only a few miles south of Smyrna, and must have spent much of his early life here. *Homer,* about B.C. 962, was perhaps born here. *St. Paul* unquestionably had one of his preaching stations at Smyrna, and here was that one of the seven churches of Asia to which "the beloved Disciple," the good St. John the Evangelist, he who bare record of the word of God and the testimony of the Lord Jesus Christ, and of all things that he saw (Rev. 1:2), and whom all loving Masons claim as a brother, wrote this thrilling epistle: "These things said the first and last, which was dead and is alive. I know thy works and tribulation and poverty (but thou art rich), and I know the blasphemy of them which say they are Jews and are not, but are the synagogue of Satan. Fear none of those things which thou shall suffer; behold, the devil shall cast some of you into prison that ye may be tried; and ye shall have tribulation ten days; be thou faithful unto death and I will give thee a crown of life." (Rev. 2:8-10.) And here that grand old evangelist *Polycarp* (what an appropriate name, the *seed-abounding!*) preached and labored for seventy-four years, making good testimony of his faith by suffering death at the stake A.D. 167, under the reign of Marcus Aurelius Antoninus. His tomb is still shown, designated by a fine old cypress-tree.

Along the east side of the city is a beautiful plain full of villages. Two lines of railway run out in that direction; one finished to Aidin (Tralles) by way of Ephesus, eighty miles; the other to Magnesia and Kassaba, sixty miles. Trains run daily over these lines at the rate of twenty-five miles an hour.

An account of the sieges this city has suffered, and the terrible disasters consequent upon its numerous captures and destruction, would fill a volume. Operative Masons will be interested to know that when Timour the Tartar (Taimour-lang) captured Smyrna, A.D. 1402, after a blockade of fourteen days, he slew all the inhabitants and demolished the houses. In rebuilding a portion for military purposes, he ordered all the heads of the slain to be *built into* the walls with mortar and stone. History fails to say what sort of materials these proved to be.

Smyrna and the country around it abound in antiquities, the best description of which I have seen being that in "The Seven Churches of Asia," by A. Svoboda, 1869, with an introduction by our good Mason brother Prof. H. B. Tristam, of England. A copy of this, with twenty photographs pasted on the corresponding leaves, is in the possession of Col. H. J. Goodrich, Chicago, Illinois. Amongst these ruins the most remarkable is the sculpture made by Sesostris at Kara-Bell, not long after those cut on the rocks near Beirut, which I shall minutely describe in their place. These were only discovered in 1839, although described by Herodotus more than 2,300 years ago. It is sculptured in relief, sunk in a panel cut into the perpendicular surface of a massive, calcareous hard rock, in height about seven feet. The image is represented in profile, *looking to the east.* The inscription, as described by Herodotus, although now obliterated by the tooth of time in thirty-four centuries, read thus: "I conquered this country by the might of my arms."

In the vicinity of Smyrna, six miles from Sardis, are the remains of the largest tomb in the world, that of Algattes, father of the opulent Crœsus, to whom the adage "rich as Crœsus" applies. This immense monument is 3,800 feet in circumference and very lofty. The base is of very large stones, the rest earth. Herodotus says it was erected by tradesmen, mechanics, and strumpets, and rather oddly adds that the latter did the most of it!

The far-famed mausoleum of Mausolus, King of Caria, erected by Artemisia, his queen, and the second of the Seven Wonders of the ancient world, was at Halicarnassus, not far from Smyrna. It was built B.C. 350. Artemisia invited all the literary men of the age to compete for the best elegiac panegyric upon the deceased, and adjudged the prize to Theopompus, B.C. 357. The statue of Mausolus, taken from these ruins, is now in the British Museum at London.

To commemorate this model of all funeral piles, I locate at this place, marked on the map "I," the names of ten eminent Masons, Grand Masters, and Past Grand Masters, viz.: Theodore S. Parvin, Samuel M. Todd, D. H. Wheeler, Hiram Bassett, J. M. S. McCorkle, John Scott, D. C. Cregier, Wm. M. Wilson, Thomas A. Doyle, William E. Pine, Philip C. Tucker, Jr.

In passing through Smyrna, the first Oriental city I had ever visited, I was struck, as all travelers are, with the unexpected variety of scenes, the people of so many colors and creeds, and the customs, so novel to an American. A few pages from my notebook will serve to show how my mind was affected, and will exhibit my method of jotting down information during my whole journey through the East:

Greek boatmen in pantalettes; they face the way they row; oars fastened to rowlocks, and weighted to accommodate feeble wrists; prices of labor, low; handkerchiefs around head; talk in strident tones as if quarreling; gesticulate like St. Vitus; *merchandise;* piles of madder on docks; cotton bales hooped with five iron bands; through whole day's ramble felt as if in lanes and by-ways, and that I should presently come out into a broad street, but never did; streets only eight to twelve feet wide; *Camel,* solemn, stately-stepping, silent, serious ship of the desert, clipper-rigged, his spongy feet sprawling all over the wide paving-stones, as though to grasp them and secure a footing; each wears a nose-bag like a huge *mouchoir;* always five camels in a row, following a little donkey who carries a bigger one on his back: the procession of six is coupled by cords six feet, tying them neck to neck; number six wears a large cow-bell, having inside of it a small bell with a clapper; unmusical sounds; camels loaded with madder in bales; also with cotton; each carrying two large round bags of cotton of about 300 lbs. each, not well compressed; these loads do not shorten the three-feet steps or reduce the stately stepping, as regular as Mrs. M——'s clock that hangs over the fireplace at home; his long, snaky neck level as *the* Level of the Senior Warden; caravan of 500 of them just in from Persia, and whole city full of them scattered in followings of five; *Turkish Carrier* with wooden frame on his back supports a great load; a barrel of flour being strapped on it, he leans forward, nearly horizontal, grasps tightly a stick fastened by a string to his neck, and walks off with a long, quick stride as silently and solemnly as the camel himself; *such* a rheumatism as he will have when he gets to be sixty; the *markets* called bazaars; no signboards; numbered in Arabic and English; every man's stock is open in front, with no counter or railing; you just sit down on the shop-floor, in front of the merchant, and trade; each stock worth from $50 to $500 all told; nobody sells more than one line of goods; first is a tobacco-store, then drygoods, thread, tobacco again, fruits, brass vessels (very bright and tasty too); jewelry, mostly of the cheap and nasty sort; fruits, tobacco, calico, woolen caps with silk tassels; small stock of drugs; hardware from Birmingham, England (such scissors! to cut your nails will take the edge off!); tobacco, matches, confectionery, four in a row;—and so on with tobacco as a *staple;* only one butcher-shop an hour; bread in loaves and rings, nice, and of good quality; confectioneries particularly well got up; no cakes nor *pison things,* as in American shops; every hundred yards or so an open court, mostly paved, with fountain in center, and trees of orange, palm, etc.; in Armenian quarters, front doors open, display hall with settees, paved elaborately with pebbles; set mosaically in cement; *Armenian Graveyard,* with drawings on gravestones, to show dead men's business on earth,—barbers' tools, tools of carpenters, stonemason, blacksmith, etc., etc.; *Turkish Mosque;* at high twelve people pray; first washing feet, hands, arms, neck and head, and scouring mouth, ears, etc.; my servant Joseph, being a Jew, debarred admission, stayed outside and watched my boots while I went in; had to go in stocking feet (stockings had holes in them); worshipers barefooted; no furniture nor seats; matted with ragged mats; galleries, but nobody there; regular barn of a place; no preaching; no singing, no nothing; those who spoke to one another whispered; kept my hat on according to orders; the door was a quilted leather affair that hung tapestry-fashion; no arrangements for warming or lighting; heard no muezzin; crescent on top of the church; *Turkish School,* all boys, no girls; noise startling, gesticulations marvelous, scholars all leave their shoes outside, perfectly safe, the fifty pairs not worth a dime for the lot; sight of my fur cap delighted the boys; *Women;* Turkish women wear cloth over face, other women not; Armenian women expose breasts indecorously; *Old Fort on hill;* built by Genoese; magnificent view from summit; Mt. Cybele with its snowy cap and many traditions; the fort a grand piece of labor and skill, but now entirely in ruins; looking southeast, imagine St. Paul coming to the top of the hill, to take a first view of Smyrna preparatory to preaching here; *Turkish Graveyard;* turban on gravestones of men; rosebuds on women; inscriptions written from right to left, and slope upwards, a modern innovation, I am told; many epitaphs in gilt; none handsome; graveyard full of broken columns, once doubtless forming parts of ancient temples, etc.; six enormous ones lately exhumed by Exploration Society, curiously carved work upon them; had stones thrown at me here by schoolboys, but only because my guide was a Jew; *Fountains;* a Turkish hobby founding fountains, and one that excited my gratitude; the city is full of them; all free; *Streets* cleaner than I expected, and well paved, but the boulders are rude, and hurt the feet; *Fruits,* etc., figs, seedless raisins, pomegranates, carob pods, garlic, cauliflowers, shelled almonds, oranges, lemons, dates, fig-paste, English walnuts, hazelnuts, dates, delicious prunes, and very many others; *Costumes;* everybody's nationality and religion recognized by his dress, handsomest race is the Armenian; but few beggars; group negroes playing cards; soldiers with French muskets, percussion locks, carried at half-shoulder shift; but little importunity among merchants to get my custom; street-brokers everywhere with a peck or two of money ready for exchange; in changing a twenty-franc piece they only charged two cents premium; gave me a pint of native money in copper and alloyed silver, very base; only two tipsy men, and they "but just a drappy in the ee'," as poor Burns used to say.

Over the old Greek church, in which Polycarp is said to have preached, are the words (in ancient Greek), *Polycarp the Divine Shepherd.* * * * * * And so on for a dozen pages for quantity.

The streets of Smyrna are ludicrous parodies on the word! More crooked than those of Boston, more filthy than those of Cairo (Illinois), they are so narrow that a loaded camel fills one up *even.* Shakespeare must have had a description of them before penning that laughable thing in the *Merchant of Venice* (Act 2, Scene 2), where one of his characters gives these directions to a sorely-puzzled traveler: "Turn upon your right hand at the next turning; but at the next turning of all, on your left. Marry, at the very next turning, turn of no hand, but turn down indirectly to the Jew's house!" No marvel at the answer: "'Twill be a hard way to hit!"

Seeing here the first caravan of camels I had ever beheld (some five hundred of them, just in from Persia, loaded with cotton), I am reminded of the Eastern legend commemorating the extreme homeliness of this beast. "The first man who beheld a camel fainted with dismay; the second one drew tremblingly near; the third roped him and put him to work!" In good sooth, he is a failure in animal architecture, reminding us, as compared with the other beasts, of the *lodge-tyler* compared with the other officers.

To commemorate the Masonic spirit manifested in this ancient Masonic and ecclesiastical city of Smyrna, marked on the map "E," nine honored names of British craftsmen, whose names will survive them, are located here, viz., Hyde Clark, Stephen Barton Wilson, W. J. Hughan, D. Murray Lyon, Charles Purton Cooper, Matthew Cooke, Charles Warren, E. T. Rogers, and V. W. Bate.

It was not in my route to visit Constantinople; but I was assured by well-informed gentlemen at Smyrna that some of the highest officials of the empire are acknowledged members of the Masonic fraternity there. Amongst these I name that distinguished officer, *Fuad Pasha,* who deceased the following year. The *Sultan* himself is an avowed *friend* to this society. A few years since he directed one of his secretaries *to become a Mason,* and the secretary's report upon the aims and principles of the institution was so favorable as to secure the imperial favor. Of this the great officers of the empire are well aware.

Constantinople is intimately associated in our minds with terrible conflagrations, especially that of 1870, which was one of a series that have devastated this devoted city for many generations. A traveler in 1610, referring to the sad fire of October 14, 1607, remarked that he did not know to what fate or misfortune this city was subject in suffering so much. At that time three thousand houses were burned to their foundations.

I left Smyrna on Wednesday, the 26th February, still one week's journey from Holy Land. Passing the island of Samos, I again recall the history and labors of the sublime Pythagoras, born here B.C. 570.

Samos, says Anthon in his Classical Dictionary, is an island of the Ægean, lying off the lower part of the coast of Ionia, and nearly opposite the Trogilian promontory. The intervening strait was about seven *stadia* in its narrowest part. (A stadium was the eighth of an English mile.) The first inhabitants were Carians and Leleges. The temple and worship of Juno contributed much to its fame and affluence. A tunnel was carried through the mountain seven stadia, to convey water from a distant fountain to the city. A mole, twenty fathoms deep and two stadia long, defended the harbor.

The circuit of Samos was 600 stadia, equal to 75 English miles. It yielded almost every kind of Levantine produce, except wine, The city of Samos was exactly opposite the Trogilian promontory and Mount Mycale. The port was secure and convenient for ships. The town stood chiefly in a plain rising gradually from the sea. The island, sailing north from Patmos, is very conspicuous, so much so that the ancients styled any very lofty place *Samos*. It is the most conspicuous object, not only in the Ionian Sea but the Ægean also. The following cut will give an idea of its shape.

MAP OF SAMOS.

At so appropriate a locality as Samos, marked "F" on the map, I place the names of Thomas J. Corson, Daniel B. Bruen, W. B. Langridge, A. H. Copeland, P. H. Taylor, John Leach, J. McCormick, Cornelius Moore, A. J. Wheeler, and John A. Morris.

Passing off the coast, a little ways west of Ephesus, I note the fact that Eleusinian Lodge No. 987, of which the venerable Brother Landon is W. M., holds its sessions here, although the city at present is but a poor place. I had promised the Smyrna Masons to return to them in June next and spend the 24th, the anniversary of our patron-saint John the Baptist, in a Masonic *picnic* among the ruins of Ephesus. It would have been a rare experience indeed. Here at Ephesus were many of the most celebrated structures of antiquity, including that third "Wonder of the World," the Temple of Diana. This noted edifice was erected B.C. 552, at the common charge of all the Asiatic States, its chief architect being Ctesiphon; two hundred and twenty years were expended in the work. The Temple was 425 feet by 225. It was supported by 127 marble columns 60 feet high, and thick in proportion, each weighing 150 tons. Each column was a present from a separate king. This building was set on fire by Eratostratus the same night Alexander was born, viz., B.C. 356. It was rebuilt, but finally destroyed by the Goths A.D. 256 to 262.

The foundations of this Temple, like those of King Solomon's, were artificial, although for a very different reason. The soil being marshy, deep beds of charcoal and fleeces of wool were laid in trenches, and so a substantial base was formed. Pliny describes the difficulty encountered in moving and raising the enormous blocks of stone wrought into this Temple, a problem which exercises the wits of all who traverse Egypt and the East, and to which I shall give attention further on. In the present instance he says: "The architect contrived to raise the architraves by means of bags of sand piled upon an inclined plane to the height of the columns (60 feet) and by gradually emptying them the blocks fell to their assigned places."

The roof of this Temple was of cedar, like Solomon's, the doors of cypress (Solomon's were of olive), and the stairway of vine-wood. As the grapevines in the East are often twelve to fifteen inches in diameter, this is credible. All the wood before using was glued together and left four years to season. So well was this seasoning executed that the wood of the Second Temple was found by Mucianus, B.C. 75, to be as good as new, although then 400 years old. So the wood in the old church at Bethlehem seems now as good as new, although more than 1,500 years old. Upon the whole, this Temple was so beautiful that Philon burst out in rapture concerning it, saying, "it is the only house of the gods; you will think when you see it that the gods have left heaven and come to live here!" Its position was at the head of the port facing me, as I sail past, and it shone there like a meteor. But now the sea has receded three miles eastward and left a reedy, miasmatic marsh between us. The very site of the Temple of Diana is in dispute, and the city itself is a vast and almost indistinguishable ruin.

The supply of marble for these works was of course immense. Three ancient quarries were open, those of Ctesiphon and Paros, to which reference has been made on preceding pages, and Proconessus. But the question of *freight* was the puzzle; the transport of so much stone would demand whole fleets of vessels, although the distance, as compared with that traversed by the fleets of Hiram, was insignificant. The difficulty was solved in the nick of time, by the discovery of a quarry of fine marble on Mount Prion, in the vicinity of Ephesus, brought to light by the butting off of a piece by the horns of a ram!

At this ancient Queen City of the Levant Ephesus, marked on the map "H," I locate the following Masonic names: Charles W. Moore, H. G. Reynolds, David Clark, F. G. Tisdall, G. F. Gouley, Henry D. Palmer, James Fenton, S. D. Bayless, Joseph B. Hough, and E. S. Fitch.

And there the people believe our good December-Saint John lies buried behind the high altar. But his tomb, when opened, was found to have lost its body; the pure flesh of the apostle of peace had turned to manna, or the body itself had been translated to heaven, leaving that Celestial bread of the Royal Arch in its place. This grave had been made under his own instructions, while alive, and in his death-day he walked there voluntarily and laid himself down in it.

Here, too, he led his adopted mother, Mary (John 19:26-27), who, at the age of seventy-two years, followed Jesus to the celestial courts.

Passing along, on the 26th, by the island of Patmos, I read with uncommon interest that collection of imagery, thrilling and inimitable, which makes up the *Apocalypse* or Revelation of St. John, in which the Apostle saw "the spiritual city and all her spires and gateways in a glory like one pearl," and where on that celebrated Lord's day he was "in the spirit," his raptured soul dwelling in the midst of opal and amethyst and chalcedony and sardonyx and gold.

Much of these figures is embodied in various degrees of the Scotch Rite. Entering into the spirit of this strange book, it reads as though a woman were peeping into a lodge-room, witnessing the ceremonies of Freemasonry, and trying, with raptured pen, to record them! How I should like to spend a week here and read it through. The aspect of the island is peculiarly rugged and bare, which explains why it was selected as a place of exile for St. John, as the practice was to choose rocky and desolate islands for such purposes. Only one palm-tree remains upon it, although so numerous were they 1,000 years ago, that the name *Palmosa* was given to the island. So Jericho, anciently called "the city of palm-trees" (Deut. 34:3), has now *only one palm* remaining. This island, now called *Patino,* in which God opened the pearly gates of paradise, is divided equally by a very narrow isthmus, making the whole something in the shape of an hour-glass. The following engraving gives a correct idea of its appearance.

MAP OF PATMOS.

Here dwelt St. John the Evangelist, a prisoner "for the Word of God and for the Testimony of Jesus Christ (Rev. 1:9), during part of the reign of Domitian, probably from A.D. 95 to 97, when he was nearly a hundred years old.

To commemorate a place so sacred in Masonic and Biblical, I locate at Patmos, marked "G" on the map, the names of ten clergymen, eminent both in Masonic and religious relations, viz., J. H. Fitch,

Hiram A. Hunter, D. H. Knickerbacker, Robert Collier, Charles Loshier, C. G. Bowdish, John Trimble, Jr., Robert McMurdy, J. S. Dennis, William S. Burney.

I arrived at Rhodes Feb. 27, and remained a few hours off the city, but not long enough to go on shore. I recalled some facts which commend the island particularly to the attention of Knights Templars. It was the refuge of the Christian Knights when they were finally driven from the Holy Land in the fifteenth century. Those gallant warriors fortified it so strongly and defended it so gallantly as to resist for a considerable period the utmost power of the Ottoman Empire; and when at last, overborne with numbers, and weakened by famine and the unending assaults of their enemies, they were compelled to surrender, they capitulated upon the most honorable conditions, being allowed to withdraw from the island with all their possessions, and to go to Malta.

Rhodes is specially worthy of Masonic study, as being the site of the fifth of the seven ancient wonders of the world, the vast brazen image of the sun, styled the *Colossus of Rhodes*. This was seventy cubits high (about sixty-five feet). It was erected by Chares of Lindus, about B.C. 290, but only stood about sixty years, being thrown down by an earthquake, about B.C. 224. St. John doubtless saw this remarkable piece of art, and it may have suggested to his mind the allegory in the tenth chapter of his *Revelation:* "And I saw another mighty angel come down from heaven, clothed with a cloud, and a rainbow was upon his head, and his face was as it were the sun, and his feet as pillars of fire; and he had in his hand a little book open; and he set his right foot upon the sea and his left foot upon the earth."

The following engraving will give a clear idea of this island.

It is about forty miles long, and one-third the same in breadth. Its population is about 25,000, largely Greeks and Jews. The modern city only covers one-fourth the area of the ancient city, whose majestic ruins fill the vista as I gaze upon them from the deck of the ship; but few traces of the glory of ancient Rhodes are visible. Instead of the innumerable galleys that once swarmed out of yonder port, like pigeons from their cotes, and commanded all

MAP OF RHODES.

these seas by their numbers and daring, nothing has come forth
during the four hours I have lain off this harbor, save a few skiffs
seeking to take passengers ashore, a flat-bottomed barge for our
freight, and a custom-house boat manned by ten red-capped
sailors, and commanded by an indolent Turk, which rows round
and round us during our stay here to see that we do no smuggling.
Probably his "fidelity to his trust" equals that of the custom-house
officer on the wharf at Smyrna, who lazily examined my box of
figs and the roll of stationery which I had purchased in the
bazaars, and compromised all informalities concerning them by
accepting two piastres (eight cents) for his own pocket! I venture
to say that that fat gentleman yonder would "pass" a whole cargo
for a moderate compensation without a blush. The name of the
island, Rhodes, was probably derived from *Ros,* a rose, referring
to the multitude and variety of that sweet blossom here.

Waiting upon the slow movements of the customs officers, I find
time to read Acts 21, where Paul, having parted the day before
with the Christian brethren of Miletus and Ephesus, "came with
a straight course unto Coos, and the day following Rhodes," and
so on through his subsequent journey to Jerusalem, Cæsarea,
Malta, and Rome!

To commemorate a place so intimately associated with the glory
of Christian Knighthood, I locate here at Rhodes, marked "K"
upon the map, the names of ten Masons, eminent in the Christian
Orders of Knighthood, viz.: J. Q. A. Fellows, William S. Gardner,
William E. Lathrop, John A. Lefferts, G. Fred Wiltsie, Orrin
Welch, A. V. H. Carpenter, E. D. B. Porter, Alfred E. Ames, and
George L. Otis.

Remaining twelve hours at Mersina, February 29 (this being
leap year), I am told that this town lies at the mouth of the river
Cydnus, and is only six miles from ancient Tarsus, the birthplace
of the great Paul, the man who was set to be a light to the
Gentiles, that he should be for salvation unto the ends of the
earth (Acts 8:47.)

From childhood I have been accustomed to consider the Apostle
Paul the man who, next to Moses, has exercised the greatest
influence upon the minds of his race. Being thus within six miles of
his birthplace, I cannot but follow, in imagination, his footsteps
hence, to the theological school of Gamaliel at Jerusalem; thence on a
fanatical errand to Damascus; thence miraculously confounded and

converted to the Christian faith; thence on journeys hither and thither, establishing churches, bearing painful testimonials "in labors more abundant; in stripes above measure; in prisons more frequent; in deaths oft; of the Jews, five times, receiving forty stripes save one thrice beaten with rods; once stoned; thrice suffering shipwreck; a night and a day in the deep; in journeying often, in perils of waters, in perils of robbers, in perils by his own countrymen, in perils by the heathen, in perils in the city, in perils in the wilderness, in perils in the sea, in perils among false brethren; in weariness and painfulness; in watching often; in hunger and thirst; in fasting often, in cold and nakedness." (2 Cor. 11.)

Whatever one may think of *the particular cause* to which this man gave his learning, labor, and life, no one can help respecting him for the fidelity he evinced in the performance of duty. And surely no Mason who has dropped the tear over the martyred Hiram can refuse the sympathetic drop to the memory of Paul; or to share the triumphant glow which inspired him when he wrote in his old age to Timothy: "I am now ready to be offered, and the time of my departure is at hand. I have fought a good fight; I have finished my course; I have kept the faith; henceforth there is laid up for me a crown of righteousness, which the Lord, the righteous judge, shall give in that day." (2 Tim. 4.) Mighty soul! hast thou not satisfied those immortal longings ere this! Gathered with the saints at the River of Life, is not thy weariness refreshed and thy thirst satisfied?

I do not fancy Renan's views upon religious subjects, whatever he may know in science and literature, but I must say that his conception of St. Paul's character is fine and just. He describes his soul as growing great and expanding without ceasing; a man of boundless vigor, unlimited capacity, will, and action. His *Life of St. Paul* might be *expurgated,* and so made a valuable book.

We sighted the Syrian shores on the first day of March, the opening hours of spring, the day being but a few hours old. At Alexandrette, or Scandaroon, I was permitted to go on shore and remain for some hours. My first act was to fall upon my knees and praise T. G. A. O. T. U. that now at length, near the going down of my earthly sun, I am permitted to stand upon a portion of earth so hallowed by Biblical and classical recollections as this. At last my desires are gratified. One of the fixed purposes of my whole life, to visit the Holy Land, is fulfilled. Since I began to read with understanding the Sacred Writings, that purpose has been kindled into a longing desire.

5

Upon my entrance into Freemasonry (March, 1846), I formed a resolution that, if the Grand Architect of the Universe would spare my life, and open a way for me, I would as surely set foot upon the sacred soil before my Masonic career should be closed.

Alexandrette is a good place at which to enter the Holy Land, being the "northeast corner" of the Mediterranean Sea, and contiguous to several localities of thrilling memory. Around yonder point, to the northwest, a short two days' journey, is Tarsus, the birthplace of Paul. A little nearer is the battlefield of Issus, wherein, B.C. 333, Alexander achieved that victory which, in effect, was the conquest of the world. South of this, and only thirty miles from me, is Antioch, "where the disciples were first called Christians." East of me, and about the same distance, is the purely Oriental city of Aleppo; beyond which is Baalbec, and beyond that, Damascus The road over those mountains, now heavily banked in snow, has been trodden again and again by the conquerors of the earth, and by the Evangelists of Jesus. It is in every respect a good beginning point for my survey of the Holy Land.

There was once a pigeon-express maintained between this place and Baghdad.

The literary history of the world—Masonic, scientific, religious,—moves toward the *Orient,* as the march of empires to the *Occident.* Unplowed lands are the search and prize of nations; destroyed lands, of scholars. In the spread and conquests of Grecian heroes, Hebrew conception found fresh expression; the thoughts of the East were wedded to the words of the West.

To commemorate this northeast corner of the Mediterranean, marked "M" upon the map, I have placed the ten following names, all well-known in the Masonic records as Past Grand Masters, viz.: Charles W. Nash, O. H. Irish, Jno. Adams Allen, Charles Scott, S. H. Johnson, John H. Brown, Thomas R. Austin, Reuben Mickel, James M. Howry, and John B. Fravel.

On Monday, the 2d March, we called successively at Latakia, the ancient Laodicea, the seaport of Antioch, a few miles in the interior, famous now, like Gebal, only for its tobacco, and Tripoli, where at this time (1872) is stationed, as Kamiakam, our good brother Noureddin Effendi, whose portrait adorns a subsequent page of this volume.

The terraced houses of Tripoli, bathed in bright Oriental sunshine and viewed through the clear ethereal atmosphere peculiar to this classical and Biblical clime, are beautiful.

The only available passage for a railroad eastward from this coast is said to lead out of Tripoli, and from here the line has been engineered to the East Indies by an English company. The highest point to be surmounted is only 1,500 feet, and the ascent is without very heavy grades.

Going southward here the Lebanon mountains rise higher and higher as we advance. We pass ancient Gebal, marked "O" on the map, from whence some of the most experienced Masons went, at the call of King Solomon, to build the Temple at Jerusalem. Going south I begin to wonder at the narrowness of the little shelf of level land, the vast and lofty Lebanon *behind,* the illimitable Mediterranean *before* it, which, under the name of *Phœnicia,* exercised such influence upon the minds and fortunes of the human race. This nation was here when Abram came down from Mesopotamia, B.C. 1921, and even at that early period was far advanced in the knowledge of the arts and sciences. This narrow shelf was then crowded with towns and cities.

The sky so pure and bright, the moon and stars shining with such celestial beauty, the morning air peculiarly bracing and tonic—this whole journey from Marseilles has been a delicious recreation.

My reflections on approaching the coast of Syria were colored by the expectations upon which my mission was founded. To trace up to their sources ancient *habits, modes of thought, forms of speech, emblems* whose original meaning is obscured in the lapse of thirty centuries; to tread upon the sites of ancient cities, from whence sprung all science and art, and even the knowledge of letters itself; to descend into rock-hewn sepulchers, whose tenants 3,000 years ago were laid in their everlasting rest with the same symbolical rites that will some day accompany my own interment; and, above all, to read the Bible, the *whole* Bible, in the land *of* the Bible, and having and *wanting no other* Guide; to travel through the length and breadth of this country with *this* Guide in my hand; such was the work for which I girded up my loins on the 1st day of March, and invoked the blessing of the Most High that I might accomplish it, *all* of it, as I had proposed.

The night-scenes on the Mediterranean are delightful to contemplate. One of them, in which I walked the steamer's deck till midnight, can never be forgotten. It is best described in the words of another: "Above a vast hemicircle of clouds shone a little crescent moon fading into her last quarter, and like a luminous summit to an immense pyramid of shade. Over the waves she traced a path of trembling light."

Early on Tuesday morning, the 3d of March, we cast anchor in the Bay of Beirut (St. George's Bay), and so this first division of my volume ends. It only remains to add a sketch of the whole route, the chapters following not being arranged in chronological order.

ITINERARY.

Left New York		February	2d.
Arrived at Liverpool		"	14th.
"	London	"	14th.
"	Paris	"	16th.
"	Marseilles	"	17th.
Left	"	"	18th.
Arrived at Palermo		"	20th.
"	Messina	"	21st.
"	Syra	"	23d.
"	Smyrna	"	24th.
Left	"	"	26th.
Arrived at Rhodes		"	27th.
"	Mersina	"	28th.
"	Alexandrette	March	1st.
"	Latakia	"	2d.
"	Tripoli	"	2d.
"	Beirut	"	3d.

Whole distance from Marseilles to Beirut, 2,093 miles.

Reached Gebal		March	17th.
"	Damascus	"	26th.
"	Tyre	April	14th.
"	The Cedars	"	26th.
"	Joppa	May	1st.
"	Jerusalem	"	3d.
"	Nazareth	"	17th.
"	Tibnin	"	21st.
"	Alexandria	June	15th.
"	Cairo	"	16th.
"	Brindisi	"	25th.
"	Paris	"	28th.
"	London	July	2d.
"	Southampton	"	7th.

Reached New York............................ July 18th.
    "   La Grange, Kentucky........... "   21st.

A note of passage-money paid for one passenger, New York to Beirut, may be interesting to close the chapter:

Steamer, New York to Liverpool, 1st class passage		$100 00
Railway, Liverpool to London, 2d	"	9 00
" London to Marseilles, 1st	"	47 00
Steamer, Marseilles to Beirut, 2d	"	125 00

$281 00

These fares being paid in gold, I have added such a premium as makes the amounts equal to Federal currency, February, 1868.

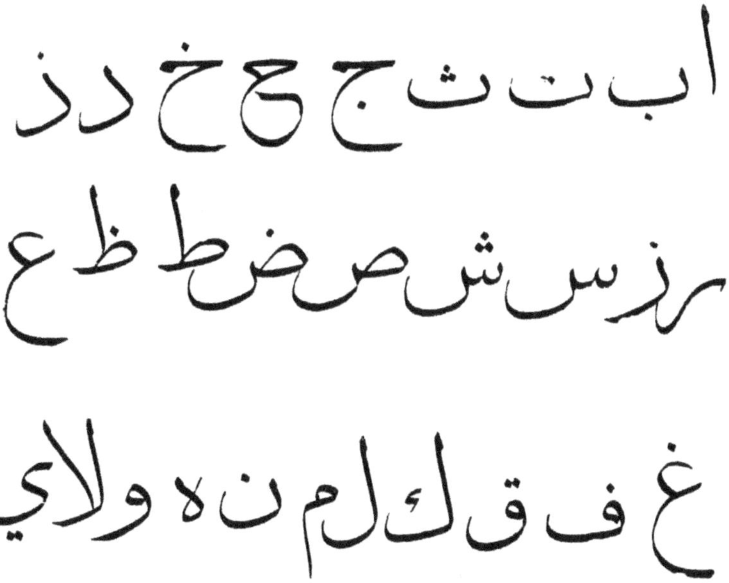

ذ د خ ج ج ث ت ب ا

ع ظ ط ض ص ش س ز ر

غ ف ق ك ل م ن ه و لا ي

THE ARABIC ALPHABET.
(Read from right to left.)

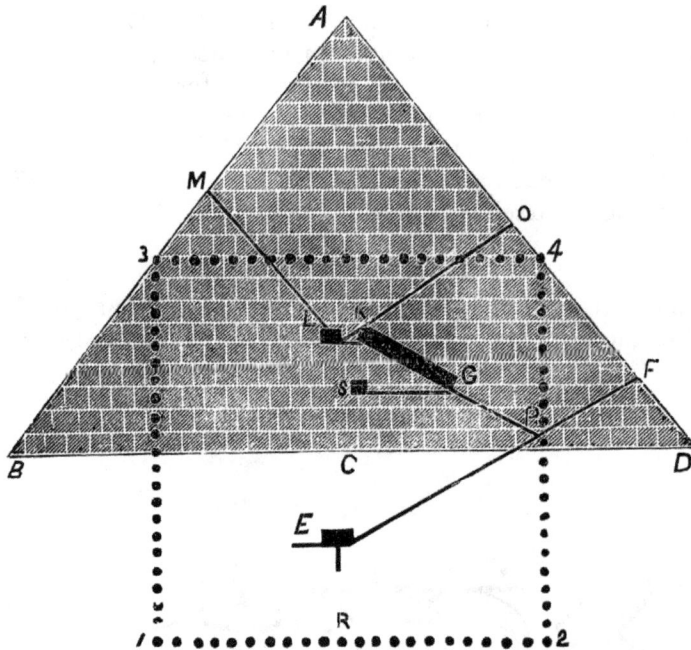

THE PYRAMID OF CHEOPS.

Original Measurements.—Length on each side is 753 feet; perpendicular height, 480 feet. 13½ acres.

Not useless: cold must be the heart
  Can linger here in critic-mood,
  And fail to recognize the good,
And look and sneer, and so depart.

Not useless: were it but to prove
  What aspirations are in man;
  Almost *divine* this mighty plan—
Almost an impulse from above.

Not useless: were it but to stir
  The sense of awe within the breast:
  What grandeur does the pile attest!
Is it a mortal's sepulcher?

Not useless: no; while life abide,
  The measure of the soul, to me.
  Its utmost stretch of thought shall be
My memories of the Pyramid!

TYRE, FROM THE SOUTH.

DIVISION SECOND.—TYRE.

Nil actum credens, dum quid superesset agendum.—LUCAN: Nothing is *done* while anything is left *undone.*

Thus saith the Lord God, I am against thee, oh Tyrus, and will cause many nations to come up against thee, as the sea causes his waves to come up.

And they shall destroy the walls of Tyrus, and break down her towers: I will also scrape her dust from her and make her like the top of a rock.

It shall be a place for the spreading of nets in the midst of the sea. Ezekiel 27:3-5.)

> Patriots were here in freedom's battle slain;
> Priests, whose long lives were closed without a stain;
> Bards, worthy him who breathed the poet's mind;
> Founders of arts that dignify mankind;
> And lovers of our race whose labors gave
> Their names a memory that defies the grave.

MOSLEM FORMS OF PRAYER.

CHAPTER V.

N Deuteronomy 34, Moses is described as taking his panoramic view of the Land of Canaan, *from the southeast,* The sacred record affirms that he "went to the top of Pisgah, and the Lord showed him all the land of Gilead ante Dan, and all Naphtali, and the land of Ephraim and Manasseh, and all the land of Judah unto the utmost sea." In a map facing a subsequent chapter may be found this stand-point of Moses, nearly east of the northeast corner of the Dead Sea, and about fifty miles east of Jerusalem.

My *stand-point* for a first view of Palestine is in the extreme *northwest* of the Holy Land, at Beirut, diagonally opposite that of Moses. Between the two lies the whole land of Canaan, our respective stand-points being about one hundred and fifty miles apart.

This city of Beirut, which constituted headquarters during my Oriental explorations, has no place in ancient Masonic history, although it is now (1872) the site of the only lodges in this country. It is indeed scarcely mentioned, if at all, in the Bible. It is interesting to Freemasons, however, as lying on the south side of the beautiful sheet of water which I shall style the Bay of the Rafts. It is called here *St. George's Bay,* from the fabulous encounter of that hero with the dragon, said to have occurred at this place. In Spencer's *Faerie Queen,* the long-drawn battle is graphically described. My name of "The Bay of Freemasonry, or Bay of the Rafts," is derived from its ancient use for making up the rafts or "flotes" of cedars provided by King Hiram for Solomon's Temple. They were sent out from this place, as I shall show in subsequent pages, to the port of Tyre, one hundred miles south. My headquarters at Beirut were in the hospitable mansion of Brother Samuel Hallock, a member of Lodge No. 9, Philadelphia, Pa., and as thorough and genuine a Mason as ever old Number Nine turned out from its busy *Atelier.* He accommodates me with a room, for which I supply myself with a few pieces of furniture; and so in all my sojourning through Holy Land I have an abode to which

I can turn as *home*. Many a profitable hour did we two stranger Masons enjoy in mutual confidences and the interchange of useful thoughts. Brother Hallock is the electrotypist of the printing-house connected with the American Protestant Mission, and a contributor to the New York *Journal of Commerce*. The condition of Freemasonry in Beirut, and the elder lodge (Palestine Lodge No. 415), will be fully detailed in a subsequent chapter.

I commence this second division, therefore, at Beirut, where I landed, March 3d, 1868. The place, as remarked above, has no particular mention in Biblical or Masonic history, yet its traditions imply that it is one of the oldest of Phœnician cities. Having the best harbor that exists along the coast (although at the best it is only third-rate), Beirut has been adopted as the seat of the general consulates of all the great powers. Being connected by a turnpike road eighty-four miles long with Damascus, and by telegraph with points north, south, and east, it enjoys the best business of the coast, and has risen rapidly from a population of 10,000 to 60,000. This growth more resembles one of our Western railroad towns than anything in this old-fogy land. Beirut has outgrown gates and walls, and is spreading abroad into the suburbs on all sides. Spelled in the geography "Beirut," it is properly pronounced *Bay-reet*. Its latitude is 33° 54' north, longitude 35° 29' east of Greenwich. On the east runs the river *Beirut,* called by Pliny, eighteen hundred years ago, the *Magoras*—in dry seasons, however, a mere creek. The town stands, like Joppa, upon a head-land, called in Arabic *Ras,* (meaning head), which projects about five miles into the sea from the foot of Mt. Lebanon.

This head-land, with the mountains behind it, is what would first strike the eye of Phœnician sailors coming, as I did from the westward. For here the mighty Lebanons exhibit their vast proportions, five to ten thousand feet high, in the most impressive grandeur. I doubt whether all Syria affords another such view as these white-capped heights, striking the clouds with their hoary tops and planting their roots deep at the earth's very center.

My first work, upon landing at Beirut, was to forward by mail to each of several hundreds of old correspondents, a specimen of the "productions of the land" in the form of an *Olive Leaf.* I learned that it was gratifying to them, both as a veritable token from the Holy Land and an appropriate *tessera* of brotherly remembrance. Upon my return home in July, I went heavily laden with "the searching of the land," even more than the twelve spies who "came unto the brook Eshcol, and cut down from thence a branch, with one cluster of grapes, and bare it between two upon a staff, and brought of the pomegranates and the figs." (Num. 13:23.) These and hundreds of other specimens I bore to my friends.

Each of the olive leaves sent from Beirut was accompanied by a copy of the following lines:

THE OLIVE-LEAF.

Lines composed to accompany olive-leaves plucked from the groves of Beirut, in the Holy Land, March 6th, 1868, by Brother Morris.

And the Dove came in to him in the evening; and lo, in her mouth was the Olive-leaf plucked off; so Noah knew that the waters were abated from the Earth. Gen. 8:11.

> Like wandering Dove, whose restless feet
> Could find no solid landing-place,
> I pluck this Olive-Leaf to grace
> A memory very pure and sweet.
>
> This was the ancient *type of peace;*
> The wrathful flood was overpast:
> The gladsome sun beamed forth at last;
> The Ark on storm-tossed ways did cease.
>
> Then from the Olive-Bough, the Bird
> Plucked this green leaf with mystic care,
> And to the Patriarch's fingers bare
> The missive with its high accord.
>
> Dear Friend, to you this Olive-spray
> I send, the Messenger of love;
> It speaks a sentiment above
> All other language to convey.
>
> The Olive,—glory of this land:
> Our Ancient Craft from this expressed
> *The Oil of Joy,* that shone, and blessed,
> In hours of rest, the laboring Band.
>
> The deadliest hands, upraised in hate,
> Before this gentle missive drop;
> The direst discord then must stop;—
> The Olive speaks, the floods abate.

> All this and more I fain would teach
> From this bright ancient verdant text;
> Take it with all the words annexed;—
> Be yours the sermon that they preach!

The "words annexed," in the last stanza, were quotations from Deut. 8:8; 1 K. 5:11; Ps. 52:8 ; 128:3, etc. A space was left in the printed copy to fasten the olive leaf upon, that so it might be framed and preserved.

At the conclusion of the last chapter I gave an itinerary of my entire travels while in Syria, Palestine, and Egypt. In the making up of this volume, however, I follow the natural order of a Masonic narrative thus:

DIVISION FIRST.—*Tyre,* the royal seat of King Hiram.

DIVISION SECOND.—*Gebal,* the home and school of Hiram the Architect,

DIVISION THIRD.—*Lebanon,* the source of the cedars.

DIVISION FOURTH.—The Bay of the Rafts where the cedars were floated.

DIVISION FIFTH.—*Joppa,* the port of trans-shipment.

DIVISION SIXTH.—The clay-grounds, the site of Hiram's furnaces and foundries.

DIVISION SEVENTH.—Jerusalem, the site of the Temple. * * * Tyre and its surroundings therefore come foremost.

On the morning of April 13th, at 7 o'clock, I started on horseback with an Arab servant, one Hassan Mardby, riding a second horse and carrying my *impedimenta* of blankets, overcoats, books, provisions, working tools, etc., etc., to visit the city of Tyre, now called *Soor* (or Tsoor). Having been nearly six weeks in the country, during which I had made four excursions, I felt posted upon the best method of travel, and the quantity of baggage, etc., essential to it. My plan, which I recommend to all travelers who do not fancy making themselves slaves to dragomans, is to hire two horses and their owner for a certain number of days (in this case, six); he to subsist himself and his horses and be his own quartermaster. The stipulated price with Hassan was twelve francs a day for the whole, equal at the then rates of gold to $3.25 per day. Besides this, my own board and lodging cost me about $2.00 per day. So, for $5.00 per day, or thereabouts, I go as an independent traveler, stopping *when* I please and *where* I please, and *as long* as I please, with none to molest me or make me afraid. Hassan stipulates to collect specimens for me, do my interpreting, and serve me in every way that he is ordered.

The road from Beirut to Sidon runs for five miles over singular red sand-hills, the only deposits of the sort on the coast. It is suggested by some that this sand is blown into the sea, near the mouth of the Nile, in Egypt, brought by the prevailing currents to this shore, where the wind seizes it when dry, and drifts it westward like snow, threatening some day to submerge the whole city of Beirut. I took considerable quantities of this desert-sand, the only link now connecting Egypt and Phœnicia, once so nearly related in religion, symbology, and all the details of ancient Freemasonry.

This road over the sand-hills was described six centuries ago, as a *good, deep road,* and never was one better named. For miles the horses stepped fetlock deep in the sand.

I had already inaugurated the practice of naming the best-marked bays on this coast after Masonic emblems, and dedicating them to American lodges. There is one such at the distance of five hours (about fifteen miles) from Beirut, shaped much like a Trowel. This, therefore, I dubbed *The Bay of the Trowel,* and dedicated to the genial and generous brethren of Manchester, Iowa; Indianapolis, Indiana; and La Grange, Kentucky, between whom there runs a line of Masonic similarity, closer than blood-relationship. This bay will be identified by travelers by the circumstance that, just south of it, as you rise the hill on the old Roman road, there is an ancient watchtower of squared stone, by some attributed to Queen Helena, but probably Phœnician in its make. Here a great battle was fought, B.C. 218, between the Syrians under Antiochus the Great, and the Egyptians under Ptolemy. Coins of these two kings will be found figured in this book. The latter was defeated with fearful slaughter. The *Bay of the Trowel* is a charming little nook of water, its shores abounding in shells and sponges, and in every way worthy its dedication.

Not far from it is a Moslem tomb, called *Neby Younas,* the tomb of Jonah; and here, in a little bay close in front of the tomb, is the traditional *disgorging place* of the disobedient prophet, who went *southwest* when ordered to go *northeast.* Close by the tomb is a Khan, or tavern, more strictly a café, or coffee-house, where several times in passing I spent a quiet hour, sipping the native coffee, and writing up my notes. Shall I record the memorandums made of "what I resolved to do every day while in this country?" For four months, I acted upon the plan following, and *fortes fortuna adjuvat,* as Pliny Senior said, just before he was gobbled up by Mount Vesuvius:

"A person visiting any strange country should possess practiced powers of observation, or his travels can present no useful results. The ordinary grade of tourists' observations upon Holy Land is scarcely above an infant's. He should be skilled in trees, plants, rocks, customs, costumes, peoples; but those who have written upon this country seem to have known nothing of such things when they landed, and but little more when they sailed away. What drivel makes up their books! I have hundreds of them in my library, and it is enough to give one the dyspepsia to look through them. For my part, I am resolved today, and for my coming four months, to bring forty years of reading, study, and travel to bear on the scenes before me. I will examine the earth and rocks, and see what they are made of. I will consider this ancient country as a naturalist's museum, and get my money's worth out of it. As a French *savant* said, when congratulated upon his vast discoveries, I will simply *look* and see things as they are made, and tell the story as it is."

But this Neby Younas Khan (literally Jonah House) is *vox prœterea nihil,* only a sound. It is a local liquoring place. All it has is coffee and smoke, the coffee coming to you in Turkish cups, Liliputian indeed, the smoke through the great water-pipe styled narghileh (nargeely), and the tomb itself recalls the old Barnum story of Captain Cook's war-club. Finding that every other museum had the club that killed Captain Cooke, Barnum procured it also! For there are already *five tombs* where Jonah is buried, besides this one, viz.: at Sephoris, Hebron, Tyre, Alexandrette, and the one near Babylon, described by Layard. Were I opening a coffee-house, near the Dead Sea, for instance, I should build a Jonah's tomb too. It would pay. I forgot, after all, to mention Jonah's tomb at Raphiah, near Egypt, where the Mohammedans report a visit from this celebrated traveler.

At Neby Younas I saw the first truly sick person I had come in contact with in the Holy Land. His broken cough, sunken eye, hollow cheek, fetid breath, and despairing face, were so many indications of rapid approach to the grave, that recalled a thousand sad memories of dying friends. These people have a perfect passion for medicine, and he insisted on having some of me. I gave him half of the ginger-root I always carry in my pocket.

The hard, smooth beach around Jonah's Bay by Neby Younas tempts me for the first time today into a gallop. How invigorating

ROMAN STANDARDS.

ANCIENT LAMP.

ANCIENT POTS AND JARS.

THE ALMOND.

METHOD OF SHROUDING A CORPSE.

the Western breeze, the solemn swash of the wave, the shriek of the gull, the flight of my sinewy horse. I am twenty years younger again. But no, my hat blows off. In dismounting to get it I turn my ankle. In remounting I break my pocket-comb, and so the rest of the day's journey is done in a slow walk.

As I sat imbibing the coffee of Jonah's Tavern in a steady draught, for nothing less than the Fellow-Craft's number will suffice a drinker from these cups in an Oriental *café*, I quietly asked the landlord: "Khanjee, where along this coast did the great fish discharge the prophet Jonah?" The Khanjee had learned this part of his lesson well. His fishy eyes brightened up. He took his hands, figuratively speaking, out of his pockets, scratched himself, and then pointing the dirtiest finger in the direction of a little bay a hundred yards in the southwest, answered, "Howadji, yonder is the spot."

It *was* a suitable place, and showed a good taste of selection either in the whale or the Khanjee. So, after looking pleasingly towards it, and emptying a few more cups, I abandoned the examination in chief and began the cross-examination:

"But, Khanjee, how do you *know* that is the place?

Here was a puzzler. The query had never before been propounded the stupid fellow. Dropping his head and returning his hands, figuratively speaking, into his pockets, he sat for a moment a monument of inanity. Then, with a spirit of repartee that I had not supposed was in him, he raised his head, and answered:

"But, Howadji, if *that* is not the place, where is the place?" And so the subject dropped.

Continuing my journey, sometimes along the hard beach of this sea without tides, sometimes in the deep sands a little ways back, sometimes across the rocky points of the hills, I came, about 4 P.M., in sight of the crenulated battlements of the Gothic chateau of St. Lois, and then of the city of Sidon itself, surrounded on the land-side by groves of fruit-trees. Sidon abounded, of old, in citrons, oranges, pomegranates, saffron, figs, almonds, sugar-cane, coriander, and other rare objects of desire. It was called of the Phœnicians *Sidon,* in regard to the abundance of fish. The neroli, or oil distilled from orange blossoms, made so abundantly here, is so far superior to that extracted from orange-peel, that thousands of trees are stripped of blossoms every season, which never go to maturity of fruit, to supply the wants of the perfume-makers.

The orange groves surrounding this ancient city are so charming

6

as to make the poor old place look by contrast worse than it should. The fruit is abundant, large, and delicious. For four months they hang on the trees ripening, and the germ, the bud, the blossom, the green fruit and the ripe fruit cluster, side by side, as I have seen an old New-England family on Thanksgiving-day grouped together in the third and fourth generation; or, more graphically, as I have seen in an old and lively lodge of Masons, working on the First Degree, the bud, the flower, and the ripened fruit in the three classes of Craftsmen there assembled. An old author, Sandys, translates from the Odyssey (2:1) an appropriate passage, which I transcribe as follows:

> These at no time do their rare fruits forego,
> Still, breathing Zephyrus makes some to grow,
> Others to ripen; growing fruits supply
> The gathered, and succeed so orderly.

Here, too, "the acacia waves her golden hair," large trees, ten to twelve inches in diameter, lining the avenues of the city on the east. In a subsequent chapter I will describe this tree, famous in Masonic uses.

I reached Sidon about 4 P.M., and spent the night, by invitation, with Rev. Wm. M. Eddy, one of the American missionaries stationed here. The father of this hospitable gentleman was made a Mason, in company with Pliny Fisk, about the year 1824, preparatory to embarking for the Holy Land as a missionary. They united with our ancient Order under the hope that through its cosmopolitan character and influence their holy work might be expedited. The present Mr. Eddy is not a Mason, although possessing the general spirit of one. He made my stay at his house, both going and returning, home-like and sweet.

In the bazaar may be seen oranges by the cargo, piled in huge heaps, figs, grapes, olives, pomegranates, dates, almonds, raisins, peaches, apricots, limes, lemons, plums, quinces, the most luxuriant bananas, and other fruits in variety and abundance.

On returning to Beirut some days afterwards, I was conducted by a smart little son of Mr. Eddy, since sent to America to be educated, to the establishment of a potter, outside the gate. A view of this ancient art, esteemed honorable in 1 Chron. 4:23, and made by Jeremiah (18.) and other Bible writers a subject of imagery, cleared up to my mind a number of Scriptural allusions. The workmen, however, were an unsightly set; three Arabs with only four good eyes among them. I observed here that every man you meet is wearing the dress in which "he lieth down at night"—a fact that explains various things, entomological and otherwise, that at first glance puzzles you in the East. As I sat there watching the chief potter, I read Romans 9:21: "Hath not the potter power over the clay, of the same lump to make one vessel unto honor and another unto dishonor?" and my answer was in the affirmative.

There is no lodge of Masons at Sidon, but quite a number of the craft live here, whom I met the following June at Beirut. It is a city well adapted for a lodge, high and ample chambers being found in abundance, and a resident population that would afford an abundance of good "timbers" (materials) for Masonic work. I hope to learn that a lodge ere long will be established here. In the hope of such a desirable consummation, I locate here the following names of worthy and eminent Masons: O. H. Main, G. B. Van Saun, Henry Hitt, George W. Chaytor, A. R. Whitney, Jesse B. Anthony, Washington Galland, B. F. Simmons, Luke E. Barber, Elwood Evans.

Spending a Sabbath-day here in the following June, I had some genial hours in that Christian family, remembering the days of old, meditating on all his works, musing on the work of God's hands, (Ps. 143:5), and heard a very lovely song of one that hath a pleasant voice and can play well on an instrument (Ez. 33:32).

Sidon has been four times taken, plundered, and dismantled. On one occasion (most memorable) it was absolutely reduced to ashes and cinders, and the privilege of sifting out the *débris* for the precious metals found in them was sold to an enterprising peddler for a considerable sum. One of these fearful conflagrations of Sidon may be compared in several points with that unparalleled fire which reduced Chicago, Oct. 8-11, 1871, to dust and ashes, turned sandstone into sand and limestone into gas, and melting the most obdurate metals as wax. Alas, when I made notes of Sidon, I little thought that the city which Miss Bremer had styled in her admiration "the home of Loki and Thor, the supernatural powers," could become in any way a parallel in desolation. At 8 o'clock, Tuesday morning, April 14, I left Sidon for Tyre. In three hours I arrived at Sarepta, named in 2 Kings 8, and believed to be the city alluded to in Matthew 15, and Mark 7., where Jesus cast out a demon from the widow's child. This is the first ground sacred to *Jesus* upon which I had trodden, and

I spent several hours at Sarepta, collecting specimens, and exploring the ruins. In my chapter on the Itinerary of Jesus I will refer to it again. There is not a house now standing at Sarepta, where was once a large city. I cut the Square and Compass with my chisel upon a huge ashlar belonging to some ancient temple, in the shadow of a tamarisk-tree, and loaded my servant with a hundred weight of marble and granite fragments, shells, bits of glass, etc., representing this once famed city.

I took occasion while here to examine the spear of an Arab sheikh, one of the Bedouin persuasion, who stopped to drink water at Ain Kanterah. It was fourteen feet long, ornamented near the top with two large black tufts feathered. It was armed with a sharp iron ferule at the lower end, so as to enable its holder to strike it into the ground at an easy blow. This is truly a formidable weapon, but its owner handled it as gracefully as a Charleston dandy handles his cane. The Bedouin himself was of low stature, raw-boned, tawny, having a feminine voice, and a swift and noiseless pace, like one of our moccasin-shod Indians of the West.

His horse was a genuine specimen of the Arab stock. He was larger than ordinary American horses, had an eye full of fire and intelligence, head well set on, forehead rather straight, fine at the withers, quarters well turned, body round and good, legs clean, pasterns long; a serviceable-looking animal. The following conversation gives a good idea of the rider:

Howadji. Where would you rather live?
Bedouin. In the desert.
Howadji. Why in the desert?
Bedouin. Because I am the son of the desert, and not the son of the city.

He said the race of horses he was riding had been four hundred years in his family, and that no money could buy this one. He was broken to travel only at the *walk* and *gallop,* the unnatural and ungraceful movement of a *trot* being deemed unworthy of an Arab courser.

The life of this Arab is one of danger and distress from his youth. He wears upon his face the features of his ancestors, "wild men," who in the days of Moses, and of Mohammed, twenty-one hundred years later, dwelt in tents and conducted their flocks to the same springs and pastures as their fathers of the earliest times.

At Sarepta I caught a view of *Jebel,* old *Jebel-es-Sheikh,* Mount

Hermon, fifty miles in the southeast. His snowy cap gives him prominence in the clear blue sky. The mountain seems from this point like a pale blue snow-capped peak peering over the intervening ranges of Lebanon. How often in Masonic lectures have I quoted the passage from David:

"Like the dew of Hermon and like the dew that descended upon the mountains of Zion; for there the Lord commanded the blessing, even life forevermore."

How often have I sung the paraphrase of the good Giles F. Yates, whom I knew so well in 1855-7:

> "Like Hermon's dew, so richly shed
> On Zion's sacred hills!"

In a future chapter I will give a full description of this mountain, Freemasonry's grandest type of brotherly love. But here I remark that the amount of moisture the earth receives from this great water-cooler and atmospheric regulator must be immense, when we consider the acknowledged fact that a single inch of water spread level over *one acre* of ground weighs one hundred tons!

To this dewy thought the poet alludes:

> When the West
> Opens his golden bowers of rest,
> And a moist radiance from the skies
> Shoots trembling down.

I am loth to lay aside the theme. Hermon is the mountain that passes into the clouds and joins to the upper air; one of "the eternal hills" raised to an elevation that cools, condenses, and returns the moisture ascending from the parched earth, sending it back in grateful dews, rains, and springs.

Sarepta, now without a winepress, a grapevine, or a winedrinker, was once celebrated for the quantity and quality of its wine. But a man hunting his morning dram in 1868 would be as badly off as at Grinnell, Iowa, where the "drummers" are said to carry full flasks with them, or do worse.

> Along this dreary waste, where once there rung
> The festal lay which smiling virgins sung;
> Where rapture echoed from the warbling lute,
> And the gay dance resounded—all is mute.

> *Macaulay*

My noontide at Sarepta did not pass without an appeal to the muse. Amidst these undecipherable ruins, the very *débris* of ruins, the sight obstructed by deep holes dug by the laborers to get materials for the buildings at Beirut, the gushing water of Ain Kanterah flowing at my feet, the shady tamarisks embowering me, the romantic mountains behind and the sea before me; withal, the affecting story of Jesus on the open page on my knee, it was easy to pen the following

LINES AT SAREPTA, APRIL 14, 1868.

Led by a hand invisible,
    I come at last to view the place
Where Jesus broke the power of hell,
    And gave the tortured child release.

And can it be my wearied feet
    Press the same earth that Jesus trod?
Oh, happy hour, oh, bliss complete,
    Oh, promises fulfilled of God!

These mountains looked on Christ that day;
    This fountain murmured in His ear;
The sky serene, the glassy bay,
    The charming flowers—all, all were here.

How looked the Savior? oh, to see
    His face divine! Was it in grief
At human pain, and misery,
    And want, and sin, and unbelief?

Beneath this tamarisk-tree I muse;
    Grant me to drink the spirit in
Of that great hour, nor let me lose
    One feature of the wondrous scene:

The mother clamorous with her plea,
    The apostle's cold, impatient word,
Faith's trial and sure victory,
    And oh, the utterance of the Lord!

Cease, murmuring fountain, cease thy flow,
    And let His utterance reach my soul:
"Great is thy faith, O woman, go!
    Already is the child made whole!"

The chain of evil power released,
    The demon's fetters broke at last;
The very crumbs of Jesus' feast
    Better than all the world's repast.

No longer to restrain my tears,
   Such gratitude these drops recount:
'Tis surely worth my fifty years,
   This noontide at Sarepta's fount!

Sing, murmuring waters, lulling streams;
   Roar, foamy breakers, on the shore;
Broken Sarepta's fleeting dreams,
   The vision will return no more.

Far o'er the western sea my heart
   Wanders from lone Sarepta's shrine;
I rise, and on my way depart,
   Never to view these scenes again.

But *I shall meet Him!* yes, I know,
   My inmost being this assures,
Where founts celestial smoothly flow,
   And perfect blessedness allures.

Onward and onward moments fly,
   My sands of life make haste to run;
Lord, grant me favor ere I die,
   To leave no appointed task undone!

Leaving the sight of that mountain, along by whose base passed the man, 4,000 years ago, in whom the whole Church was contained, and the sweet spring that to the latest hour of my life will be associated with romantic memories, I passed on southwards over Phœnicia, a narrow strip of plain rarely extending more than a mile or two in width from the shore, backed by ranges of mountains, piled tier upon tier to the snow-covered crests of Lebanon; remembering that between Sidon and Tyre, where there is now not only no city nor village, but *not even a house,* there were once sixteen prosperous towns! As the distance is a scant twenty-five miles, the suburbs of these contiguous towns must have been very much restricted, the wall of one city almost meeting that of the next.

The sight of fishermen standing naked in the hot sunshine, waiting to cast their hand-nets at the approach of schools of fish, interested me greatly. A basket of the Mediterranean fish had been shown me at Khan Younas. When I saw what severe labor the poor fellows undergo, I sung my favorite lines:

God bless the laboring man, I pray;
Make sure his wages every day;

> Afield, afloat,
> Afloat, afield,
> Make honest work its wages yield.

I think there is always a group of gazelles feeding in the meadowlands a few miles north of Tyre—meadows so rich that one of the old pilgrims declared that those bad roads were fully recompensed to him by the fragrant savors of rosemary, bay, hyssop, marjorum, and other perfumed plants. Altogether, I passed here three times, and always found gazelles. They are the *Gazella Arabica,* two feet high at the shoulder. The Scriptural names are Ariel, Dorcas, Tabitha, etc. Their airy and graceful forms are very attractive. The first group of them that I saw stood motionless, sharply defined against the background of the sky and hills. After a moment they threw their heads up, and bounded away like the flight of birds.

A few miles north of Tyre I crossed the "willful headlong river," called now Nahr-el-Kasimiyeh (but you will not pronounce it as the Arabs do in fifty times trying! I got a sore throat and wasted two miles trying to catch it from Hassan.) The words mean, "the Dividing River." It is, no doubt, the old Leontes, and a beautiful stream it is, closely resembling the Jordan, as I afterwards saw, and about thirty feet wide. The bridge is a single arch, very neat and strong. The current is so swift that, seeing a dead duck floating under the bridge, I ran to the other side, but the duck had got past me on its way to the sea.

The heavy load I had imposed upon Hassan necessitated the poor fellow's walking all the way from Sarepta to Tyre, some eighteen miles' distance. I named a charming little bay, distant about six miles south of Sidon, *the Bay of the Square,* from its peculiar form, and dedicated it to the Freemasons of Wheeling, Western Virginia; Omaha, Nebraska; and Waterloo, Iowa. This bay may be known from an ancient watch-tower standing directly on the edge of the bay at its southwestern extremity.

Arrived at Tyre about six o'clock. Found accommodations in the house of a native family, who were extremely attentive to my wants, for a moderate price. In my visit to Damascus, two weeks before, I had procured from the Governor-General, Mohammed Raschid, a document directed to all governors of towns and villages throughout Syria, commanding them to see that I was furnished with suitable accommodations for myself and servants, together with guards in going from place to place, etc.. and all at reasonable prices. This document, called a Buyuruldi, which was secured strictly through Masonic influence, was of service to me in every place I visited. I have also a Firman from the Sultan himself, at Constantinople, *Abdul Aziz,* sent me through the kind influence of Brother John P. Brown, Secretary of the American Embassy there. The two together never failed to secure for me all the attentions I needed, for a reasonable consideration.

The following is a translation of the Firman referred to. It is written upon a thick and substantial sheet of paper, about twenty-four by thirty inches in dimensions, at the top of which is the name of the Sultan, Abd-ul-Aziz, in a peculiarly complicated anagram, called a *Toogra:*

"Imperial Traveling Firman of Sultan Abdul Aziz Khan, granted in favor of Robert Morris, addressed to H. E. Mohammed Raschid, Pasha, Governor-General of the Vilayet of Syria.

"To my Minister and very glorious Councilor, the model of the world; the regulator of the regulations of the universe; he who directs the public interests with rare wisdom, and settles all important affairs with singular judgment; he who strengthens the edifice of the Empire and secures its prosperity; who invigorates the columns of felicity and magnificence; in fine, who is the especial recipient of the power and favor of the Most High Sovereign of the universe; the Governor-General of the Vilayet of Syria; wearer of the First Class of the Decoration of the Mejidiah, Mohammed Raschid, Pasha and Vizier; may the Most High prolong his grandeur!

"When the present sublime Imperial Document reaches you, know that the American Legation at the Capital of my Empire, has reported that an American citizen, Robert Morris, a traveler, is desirous of traveling from Constantinople to Syria, *via* Beirut, Sham Shereef (Damascus), Khuds Shereef (Jerusalem), Yaffa (Joppa), and their vicinity, and asks that while on his way, or residing in any place, he be protected and aided. In each point of view, I have therefore issued the present Noble Order. You, therefore, the Governor-General before mentioned, will see that the aforesaid traveler, wherever he may go or desire to stay on his journey, be treated with respect and regard; that he be provided with horses, according to the regulations, and receive guards to enable him to pass through all dangerous places. Be careful to provide for the execution of my present Sublime Command. Written on the 7th of moon of Zil, etc., etc., A. H. 1284."

CHURNING BUTTER.

DANCING DERVISHES.

CHAPTER VI.

THE CITY OF KING HIRAM.

RRIVED at the city of Tyre about sundown, I entered through the opening where until recently a thick and strongly guarded gate stood, and I felt the force of the expression of Isaiah: "Her gates lament and mourn" (3:26). Many of her houses are desolate, even great and fair, without inhabitants (5:9). Her fleets of richly burdened ships and ranges of strong forts were but so many incentives to the Grecian conqueror, Alexander, who, flushed with his conquest over Darius, came down here, B.C. 332, with that army well styled "Invincible," the rich and powerful city of Sidon surrendering to him without a struggle, and even joining her fleets to his to aid in the subjugation of sister cities, and these massive buttresses of Tyre and the hosts of gallant men behind them could not preserve her from her predicted doom. As Isaiah had written nearly four centuries before, "The day of the Lord was upon every high tower, and upon every fenced wall, and upon all the ships of Tarshish" (2:15). *Gravis ira regum semper*—the wrath of kings is always dreadful; and so this magnificent city proved under the hand of Alexander. She had been a stronghold, in which silver was heaped up as the dust and fine gold as the mire of streets; but the Lord cast her out and smote her power in the sea, and she was devoured with fire (Zech. 9:2).

I was lodged, after vacillating between the military barracks, the room over the blacksmith's shop, and somebody's convent of male sisters, in the house of a very clever man, a Christian, who lived in his second story, to which you go up by stone steps on the outside, and divided the ground-floor between stables for his asses and a drinking saloon, in which his oldest son sells arrack and brandy to the soldiers. It was a private house, but for a very moderate price he took me in and provided well for my wants.

Tyre is practically a city *under ground*. It lies, like Jerusalem, twenty to fifty feet beneath a *débris* of many centuries. Formerly

separated from the shore about one half-mile, this space was
filled in by Alexander the Great when he captured the city, B.C.
332, and so became an isthmus. I saw the place on the beach
where that fearful butcher of his fellow-men crucified 3,000 of the
gallant and patriotic defenders of Tyre. The location is now a
peninsula joined by a long sandy isthmus to the mainland. Its
latitude is 33° 18′ N., longitude 35° 12′ E. from Greenwich. The
ancient word "Tzur" means *a rock*. The city is said, by Josephus,
to have been founded 230 years before the corner-stone of
Solomon's Temple was planted, that is, B.C. 1242. It was never a
republic, like most of the ancient commercial cities, but always a
monarchy. As early as the time of Solomon its people had became
famous for their skill in manufactures and arts; and Hiram, the
widow's son, was called from Gebal by King Hiram, of Tyre, to
prepare all the sacred emblems for King Solomon's Temple. The
distance traveled by him from Tyre to Jerusalem, by way of Joppa,
was about 130 English miles.

I advise my readers to take the first Sunday afternoon they
have at command, and read critically the following passages
giving the best *biblical history* of Tyre. This is better than for me
to crowd so many quotations into my book.

Joshua 19:29; Judges 1:31-32; 2 Samuel 24:7, and 5:11; 1 Kings
7:13-45, etc.; 2 Chronicles 11:16; Joel 3; Amos 1:9-10; Jeremiah
25:22, etc.; Ezekiel 26, 27, and 28; Zechariah 9:3.

I collected very large quantities of relics, coins, funeral lamps,
tear-bottles, and specimens of various kinds, at Tyre and vicinity.
Having the friendship of the American Vice-Consul, Mr. Jacob
Akkad, and of the commanding officer of the garrison, Captain
George Demetry, and being well posted in the objects of which I
was in search, I let no opportunity escape me to secure both facts
and things. I could not hear of a single Freemason at Tyre.

About three miles southeast of the city there is a remarkable
spring of water, styled, in Arabic, Ras-el-Ain, the Head of the
Fountain. There is also a fountain of this name at Baalbec. The local
tradition at Tyre is, that when Hiram had done all the work which
he contracted to do at Jerusalem, and received the wages of "corn,
wine, and oil" stipulated, King Solomon showed his gratitude for the
skill, patience, and fidelity of his Phœnician allies by building, at his
own expense, this fountain-head, with a costly aqueduct, to convey

the water into the city. Sufficient portions of the aqueduct remain to prove that it was a magnificent structure. Amongst the rest, there is a fragment comprising *three perfect arches,* beautifully devised, and finely preserved, which stand at the eastern point of the isthmus that connects Tyre with the mainland, and attract the eye of every traveler approaching Tyre, either from the north or south. These three arches, erected according to tradition by the Masonic Pillar of Wisdom, King Solomon, for the Masonic Pillar of Strength, King Hiram, I have ventured to dedicate as follows:

I. The Eastern Arch to De Witt Clinton, first G. G. High-Priest of the G. G. Royal Arch Chapter of the United States.

II. The Middle Arch to Albert G. Mackey, in 1859-65 G. G. High-Priest of the same body.

III. The Western Arch to John L. Lewis, in 1865-8 G. G. High-Priest of the same body.

The present population of this renowned city is between 3,000 and 4,000; about one-half being Arabs of the Metawileh tribe, the other half Christians of various Roman Catholic sects, and a sprinkling of Protestants. The old wall is built across the isthmus, and its gate is still in use, more as a convenient military post than anything else, for the town is in no sense protected by it. Among the ruins is a block of stone bearing the unmistakable mark of the Phœnician architects (the *bevel* or *rebate*), which measures seventeen feet in length. A double column of red granite lies among the ruins of the ancient cathedral at Tyre, six feet in diameter and twenty-six feet long! This is the largest single piece of stone, artificially wrought, that I saw in the Holy Land. One of the former governors of Acre, twenty-five miles below here, about seventy years ago, undertook to have it removed there, but all the skill and machinery his engineers could apply to it failed to stir the monument. Do not let the visitor to Tyre fail to visit this pillar.

Never, surely, was a country where money is *worshipped* as here. It is the true *idol* that Mohammed left after destroying the others. The poet Virgil, had he known it, would have located his *auri sacra fames,* the accursed greed of gold, in these Oriental parts; and we may well propound Virgil's inquiry, *Quid non mortalia pectora cogis?*—to what crimes dost thou not impel a mortal's breast? Propertius justly embodies the thought in the words, *Auro pulsa fides, auro venalia jura, Aurum lex sequitur;* for such is the condition of Syrian morals, as all writers, native and foreign, admit. Those who have heard our good brother, the moralist, Abd-el-Kader, preach to his theological classes at Damascus, affirm that his denunciations against this *greedy covetousness* of the people are severe. The derision in which he holds up the miser to his auditors is terrible, while the consolation he gives to the generous is inspired both by the precepts of his own Koran and the Holy Scriptures of Masonry.

We perceive, in Acts 9:19, that a church was established here dating from the martyrdom of St. Stephen, proto-martyr; and the only edifice whose ruins have not been entirely removed, or so much disarranged that the plans are entirely lost, is the old Christian Cathedral built about A.D. 310,

In this now ruined but once glorious church, whose apsides are used by the natives for privies, once lived the historian, *William of Tyre.* Among all the great men whose names are associated with this Phœnician, Roman, and mediæval city, none are more worthy of remembrance than William. Here, too, preached Eusebius, and his Dedication Address, still preserved in his works, reads like the hundreds of Masonic dedicatory effusions, to which pile I myself have added some weak specimens.

The Christian Father Origen is also buried here, and here molder the bones of Frederick Barbarossa, of Germany, whose splendid career was brought to an ignominious close by a trifling accident. The funeral procession of Frederick, as it came down from Tarsus, past Gebal, Beirut, and Sidon, some three hundred miles, must have awakened memories among the Freemasons of that grander funeral of Hiram of Tyre, two thousand years before.

Many natives of Tyre are afflicted with sore and inflamed eyes, either by reflected heat upon this calcareous soil, or by the sharp, acrid nature of the soil itself, when raised in dust. Judging from the exquisite specimens of engraving on precious stones that are dug up here, I should think the old artists had better eyesight than I see here now.

A writer has accumulated in one sentence a strong sketch of Tyre: "Prostrate and broken columns, dilapidated temples, mounds of buried fragments, mark the once proud and populous city."

I saw in the bay, north of the town, the graceful, gull-billed *tern* (*Sterna Anglica*), which loves calm and shallow water, and in its presence gives omen of fine settled weather; also, the Adriatic gull (*Larus melanocephalus*), quietly riding in the scarcely perceptible swell. These natural history facts and others I derive from Brother

H. B. Tristam's most readable work, "The Land of Israel," not republished in this country. It is full of allusions to birds, beasts, flowers, and reptiles. He has also published a "Natural History of Palestine," which I bought in Jerusalem.

About a century ago, Tyre was destroyed, with its inhabitants, by an earthquake. In the rebuilding, the houses are mean, both in style and composition; low, built of rough stones, arched within, flat on the roof, and inclosing a quadrangle. The walls surmounting the roof for battlements are wrought through with pottery tubes to catch and strike down the refreshing winds, at the same time they conceal the persons on the roof from neighboring eyes. Often the roofs are covered with mats and hurdles. Since the awful convulsion of the last century, the houses are built smaller and lower than formerly, recalling forcibly the passage relative to Zacynthus, "The streets unpaved, the buildings low, by reason of the often earthquakes whereunto the town is miserably subject."

Somebody had presented an Arab here with a phrenological bust (or may-be he stole it), endorsed on the back, "Description of character, with advice as to best pursuit, self-improvement," etc., and had told him it was a likeness of *Jeff. Davis,* leader in the American rebellion, and it was pleasant to see the fellow's *awe* as he pointed it out to me. But it was useless to explain the "sell" to him, although I, who have known Mr. Davis ever since 1848, could enjoy it.

Esculapius was associated with the city of Tyre, and so every barber's pole in the universe is in some sense a Masonic emblem referring to this place. The god of medicine and patron of the barber's pole had listened to the rustling of leaves, the tones of water-fall and wave, the songs of birds, and the hum of insects, in this then beautiful land, until he learned to make music for himself. I thought of him as I sat on the rocks one twilight evening, the sea and sky of such even and utter blueness that any visible horizon is out of the question.

Among my pleasant memories of the days spent in Tyre was a visit to the good Jacob Akkad, for very many years United States Vice-Consul of Tyre. He signalized my call upon him by raising the flag of our country upon the staff that dominates the roof of his two-story house. As in all these dwellings, his family reside in the second story, the lower being used for stables, etc. In a neighboring house a woman was having that sorrow in travail because her time had come (John 15:21), which so moves the sensibility of every feeling heart. I sent up a heartfelt petition that she might have a safe delivery.

In the center of Akkad's room was a stool (souffra), with as many cushions around it as there were guests. The servant brought in sweetmeats, sherbet, coffee, and cigarettes. Each of us took a mouthful of the jelly from the common spoon, drank a mouthful of sherbet, and supped a cup of the thick, black, highly-sweetened coffee, very aromatic. These people never parch coffee until about to use it, and make it as muddy as chocolate, because they *pound* the grains instead of *grinding* them. They stir it up slab with a spoon. The coffee-cup is a trifle larger than half an egg-shell, and, being very hot, is placed for use in a metal receiver called a *fingan,* so as not to burn the fingers.

In the Vice-Consul's office I saw a sheikh (pronounced *shek*) signing an agreement with another sheikh (pronounced *shek* also), by simply dipping his finger in the ink and pressing it on the paper, as I did many a time in boyish days. The *seal* thus formed resembled a squashed bed-bug. Somehow, it reminded me of Mephistopheles and the fellow who sold his soul's salvation, and sealed the parchment with a drop of blood. I should like to see the original papyrus agreement between Solomon and Hiram, doubtless signed and sealed in this very town, and compare it with the sheikhs' contract, which was something concerning a sucking colt and a small patch of barley.

But the good Yacob Akkad, intent as he was on hospitable cares, was not unmindful of the adage, *oculus domini saginat equuum—* the eye of the master fattens the horse, as his frequent visits to his laborers in garden and orchard testified. He works quite a number of hands, and, it is said, gets his money's worth out of them.

Leaving his house, I met four men walking in a line behind each other, each one barefoot and with drooping head. The leader had lost a friend by death, and his companions were mourning with him for company. This was like David when he walked barefoot with his head covered, in his sorrow, up the Mount of Olives (2 Sam. 15:30).

There is no end to the legends related of Tyre. One was told six hundred years ago of a stone still lying in front of the gate on which Jesus *sat* when he preached (for all Oriental discourses were and are preached *sitting,* and so the Worshipful Master should always remain *seated* while giving instructions to his lodge!), and as He sat there He forgave the Canaanitish woman, as the Scripture sayeth.

In times of old, Tyre was the metropolis, the New York of the Mediterranean coast. Everything to be shipped was shipped from this port, and what they could not purchase they made. Commerce, for ages, could only be done by these people; they were truly what the British for some centuries claimed to be, *lords of the seas*. The perusal of the 27th chapter of Ezekiel illustrates this point thoroughly. Written about B.C. 590, it is as minute as a Philadelphia merchant's invoice of goods shipped, and, had I space here, I would insert it entire. It was from Tyre that the *itinera mercatorum*—the roads of the traders, all diverged, and in the oldest atlas they are marked in red ink. They ran from Tyre into the heart of Africa, skirted the Mediterranean coast, wound through the Straits of Gibraltar along by Portugal and France, penetrated Arabia; in short, searched out every place in the world where products could be exchanged for products, and profits made.

As a fitting group of American Craftsmen to associate with this illustrious locality, I enroll the ten following: John J. Crane, Robert D. Holmes (deceased), Robert Macoy, C. M. Hatch, H: J: Goodrich, H. D. Hosmer, Albert G. Hodges, James R. Hartsock, Rev. C. F. Deems, R. F. Bower.

I ought to be sorry to record that I gave utter and irreconcilable offence to a Roman priest here, a man with both feet bare, a cable-tow four times round his unwashed body, and his head shaved, by asking him why it was that he was called *Father* when he had no children. The disgust with which he contemplated my question prevented him from waiting for the *backsheesh* which I was about to give him.

A story more modern and better established than that I have just given, illustrates the biography of a former governor of this district, whose name, I am sorry to say, I have forgotten. He had orders from the Vali (Pasha) at Damascus, to secure a certain number of conscripts for the army, but could contrive no ordinary way to catch them. So he gave out that he was opening the old water-channels that connect the city with Ras-el-Ain, and offered large wages to all who would come and dig. In this way the unsuspecting and hard-fisted farmers of the locality were deluded. They came in a hundred strong, and just as they got fairly into the trenches digging, a detachment of troops surrounded them, seized, bound, and brought them before the Regimental Surgeon for inspection. To his credit, it is said, he *passed* them all except two, who had but one leg each, and one who had *psoriasis* (if that's the word for itch) horribly; the latter was put in jail till he got well. The rest were "grafted into the army," and are probably there yet. The whole thing, as a joke, was considered a success.

On another page I have alluded to the great Syenite column, six feet by twenty-six, that lies in the courtyard of the ancient Basilica. This glorious shaft, a worthy representative of the Broken Shaft buried with such mourning rites at Jerusalem, is own brother to those in Egypt, proceeding from the same quarry of Syene, and equally related to the granite beams of the King's Chamber in the Great Pyramid of Cheops. The Egyptians seem always to have thought of *gigantic* constructions when they used this Syenitic granite. The measurements of those beams just named will be given hereafter.

It is a very singular fact that in the ruins of Konyunjih, near Mosul, in Mesopotamia, there still exists a slab of stone on which is delineated this ancient city of Tyre, with its palm-trees, fishes, a man carrying a banner, etc., etc., with really artistic minuteness.

It is pleasant to see how little *language* a man can get along with when he tries. The first time I was at Tyre, I always had to call Hassan to communicate my most familiar wishes to the family and visitors. The second time I came to Tyre, Hassan had been left behind at Tibnin with a foundered horse, and I can say in strictness that there wasn't a man in the place with whom I could exchange a single thought. But it made no particular difference.

I shall never forget the second night I spent in Tyre. The officers of the garrison, very friendly and courteous men they were, had come up to smoke their pipes and talk to the great American Howadji. After entertaining them as well as I could, I played the *Freemasons' March,* that oldest of Masonic tunes, to which many generations have stepped briskly, returning from fraternal graves, my flute being the same silver-lined instrument inscribed, "Presented to Rob Morris, K. T., May, 1855, by the Freemasons of New York," an event that elicited the since celebrated flute-story from John W. Simons, and a good many other stories from the genial fellows who were gathered round Thayer's table that night at 383 Broadway. Will the reader believe me, after those heathens had admired the silver bands of the flute, and amused themselves with the way I puckered up my lips in making the *embouchure,* they turned away without being in the least impressed with the music itself! This was my first and last attempt at emulating Ossian E. Dodge while in the Holy Land.

During my stay here, I experienced a touch of the *Khamseen,* that celebrated desert-wind known in its perfection as the *Simoom* and *Sirocco.* Afterwards, at Beirut, I felt its effects more severely. It excited nervous irritation, made me dyspeptic, shortened my sleep, and gave me slow fever. Its name, denoting fifty, implies the length of time it usually traverses the desert. The amount of dust carried before it is suggested by a storm December 24, 1870, in Clinton County, Indiana, in which 600 tons of dust fell within a radius of twenty miles; so says Prof. J. Twigley, before the American Association for Advancement of Science, at its session in 1871.

The custom of keeping a lamp burning all night in the house is universal throughout the East, and to me quite disagreeable; so I blew mine out at Tyre every time. Stevens describes a man living in a tomb on the banks of the Nile, who keeps his night-lamp going as steadily as the one in the lighthouse on the Skellig rock. An irreverent friend has suggested, in view of the *buggy* condition of the native houses, that may-be this lamp is burned to deceive the insects as to the time. If so, it was a failure.

An hour's nooning, seated upon the tradition-stone I have named, in the shade of the fountain outside the town, was spent in making notes, some of which I group together here for want of space.

An old man coming for water, so very ancient that, in Tennyson's words: "The man was no more than a voice in the white winter of his age." The sight of the prostrate columns yonder covered with nets placed there to dry, recalls the lines:

> Like the stained web that whitens in the sun,
> And purer grows by being shone upon.

The extremely fine work I see upon the ancient gems exhumed here every day, cornelian, jasper, emerald, chalcedony, etc., remind me that recent researches at Konyunjih show the use of *the microscope* in ancient times. Minute lens and specula of magnifying lens have been found. A cone engraved with a table of cubes, too small to be visible by the naked eye, is now in the British Museum, found in Persia, and attributed to a very ancient date. Some of the lodges in America are named after those Oriental gems, viz., Cornelian, 40, Minn., etc., far more appropriate than that of High Log Lodge, Grasshopper Falls Lodge, Bear Wallow Lodge, and the like. Maundeville, A.D. 1322, wrote that here, at Tyre, was once a great and good city of the Christians; on the sea-side many rubies were found, and the well is here of which Solomon wrote, "a fountain of gardens and a well of living waters." (Song 4:15). The great use made of blue dye in this country, in coloring the cotton and woolen fabrics so universally worn, dates back to B.C. 1500, and is suggested in the Mosaic code, where the lawgiver requires every Jew to wear a fringe of blue. The poet has referred to this color in the lines—

> The deep, deep blue, the melancholy dress
> Bokhara's maidens wear, in mindfulness
> Of friends or kindred, dead or far away.

A fellow passed me, so small, he ought to carry weights in his pockets to keep from being blown away, as the poet Philetas of Cos did, B.C. 330. The style of Arabs who people this place, called *Metawely,* very much resemble the Jew in features; but they are more fanatical than the descendant of Abraham ever was. I had picked up a plow one day belonging to a Metawely, and he cursed me by all his gods for touching it, swearing that he would never use it again. He called me *kelb* (dog), and I called him *kelb* back again. The hatred of this miserable race against the Christians is foreshadowed by David, in the expressions, "They that sit in the gate speak against me; and I was the song of the drunkards" (Ps. 69:12); "a brutish man knoweth not" (92:6), and scores of others. But it would do no good to quote David against a Metawely, so I simply called the fellow *kelb.* Methodius, Bishop of Tyre, was martyred here A.D. 1311. They tell a story of the "Ladder of Tyre" yonder, that a bold fellow once jumped from the top of it, in the style of our Sam Patch, and swam to Tyre! I was offered today an ancient marble statue dug up here a few years since. It is that of a female figure, a matron, full size, moderately robed, and in admirable preservation. Were it not for the difficulty of transportation I would not have begrudged the price. The number of lodges in America named from *Tyre* is very large. I instance a few, as derived from my "Old Prudence-Book" of 1868: No. 73, Maine; Nos. 187 and 198, Texas; No. 18, Michigan; No. 5, Mississippi. In England, No. 315 derives its title from the same source.

The name of *Hiram* has been still more extensively adopted in lodge nomenclature, as witness No. 4, Kentucky; No. 28, Illinois; No. 21, Virginia; Nos. 18 and 88, Ohio; No. 70, Louisiana; No. 42, Indiana; No. 10, D. C.; No. 7, Tennessee; No. 5, Florida; Nos. 21 and 51, Georgia; Nos. 40 and 98, N. C.; Nos. 105, 144, and 449, New York; No. 103, Maryland; No. 51, Wis.; No. 7, Iowa; Nos. 1 and 12, Ct.; No. 43, Cal.; No. 110, Michigan; Nos. 37, 78, and 89, Canada; No. 42, Alabama; No. 9, New Hampshire; Nos. 81 and 261, Pa.; Nos. 14, 30, and 95, Mass., etc.

I spent a quiet and solitary hour on the sea-shore reading Acts 21, in which the visit of Paul to Tyre, some 1,800 years ago, is described. I had been in Paul's tracks for several weeks, and become somewhat familiar with his movements. In the present instance, he was on his way from Miletus and Rhodes to Jerusalem, and had "landed at Tyre, for there the ship was to unlade her burden." He remained here seven days, and as he departed all the Christian people followed him out of the city with their wives and children, and kneeled down on the shore and prayed. To peruse the account on the spot gives it a reality.

In closing this chapter, I would say that, while there are no members of the Masonic society resident here, quite a number of native gentlemen, civil and military, and some foreigners, "have long entertained" the necessary "opinion," and were a lodge opened, either in *Sidon*, twenty-five miles north, or *Acre* (or Caifa), the same distance south, these would become petitioners. And while Tyre is scarcely adapted, by the character of its population, for a permanent lodge, those who, like myself, feel that the home of Hiram should not be entirely overlooked, could unite in the plan in regard to Ephesus, which resembles Tyre in the same particular. There, while the lodge is nominally located at Ephesus, the members all live at *Smyrna,* twenty-five miles north, and go together, by day, on the regular occasions, to open the lodge at Ephesus and do its regular work. So the brethren at Sidon, Acre or Caifa, might have a lodge at Tyre without being residents here.

COIN OF ALEXANDER. STRUCK AT TYRE.

KABR HAIRAN.

CHAPTER VII

N Tuesday, April 14th, as I have said, I arrived at Tyre, after two days' hard horseback exercise from Beirut, and early next morning, April 15th, went out five miles east, to view the celebrated monument of antiquity, called by the natives *Kabr Hairan,* meaning Hiram's Tomb. In the survey of this old relic I spent the day, returning late in the afternoon to Tyre, and made a second visit to it a month later.

The way thither is through the only gate of Tyre now in use. There all day long a group of men sit smoking, chatting and enjoying their *dolce far niente,* as the Italians have it. Nobody reads newspapers in Tyre; this group of observant idlers is so thoroughly posted in all Tyrian news, that what they do not know isn't worth knowing. They discussed me for several days in all my bearings, and I hope came to favorable conclusions. A splendidly carved marble sarcophagus, once of large cost and rare beauty, lies a hundred yards in front of the gate, degraded now to the uses of a horse-trough! On its four corners are rams' heads beautifully carved. It much resembles a sarcophagus that I saw at Gebal a few weeks since.

Everybody I meet here has a welcome word and sign for me, except those ill-conditioned brutes, the *Metawelies.* They are on a par with the publicans, of whom the Great Teacher said, "if ye salute your brethren only, what do ye more than others?" (Matt. 5:47), for they pay no sort of attention to my most graceful of *salaams,* or my cheeriest of "how are ye, my bully boys?" with which I greet them day after day, with unwearying patience.

I crossed the isthmus connecting the island, on which Tyre was originally built, with the mainland, now only a dreary waste of white sand, drift upon drift. This isthmus seems to have been crowded as far into the water as it can be. I do not think that even the display of fishers' nets spread over the costly marble and granite ruins of Tyre affect me so much as this cheerless waste of sand. If a man would have a lesson of the mutuability of earthly things, let him stand upon the eminence where the sand-billows have drifted the highest, and read from the twenty-seventh and twenty-eighth chapters of Ezekiel such passages as these: "Thou sealest up the sum, full of wisdom and perfect beauty. Thy borders are in the midst of the seas, thy builders have perfected thy beauty," and other paragraphs of this nature; then cast his eye over yonder poor crumbling ruins called *Tyre*, its magnificent church reduced to fragments of walls whose enclosures are used for the vilest purposes, its triple walls broken down, its incalculable traffic comprised now in a few small boats. But the theme is too painful to contemplate this charming April day, so I turn my back upon it and ride eastward, cheerily whistling "Over the hills and far away."

I have nowhere seen such a number of camels as throng this road. They are loaded chiefly with charcoal from the mountains, each of the huge beasts carrying two immense hampers filled with it. Fuel is so scarce in this country that no one thinks of making a fire for any purpose save cooking, and for that charcoal is the cheapest. It is shipped from here, up and down the coast in considerable quantities by the small coasting-boats. Many of these camels, however, are loaded with millstones, made of the hard, black, indestructible basalt that lies heaped in petrified billows east of the Sea of Galilee. These are also shipped in different directions, and form one of the leading articles of Tyrian traffic. As the daily "Prices-Current" of Tyre are not published, I could not find out the *ruling* prices of millstones.

The plain of Tyre, after I passed the sand-drifts, is extremely beautiful. The barley, the principal grain raised upon it at the present day, is at this time about a foot high, and looks promising. Doubtless a good system of farming would develop immense crops here; but the native plows only *tickle* the ground; no manure is used, the seed is scantily sown, and everything is done in a barbarous way. Many groves of mulberry-trees, attract the eye, and I learn upon inquiry that an attempt is making to raise silk here. I apprehend, however, that the unhealthiness of the neighborhood will always make against that. They have the "chills and fever" around Tyre as bad as in the Wabash swamps of Indiana.

In about one hour's ride I begin to ascend the hills, the snow capped Lebanons seeming to rise just before me, though I know very well that a day's hard riding will not more than reach them. This is one of the most charming days I have seen in Palestine, and my very soul and lungs expand as I draw in this invigorating breeze from Lebanon. The mountain-sides are black with goats, the valleys are white with sheep; the voices of their keepers, calling to each other, reach my ears, mellowed in the distance; and as I observe the little lambs tenderly cared for by their rude Arab keepers, I feel involuntarily to burst forth, as the shepherd-poet at Bethlehem: "The Lord is MY shepherd, I shall not want. He maketh ME to lie down in green pastures; he leadeth ME beside the still waters. He restoreth my soul." May I never be less submissive to HIM than these poor creatures are to their shepherd.

Seeing a large upright stone on the top of a high hill on the left, I leave my horse with Hassan, and scramble up to it through a field of barley. It is an immense block, having a chiseled groove down the side, and, as I afterwards learned from the well-posted missionary, Dr. W. M. Thomson, at Beirut, author of *Land and Book,* it is part of an *olive-press.* But the very olive-trees that supplied the fruit for this press have disappeared; even their stumps are gone, and the press has been, perhaps, a thousand years out of use. Near it is a large cistern cut in the solid rock, well cemented on the sides and bottom. A few steps lower down are the remains of a house in which, to my delight, I found large patches of a Mosaic pavement, so interesting to a Freemason. This led me to call for my chisel and hammer, and I soon collected enough of the *tesseræ* from this *checker-work* to fill my carpet-bag. I afterwards collected stores of similar objects from Mount Zion at Jerusalem, Mount Olivet, and other places. There are no remains of Hebrew, Greek and Roman periods so numerous as patches of the Mosaic pavement.

Going on eastward I open my eyes widely to catch the first view of Hiram's Tomb. I make my two servants fall behind me in the road. No one shall point it out to me. I press on, having two eagles a mile or so overhead, leaving on my right and left great fragments of pillars, and chapters, and sarcophagi, and deep pits cut in the solid rock for the reception of water for Hiram's men in the older times. I pass by groves of olives and figs, my kingly birds watching me keenly. I see, upon a steep hill to the right, the town of Hanaweigh, built, as Dr. Thomson informs me, out of the ruins of the country seats   and   summer   residences   of   Tyre's   merchant-princes that once crowned these hills. I meet caravan after caravan of camels, with their loads of charcoal, so suggestive of that Masonic *fervency* on which I have so often expatiated. But I have no eyes for these things; I am watching out for Kabr Hairan, the sepulcher of Hiram.

Yonder it is! It is worth coming all the way from the United States to see it. There is no mistaking it. Nowhere in all the world have my eyes beheld anything like it. A little to the right of the hill I have been ascending, and a little beyond its apex, the regal fowls looking down upon it so knowingly, it stands out clear and sharp against the mountains beyond; its grand sepulchral stone crowning the structure with a massiveness proportioned to the whole. At last I see the burial-place of the great *Huram,* who was ever a lover of David (1 Kings 5:1), and who rejoiced greatly when he heard the words of Solomon, and who wrote generously in acknowledgment of the royal missive announcing Solomon's intention to build an house unto the name of the Lord his God: "Because the Lord hath loved his people, he hath made thee king over them. Blessed be the Lord God of Israel that made the Heaven and the earth, who hath given to David the king a wise son, endued with prudence and understanding, that might build an house for the Lord, and an house for his kingdom" (2 Chronicles 2:11-12). Here lies the Master of the Widow's Son, whose tragic history seasons every instruction of the Freemason's lodge.

Riding more slowly towards the resting-place of "this friend of Solomon," my legionary birds drawing still nearer to me, I love to think that the Phœnician monarch selected his burial-spot in his own lifetime, in accordance with the customs of his country; that the plan of the structure itself was drawn by the pencil of Hiram, the Widow's Son; and that the munificence of King Solomon bore the expense of its erection. Thus our first three Grand Masters were united in this as in other matters interesting to all Masons.

Kabr Hairan bears about it unmistakable marks of extreme antiquity! So says Dr. Thomson, and so say I. It is impossible to disprove the local tradition which assigns this tomb to the great Tyrian King. So says Prof. H. B. Tristam, and so say I. Much more will be *felt* than *uttered* by a Masonic visitor. Standing on the farthest point eastward, from which a clear view of the sea-coast is obtained, and at a spot where the brightest Orient rays come down from the Lebanon ranges, it is the place of all others for the Tomb of Hiram. The *genus loci,* the spirit of the locality, is worth a hundred cold arguments based upon tape-lines and parchment records. This *is* the monument of Hiram; yonder eagles know it, and I know it.

This remarkable structure consists of fifteen stones arranged in five layers of the ordinary hard cretaceous limestone, solid, firm, and durable, without any marked lines of stratification, and inclining to a crystalline structure. As I know very well from having cut into it with my chisel, it is very hard, the outer surface blunting the edge of the chisel much like glass.

I. There is a layer of stones, about fifteen feet by ten, resting upon a bed of *grout* (that is, small pebbles intermixed with mortar) six or eight inches deep. There is only one stone (near the northwest corner) belonging to this foundation exposed; but I take it for granted that this layer extends equally under the whole monument. This one stone is thirty-four inches in height, and four feet long. No one would have supposed that this underground layer existed but for the fact of there being a deep-arched well or cistern on the north side of the monument, in digging which a part of the substructure was exposed, together with the bed of *grout* on which that first tier of stones rested. Not finding any accurate measurements of Hiram's Tomb in the books, I took them myself, and verified them on my second visit here.

II. The *first layer* of the monument aboveground consists of four stones, numbered in my plan A, B, C, D. This tier is four feet high.

III. The *second tier* consists of five stones. These exactly cover the lower tier, breaking the joints, as will be seen in the plan, in an artistic manner. They are numbered in my plan E, F, G, H, I. This tier is two feet ten inches high.

IV. The *third tier* consists of four stones. These extend in every direction several inches outside the tier below, forming a pleasing sort of ledge or cornice. These are numbered K, L, M, N, in my plan. This tier is two feet eleven inches high.

V. The *fourth tier* is monolithal, consisting of *one great block* of stone. It is numbered O in my plan. Out of the center of this, in the top, was hewn a huge cavity for the reception of the corpse. Elevated as this sarcophagus is—more than ten feet from the ground—it presents a majestic appearance. I climbed up to it by the help of an Arab, who mounted before me, gave me his hand, and by nature's own grip assisted me to rise, my two eagles looking curiously down upon the effort. Walking round to the eastern end of it, upon the cornice already described, I found that the burial-place had been burst open and was empty.

VI. The *fifth tier* aboveground is also monolithal, making the lid of the sarcophagus. This lid was made with a tenon on the under side, which fitted into the cavity or coffin of the sarcophagus. I could not tell whether cement was used in fastening down the lid, but presume that it was. The dead body was reached by those who rifled it by going to the top of this lid, bursting down a large piece at the northeast corner, then breaking out the end of the sarcophagus immediately below it; so an entrance was effected. By this hole I looked immediately into the place where once lay the body of King Hiram, empty, no doubt, more than two thousand years. Afterwards I crept into the coffin itself, and measured it.

The great stones of this monument being considerably shattered, probably by earthquakes, I found it easy to procure pieces of them, and did so abundantly. I cut the *Square and Compass* deeply on the monument, on the second tier, eastern end, near the northeast corner. My Arab servant, Hassan, having seen me do this at other places, labors under the impression that *it is my name,* and tells everybody so. I also exposed my Masonic flag there. I sum up in the following tables all my measurements of this curious relic of antiquity:

SIZES OF THE FIFTEEN ASHLARS IN KABR HAIRAN.

[See Drawings.]

		FROM EAST TO WEST.	FROM NORTH TO SOUTH.	HEIGHT.
First Tier.	A	3 ft. 0 in.	8 ft. 8 in.	4 ft. 0 in.
	B	7 ft. 1 in.	4 ft. 4 in.	4 ft. 0 in.
	C	3 ft. 11 in.	8 ft. 8 in.	4 ft. 0 in.
	D	7 ft. 1 in.	4 ft. 4 in.	4 ft. 0 in.
Second Tier.	E	5 ft. 0 in.	6 ft. 0 in.	2 ft. 10 in.
	F	6 ft. 4 in.	2 ft. 10 in.	2 ft. 10 in.
	G	7 ft. 8 in.	2 ft. 11 in.	2 ft. 10 in.
	H	4 ft. 1 in.	5 ft. 9 in.	2 ft. 10 in.
	I	4 ft. 9 in.	5 ft. 9 in.	2 ft. 10 in.
Third Tier	K	3 ft. 9 in.	9 ft. 11 in.	2 ft. 11 in.
	L	4 ft. 0 in.	9 ft. 11 in.	2 ft. 11 in.

	M	3 ft. 9 in.	9 ft. 11 in.	2 ft. 11 in.
	N	3 ft. 7 in.	9 ft. 11 in.	2 ft. 11 in.
Sarcophagus.	O	12 ft. 11 in.	7 ft. 8 in.	6 ft. 0 in.
Lid.	P	12 ft. 11 in.	7 ft. 8 in.	3 ft. 6 in.

DIMENSIONS OF THE RESPECTIVE TIERS.

	FROM EAST TO WEST.	FROM NORTH TO SOUTH.	HEIGHT.
First Tier.	14 ft. 0 in.	8 ft. 8 in.	4 ft. 0 in.
Second Tier.	14 ft. 0 in.	8 ft. 8 in.	2 ft. 10 in.
Third Tier.	15 ft. 1 in.	9 ft. 11 in.	2 ft. 11 in.
Fourth Tier.	12 ft. 11 in.	7 ft. 8 in.	6 ft. 5 in.
Fifth Tier.	12 ft. 11 in.	7 ft. 8 in.	3 ft. 6 in.

Total height .... 19 ft. 8 in.

CONDITION OF THE RESPECTIVE BLOCKS.

A, considerable piece out of the upper and northeast corner. B, piece out of upper and southwest corner. C, piece out of the upper and southwest corner, and lower and northeast corner. D, in good condition. E, northeast and southwest corners much shattered. F, cracked through by earthquake. G, broken at upper and northwest corner. H, best condition of all. I, cracked by earthquake. K, very large piece gone at north end under side. L and M, in good condition. N, shattered at south end. O, broken open at east end. P, large piece burst off northeast corner. My chiseling of the Square and Compass was done on block E, on the east face.

The coffin or cavity in the great sepulchral stone is in length 6 ft. 3 in.; width, 1 ft. 10 in.; depth, 2 ft. 2 in.

DEDICATIONS OF THE FIFTEEN ASHLARS.

A   William Preston, of England, Masonic Ritualist.
B   William Hutchinson, of England, Masonic Moralist.
C   Thaddeus Mason Harris, of United States, Masonic Moralist.
D   Thomas Smith Webb, of United States, Masonic Ritualist.
E   George Washington.

F   Benjamin Franklin.
G   The Duke of Sussex, long Grand Master of England.
H   Pliny Fisk, first (Masonic) Protestant Missionary to Palestine.
I   Wellins Calcott, of England, Masonic Moralist.
K   Edward A. Guilbert, of United States, Masonic Journalist.
L   John W. Simons, of United States, Masonic Jurist.
M   D. Murray Lyon, of Scotland, Masonic Journalist.
N   The Earl of Zetland, long Grand Master of England.
O   The Illustrious Dead of the Masonic Craft.
P   The Zealous Living Workers of the Masonic Craft.

The honor of these dedications has, I think, been fairly earned by their respective recipients, as the history of Freemasonry, in earlier and later times, abundantly proves. The workmen themselves are such as the Royal Grand Master would have hailed worthy associates, and "their works do follow them." Will it not bring many Masonic pilgrims to this sacred locality, when there may be grouped together around the great pile so many of the richest associations in our history?

I am confident of having the approving sentiment of every Mason of intelligence in adopting *Kabr Hairan* as the best remaining monument of the most ancient Masonic period. Here, I think, was laid the body of our Grand Master, Hiram, King of Tyre. The resting-place of Solomon is lost; that of the Widow's Son (like that of Moses) "no man knoweth;" but here, in these fifteen huge stones, we have the burial-place of the *Pillar of Strength!* Surely it was good for me that I came here; and I cannot but approve the enthusiasm of that thoroughly good Mason, Brother E. T. Rogers, Master (in 1868) of the Palestine Lodge, No. 415, at Beirut, who projected, years ago, a Masonic visit and picnic to this memorable fane.

I lump together a number of notes of measurements and descriptions made on the spot. The accumulations of earth and *débris* from the field on the north have been walled up around the monument a few feet distant, leaving an alley on the three sides of it. Otherwise the tomb would be concealed (as the great wall of Mount Moriah is) one-half its height. The object of this extraordinary care, so different from what we generally observe in this country, was to preserve the water-cistern for use. This cistern is six feet north of the monument, and reached by stone steps from the northwest corner of the tomb. Go down eastward by four narrow steps to a platform, six by

four feet; continue eastward by four broad steps, six feet long;
then turn northward and go down five narrow steps to the water,
two feet deep. Arched entrance to the cistern is four by ten feet.
Cistern itself is nearly hemispherical in shape, fifteen feet from
north to south, by ten feet. It is plastered with gravel-stones, set
in cement and shards of old pottery. Water cool and good, much
liked by the villagers of Hanaweigh. No signs of tools can be seen
where the break was made into the sepulcher. The sides of the
coffin or cavity have three notches on the north side and one on
the south, but none overhead. I readily crept in there, through the
break made by the robbers, perhaps of Sennacherib, B.C. 715, or
thereabouts. No hieroglyphics of any kind are on the monument,
so far as I could discover. From the top of the monument there is
a fine view of Tyre, the plain of Phœnicia almost to Sidon, and the
Great Sea beyond. A steamer was passing southward, bound for
Egypt, and quite a number of sail-vessels. Lizards abound in the
tomb, and Brother H. B. Tristam (in *Land of Israel*) killed a large
adder that lay asleep, with its head exposed, at the joining of the
tiers. But I saw no snakes around here. Hyssop grows abundantly
in the cracks, and makes quite a green and tufted appearance for
old Hiram.

Kabr Hairan is usually described as standing due east and west,
but by the aid of the compass furnished me by my old friend,
Brother Edward Jewell, of Louisville, Ky., I conclude, either that
the variation here is fifteen or twenty degrees from the true
meridian, or that the monument is not oriented to face the four
points of the compass.

While taking measurements and making notes, an old man,
head of a party of camel-drivers, stopped and looking on for a few
minutes, asked, through my servant, "what for all my writing?" I
told him I had come six thousand miles over yonder blue sea,
pointing to the Mediterranean, which stretched out majestically
at our feet, and that when I return home I shall tell my friends all
about the great and curious Kabr Hairan. This pleased him, and
he cried out, with the accompanying gesticulation, "*Tyeeb, Tyeeb*"
(good), and went on his way to tell his companions of the *Melican
Howadji* who had come so far over the sea to look at Kabr Hairan.

In the hot hour, at high twelve, I sat in the shadow of the tomb
and wrote these lines:

KABR HAIRAN.

(Written April 15th, 1868, at the Tomb of Hiram.)

Eastward from Tyre, where the sun
    First gleams above gray Hermon's side,
They brought thee, when thy work was done,
    And laid thee here in royal pride:
They brought thee with the noblest rites
    The wisest of our Craft enjoined; (1)
Before thee soared the mountain heights,
    And thy loved ocean-isle behind.

The Cedars bowed their kingly tops
    As Hiram, Chief of Masons, passed: (2)
O'er Lebanon's all-snowy slopes
    The eagle screamed upon the blast: (3)
Westward the foaming sea was crowned
    With snow-white sails returning home:
Their Sea-Queen (4) glorious they found,
    Where thou, their King, should no more come.

Where in thy lifetime thou hadst reared
    This Tomb, befitting one so great, (5)
They bore thee, Monarch loved and feared,
    And laid thee in thy bed of state: (6)

---

(1) See note 10 for an explanation of this. King Hiram was traditionally buried with the Masonic Honors, as prepared by the pen of King Solomon.

(2) Formerly all these offshoots and spurs of the Lebanon Mountains were probably covered with cedars, though now the nearest grove of which I have any knowledge is thirty or forty miles north of Hiram's Tomb.

(3) As I write these lines, two of those noble birds are soaring in the clear sky above me.

(4) For many centuries the City of Tyre was the commercial metropolis of the world. The title "Sea-Queen" is therefore highly appropriate.

(5) It was the custom of the princes and rulers of Phœnicia to prepare for themselves great and costly sepulchers, even while living; the hills around KABR HAIRAN are full of these, but all shattered and empty.

(6) To comprehend the splendor of Hiram's burial procession, read that of Alexander the Great, as detailed in Rollin's Ancient History.

They closed thee in with cunning art
    And left thee to thy well-earned fame:
"Twas all the living can impart,—
    A tomb, a pageant, and a name.

Loud was the wail on Zidon's hill,—
    Her Sages mourned thee as their own: (7)
Loud the lament on far Jebale
    Her wisest Son of Light was gone: (8)
The ships of Tyre bore the word
    On every wind across the main,
And white-robed craftsmen wept their lord
    And strewed the mystic leaves again. (9)

Nor these alone;—on Zion too
    A Brother joins his tears with theirs:
King Solomon, to friendship true,
    The grief of Tyre fitly shares:
His matchless pen such words indites
    Of true report and sacred woe,
That to this hour, Freemasons' rites
    Within his wise direction go. (10)

The centuries wore apace; and changed
    The kingdom of each royal Sire:
Ephraim from Judah was estranged,
    And Zidon separate from Tyre: (11)

---

(7) At the period of Hiram's reign, the city of Zidon, which lies about twenty-five miles north of Tyre, was under his rule.

(8) Jebale (styled in the Scriptures Gebal) is about seventy-five miles north of Tyre, and once marked the boundary of Hiram's possessions. It was the seat of the Architectural and Philosophical Schools of early ages.

(9) The various colonies of Tyre were established at all the prominent points on the Mediterranean Sea.

(10) According to Masonic tradition, the funeral rites under which King Hiram was buried were composed by King Solomon: they were substantially the same as those in use at the present day.

(11) It was but a few years after Hiram's death that his own kingdom, as well as that of his royal friend Solomon, was rent in twain by internal convulsions.

Then swept the deluge over all;
    The Conqueror came with sword and flame,
And templed shrine and kingly hall
    Are but the shadow of a name. (12)

Yet here thy burial-place is kept,—
    Still this Memorial appears,
Though shadows of old time have crept
    Along these stones three thousand years.
The frost and rain have gently seared;
    The Orient-sun hath kindly blest:
And earthquakes shattering have spared
    Our Kabr Hairan, Hiram's rest.

Still warm thine eastern front the rays
    That call the Craftsmen to the wall:
Here let me chisel this device,
    The oldest, holiest of all! (13)
And as the western sun goes down
    To give the wearied Craft release,
His latest gleam, in smile or frown,
    These time-stained ashlars still doth kiss.

The lizard darts within thy walls,
    The Arab stalks indifferent by,
Vast relics once of lordly halls
    Around in mute suggestion lie:
The hyssop springs between the stones,
    The daisy blossoms at the foot,
The olive its peace-lessons owns,
    Best moral where all else is mute.

Stand thou, till time shall be no more,
    Great type of Masonry divine!
From eastern height, from western shore,
    Let Craftsmen seek this ancient shrine

---

(12) Referring to the Chaldean monarch Nebuchadnezzar, who conquered the kingdoms of Phœnicia, Israel, and Judah, about four hundred years after Hiram's death.

(13) I chiseled the Square and Compass deeply on the tomb near the northeast corner.

> And from each pilgrim this be heard,
>   As from one humble voice today:
> "Honor to Hiram,—Masons' lord,
>   "Honor and gratitude we pay!"

Sitting on the north side of this old structure, "the place of *darkness,*" and what is better just now, of *coolness,* my eye is again attracted by that pair of mountain eagles who started across the isthmus of Tyre with me this morning, and have been watching me with unwearying patience, while I examined olive-presses, collected mosaic *tesseræ,* culled anemones and poppies, and browsed generally along the way. Grand old fellows! how they hang up there in the sky on their broad wings, extended sail-like six or eight feet horizontally! Whatever their *intentions* in thus following me, their *patience* is most praiseworthy; and I feel it to be a good omen that King Hiram's Lebanon has sent down two of its *aquilæ auræ,* its golden eagles, to guard my way by old Hiram's sarcophagus. And now is my best time to embody Scriptural references to the *Eagle* in these pages. Come, ye inspired prophets, around me, and let us study the *Bird of Jove* together. Roman cohorts and Roman legions have often enough displayed *their* eagles along this rocky road, running eastward from Tyre, and the Germans, a thousand years later, exhibited *theirs,* the double-headed one, as they came down from Antioch, A.D. 1099, to the capture of Jerusalem. But what use did you prophets make of the eagle when "inquiring and searching diligently, and prophesying of the grace that should come" to fallen men?

Who of you all have made the "unclean bird" (Lev. 11:18) your emblem?

Moses: I used it in threats against my people, in case they should refuse to hearken unto the voice of the LORD their God. Observing its swiftness of flight, I declared that the nation whom God should send against Israel, from the end of the earth, should come "as swift as the eagle flieth." (Deut. 28:49.)

Habakkuk: I took up the figure of Moses 885 years afterward, and compared that bitter and hasty nation, the Chaldeans, to yonder bird, saying, "they shall fly (against Israel) as the eagle hasteth to eat." (1:8.) This prophet had doubtless seen the swoop by which the eagle descends upon its prey, so graphically described by W. M. Thomson. "They poise themselves for a moment, then, like a bolt from the

clear sky, down they come, head foremost, with wings collapsed,"
and snatch the defenseless lamb from under the very eye of the
shepherd.

Jeremiah: I denounced the pride and self-confidence of the
Edomites at Mt. Seir, and declared that, though they should
make their nest on high, as the eagle that has established his
eyrie in yonder inaccessible crag of Lebanon, yet the Lord will
bring him down. (49:16.)

David: I sung of God's bounty, declaring that he renews the
youth of his saints as the moulting eagle renews his glorious
pinions. (Ps. 103:5.)

Moses: In promising the tender mercies of God to an obedient
race, I reminded them of the eagle's care for her young: "As an
eagle stirreth up her nest, fluttereth over her young, spreadeth
abroad her wings, taketh them, beareth them on her wings, so the
Lord alone did lead him." (Deut. 32:11.)

EAGLE AND PREY.

The voice of Jehovah, showing his almighty power to Job
condescends to introduce this bird into the lesson, in these grand

words: "Doth the eagle mount up at thy command, and make her nest on high? She dwelleth and abideth on the rock, upon the crag of the rock, and the strong place. From thence she seeketh the prey, and her eyes behold afar off. Her young ones also suck up blood, and where the slain are, there is she." (Job 39:27.)

But my hour is exhausted, and I must to my measurements, although my Scriptural references to the eagle are not half exhausted. I have left out "mounting up on wings as eagles" (Is. 40:31), and a score of passages. I imagine the imperial bird descending from these heights upon the scepter in the left hand of the statue of Jupiter Olympus, on the Acropolis, far in the northwest.

And I must not forget what Mrs. Ellet says:

> "Imperial wanderer! the storms that shake
> Earth's towers, and bid her rooted mountains quake,
>   Are never felt by thee!"

Could I question the mighty bird, it would be an interesting inquiry with what sentiments he viewed the dreadful earthquake that racked all this country, on New Year's day, 1837; when Safed was shaken together as a heap; when El Jish was totally destroyed; Tiberias cracked and shattered; and the death-cries of three thousand souls went up to heaven from yonder eastern range; when every hand was faint and every heart melted, and pangs and sorrows took hold of them, and they were amazed one at another (Isaiah 13:8); when the earth reeled to and fro as a drunkard, and was removed like a cottage (24:20); when the great house was smitten with breaches and the little house with clefts (Joel 6:11). A number of our American lodges are named *Eagle Lodge.*

To compare my measurements and descriptions with those of other writers, I have looked up Van der Velde's, and copy what he says: "Hiram's tomb stands on an oblong, four-sided pedestal, of two layers of huge stones, 14 feet long, 8 feet 9 inches broad, 6 feet high. The third layer is 15 feet long, 10 broad, 3 feet 9 inches high. Above this is a truncated pyramid, hewn out of a single rock, 12 feet 1 inch long, 8 feet 6 inches wide, 6 feet high. This is surmounted by an oblong stone of the same dimensions, 5 feet high. The entire tomb is about 21 feet high. There is nothing to prevent passengers from approaching the monument, no peculiar sanctity being ascribed to it, as in the numerous *welies* (tombs) of the Moslems." Van der Velde admits the tradition that claims this as the monument of Hiram,

Solomon's friend and ally, and thinks the popular belief well founded. No heathen king, he says, was ever in such close relationship with Israel as the King of Tyre, and nowhere else in this country, except at Jerusalem, is there so large a monument as this, or one so appropriate to such a king. He sees in this remembrance of Tyre's great monarch, thus visibly preserved in this monument, a confirmation of the Lord's words, in 1 Sam. 11:30, "Them that honor me, I will honor."

Brother Capt. Charles Warren, so long in charge of the Jerusalem Explorations, makes a note of Hiram's Tomb, under date July, 1869, as follows: "We passed out of our way to visit Hiram's Tomb, as I was anxious to see if there were any masons' marks on the stone. I could only see two,—one is a Christian Cross, of the Byzantine type, at the western end; it appears to be ancient. The other consists of a square and compass, very recently cut." As I saw nothing of this "Christian Cross," I fancy it must have been put there since May, 1868.

Some sort of a fair, I think, was going on at Tyre the day I first visited Kabr Hairan, something like the one at Bint Jebale, which I shall describe in another chapter, and the number and variety of travelers was no doubt beyond the ordinary. I took down a score or two of notes, sitting in my stocking-feet on the cornice at the east end of the monument, and here are specimens of them:

A party of Arab charcoal-dealers, all mounted on camels, eighteen in all. As the wind blew in their faces they had all turned themselves to the rear, except the leader, and so avoided the draft. These Arab saddles are just like a sawhorse, an old-fashioned X, on which you can face either way, and suffer, I should think, excruciating pain, no matter which way you sit. I was never on a camel in my life, but I *have* sat for ten minutes at a time on a sharp-edged fence-rail, and I remember it. The sheikh of the little village has come over to ask Hassan what I am doing up there. I told Hassan (sarcastically) to say that I had bought this tomb from the Pasha, and was going to ship it to America, but he evidently told him something else. The sheikh is a short man, with the darkest shade of bronze; eyes keen, roving, and unsettled; teeth white; skin so dried and withered it seems cleaving from the bones. Here passes a man in, or just out of, an ague fit. How well I know how he feels. He may say as the prophet of Anathoth did: All my bones shake; I am like a drunken man, a man whom wine overcometh (Jer. 23:9). And the word *wine* reminds me to offer him some *arrack* from my leather bottle. But he loathes it, and (I judge by the sound) curses me inwardly (Pa. 62:4). Truth is, all Moslems are Rechabites (Jer.

35:2). Some cows pass by from the pastures of Kanah, just over the hill yonder. One is what Jeremiah calls (40:20) a very fair heifer. Some are fat as heifers at grass, and bellow as bulls (Jer. l:11). The long line of telegraph poles between me and Tyre yonder, suggests how differently certain passages of Scripture would read had Morse only appeared 3,000 years sooner. Jonah need never have gone *personally* to Nineveh; Joseph need not have come to Palestine before finding that Archelaus did reign in place of his father Herod; the movements of invading armies would have been telegraphed, and time given the natives to prepare for defense; and so all through the sacred pages. And here, on a certain day blessed in all the history of this country, if the miserable people only knew it, there passed one who, though rich, yet for our sakes became poor. On his way to Sarepta, as I will show in a coming chapter, Jesus and his disciples passed this monument, doubtless looking up to it and passing comments upon it, even as travelers do now. It is easy to recognize a Christian village, both by the unveiled faces and black, sparkling eyes of the females, and the neater houses and cleaner streets. How truly that city of Tyre, five miles yonder in the west, was said to have been planted in a pleasant place! (Hos. 9:13.) A sheikh is passing by, gorgeously appareled, as the Scripture expresses it, and doubtless as "full of all subtlety" (Acts 8:10) as his progenitor in the days of Peter. The purity of the atmosphere and gentle freshness of the air, as it comes down from the hills in the east, high, broken, and rugged, makes everything delightful up here. That old camel-sheikh, with his eye like a hawk's, can see ten miles off. But he cannot reverse the telescope; the pencil-marks on my notebook are invisible to him; the copy of my Arabic newspaper, *El Hadekhat,* is a sheet of white paper. A chap climbed up side of me for purposes of instruction. He told me a great deal; and when I had paid him for his information and dismissed him with thanks, he remembered a great deal more and came back again. Like the eccentric Wors. Master, L. O. B.,—who, having told the candidate "all he knew" and closed the lodge, summoned them together again "in called communication" a few minutes afterwards, explaining that he had just then remembered something else, and was afraid he would forget it if not promptly disbursed! As the body of King Cheops is probably resting, not in the King's Chamber, nor Queen's Chamber, nor Chamber of Projection (subterranean), but in a vault far below the last, so I suggested the theory to Capt. Warren that the *body* of the great Hiram was never laid *in* this sarcophagus, but *underneath,* perhaps far underneath, and when the time for great explorations in this locality arrives, it may be found there. To bring to light the remains of Abraham from Hebron, David and Solomon from Sion, Hiram from this hill, and Cheops from that subterranean chamber "forever flowed about by water," are among the works reserved for Masonic explorers. An ungainly, wobbling creature, with a withered hand, as in the story of the miracle at Capernaum. The next is a party of Swedes, judging from dress, eyes, and hair. One of them recalls the portrait of Gustavus Adolphus, tall, vigorous, graceful, yellow hair flowing thick and plentiful, expression mild, manners singularly engaging. I was sorry he knew so little English, for what little he *did* know did him good. Now come two men with silver beards, walking staff in hand, who do not even deign me a nod. The next is a grave, patient-looking Rabbi, whose philosophy is good enough for Socrates. Replying to my remark, that the oppression the Jews had received from the world would naturally sour them against their tyrants, he said, "Hakeem, but it is noble and god-like to bear with calmness and observe with pity the failings of others." Whereupon I (figuratively) gave him my hat. Next there comes a fine, comely girl, in the beautiful costume of the Lebanons, with bracelets round her arms and ankles. The trees that I observed this morning are the olive, palm, orange, lemon, cypress, oleander, tamarisk, etc.; the flowers (as I gather the class-names from other authors), *Ranunculus myriophyllus, Draba verna, Reseda suffruticosa, Zizyphus vulgaris, Senecio vernalis, Anchusa italica, Parietaria officinalis,* and the like. The little Scops owl, called here *Maroof,* stares at me from an olive-tree close by, in his own inquisitive style; and the lazy people, by a stare equally persistent, but not half so wise, prove that, however they may value *money,* they have no real appreciation of that which money only represents—*time.* And now a whole party, of divers ages and sexes, gather on the bank in front, almost level with my face, and take a long stare at me. Klauber can't make a photograph of me half so accurate as they will. The old man, with "childish treble," leads off in the hated dissyllable *backsheesh.* He is followed in coarser tones by another and another of the crowd, until every gullet is croaking with that abhorrent password of beggary. In this vicinity this morning, looking up the almost illegible carvings on old stones, I stirred up a number of partridges, larger than ours at home, and of different color. Their beaks and feet are red, and plumes ashy gray, like the color of the dust. The country around is rocky and impracticable, and much overgrown with thorn. The caravans that go by kick up a dreadful dust. The dust of these roads, powdering the face, irritating the eyes, and leaving a taste of *hyd. cum creta* in the mouth, recalls a host of Scripture passages, showing that *Holy* Land was always *Dusty* Land. That we were made of "dust," according to the expression (Genesis 2:7), "And the Lord God formed man of the dust of the ground," and other passages, seems plain enough this morning, and that "unto dust" all the generations of this country have, literally, returned, perhaps explains the peculiarly acrid and unpleasant flavor to which I have referred. Jesus told his disciples to shake the dust off their feet at the doors of inhospitable men as a testimony against them. It may be that explains the dust-heaps I have seen at so many thresholds! In the fourteenth century the English government instituted a court styled The Court of Dusty Feet (pie-poudre), to be held at markets, to settle difficulties

between buyers and sellers on the spot. I should think Raschid
Pasha might introduce it here with equal regularity and propriety.
A fakir, or native beggar-priest, of the class that subsists on
charity. A wild-looking man, naked to the waist, having in fact no
clothing save a sheepskin tied around his hips, long, matted hair,
shading a wild, haggard face; he is, in all the uses of the word, a
grim fanatic. Who is it wrote these lines, that occur to me in my
survey of old Kabr Hairan?

> As if time had been to it all sunlight and soft dew,
> As if upon its freshness the cold rime
> Of decay should never fall.

Gathering up my effects at 4 P.M., I started to return to Tyre,
taking upon my way the celebrated fountains called Ras-el-Ain, or
"Head of the Spring," four miles from Tyre, and said, in the native
traditions, to have been erected at the expense of King Solomon,
as a present to his royal friend Hiram. These fountains are the
finest I saw in Syria. Originally there was a large spring broke
out here. This was enclosed by immense stone walls until the
water rose about twenty feet, in one great reservoir, from which it
was carried off by aqueducts towards the city. This abundance of
sweet water makes everything around a mass of vegetation,
recalling the beautiful expression, "Whereupon there grow roses
and lilies, flowers of unchangeable color, from which are emitted
odors of wonderful smell." (2 Esdras 6:44.)

At the top of this fountain, I was accosted by one of the officers
of the Protestant Church at Kanah, six miles east, with a
subscription paper, asking aid towards purchasing a church-bell.
I was glad to give my *mejeedia* (ninety-four cents) to this
desirable end, and I hope the echoes of Lebanon have, ere this,
been stirred by the suggestive sound. It is but a late thing that
the Turkish government has permitted the use of bells in
churches; a timber of heavy, porous wood, struck with a setting-
maul, having heretofore answered the purpose of a bell in calling
God's people together. In all Asia Minor there is only one
Christian church supplied with a bell, viz., the old city of
Philadelphia. The Turks themselves employ men with loud voices,
styled muezzins, who station themselves in the minarets (steeples)
of the mosques and roar out the holy news with incredible force.
The last association, therefore, connected in my mind with these
abounding waters of Ras-el-Ain, is the presenting that man with
a Turkish dollar for the purpose of buying that church-bell at
Kanah. And so I quietly go back to Tyre, to dinner and to bed.

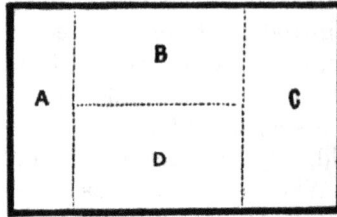

1st.

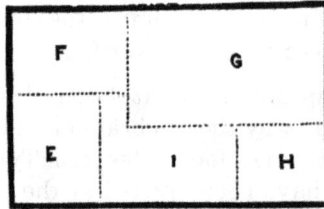

2d.

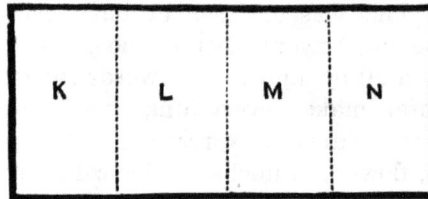

3d.

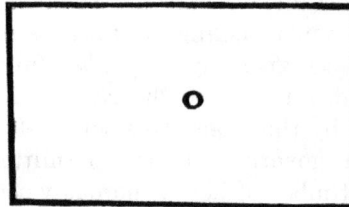

4th.

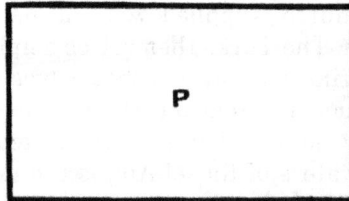

5th.

THE FIVE TIERS OF STONE IN HIRAM'S TOMB.

WILSON'S EXPLORATIONS AT JERUSALEM.

BATTLE-GROUND OF HATTIN.

DIVISION THIRD.—GEBAL.

Loud wind, strong wind, blowing from the mountains,
Fresh wind, free wind, sweeping o'er the sea,
Pour forth thy vials like torrents from air-fountains,
Draughts of life to me.

A field of ruins, a scene of unutterable desolation.

Thorns coming up in her palaces, nettles and brambles in the fortresses thereof, a habitation of dragons and a court of owls.

There is a tongue in every rock, a voice from every leaf, which witnesses, to all who visit here, of the eternal truth and majesty of Him who is working here the melancholy penalty of sin, in the sorrow and degradation which surround him.

Sacred land by blood and tears of God,
Instinct with thrills of consecrated life.

The quaint, enameled eyes
That on the green turf suck the honeyed showers,
The ground all purpled with the vernal flowers:
These bells and flowerets of a thousand hues.

Here rest the great and good; here they repose,
After their generous toil; a sacred band,
They take their sleep together, while the year
Comes with its early flowers to deck their graves,
And gather them again as winter frowns;
Theirs is no vulgar sepulcher; green sods
Are all their monument; and yet it tells
A nobler history than pillared piles
Or the eternal pyramids. They need
No statue nor inspiration to reveal
Their greatness.

CHAPTER VIII.

HE Second of the Seven Grand Masonic Localities that my visit to the Holy Land enables me to identify and describe, is Gebal (pronounced Jebale, accent on the last syllable). I went there from Beirut, a distance of about twenty-four miles, March 17, and remained three days, returning on the 21st. My expeditionary force consisted of one *man,* Hassan, a stout, good-natured Arab, described in Chapter V., who knows considerable English of the hassanic quality (the joke here consists in the fact that the word hassan means a horse); one *boy,* Yasoof (meaning *Joseph,* I am told), two horses and a *donkey;* the latter (whom I had named *Boanerges,* because I do not remember the singular form of the word), addicted to lying down without the slightest warning, and to making the most excruciating noises that organized nostrils ever projected. These three persons and animals bore with them all needful supplies of blankets, overcoats, working-tools, such as chisel, mallet, etc., and a good quantity of provisions for my personal use, for five days.

In view of this five days' trip I had consulted a professional dragoman, who generously offered to convey me to Gebal, feed, lodge, and find me for five days, and all for the insignificant sum of $125! When I asked him what sort of accommodation he could afford for that trifling remuneration, he replied that he should take nine horses and mules, twelve servants, a cook, three tents, one for me, one for himself and servants, and one for the kitchen, and that my dinner should consist of five courses. I asked him if he thought I had come all the way from Kentucky to eat dinners of five courses. The conundrum remains unanswered to this day.

This was the third visit I had made up the coast from Beirut, as far as the month of Nahr-el-Kelb (Dog River), a place all travelers visit, to inspect the ancient inscriptions on the rocks there. These will be fully described in my account of the Masonic Bay, or Bay of the Rafts, in Division Fourth. But I shall not find so good a place as this to describe a thunder-storm in which I was caught, the first visit I made to the place. It was on the 5th of March, 1868 (the twenty-second anniversary of my Masonic Initiation), and my purpose was to inspect those ancient proofs of human pride and grandeur. I had scarcely got out of Beirut on the sea-shore, when the bay became lashed into fury by a gale. A tremendous thunder-storm swept grandly a little way before, and as I was congratulating myself on escaping its fury, I was startled by the roar of thunder in the rear. Looking back, I saw myself pursued by one of Mount Lebanon's blackest clouds, that bellowed a thousand times worse than Spenser makes the dragon bellow who was killed right at this spot, if report is true, by St. George. I was riding a donkey a trifle larger than the conventional goat of the Masonic lodge, and my prospects of escaping a drenching and a pelting were solely based on his speed. Capricornus did his utmost, and I reached a native khan, or tavern (like the one described at Neby Younas), and entered, thanks to my goat and a gum-coat, not all wet. A dozen people with their beasts were in there before me, the old khan proving to them, as to me, a place of refuge and covert from storm and from rain (Isa. 5:6). The storm being over, I went on to the inscriptions, a mile or more further north, and while making notes there a second cloud swept through the passes of old Lebanon and poured its contents, true as the plumb-line, on me, as I cowered under shelter of the overhanging rocks. This convulsion of nature was inconceivably grand and awful. I have nothing parallel to it in all my memory. The gorge through which Dog River runs separates two mountains, a thousand feet in height, by an interval of about 300 feet. The sides of these tremendous heights gave back the awful thunder-peals in countless reverberations. The lightning flashed across the defile with a vividness blasting to the eyeballs. I could conceive that the spirits of the mighty dead were revisiting these scenes of their earthly grandeur, and speaking, as they once addressed the world, in tempest and fire. In these terrific passages of sound I learned the propriety of the Hebrew name for echo, "the daughter of the voice." I was so impressed with the unparalleled sublimity of this scene, that, on my return that night to the shelter of Hallock's hospitable (flat) roof, I was unable to sleep, but spent the hours composing the following verses, together with music to them:

THE GLORY OF LEBANON.

That goodly mountain, Lebanon (Dent. 3:25). He maketh
Lebanon to skip like a calf (Ps. 29:6). The fruit shall shake like
Lebanon (Ps. 72:16). The righteous shall grow like a cedar in
Lebanon (Ps. 92:12). Like the smell of Lebanon (Cant. 4:11).
Lebanon shall fall like a mighty one (Is. 10:34). The glory of
Lebanon (Is. 35:2 and 55:13). The head of Lebanon (Jer. 22:6). His
smell as Lebanon; the wine of Lebanon (Hosea 14:6-7). The flower
of Lebanon (Nahum 1:4). The violence of Lebanon (Hab. 2:17).
Open thy doors, O Lebanon (Zech. 1:10).

Oh charming Mount! thy flowery sides,
    Thy heights with cedars crowned,
Thy gushing springs, and painted wings,
    And birds of sweetest sound!
Oh Lebanon! oh roseate throne,
    The church of God shall be,
In days to come, a flowery home,
    A roseate mount like thee!

Oh fearful Mount! thy stormy Crown,
    Thy echoing tongues of flame,
Whose awful word proclaims its God,
    And bids adore His name!
Oh Lebanon! oh darkened throne,
    The church of God shall be,
In days to come, an anchored home,
    A solid mount like thee!

Oh mighty Mount! thy stony gates,
    Thy heights in walls secure,
Thy dizzy hills, and sheltered dales,
    And guardians tried and sure!
Oh Lebanon! oh guarded throne,
    The church of God shall be,
In days to come, a castled home,
    A forted mount like thee!

The road to Gebal is fearfully bad. You go a few miles painfully
through deep sand, strewed with boulders, until you look longingly
up the mountain-slopes on your right, and wish you were ascending
the steepest of them. Then you come to a spur of the stony hills,
so rough and difficult that the heaviest sandbanks appear as
green meadows in the comparison. One of these rocky passes,
about six miles from Beirut, occurred to me as a capital place to
work the Royal Arch degree! It presents a regular succession

of difficult passages, increasing in roughness every step, and ending in a frightful climax, delicious to the heart of a Principal Sojourner. The Chapter room at Akron, Ohio, reminds me of it.

Yet this is one of the most noted highways in the world. It has passed great men along this way, north or south, going to conquest, or going to defeat. I cannot even sum up those great names; but Rameses came here from the south about B.C. 1500, and Sennacherib from the north, 700 years latter. It was equally the turnpike-way of Alexander, B.C. 332, and of Vespasian, 400 years later; of Sesostris, and Saladin. It was the apostolical highway, all the missionary apostles traversing it again and again, as they went to and from Antioch, and up and down, preaching to a sinful world. By this highway, about A.D. 320, came the venerable mother of Constantine the Great, Hellena, at an extremely old age, yearning to behold the places that Christ had sanctified by His corporal presence. By this route had come the Assyrian with his shadowy shroud and high stature (Ez. 31), and along this road, in the summer of A.D. 1099, the armies of the Cross slowly worked their way southward towards Jerusalem, yet 200 miles in the distance.

About-half way between Beirut and Gebal, and close to the road, there is a beautiful sheet of water styled Junia Bay (the word *Junia* meaning a plain). Near the middle of the curve of this bay stands a large Stone Column, broken in the midst, the lower part about ten feet long, yet standing erect, originally erected probably as a Roman milestone. Upon this I engraved with my chisel the memorial *Square and Compass,* cutting it in the sea-ward side, so that ordinary travelers may not observe it, and dedicated it to the lodges at Des Moines, Iowa, who gave me such a royal reception, Thanksgiving night, 1867; Elizabethtown, Kentucky, and Dubuque, Iowa. If ever those members come along this way, as I hope some of them will, let them stop and see how upon the face of the everlasting rock here I imprinted this mark of loving remembrance. I also locate, at this fitting place, the following names of Masons who have emulated the fortitude of him whose emblem was *the Broken Column:* W. W. Goodwin, Charles Marsh, Solon Thornton, George R. Fearn, B. Perley Poore, N. P. Langford, R. W. Furnas, Alex. H. Newcomb, Richard Vaux, and J. P. Almond.

Walking aside from this great milestone, I see something fluttering among the rocks, and on strict examination discover, nor lizard nor snake, but a wounded dove, its sweet love-notes changed to piteous

9

moans, a regular *Jonath elem-verhobim,* as the ancient Hebrew would have called it, "a dumb dove in distant places." The best I can do for this poor Noah's messenger, with its great flutter of wings, is to put it out of its misery; a broken side and a useless wing being very far above my powers of surgery. Am I mistaken in thinking there is a passage in David's life recalling this incident? No; here it is, in the caption of the 56th Psalm, "When the Philistines took him in Gath."

At the distance of about three miles south of Gebal, I crossed the Nahr Ibrahim, or River of Abraham, famous in mythology as "the River of Adonis," which, according to tradition, annually *ran blood,* in commemoration of the death of Adonis, which occurred on the heights near the head-waters of this stream. I will refer to the subject again. The waters of Nahr Ibrahim were unquestionably tinged with *red* the day I crossed it, as I presume they always are after such a severe rain-storm as we had had the night before. The river was quite full, about one hundred and fifty feet wide, ten or twelve deep, and fringed with the usual willow, cane, and oleander-growth of the country. Just beyond the bridge, and on the right hand side of the road, I observed a handsome piece of Mosaic Pavement, part of a splendid edifice once standing there. This is the first I had seen. Travelers also describe the remains of an ancient aqueduct, running from this river towards Gebal, by which the old city was supplied with water; but I did not observe this.

On my way I stopped frequently to rest and refresh myself, studying human nature, of which there is a great deal existing in this country. At a blacksmith-shop I had a good time. To say it was the dirtiest house I had ever seen before, but imperfectly describes the loathsome squalor in which that Tubal-Cain, with Mrs. Cain, and a number of juvenile Cains, existed. (They raised cain at the rate of seven every ten years!) To say that this *atelier* was more infested with fleas and lice than other places in Holy Land, might be considered invidious; but I am sure I counted five *species* of lice on my coat-sleeve as I came out, and of each species, varieties. They asked me questions *and* questions. I answered through Hassan. I showed them my pistol, eighteen-bladed jack-knife, the portrait of my wife, my india-rubber bottle full of coffee, my self-folding measuring tape (a startling piece of ingenuity to them; they never wearied of it), and even pulled out my Firman, a dreadful piece of Arabic writing, large as a table-cloth, of which I gave a translation in a preceding chapter. A Syrian gentleman, who sat with us, amused at my efforts to please the blacksmith and his family, recalls the description of such, with which I am familiar: manner, alert, easy, graceful, cordial, insinuating; smile, ready and sultry as the Syrian sunlight; quite a young man, but life comes early under the sun which fondles the fig, olive, vine, and palm.

Another of the company was a tall, thin man, with dark face, almost covered with a black beard. He went barefoot usually. He had really a fine beard, and an expression of earnestness and simplicity of character. But his ignorance was startling. He actually seemed to know less than the blacksmith, and but little more than the blacksmith's wife.

In this blacksmith's shop, the exceedingly loquacious natives all talked at once. Either they possess the faculty of talking and hearing at the same time (a thing I cannot do), or they are so disposed to garrulity as to talk without caring to be heard. I had noticed this same peculiarity among the French officers of my steamer, *L'Amérique,* in Marseilles. As we came out, Hassan stigmatized the whole crowd to me in an undertone as *Shaitan,* meaning *devils.*

Everybody who visits this country notices the dogs, so often and so much in the way. The blacksmith had nine of them. Strange that the Bible-writers, from first to last, have made the dog the image of scorn and contempt. Moses in the Pentateuch; Job in his noble allegory; David in his matchless psalms; our Savior in His parables; Paul in his Epistles; John in his Apocalypse, uniformly agree in this; and the Koran of Mohammed fully confirms the Oriental idea of the dog. And yet, if the tradition is true, it was a dog that discovered the use of the celebrated Tyrian dye that became so world-renowned. And Dr. Barclay gives to his dog the credit of discovering the great quarry under Jerusalem. However, I mustn't say too much in favor of the dog, as the Masonic word *Cowan* is probably derived from it; and what is worse than a cowan!

At parting I gave the good fellow several paras (a para is one-fourth of a cent), and promised to call again. He has some fine fig trees around his house; a tree which flourishes best in stony, barren places, where "there is not much depth of earth." It does not like the companionship of other trees; nothing but the olive is congenial company to the fig on these stony bills. The shade produced by its succulent, five-lobed leaves and spreading branches is very fine. I noticed today that while the earth under my feet was really hot, and made the soles of my shoes uncomfortably warm, the ground under this large fig tree was cool and pleasant; I felt the force of the expression in 1 Kings 4:25: "And Judah and Israel dwelt safely, every man under his vine and under his fig tree." In this verse the fig tree is named as a symbol of peace and plenty, for which it is elegantly adapted. So in Micah 4:4; Zech. 3:10; John 1:49, etc.

I shall have so much advice to give to Masonic travelers all through this volume, that it will be politic to scatter it along in *chunks*. A few chunks, then, right here. As to the difficulty or danger in traversing this country, the mere tourist who only wants to *see* and pass along will find not the least. He can ride over the sacred hills, and rest himself under the offered shelters of Palestine, with as much security as at home. The fanaticism of the Mohammedan has given way to the craving for gold; the cry of *backsheesh* drowns the old clamor of *Allah il Allah*. It is the *explorer* only who experiences any difficulty in pursuing his aims. To excavate, to pull down, to expose the ancient foundations, where alone can anything valuable be looked for; it is this that revives the ancient hatred, and exposes the seeker for light to delays, extortions, and sometimes worse. For this reason it is best, in general, for several to go in company, both for mutual protection in digging, etc., and encouragement.

The most careless traveler in the East is constantly reminded that he is in the *land of the Bible,* and it is in poor taste to make such tours as Browne and Clements did for the sole purpose of making sport. The latter ("Mark Twain," as he likes to call himself), facile humorist as he is, might have recalled the school-day adage, *ludere cum sacris,* not to jest on holy themes. It is the easiest as well as the least praiseworthy effort of wit, and every admirer of Mark Twain must regret that "Pilgrims Abroad" did not terminate their journey where they began it, in Europe.

In regard to the Arabic language, I really would not advise any American to learn it, unless he is qualifying himself for a Professor, a Dragoman, a Consul, or a Missionary. If, in spite of my warnings, you undertake it, I am afraid you will say, as an irreverent friend did under the same circumstances, that when "God created the fruit of the lips" (Isaiah 57:19) it was only for *Arab* lips that he created *this particular* fruit! And yet, you might learn enough of it (some travelers do not) to call the plural of dragoman dragomans, and of

Moslem Mos*lems*. Drago*men* is as near right as *pen* is the plural of *pan*. About one hundred words in Arabic are enough for any one to travel on here. If you wish to talk to respectable people, learn French.

Do not disparage too much the race who now inhabit this country. See what they have produced when temporarily released from the iron grip of despotism, and consider that in the minds of many a peasant here, whose every moment is bestowed in wringing from the soil a scanty subsistence, there slumber powers which might have elevated their possessors to the bead of armies, to thrones, to the rule of literary coteries, to the guidance of religious sects whose debates shake the world, had fortune been more propitious to them.

It is a merit in an Oriental traveler to have muscle—bodily vigor. Our good Masonic brother, Belzoni, who became one of the most famous of Egyptian explorers, began *as a circus-rider,* for which his great size and muscular developments well adapted him. His Egyptian travels began in 1815; his death occurred in 1823.

The natives say there is a plant grows here which, when powdered, is grim death to fleas. But I think they never powder it. Costar's Exterminators (cat, rat, and roach) have never been introduced into Syria! The flea, in fact, reigns here, unsubdued as yet. The very earth teems with them. Is it possible, asks a pious lady over her Bible, that it was so in ancient times? Did Deborah, Miriam, Abigail——but the theme becomes too affecting! I will say, however, that if the plowmen here would only scratch the *earth* as deeply, vigorously, and persistently as they do their calloused bodies, their granaries would enjoy the results of it.

Make a point of comparing daily objects with those Scriptural facts that enter into our prayers and sermons; see how bread is made "daily;" how the native salt "loses its savor;" how the goaded cattle "kick against the pricks;" how the south wind blows heat and the west wind rain;—but there is no end to these analogies.

The indolence of these people is like the offence of *contumacy* in the Masonic code; it is unpardonable, because embracing all other faults. To give an instance of native laziness which annoyed me greatly: I hired a man in Beirut, at daily wages, to saw up a lot of seasoned olive-wood which I had purchased. By the third day he had gathered round him all the idlers in the place, and I venture the assertion that the eight hours' work for which I paid him, done, too, with his miserable little back-action hand-saw, seated on the ground, and holding the wood with his toes, could all have been done in one hour by an American competitor.

They are, generally, an incurious race, and, of course, an ignorant one; they have yet to understand the first principles embodied in the degree of "Grand *Inquisitor* Commander," as the old translators rendered it.

You must not be disappointed, in a country so unfortunate in its history as this, to find the low, mean vices of lying, swearing, petty theft, and vulgarity, extremely common. But the better opening remains for you to teach them a better way. An American Mason, who is not addicted to these degrading habits, becomes an effective missionary of morality to these heathen, reflecting honor upon the craft, his country, himself, and his God.

That experienced Masonic traveler, Dr. Livingstone, fittingly rebukes that class of tourists who hurry over the ground, abuse and look ferocious at their companions, merely to show how fast they can travel. He styles such characters "combinations of silliness and absurdity."

This is a good field to disseminate Sunday-School ideas. Anything so practical and fruitful in good results as the American Sunday-School system is bound to succeed among such people as these. I met a man in England who appreciated it. He was from Stockport, England, where the largest Sunday-School in the world is maintained (300 teachers, 1,500 scholars), and he admitted to me, in confidence, that the Americans are far ahead of them in this department of instruction. I had an agreeable hour describing to him my old "Berean Bible-Class" in the First Presbyterian Church at Chicago, Illinois.

Those who have read Robinson's *Biblical Researches,* three large volumes, with a fourth volume of maps, must suppose Robinson had spent the years of an active life traveling and making all those discoveries. No such thing. He was here only a few weeks! but his companion, Dr. Smith, had spent very many years here, was perfectly familiar with the people, the country, and the language, and it was *his* knowledge, sifted and crystallized by Robinson, that made up those valuable books. That which gave the books their real value was, there was nothing in the field before them except works written by Catholic travelers, who only know what "the Church" tells them, or small sketch-books not worth shelf-room in a library.

CHAPTER IX.

GEBAL.

ARRIVED at Gebal a little before night and was lodged in the Bachelors' Hall of some Maronite (Roman Catholic) priests, who have charge of an ancient church here, which is considered a curiosity by all lovers of ecclesiastical architecture. It was built about 800 years ago, and, except for exhibiting the marks of old age, given by King Solomon in the twelfth chapter of Ecclesiastes, is none the worse for its years. The roof, floor, walls, and supports are all of stone. In fact, there is nothing *wooden* about it. I was so much interested in this ancient relic that I gave a Napoleon ($4.00) of Masonic money towards its conservation and repair.

The town of Gebal lies about twenty-five miles up the coast (north) from Beirut. It stands upon an easy and regular slope from the sea eastward, the slope extending about two miles along the coast, and from one to two miles back. All this space and more was once thronged with temples, palaces, and other splendid erections, the remains of which, in granite, marble, and Lebanon limestone, are visible in every stone-fence upon the surface, and appear in excavations at depths varying from ten to thirty feet. But now Gebal is a poor and forlorn little village of five hundred inhabitants. There is not one edifice standing now that has the least attractions, unless it be the old Maronite Church, already alluded to, and that does not date beyond the Crusades. There is a force of about one hundred and fifty soldiers, red-legged Turkish Zouaves, who live in some new buildings, the remnants of more costly structures, while the grand old castle next the sea is suffered to fall into irreparable decay. Desolation and neglect are written upon all the remains of Gebal.

My time during three days at this place was spent between visiting the more prominent localities, purchasing coins and antiquities, and writing up my notes for preservation. It is one of my peculiarities that I cannot think freely unless I have *pencil in hand;* hence my large use of white paper upon occasions like these. The Oriental custom of crowding the traveler's room by day and night with guests, bidden or unbidden, made it so well-nigh impossible for me to write by daylight that I soon took to the free use of candles, purchased in the bazaars, and so wrought out my plans in ink after all Gebal had succumbed to the dominion of slumber. The objects collected here are numerous and varied, such as coins in great numbers; sea-shells; specimens of the red and gray granites and porphyry, imported here at incalculable expense in the olden times; funeral lamps; tear-bottles and beads from the Phœnician tombs, etc., etc. I longed to make good collections of the early spring-flowers that paint this beautiful site of Gebal; but this is a matter requiring a longer stay, more active limbs and flexible spine than I can boast of at the age of fifty. I found I was not able personally to make many botanical collections in the Holy Land.

Gebal derived its name originally from the hill on which it stood. The Greeks changed the name to Byblos, but in this case, as in many others, the title imposed by the conquerors fell into oblivion, while the original name was retained. Gebal also gave its name to the country around it, which, in Joshua 8:5, is termed "the land of the Giblites." This, it will be remembered, was more than fourteen centuries before Christ, or 3,300 years ago. In the days of Solomon, the people of Gebal were the most skillful sailors and artists under the dominion of King Hiram. So eminent were they in architecture, that the word *Giblites,* in Hebrew, is translated *stone-squarers,* a most remarkable circumstance (1 Kings 5:18). In the tremendous denunciations by Ezekiel against all Phœnicia, he says "the ancients of Gebal and the wise men thereof were in thee thy calkers" (Ez. 27:9). This was written about 400 years after the building of Solomon's Temple, and refers to the city I am now describing.

My visit to Gebal, as it was the first of my more extended Masonic explorations, has impressed itself more deeply upon my mind than any future visit could be expected to do. Here I find upon the monstrous ashlars of Phœnician ages (hewn stones eighteen feet long and upwards) the distinguishing mark, the *rebate* or *bevel,* of which I have so much read, but now for the first time in my life I see. This is the Masonic mark of ancient-craft Masonry. As I have told the thousands of brothers and fellows who will read these pages, all stones having this mark upon them belong to us! Our fathers wrought them, and set them up in useful places in great edifices, and we, their lineal descendants in the mystical line, must not forget our inheritance therein. The stones themselves strike an American, unused to such architectural prodigies, as enormous. They are twice as heavy as any wrought ashlars I had ever before seen, but of course do not compare with some at Baalbec and Jerusalem.

And this deep-plowed furrow upon their edges—what a hopeful thought does this convey to a Freemason! So long as that mark remains—so long as the main surface of the wall stands out far enough to protect and shield that mystic device of the Phœnician, so long the institution of Freemasonry will survive! This is the lesson they inculcate to me as I turn away silently from them and draw my breath with amazement. Let the *Blanchardites* note it with dismay.

Gebal is full of the "Handmarks of Hiram." Hundreds and thousands of granite columns are here, both of the red and white varieties, taken from the quarries of Egypt, with all the enormous labor which the working of that primitive stone requires; brought a thousand miles down the Nile; shipped thence on Phœnician vessels or rafts to this coast, landed here, drawn up this steep hill by human hands, and finally reared up, doubtless with shoutings and rejoicings Thousands of them, I say, are here, from twelve to thirty inches in diameter, and from ten to forty feet in length, their surfaces often as smooth and unaffected by the weather as on the day they left Egypt, two, three, or four thousand years ago. They prop up the stalls in the bazaars; they sustain the filthy roofs of stables; they are built into the military castle, and other public edifices in numbers; they are worked into stone walls; in short, they are used with a profuseness that shows the inexhaustible quantities of them that now lie concealed among the ruins.

It is but a brief seven miles east of this place that Aphaca, the principal seat of the worship of Adonis, or Tammuz, stood. This worship was the Freemasonry of the heathen, and the system upon which King Solomon engrafted the revealed precepts given his fathers upon Sinai. As the wild stock into which the inspired Word was engrafted, these Rites of Tammuz deserve the attention of Masonic writers. This is not the place to enlarge upon the theme; but I must be permitted to say that a system which had the favor and support of the wisest and best-cultivated of the human race for two thousand years; that led to the cultivation of the fine arts as they have never been cultivated since; and that was thought worthy, by so far-reaching a mind as King Solomon's, of adoption and incorporation into the inspired theology, cannot have been altogether vile. That, by the age of Constantine, A.D. 306, it may have become so corrupt that that zealous reformer thought it necessary to uproot the last traces of it, is quite likely. But the same thing may be said of the prevailing system of Christianity at the same period. By the age of Constantine the Rites of Adonis had probably accomplished whatever good was embodied in them; but they must have presented many innocent and pure traits to attract the admiration of a Solomon. It was then, doubtless, that this wide-spread system of worship gave to the poet his idea of the *Age of Gold.*

I reserve to this place, however, to justify Freemasons in selecting Gebal as one of their seven prominent Masonic localities. It is, that here was the great *School of Architecture* and of the seven liberal arts and sciences. Here, in the days of Hiram, the Widow's Son, was a congregation of earth's wisest, let us believe earth's *best* spirits, to whom a seeker of knowledge like himself could come for instruction, and where such a genius as his could be fitly schooled. From this center of learning went the men who planned that unparalleled Temple across the hills eastward, that crowns the plateau of Baalbec, just as from here fared the Masters of the Building Art who went southward down the coast to build a matchless Fane on Mount Moriah, at Jerusalem. The Paphian Temple, on the Island of Cyprus yonder, in the west, which was thought unapproachable for beauty, doubtless received its inspiration from the same men, as many another temple, palace, and stronghold did, during successions of ages. I stood within the tombs of some of these Giblites, excavations painfully chiseled in the hard blue limestone of the hills. I saw a row of their stone coffins (sarcophagi) opened. I purchased many of their funeral lamps, scarabæi and other tokens of their faith, and coming back to my housetop I walked and mused upon the hopes embodied in these emblems. Hopes of some kind (the resurrection and the soul's immortality) we know those old Masons had; the rites handed down through so many generations from them to us clearly prove that. But a resurrection to what? and immortality for what? what secrets were so held within their emblems? what made them so anxious to express them in outward marks, but to *conceal* them even at the risk of their being forever lost as to their esoteric meaning? I find in my notebook this acrostic:

Gone, gone thy glories, city of the wise;
   Extinguished all thy lamps above, below;
But from this dust a viewless spirit cries,
   Announcing to the ages as they go,
   Life from the tombs and light in Heaven's perpetual glow!

Did he who prepared the rituals of the Select Master's Degree have in mind that exquisite passage from an English poet—

   Silence and darkness, solemn sisters, twins
   From ancient night, who mark the tender thought,
   To *reason,* and on reason build *resolve,*
   That column of true majesty in man.

The "twenty-two from Gebal," who constituted so large a portion of the mystic number twenty-seven in a Lodge of Select Masters, were, of course, drafted from this city, and each of them must have seen, as I see today, this enormous ashlar that forms the base of the old castle-wall near the seashore. It is nearly twenty feet long, and broad and deep in proportion. To whom can I dedicate it with so great propriety as to King Solomon himself, who, it is said, ordered a number of stones cut upon this model, beveled as this is, and built on this the foundation of the Temple-wall in Mount Moriah, as is seen to this day.

And here at Gebal I am insensibly reminded of the reflection made by a distinguished poet (Lamartine), while visiting another spot famous in history. Let me quote it: "I pass delicious hours, recumbent beneath the shade, my eyes fixed on the falling pediment of that Parthenon. Its aspect displays, better than history, the colossal grandeur of a people. What superhuman civilization was that which supplied a great man to command, an architect to conceive, a sculptor to decorate, statuaries to execute, workmen to cut, a people to pay, and eyes to comprehend and admire such an edifice as this! Where again shall we find such a people, or such a period? Nowhere!"

The same poetical writer records his impressions of Gebal in these words—(he was here April 13, 1833): "I slept at Gebal, in a khan (tavern) outside the city, on a rising ground overlooking the sea Gebal is supposed to be the country of the ancient Giblites, who supplied King Hiram with *squares* of stone for the building of the Temple of Solomon. The father of Adonis had a palace here. The worship of the sun constituted the religion of all the neighboring countries of Tyre." My readers will readily correct the mistake into which our French brother, or his translator, has fallen, in writing *squares* of stone for *squarers* of stone.

Before leaving Gebal, I sought out the entrance of one of the great Phœnician tombs, carved out of the face of the cliffs high above the town, and there cut deeply with my chisel the *Square and Compass,* dedicating it to a number of active working and renowned members of the Craft, named below. There, too, I waved aloft my Masonic banner in the strong breeze blowing from the sea.

On this cliff, in the pure air of this mountain region, sounds move with the greatest freedom. I hear the *muezzin* in the minaret of the mosque, a mile away, with perfect ease: *Il Allah— ah—ah—ah,* "No God but God," and my heart answers: "Amen: So mote it be!" So the trumpets of the Crusaders sounded as they came down this coast from Antioch, A.D. 1099, on their way to the Holy City. So the "procul, procul" of the priests of Adonis rang through this clear air, many centuries before.

In selecting appropriate names of Masons worthy to be associated with this School of Hiram's builders, I anticipate the general approval of the following: L. E. Hunt, John S. Perry, A. G. Abell, Winslow Lewis, John Augustus Williams, J. Emmet Blackshear, William M. Cunningham, Thomas H. Logan, A. R. Cotton, James Gibson.

I found no member of the Masonic fraternity here, but among the officers in the garrison several, who have probably since united with the lodge at Beirut. In the nomenclature of American lodges some are named *Hiram Abiff Lodge,* as, for instance, No. 90, Maine, etc.

In my preface I alluded to the provocations to laughter that meet the traveler here. Will my readers accept a little nonsense that I wrote from Gebal for that genial brother, Robert D. Holmes (now, alas! silent in the grave), to publish in the *New York Sunday Dispatch?*

"I would fain disport me in this exceedingly solemn and un-hilarious country, where the only thing that ever *seems* to smile is the camel; and this is only a pretence, as I verified today, when, attracted by the pleasing manner in which he threw his lower jaw around his upper one, I went up to pat him and he bit me. Such is life. I haven't had a good laugh since I landed on the Syrian coast.

"I came from Beirut to Gebal the other day, chiefly to collect relics. I was also slightly in hopes of finding the remains of the Christian tribes of Israel, long lost, and probably the murderer of Helen Jewett. Nobody seems to have been here before, at least I could not find anybody that knew anything about it, and the only guide-book that speaks of it is the Holy Writings—good authority, but rather ancient as a book of travels. However, I got here easy enough, because all you have to do is to *follow the coast.* If you undertake to turn to the right you go over Jebel Sunnin, some eight thousand feet high (one thousand of it solid snow-banks), and if you would deviate even slightly to the left, you experience Jonah's fate, without the intervention of Jonah's whale. I came in eight hours, and took lodgings in a house kept by three priests, who, no doubt, would have been extremely shocked had they understood my question when I politely inquired as to the health of their wives and children.

"My arrival was the signal for all Gebal to gather at my quarters with what they call 'anteeks.' And such antics as the bare-legged fellows do cut when they call on you! Try to realize the condition of the American Howadji trading for 'anteeks.' Poor, but proud, as you know, I rigged up a seat upon an upright stone by covering it with all my overcoats and blankets, and upon that I sat in state. Dignity is not wasted even on Arabs. Intelligence of expression, firmness mingled with suavity (*suaviter in modo,* etc., you have the rest); the strictest honor in dealing out small change, yet the severest decision in requiring an honest compensation; these are the true principles for traffic in 'anteeks,' and these the American Howadji (if the court knows herself) *has* displayed, as all Gebal will testify.

"My first purchases of 'anteeks' were curious. A number of decanter stoppers, avowedly from Phœnician tombs, cost me quite a handful of ten-para pieces. Buckles, cast off by the military, I secured in good supply. I think I should have gone on purchasing buckles to the last had I not found the trade-mark "Smith & Brown" on one, and this made me skeptical. Broken crockery, several crates full. This, I felt, I was getting cheap, viz., one para for ten pieces (now, one para is one-fortieth part of ten cents); I, therefore, secured the golden opportunity, and if I can get it all shipped to America, you must advertise for me, for I shall open a wholesale establishment of Syrian shards. The next day, however, I took an extensive walk across, around, and *under* Gebal, and I should testify, if upon oath, that one-half the soil is broken crockery. Query: Did the ancient Phœnicians slosh around and break things as they do in Alabama? If not, why so many broken vessels? But this discovery stopped further purchases of shards.

"Having bought up all the buckles, tops of pewter buttons, brass tacks, glass beads, etc., together with a considerable quantity of musket-flints, which I was assured had curious inscriptions on them, I saw that I was making no headway, and began to inquire for ancient coins. At this, the modern Giblites sneered. Coins? Why, they told Hassan the very earth was old coins, in various stages of dilapidation! Still, I insisted that, salable as the articles they had been furnishing me admittedly were, yet the old coins of Phœnicia and her conquerors were what I had come for. Then they went out for a few hours, and brought them in. I must honestly aver that I did not know there was so much specie of the copper coinage in the whole world as there is here among the ruins of Gebal. Every object in nature, and a great many objects *out* of nature, are stamped on them. Names, portraits, inscriptions, and emblems abound, often in the best state of preservation. The Howadji was amazed, and began to ask himself what conveyance, under the elephants of Antiochus, that used to come down this road some 2,300 years ago, could convey such burdens, if I bought them all. I bought, and bought, and bought, until nature and my small change were exhausted, and then I closed my purchases.

"Of genuine relics and antiques (let me be serious for a moment) I procured a good supply, in the form of tear-bottles, funeral lamps, cornelian scarabæi, seals of various devices, and several elegant carvings in marble, but sadly mutilated.

"In making my daily tour around and beneath the place (I mean the tombs so wonderfully excoriated beneath the surface), I was guided by an old, bare-legged barnacle, who clung to me from first to last with unwearying devotion. Had the mainspring of his zeal been the love of science, Agassiz himself might well defer to him, but alas, it was the love of backsheesh. It was the funniest sight in the world to look at my procession, and I wonder that even that fellow who goes out on the top of the Mohammedan mosque every little while to scream out 'Hu Mah!' did not stop to laugh as he saw it. First went the bare-legged old gray-beard, in his right hand a long-stemmed pipe. He had but two passions, one to get me to the interesting localities, the other to get me away from them before I could see anything. This Howadji never did so much tall walking to so little purpose in his life, as in following old Backsheesh the first day. Afterward, however, he took matters more into his own hands. Next to the guide came the subscriber. He was ornamented with a red cap, which he bought at Smyrna, because everybody buys one of them for his sins; he wore it five days in succession. That sunstroke, or at the least ophthalmia, did not supervene, is a subject of gratitude. Next came Hassan, my interpreter, who was all the time interpreting Arabic into hassanic English. This dialect of our common tongue is formed chiefly out of nouns, with a few adjectives. It has every element of sublimity near to profundity; and certainly no living man can beat it. Let me give you a specimen. Hassan is telling me how to smuggle a few *okes* of Gebal tobacco into Beirut. He says, 'Sojer man come to me—say, you tobakky got? Me say no. Then he irons, big irons on my leg. He say to you, you tobakky got? You tell him go way dam fool—go hell—*he go.*' And all this the fellow tells me with perfect gravity, not having the least idea but that the language is eminently chaste and proper.

"Next to Hassan come the rabble. I dare not tell you how many persons have followed me about Gebal, people are so skeptical of travelers' tales. But as there are only six hundred people here, you can easily make the estimate. I fear that some of my company were disreputable characters, but as there is no Sunday paper published at Gebal (nor for that matter any other), and as no strangers ever visit the place, it is of less importance. You will, of course, make no mention of it to the discredit of the American Howadji. So from ruin to ruin we wandered—now looking sadly at a group of sarcophagi wherein once lay the beloved dead, broken to pieces, or, still worse, used only for water-troughs and baser purposes; now plucking an extraordinary specimen of the *anemone,* which crimsons all these hills as with the blood of Adonis; now chaffering for an 'anteek' now twisting my lame ankle round a boulder until I seem to have more than the usual number of joints in it; now creeping into an excavation lined with loculi or places for the dead, all cut into the solid rock; now sipping coffee with some Giblite gentleman, who invites me to his house, courteously excuses me from taking off my boots, and seats me in the Lewan, the place of honor; now standing by some high wall anathematizing the barbarism of its builders, who destroyed chapters, pillars, and sarcophagi, with ruthless hand, to

build it, undoing in a day what years of labor was necessary to
construct; now from some high place looking over the blue sea and
heaving a homesick sigh after that steamer whose prow points
westward; now walking over the piles of granite columns in the
harbor; now sitting, to relieve aching foot, and conning over the
past and the glories of Gebal till the sun goes down and the jackal
begins his cry, and I return to my room to write out the
adventures of the American Howadji for the *New York Dispatch*
and its million readers.

"As you or some friend may desire to call on me while I am
domiciled here, I will give you explicit directions for finding my
boardinghouse. Let us suppose you starting out at some well-
marked locality in the city—say at the corner where the blind
beggar sits, near the three granite columns, a little east of the
narghileh establishment half-way up the hill. Now you will have
no difficulty in tracing the way to my residence, if you will only
'follow the directions.' The embarrassment experienced by some
people in getting round our Oriental city is greatly exaggerated
by their neglect 'to follow directions.'

"Well, then, take the blind beggar on your left shoulder, and
come round the new barracks, avoiding as far as you can those
eight donkeys that are always coming round that particular
corner with their loads of stone from the quarry. So far you have
made a good start. Now enter that street—do not call it a mere
drain; it is a good six feet wide—until you meet the camel with
his two bales of cotton. Avoid that camel; he snapped at me one
morning. On now to where the boys are playing marbles. If they
throw stones at you, smile and pass on. The darlings; their little
arms are not strong enough to hurt you much, though they may
break your spectacles, as they did mine. Look back. They are
saying something in Arabic that is doubtless a blessing on the
stranger's head. On again to the second or third turning to the
right—usually you will find there a man who sells bread. Ask him
(in Arabic) to direct you to my house."

While I was at Gebal, a native musician of some note was favoring
the people with his performances, and I took advantage of the
opportunity to increase my stock of knowledge. He was evidently in
partnership with a coffee-seller, who had a little dark cellar near the
castle; for while the audience enjoyed the *music* they were naturally

stimulated to buy *tobacco* and *coffee.* I stumbled on the establishment one morning, and was so entertained thereby as to return to it frequently. It was rather expensive to me; for in the spirit of Kentucky hospitality I always "treated the crowd" with cigarettes and coffee, and this involved an outlay, sometimes as high as fifteen or twenty cents for the lot. But I did not begrudge it. It was a real treat to watch that fellow and his proceedings. He sat on an earthen platform, raised about four feet from the floor. A stool was always brought for me, and I sat facing him. The rest of the company squatted on the ground, and sipped and smoked at my expense. Just such men had sat and sung and listened here ages before Romulus with his copper plowshare drew the boundaries of Rome.

He had a sort of fiddle with one string. But *such* a string! It was an inch or two wide. And such a bow! the wooden part of it like an ox-bow; and *such* hairs with which it was strung! From a donkey's mane and tail every one of them; else whence the hideous bray that fiddle made? The man had one eye, front teeth missing, a shirt on—only this and nothing more. On his knees, as he sat, lay an Arabic book, folio, on which his *blind* eye was steadily fixed; the *good* one watching me. He would sing a minute or two (I shall describe Arabic music in future chapters) at the top of his voice, until he turned purple in the face, and I *had* hopes he was going off into an epileptic fit, when he would suddenly stop, smile, and rasp that broad string. Then my hands went up to my ears. Then I thought of all the bad things I had ever done, and repented of them.

Hassan translated for me. One of the songs, of which I made notes, I found afterwards in Brother W. R. Alger's poetical version of Eastern poems.* He gives it thus—but I must say it did not *sound* at all like it:

My God once mixed a harsh cup, for me to drink from it,
And it was full of acrid bitterness intensest;
The black and nauseating draught did make me shrink from it,
And cry, "O Thou who every draught alike dispensest,
This cup of anguish sore, bid me not to quaff of it,
Or pour away the dregs and the deadliest half of it!"
But still the cup He held; and seeing He ordained it,
One glance at Him, it turned to sweetness as I drained it!

---

* The news that comes to me in November, 1871, that this amiable gentleman and marvelous scholar has gone deranged through excessive study, has excited the sympathies of a great circle of friends and brethren.

The subjects selected were more usually amatory, and, I suspect, from the leering and sensuous smiles of Hassan and the other auditors, were such as a married man ought not to hear. Yet this is characteristic of Eastern verse, and the dirty sans-culotte who thus afforded merriment connected us by a simple tie with El Mamoun and the Pyramid of Cheops on the one hand, and Haroun-al-Raschid and his Nights' Entertainment on the other. For El Mamoun was the son and (unworthy) successor of *Aaron the Great* (Haroun-al-Raschid).

I spent a good many hours in the old Church of St. George, to which I have before alluded. When I explore one of these ancient churches, I am affected by the thought that it presents a parallel to the Scriptures in this: the thought it embodies is *divine,* though the *materials* of which it is composed are of the coarsest, only stone and wood, fastened together with lime and iron. So the material facts making up the inspired narrative are but commonplace, but the *theory* is divine.

In this venerable fane have stood the feet of Godfrey, first King of Jerusalem; he who "increased the glory of his people when like a giant he put on his arms for the fight;" and Tancred, and Gerard the Crusader, who chose rather to die than inflict dishonor on the holy cause he professed. Glory gilds their sepulchers and embalms their memories. Into this church has entered Salah-ed-deen (Saladin), chief of the Saracens (born at Takreet, on the Tigris, A.D. 1137), of whose death-dealing arm we shall read when we come to the field of slaughter, Hattin—fatal Friday of July, 1187, never to be obliterated on the page of history.

The cemetery of Gebal was right under my windows. In the middle of it was a small summer-house which, at certain hours of the day, was thronged with women, who have a practice here of praying by the graves of husbands, parents, children and friends. In one sense the custom works well; for they always wear clean white clothes in the graveyard, and really look handsome at a distance. One evening, about sundown, I was hurrying to dinner, and found my pathway through the cemetery blocked up by these mourning women. It is considered bad manners for a man to interrupt women in the graveyard. In fact, they throw stones at you if you do. And there they "sot and sot," entirely enveloped in their concealing garments, occupying all the eligible hollows and shady places, until it became almost dark. The ordinary dress of the women has much in common with that of the men; a dirty white tunic (vulgarly called shirt) bound round with a leathern girdle, somewhat in the style of our Patron-Saint John the Baptist. I was glad when they left and I could proceed to my dinner.

I remarked before, that I boarded, or, rather, hired a room, while in Gebal, of some Maronite priests. This was in the second story of the house, the lower being the stables. A large wooden door opened from the street. No house in the Holy Land has more than one door. A heavy iron knocker adorned that door. When I wanted to enter, I struck the knocker three times. One of the priests, generally Father Yusef, or his assistant Latoof, "looked out of the window" (as Jezebel did at Jezreel, 2 Kings 9:30), and seeing who it was, pulled a cord which lifted a heavy wooden latch, and then, with some muscular effort and fearful squeaking of hinges, I pushed the gate open, mounted the stone stairs to the top of the house, first story, and so entered my room.

The private room of my landlord was furnished scantily enough. I looked in upon him one morning, and saw three old presses, a lamp, a small box, and the mat on which Father Yusef sat, reading his breviary and keeping time by the motion of his body and the droning of his voice.

My host had a visitor, a reverend old gentleman, with voluble tongue and winning behavior, who used to show me through the bazaars and persuade me to buy things. But I discovered he was allowed his little commission on my purchases, and so confined myself to a few pounds of the tobacco for which Gebal has been famous ever since tobacco was introduced here, a few centuries back. These Oriental bazaars shall have full description in future chapters. I saw in this one an old man wrapped in a coarse, tattered garment, sitting on the ground, with a bushel of dirty wheat lying on a fine cloth before him, selling it by the gallon. Close by him women were seated, one with a few oranges, another having a small quantity of rice, etc., etc.

The variety sold in these miscellaneous collections of shanties called bazaars, is something remarkable; cotton and silk clothes; beef, mutton, fish, and eggs; poultry, skinny, small and cheap; quinces, pomegranates, apricots, figs, raisins, olives, grapes, and other fruit; domestic utensils;—the list is as long as my arm.

I bought of a man here a simple, plain cross, out in marble, perhaps marking the resting-place of some early disciple of the Crucified

One. Also, a fragment of an elegant statuette, a faunus, in Parian marble, exquisitely wrought. Both these rare objects were burned three years afterward in the great fire at Chicago.

It is a charming memory of Gebal, of the evenings, about sundown, when I was accustomed to walk alone around the old phœnician harbor. The sound of a convent-bell high up in Lebanon sometimes affected me to tears. The sea, smooth as the clearest mirror; the sun descending magnificently into it; the evening star, soon followed by the whole host of the heavenly lights, and a glorious night breaking in around me. I can never forget it. The sea-line here presents a constant succession of novelties. Now a jelly-fish, strangely out of its element, and soon to be swallowed by the gulls as one would gulp down a mouthful of *blanc-mange.* Now the jaws of a shark, not very large, but so abundantly supplied with teeth that I sawed my riding-stick through upon one of them in a jiffy; even as Talus performed that exploit with the jaws of a *serpent,* and was so pleased with the experiment that he kept trying until he invented the first iron saw. Now an oyster-shell (the *ostrea edulis*), but what business it has here, is more than I can describe. Certainly, I had no idea that the Baltimore oyster lives near Gebal. On one occasion I found the dead body of that enemy of flocks and herds, that gourmand of the flesh of asses, that eater of grain when meat cannot be had, the hyena. On another occasion the waves were rolling, foaming, and breaking in the most beautiful and majestic manner, the creamy mass of foam tossed by the sparkling waves, as again and again they roll majestically in to the shore, rapidly pushing each other, and riding over each other in merry play like the sea-gods of old gambolling among the isles of the Ægean. The world retires with its noisy discords, its poor shows, its empty glories, and gives way to the solemnity of the seas constantly doing their work.

It was a constant source of interest to me to watch the fishermen who stood, naked, a little ways in the sea, or on a jutting column. Of one I made this note: his net is gathered on his left arm, crooked, cleared and prepared for a throw with one turn of his right hand. Taking advantage of the ripples made by the wind, the sun throwing a shadow behind him, he runs along the shore until he sees a school of fish. Then, noiselessly and with much dexterity, he makes his throw. The net opens and spreads as it goes, so that a bag that could be compressed in my hat covers a space of twenty-five feet in circumference. I have not time to learn the art, but think I could do it with practice. This labor promotes meditation, as old Izaak Walton so often acknowledged, and this may be seen, perhaps, by a shrewd discerner, in the character of Peter, James, John, and those other "fishers of men," born on the shores of Galilee.

I made hundreds of notes under the excitement of the moment, some worthy of record, though not to be dovetailed with connected subjects. I append a page or two.

Of the jackals I write, late one night, getting up, lighting a candle, and fumbling for my pencil expressly to do so; that my slumbers on that stony couch were disturbed by the jackals, whose dismal howlings rent the air, seeming to threaten me with a penalty for intruding on their ancient dominion. From a hilly knob just above the town I write: it is a stirring scene—the gazelles playing in the valleys, partridges running up the hillsides, along these territories of the old Phœnician—

> Whose iron arm did make the mighty world
> A reach of beauty, and subdued the wave.

Of a sarcophagus, elegantly carved, I quote:

> "Faith, with her torch beside, and little cupids
> Dropping upon an urn their marble tears."—*Southey*.

Of the boys in the bazaars, I say, they prove themselves apt scholars. One of them has learned a compound English oath of four hundred horse-power, which none but a sailor could have taught him, and hard enough to raise the sheet-anchor without a windlass; another one repeated to me an expression so obscene, that I was glad to believe he himself did not know what it meant. Some tourists delight to corrupt these unsophisticated youth. Of the effect of the sunlight upon this cretaceous stone and soil, I say, I soon had to stop looking for specimens after 10 A. M., the glare of "the sun waxed hot" upon the calcareous rock seeming almost to blear my eyeballs. No wonder these people have weak eyes. Our missionary friends down there at Beirut, in printing books for them, use a type extremely large; anything smaller than four-line pica fails to serve them without glasses. I notice, when I show these people my pocket Bible, they scarcely distinguish the letters. The natives suppose every American to be a *hakeem* (doctor), and a very little surgical and medical skill makes the traveler extremely useful to them. As the Giblites know I am a Doctor (*not* M.D., but how should they appreciate the difference?) they often came to me with their wants. All I could do, however, was to look serious, feel the pulse, and divide my piece of ginger-root with them. Even for this they seemed thankful, always acknowledging my kindness by the tender

word *backsheesh*. Amongst the flowers most common here I note
the cyclamen, and recall the lines—

> "Tis cyclamen I choose to give,
>   Whose pale white blossoms at the tips
> (All else as driven snow) are pink,
>   And mind me of my true love's lips.
>   *   *   *   *   *   *
> Old, kept, and kissed, it does not lose,
>   As other flowers, the hues they wear;
> Love is triumphant, and this bloom
>   Will never whiten for despair.
> Rather it deepens as it lies,
> This flower that purples when it dies.

Of the uncounted mass of art-treasures, fragmentary and
heaped up on every hand, I say: these elegant moldings, cornices,
and entablatures are thrown together with common stone to
make walls for the fields. In giving my measurements of distances,
etc., it is well to compare the standards used at different times in
this country, with our own:

The Roman mile was .... 0.710   of a geographical mile.
Arabic mile .... 1.055   "
Turkish mile .... 0.689   "
German mile .... 4.000   "

The average caravan journey with camels is reckoned at about
sixteen miles per day; mules make about eighteen miles. All
travel here is ordinarily so slow that the dromedary who carries
the mail at the rate of six miles an hour, and the blooded Arabian
who gallops one hundred a day, are prodigies in comparison.

The sight of a great cavity bored in the monstrous ashlar in the
castle, by some stupid treasure-seeker, recalls Sveboda's description
of a similar attempt to find gold and silver, by boring into *the head* of
the stone statue at Pergamos, Asia Minor, under the belief that in
the center of the skull is a rich deposit. The fellow who did it hadn't
much in the center of *his* skull. The people below here are cutting
and planting joints of sugar-cane. The Crusaders, as they came to
Antioch, in 1098, first ate and described sugar-cane. Afterwards they
became so fond of it as to cultivate the plant and erect large mills for
grinding and purifying it, near Jericho. One man, today, was plowing
with two little oxen, scarcely larger than a pair of *yearlings* in
Kentucky. Numbers of camels were winding down the mountain-side
laden with squared stones for buildings at Beirut. Hassan says the
camel here is worth from $100 to $125 for a good one. The fair horse,
such as I am riding, cost him twenty napoleons— about $80. The
old Roman road, running north of Junia Bay, still shows the rats
worn into it by Roman chariots in the days of the empire. A
wheelbarrow could not now be trundled over it without

danger to the wheel. The town of Junia is beautifully located, and I do not wonder the rich citizens of Beirut like to reside here in warm weather. A mile north of it is a place of romantic interest. A cave, partly artificial, is in the hillside, about three hundred feet from the beach, traces of an arch inclosing it with faint lines around the top; the thundering roar of the breakers making its walls quiver; the blue and grand sea, with four sail-vessels in sight; an ancient ruin crowning a high point near by; a palm-tree on another eminence; the magnificent Lebanon in the rear; the interminable line of telegraphic wire connecting this retired nook with the outer world;— why was I not an artist?

Today I first saw that the ancient custom of hauling the coasting vessels on the shore for repairs, or for wintering and storms, is still kept up. A number of them were thus disposed of a few miles from Gebal, in a sheltered cove, where the workmen were calking and repairing them. On a coast like this, where no docks can be built, such a method is indispensable.

I watched the exercises of the soldiers here today, particularly in the *Manual of Arms,* which they went through well enough. Could they have kept their eyes off *me,* they would have done better; but every time the drill-master rested for an instant, one hundred and fifty pairs of eyes made me their focus. As I saw they wanted me to *smile* in token of approbation, I smiled every time. This made the lance-corporal so happy that he snickered, and got a cut for it from the drill-master's ratan, and good enough for him. As I saw the drill-master wanted an excuse to speak to me, I offered him one of Hassan's cigarettes (I do not smoke myself), and it would have shocked old Baron Steuben to see how quick he (the drill-master) lighted it and commenced smoking, while one hundred and fifty mouths watered to do the like. I told him to invite the soldiers to coffee at my expense, which he did, at an outlay to me of a trifle less than a dollar (6 mills a cup, for 150 cups, is how much?)

SILVER PENNY OF TIBERIUS

PAPYRUS IN LAKE HULEH.

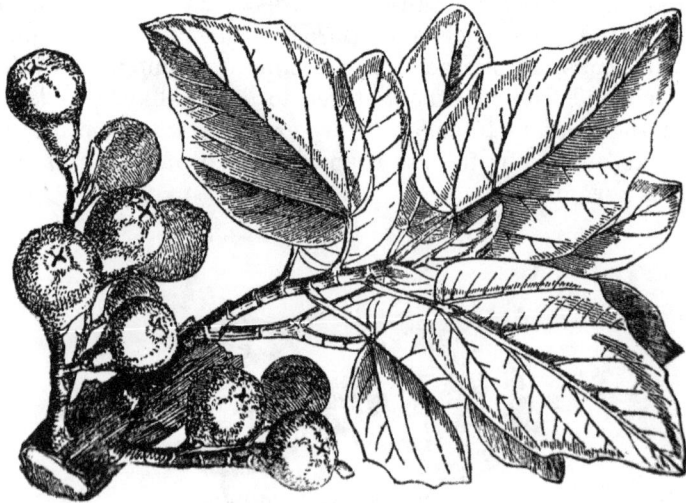

THE FIG.

THE TALL CEDARS OF LEBANON.

DIVISION FOURTH.—LEBANON

As Lebanon's small mountain-flood
Is rendered holy by the ranks
Of sainted cedars on its banks.

Like a glory, the broad sun
Hangs o'er sainted Lebanon,
Whose head in wintry grandeur towers,
And whitens with eternal sleet,
While summer in a vale of flowers
Is sleeping rosy at his feet.

Lifting their dreamy tops far into the heavens, there seems to be a conscious majesty about them: keeping ward and watch over the world below, they stand,

Like earth's gigantic sentinels
Discoursing in the skies.

How calm, how beautiful comes on
The stilly hour when storms are gone.

Palestine sits, as represented in the well-known coin of Vespasian, desolate, robbed, and spoiled, a widow amidst the graves of husband, children, and friends.

And the trees, once so numerous that everybody in the land had heard of them, and almost every one had seen them, are now so few that, as Isaiah predicted (10:19), a child may count them.

Lebanon is ashamed and hewn down (Isaiah 33:9).

CHAPTER X.

HE third of the Seven Grand Masonic Localities, according to my system, is Mount Lebanon, the site of the cedars. First, I took my readers to *Tyre,* whence came the Pillar of Strength, King Hiram, and his multitude of skilled employees, to whom the work of temple-building was familiar. Second, I led them to *Gebal,* the seat of the Schools of Architecture, whence came out that wisest of ancient Builders, Hiram Abif. In the present division I shall discuss *Lebanon,* the source of the cedar-trees, of which such large quantities were used by King Solomon, not only for the construction of the Temple, but for his palace in Zion, in which this material was so largely employed that the edifice was called "the house of the forest of Lebanon." Following the order already commenced, the reader may expect to be conducted successively to the bay in which the cedars were gathered into rafts ("flotes"); to Joppa, where they were drawn ashore for land-shipment; to the clay-grounds in the plain of Jordan, where the foundries were established, and finally to Jerusalem, where everything was consummated, both in operative and speculative Masonry. Until within a few years, it was thought that the only remains of the once abundant forests of cedars that crowned the caps of Lebanon, in its entire range, were at a point about three days' journey northeast of Beirut, and nearly due east of Tripoli. It was there that travelers sought them, and many a glowing account of their immense trunks, their lofty tops and spreading foliage, has been transmitted to us through travelers' journals. There are about five hundred trees, great and small, in the grove at that place, on the head-waters of the Kadisha (the Sacred River), that flows into the Mediterranean Sea near Tripoli. Latterly, however, large groves of the same trees have been discovered, particularly one within a day's journey of Beirut. The trees here, though not quite so large as the others, are of the same species of cedar, viz., the *Cedrus Libani,* or *Pinus Cedrus,* as another botanist styles it, and amply repays the visit of the tourist. I started from Beirut to see them, April 25th, in company with Brother Samuel Hallock, and propose now to make report of my journey.

The way out of Beirut is by the French turnpike towards Damascus. This I followed for twenty-five and a half French miles, equal to about eighteen of ours. It is an excellent road, perfectly smooth, ascending the whole way in a romantic serpentine, in which the traveler is never out of sight of the sea. The thick groves of olive and mulberry trees around Beirut, with the heavy snow-banks that crown the mountain-tops before you, and the increasing coolness of the breeze, afford delightful sensations. Some of these valleys around which the road winds, are deep and impressive, while the variety of travelers, the cultivated terraces, and the thousand novelties of which one never gets weary, take away from the monotony of ordinary travel, and give a delightful zest to the undertaking.

To give an accurate account of travel upon these mountains, I insert here, as the most fitting place, a description of my stage-ride, a month earlier, from Beirut to Damascus. There is only one stage-line in all Syria and Palestine, and for this good reason, only *one road* on which a stage could travel. *Wheels* are a superfluity here; *legs* have the monopoly. Over this one stage-road I passed, March 26th, 1868, on my journey from Beirut to Damascus. The road is 110 French miles in length (equal to about seventy-five American miles) and is passed over in fourteen hours; the way, of course, being extremely mountainous. The stage (or, as termed here, *diligence,* pronounced dily-*zhonce*) starts for Beirut at 4 A.M., and arrives at Damascus at 6 P.M. I arise at 3 A.M., being called by my host, Brother Hallock, who has insured his own waking up by the primitive process of *sitting up all night;* get a good cup of coffee and a bite, and go, followed by his faithful servant Asaph (pronounced Hasaf, accent on the last syllable), down to the stage-office, lantern in hand. A person in any Oriental city caught out after dark without a lantern goes to prison, or only avoids that penalty by a heavy *backsheesh* to the officer who arrests him. As we walk down the narrow *lanes* (which are over-honored by being called streets) the only living objects met by us are the police (who are soldiers carrying muskets, so very useful a weapon in the dark!) and the dogs. The latter, having no owners, lie out at nights and bark at all who approach them.

The stage-office is a room twelve feet by eight, in which the baggage is weighed. I am allowed a weight of ten *okes* (whatever that means), and as mine weighed eleven I pay a piaster and a half (nine cents) extra for that. My stage-fare, 101 piasters, is equal to about $4.00 in our currency. At this season the stage is so much in demand by travelers that seats must be engaged several days in advance. Seven mules, three abreast, draw the *diligence.* Seats are arranged in four compartments, and tickets sold accordingly. The lower story is divided into two rooms. On top there is a seat for four immediately behind the driver, and a place still further back among the baggage where a dozen or more can sit, *uncomfortably.* The whole diligence is nearly as large and quite as heavy as an ordinarily sized Masonic lodge-room in the United States. My seat is *on deck,* beside the driver, the pleasantest berth of all, and cheaper than in the lower cabin. The front room below is occupied by a Syrian, his wife, servant, and child; the back room by a Turk with his hareem. By the way, I got a sight at the women at breakfast-time, but am not tempted to a second peep. Pale, sickly, and faded, like bundles of old pinks – that is about the way they look, to me.

The seven mules are started by the driver coming down in his seat with a concussion like a heavy rock, and screaming out in French "heep." If that word has the same effect upon horses accustomed to the English language, I recommend my readers to try it; it will stimulate into motion even the most obdurate. Our seven quadrupeds go off like a shot; the assistant driver, whose business it is to manage the brakes, shouts *yellah, yellah,* at the top of his voice. This word, I am told, was originally intended as blasphemy, but in modern parlance it only means *go ahead.*

YELLAH! right through the public square, where in the day-time all manner of professions are followed, from trading horses to cheating us Franks in the purchase of antiques.

YELLAH! into a narrow lane and up a hill, with the tail-end of the constellation *Scorpio* right before me, as I peer over the driver's head upon the morning sky beyond.

YELLAH! past the stonecutters' shops where yesterday I saw the descendants of the ancient "Giblites" at their devices, each one squatted upon his hams in true Oriental style.

YELLAH! past the office of the American Consul, the kind and gentlemanly Mr. J. A. Johnson, his national coat-of-arms appearing faintly over the gate, near which all day sits his military guard, sword in hand, as becomes the armed defender of so great a nation.

YELLAH! past the dwellings of Beirut's aristocracy, each with its verandas with galleries, and queer eyelet holes, its orange-groves in the trickling grounds of water from the fountains in the court.

YELLAH! past the big sycamore trees holding their great limbs horizontally out, each strong enough for a dozen of Zaccheus.

YELLAH! past the last military station on the borders of the city, and along the lanes lined with the great cactus-leaves, faithful to their trust as any lodge-tyler, and through the interminable mulberry groves with which the suburbs of Beirut are planted.

YELLAH! past the three palm-trees on the left and the two on the right, and skirting the forest of pine-trees planted here centuries ago by the great Fakah-ad-din, and past those carob-trees, reminding me of the Prodigal Son, and through more lanes of the prickly-pear and past more palm-trees and more sycamores, and now at the foot of the mountains, we address ourselves, about 5 A.M., to the ascent of Lebanon.

Let me read a Biblical passage; it is good to go up the sides of Lebanon with the Word of God in one's mouth: "The glory of Lebanon shall come unto thee, the fir-tree, the pine-tree and the box together to sanctify the place of my sanctuary; and I will make the place of my feet glorious." And shall I this day in good truth pass over Lebanon? Forty-five years ago I read that passage in Isaiah, when a little boy at my mother's knee.

"At last; all things come round at last!"

The French engineers did their work well in building this road. Its grade is nowhere (except in one place) more than the ordinary road-level of a good highway, though to get over the range, which is some 8,000 feet in altitude, the task is a serious one. The road, in fact, winds like a serpent, often returning almost into itself, and traversing a mile of length to gain a quarter in height. A milestone (of French measure) is set for every mile. A telegraph-line, with two wires, accompanies it in the main, but often leaves it for a while, to gain the short cuts. Lightning, I discover, can go up hill by a steeper grade than the most diligent *diligence.* In three hours we have attained to the twenty-fifth milestone. By this time the toiling world has fully commenced its day's work, and we are meeting it in endless variety. First an old man driving his loaded donkey; then a cavalcade of mules heavily laden; then a lot of camels piled up with rawhides; then a long succession of covered wagons belonging to the telegraph company, each drawn by three mules tandem.

We change our own team every hour, usually putting on six horses or mules, sometimes only five, in one instance eight, according to the character of the grade. At the stations all the Arabs of the vicinity gather in, and every one helps, with tongue and hands, to shout and fasten the rope-harness used in this country. The horses are in general miserable, worn-out, half-fed beasts; the mules look better.

At the foot of the mountain I had observed the snowy top in advance, apparently quite near; but it was not until nearly nine o'clock, and I had come thirty miles, that I reached it. Snow has fallen enormously deep up here, and even now the banks are very thick, and the snow so hard as to bear the weight of a horse. No wonder it is so cold here as to require gloves, overcoats, and wrappers, although at Beirut it was too warm for any of them.

About daylight we see a jackal sneaking into a ravine from his dirty deeds of darkness. He reminds me for all the world of a prairie-wolf.

Looking up the mountain-flanks, all seems desolate and uncultivated; but, looking backwards from this height, what a mistake! every square rod of ground is cultivated, mulberry-trees, fig trees, olive-trees, etc., by millions striking their roots into this soil, the latter especially "sucking oil from the flinty rock," as the Scriptures figure it. The picture is the reverse of the *locust* image; for, as you ascend the mountain, *before you* seems the desert, *behind you* the garden. Grain is shooting greenly from every flat, and promising its owners an hundredfold. 'Tis curious, however, to ask where these people live, for while surveying a vast area of cultivated land you do not see a single house. The reason, however, is, that the houses are built of stone, with flat roofs covered with earth, on which, at this season, grass is thickly growing. They are not distinguishable to the eye for want of chimney-smoke, windows, etc., etc., as in our country.

By nine o'clock I am nearly at the top, after five hours of steady climbing. What a magnificent valley is this on my left! grand indeed; and here the fig tree takes the place of the mulberry. The two classes are easily distinguished from each other, as the mulberry is always pollarded and trained to a few horizontal limbs near the ground, being raised only for the leaves.

Now the driver and his assistant eat their breakfast; nothing but a few of the thin, black, heavy, unleavened cakes, which is the native bread. No meat, no cheese, no drink of any kind; cheap boarding!

The culverts on this road are of splendid mason-work. The heavy torrents of these mountains demand the strongest kind of conduits to resist their erasive power. An immense machine, made to press the surface of the road into compactness, meets me.

We pass the crown of the mountain about half-past nine; here eight horses are scarcely able to drag us up, with two assistants to run along and whip them. Great crowds of travelers. An officer with thirty foot-soldiers, all in gay spirits. Camels, horses, donkeys, and mules. No private conveyances are met on this road.

Going down Lebanon. Good gracious, what speed! ten miles in forty minutes. Full gallop, and everybody bawling *yellah* at the top of his voice. It quite takes my breath away to look out from my elevated seat in the *parquette*. In meeting the loaded animals their conductors have great difficulty in dragging, pushing, and cursing them out of the way. These Arabs do *cuss* amazingly. One poor donkey, staggering under a load of sacks that almost concealed him, was knocked endwise by our carriage over the parapet, and, for aught I know, may be rolling down Mount Lebanon yet. The assistant, however, holds the handle of our brakes, and so regulates the motion that we arrive safely in the valley of the Bukaa, the ancient "Cœlosyria," a magnificent prairie-plain, from ten to fifteen miles wide, of the richest soil, all in cultivation. Here, at the stage-barn, I get my "déjeuner," or breakfast, for which I pay twelve piasters (they call them *herrish;* five of them make a French franc). It was worth it. The courses were fish, stewed meat, fried meat, oranges from the Sidon gardens, Lebanon figs, small but excellent, the large walnuts (what we call *English* walnuts), wine of the best, and coffee. A half-hour to eat it in. No other passengers partake, they having basketsful of their own.

Here in Cœlosyria I hope to catch a glimpse of Mount Hermon, which lies under the sun from my position, and about forty miles off. "As the dew of Hermon and as the dew that descended upon the mountains of Zion;" how often have I read that passage and longed to cast my eyes upon that memorable height. But I look in vain, nor in all the day's ride can I feast my vision upon it.

YELLAH! a caravan of camels, to which the sight of a stage-coach drawn by six horses is a novelty. They are greatly disturbed at our appearance. They twist their long curly necks in every direction, as if to find a retired spot for escape, and with difficulty are made to obey their masters' voices and keep the road.

11

A company of gentlemen, mounted on splendid Arabian horses. Their saddles are gaily decorated with yellow tasselling; their large shovel-stirrups ring out a merry music; their riders are proud to put them to their paces. Everybody here rides with short stirrup-leathers, which do not add to equestrian gracefulness.

The women whom I meet are generally barefoot, and carry their shoes in their hands; their lords shuffle along, however, with all the dignity of slippers. Both sexes have their legs bare to a height that I dare not measure with the eye. These women trudging over the highways of Lebanon are about as good-looking as Indian squaws of the squaw-class. Five out of six of them have children in their arms.

One of the Syrians, who has his family in the "coupée," comes up and sits by my side. He sings for an hour in the monotonous style usual in this country, and of which no language of mine can afford the slightest idea. Mostly an entire song is limited to three full tones, with its accompanying semitones. It abounds in shakes, in which a particular syllable is made to do service for a whole bar or more of each. I do not understand the words, and I do not want to. It is the very infancy of music, such as would occupy a child at the very earliest age when melody attracts his mind. Accompanied, as it sometimes is, by an instrument of one string, played upon by a bow, and capable of only three notes, these Arabs will continue it in a long, drawling, melancholy monotone for half the night. My Syrian evidently enjoys his own gifts, and so do the driver and assistant, who occasionally pitch in, in a sort of chorus, but all singing the same notes, either in unison or in octaves. Considered as music it is fearful.

People here smoke all the time when not compelled by some urgent necessity to intermit the amusement. In traveling they smoke cigarettes, occupying their valuable time in making one while they are smoking another. The tobacco is about the average strength of dried cabbage-leaves; and as much annoyed as I am when people puff tobacco-smoke into my face, I can really scarcely tell now when this millet-flavored weed is consuming around me. Everybody carries cigarette papers and a box of matches. At home they smoke the *narghileh,* in which the smoke is drawn through cold water, still more reducing its strength of nicotine, and rendering the habit less deleterious. Was it not that I have been so loud in denouncing the use of tobacco all my life, I might even use a *narghileh* ("hubble-bubble," as the machine is called) myself. But there is nothing like consistency.

Leaving my breakfast-place, where I had been studying the Scriptural image of "the sparrow on the house-tops," away we go at a gallop through Cœlosyria. We cross the memorable River *Litany* (which I shall see again near the city of Tyre ere long), upon a wooden bridge with iron railings. What would the mighty conquerors of antiquity think of that? Meet the western-bound stage from Damascus at 11 A.M., full of passengers. Foreign travelers this year very numerous. This is at the forty-seventh milestone. People plowing on every side, generally with two heifers yoked together. The plow is a crooked stick, forked, the short end having an iron coulter. One hand of the plowman holds the end of the stick, the other prods the poor little *cows* along at the rate of a mile an hour. Such caricature of plowing! The wheat and barley not advanced here as in the valley of the Mediterranean, which indeed is very much lower, and consequently warmer.

Opposite milestone No. 53, pass a "tell," or hill, such as often occurs in Scripture history. It is black with browsing goats. This magnificent plain is a very garden of the Lord's own spreading forth; but with such want of agricultural skill it yields scanty returns. Oh for a colony of good American or European farmers, with cattle, and implements of modern make! I observe that the skirts of the Lebanon mountains that slope towards this beautiful valley are not terraced or cultivated at all.

Near the east end of the valley is another "tell," green with springing grain. Near it is a Mohammedan wely or tomb, as I should guess from its appearance. The streams that run along this valley are all full to overflowing from the melting snows in the heights above.

At the sixtieth milestone, at noon, we begin to rise the mountains of anti-Lebanon, nothing like so high or steep as the other, yet high enough, and wanting in all the beautiful terrace-cultivation, etc., of the forepart of the day. For four hours we scarcely meet a person, or observe any signs of human life, save the numerous laborers on the road, and one little town on the left. I forgot to mention several crowds of English and American tourists, hurrying to Beirut to catch the steamer of Sunday next. The Oriental lives of these amiable and helpless beings is divided into two anxious parts, one to *get to* a place, and the other to *get away*. These folks got to Damascus, a hundred of them, night before last. All day yesterday they spent in contriving the means to *get away* from there this morning They pay fabulous sums of money to accomplish these two objects, and when they get home all they can with truth tell, as the reward of *their travels,* is the dust, the lies, the swindles, the fatigues, and the great expenses of their tours. I shall grin with fiendish look for the rest of my life when I hear them talk of their *travels.* Travel enough they have, in all conscience, but all that they see except vanity and vexation can be put into a pomegranate-seed.

At the change of horses at milestone 85, I walked on ahead for a half-hour. Saw an enormous lizard, out-lizarding everything I had conceived of in the lizard line. Saw an old-fashioned home, which a family had established for itself by setting up thorns round the mouth of a cave. It is the "camel-thorn," so called, and a terrible thorn indeed. Here, too, I first observed the basaltic rock of this range, black, metallic, and sonorous when struck. The bright crimson anemone waves in charming contrast with it.

Ten miles further, and I am approaching Damascus, called by the French "Damas," without the *cus,* and by the natives, "Es Shems." Here the fence-walls, out-buildings, and finally the buildings themselves, begin to be made of clay-bricks, cut out about four feet square, dried in the sun and set upon their edges. These are the *adobes* of the Mexican people, and, I am told, make quite durable material for building purposes; certainly they are cheap.

Crows in great abundance are calling to each other, in the purest crow-English, just such as I remember from a boy. If a certain distinguished Iowa gentleman were here, he could sing his "crow song," and be respected.

Vast apricot and peach orchards in full bloom. Fig trees in abundance. No more prickly-pears. The sycamore-trees gigantic. A straight wet-land tree in close clusters. Another jackal creeps up the hill, followed by the curses, both loud and deep, of the driver. I do not know enough of the language to inquire why he is so *down* on the jackal: probably his folks have been foully dealt with by them.

At 105th milestone we begin to strike the River Barada, one of those lovely streams of which the proud Naaman declared "it is better than all the waters of Israel." I think so too. Filled to overflowing from the mountains in which it rises, it pours through its narrow channel brim-full, and we follow it clear down to Damascus, now crossing it upon a wide constructed bridge of French masonry; anon galloping along its beautiful banks under the shadows of these dense orchards; now leaving it for a short distance to take advantage of some short cut; now pressing closely upon it, almost into its waters, so narrow is the glen through which it flows; thus we go at headlong speed, until the river Barada and our stage-coach burst forth together into the plain of Damascus, the oldest city in the world; the city of Abraham and Elisha and Paul; the beautiful gem where two of Mohammed's daughters lie interred; the gateway to the road to Palmyra; the object of one of my life-long dreams—*Damascus.*

At the point where I left the turnpike, I engraved, on the surface of a large, smooth stone on the left-hand side of the way, the device of the *Square and Compass.* The extreme hardness of this material, so long exposed to the weather, made the task a painful one to wrist-muscle, and explains the perfect preservation of such monuments as Hiram's tomb, the great inclosing wall of Mount Moriah, the Fountains of Solomon at Etham, and others.

Leaving the turnpike, the change to a Lebanon bridle-way is at once painfully evident. You begin to descend a hill so steep that you involuntarily stop and look around to see that the road before you has no been abandoned. At first sight it resembles those deep gullies some times observed in our own country, washed out by wintry storms from a forsaken road. Finding that there is no other way, you get down and attempt to lead your horse. But a Syrian horse is accustomed to be *ridden* or driven, not *led.* If you are alone, there is no other remedy but to remount and let the animal bear you down the hill at his own discretion. Here the peculiar training of the horse is seen in the perfect caution and safety with which he does his work. Teetering from rock to rock, springing up a long step, dropping down on two feet at a time when the descent is too great for *one,* placing his feet successively into crevices barely large enough for them, and taking the worst places he comes to so cheerfully as to show he is accustomed to it, the horse soon brings you to the foot of the first hill, and prepares to mount the second. That day's journey gave me a new idea of the intelligence of a Syrian horse. Sometimes we rounded the sides of precipices so high and steep that I was fain to shut my eyes in dismay. Sometimes we meandered among gigantic masses of rocks shaken from the mountains by some old earthquakes. Sometimes we crossed stone bridges so narrow and rough that nothing but the peculiar construction of the horse's shoes (made to cover the whole foot) prevented him from slipping. Finally we arrived at the village of Ain-Zehalteh and closed our first day's stage.

A few memorandums that I made on the point of a precipice will come in very well here. If the reader could only see how my hair stood on end with fright while writing them, the picture would be complete.

The experience of a *ride up Lebanon* is something never to be forgotten. Roads tortuous and rocky, over a country wild of aspect, stony and wooded; roads winding to all points of the compass, up and down among the hills; roads rocky and bad, with many twistings up and down, but romantic and picturesque; hardly prudent to remain on horseback, as the precipices are frightful, and the risk of rolling over with the horse is imminent; as the Latins used to say, *a fronte precipitum, a tergo lupus,* the cliff before and the wolf behind; ways very narrow, one side dropping down upon high, perpendicular rocks, the other an inaccessible wall; *mutum est pictura poema,* it is a poem without words; paths tortuous and fatiguing; a frightful mountain-pass; the crest of a steep hill in the midst of a wilderness of rugged ravines and impracticable crags; a bitter, sharp, cold wind sweeping down from the snow-clad heights of Lebanon; going high up where "the hay withers away, the grass fails, and there is no green thing" (Isaiah 15:6); past beds of iron-stone, recalling the "one hundred thousand talents of iron" (1 Chron. 29:7) which Israel gave for the service of the house of the Lord; toiling far beyond my strength until "my face did wax pale" (Isaiah 29:22);

Where the summits glitter with streaks of snow,

And the villages crown the knobs below,

bare and stony, cut by every rain. A hill that none but man can climb, covered with a hundred wintry water-courses. "A lowly vale, low as the hill is high," where the hardy pine-tree thrusts its roots deep into the rocky side of the mountain; this is the *pinus allapenses* of the botanist. "As when the winter streams rush down the mountain sides and fill below, with their swift waters, poured from gushing springs, some hollow vale." Here rises the Damoor, which I crossed the other day going from Beirut to Sidon, and not far from here the Owely. My view from this point suggested a thousand passages referring to height. It seemed if I was on "the highest part of the dust of the earth" (Proverbs 8:26); when the Lord of hosts lopped the bough with terror, and the high ones of stature were hewn down with iron, and Lebanon fell by a mighty one (Isaiah 10:34).

In the destruction of Assyria, even Mt. Lebanon is said to rejoice. One of the finest thoughts in Isaiah's prophecies (14:8) is that in which the mountain that had been widowed of its noblest trees by Sennacherib and other Assyrian tyrants, joins in the cry of exultation that goes up to heaven at the downfall of the kingdom.

When a boy, I read of an herb growing along this road that colors of a golden hue the teeth of animals that browse upon it, but I can find nobody here who ever heard of it.

The men living among these crags are considerably larger and far more muscular than the dwellers in the plains. Doubtless it was so in Hiram's day, and the work of cutting and removing the cedars was entrusted to the mountaineers. Old Sandys remarked, in 1610: "Perhaps the cause of their strength and big proportions is that they are bred in the mountains; for such are observed to oversize those who dwell in low levels." At the interment of Past Grand Master Henry Clay, at Lexington, Kentucky, in 1852, a company of 100 men came down from the mountain, riding blood-horses. Not a man in the company was less than six feet, and their *average* weight was 240 lbs.!

A man has just passed me with yellow slippers and red shoes over them. His sash holds his pistols and sword. He has a long venerable beard, a thing from which military officers and soldiers are debarred. These regular Turks seem to me generally to wear a light and florid complexion. Scanning this man's dress I observe, what other writers have remarked before, that the Turkish dress hides all deformities of limb and person, while the variety of color, arms, and flowing beard, naturally divert attention from close examination of the features.

Another man passes us, an ill-favored, slovenly fellow, of whom I inquire what part of these mountains no man can pass over. The mountaineer replies that he can go up or down any *wady* on horseback that water can run through!

A female school recently opened here, under the patronage of the Protestant Missions of the country, enabled me to secure pleasant accommodations with the teachers. They gave us the best fare at their command, spread for us on the floor, in the preacher's room, sufficient bedding, and left us to a repose needed after the day's ride. At the village of Ain-Zehalteh there is an old fountain, now disused, which has a pair of carved leopards on it, resembling the lions graven on the side of St. Stephen's Gate, at Jerusalem, supposed to be remains of the Crusaders' period. There are here, also, several tombs of that singular people, the Druses, to whose particular form of Freemasonry I will call attention in a subsequent chapter.

Early the next morning we took a guide and started for the cedars, which, however, were in plain view, standing in the snow-drifts, high up on the mountain-side. It took us two hours' hard riding even to the foot of the slopes below them. Here we left our horses and made the ascent on foot. This is the first time I discovered that a man's knees at fifty are not the same machinery as at thirty. I used to be noted as a good walker and climber; but that piece of work took the conceit out of me forever and a day. We mounted mile after mile. We passed the highest barley-fields, which occupied a slope of ground almost perpendicular. We passed the line of scarlet poppies and other gay flowers, and the line of singing-birds, and finally the line of vegetable and insect life.

The mountain-air revived me in my heat and fatigue, as I stopped occasionally to look back and enjoy the splendid panorama of the Mediterranean Sea seen from Mount Lebanon, which once beheld can never be forgotten. Again I went on, with tottering knees, and muscular system so paralyzed by the unwonted strain that I seemed to have no control over it. Looking above me, the cedars appeared to mock my desires, and withdraw as I advanced. Now I came to the line of the snow-drifts, across which the winds sobbed, cold as winter.

At last I reached the lowest, and as it proved, the largest of the grove, a cedar-tree fifteen feet in circumference, and divided symmetrically into four noble trunks. Here I threw myself exhausted, and devoted the first hour reflecting upon the time, place, and occasion: high 12—Lebanon—visit to the cedars! While recovering my breath I referred to some of the authorities concerning these memorable trees—such as these: An house of cedar (2 Sam. 7:2). He spoke of trees, from the cedar (1 Kings 4:33). The thistle sent to the cedars (2 Kings 14:9; 2 Chr. 25:18). Grow like a cedar (Ps. 92:12). Beams of our house are cedars (Cant. 1:7). Boards of cedar (8:9). Some forty other references may be traced through the concordance.

The particular connections between the cedars and the mountains are these: Devour the cedars of Lebanon (Jud. 9:15). The cedars of Lebanon (Ps. 104:16). Upon all the cedars of Lebanon (Is. 2:13). The cedars of Lebanon rejoice at thee (Is. 14:8). The cedars of

Lebanon to make masts for thee (Ezekiel 27:5), and various others.

The Hebrew name erez, is preserved still among the Arabs. I asked my guide the name of the tree that bent so grandly over me; and he replied, in his corrupt vernacular, *arruz,* equivalent in good Arabic to arz. The word is applied in Scripture, as it is in the vernacular Arabic, generally, to the trees of the *pine family,* but especially to the *cedar of Lebanon (Cedrus Libani).* The cedar-tree named in Lev. 14:4, etc., was probably the timber of a fragrant species of juniper growing among the rocks of Sinai; but in most of the Biblical references this tree which is now shading me is doubtless meant. Everywhere the symbolic expressions of the cedar of Lebanon are lofty and grand: it is the glory of Lebanon, the tree of the Lord, the high and lifted up, etc., etc. The Amorite in his arrogance and the Assyrian in his greatness were compared to cedars. It is also the model of expansiveness. The constant growth of the righteous man is described under this similitude. Its fragrance is not overlooked in such expressions as "the smell of thy garment is like the smell of Lebanon." The cedar was the prince of trees. Every one who has seen it amongst the snows of Lebanon will recognize the force of the glorious and majestic imagery of the prophets. This great monarch of twenty or thirty centuries, under which I am sitting, with its gnarled and contorted stems and its scaly bark, with massive branches spreading their foliage rather in layers than in flakes, with its dark-green leaves, fully asserts its title, Monarch of the Forests.

Of the quality of the wood I need not say much; hundreds of my patrons are enabled to judge of that for themselves, as I have served good specimens to them. The roof of the Church of the Nativity, at Bethany, is made of it. It is certainly close in grain, as well as dark in color. The King's House on Mount Zion was made of it, and Solomon used it very largely in the Temple, as well as in his own palace. The second and third temples were equally constructed of cedar. It worked well in carvings, and was used by the Tyrian shipwrights for their masts. In the days of the Old Testament writers, the whole of this great range of mountains, probably, abounded in this noble tree, now so scarce, and found only upon spots nearly inaccessible to visitors.

I am here just on the level of Wyoming Territory, in the United States, 8,262 feet above the sea-level, and will quote from the description of a traveler there: "For nine months in the year, the sides and summits of these everlasting hills are bedecked with the greatest variety and the grandest display of flowers that ever grew. Gorgeously arrayed in countless numbers, they present every color, form, and size. The higher the peak, the lighter and more delicate the colors; at the very loftiest summits grows the *palmito nivalis,* or snow-plant, an exquisite gem of floral beauty."

> Gradual as the snow at Heaven's breath
> Melts off and shows the azure flowers beneath.

The view of the great mountain-eagle, through the broad spreading branches of the cedars, is inspiring. Serene as the sublime untrodden heights around him, he sails alone where the eye of man cannot pierce, and, in an untroubled atmosphere, sees the lightning leap and play, and hears the thunder burst, and the hurricane roar far, far below him. Doubtless the prophet Obadiah was regarding him under this aspect when he wrote, "Though thou exalt thyself as the eagle, and though thou set thy nest among the stars, thence will I bring thee down, saith the Lord" (1:4).

Ten thousand axe-men are now (the winter of 1872) chopping pines in the forests of Michigan alone, and, with their improved steel axes, every blow struck must be equal to six of Hiram's choppers, using the clumsy copper axes.

The throne on which the statue of Jupiter Olympus sat, in his statue by Phidias, at Athens, was made of cedar-wood, adorned, of course, with gold, ivory, ebony, precious stones, and colors.

From my present standpoint, were the sun setting so that I might have the full benefit of his light, I could see the island of Cyprus, eighty miles in the northwest; were it not for yonder projecting point, I could see Sidon, twenty miles nearly in the west.

After a good rest, my companion and myself left our overcoats at the foot of this grand old cedar, and mounted to the top of the range, crossing deep snow-drifts, piles of rocks, loose gravel-beds, and other varieties of mountain surface. With the exception of a few pheasants or partridges that whirred out of a pile of rocks before me, and a few insects, I saw no signs of animated nature, and a few specimens of flowers exhausted the botanical exhibit. The view from the top of the range, which is here about 8,000 feet high, is extremely grand, and had not the wind been blowing so excessively cold, I should have enjoyed a longer tarry. Villages by scores and hundreds dot the hillsides in every direction, though, at so great a distance, no signs of inhabitants can be detected, save a single plowman far beneath me, who is turning up the earth between two snow-drifts, preparatory to sowing his late barley. How he has managed to climb so high with his poor little cattle, and what he expects to raise in this mountain-zone, I cannot tell.

I return to my great cedar, which, of all the trees around me, I had chosen to be my Goliath of Gath, the very one which Daniel might in spirit have seen and described as his "tree in the midst of the earth, and the height thereof great, reaching unto heaven, the sight thereof to the end of all the earth; the leaves fair, the beasts of the field having shadow under it, and the fowls of heaven dwelling in the boughs thereof" (4:10). Returning, I say, to this tree, I named it, on account of its four prominent divisions, the *Tree of the Four Cardinal Virtues.* I ate heartily of the victuals we had prudently provided before leaving Beirut, and then, snug myself in a nook on the leeward-side of the tree, and call up in succession the names of seventeen persons whom I have reason to remember with gratitude or kindness. To each one of these I wrote a letter, dated "On Mount Lebanon, April 26, 1868." If these epistles were received and read with half the pleasure they afforded me in the composition, my frozen hands and feet and general discomforts were amply compensated.

To the four great divisions of this tree, shooting its branches so magnificently abroad, after carving the Square and Compass deftly upon its root, I apply four names of earth's monarchs, who in their day did not deem it derogatory to their greatness to patronize the Masonic assemblies, viz.: Frederick the Great, of Prussia; Napoleon the Great, of France; the present Charles XV., King of Sweden; and William, present Emperor of Germany.

The number of trees in this grove is probably a thousand, mostly of good size, but none of them tall enough to furnish a mast or beam, still less good boards. From all of them the Arabs have lopped off the superfluous branches, and indeed so many others as to give the entire grove a stumpy appearance, perhaps not natural to it. Upon only one did I discover any cones, those large and handsome seed-vessels, so much sought after by travelers; the natives had doubtless gathered the best for fuel. My guide, however, afterwards collected one thousand for me, and sent them down to Beirut. With these I supplied my patrons, as valuable additions to their cabinets. Of the wood, I secured a large trunk of a tree, long since felled; had it rolled down the mountain-side the day following my departure, cut in two, and brought to me on the back of a camel.

As soon as this grove is thoroughly "discovered," and gets into Porter's *Hand-Book,* which is the Bible of all English-reading tourists, it will take no time at all to people it with legends. Monks will come here and build their shanties, and retail their *shenanegan* around it. Every tree will have its name, yes, a hundred names; in fact, will be carved all over with names. From my own cognomen, back to that of Lamartine, Willebald, and—I forget the list, the same as seen in the "Sacred Grove," at the head of the Kadisha—a regular itinerant directory, worse than the one on Cheops' pyramid, will be engraved here.

The extreme cold of the mountain-air warned me away. So, after cutting a good stick, and collecting an abundance of sprigs and leaves, and waving my Masonic flag to the winds of Lebanon, I started upon the descent, only less adventurous and even more tedious than the ascent. My very knee-caps twinge now with the remembrance as I write of that slipping, scrambling, tumbling journey to the base of Mount Lebanon. How glad I was to have the relief of my saddle I need not say. I again spent the night at Ain-Zehalteh, surrounded with the dwarf round-topped pine and umbrageous carob (the name means "The spring that has moved"), and returned next day to Beirut, highly gratified with my successful and invigorating visit to Lebanon.

In the opening of this article, I alluded to the great cedar-grove at the head of the River Kadisha. Those are much the largest specimens of the *Cedrus Libani* known to be in existence, and it is quite probable that some of them even antedate the time of the Hirams. Professor Tristam says of them: "The trees are not too close, nor are they entirely confined to the grove. Though the patriarchs are of enormous growth, they are no higher than the younger trees, many of which reach a circumference of eighteen feet." Dr. Thompson says: "The platform where the cedars stand is many thousand feet above the Mediterranean, and around it are gathered the very tallest and grayest heads of Lebanon. The forest is not large, not more than five hundred trees, great and small, grouped irregularly on the sides of shallow ravines, which mark the birthplace of the Kadisha or Holy River. Some of these trees have been struck by lightning, or broken by enormous loads of snow, or torn to fragments by tempests. Young trees are constantly springing up from the roots of old ones, and from seeds of ripe cones. The whole of the upper terrace of Lehanon might again be covered with groves of those noble trees and furnish timber enough, not only for Solomon's Temple and 'the house of the forest of Lebanon,' but for all the houses along this coast. They have been propagated by the nut or seed in many parts of Europe, and it is said there are more of them now within fifty miles of London than on all Lebanon."

It is said also that these groves of cedar east of Ain-Zehalteh, which I have just visited, could, a few years ago, boast of their ten thousand cedars; but the sheikh sold them to a native, who cut them down for *pitch*. Vigorous young plants, however, are springing up on every side; one stump has been measured which was thirteen feet in diameter. I can only say that the largest tree *I* found there was but five feet in diameter (fifteen in circumference). The so-called California pine, thirty feet in diameter, a branch that springs out at a height of fifty feet being six feet in diameter, is of course a much larger tree than any of these.

And now for a few desultory passages from my diary:

Sitting under this "Tree of the Four Cardinal Virtues," let me summon up one of that cloud of witnesses who found the cedar a worthy type of inspired truth, he who noted the rush of the workmen that poured up these slopes at the command of Hiram to cut the great trees. Jeremiah: "When I prophesied of the hosts who should swarm under Nebuchadnezzar to destroy Jerusalem, I said, They shall march with an army, and come against her with axes, as hewers of wood. They shall cut down her forest" (46:22). Seeing how few and comparatively dwarfish these are, as compared with the size and abundance of the cedar forests in olden time, we see the force of Isaiah's expression (2:12): "The day of the Lord is upon all the cedars of Lebanon that are high and lifted up." Down at Bethlehem, a hundred miles southward, the rows of unpainted beams in the old church acknowledge this forest as their source. An old pilgrim who was here A.D. 1322, wrote that cedar-trees grow very high in these hills and produce apples as great as a man's head. This was, of course, what we commonly style *cones*.

As Joshua, when he had waxed old and was stricken in age, called all Israel together at Shechem (B.C. 1427), and made a covenant with them, and recounted all that God had done for them since the call of Abraham (B.C. 1921), nearly five centuries before; and then "took a great stone and set it up there under an oak," and made it a witness unto them, "lest they should deny their God" (Joshua 23-25.) so let me set this rude ashlar on its end, and gratefully recount what God has done for me since I left my native land two months ago. At

Ain-Zehalteh, I remarked that nothing is so painful among these grand historic mountains as to see the degradation of the women of the Lebanon villages. Descending from the steeps in lengthened files, with heavy loads of wood upon their heads, bending under burdens which their weak frames can ill sustain— here are the women of the Koran. It is humiliating to be the object of their silly stare and rude laughter, and compelled to witness their unseemly deportment, clothed as they are in filthy, coarse, and scanty garb.

A generation back, the Druse women of Lebanon wore the *tantura,* or silver horn, often two feet in length, fastened to the forehead by a strong cushion, and supporting a white veil which concealed the face. Assumed at her marriage, she never laid this aside until prepared for the grave. But this strange and characteristic ornament is now dispensed with. As I do not know why they wore it, neither can I explain why they have discontinued it. The horses I meet are lean and poor in flesh, but sinewy and patient of labor. Their nimbleness at a stumble is only inferior to a goat's. Evidently they are accustomed, when stepping on a stone, to calculate on its rolling, and govern themselves accordingly. The incalculable quantities of cedar transported by the mariners of King Hiram, from Lebanon to Jerusalem, contrast so widely with the scanty yield of the present day, that the reader is almost tempted to suggest an exaggeration in the figures. Yet, as late as 1837, the Pasha of Egypt sent to these same mountains with an order for 1,052,000 trees of different sorts. Of these, 70,000 were required to be thirty-five feet long and eight inches square; the rest smaller. Year by year from that time from 50,000 to 60,000 trees were shipped thence to Egypt. From the vicinity of Alexandrette they furnish yellow pine and other sticks, of the following dimensions:

Yellow pine,	80	feet long,	18 to 20 inches square.
Green pine,	20	"	9 inches square.
Beech,	35	"	15 "
Linden,	50	"	27 "

The allusions to the use of the Lebanon cedar in the construction of Solomon's various works are frequent. The same appear in the Zerubbabel constructions, 500 years later. In 2 Samuel 7:2, David says to the prophet Nathan: "I dwell in a house of cedar," and he asked leave to build "a house of cedar" for Divine worship. The material for his palace had been secured through the friendship of the King of Phœnicia, the same who was afterwards so munificent to Solomon. To facilitate the work of constructing a temple, which was reserved for his son Solomon, he collected "cedar trees in abundance for the Zidonians, and they of Tyre brought much cedar wood to David." The cedars of Lebanon are ever a symbol of beauty, loftiness, and grandeur. In Psalm 104:16, we read: "The trees of the Lord are full of sap; the cedars of Lebanon which He hath planted, where the birds make their nests." In Isaiah 2:13: "The cedars of Lebanon are high and lifted up." In Ezekiel 27:5: "They have taken cedars of Lebanon to make masts for thee." Many other references of this sort may be found in the Old Testament by the aid of a concordance.

In the construction of the great temple upon Mount Moriah, such quantities of cedar were used as surpass all computation. The labor necessary to fell these upon the high mountains; to bring them down 6,000 to 8,000 feet of perpendicular height, through frightful passes and down giddy chasms, to the plain; to make them up into rafts in the coves and inlets of the coast; to float them seventy-five miles along the shore; to draw them, water-sodden, up the acclivity at Joppa; to bear them by land thirty or forty miles across the country, ascending some 2,600 feet by the way; and, when arrived at Jerusalem, to shape them into the various uses demanded by the great builder—this labor, we say, was truly immense, and defies calculation. It is, indeed, well said in 1 Kings 9:11, that "Hiram, King of Tyre, had furnished Solomon with cedar-trees according to all his desire."

In two minute accounts of the temple-building, contained in 1 Kings and 2 Chronicles, are seen these references to cedar material: "He covered the house with beams and boards of cedar;" the chambers, five cubits high against the house, "rested on the house with timber of cedar;" "He built the walls of the house within with boards of cedar;" "He built twenty cubits on the sides of the house, both the floor and the walls, with boards of cedar;" "The cedar of the house within was carved with knops and open flowers; all was cedar; there was no stone seen;" the altar in the holy place was of cedar, covered with pure gold.

But his own house, on Mount Zion, still more profusely abounded with this costly wood. It was, indeed, termed "the house of the forest of Lebanon," for this very reason. It stood "upon four rows of cedar piliars, with cedar beams upon the pillars, and it was covered with cedar above upon the beams that lay on forty-five pillars, fifteen in a row." The porch of judgment "was covered with cedar from one side of the floor to the other." To sum up this profusion in a few words, the sacred historian says (1 Kings 10:27): "The King made cedars to be as the sycamore trees that are in the vale for abundance." In an excellent volume by Mrs. Forbes, lately published, under the title of "A Woman's First Impressions of Europe," the following passage occurs: "Down the long vistas of the park of Warwick Castle, England, stand cedars of Lebanon, stretching their wide branches over English earth, perhaps brought from Palestine by the great Earl Guy himself."

In the re-construction of the temple, commenced about B.C. 535, by Zerubbabel, we read that "they gave money, and meat, and drink, and oil unto them of Zidon, and to them of Tyre, to bring cedar trees from Lebanon to the sea of Joppa, according to the grant they had of Cyrus, King of Persia." The same thing occurred about 500 years later, as we learn from the writings of the Jewish historian Josephus, when Herod, that renowned builder, undertook to restore the house of the Lord, which was by that time greatly decayed, and procured, through the Phœnicians, who then possessed the defiles of the Lebanons, the needed wood for the reparation.

A very large number of American Lodges are named after this mountain, either Lebanon, Libanus, or Mount Lebanon. Among them I instance No. 86, Ky.; No. 26, Ohio; No. 104, La.; No. 46, Vt.; No 7, D. C.; No. 59, Tenn.; No. 117, N. C.; No. 191, N. Y.; No. 104, Md.; No. 229, Ala.; No. 97, Ark.; Nos. 32 and 49, N. H.; No. 226, Pa.; No. 35, Mass., etc., etc.

As names appropriate to lay upon this great Masonic locality, the following are selected, viz.: Fred Webber, Stephen Merrill, L. A. Foote, Oliver George, Royal G. Millard, J. W. Clayton. Rev. W. H. Makeany, J. C. W. Bailey, Jacob H. Medairy, M.D., and William Mead.

ANCIENT ALTARS.

GRAND PORTAL AT BAALBEC.

12

GENTLEMEN DINING.

CHAPTER XI.

BAALBEC AND PALMYRA.

I T was not in my power to visit Baalbec and Palmyra without neglecting more important interests. I am therefore chiefly indebted to Brother A. L. Rawson, the Oriental artist and scribe, for my notes upon those wonderful (*wonder full!*) localities, interesting especially to the Masonic antiquary, because doubtless built by the same hands whose chisel-marks are found today indented upon the walls and ashlars in the great quarry at Jerusalem. In other words, the remains of Baalbec and Palmyra are covered with the "Handmarks of Hiram's Builders!"

Baalbec, or Heliopolis, the City of the Sun, is situated about thirty miles to the left of the route between Beirut and Damascus, described in my last chapter. It is usual for travelers to go first to Damascus by stage ("diligence," so called in French, because an exceedingly "slow coach"), and there hire horses and servants, with that inevitable and dreadful bore, the dragoman, to torment you, and be paid for it. Not that there is the least need of this fellow. There is not a horse in Damascus that could not keep the track between that place and Baalbec with his eyes shut; but it is fashionable here to have a dragoman, just as it is to tie a piece of (dirty) white cotton cloth around your hat, and buy a "yaller" silk scarf in the bazaars to carry home. The site of Baalbec is a pleasant one, though the mountain-ride across from Damascus is very rough and disagreeable. I noticed, at my dining station in the Bukaa valley, a party setting out from there to Baalbec, thus avoiding three times crossing the hills between that and Damascus—a sensible procedure. Baalbec lies well up the valley, near some charming rivulets of water, at the opening of a little nook leading into the main valley. For all particulars of the history, etc., of the place, I refer the reader to the larger works of Thomson, Porter, Robinson, etc. At what period, or by whom, the city was founded is unknown; but it is probably coeval with the most prosperous period of Phœnician history; local tradition associates it with King Solomon. A slight examination shows that, while the colossal platform of the Temple and the beveled masonry under the great peristyle point to the Phœnician architects, the Greeks, Romans, and Syrians have all, in turn, had a hand in the erection of the later structures, just as we know that many of the inscriptions are Saracenic, and therefore comparatively recent. Julius Cæsar, about B.C. 47, made it a Roman colony, under the name of Heliopolis. On the coins of Augustus Cæsar, about B.C. 31, we find the corroboration of this fact in the inscription, "Col. Julia Augusta Felix Heliopolis." A sacred oracle was established here a century later, which the Emperor Trajan, A.D. 98, consulted prior to an expedition against the Parthians.

The city of Baalbec was irregular in form, covering an area of about a mile in diameter (more accurately, two miles in circumference), and this whole space is piled up with *débris* of costly and exquisite architecture in marble, Lebanon limestone, granite, and porphyry, Some extremely large and elegant columns of porphyry were taken from here 1,500 years since, and now form portions of the Mosque of St. Sophia, at Constantinople. The whole ruin may be best divided, for examination, as Professor Rawson has done, into the Great Temple, the Peristyle Temple, and the Temple of the Sun. Weeks and months are profitably spent by architectural students in the study of these three monuments. Fortunately, there are extant, in the great American libraries, copies of the accurate works of Wood and Dawkins, who explored, figured, and wrote up the place in the last century, when many more of the great columns, etc., were standing than now.

If an American reader, who has never seen any erections larger or finer than the Capitol at Washington, will set his imagination to work as to the designs originally drawn on the trestle-board by the Grand Architect of Baalbec (perhaps Hiram Abif himself), let him be supposed to be standing on the eastern edge of a platform, looking west. First comes the portico, one hundred and eighty feet from north to south, and thirty-seven feet deep. The platform itself is elevated twenty feet, the wall below being built of large undressed stones, and showing that formerly a grand and massive stairway, now absent, led up to it from the direction of the rising sun. Only the bases of the columns of the portico remain, the columns themselves having been removed or destroyed. But the wings of the portico, built of stones from twenty to twenty-four feet long, and broad and high in proportion, remain almost intact. Into each wing you may enter from the portico into chambers thirty-one by thirty-eight feet, which have been used by the present government as forts; stairways lead down from them into the body of the massive platform below.

Passing westward from the portico through a triple gateway, we enter a hexagon (six-sided) court, two hundred feet deep by three hundred wide (from north to south). On the east, north, and south sides of this vast court are right-angled recesses, each having four columns in front of it. Still passing westward, we find a portal fifty feet wide opening into the second court, which surpasses all of human grandeur that the world contains, except some Egyptian edifices. It is four hundred and forty feet from east to west, and three hundred and seventy from north to south. It was entirely encompassed by recesses and niches which, in their very ruin, are overpoweringly magnificent. Great rows of columns surrounded this enormous court, their bases being seven feet three inches in diameter, and their height, including base, capital, and entablature, eighty-nine feet! Each of these tremendous works, a portion of them being of that hardest and heaviest of stone, Syenite, is composed of six pieces, viz.: the base is one, the shaft three (fastened together inwardly by massive iron cramps), the capital one, and the entablature crossing from pillar to pillar, one. The style is Corinthian. The entablature is exquisitely done, "the moldings being deep, and filled up with the egg and dice ornaments. The frieze has garlands hung between projections, each of which is adorned with an acanthus leaf and a bust."

But we are yet only in *the outer court* of Baalbec's vast temple. Still continuing westward, we come now to the real edifice for which all these costly approaches were made. It is a vast peristyle, measuring two hundred and ninety feet from east to west, by one hundred and sixty. On each side of it were nineteen columns, at each end ten; the dimensions, etc., of these columns have just been given. This temple stood on massive walls fifty feet high, so that a person mounted on the highest projection of the wall is one hundred and thirty-nine feet above the surrounding plain. Thus the whole distance from the eastern edge of the platform, through the portico, the two courts, and the temple itself, is nearly three hundred yards.

And even this does not express the greatest architectural wonder of Baalbec. That which my readers will view with the greatest astonishment is the collection of enormous ashlars, of which the western part of the platform is composed. Here are the three great stones, so long and justly celebrated, one being sixty-four feet in length, one sixty-three feet eight inches, the third sixty-three feet, making their combined length one hundred and ninety feet eight inches. Their height is thirteen feet, and depth eleven, and they are twenty feet above the ground, in the heavy masonry of the wall. From these great ashlars the building was named by the Greeks "the Three-stoned" (*trilithon*). In the northern part of this platform are nine stones, each about thirty-one by thirteen feet, and nine feet seven inches wide.

Near this wonderful building I have just described, but on a platform considerably lower, there stands, to the south, the most perfect and most magnificent monument of ancient art in Syria, *the Temple of the Sun, or Apollo*. Like the other, it faces the east, and is two hundred and twenty-seven feet by one hundred and seventeen, something larger than the Parthenon at Athens. The style is also Corinthian. In 1751, Wood and Dawkins found nine columns standing on the south side of this edifice; but the earthquake of 1759 threw down three of these, and nine from the temple first described. The portal to this temple, when entire, was probably the most striking and beautiful gateway in the world. It was ornamented, says Rawson, with every device that could be used, in the most florid Corinthian style. Ears of grain, vine-leaves, and grapes, with little figures of genii or elves hid among them, and many choice touches of scroll-work, attract the eye and gratify the taste. Near the southwest angle of this temple is a heap of ruins that form a most striking image of the desolation of architecture; in one confused mass, colossal columns of shafts, huge capitals that look, when on the ground, out of all proportion with the airy columns that rise up beside them, gigantic architraves, friezes, and ceilings.

The third of these ancient structures to which the traveler will give attention is the Circular Temple, situated about three hundred yards from the others. From the center of all these ruins the great quarries, from which the material for the underlying walls was procured, lie under the base of the hill, one-half mile west. Here is a stone, finished in the quarry, but never used, and the largest of them all. It is sixty-eight feet in length, fourteen feet two inches high, and thirteen feet broad. It contains, therefore, more than thirteen thousand cubic feet of stone, and weighs about one thousand two hundred tons. To a student of the human intellect, it was worth a visit to Baalbec, to muse upon this ashlar! It would be an interesting study to compare it with a few of the great stones wrought in different parts of the world by ancient builders; at Sais, in Egypt, for instance, there is a chapel, cut from a single block, that is eighteen feet long, thirteen broad, and seven high. It was brought from Elephantine. Two thousand men were employed for three years in carrying the mass down the Nile. It was finished about B.C. 569, under King Amadis, the man who was visited by Pythagoras, with letters of introduction from the governor of Samos, by means of which he was initiated into the mysteries of Egypt, and whatever was abstruse and important in their religion. A block of granite was quarried a few years since, at Monson, Ms., three hundred and fifty feet long, eleven wide, four thick, calculated to weigh about one thousand three hundred tons. To detach it from the matrix, eleven thousand and four holes were drilled in a line parallel with its front edge. The corner-stone of the State House of Illinois, spoken of in the papers as something ponderous, weighs fourteen tons! In the Emporium Romanum, within a few years, a block of Syenite granite has been found that measures one hundred cubic meters (a meter is about two feet). Gibbon describes an obelisk of the same material, as being removed from Egypt to Rome, that is one hundred and twenty-five feet in length, and twelve feet diameter at the base. The Luxor Obelisk, now in Paris, which is seventy-two feet high, is estimated to weigh one hundred and twenty tons. The column of Alexander, at St. Petersburg, a granite monolith, is eighty-four feet high and fourteen in diameter, and estimated to weigh four hundred tons. The sarcophagus of King Hiram, described in a previous chapter, weighs about fifty tons. The corner-stone at the south western angle of Mount Moriah, thirty feet by eight, and six high, weighs about one hundred and fifteen tons; another in the same wall is reckoned at two hundred and thirty tons. One of the ashlars in the ancient work at Stonehenge, England, weighs forty tons; another seventy.

How well it may be said of all these grand buildings:

> They dreamed not of a perishable home,
> Who thus could build!

And yet the ancients had no mechanical powers other than those we possess; nor theirs half so perfectly at command as our builders have. Of the largest ashlar I have mentioned, Mr. Charles Buckle calculates that if only muscular power was applied to it, 20,000 men would not be too large a force, allowing one hundred and seventy-six pounds to each.

A poet-author suggests good thoughts in these lines:

> These lonely columns stand sublime,
>   Flinging their shadows from on high;
> The dial which the wizard time
>   Has raised to count his ages by.

Dr. W. M. Thomson very forcibly suggests that, being on the road from Tyre to Tadmor (Palmyra), the Phœnician masons who were employed to construct that wonderful vision of the Desert, could refresh their memory in the grandest architectural details, by an examination of these unexcelled productions, these perfect gems of human art.

The coins struck here, in the time of Septimius Severus (crowned A.D. 222) have on the reverse this temple, now in ruins, with the inscription *Colonia Heliopolitana Iovi Optimo Maximo Heliopolitana.*

Some writer has elegantly said here, that time carries his *secrets* away, leaving his *enigmas* to perplex us. I have already remarked that popular tradition attributes these stupendous works, as indeed all other extraordinary things in this country, to King Solomon. They are themselves but a stupid race, though, three hundred years ago, travelers reported them as exhibiting a skull so large that man could put his head in it. It surely was not of any member of the races now inhabiting this valley. The story they tell of the Great Ashlar is, that the devils (*genii,* or evil spirits) being subjugated by King Solomon, were compelled by that remarkable executive to excavate these majestic stones, and lay them in order in the platform at Baalbec; but, just as the largest stone was about to be cracked from its native matrix, the death of the Great King was announced to them, B.C. 975, and they incontinently refused to work any longer. So far as I can ascertain, they have done nothing in the architectural way since. Of their flight the Arabic poets say, "they filled the air with the sound of their chains."

I remarked before that the eight porphyry columns seen in the Mosque of St. Sophia, at Constantinople, were taken by the Roman Emperor Aurelian, from the temple at Baalbec, in Syria. When that great Church of St. Sophia was dedicated by Justinian, long afterwards, he is said to have cried out, "Solomon, I have surpassed you!" This was hard on Solomon, who, having been in his royal sepulcher for some thirteen centuries, was not in a condition to silence the braggadocio. After all, when we come to charge our thoughts full of these stupendous proportions, we may bear in mind that they do not at all equal those of the Pyramid of Cheops, to be described in a later chapter.

Quite a number of American lodges have names suggested by this place, or by particular objects found in its ruins, as, for instance, *Ashlar* Lodge No. 203, Georgia; 111, Iowa; 91, Michigan; 70, Massachusetts; also, *Baalbec* Lodge No. 71, Massachusetts; *Hobah* Lodge (from a Biblical locality between Baalbec and Damascus) is No. 276, Pennsylvania. From *Naphtali,* the Hebrew tribe that possessed this end of the country as far as David's kingdom extended, Lodge No. 262, Ohio, is named. We enlarge the circle of association, by planting amongst these grand old Masonic ruins the names of ten brethren, honored on the register of American and Canadian Masons, viz., W. J. B. McLeod Moore, Solomon W. Cochrane, X. J. Maynard, William C. Mahan, Charles Spaeth, R. A. Whittaker, M. E. Gillette, T. Boyd Foster, William Storer, and Enoch P. Breed.

Our good brother Mason, Lamartine, set out for this place from Beirut, March 28th, 1833, with twenty-six horses and a whole company of natives for servants and escort. The French poet made a noise in these mountains, and his name is even now a household word for liberality and largeness of idea. His descriptions are unparalleled for elegance of language, and I regret that I have not more space to give them. I have never seen a work that the student of the French language can read with so much profit as his "Souvenirs, Impressions, Pensées et Paysages pendant un Voyage en Orient, 1832-1833, on Notes d'un Voyageur, par M. De Lamartine." In the life-long sorrows of this remarkable man was exemplified the truth of the adage *Cuivis dolori remedium est patientia*—the remedy for every sorrow is patience.

The ruins of *Palmyra,* or *Tadmor,* which is the Bible-name of the place, are only second in extent and grandeur to those just described, and are best delineated in the splendid work to which I have already referred, that of Wood and Dawkins, published in England about one hundred and twenty years since. To visit the place at present involves so heavy an expense, in purchasing protection from the

Arabs, that but few travelers care to attempt it. I was within the
turn of a hand in securing a free and safe passage, on the staff of
the Pasha, in April, 1868, but failed at the last moment, for
reasons I will detail in my chapter on Damascus. It is a journey,
from Damascus, of five days by the ordinary mode of travel. The
sheikh who furnishes the required escort is named Miguel, a fine
specimen of the Bedouin; for, although his charges are
exorbitant—$100 to $150 a head—yet when he has your money in
his belt and your life in his power, he will be found, it is said, kind,
generous, and faithful. The tribe to which he is attached is that of
El Besher, the most numerous of the Anazeh tribes. The Anazeh,
by the way, is a nation of itself, the most powerful of the Arab
clans, covering the desert from the River Euphrates to Syria, and
boasting of 10,000 horsemen, 90,000 camel-riders, etc., etc. The
sheikh Miguel married an Englishwoman, Mrs. Digby, whom I
met twice in the Protestant Church at Damascus. She lives part
of the year in the deserts with her husband, and the rest of the
time among civilized people in Damascus, where she is attentive
to religious duties, and bears a good reputation among the
Protestant missionaries with whom I made acquaintance there.
So much was said in the papers against Mrs. Digby, a few years
since, that I am constrained to record this testimony in her favor.
I saw members of her tribe (the Anazeh) in Damascus, all
wearing the conventional dress of the clan, viz., an undergarment
of calico, gray or blue, extending to the mid-leg, and fastened
round the waist by a leathern girdle, in the fashion of our June-
saint, John the Baptist. The sleeves are wide, and have very long
pendant points. Over this is thrown the cloak (*abah*) of goats' hair,
having usually broad, vertical stripes of white and brown. On the
head is the handkerchief (Kafeeyah) of yellow silk or cotton, tied
round the temples by a cord of black camels' hair, passed twice
round. The chiefs wear a short scarlet pelisse, lined with fur, and
large red boots; but the common people go barefoot. These people
are small and low of stature (about five feet six inches), but walk
erect, step light, and are as graceful in movements as our
Western Indians before they learn the mysteries of "tangle-foot."
On their faces is the expression of a wild, free nature; the piercing,
fitful, daring flash of the eye is startling, while their abrupt
speech, as a writer says, is like the sudden bark of a dog. I hailed
a squad of them on the mounds outside the east gate of Damascus
one morning, by making use of some friendly expression, and the
manner in which they turned on me and snapped their jaws

together would have been alarming, only that I do not scare worth a cent. I only laughed at them, and twiddled my fingers gracefully from the end of my nose. Whereat, after a moment's exchange of glances with each other, they laughed too, and asked me for *backsheesh*. Which they did not get. Each of those ruffians of Anazeh had a gun, horse-pistols like blunderbuses, and a dagger, and looked about as dangerous as a corner-group of Five-Points loafers.

The way to Palmyra (I had almost forgotten my subject) is by Kuryetein, where a supply of water must be taken to cross the desert. This is quite a town, containing a large Christian church. Here you are forty miles from Palmyra, and on what was once the highway from Mesopotamia to Syria. All roads in this country must be regulated by the water-supply, and the fountains of Kuryetein and Palmyra, established these as essential points on the journey. Abraham must have come this way B.C. 1921. Jacob went to Padanaram by this route, and returned again twenty years later. The exiles of Israel and of Judah well knew this weary road. When Palmyra was in its glory, the wealth of the east and the commerce of the west were conveyed along this highway. But Jim Fisk's old peddler-wagon could carry all the goods that pass along here now.

The appearance of Palmyra is said to be startling and romantic. Syria, it is claimed, has nothing to compare with it. Ruins so extensive, so desolate, so bare, exist nowhere else. Long lines of columns, in irregular clumps and single pillars, rising up out of huge piles of white stones; fragments of gateways, and arches, and walls, and porticoes; such is the general view of the great "Peddlers' city" of King Solomon. Here that far-seeing "Merchant-King" established a vast depot for the exchange of commodities. Out of the enormous developments of the trading spirit in those days, the poets derived many of their keenest jests. The reader will particularly recall that of Ovid:

> *Da modo lucra mihi da facto gaudia lucro;*
> *Et face ut emptori verba dedisse juvet:*

—only let me have a profit, let me enjoy the delight of making a bargain, and impose on my customers!

The situation was the best in the world, half-way from the Euphrates to the Jordan. An abundance of good water was here, and so, for 1,500 years, Palmyra vindicated the forethought of Solomon in wealth, power, and political importance. With this city the history of Zenobia is associated—Zenobia, Queen of the East, who, leading her armies from these deserts, A.D. 274, conquered Syria, Asia Minor, and Mesopotamia, and defied the Roman himself. She was overcome, however, and taken a prisoner to Rome. From that period the decline of Palmyra began, and now its population is scarcely three hundred souls, who reside in some fifty wretched hovels built within the court of the temple.

The Temple of the Sun, which is one of the great attractions of Palmyra, is contained within a square court, 740 feet on a side, with walls seventy feet high. The entrance to this was on the western side, through a triple gateway, ornamented by a portico of ten columns. The central door was thirty-two feet high and sixteen wide. Its sides and lintel were monoliths, richly sculptured with garlands of fruits and flowers. Nearly 100 of the grand columns of this court are yet standing.

In this court, and near the southeastern corner, was the temple itself. A single row of fluted Corinthian columns, sixty-four feet high, with bronze capitals, encompassed the *Sanctum Sanctorum,* supporting an unbroken entablature, ornamented by festoons of fruits and flowers, held up at intervals by winged figures. The sculptures are much like those at Baalbec, and not inferior in design or execution. The signs of the Zodiac are seen on a portion of the remaining wall.

But, as Dr. Porter observes, it is the Great Colonnade that constitutes the chief wonder of Palmyra. It was originally composed of rows of columns, thus forming one central and two side avenues, which extended through the city about 4,000 feet. Each column, on the inner side, had a bracket for a statue. There are remaining about 150 of these columns out of the original number, 1,500. Their height, including base and capital, is fifty-seven feet. Two or three columns are still seen here of the Syenite (red Egyptian) granite, brought, of course, all the way from the quarries of Syene, high up the Nile. All the other columns, however, together with the buildings and walls, are of compact limestone, so fine and firm in texture as to receive a polish nearly equal to marble. It is of a yellowish white color, and was doubtless quarried near by.

The names *Tadmor* and *Palmyra* have been used in the distinctive titles of American Lodges, viz., Lodge No. 108, Kentucky; 55, Virginia; 147, North Carolina; 248, New York; 68, Wisconsin, and others. From the river, a little way east of Tadmor, we have the name of *Euphrates* Lodge No. 157, England.

To make a still closer union of Masonic names with this, so honored in history, the following list of American Masons is associated with Palmyra: Martin H. Rice, O. H. Minor, Noble D. Larner Alfred W. Morris, A. R. West, John Hoole, D. B. Tracey, A. S. Wadhams, George W. Harris, Alfred Burnett.

It is a strange neglect of those rich and powerful associations, the London Palestine Fund, etc., that they do not visit Palmyra, and bring modern learning and skill to bear upon this ancient and renowned city of the East.

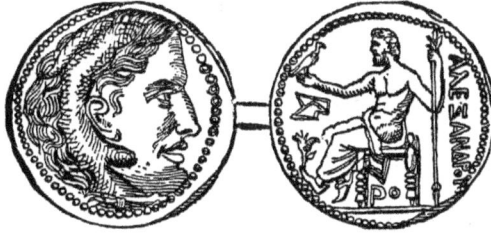

COIN OF ALEXANDER THE GREAT.

COIN-NOTES EXPLANATORY OF PAGE 362.

The coins so forcibly delineated on page 362, are thus named, beginning at the top and reading the lines toward the right hand: Messina; Trapane; Catania; Syracuse; Syracuse; Seg esta; Agrigentum; Megara; Panormus; Lentini; Unnamed; Egypt; Egypt; Al. Severus; Macrinus; Egypt.

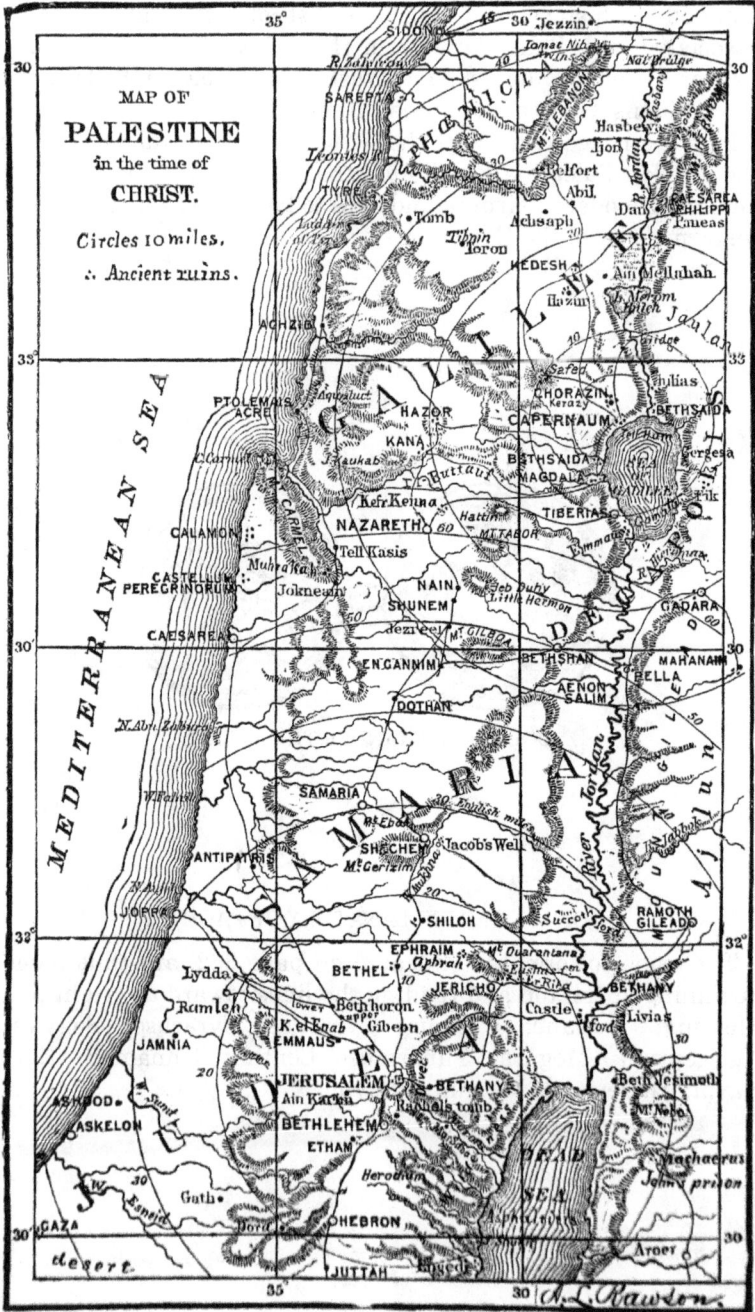

MAP OF
PALESTINE
in the time of
CHRIST.

Circles 10 miles.

∴ Ancient ruins.

MEDITERRANEAN SEA

PHŒNICIA

GALILEE

SAMARIA

JUDEA

DECAPOLIS

SIDON
Jezzin
Tomat Nihain
Nal Brülpr
SAREPTA
R. Zahirani
MT LEBANON
Hasbeya
Ijon
Belfort
Abil
TYRE
Dan
CAESAREA
PHILIPPI
Paneas
Tomb
Achsaph
Tibnin
Toron
KEDESH
Ain Mellahah
Hazur
Waters of Merom
Huleh
ACHZIB
Jaulan
Bridge
Safed
Julias
PTOLEMAIS
ACRE
CHORAZIN
Kerazy
BETHSAIDA
HAZOR
CAPERNAUM
KANA
BETHSAIDA
MT CARMEL
Buttauf
MAGDALA
Gergesa
KefrKenna
TIBERIAS
NAZARETH
Hattin
MT TABOR
Tell Kasis
Emmaus
CALAMON
CASTELLUM
PEREGRINORUM
Muhrakah
NAIN
Jokneam
SHUNEM
Neb Duhy
Little Hermon
GADARA
Jezreel
MT GILBOA
CAESAREA
EN GANNIM
BETHSHAN
MAHANAIM
AENON
SALIM
PELLA
DOTHAN
River Jordan
SAMARIA
ANTIPATRIS
MT Ebal
English mile
SHECHEM
Jacob's Well
MT Gerizim
JOPPA
SHILOH
Succoth
RAMOTH
GILEAD
EPHRAIM
MT Quarantana
Lydda
BETHEL
Ophrah
Fishon Riv
BETHANY
Ramleh
JERICHO
Castle
Livias
lower Beth horon
upper
K. el Enab
Gibeon
JAMNIA
EMMAUS
Beth Jesimoth
ASHDOD
JERUSALEM
BETHANY
MT Nebo
ASKELON
Ain Karim
Rachel's tomb
BETHLEHEM
ETHAM
DEAD
SEA
Machaerus
John's prison
GAZA
Herodium
Gath
HEBRON
Aroer
desert
JUTTAH
Engedi

A. L. Rawson

MASONIC BAY, OR BAY OF THE FLOTES.

DIVISION FIFTH.—THE BAY OF THE FLOTES.

The land of patriarchs and prophets; the land of apostles, and martyrs, and confessors; the land of Emmanuel,—the HOLY LAND!

The antiquities of this country display less beauty than those of Greece, but far more of arduous labor. They remind us greatly more of the *people* than the *artist.*

By its constant reference to localities,—mountain, rock, plain, river, tree,—the Bible seems to *invite examination;* and indeed it is only by such examination that we can appreciate its minute accuracy, and realize how far its plain, matter-of-fact statements of actual *occurrences,* to actual *persons,* in actual *places,* —how far these raise its records above the unreal and unconnected rhapsodies and the vain repetitions of the sacred books of other religions.

The Holy Land is a country of ruins, of fragments. All those objects referred to in the Holy Writings, as well as the Masonic lectures, are *in ruins,* and it is necessary to go *under ground* and see what "mother-earth" has "heled" there, before any labors of the past ages can be established. As the bodies of the ancient craft lie in dust in their stone coffins, so of their works; "dust and ashes" symbolize them.

Of the signs and ceremonies of Freemasonry, the remains of ancient mysteries, fragmentary remains are preserved here in the customs of the common people, especially in their religious and burial ceremonies.

13

CHAPTER XII.

THE MASONIC BAY.

THE fourth of the Seven Grand Masonic Localities visited and identified during my researches in Bible lands, is the MASONIC BAY, on the shores of which the materials of cedar and fir were made up into rafts ("flotes"), and embarked for Joppa. This is the sheet of water in modern times known as the Bay of Beirut, or more commonly *St. George's Bay,* this title referring to the fabled encounter of that hero with the dragon, so graphically described in Spenser's Faerie Queene, (Book 1, Canto XI). To amuse strangers and extort from them their loose piastres, the Arab guides even now will show the cave from whence the dragon issued on that memorable occasion, and for a suitable consideration, his very scales and bones.

I have modernized Spenser's language, to give a verse showing how *hard and heavy* the beast died:

So *down he fell,* and forth his life did breathe,
That vanished into smoke and clouds all swift;
So *down he fell,* that earth him underneath
Did groan, as feeble do great load to lift.
So *down he fell,* as a huge rocky clift
Whose false foundation waves have washed away,
With dreadful poise is from the mainland rift,
And rolling down, great Neptune doth dismay;
So *down he fell,* and like an heaped mountain lay.

After repeatedly exploring the Bay of St. George, and comparing it with all the other bays upon the coast near by, I came to the settled conclusion, which fire cannot burn out of me, that here was the chief of those natural coves or harbors used by our ancient brethren in making up "flotes" of the cedars, which they felled from the sides of the hills, that rise above it, and shipped to Joppa (1 Kings 5:2, Chron. 2). Hiram, in his celebrated letter to Solomon, says: "My servants shall bring them (the timbers) down from Lebanon to the sea in flotes, unto the place that thou shalt appoint me, and will cause them to be discharged there, and thou shalt receive them."

A charming place indeed is this Masonic Bay, with its beautiful curves and coves, its deep blue waters, its clean white sands, and the unparalleled grandeur of the overhanging hills upon the east. On the day I first rode around it (March 5) the bay was lashed into fury by a gale, as I have described in a preceding chapter. And I saw that, while it is the *best* of the Syria harbors, it is at the best but an insecure anchorage. I succeeded, however, in reaching the foot of the mountain, and entering the little khan, where some ten or twelve other persons, weather-bound, with their beasts of burden, had collected before me. The Masonic Bay is famous at the present day for its wrecks, of which four, one of them quite recently stranded, met my eyes as I rode along the beach. Near the northern extremity of the bay is the celebrated military pass of Nahr-el-Kelb (Dog River), by the side of which may be seen the most remarkable collection of ancient emblems and inscriptions in the world. That the reader may understand the subject perfectly, I will explain that through this maritime country (Phœnicia) lies the only great military road formerly connecting Asia with Africa. As such it was used for more than three thousand years. When Rameses, or Sesostris, the mighty Egyptian conqueror, passed up this coast, about B.C. 1400, say 3,300 years ago, on his way to the conquest of Assyria, he found his progress impeded by this spur of Mt. Lebanon running into the sea, just north of the Bay of St. George. Through the hard limestone of Lebanon, on which my chisel has rung so often, his engineers cut a military road, a work, considering they only had copper or bronze tools, of immense labor. On his return to Egypt, after achieving great victories in the East, he engraved upon large smooth panels, chiseled in the sides of the native stone for that purpose, hieroglyphical records of his victories. Those inscriptions *are still here,* though thirty-three centuries have passed since the edge of the chisel indented them! As I sat and made drawings of them, the sea-breeze whistled mournfully through the insulator of the telegraph-pole that is fixed in a crevice of the rock, right in front of it.

Again, when Sennacherib, the Assyrian conqueror, came down this way to the conquest of Egypt, about B.C. 700, say 2,600 years ago, he ordered panels of the same character cut by the side of the last, on which his name and his victories were, in the Assyrian cuneiform characters, duly recorded, and these, too still remain! After I had copied them, I read in Isaiah 37 of the haughtiness of this monarch, his great victories, the terrible destruction of his armies by a simoon, and his murder at the hands of his own sons.

Again, when the Roman Emperor Aurelian had completed his conquests in this country, about A.D. 173, say 1,700 years ago, finding the old Sesostris-Sennacherib military road in disrepair, he caused a new one to be excavated from the solid rock, about twenty feet lower down the mountain-spur than the other; it is this which is now used. Aurelian commemorated the act by an inscription that still remains, in square, beautiful Roman letters, giving *his* name and *his* exploits. Here it is, just as I copied it, on my fifth visit there:

Imp. Cæs. M. Avrelivs
Antoninvs Pivs Felix Avgvstvs
Part. Max. Brit. Max. Germ Maximvs
Pontifex Maximvs.
Montibvs Imminentibvs
Lyco Flvmini Cæsis Viam Delatavit
Per   *   *   *   *
Antoninianam Svam.

The portion after *Per* was carefully erased by somebody long since. It is probable, says Porter, that this work was constructed about A.D. 173.

Again, one of the Saracenic conquerors, about A.D. 1400, left an inscription here, cut elegantly in a stone panel, on the same plan as that adopted by his predecessors, and this also remains. And so finally did the French soldiers who were here in 1860 and 1861. Now, my visit to Nahr-el-Kelb, March 5, 1868 (which, by the way, was the twenty-second anniversary of my own initiation into Freemasonry), was made for the particular purpose of inspecting these ancient emblems and inscriptions. I found nine of them on the old or upper road (that of Sesostris), which to reach now requires considerable climbing. No doubt there were originally more of these carved panels—lost by the breaking away of the cliffs on the south side. Three are considered to be Egyptian, and six Assyrian. When the light strikes the ancient carvings properly, they stand out plainly enough to the eye. I found it necessary, however, to stand off fifteen or twenty feet from them, to gather the original idea satisfactorily.

Beginning at the south, or upper end of the road, the carvings are thus arranged, viz.:

1st. *Assyrian.* King Sennacherib at full length. A fine figure of a bearded man, his left arm grasping a club, and bent across the breast; the right arm raised. In Layard's *Nineveh* you see this figure again and again repeated. The whole tablet or panel is covered with an inscription in the Assyrian cunei characters, which Rawlinson and Lepsius have read without much difficulty.

2d. *Egyptian.* Two small figures at the top, and inscriptions below; the whole rather indistinct.

3d. *Assyrian.* Rounded at the top, with a border encircling it. A figure like No. 1; no inscriptions.

4th. *Egyptian.* Square-topped, with a cornice. Figures like No. 2.

5th. *Assyrian.* Much like No. 1; in good preservation.

6th. *Assyrian.* Round-topped. A figure like that in No. 5.

7th. *Assyrian.* Square-topped. Figure indistinct.

8th. *Assyrian.* Square-topped. Figure like that in No. 1; the outline only discernible.

9th. *Egyptian.* Square at top; ornamented with a cornice, with the design called *cavetto.*

In the corners of the three *Egyptian* tablets are holes, apparently made to insert staples for hinges, showing that doors, probably of bronze, were constructed to protect the carvings from the weather.

Near the tablet marked No. 1, I selected a spot a few feet south of the Human Image, whose right hand is raised in such a suggestive attitude towards heaven, and cut in the solid rock an emblem more expressive and glorious than all the symbolisms of Egypt, Assyria, and Rome combined, viz., the *Square and Compass.* The place of this inscription is a romantic one. Nearly on the apex of that spur of Lebanon through which the engineers of Sesostris made their arduous way, it overlooks the Mediterranean Sea for twenty miles out, giving an outlook towards Gebal northward, and over the Masonic Bay beyond Beirut southward.

After cutting this emblem, I solemnly consecrated the place to a suitable number of those Masonic brethren whose patronage enabled me to set about this mission. This was to the intent that a Masonic interest might attach to the place, and that the future tourist, looking upon the Square and Compass conspicuously engraved here, may recall those names which our institution "does not willingly let die.' A few weeks after this was done, Admiral Lord Paget visited Beirut with a squadron of ships; and in company with the British Consul, E. T. Rogers, Esq. (the Worshipful Master of Palestine Ledge,

No. 415, at Beirut), made an examination of these ancient localities. Seeing the Square and Compass chiseled upon that hillside, the old mariner, it is said, put on a knowing look, and made a remark which my readers would have perfectly understood had they only heard it.

The names of Masons located here, and associated thus intimately with Hiram, King of Tyre; Hiram Abif, the Widow's Son; Adoniram, Prince of Judah; and Zabud, the King's Friend, are the following: Thomas H. Benton, Jr., Rev. William Leas, J. M. Griffith, M. W. Robinson, William Potts, R. J. Chesnutwood, B. H. Dewey, Luke Lockwood, James Walsh, Charles E. Blumenthal, M.D.

In consecrating this spot, first of all to the memory of "the Widow's Son," I do not forget that he must many a time have "gone this way," journeying to that school of architecture, *Gebal,* twenty miles up the coast. Passing where I passed this morning, he must have halted and stood where I now stand, to examine these three ancient Egyptian tablets, then scarcely five centuries old, and, doubtless, perfectly distinct to an eye like his, skillful "to find out every device" (2 Chron. 2:14), and probably learned in all the knowledge of the Egyptians, as Moses was. It was easy for Hiram, then, to read all these hieroglyphics, which only by taking the utmost advantage of the sunlight I can now barely trace out.

One of the most elegant myths connected with the history of Freemasonry in the Holy Land is associated with this spot. It is to the effect that, when King Solomon had forwarded to King Hiram of Tyre his royal request, "to send him a man cunning to work in gold, etc., and skillful to grave with his own cunning men" (2 Chron. 2:7); and when that monarch had chosen his own namesake, the renowned Hiram Abif, the latter promptly accepted the trust, and set off for a tour through the Lebanons, to designate the most accessible groves of cedar, and the best natural coves in which they could be made up into flotes and embarked. A number of bays met his view, but none that presented such a combination of favorable circumstances as this, which I call *Masonic Bay,* at the mouth of Nahr-el-Kelb. Just above it the overhanging mountains, now so bleak and unclothed, abounded in the finest groves of cedar and fir. The natural avenues to the sea which were presented by the ravine of Nahr-el-Kelb, at the north end of the bay, and Beirut River at the south end, afforded the most desirable inclines down which the cedar-trunks could be moved from the mountains. This place was therefore selected; and during the seven years in which the best science and skill of Phœnicia were expended in the erection of King Solomon's Temple at Jerusalem, the shores of this bay presented an appearance only paralleled, at the present time, by those vast depots of pine-timber in which the supplies of Maine and Wisconsin are hoarded up.

And now to recall the myth alluded to. It seems, from the traditions of the craft, that various questions in regard to the construction of Freemasonry, or "speculative masonry," as we call it, were made subjects of discussion by the three Grand Masters, and settled from time to time at their conferences in Jerusalem. One of the most interesting of these was that of an appropriate *color*. Upon this point the minds of the three philosophers were strangely diverse. King Solomon preferred *red*, or *scarlet*, emblematic of that fervency and zeal so strikingly illustrated in his own character. King Hiram expressed his choice of the royal color, *purple*, a hue associated with his own metropolis, Tyre, ever since the purple-shell had been utilized as emblematic of the noblest precepts. Hiram Abif was partial to *blue*, as suggestive of that expansion and universality which, they all hoped, would become characteristics of the new society. Standing here on this lofty point of rocks, and gazing over the vast sea before him—a sea famed in all ages for its *depths of blue*, the boundary of his vision only limited by a clearness of blue, Hiram stored his mind with so many arguments in favor of *the adoption of that color*, that when the three Grand Masters held their next conference at Jerusalem his logic proved irresistible, and so the "cerulean hue" was adopted as the unchangeable type of Masonry.

The following lines were written at this locality:

> Thoughtfully gazing on this wall,
>   By Egypt carved for Egypt's glory,
> I strive to call before me all
>   The sum of this symbolic story:
> It is, that in the human heart
>   There ever is a deathless longing
> For life eternal; from death's rest
>   The immortal soul expects returning.
>
> These conquerors, in blood and flame,
>   Wrote on earth's history their hope
> To have eternity of fame!
>   Traveler upon these mountains, stop

And pay obeisance! 'twas a good
   And worthy hope,—the same that fires
And animates your generous blood,
   And to all noble deeds inspires!

The examination of this beautiful Bay of the Rafts was the subject of numerous explorations, both along the beach and at the foot of the mountains. Here, as Porter says, the terrace-cultivation, to which I alluded in my description of a stage-ride from Beirut to Damascus, is seen in perfection. What an amount of time and industry has been expended in these terraces! But they show, better than anything else, how a dense and industrious population like that of the Jews, from B.C. 1450 to A.D. 70, succeeded in turning the hillsides of Palestine into gardens, and orchards, and fruitful fields. These terraces typify the golden future of this country. What richness must be in this disintegrated limestone-soil, where a few handfuls of dirt scattered among the rocks can produce such vines, fig trees, mulberries, and olives, as I see here!

And it was here, too, that I first learned to view with infinite scorn and contempt the practices of ordinary tourists who throng this country. After meeting and greeting the first dozen or two of them, I accustomed myself to avoiding them as the genuine *bores* of the land. Their "beastly-looking place, you know," became more disagreeable to my ears than a whole volley of Arabic gutturals. They skim the country like a bird, but without the bird's powers of perception. They ride all day to sleep soundly all night, that they may ride all next day, and sleep soundly all next night. That is the history and the pith of their diaries, if they keep diaries while in Palestine.

But, oh, the laziness of the natives! *Ignavis semper feriæ sunt* is their motto—it is always holiday to the idle. It gave me the *fidgets* to see one of them hoeing in his garden. He stood so long in one place that, if he had worn a broad-brimmed hat instead of a *tarboush,* the shade might affect the growth of the plants. (This, by the way, is an old Kentucky joke; a neighbor of mine *did* kill his tobacco-plants in that way, or report lies.) Riding one day in search of shells, near the mouth of Nahr-el-Kelb—

I found a wild and strange retreat
As e'er was trod by outlaw feet;
The dell beneath the mountain's crest
Yawned like a gash on warrior's breast.
                         —*Scott.*

Riding, I say, along the mouth of that grand gorge through which the Dog River flows, under the aqueduct, where the spider sparkles like a rich setting of pearls and rubies, and makes his web a marvel of geometric preciseness, I met an Arab sheikh, small of stature, about forty, keen as a fox, with whom I had a long talk about farming. I told him all that Horace Greeley "knows about farming;" all my own experience in raising corn, and cattle, and hogs; described the success of my (much) "better half" in butter-and-milk raising, and chicken-raising, and cabbage-raising. By means of Hassan, whose powers of interpretation are sorely tried when I tell these people things they never heard of before, but whose faith in "General Morris" is of that sort which "removes mountains," I really did expatiate and spread myself before the eyes of that Arab sheikh, who all the time was drinking my coffee, and smoking cigarettes at the expense of the "Masonic Exploration Fund." And, you will ask, what impression did all this make on his mind? Why, he arose, after imbibing the last drop of coffee in my rubber-bottle, smiled a smile of contempt, and said in three or four jaw-cracking words (in Arabic) "No keef," and so left me without a thank-you. The word *keef* expresses comfort, quiet, the *dolce far niente,* which is the celestial idea of these Orientals. To lie back in cushions, sip coffee, and smoke *tombac,* is *keef*—heaven on earth.

The fencing to the fields and gardens around this bay is usually the large cactus or prickly-pear, which reminds me that our *agave americanus,* used for fencing in Florida, makes an impenetrable *chevaux-de-frise,* with its long pointed leaves interlocking, and forming a most formidable barrier against stock.

How much the traveler will miss who journeys through these Oriental lands without a Bible in *hand,* and a Bible in *head,* and a Bible in *heart,* can only be estimated by one who has seen what floods of light are shed by Holy *Writ* upon holy *scenes.* To read a passage, however graphic, of the Old or New Testament, sitting by the fireside, or in the class at school, is one thing, and, as far as it goes, it is a *good* thing. Truth is *cosmopolitan,* and is equally truth in Occidental as in Oriental lands. But to read it amidst the same surroundings in which it was written, is *quite another* and a *better* thing. *Then* the casual allusions, which may have seemed clear before, will appear doubly clear; while many passages that the language of nature, and not human language, must clear up, will be illuminated.

From my notebook I propose to illustrate this subject by a few scenes in Holy Land, examined *Bible in hand*. I begin with an incident that struck me as I went from Beirut to Gebal. The *location* of the fact was at the northern end of the Bay of St. George, just as you begin to mount the pass before arriving at *Nahr-el-Kelb*, or Dog River; the *season* is the sowing-time of grain.

Here, as I ride slowly through this petty enclosure of an acre or two, whose "landmark," a stone wall, is scarcely high enough to confine a skipping lamb, let me read the narrative in Mark 4, and watch the husbandman's operations while he sows his grain: "There went out a sower to sow." This poor *fellah,* or native farmer, has also *come out* from yonder village, in the nook of the mountains, several miles away, for he dare not sleep, nor keep his little pair of plow-heifers outside of stone walls, lest the robber come upon him unawares and impoverish him.

"And it came to pass, as he sowed, some fell by the wayside, and the fowls of the air came and devoured it up." Look how busy they are yonder. There are the sparrows (called by naturalists the *passer salicicola* and the *passer montanus* and the *passer cisalpina)* and other grain-eating birds.

"And some fell on stony ground, where it had not much earth; and immediately it sprung up, because it had no depth of earth; but when the sun was up, it was scorched, and because it had no root, it withered away." Look in the skirts of the enclosure yonder, next the fence. The earth is but a half inch deep on those rocks. And how warm the soil is to the feel. Doubtless this grain will spring up most quickly of all that he is sowing; but there is no *depth of earth;* it can have no root; it must wither away.

"And some fell among thorns, and the thorns grew up and choked it, and it yielded no fruit." Look yonder, in that recess of the hills, how dense the thorns. The withered old woman whom we met a few minutes since, bearing her bundle of sticks, gathered them from this thicket of the "camel's thorn," supposed by some to be even the same spiny growth of which our Savior's plaited crown was woven. Think you that the grain which our sower is scattering there can ever come to maturity? Surely no; it will be outgrown by the thorns; chocked by them; rendered fruitless.

"And others fell on good ground, and did yield fruit, that sprung up and increased and brought forth; some thirty, some sixty, and some a hundred." Look at this fat soil. A generation back it was hard, blue limestone, like the stony cliffs overhanging it. Under the bright showers of heaven, and the quickening sunshine, it has kindly yielded as we now see it. For, as Pope says,

> "The seas shall fail, the skies in smoke decay,
> Rocks fall to dust, and mountains melt away."

All the fertilizing phosphates and carbonates, and other chemical elements that mother-earth so covets in her transforming processes, are here; and upon these level flats, where the birds *dare not* alight, where the thorns *cannot* encroach, where there is ample *depth of earth;* here in this "good ground," the poor man's grain will spring up; will increase; will bring forth. Here the beautiful language of our Masonic Monitor concerning mother-earth will be realized.

Has not the quarter-hour been well spent? As I mount and ride forward upon my way, let me try my memory upon a paraphrase of this divine narrative, which I composed many years ago.*

> He that hath ears to hear
> May listen now,
> While I shall tell, in mystic words indeed,
> Of a good husbandman who took his seed,
> And went to sow.

> Some by the wayside fell;—
> On breezes borne,
> The fowls of heaven flew down, a greedy train,
> And snatched with hasty appetite the grain,
> Till all was gone.

> Some fell upon a rock;
> And greenly soon
> They sprouted as for harvest, strong and fair;
> But when the summer sun shone hotly there,
> They wilted down.

> Some fell among the thorns,—
> A fertile soil;
> But ere the grain could raise its timid head,
> The accursed weeds luxuriantly o'erspread,
> And choked them all.

> But some *on the good ground,*
> God's precious mould,
> Where sun, breeze, dew, and showers apportioned well;
> And in the harvest, smiling swains did tell
> An hundredfold!

---

* The text of my paraphrase is that in the eighth chapter of Lake.

Need I say that all this comes naturally to mind, while journeying through these Bible lands? I pity the traveler who has enjoyed such opportunities as a visit to Palestine at the present day affords, and yet has not increased his knowledge in, and his love for, the Holy Scriptures.

ANTIOCHUS VII., KING OF SYRIA.

COIN-NOTES EXPLANATOY OF PAGE 498.

The coins so forcibly delineated on page 498, are thus named beginning at the top and reading the lines toward the right hand: Dentella; Palermo; Seleucus; Antiochus II.; Antiochus III.; Alexander II.; Demetrius Nicator; Antiochus VI.; Seleucus Callinicus; Heraclea; Seleucus III.; Mamerco.

CHAPTER XIII.

BEIRUT.

BEGIN this chapter by describing my visit to the Protestant Cemetery, where the black cypresses shoot up their pyramidal cones into the sky, and where, of all places on earth, lies our brother, the man of eloquence, earnestness, and deep piety, Rev. Pliny Fisk. Among the dead who calmly repose under the thick shade of these mourning cypresses, this man is most worthy of honor in Masonic memories. When this earth shall restore those that are asleep in her, and the dust those that dwell in silence, and the secret places shall deliver those souls that were committed unto them (2 Esdras 7:32), the form of our first Protestant missionary, who gave his young life here to his work, will lead all the rest.

We may not be able to understand the fascination that draws us to the graveside of such men and holds us solemnly there; but it exists, and often men of the greatest intelligence are most free to acknowledge the influence.

I cannot do better, in this connection, than to insert an article, written in pencil, sitting upon this tomb, and afterwards published in an American journal.

THE MASON-MISSIONARY.

In the Protestant graveyard at Beirut, in the Holy Land, is a modest structure, built of the Lebanon limestone, inscribed at the top, "Rev. Pliny Fisk, died Oct. 23, 1825, Æ. 33 years." The writer, in company with Brother Samuel Hallock, first visited this hallowed spot on the 23d of March, 1868, and plucked a sprig from the funeral cypress-tree that grows straight and tall at the head of the grave. His emotions are expressed in the lines following.

The Rev. Pliny Fisk was the first American missionary to the Holy Land. He came here full of hopes and holy impulses in the

Master's work. His youth, his zeal, his lovely spirit, overflowing with kindly sentiments, won him hosts of friends, and, had he lived, doubtless the mission here had been in advance of what it now is. But it was not so to be. The Master called him up "higher," and he passed beyond.

Brother Fisk was a Freemason. At the period of his entrance upon this work, as the records of the Grand Lodge of Vermont show, the fraternity assisted him with money and moral encouragement. I have thought recently that perhaps my own mission to the Holy Land was partly suggested by reading, several years ago, this Masonic history of Pliny Fisk:

'Neath our weeping, 'neath our weeping,
Lies the young disciple sleeping.
  Jesus moved him with his story,
  Promised him the heavenly glory,
While his vows of service keeping.

Earnest spirit, earnest spirit,
How he did that fire inherit!
  How, to seek the lost, did wander,
  Rent his home-ties all asunder,
And his martyr's crown did merit.

Oh, to see him; oh, to see him;
When the stroke of death did free him!
  Burst the chains that long impeded,
  Quenched the sorrows he had heeded;
Angels to his home convey him.

Blessed resting, blessed resting,
Not a jar of earth molesting;
  Leaves of cypress sigh above him,
  Breathe the faith that once did move him,
Green and fragrant life attesting.

A friend, after reading this article, gave me a quotation, which add to the rest:

So may some gentle muse,
  With lucky words, favor *my* destined urn,
  And, as he passes, turn
And bid fair peace be to *my* sable shroud!

After composing these notes concerning the man of God, I discovered, in old files of the Missionary Herald, copious extracts from Fisk's own diary, together with biographical details, from which I cull some additional thoughts. Every Freemason feels interested to know that the American Mission to Syria, now the most prosperous and successful of all the missionary operations upon the face of the earth, was initiated by a Freemason, assisted by Masonic funds and other encouragements from the "great fraternity." Will not the time come when Freemasons will unite in erecting a monument to this Masonic apostle?

Pliny Fisk, the fourth son of Ebenezer and Sarah Fisk, was born at Shelburne, Franklin county, Massachusetts, June 24, 1792. From early youth he was distinguished for an engaging disposition and unusual sobriety. Persevering application was a prominent trait in his disposition. As a son, he was faithful, dutiful, and affectionate. He diligently improved his scanty literary advantages, and entered Middlebury College, Connecticut, in 1811, graduating August, 1814. In January, 1815, he was licensed to preach the gospel. From 1815 to 1818 he pursued a regular course of divinity in the Theological Seminary at Andover, and was then appointed, in connection with Mr. Parsons, to the Palestine mission. On the third of November, 1819, he sailed for that country. He engaged in Oriental studies at Smyrna, while Mr. Parsons made a preliminary survey of the Holy Land. In April, 1823, Mr. Fisk entered Jerusalem, and pursued his labors there during the first year. Then he established his mission at Beirut, where, on the 23d of October, 1825, he expired, a victim to one of the fevers of the country.

Among all who have given their lives to missionary labors in foreign lands, few possessed so happy a combination of qualities for the work as Mr. Fisk. The pointed and inveterate hostility of the enemies of the Gospel, were met with that union of firmness and gentleness best calculated to subdue them to the obedience of the faith. The instructions given him by the society under whose charge he was operating, strike the keynote of all his labors.

"From the heights of the Holy Land, from Calvary, from Olivet, and from Zion, you will take an extended view of the wide-spread desolations and variegated scenes presenting themselves on every side to Christian sensibility; and will survey, with earnest attention, the various tribes and classes of fellow-beings who dwell in that land and in the surrounding country. The two grand inquiries ever present to your mind will be, What good can be done, and by what means? What can be done for the Jews? what for the Pagans? what for the Mohammedans? what for the Christians? what for the people in Palestine? what for those in Egypt, in Syria, in Persia, in

Armenia, in other countries to which your inquiries may be extended?"

Upon his death-bed, Mr. Fisk dictated the following letter to his father:

"BEIRUT, Oct. 20, 1825.

"My beloved, aged father: I compose a few lines for you upon a sick, probably a dying bed. When you gave me up for this mission, you gave me up for life and death. You know to whom to look for consolation and support. The same God who has comforted you so many years, under so many troubles, will comfort you under this. You know His consolations are neither few nor small. I leave these lines as a pledge to you, and my brothers and sisters, my nephews and nieces, that I love you all most dearly, though so long separated from you. I hope all, or nearly all, our number have been enabled to give themselves to Christ, and that we shall meet with our departed mother in heaven."

He died on Sabbath morning at 3 o'clock. As soon as the news of his death was announced, all the flags of the different Consulates were suspended at half-mast. His funeral was attended at 4 P.M. the same day, in the presence of a numerous and orderly concourse of people.

And now for some account of the city of Beirut. A writer describes it as exceedingly beautiful. The promontory upon which it stands is triangular, the apex projecting three miles into the Mediterranean, and the base running along the foot of Lebanon. It occupies the *southern* horn of the crescent of the Masonic Bay, as the rocky pass at the mouth of Dog River occupies the *northern* horn. The southwestern side of this promontory, which I perambulated one day on foot, is composed of loose drifting sand, with the aspect of a desert; but the northwestern side is very different. The shore-line, which I frequently traversed in search of shells and general information, is formed of a range of irregular, deeply-indented rocks and cliffs. Between these rocks the ground rises gradually, for a mile or two, to the height of 200 feet. In the middle of the shore-line stands the city; first, a dense nucleus of substantial buildings; then a broad margin of picturesque villas, embowered in foliage, running up to the summit of the heights; then the mulberry groves, covering the acclivities, and here and there groups of palms and cypresses. The population of the city is about 75,000, one-third of them being Mohammedans, the rest Christians and Jews. It is growing fast in size and importance.

As my headquarters were at Beirut, and for nearly four months

I was passing in and out of the city, I am competent to affirm that the only city in Palestine or Syria where there is any "social life," in the sense that Americans attach to the term, is *Beirut*. At Jerusalem there are but a few foreign families, not enough to form a circle for social life, while in no other Syrian city is there even so much as at Jerusalem. But at Beirut are found all the materials for society, as genial and cheerful as those at home, and well are they manipulated.

There is given, through the cooler seasons, a weekly series of lectures upon historical, educational, and scientific subjects, that would bear honorable comparison with those in any country. During the winter of 1867-8, among the topics handled were "Petra," by Rev. Mr. Dodge; "Abyssinia," by Bishop Gobat; "Turkey in Europe," by Rev. Mr. Washburn, and other subjects by Col. Churchill, Mr. J. Aug. Johnson (the American Consul-General), and other gentlemen of repute. These were given at private houses, thrown open to all respectable visitors. The lectures occupy about an hour each, and are followed by a distribution of tea and cakes, offered with a hospitality that is truly refreshing. I attended several of these *séances* with ever-increasing pleasure.

A society of young gentlemen was formed at Beirut, in 1867, entitled, "The Once-a-Week Club," which met every Wednesday evening, at the house of Brother Samuel Hallock. Modeled partly upon the old-fashioned system of debating societies, this club embraced other features that made its assemblies pleasant to all concerned. There were about twenty members, and various honorary members, of whom I was one.

But these superficial demonstrations of social life are only slight indications of the great under-current. The truth is that, in a foreign country like Syria, people lay aside, to a great extent, those social distinctions which, at home, form an almost impassable barrier between them and their neighbors. "The nobility and gentry," as they are so magniloquently designated in the English papers, or the "upper classes," as the American press somewhat vaguely styles them, finding no other members of the "upper classes," still less of the "nobility and gentry," with whom they can associate, come gradually down from the upper and mysterious atmosphere in which they were born, and cultivate the social spirit with people who are their equals in all but the accident of birth. Very gracefully do they develop themselves. No persons can make themselves more agreeable.

14

At Beirut, this blending of respectable people, regardless of other distinctions, forms the principal charm of society. At church, at funeral, at lecture, and in family parties, they mingle, each bringing his share to the enjoyment of the whole; some of music, some of conversation, etc.

The religious circles are equally free and social. A Bible-class, under the superintendence of Rev. Mr. Robinson, a Scotch minister, who has charge of the Beirut church, included some of the best-instructed spiritual minds that I ever met in such a circle. At the regular Sunday morning service, in English, all attend and blend their voices in the psalmody, as, doubtless, their hearts in the prayers. So many ministers, of so many denominations, are found among the tourists to this country, that the variety of pulpit gifts is uncommonly great, while, it is to be presumed, each one who is thus called upon to officiate, exerts his best efforts.

The best English and American periodicals, religious and secular, are taken by the English-speaking population here in great numbers. These are exchanged and loaned or distributed, in a manner partaking of the free-and-easy spirit that animates the whole circle, until there is no lack of good reading for all. A considerable library is attached to the American Mission, and there is a kind of *Reading Club Subscription,* for the purchase of periodicals and cheaper literature.

But one of the most agreeable features of "social life in Beirut" remains to be described. During the hot season, say from June 15th to October 1st, existence in Beirut is intolerable to foreigners. Every family, therefore, has a summer residence in some one of the innumerable villages that dot the cool and breezy mountainsides overhanging Beirut on the east. Here an unbounded hospitality is maintained, that goes right to the heart of the stranger. Here he can find, among the most refined classes of people, a yielding of social position, an open hand and heart, a blending of luxury with plainness, and generosity with all, that would be hard to find anywhere else. Those who have spent a summer among these people, in the range of the Lebanons, have nothing further to look for to realize the perfection of hospitality.

From the highest point of Bassoul's Hotel the view by starlight is a charming one. Below are the gleaming roofs, the dark shadows of winding streets, the outlines of a battlemented wall, a castle by the sea, the waters of the harbor, silvery with the starlight, a faint view of prostrate pillars of Egyptian granite at the landing-place, the dark sweep of the pines beyond the city, and all closed in, on the east, by the somber, solemn ramparts of Lebanon.

As life in Beirut is analogous to all Oriental experience, I give here quite a number of extracts from my diary, mostly made in a day's stroll through the bazaars, and amidst the din and turmoil of the streets. I was under the effects of that southern wind called *Khamsin,* which Dr. W. M. Thomson has so well described in his *Land and Book,* and viewed things in a cynical mood, yet not so much so as to prevent accurate details.

Behold my notes, scratched amidst the bustle and yells of an Arab market-place! *Saffron:* piles of it sold here; name from the Arabic *saphor,* signifying *hot;* carried by pilgrims to England, A.D. 1539. After turning half a dozen corners in these narrow lanes, it will defy anything but an intelligent dog to tell where you are. I have already lost my way on three several days going from Hallock's to the American Consulate. The tools used by these mechanics would give an American artisan the horrors. The ancients used saws for wood-cutting, made, probably, of iron; though the saws from the Egyptian tombs of the same period are of bronze (that is, copper and tin alloy). The stones for the Temple of Solomon were cut with saws (1 Kings 7:9), just as the blocks of stone from the old Temple quarry under Jerusalem, which I brought home with me, were taken out with saws, so soft is the rock in its native condition. Saws were used in punishing criminals (2 Sam. 12:31, and 1 Chron. 20:3), and these, as the text shows, were of iron. The saws of the Egyptians were single-handed and straight, and this is the only pattern that I noticed in Palestine; but in Nineveh the sculptures, nearly as old as Solomon's time, prove that the Assyrians used the cross-cut or double-handled saw. *Hyssop:* it "springeth out of the wall" abundantly here, and awaits such a botanist as Solomon to describe it (1 Kings 4:33), for I notice that no two writers agree as to its identity. *Sparrow:* this bird is on every house-top, building nests on every jutting, and stuffing materials of nests into every crevice. Lucky there are few *cats* here to worry them; cats are only once mentioned in the Bible, and that in the apocryphal book of Baruch. *Blindness:* blind "beggars by the wayside" in sufficient abundance to deplete my spare change; I find the eighth-piastre pieces capital coin for this purpose; being worth only half a cent a piece, I can give to a score of applicants without impoverishing myself. *Battlements:* every roof more than six or eight feet above the ground has a battlement, according to the requirements of the old Jewish law. *Bazaars* these and the mechanics' shops are unending sources of curiosity and instruction. *Meal-times:* awkward hours to Americans, to eat at 8 o'clock; nothing but bread, jam, fruit, and coffee, and then wait until noon for breakfast; I notice strangers seem wolfish about 10 A.M. for want of their steak. *Dr. Thomson:* a bluff, genial, weather-beaten old Buckeye (Ohio) American, ready to communicate all that he knows, in the most affable and unpretending manner. His wife (second wife, the first died at Jerusalem), an Italian lady, cordial and kind. *Clothing:* had full suit made of French cloth, worth in New York $8 per yard, for $28 the entire suit. *Palestine Lodge* is in a low condition—want of harmony among the brethren; scarcely had a meeting for a year; Dr. Brigstock, a most intelligent physician lately W. M. One of the Past Masters is an Israelite. *Women.* under the white, enveloping sheet they spread out their arms cunningly, to appear corpulent, thinking it "an especial honor," as the old traveler Sandys remarked, "to be fat; and many of them are fat!" So far as their faces are concerned, I can say nothing, for I did not see the face of a Turkish woman all the time of my pilgrimage in the Holy Land. But among the lower classes of the Arabs less care is taken to conceal the countenance from strangers, and of them I can repeat another observation of the same ancient, accurate traveler: "I saw divers of the women with their chins stained with blue knots and flowers, made by pricking the skin with needles and rubbing it over with the juice of an herb (*henna*), which will never wear out again." *Snails:* a wonderful place for them; very large and edible for those who hanker after them. Their firm, crescent-shaped jaws, and tongues, with sharp, hooked, rasping denticles to the number of 10,000 or more, on a bit of membrane not a quarter of an inch long nor half so wide,—all this is very well in natural history, but when it comes to *eating them,* I prefer sardines. *Freemasons:* I found here Brother Todd, a member of the lodge at Newburyport, Massachusetts; Gen. Starring, a Chicago Mason; and Brother J. M. Himes, of Atlas Lodge, New York; all nearly through with their Syrian travels. The snows on Mount Lebanon, always an obstacle to travel in the month of March, were deeper in 1868, as I was informed by Dr. Thomson (who has been in this country thirty-six years), than he had ever known them before. A number of travelers were detained at Beirut on this account, desiring to visit Damascus, but unable to cross the mountains. I made early and frequent calls upon the United States Consul-General, J. Augustus Johnson, favorably known in American journals as a vigorous writer. He returned to New York in 1870. I brought him letters from his wife, then visiting Bethany, West Virginia, the residence of her father, the veteran Jerusalem explorer and missionary, Dr. J. T. Barclay. Mr. Johnson met me cordially, and tendered me all the aid in his power to further the purposes of my visit. He ought to be a Mason, as all the English Consuls are. Fortunately, there is a library, well-selected and well-filled, attached to the Protestant mission here, and I shall read, while in this country, Kenrick's Phœnicia, Lamartine's Pilgrimage, Hasselquist's Oriental Botany, Anderson's Geological Survey of Syria, and Renan's new work on Phœnicia, just coming out in parts.*

---

* Since returning home, I have purchased the numbers of this splendid production so far as issued, *Mission de Phénicie,* and can heartily recommend it to all who read French, as a noble contribution to Oriental literature.

An educated Syrian, in the provision-store here, described the Dead Sea to me with accuracy, spreading meal upon his hat and delineating the topography with his finger, just as the plan of the city of Alexander was first drawn by the architect when inaugurating that work. In looking at the antique weights and measures used by these people, it is a good time to commence the inquiry, how far they can be traced to that one necessarily material center (the Great Pyramid of Cheops, in Egypt), from which those material things called *weights* and *measures,* in a primeval age, were divinely distributed to every leading people. Groups of women returning from the cemetery, wrapped in shrouds, white as the "White Lady of Avenel." No wonder they catch catarrhs, rheumatisms, fevers, blindness; sitting through such damp days as these on the cold ground upon the graves. The hired mourners, who weep, howl, beat the breast, etc., by contract, are wiser. They only go out professionally, and remain but a few minutes. One hundred of these drygoods stores would not make one such establishment as in the Bowery, New York, constitutes a fair retail store. It was here at Beirut that Gregory was coming, A.D. 231, to attend the famous law-school, when he met Origen, and was converted to Christianity. Three fine columns of gray granite are standing behind the donkey-stables of Beirut, representing three of the angles of a perfect square, the fourth being absent; these noble pillars are some thirty feet long, and thick in proportion. I have dedicated them to Freemasonry, and styled them *Faith, Hope,* and *Charity,* the three theological virtues of our order. Beirut is said to be the cleanest place in Syria. A fountain with an Arabic inscription, said to be an invocation to God for a blessing to him who drinks; in this spirit, I took often and copious draughts. But there *is* a blessing in cool, sweet water everywhere, and especially in the East. The presbyter, Pamphylus, was born here A.D. 275, and martyred A.D. 300. He had collected a very complete library of Christian literature, all destroyed long since. The weather here has had close observers. Dr. Klein, comparing the mean annual frequency of thunder-storms throughout the world, says that while Java has from 159 to 110, and Sitka 1 ½ per annum, Beirut has 4. "Bark from Boston, 3,200 bbls. capacity, freighted with kerosene in barrels and cases." *Adv.* Sept. 12, 1870. This advertisement reminds me that the only merchantable commodity sent by the United States to this country is *kerosene,* of which three or four cargoes are landed here annually from Boston. The return freight is wool. 'Twas a droll sight to see my French tailor's row of Arab journeymen, squatting in the street, outside the shop, stitching away for dear life. Hallock particularly requests me, when I walk on the flat roof of his house, not to look down into the adjacent courtyard. His neighbor, a chaste Mohammedan, has his *hareem* there, and I might possibly catch a glimpse of the faces of some of his wives. Of course, after such a warning, I spend considerable time every day, *looking,* but thus far in vain. Josephus, in his Wars of the Jews (Wars, VII., iii. 1), gives interesting details concerning Beirut. Everybody who reads travels in the Holy Land, expects to see something upon the subject of Turkish baths. I made an article, spiced with some exaggeration, that was published in the Masonic department of the New York *Sunday Dispatch*. In reading it, three years afterwards, I recognize its general accuracy. Only I forgot to say that one of those bath-servants has been in the profession, it is said, for forty years. He looks it. He is a Calvin Edson, as I remember Calvin, the "Living Skeleton" of Barnum's time, a dried-up old man, washed away by palm-fiber and olive-oil soap.

COIN OF SARDIS.

CHAPTER XIV.

FREEMASONRY IN BEIRUT.

I WAS disappointed by finding that none of the American missionaries in the Holy Land were Masons. The first two to that country, Mr. Pliny Fisk and Mr. Eddy, became members of the Masonic Order before leaving the United States, in 1818, rightly judging that nothing would bring them so near to the hearts of the Mohammedans. The consequence was, they enjoyed an intimacy with the natives such as no missionary has done since; and when Mr. Fisk died, in 1825, after a short and brilliant career, he was mourned for by them with regrets that no missionary now operating there can expect to inspire among that class. And this, simply because, in addition to zeal, piety, and learning—all of which our missionaries have abundantly—Mr. Fisk had the Masonic claim, which they have not.

The first two men, not natives, whom I met in Beirut, were Masons, guests at Bassoul's Hotel, where I stopped. I have given their names in a preceding chapter. The following day I made the acquaintance of Brother Hallock, already alluded to more than once, an ardent devotee of the order, and afterwards fell in for a moment with Brother General Starring, who was passing hastily through the city. A few weeks before my arrival, Brother John C. Breckinridge, of Kentucky, with whom I was associated in the Grand Lodge of that State as far back as 1853, spent a few days here. From time to time, I enlarged my circle of fraternal acquaintance, and at last, visiting a company of white-aproned brothers, "where the lambs feed after their manner" (Isaiah 5:17), I am enabled to examine and describe their lodge-room.

An account of the origin of Palestine Lodge, No. 415, Beirut, is given me by Brother D. Murray Lyon, of Ayr, Scotland, to whom I wrote for information on the subject. Extract from the records of the Grand Lodge of Scotland: "In Grand Committee, March 4th, 1861, the M. W. the Grand Master stated that he had received an application for a charter for a new lodge in Syria, to be called *The Lodge of Palestine,* at Beirut. That the application had come to his son, the Marquis of Tullibardine, by the hands of Lieutenant Colonel Burnaby, Commissioner of the British Government to the French Army of Occupation at present in Syria. That Colonel Burnaby intended to return to Syria immediately, and the parties were most anxious that the charter should, if possible, be taken out by him. The M. W. the Grand Master thereupon moved that, in the special circumstances of the case, the Grand Committee should authorize the issue of the charter in question, and he felt confident that the Grand Lodge would confirm their resolution. It was therefore unanimously resolved to issue the charter, under the peculiarly pressing circumstances of the case; but this should form no precedent for the future." This action *was* confirmed by the Grand Lodge at its next session. On the occasion of my visit, in 1868, the lodge had a membership of about seventy-five, scattered as far as Gaza on the south and Baghdad on the east, and included brethren at Sidon, Acre, Nablous, Damascus, Aleppo, Hums, etc., etc.

Since my departure, June, 1868, the Grand Lodge (Orient) of France has established a second lodge here, entitled *Le Liban.* This lodge set out with a feature peculiar to itself, described in the Grand Lodge records thus: "Your Committee on Administration proposes to you to sanction the remarkable by-law of the Lodge Liban, at Beirut, which comprises the creation of an establishment of relief (Relief Lodge, or Board of Relief) for Masonic travelers; also a library and a Masonic Tribunal of Conciliation, to settle differences between the brethren, and in their relation with the outside world." I cannot discover whether this idea was made practical or not. This lodge was installed January 4th, 1869; Brother Lambert, W. M.; Brother Haggy, S. W.; Brother Mossip, J. W. My informant says: "It is destined to throw out deep roots into the Syrian soil; to spread abroad bright rays amidst ignorance and superstition, and to spread the protecting shadow of peace and fraternity over all." I hope it may.

The order of Freemasonry at Beirut is not, I regret to say, in a condition satisfactory to the members there, or creditable to the great cause in which the fraternity are engaged. The reasons for this need not be enlarged upon; they are such as do not in the least compromise the honor of the individual craft at Beirut, nor will it require any extraordinary effort to remove them. Personally, there is the best of feeling amongst the brethren concerning future operations, and I feel confident that the opening of a new era for Masonic progress upon the Syrian coast is not distant.

I had postponed my intention to have the good fellows of Beirut called together, owing to the protracted absence of Brother G. J. Eldridge, H. B. M. Consul-General of Syria, late Master of the lodge here (Palestine Lodge No. 415) and who had been endowed, it was understood, with special powers for the extension of Freemasonry in this country. That functionary had been away on leave of absence to his native country for nearly a year, during which period little or nothing had been accomplished in the affairs of the lodge, the actual Master, Brother R. W. Brigstock, M.D., being much engaged in the engrossing duties of his profession, and the other officers declining to act in his absence. But upon the return of Brother Eldridge, a general wish was expressed by the fraternity of Beirut that we should have a meeting, and one was called for Saturday, the 6th of June. The night, of course, was oppressively sultry, yet the attendance embraced nearly all the resident members of Beirut, about thirty. Amongst them were Brother Eldridge, just named; Brother E. T. Rogers, Master-elect of this lodge; the present Master, Dr. Brigstock; Brother Ridley, an old and highly-respected merchant here, etc. The visitors included Brother Samuel Hallock, of Philadelphia, Pa., and others.

The extreme heat rendering the lodge-room insupportable, we used the parlor of the lodge for our meeting. This is a well-furnished apartment, very tastily arranged, similar to those I saw in Smyrna, Alexandria, Paris, and elsewhere. Here, after an introduction to the brethren, most of whom spoke Arabic only, I opened the purposes of my mission to Palestine, my remarks being excellently interpreted by Brother Rogers, one of the best Oriental scholars upon this coast. I said, in brief, that I had come to the land of historical and Masonic associations, representing a large number of the enterprising members of the fraternity in the United States; that, in pursuance of my mission, I had visited all places particularly memorable in the history of our society, especially Tyre, Gebal, Mount Lebanon, the Bay of Rafts (St. George's Bay), Joppa, and Jerusalem, and had collected relics from every part of the land, that would serve as tokens to our friends at home; that the most profound interest is felt in the United States in all matters relative to Syria and Palestine; that no questions will be propounded me, on my return, with more earnestness than those relating to *the condition of Freemasonry* here.

Then I pointed to the world-wide reach and extent of our ancient associations, showing them that I had found a group of the members of this fraternity upon the steamer that brought me to Liverpool; another upon the Mediterranean steamer; a large body of Masons, representing seven or more lodges, at Smyrna; a company of sixteen Masons in Damascus, and a goodly number at Sidon, Jaffa, and Jerusalem; that all these, without exception, seemed earnest and zealous in the cause, and glowed with the desire to extend the honorable and useful reputation of the fraternity; that the prospects were now bright for the establishment of lodges at Damascus and Jerusalem.

Then I sketched the principles and aims of the Masonic Institution. I showed them that a prudent reticence, so rare in this country, where men talk more freely of each other than anywhere else, is one of the fundamental principles of the order. That *obedience* to the laws and regulations of the society; *charity* in relieving the wants of the distressed; the most scrupulous *honor* in our dealings with each other; *promptness* in recognizing Masonic summonses; *secrecy* in preserving the fundamental esotery of the order; *fidelity* in regard to exchanged confidences, and profoundest *caution* in the admission of members to the lodge, are essential to the successful workings of the institution anywhere. I assured them that Freemasonry stands very high in the opinion of the better classes in Syria and Palestine; that is to say, amongst the governing classes and those who would do more credit to its affiliation; and that it only needed for the Masons of Beirut to strengthen themselves; to establish a few more lodges in the city; to establish regular meetings; to publish their laws, aims, and principles, for the reading of their own members and the outer world, and the benefits of the royal order would be increased an hundredfold.

I told them of our methods of operation in the United States; that our lodges held regular meetings in places well-known to every one; that they let the surrounding community know *who* they are and *where* they are, and *what they are endeavoring to do;* that they publish a number of journals devoted to the interests of Freemasonry; that when a stranger calls at one of their assemblies there is an officer, the Senior Deacon, specially charged with the duty of welcoming and accommodating him, and introducing him to the officers and members of the lodge; and that his stay in the place is made pleasant in consequence of the Masonic associations thus formed. On behalf of the great American fraternity, representing more than one-half of all the Freemasons in the world, I invited them to come and see us and verify the statements I had made.

By special request, I then recited "The Level and the Square," following after, "Our Vows." Both seemed to give satisfaction. An hour was then spent in the interchange of friendly sentiments. There is a fervor about these Syrian Masons that is extremely pleasant to a stranger. I was overwhelmed with kind wishes, invitations, and solicitations "to come again," and "to come often," and if anything can tempt me once more to undertake the long journey from La Grange to Beirut, it will be to duplicate the agreeable sensations of that evening among the Masons of Beirut.

Before dissolving the meeting, one of the lodge-officers suggested that, as few of the craft there had ever received a "side degree" of any kind, they would be pleased, and perhaps benefited by the communication of the *Secret Monitor*. Anxious to gratify them, I explained what a "side degree" is, and the object of this one. All expressed their wish to receive it; and certainly, if its uses are at all commensurate with the enjoyment it gave that good set of fellows, the *Secret Monitor,* whoever got it up, is not to be sneered at. In this, as in all other inculcations of the evening, my words were interpreted into Arabic to them by Brother Rogers. My general statements were substantiated by Brother G. J. Eldridge, now Deputy Grand Master for the District of Syria, and by the other English-speaking Masons present. This assembly was one of unmingled enjoyment, and will, I think, do well.

I cannot close the chapter without pointing out the chief difficulties with which the Masonic devotee in this country must necessarily contend. It is the necessity of working the rituals both in French and Arabic. A portion speak French only, and all *foreigners* in Syria speak French, no matter what may be their nationality. But the natives generally only speak Arabic. No one in Syria has the rituals in the Arabic language, and this compels the Worshipful Master to extemporize the lectures, covenants, etc., as he goes along, a task immensely difficult. In a lodge that I visited at Alexandria, Egypt (the *Loge des Pyramides*), the work is done alternately in

French and Arabic, and the record-books, which I examined, are kept correspondingly. But even there the rituals—(in all French lodges the rituals are printed and laid out on the pedestals for the officers' use)—are printed in *French,* not in Arabic, and this reproduces the difficulty above alluded to.

Let one of my readers, who is Master of a lodge, conceive, if he can, the labor of being compelled to translate into a foreign tongue, clause by clause, the language of the rituals, so that the candidate may understand it. This embarrassment, too, is increased when that foreign tongue is the *Arabic,* an Oriental tongue whose phrases and trains of thought are essentially different from the French and English. I think I have said enough to show that, instead of blaming our Syrian brethren for their want of progress, we should give them credit for what they have done, and lend them warm wishes and sympathy in their future operations.

The Masons of Beirut, and generally of Eastern lodges, know nothing of demitting. They may transfer their membership to other lodges, or become members of as many other lodges, at the same time, as they choose; but, like the Masons of Connecticut, they are charged no dues, and running no risk of suspension, retain affiliation with their *alma mater,* their mother-lodge, as long as they live. In conversation with them during my various visits to Beirut, I learned much of the high claims that *charity* makes upon them. I think that in foreign countries the society is not so much a moral institution as with us, but has more of the social and benevolent features.

> Fatherless, motherless, sisterless, brotherless,
> Houseless and homeless, the wanderer here,

having any claims upon Masonic charity, will realize them with less difficulty than with us, while the discipline due for unmasonic conduct will not fall so promptly as in American lodges. One of them quoted to me—

> "The drying up of a single tear has more
> Of honest fame than shedding seas of gore,"

and evidently considered that this expresses the whole theory of Freemasonry. Although Lebanon Lodge, No. 415, is of Scotch parentage, yet it has been worked under some of those new-fangled whimseys, as Southey calls them, those bizarre ceremonies, the product of the French mind, which, as they could never be adapted to a cosmopolitan system, are as impracticable as they are trifling.

With the Oriental dislike to change, these craftsmen will be strong advocates of *uniformity,* and stern opponents of innovation, saying with Southey:

> "It do not look well,
> These alterations, sir! I'm an old man,
> And love the good old fashions;
> I like what I've been used to."

The eunuch, that dry-tree of Freemasonry, as Isaiah terms him (56:3), artificially made, is common here, readily distinguished by the imbecility of his countenance and moroseness of manner. He is the conventional *non-Mason* of this as well as all jurisdictions.

The only innovation possible to Oriental Masons is that of *omission* They may (and do) drop out, lop off, more or less of the work, and so fail to exhibit the great principles in as heavy relief (*basso-relievo*) as we do in America. This is too clear to an observer in one of their lodges to bear contradiction. But they never "put new cloth upon the old garment," tattered as it may be.

The holy nature of our obligations to the wife, daughter, widow, sister, and mother, of the Master Mason, growing out of that respect for the sex which colors all our communications with each other, is carried here to excess. Even to ask a Moslem if he has a wife or daughter, or to inquire after her health, or to make any allusion to her existence, is a violation of social etiquette; therefore a violation of one of the landmarks of Oriental society!

In relation to the NAME of DEITY as a Masonic emblem, strangely disputed by some American reformers, I found no variety of opinion in the East; and the following English translation of a Russian poem by Derzhaven embodies *their* views as well as ours:

> Oh thou eternal ONE, whose presence bright
> All space doth occupy, all motion guide;
> Unchanged through time's all-devastating flight,
> Thou only GOD,—there is no GOD beside!
> Being above all beings, Mighty ONE,
> Whom none can comprehend and none explore,
> Who fill'st existence with Thyself alone,
> Embracing all, supporting, ruling o'er;
> Being whom we call GOD, and know no more!

And yet if there is any one precept in Masonry more persistently violated by these people than another, it is that Masonic injunction "Never to mention the name of God, but with that reverential awe which is due from a creature to his Creator." The Mosaic prohibition against profanity was as positive as human language could make it, and equally forms a part of the Mohammedan's Koran as of the Book of Exodus; yet the name of God is persistently, irreverently, and even ridiculously used here, by old and young. It is always ringing in your ears while traveling among Mohammedans. The expression to your horse or ass, "Get up; go ahead," is *Yellah* (Ya Allah), oh God! and in a hundred, yea, a thousand other forms the Divine Name is made contemptible among them. The Jews, I suppose, had got to the same point in the days of Jesus; for Peter, in his shameful fall and denial, "made imprecations and swore," taking heavy blasphemies on his tongue when he cut loose his friendship for the MAN who had fallen into evil hands. The Crusaders swore like Trim's "army in Flanders," and the Oriental Catholics and Greek Christians are as bad as the Mohammedans. "For swearing the land mourneth," may well be said of the Orient. This is a subject to which the Masonic moralist here should turn his first attention.

It is peculiarly gratifying to know that, in spite of Gallic influences, the Open Word is yet spread out on the altar in Palestine Lodge, No. 415, to gladden the first sight of the Masonic Candidate "brought to light;" and the Emblem of Deity, author of the Bible, still greets his first upward glance to the Orient. Long may these ancient landmarks of the craft be maintained! Every Freemason, whether Christian, Jewish, or Mohammedan, is willing to abide by the precepts, admire the beauty, revere the mysteries, and practice the principles, so far as he has the power, of this sacred volume; and these genial craftsmen, with all their lack of skill in rituals, have not transgressed the fundamental laws of Masonry, or changed its ordinances, or broken its everlasting covenants (Isaiah 24:5). Occidental reformers may encourage their Oriental brethren with the hope that though "the bricks are fallen down, we will build with hewn stones; though the sycamores are cut down, we will change them into cedars" (Isaiah 9:10).

But as it used to be said so often, by our Masonic authors, that the Koran has been, or will be, or may be, substituted for the Hebrew Scriptures, in lodge-use, this is a good time to consider the subject. An entire chapter, had I the space, would not be too much to dissect that singular work, which some Masonic writers have suggested as a fitting substitute on Masonic altars, in Mohammedan countries, for the Hebrew Scriptures, and illustrate the numerous topics introduced into this volume. That it is *the Bible* of Mohammedan Masons may be admitted in one sense, and Preston seems, in his *Illustrations,* to take it for granted that as Freemasons we may so recognize it.

Is the Koran a book to support the hands of a Freemason? The perusal of it will show—

1. That all the *doctrines* (as distinguished from the *legends*) are sound and good.

2. That nearly every maxim, religious precept, and doctrine, strictly so called, is quoted from the Hebrew Scriptures, and notably from the Ten Commandments, and is then sound and good.

3. That the larger portion of its legends (traditions, historical passages) are borrowed from the same source, and are therefore reliable.

It follows, then, that the so-styled "True Believers" are qualified, as to religious belief, to receive the mysteries of Masonry.

About twenty years since I made a critical commentary on Sale's *Koran,* with special reference to the question, "May this book (or the original) be used on the Masonic altar as a substitute for the Hebrew Scriptures?" From that essay the following is extracted:

1. The Bible is to be judged by its general scope and intention,— not by a few isolated passages, and these, possibly, misconceived in the process of translation from a language highly idiomatic and poetical to one extremely practical. Many of its traditions and teachings were delivered orally, and awaited for years the pen of the historian. How easy, then, to mistake their meaning! As believers in its authenticity, we are unwilling that it shall be treated harshly. Let us only have like charity for the *Koran,* and it will not stand so much condemned. The history of the one, in these respects, is very similar to that of the other. It inculcates the mode of life exemplified by its giver; and of him *Spanhemius* says: "He was richly furnished with natural endowments; beautiful in his person; of a subtle wit; agreeable behavior— showing liberality to the poor —courtesy to every one—fortitude against his enemies—and, above all, *a high reverence for the name of God;* severe against the perjured, adulterers, murderers, slanderers, prodigals, covetous, false witnesses, etc,; a great preacher of patience, charity, mercy, beneficence, gratitude— honoring of parents and superiors; and a frequent celebrator of the divine praises."

2. That it is principally derived from the Holy Scriptures, can only be proved by a more extended comparison than can be made here, and, after a thoughtful examination of the quotations that follow, the student is referred to the body of the work.

3. That its traditions are mainly true, follows as a corollary upon the establishment of the second proposition; therefore, reference is only made here to the Scriptures of the Old and New Testaments, and to Masonic tradition.

4. Faith in God, a belief in a revealed Word, is the first requisites of a candidate for Masonic honors and privileges. Unless he possess the former, no pledge, obligation, or covenant, can be considered binding upon him. Without the latter, he can know nothing, spiritually, of the former. With both, he possesses that veneration for truth which the Institution requires, and that horror of falsehood so eloquently illustrated in Masonic rites. The proof that the *Koran* is such a Revelation to those who believe it, is found in its pages, from which the following extracts are taken.

5. The fitness of the Koran for Masonic uses, may be considered from the first of these propositions. It is the *Bible* of the Moslems, and they are many millions; nations are governed by its precepts, religious and civil; they neither have, nor desire to have, any other law; it is as fully the standard of Mohammedan brethren as are the Holy Writings to the Hebrew and the Christian.

"Thee do we worship, and of Thee do we beg assistance. Direct us in the right way, in the way of those to whom Thou hast been gracious—not of those against whom Thou hast been incensed, nor of those who go astray.

"God is almighty; God is omnipresent and omniscient; God is easy to be reconciled and merciful; God is gracious and merciful unto men; God is mighty and wise.

"GOD, there is no God but He, the living, the self-subsisting; neither sleep nor slumber seizeth Him; to Him belongeth whatsoever is in heaven or on earth. He knoweth that which is past and that which is to come.

"Who forgiveth sins except God? God loveth the beneficent. Truth is from the Lord. As for him who voluntarily performeth a good work, verily God is grateful and giving. God is bountiful unto whom He pleaseth, without measure. They who believe, and who fly for the sake of religion, and fight in God's cause, they shall hope for the mercy of God; for God is gracious and merciful. Unto God belongeth the kingdom of heaven and of earth; He giveth life, and He causeth to die; and ye have no patron or helper beside God. God is easy to be reconciled and merciful. O, true believers, fear God and be sincere. If ye attempt to reckon up the favors of God, ye shall not be able to complete their number. God is surely gracious and merciful. If it be asked of those who fear God, What hath your Lord sent down? they shall answer, Good!—unto those who do right shall be given an excellent reward in this world. But the children of the next life shall be better; and happy shall be the dwelling of the pious, namely, gardens of eternal abode, into which they shall enter; rivers shall flow beneath the same; therein shall they enjoy whatsoever they wish. Thus will God recompense the pious.

"Praise be unto God, the Creator of heaven and earth. The mercy which God shall freely bestow on mankind, there is none who can withhold; and what He shall withhold there is none who can bestow. O men, remember the favor of God towards you!—is there any Creator besides God, who provideth food for you from heaven and earth? The promise of God is true. Let not, therefore, the present life deceive you. Whosoever deviseth excellence, unto God doth all excellence belong; unto Him ascendeth the good speech; and the righteous work He will exhort. Oh men, ye have need of God, but God is self-sufficient. Whosoever cleanseth himself from the guilt of disobedience, cleanseth himself to the advantage of his own soul, for all shall be assembled before God at the last day.

"The pious distribute alms out of what God has bestowed on them.

"Ask help with perseverance and prayer.

"Surely those who believe, and those who Judaize, and Christians, and Sabines, *whoever believeth in God and the last day, and doth that which is right,* they shall have their reward with the Lord; there shall no fear come on them, neither shall they be grieved.

"Ye shall show kindness to your parents and kindred, and to orphans, and to the poor, and speak that which is good unto men, and be constant at prayer, and give alms.

"They who purchase this life at the price of that which is to come, their punishment shall be complete, and they shall be without help.

"Be constant in prayer, and give alms; and what treasures ye have laid up in heaven, ye shall find them with God. He who resigneth himself to God, and doth that which is right, he shall have his reward with his Lord.

"Beg assistance, with patience and prayer, for God is with the patient.

"Righteousness is of him who believeth in God and the last day, and the angels, and the Scriptures, and the prophets; who giveth money, for God's sake, unto his kindred and unto orphans, and the needy, and the stranger, and those who ask, and for redemption of captives; who is constant at prayer, and giveth alms; and of those who perform their covenant, when they have covenanted, and who behave themselves patiently in adversity and hardship, and in time of violence,—these are they who are true, and these are they who fear God.

"He who voluntarily dealeth better with the poor man than he is obliged, this shall be better for him.

"Make not God lightly the object of your oaths, and deal justly, and be devout, and make peace among men.

"God will not punish you for an inconsiderate word in your oaths, out for that which your hearts have assented to.

15

"Let there be no violence in religion.

"Whatever alms ye shall give, or whatever vow ye shall vow verily God knoweth it.

"If there be any debtor under a difficulty of paying his debt, let his creditor wait till it be easy for him to do it.

"Whoso keepeth his covenant, and feareth God, God will surely love. . ." But they who make merchandise of God's covenant and their oaths, shall suffer a grievous punishment.

"He who cleaveth firmly unto God, is already directed in the right way.

"Fear God that ye may prosper.

"What is with God shall be better for the righteous than short-lived worldly prosperity.

"Observe justice when ye appear as witnesses before God, and let not hatred towards any induce you to do wrong.

"Since ye were dead, and God gave you life, he will hereafter cause you to die, and will again restore you to life; then shall ye return unto him.

"God said, O Adam, dwell thou and thy wife in the garden, and eat of the fruit plentifully wherever ye will; but approach not this tree, lest ye become of the number of transgressors. . . . But Satan caused them to forfeit Paradise, and turned them out of the state of happiness wherein they had been.

"Remember, when God delivered you from the people of Pharaoh, who grievously oppressed you, and slew your male children; and when He divided the sea for you and delivered you.

"God raiseth the dead to life.

"Solomon was a believer.

"God shall judge between us, at the day of resurrection, concerning that about which we now disagree.

"The dead have what they have gained, and ye shall have what ye gain; and ye shall not be questioned concerning what others have done.

"Wherever ye be, God will bring you all back at the resurrection.

"God shall lead the believer out of darkness into light.

"God created you out of one man, and out of him created his wife, and from them two hath multiplied many.

"God formerly accepted the covenant of the children of Israel, and appointed out of them twelve leaders.

"God sent down the Law and the Gospel, a direction unto men; and also the distinction between good and evil.

"Do you believe in part of the Book of the Law, and reject other parts thereof? Whoso among you doth this, shall have no other reward than shame in this life, and on the day of resurrection shall be sent to a most grievous punishment.

"He delivered the Book of the Law unto Moses, and gave evident miracles to Jesus, the Son of Mary, and strengthened Him with the Holy Spirit. The Scriptures descend upon the heart, by the permission of God, confirming that which was before revealed, a direction and good tidings to the faithful. Oh God, punish us not if we forget or act sinfully. Oh God, *lay not* on us a burden like that which Thou hast laid on those who have been before us; neither make us, oh Lord, to bear what we have not strength to bear, but be favorable unto us, and spare us, and be merciful unto us. Paradise is prepared for the godly, who give alms in prosperity and adversity, who bridle their anger, and forgive men. They who have committed a crime, or dealt unjustly with their own souls, who shall remember God, and ask pardon for their sins, and persevere not in what they have done, their reward shall be pardon from the Lord.

"Whosoever believeth not the Scriptures shall perish. They who conceal any part of the Scriptures, God shall not speak to them on the day of resurrection, and they shall suffer a grievous punishment."

The Scriptural doctrine of a future state of rewards and punishments is everywhere taught in the Koran: "Whosoever doeth maliciously and wickedly, God will cast him to be broiled in hell-fire," is startling enough for the firmest believer in eternal punishment. "Their couch shall be in hell, and over them shall be coverings of fire; they shall be companions of hell-fire; they shall taste the punishment for that which they have gained. On a certain day God will call all men to judgment, with their respective leaders; whoever hath been blind in this life shall also be blind in the next; the righteous shall be rewarded with the highest appointments in Paradise, because they have persevered with constancy, and they shall meet therein with greeting and salutation; they shall remain in the same forever; it shall be an excellent abode and a delightful station. Those who shall believe, and shall work righteousness, God will *surely* introduce into Paradise among the upright."

Injunctions to believe and obey the Scriptures abound everywhere in the Koran. For instance: "If they who have received the Scriptures believe and fear God, He will surely expiate their sins from them, and He will lead them into gardens of pleasure; and if they observe the Law and the Gospel, and the other Scriptures which have been sent down unto them from their Lord, they shall surely eat of good things, both from above them and from under their feet. O, ye who have received the Scriptures, ye are not grounded on anything until ye observe the Law and the Gospel, and that which hath been sent down unto you from your Lord."

But of all the matters of Masonic interest in this parallelism between the Koran and the Bible, perhaps none is so striking as the introduction into the former, though often in a distorted state, of the historical facts and narratives that make up so large a portion of the latter. Nearly every incident is transferred, with more or less accuracy, and those of chief importance are repeated several times

Concerning Adam, for instance, we have many facts—some, it must be confessed, fanciful enough—yet generally agreeable to the Bible. They refer to his creation, his being worshipped by the angels, his grievous fall, his penitence with prayer, his meeting with Eve, retirement with her, their stature, etc., etc.

Concerning Abraham, the Koran is even more diffuse. We have the facts of his idolatrous youth, his conversion, his destruction of the idols of his father's family, his preaching to the people, disputations with Nimrod, escape from destruction, prayer for his father, plea to God for evidence of the resurrection, sacrifice, entertainment of the angels, God's promise of Isaac, he is called the friend of God, is fed with a miracle, his offering up of Isaac, etc., etc.

The Old Testament relations concerning Moses, Aaron, Mount Ararat, the Deluge, Pharaoh, the tower of Babel, Balaam, the Queen of Sheba, Solomon, Jacob, and several of his sons, Cain, and Abel, Joshua, Caleb, the Golden Calf, David and Goliath, Elijah, Elisha, Enoch, Ezekiel, Ezra, the Angel Gabriel, Jonah, Ishmael, Lot, Nimrod, Sennacherib, etc., etc., are detailed with minuteness. I give specimens:

"Solomon was David's heir, and he said, Oh men, we have been taught the speech of birds, and have had all things bestowed on us; this is manifest excellence;" and of Moses—"Now Pharaoh lifted himself up in the land of Egypt: and he caused his subjects to be divided into parties; he weakened one party of them by slaying their male children and preserving their females alive; for he was an oppressor. And God was minded to be gracious unto those who were weakened in the land, and to make them models of religion,— and to make them the heirs of the wealth of Pharaoh and his people, and to establish a place for them in the earth; and to show Pharaoh and Haman, and their forces, that destruction of their kingdom and nation by them, which they sought to avoid. And God directed the mother of Moses, by revelation, saying, Give him suck; and, if thou fearest for him, cast him into the river, and fear not, neither be afflicted; for we will restore him unto thee, and appoint him one of our apostles. And when she had put the child in the ark," etc. See chapter 28 of the Koran for a minute history of these transactions.

"Your God is our God; there is no God but He, the most merciful. All power belongeth unto God, and He is severe in punishing. God contracteth and extendeth his hand as he pleaseth. God is our support, and the most excellent patron. God knoweth the innermost part of the breasts of men. Oh men, serve your God who bath created you. Ye shall not worship any other except God. Dost thou not know that God is almighty? that unto Him belongeth the kingdom of heaven and earth? that ye have no helper or protector except God? To God belongeth the east and the west; therefore, whithersoever way ye turn yourselves to pray, *there is the face of God.*"

So many Mohammedans are Masons, and the seed of Masonry has proved so congenial to the soil of Mohammedan lands, that I trust the space I have given this subject will be considered fitly occupied.

As a specimen of the style in which this singular work is composed, let us take the third chapter, entitled *Abu Laheb*. Mohammed had become incensed against his uncle, Abu Laheb, for refusing to accept his prophetic mission, and launched the following missile against him: "In the name of the Most Merciful God,* the hands of Abu Laheb shall perish, and he himself shall perish. Neither his riches nor his gains shall be of service to him. He shall go down into the flaming fire of hell, and there be burned. His wife also shall go there, carrying fuel to feed the infernal flames. And she shall have on her neck a rope twisted of the fibers of the palm-tree." The name of Mohammed's aunt, to whom he threatened such diabolical penalties, was Omm (mother) Jemeel.

The titles of some of the chapters of the Koran afford a hint of their contents, and show how florid is Oriental imagery: The Helping Hand (107), The Gloomy Veil (88), The Swift War-Horses (100), The Breath of the Winds (51), The Frowning Brow (80), The Unjust Measure (83), etc.

In the presence of the priests, the chiefs of Arab tribes meet together on the eve of a military expedition, and *putting their hands upon their sacred book* (the Koran), they say: "We swear by God (Allah) that we are brothers; and will fight with one and the same weapon; and if we perish, it shall be with the same sword."

* All the 114 chapters of the Koran, except one, commence with the passage, "In the name of the Most Merciful God"

EGYPTIAN WILLOW BASKETS.

CHAPTER XV.

THE AMERICAN MISSIONARIES.

EVERY American Mason must feel a national as well as religious interest in whatever proposes to elevate the Oriental races, and paves the way for the lifting up of this long downtrodden land. Nothing has conduced so much to this as the labors of the Protestant missions of the A. B. C. F. M., operating in this country for about half a century. Going out through the narrow, gloomy, noisy, noisome streets; through winding ways of the magnificent amphitheatre of gardens; through the pines which cast their thin shadows over the surrounding flats of sand; through the vast grove of olives which silver the shallow valley at the base of Lebanon; then, looking back over this thriving city, with a present population of 75,000 souls, and the promise of thrice the number, we may proudly point to the *Syrian University*, built by American money, and conducted by American learning and intelligence, as the only institution of the class in the East. And this is but one of the many fruits of missionary labors here. As I read the corner-stone speech of Mr. Wm. E. Dodge, delivered here December, 1871, I could not help inquiring with the poet: *An erit qui vellit recuset os populi meruisse, et cedro digna locutus linquere?*— Is there any one who does not wish to deserve popular applause, and to leave words worthy to be preserved in cedar? For I felt that I would rather have filled *his* place that day, as the chief benefactor of the Syrian University, than that of any other living man!

I associated with the different families of the missionaries a good deal, and my personal views of them as a class are admirably expressed by another writer, who says: "They are pious, sober, benevolent; devout in the offices of religion; in conversation, innocent and cheerful; exhibiting in all their actions those best and truest signs of Christian spirit, a sincere and cheerful friendship among themselves, and a generous charity to all." This witness is true. Of Dr. Van Dyke, whose professional labors, especially in the Department of Ophthalmy, have been something unprecedented in extent, I have written; he has much grace and ease, with a sub-flavor of gentle and sportive humor, hinting at possibilities. Whenever I returned to Beirut, loaded down with specimens and notebooks, his salutation, "Well, Doctor, have you discovered Jachin and Boaz yet?" was the first that greeted my ear. Of Dr. Bliss, I noted he has an air of engaging frankness. His language is always simple and unaffected. He is a hard student, and an industrious man.

It is the part of these men to contend with the bigotry, intolerance, unreasonableness, and wordly-mindedness of the Latin and Greek priests, who oppose schools, books, printing, and everything not under their own control. Among them I enjoyed the excellence and amiableness of the Lord's house. Another has given my idea in almost the same words: "What they chiefly have to contend with is not so much the heathenism that surrounds them, as the pompous and imposing ceremonies in which the remains of Oriental Christianity are enveloped. At the same shrines of idolatrous superstition, in Jerusalem, bow the subtle and exclusive Jesuit, the pompous Greek, the austere and zealous Armenian, the poor Copt, and the timid Abyssinian; their worship in all essential features similar; *heat* without *light, sound* without *sense, form* without *power,* the *body* without the *soul.*"

Since Father Jonas King (who deceased 1870) brought his own bread and wine here from Paris, to celebrate the sacrament, more than half a century since, nearly two generations have participated in the mystic repast with these missionaries, at Beirut.

They recognize no denominational names, such as Presbyterians, Congregationalists, and the like, but call themselves missionaries, as the disciples just above here, at Antioch, first called themselves Christians.

They are of opinion, and so are many of us, that one great result of the awakening in missionary effort, here and elsewhere, has been to kindle the religious fire in the churches, and increase the harmony of the Christian body *at home.* At first Smyrna and Malta were made their centers of labor, and certain persons in Boston, Massachusetts, agreed to give $3,000 per annum for five years to establish a Christian press at Malta. Then it was moved to Smyrna, and finally here.

They are making gradual but sure progress towards raising, from a degraded and vicious level, these people of the East, just as the nations of Europe were raised from a similar plane by missionaries from the East. They find, with Cicero, *Dei plena sunt omnia*—all things are full of Deity, and they lean heavily and faithfully on the Divine arm.

They have their romances, their episodes of terrible interest, their history of times when a man's heel could have stamped out the little spark they had kindled. The story of Assad-esh-Shidiak, as told in the *Missionary Herald* of Feb., 1833, is one of these. But fidelity and heroic resistance have thus far overcome all obstacles.

Some tourists have foolishly exaggerated the *comforts* they enjoy, and depreciated the effect of their labors upon the uninstructed masses around them. Both these errors, it is charity to believe, spring from thoughtlessness alone. The sight of educated, delicate ladies, like those whom I saw gracing the Protestant missions at Beirut and Sidon, who have buried themselves beyond the reach of congenial society, or that of earnest Christian gentlemen, thoroughly instructed to adorn any profession in life, but giving their whole lives to a most arduous, thankless charge; these things suggest nothing to my mind but *self-sacrifice*. Their manner of living is simple and economical, the only deviation being the necessary care of strangers who claim their hospitality, sometimes in inconvenient numbers, and add greatly to their domestic expenses.

The principal work of the mission has been, until quite recently, printing books, establishing schools for teaching Christianity to the young, and healing institutions for the sick. The number of their printed publications is large, including, in addition to hymnbooks and theological works, a complete copy of the Holy Scriptures in Arabic. For this, the first matrices were cut by the elder Mr. Hallock, and the electrotype plates made by his son, Mr. Samuel Hallock, of whose name I am making such frequent use in the present volume. He told me that the lead of which the first type-metal here was made was sheet-lead torn from the old Roman coffins, and sold to them by the natives! Several steam-presses are now kept busy by this printing-house at Beirut.

In the way of establishing schools, their labors have been abundant. Their hospital and infirmary at Beirut have a reputation that extends even to Baghdad and Egypt. For diseases of the eye, which Dr. Van Dyke makes a specialty, there is perhaps no institution in the world that excels his in the number of cases treated, or the success of operations and treatment. I used to see a regular *string* of applicants waiting their turn at his door, and was informed that during the spring I was there (1868) Dr. Van Dyke treated largely over one thousand ophthalmic cases! I shall refer to this subject again.

When the first of them landed here, November 17, 1823, they were objects of curiosity, many natives following them to the house, and the boys running before to secure a good view; now they are as much a landmark of Beirut and its history as the very pine-groves in the suburbs.

Amongst other works, they have published *The Pilgrim's Progress,* and Oriental readers are now enjoying acquaintance with *Worldly Wiseman* and other characters of good old John Bunyan, as I did twoscore years ago, and equally, I hope, to their profit. The American Protestant press, first established A.D. 1822 in Malta, printed the amount of 287,150 copies of religious matter, in Italian, modern Greek, Armeno-Turkish, and Greco-Turkish. December 23, 1834, this press was removed to Smyrna, Heman Hallock and Daniel Temple being the printers. It has been the very fulcrum of Archimedes to move the world of Oriental ignorance. It arrived here May 8, 1854, at which time there were eight presses in the Holy Land, all given to the promulgation of sectarian error.

My note of Dr. W M. Thomson is this: Something over seventy, portly but vigorous, florid face, courteous expression. Reminds me of old Zach. Taylor, with whom I once traveled on the Mississippi river. Paces his parlor in his red-painted Damascus slippers, smokes and talks, all at the same time. For this veteran missionary, to stand by the grave of Pliny Fisk, the mild and mellow light of these Mediterranean shores flowing through the cypresses, must bring a gush of devotion which memory will retain forever and forever.

I throw a few notes together here, preferring to insert them in this chaotic state than to omit them altogether:

At the mission-press, they are completing a thorough concordance to the Holy Scriptures, in the Arabic language. Sitting in their house of worship at Beirut, on my first Sabbath here, it was startling, in the midst, to hearken to the sound of the trumpet (Jeremiah 6:17) blown by the Turkish troops in the garrison, recalling the unpleasant fact that the Moslems, the Jews, and the Christians each have a different day called *Sabbath.* A society was established in

1861, entitled *Women's Union Missionary Society of America for Heathen Lands,* designed to extend Christian blessings to heathen women. A missionary, returning to his field in Turkey, writes to one of our papers of the joy and pride with which he looked upon the new American College at Constantinople. It stands perched high on the northern bluff of the Bosphorus, just above the old fortress of Europe. The site is the finest in the whole length of that classic strait. The wonder is that the Turks should ever have surrendered so choice a spot for such a use. The building is a very handsome one, of stone, with Mansard roof. But even now it proves insufficient for the pupils who apply, even at the rate, for tuition and board, of $200 for one year. They reckon every Jew converted in Palestine as worth, to Christianity, a thousand converted anywhere else. In 1835, the editor of the *Missionary Herald* wrote pathetically that the managers of this mission had sought in vain for a pious and competent physician. C. N. Righter, devoted to Bible distribution, died in the Oriental field December 16, 1856. His theory of labor was to bring back to the East the same Bible and Gospels, in their purity, whence we received them 1,800 years ago. The missionaries teach that the Word of God is fire and the hammer; when it goes forth it will accomplish that whereunto it is sent. In educating orphan children, the teachers often give them the names of their benefactors in America who assume the payment for *protégés,* and it is not uncommon to hear such names as Peter Jones, John Brown, etc., applied to a boy who carries "Ishmael" on his every feature.

The *Syrian University* was incorporated a few years since, under the laws of New York. It has a literary course of four years, and a medical department; the language of instruction is Arabic. Its first class graduated July, 1870. It has a fine *campus* of twenty acres, valuable philosophical, chemical, and medical apparatus, a good telescope, a respectable library, an herbarium of 6,000 Oriental plants, and fair collections in geology and mineralogy. In February, 1871, they received four Copt students, from a town 500 miles up the Nile. These are well supplied with funds, and promise great usefulness on their return home.

At the laying of the cornerstone of their new building, Dec. 7, 1871, the weather was charming. The warm Syrian sun beamed down with cloudless brightness, and throngs of the American, English, German, and Syrian population assembled on the site of the new College building. This site is a noble, elevated promontory on the north side of Cape Beirut, a mile west of the city, commanding an unobstructed view of the sea, the Lebanon range, and a portion of the city.

The exercises were opened by an introductory address by the Rev.

Dr. Bliss, President of the College, who made a brief statement of the design of the Syrian Protestant College; its scope, and especially the religious element in its course of instruction. He urged that although direct proselytizing is not aimed at in the institution, yet it is the intention of its Faculty that no young man shall enter its halls and complete his studies without a thorough knowledge of the Christian system and of the way of salvation in Jesus Christ. He may enter as a heathen, but he cannot leave without seeing and knowing what it is to be a Christian. These halls will be open to Christian and Pagan, Moslem and Jew, Druse and Nusairy; but all will learn that there is one, and one only, Inspired Volume of Divine Revelation, and one Savior for lost and ruined man.

The Rev. Dr. Thomson then offered prayer, and the Scriptures were read by the Rev. Jas. Robertson of the Kirk of Scotland, in English, and by the Rev. Professor Wortabel, in Arabic.

An address was then delivered by the Hon. Wm. E. Dodge, President of the Board of Trustees in New York, who stood on a platform of six narrow joists of Cilician pine (from the Taurus range, above Tarsus), which had been laid across the stone heaps near the foundation wall. The following are extracts:

"We are assembled this afternoon to lay the corner-stone of the Syrian Protestant College. It may seem to some a very small matter of itself; but there is connected with its future, we doubt not, most important results. For more than forty years the American and other missionaries have been patiently laboring to promote the best interests of the people of Syria, trying by their schools and seminaries to awaken a desire for education; and they have been encouraged by a growth from year to year, which has now assumed such importance that we find in this city, and throughout the greater part of Syria, schools, more or less extensive, for training boys and girls, which, we cannot doubt, are destined to great enlargement within a few years. This fact has led the friends of the American and English missions to feel that the time had arrived for establishing a classical institution of a high grade, to be presided over by men of superior education and experience, where young men from the various preparatory schools of the country could have an opportunity of obtaining a thorough classical education, equal in all respects to such as is furnished in Europe and America, fitting them to fill with honor the highest positions, as instructors, physicians, ministers, lawyers, as well as the various civil and political positions under the government; and, in fact, offering young men of all classes the opportunity of securing a thorough classical and medical education.

"For several years the institution has been in partial operation, and the friends of the College have been so much encouraged by the success of the beginning, that they resolved to secure a site, and, if possible, the necessary funds to erect suitable buildings. I am gratified in being able to say that, through the liberality of friends in America and England, sufficient funds have been obtained to warrant a commencement; and having secured this beautiful situation, the Board of Trustees have decided at once to commence the erection of the buildings for the classical and medical departments, and we are here today formally *to lay the corner-stone* of the first building. Here it will rise in commanding proportions, in accordance with plans designed by an eminent American architect; and like a city set on a hill, or as the lighthouse at the entrance of your harbor, it will be one of the first objects which will meet the eye of the stranger entering your port. But more than that, we trust it will be a center of light and influence, which, like streams in the desert, shall give moral life and beauty to the hills and valleys of Syria, as from year to year there shall go forth the young men graduated with honor, and filled with a desire to communicate to others the knowledge they have acquired.

"To those connected with the education of youth in Syria, this must be an occasion of interest, for the erection of this building will increase the desire for higher attainments, and act as a stimulus to other schools. I am very happy to be with you at this interesting time, and mingle my congratulations with yours, and be able to convey to the friends in America the good news that the College building is fairly under way. May the blessing of God attend the effort, and prosper all engaged in the work of erection, giving wisdom to carry out successfully the plans till 'the top-stone shall be laid with rejoicing, crying, Grace, grace, unto it;' and as years shall go by, and those of us who have been permitted to aid in its erection shall have passed away, this University shall still go on increasing in usefulness, and thousands of young men go forth from its halls to aid in redeeming and blessing this land, so full of Bible and historic interest.

"Let me invoke the prayers and influence of all present in its behalf. This is not a money-making enterprise. It has been conceived in the spirit of Christian philanthropy, and those engaged in it have made great sacrifices, have left home and friends to secure to this people the inestimable blessings of a thorough classical education. Appreciate their motives, and give them every encouragement. And now, in accordance with the custom in America and England, I proceed to lay the corner-stone of the 'Syrian Protestant College;' having placed in a leaden case, imbedded in the foundation, a copy of the College charter; an annual catalogue, containing the names of the Faculty, Directors, Trustees, and students, and the rules and regulations; also copies of the local papers of the latest dates. And now may the blessing of God ever rest on the building whose foundation has now been laid! And to His name be all the praise."

This address was then translated into Arabic by Dr. H. H. Jessup, and after the laying of the stone, prayer was offered in Arabic by Rev. Dr. Van Dyke, when a young native physician, Dr. Selim Fray, a Greek Catholic, and a member of the first graduated medical class, asked permission to say a few words. He spoke in Arabic as follows:

"I must ask your pardon, sirs, in giving utterance to these few words, which the emotions of my heart impel me to offer, regretting the impotence of my tongue to do justice to such an occasion.

"This stone, laid before us as the corner-stone of this structure that is destined to rise in noble proportions, expresses a type of two things that ought not to escape the notice of the sons of our native land. It is not only an earnest for the upbuilding of this noble College which has diffused, as a sweet fragrance, science and virtue throughout all our borders, but also it should be held in veneration as an earnest of the return of science and civilization from the West to our land, in whose courts the raven of ignorance and folly is ever croaking. Yes, and every one who does not darken his vision by the veil of envy or partiality, will most clearly discover that the laying of this stone is the positive assurance for the beginning of a return of science and knowledge to this our native land.

"Who, before the foundation of this College, taught us algebra and arithmetic, astronomy and geometry, chemistry and natural philosophy, and the other mathematical sciences? Who, before her, taught botany, mineralogy, natural history, and medical science? To what shall I liken thee, O noble College? To the Star of the East? in that thou art scattering by thy rays the mists of the gross darkness of ignorance which has enveloped our native land. To the life-giving fountains? for thou hast changed the wild desert wastes of mind, in the sons of our land, to gardens in which resound the songs of science, which teem with the flowers and fruits of knowledge. To a tender mother? because thou dost bear in thy bosom youth from whatsoever sect or faith, nourishing them by thy life-sustaining milk, polishing their minds and understandings, and making them worthy to be numbered in the ranks of civilized nations. Come, then, ye sons of fatherland! hasten with rapid steps to the arms of this tender mother. Come, let us drink deep draughts from her milk; for it will give life to our barren minds. . . . Let us entreat the high and holy One to establish and jealously guard our beloved Alma Mater. O Thou our God! cast Thine eye in favor upon the upbuilding of this noble College, our Alma Mater. O God, environ her by Thy angels, that they may shield her from all evil, and from every evil eye. May the plots of her envious opponents be baffled by her immovable foundations, and return upon them in disappointment. O God, bestow an abundance of blessing upon those benefactors who are giving their aid in the erection of this College. O, our God, bestow upon this high-minded and excellent man, the Hon. Wm. E. Dodge, who has so honored our country, a supporting hand; for he is chief among her benefactors. Restore him, O Lord, with his family, to his native land in peace and safety. Grant them long life, and happy days, overflowing with blessings and good fortune. . . . O Thou, our God, richly impart Thy blessing to the President of this College, and to her distinguished instructors. Grant them Thy helping hand, that they may perfect this good and glorious work. Multiply their benevolent aims, and prepare for each one of the Board of Trustees and Managers, and each of the teachers of this College, and of her benefactors, a glorious portion in Thy heavenly kingdom."

At Beirut, in 1872, are Dr. Bliss, Rev. W. M. Thomson, C. V. A. Van Dyke, and Henry H. Jessup, and their wives, with three single ladies, Misses Eliza D. Everett, Ellen Jackson, and Sophia B. Loring, assisted by one native teacher and two native helpers. At Tripoli, fifty miles up the coast, are Rev. Samuel Jessup and wife, and two native assistants. At Abeih, a few miles southeast of Beirut, are Rev. S. H. Calhoun and Wm. Bird, with their wives, and five native assistants. At Sidon, Rev. W. W. Eddy and wife, Rev. James S. Dennis, and three assistants. Thirty-one outlying stations, all within sixty miles of Beirut, are connected with this great mission, which may God in power and mercy greatly bless. Other missions, for which I have not space here, are also at work throughout these mountains of old King Hiram. One pious lady, Mrs. Bowen Thompson, for many years devoted to establishing Christian schools for girls, had succeeded in organizing nearly one hundred of this class when, November 14th, 1869, she was summoned to her reward.

THE TWO SIDES OF THE RINGS OF PHARACH THOTHMES.

CHAPTER XVI.

T was strictly in accordance with my original pledge to the generous Masons who furnished me the "sinews of war" for these explorations, that I should follow the ancient raftsmen of Hiram, from the shores where they made up their "flotes" in the Masonic Bay to the place of debarkation in the port of Joppa. The timbers were all felled and prepared in the forests of Lebanon, says the old writer, conveyed by sea in "flotes" (*sic*) to Joppa, and from thence by land to Jerusalem. On the last day of April, 1868, therefore, I undertook this part of my pilgrimage.

My notes here are of course sketchy and desultory. The day of my passage was fair, and nothing on earth can be grander to the voyager than the passage down this historical coast. Eye, mind, pencil, all were busy; and if my readers can enjoy a dish of *hash, Voila!* here it is.

Moving out of the Bay of St. George on the Austrian steamer—I forget the name, a miserable affair, table poorly supplied, officers as incommunicable as the Royal Arch Word—I had a good view, through old Bishop Gobat's field-glass, of the town of Gebal, about twelve miles in the north. From its stony caskets (sarcophagi) I had procured hundreds of seals, signets, and beads, composed of opal, cornelian, jasper, agate, chalcedony, and other hard and precious stones, of all colors and compositions. As in olden times, the signet was used to ratify such social and religious transactions as called for a sacred pledge, so every person of the least note or consequence possessed one; and, like the spear and pipe of the American Indian, it was deposited with its owner in his tomb. Herodotus, speaking in his day of the Assyrians, declares that every man possessed one, even as every Arab sheikh does now. Ledvard, who found numbers of them among the ruins of Nineveh, etc., says they were anciently used by inserting them in a metal axis, and applying them like the garden rolling stone. But at present they are made flat, and applied by one firm pressure of the hand to the wax, as I saw Mohammed Raschid Pasha and Noureddin Effendi apply theirs.

So exquisitely are some of these objects engraved, that we must conclude their artists understood the use of the microscope, although history is silent upon the subject. A cylinder one half-inch high, and the same in diameter, has five human figures upon it, with accessory matters, each perfectly drawn. The story of stout old Charlemagne sounds well in this connection. He inserted his signet in the hilt of his sword, and swore, "What I sign with the *hilt* I will maintain with the *point!*"

The question as to whether the raftsmen of Hiram encountered dangerous winds along this coast, cannot be answered until we are told at what seasons of the year the work of "logging" was done. If in the *summer,* the gales are always auspicious between Beirut and Joppa; and with a moderate spread of sail, such as the artist has displayed on the rafts in my Masonic map, the distance, 150 miles, was rapidly and pleasantly accomplished. By steamer it takes only fourteen hours.

One must withdraw from the Phœnician coast about ten miles, to appreciate how narrow a *shelf* of land that kingdom was. I could imagine that once the sea ran close under the mountain's massive rocks, but that, in process of ages, they disintegrated sufficiently to compose the scanty soil we see.

Past the mouth of the Damour River, with its great grove of mulberry trees. Past Sidon, to be remembered for the hospitality of the missionaries, which I had enjoyed so recently. I can almost select their house from the mass of flat-roofed buildings facing the sea. May God bless *that* house!

Bishop Gobat talks with me about Freemasonry. He preached last Sunday against the Abyssinian war in which England is now engaged. The old man was long a missionary to Abyssinia, and the way he denounced the British government for this unprovoked and uncalled-for invasion of an innocent people, was hard on the group of British officials in the congregation. He asks me now what is there in Syria and Palestine for Freemasons to do. I reply that much illustrating the doctrine and history of ancient Masonry is yet to come to light. On coins, on broken statuary, on fragments of pottery, in the recesses of caves, anywhere, at any hour, without a moment's warning, the greatest and most important evidences of Masonic antiquity may spring forth to view, to confound the skeptic, confirm the wavering, gladden the faithful, and gag the mouths of those within our own affiliation who are trying to break down our traditional claims. After eight centuries of researches, the world of Bible-believers and Christian-believers have brought more genuine evidence to light during the past ten years than in all previous ages. What, then, may *we* not hope from Masonic researches now, in the latter half of the nineteenth century, but just begun? The great Barclay quarry under Jerusalem should be explored, every inch of it, walls, ceiling, and floor. . . . But here we are interrupted by a call to as poor a steamship dinner as I ever sat down to. Either the cooking or the motion of the sea so disagrees with my stomach, that when we get about opposite *Khan Younas* (where Jonah was vomited on shore) I give up the unsavory mess to the sea, and resume my pencil.

Past Tyre. I am reminded that all along this coast large pieces of glass, and the dross and slag of glass furnaces, lie among the ruins. I carry home a very considerable quantity of these for specimens. What Pliny says of the origin of glass manufactures, applies strictly to this section of the country. At the present time, some of the most beautiful glassware in use is made at Sandwich and East Cambridge, Mass. This is remarkable for its clearness and lack of color, and much of it is exported to Europe. Josephus, in his Wars (IX., 45:2), refers to the glass of Tyre. In the Beni Hassan tombs of Egypt, glass is found of the period B.C. 2000 to 3500, according to different chronologies. Among my most curious specimens gathered at Tyre, is a glass bottle, evidently of the very earliest period of the manufacture, and now in my office at La Grange, Ky. There is nothing directly said in the Scriptures of *glass,* though no doubt allusions to it may be found. The word only occurs once, in Job 28:7, as "crystal." It comes from a Hebrew word, signifying "to be pure," and refers to a species of glass formerly held in high esteem. The skill of the ancients in the manufacture of glass was such that they not only made it of a crystalline purity, shaped it by blowing, ground it by lathes, and carved it like silver, but by its use imitated every known marble and every sort of precious stone. In the *Museum Victorium,* at Rome, there are two ancient gems, both counterfeits, one a chrysolite, the other an emerald, but perfectly well executed, perfectly transparent and colored throughout, and both externally and internally free from the smallest blemish. The mixture used by ancient glass-makers, according to Pliny, was three parts nitrum to one part sand; and the Belus-sand, just below Tyre, near Acre, was held in such repute for its purity and cleanliness, that great quantities were exported to Europe and elsewhere for this manufacture. Glass was formerly used for wainscoting churches and dwellings, also for coffins, personal ornaments, drinking-vessels, mosaic work on walls and pavements, figures of deities, etc. The Egyptians had learned to permeate the materials with designs of ancient colors. Among the *tesseræ* of mosaic pavements which I brought home to America, many are of glass. While in the minaret of the great mosque in Damascus, I purchased quite a handful of these, which are beautiful. At Pompeii glass windows were found. . . . So much on the vitreous theme.

Past *Scala Tyrorum,* the Ladder of Tyre. As old Samuel Johnson says, on these shores were the four great empires of the world —the Assyrian, the Persian, the Greek, and the Roman. All our religion, almost all our law, almost all our arts, almost all that sets us above the savage, have come to us from these shores. Here, at *Promontorium Album,* this White Cape (*Ras-el-Abyad,* the Arabs call it), the mountains close into the sea much as they do at the mouth of Dog River, where the inscriptions are. A military road was opened across this point, which, ascending in zigzags, is named the *Ladder of Tyre.* The pass is styled Ras-en-Nakoorah, and there is a town in ruins near by, to which the great name of Alexander (*Scanderoon,* as pronounced here) is applied. At the top of this pass is a tower called Candle-tower, or Lighthouse (*Kulaat-esh-Shema*). What a landmark this white cape must have been to the raftsmen whose course I am pursuing, and how useful to them in dark nights the Candle-tower on the top!

In full sight of Mount Hermon, bearing now not far from due east, and some forty miles distant. Its isolated cone, tipped with snow, presents a noble appearance. A small hill near it, borrowing some of its peculiar claims, is styled *Abu Nedy,* the Father of Dew, because the clouds seem to cling with peculiar fondness round its wooded top, reflecting the genial influences of the grand mountain-sire above.

Passing the Plain of Acre, old Accho of the Bible, the St. Jean d'Acre of the Crusaders. I have just looked through a copy of the

London *Times,* so dear to every Englishman's breast, which lies
on the cabin-table, and have tried, as I have a hundred times
before, to interest myself in it. I took it for six months, in 1859,
and can only repeat now what I said then, after paying an
exorbitant bill of subscription: "It is the dullest newspaper I ever
came across." It was started in 1788, and probably got enough *vis
inertiœ* at that time to keep it running these eighty years;
certainly the motive-power is not *inside* of it.

But Acre, city of glorious associations! I will devote some pages
to its history in my chapter on Knights Templars, and at present
only note the current thoughts that arise. The sight of the British
flag, always a pleasant one to me, recalls the wonderful defense of
Acre made by our gallant brother Mason, Sidney Smith, in 1799,
against the French army, under that other gallant Masonic
brother, Napoleon Bonaparte. The union jack, denoting the
British vessels here, was adopted in their naval service January,
1, 1801. Before that it was a union of the old banner of St. George,
white, with a red cross. This was joined, April 12, 1606, with the
banner of Scotland, *blue, with a white diagonal cross.*

This historical Plain of Acre is connected yonder with the big
prairie-land of Esdraelon by a narrow pass, swampy and full of
rushes and alder, through which the Kishon, "that ancient river,"
flows, and there a genial English writer, in 1869, professes to
have found a crocodile! The map shows that if you set a compass
at the gate of Acre, and sweep a semicircle from north, eastward
to south, you include the whole plain. Every movement of these
billows recalls the throb of friendship's heart; every voice of these
waters, the whispers of love which made the bond of the Christian
crusades.

But the Governor of Acre, with whom our good brother Sidney
Smith so genially hobnobbed while warding off the assaults of
the French army. It was no other than "the Butcher-Ruler,"
Djezzar Pasha, who, in the old Hebrew allegory, would have
been justly named *Magor-missabib,* "fear round about"
(Jeremiah 20:3), one of those whom the prophet Isaiah
describes (10:2) as decreeing unrighteous decrees, writing
grievousness, turning aside the needy from judgment, taking
away the right of the poor of the people, making widows their
prey, and robbing the fatherless. The Turkish system of
government opens the broadest way for injustice, in such hands; all
responsibility to mortal power being taken away, we cannot but
rejoice that there is such a thing as death to break the staff of the

wicked, and the scepter of the rulers (Isaiah 14:5). Djezzar seems to have taken for his model the Governor Felix of Paul's time, the man who ruled Judea with the power of a king but the soul of a slave, the tyrant capable of every crime; and he well illustrates the dog-like rage and arrogant folly of idiots advanced to be governors. How many cases of poisoning, how many mutilations, what untold floods of human misery, has yonder city witnessed.

Past Caifa. Here Mr. G. D. Hardegg has his German colony, in which I am the happy possessor of a "lot," bought in 1871. I will refer to it again. A traveler describes the gates of Caifa covered, in 1836, with bulls' hides, like the shields of Homer. That best of Oriental Masons, E. T. Rogers, was British Consul here for many years, and here his intelligent sister, Miss Rogers, wrote her best of books, on "Domestic Life in the Holy Land."

And here is Mount Carmel, greatly admired for the regularity of its form, shaped like a sugar-loaf, having rather the appearance of *art* than *nature*. Stewart says in summer this promontory is undisturbed by storms. This fact has its bearing, as I have before hinted, upon the amount of skill and daring necessary to float the cedar-rafts from Beirut to Joppa. Just below are those mountains of masonry that even now afford an inexhaustible supply of material for the masons of Beirut, called *The Castle of the Pilgrims,* built during the crusades. Lynch referred to this view when he was here in 1848.

Off "the nose" of Carmel is a group of pelicans solemnly fishing. I always admire the piscatorial gravity which a pelican puts on when he goes a-fishing. No chatting, no loud laughter. If he gets a hook in his fingers, or a sculpin steals his bait, or he breaks his fishpole, he takes the thing as a necessary incident of the sport, and tries again. I have had so much trouble with noisy companions while out fishing on Saturdays, that I shall ever respect the pelican as a model fishist. Counting three hundred and sixty-one of them in the gang, I fall to reckoning how many pounds of fish are necessary for the daily rations of these voracious fowl. The name, if my natural history is not all afloat, is *Pelicanus onocrotalus;* a very appropriate title, too, for that forlorn one yonder, sitting on a floating piece of wreck, in a *pensive* attitude, if ever I saw pensiveness. He reminds me for all the world of the Grand Treasurer of the Grand Lodge of —— in *his* pensive attitude, when the Grand Lodge is voting away all its funds in spite of his protests.

Mount Carmel is intimately connected with the life of the great Masonic Ritualist, Pythagoras, of whom I spoke in the fourth chapter. This wonderful man founded the third school of philosophy, following that of Thales of Miletus, and Xenophanes

MOUNT CARMEL.

of Colophon. He was born at Samos, B.C. 580. He was emphatically a *born student,* receiving knowledge successively from Thales, Anaximander, and other Greek philosophers. He left no *written* instructions, but strictly followed the Masonic idea of *oral* communications; but it is certain he believed in the transmigration of souls. His knowledge of geometry and arithmetic was pre-eminent, and some of his pupils taught that *numbers* were the basis and essence of all things. He was emphatically a *religious teacher,* and some of his contemporaries believed him to be a god.

At the age of forty (B.C. 540) he opened his school at Crotona, and met with wonderful success. He formed a religious brotherhood, the members being bound together by peculiar rites and observances. Various degrees were established among them, and a period of probation, in which the mind and morals were severely tested. Everything done and taught was kept profoundly secret from the world without. The Pythagoreans had Masonic signs by which they recognized each other. Temperance was strictly observed, and the other three cardinal virtues insisted upon. The members at Crotona were usually of the noble and wealthy class, three hundred of whom formed the Grand Council of the Society. These were bound to Pythagoras and each other by a special vow, a considerable resemblance being found between this and the Jesuit Society founded by Loyola. In his eastern travels he is known to have visited the oracle then established in Mount Carmel, just as Vespasian, the Roman general, did seven centuries later.

Numerous American lodges are named from this memorable mountain, viz., Ohio, No. 303; Georgia, 150; Massachusetts, 144, etc. Among those to whom the name of Pythagoras and his school at Crotona are given, I cite Kentucky, No. 339; Georgia, 41; New York, 86; Mississippi, 48, etc. To connect the place still more intimately with our American brotherhood, I write here the names of ten genial and enlightened craftsmen, viz., John P. Brown (of Constantinople), Thomas Byrde Harris, Edward Jewell, Charles Roome, John Ransom, Henry Clark, John D. Caldwell, J. F. Brennan, John M. Bramwell, and J. C. Batchelor.

The adage of Pythagoras, *Abstineto a fabis,* Do not eat beans, which has puzzled commentators so long, refers, no doubt, to one of his doctrines of metempsychosis, that departed souls were enshrined in the center of beans. His peculiar views on that subject are well expressed in the following lines:

> *Errat et illinc*
> *Huc vinit hinc illuc et quoslibet occupat artus,*
> *Spiritus: eque feris humana in corpora transit,*
> *Inque feras noster.*

That is to say, the human soul wanders about, and comes from that spot to this, and from this to that, and takes possession of any limbs it may; it both passes from the beast into human bodies, and from us into beasts.

Passed the mouth of Crocodile River. Dr. W. M. Thomson suggested twenty years ago that crocodiles might still be found there, and in 1869 (the year after my visit to the country) an English tourist avers that he saw one in the Kishon, close by. This need not astonish us too much. In the *American Journal of Science,* January, 1870, Prof. Wyman describes a crocodile killed recently in Florida, where nobody would think of looking for them.

Passed Cæsarea as the sun was setting quietly under its canopy of crimson, gold, and blue. In these sunsets, of which I never weary, there is a splendor peculiar to these Oriental climes. Here at Cæsarea preached the great missionary apostle Paul, for two years chained, "an ambassador in bonds." His seventeen links taught, in his figurative imagination, these seventeen Christian principles: Charity, without hypocrisy; fraternity, politeness and civility, fervor, hope, joy, patience, amiability, concord and humility, pardon of enemies, love of neighbors, eagerness for the wants of the saints, a blessing upon persecutors, rejoicing with the rejoicing, weeping with the weeper, overcoming evil with good. What lessons have these fifty generations learned through that Roman chain! Sandys says, the houses in Cæsarea are now level with the floor, the haven is lost, and the situation abandoned.

A passenger describes a pilgrim caravan that landed at Joppa a few weeks since, as a small vessel loaded with seventy-two passengers, Greeks, Armenians, Turks, Arabs, both white and black, baptized Jews, a Greek woman, and a missionary, hadjis, soldiers, officers, all colors, bond and free.

At midnight our anchor drops. I come on deck; yonder two miles south is Joppa, sprawling all over a round hill, "a moderate hill, rounded off at the summit," the stars shining so brightly that I can almost count the houses in it. The view is sublime. The great constellation *Scorpio,* with its forty-four stars, hangs directly over the city, sparkling with a brilliancy that is surprising. Its principal star, *Antares,* always exhibiting a remarkably blood-red appearance, seems exactly in the range of the expanded tuft of a palm-tree that crowns the hill in the center of the town. I shall never look at that starry group again without associating it with the tree, the town, and this glorious midnight hour. It is a strange coincidence that the Jewish astrologers, mapping out the heavens among the twelve tribes of Israel, apportioned the constellation of Scorpio to *Dan,* the tribe to which yonder town of Joppa belonged. Did Jonah, when he fled from this port towards Tarshish, see that crimson star, Antares? It must have appeared to him an avenging meteor, the eye of insulted Deity! Yonder too is Andromeda, in the constellation of Taurus. Her adventures with Perseus and the sea-monster occurred here at Joppa, else history is at fault; and

> "Still in the heavens her captive form remains,
> And on her wrists still hang the galling chains."

How the raftsmen of Hiram must have reveled at the end of one of their arduous tasks. I imagine them gazing from this bay upon that concave of celestial imagery, such as American skies never present, and bursting into songs of praise to the powers that had brought them safely to the close of their journey. Let me in like manner praise the Lord, who has thus far led me on my appointed way, and then retiring to rest, gain needed strength for to-morrow's work.

Bless the Lord, oh my soul; and all that is within me, bless his holy name.

Bless the Lord, oh my soul: and forget not all his benefits:

Who forgiveth all thine iniquities; who healeth all thy diseases;

Who redeemeth thy life from destruction; who crowneth thee with loving-kindness and tender mercies;

Who satisfieth thy mouth with good things; so that thy youth is renewed like the eagle's (Ps. 103).

COIN OF LYSIMACHUS: HEAD OF ALEXANDER, WITH THE AMMON HORN.

JOPPA. FROM THE NORTH.

DIVISION SIXTH.—JOPPA.

Land of antiquity and tradition,—land where customs are landmarks—where the dress, the food, the highways, the nomenclature, the salutations, the marriage rites and the burial rites—all that make one people different from another— are continued as they originated, forty or fifty centuries since, in the very beginning of human history,—land whose very dust on which travelers' tread was once sentient, the atoms of nations long destroyed,—where each hill and valley has its tale of horror and mortal woe;—land of Judaism, Freemasonry, Christianity, and Mohammedanism!

I have considered Bible emblems as Masonic property. All emblems of divine origin are Masonic property; wherein they teach threatenings or praises, penalties or rewards, encouragement or discouragement, faith, hope, or charity, brotherly love, relief, or truth, temperance, fortitude, prudence, or justice,— they are, as an old Scotch writer calls them, "the surprising eloquence of heaven" to the Freemason's soul. Things apparently carnal and trifling are made, in the Holy Writings, to foreshadow the wisest purposes of God. Almost every object in nature is an illustrator of inspired truth, truth such as forms the light, warmth, and salt of the Masonic rituals. In this sense, I have incorporated them into my book, and so, I trust, given a new direction to Masonic study.

As the first three Masons, Solomon, Hiram the King, and Hiram the Architect, are associated with and have made illustrious their respective cities, Jerusalem, Tyre, Gebal, so I have felt at liberty, being the first Masonic traveler and author in this field, to locate, at marked and important points, the names of many persons known to me as eminent in the theory or practice of Freemasonry. Thus I have given to the *genus loci* of each site one or more worthy companions, and dotted the Masonic Map of Palestine here and there with illustrious moderns

CHAPTER XVII.

THE PORT OF JOPPA.

HE fifth of the Seven Grand Masonic Localities visited and identified during my researches in the Holy Land, is Joppa, at which ancient and far-famed port I arrived May 1st, a few minutes after midnight, it being then about 4.30 P.M. at La Grange, Kentucky. To secure a bountiful supply of relics and specimens from Joppa, I had sent my assistant there, and he had given uninterrupted attention to the locality for several weeks.

Joppa, now termed *Jaffa,* is a port of little importance in modern times, save as being the landing-place of pilgrims to Jerusalem. Steamships and war-vessels cannot approach within two miles of it. It lies in latitude 32° 3′ north, longitude 34° 44′ east of Greenwich. The population is about 7,000 souls, nearly one-half of them Christians. Formerly it was, next to Jerusalem, the most important city in the possession of the Jews. There being no other harbor on all this coast, Joppa was, of course, the place of transit for the immense accumulations of wood and metal collected in various parts of the world for the construction of King Solomon's Temple.

In the Masonic system, the port of Joppa holds a conspicuous place, occurring in the lectures of the Entered Apprentice, still more prominently in those of the Master Mason, and most of all in those of the Mark Master. It was to Joppa that Jonah fled from the presence of the Lord and embarked for Tarshish. In the building of the Second Temple, under Zerubbabel, B.C. 533—515, this city bore the same relationship to the work of the architect as in the first; but when Herod constructed the *third* Temple, he made some use of the port of Cæsarea, a few miles further north, and this rendered Joppa a place of only second-rate importance.

Joppa is reckoned one of the oldest cities in the world. Tradition ascribes its establishment as *antediluvian,* and associates it with mythological narratives of the very earliest periods. At present it is chiefly celebrated for its orange groves and gardens of Oriental produce. The oranges are the finest in the world; and as they are, unfortunately, seedless, so that I cannot collect their seeds for my patrons, as I desired, I put up and secured a supply of their *leaves* for my cabinets; and the same with regard to the lemons of Joppa equally famous for size and flavor.

In the best days of the crusades, A.D. 1099—1187, pious pilgrims departing from Joppa went out upon the sea-shore and selected shells, in which this beach largely abounds; and these they ever after-wards wore as symbols of pilgrimage and testimonials of their having performed it. I found so general a desire, among my patrons at home, to secure specimens of *the pilgrims' shell,* that I brought away several thousands of them for distribution. They are of the family and species *Ostrœa pecten* and others.

Agreeably to the lectures of the Mark Master, I find that Joppa is built upon a dome-shaped hill, rather steep, its western base washed by the Mediterranean Sea, and presenting a fine appearance from the sea. The present harbor, however, is very poor, and even dangerous; so much so, that in stormy weather the regular steamers of this coast are compelled to pass by, much to the disappointment of passengers, who are carried on to Beirut or Alexandria. An instance of this sort occurred during my first week in Beirut. The city is surrounded by a wall and ditch, scientifically constructed and well fortified.

Having a letter to the Governor (Kaimakam) of Joppa, Noureddin Effendi, from Brother E. T. Rogers, Master of Lebanon Lodge, at Beirut, I made haste to call upon that official, and was at once honored with his fraternal confidence. This gentleman is a Mason of some fifteen or twenty years' standing, initiated, as his diploma shows, in a French lodge on the Island of Corfu, but now a member of *Lodge Amitié Clemente,* Paris, France. He is about forty-five years of age, and a bachelor. He favored me with an invitation to dine with him, which I readily accepted. I found him anxious for the extension of the Masonic craft in Syria and Palestine; but, like all other Masons I have encountered here, he is but poorly posted as to the ways and means of Masonic dissemination. In fact, he has in his possession the amplest authority from the Grand Orient of France, in the form of a commission some ten or twelve years old, but never used, to establish lodges, confer degrees, etc.; and it was one of my privileges to instruct the good brother how to proceed in its use. The results, I trust, will some day be visible in the establishment of lodges either here or elsewhere.

The American colony near Joppa, of which so much has been said in the papers the past two years, is entirely broken up. Four of the colonists who were there on my arrival in May, I found to be members of the Masonic order, viz., Brother G. J. Adams, who is the Bishop and projector of the colony, and Brothers George W. Toombs, Rolla Floyd, and Joshua Walker. This rendered my acquaintance with them highly agreeable. Besides these five gentlemen, I found no Freemasons in Joppa.

In accordance with my custom elsewhere, I selected an appropriate spot at the southwestern angle of the city, and chiseled the *Square and Compass* as a token of the Masonic identification of Joppa. In doing so, I dedicated it to the following group of good Masons, viz., William B. Hubbard, G. H. C. Melody, E. J. Carr, W. W. Storey, Augustus Rowe, Andres Cassard, William Manby, E. W. H. Ellis, Edward Brewer, and Tal. P. Shafner.

Numerous lodges are named from this locality, such as No. 167, Kentucky; 152, Georgia; 201, New York; 65, Texas; 136, Iowa; 223, England, etc. The Plain of Sharon, on the verge of which the city stands, is also perpetuated in lodge nomenclature by Lodge No. 95, Texas; 116, Wisconsin; 97, Canada; 250, Pennsylvania, etc. The name of the country itself, *Palestine,* on which I am now entering —for thus far my explorations have been in *Syria,* of which Palestine is the southern extremity—has been still more frequently used in this way, as in Lodge No. 158, Ohio; 120, North Carolina; 208, Missouri; 204, New York; 31, Texas; 114, Wisconsin; 143, Iowa; 109, Arkansas, etc. The future visitor to this ancient port will find his stay made the more agreeable the more the spirit of our fraternity pervades it.

Traces of an ancient harbor are detected on the north and east sides of Joppa, which gave the city, in Solomonic times, the best protected harbor on the coast. Lieutenant Lynch, who was here about twenty years ago, was sanguine as to the feasibility of reopening this roadstead, now choked with sand, and giving a splendid revival to the old city. This is much to be desired. Traces of the ancient Roman road from Joppa to Jerusalem are plainly identified; and, as the Romans were the best road-builders in the world, it is most likely that the original causeway made by Hiram's men, for the transportation of the almost incalculable supply of materials required for the Temple, ran over the same ground. While this cannot yet be proven, I am satisfied, as the result of all my observations, that such was the fact. The distance between the two cities, on a straight line, is about twenty-five miles, but as the road runs, thirty-five miles. After running about twelve miles, it mounts to a hilly region, as will be seen by recalling the fact that Jerusalem stands 2,600 feet above Joppa. The Pasha of Jerusalem, Nazif Pasha, has opened a turn pike-way recently, connecting the two cities.

It is perhaps only an accidental circumstance, yet it struck me with some force, that in no town in Palestine have I seen so many and such ingenious combinations of *arches* as in Joppa. I copied in my notebook quite a number of them that particularly attracted my eye. The builders in our country, who seem to be restricted to a few simple forms of arches, might take lessons from these Arab builders. A few palm-trees grow here and there among the buildings, and in the suburbs of Joppa.

I remarked before that the hill at Joppa is quite steep. A friend, with myself, "tried our hands" at assisting each other to climb it; this, however, was more for speculative purposes than practical ones.

A sketch of my first day in Joppa is given from my notebook. I landed at the ancient port of Joppa, now called Jaffa (sometimes Yaffa), early on the morning of May 1. It is truly a charming day. The sea is only slightly agitated, not more so, indeed, than I am at the thought of at last treading the shores so renowned. It was hard, indeed, to conceive that this harbor, so restricted now in its marine accommodations, having only a few fishing vessels or small craft engaged in the orange-trade, was once the great port of the Jewish kingdom—their only harbor. It was difficult to recall the former glories of Joppa under the reigns of David and Solomon, when the commercial alliance with Tyre filled this bay with vessels, and brought the products of the whole earth to the foot of this hill. Yet the place is a sightly one for all that, and gratified my curiosity quite as much as I had reason to anticipate. The town covers the sea-end of a promontory that juts out for half a mile into the water, leaving a small bay upon each side. The hill being steep, the houses are built one above the other, and the narrow streets rise from the shore by broad stone steps, adapted only to camels, donkeys, and the native horses, who, I believe, could climb a ladder if required.

Approaching the shore, I called to mind all the Masonic and
Scriptural references to Joppa, those of Solomon's time, of Jonah,
etc., being prominent. As the boatmen forced their way through
the reef of rocks that runs parallel to the shore, I observed a
granite pillar upright upon a rude, stony ledge, used now for
fastening the small craft of the port, but once, doubtless, a part of
the architectural glories of ancient Joppa. At this point of my
entrance, a difference arose between the chief boatman and
myself as to the rate of compensation for bringing one person
from the ship. Had I been sufficiently acquainted with Arabic to
understand their loud and boisterous arguments, it is possible
that I should have paid their price, viz., seventy cents. As it was, I
handed them *twelve* cents, turning a deaf ear to their clamor. I
fear that my indifference left a bad impression upon those "sea-
faring men," but I could not help that. "Where ignorance is bliss
'tis folly to be wise." I have long since learned that your only way,
in this country, is to give what you think is right, and turn
contemptuously away from all protestations. One thing you may
be sure of, an Arab will never refuse to take your money, or be a
bit the less civil when he meets you again.

But oh, how the Joppanese bleed the general traveler! Some
tourists are so flush of money that they do not seem to care what
they give. Some become excited by the loud clamor of the demand,
and give *a dollar* when they mean *a shilling*. Some are
perpetually ignorant of the denomination of current coins. Many
fail to provide themselves with small change, and not until they
have spent a good many dollars in *backsheesh* do they discover
that plenty of *halfpiastre pieces* (two cents) will go just as far and
be as thankfully received in this way as francs (twenty cents) or
shillings (twenty-five cents). There is a class of tourists here
whose extravagant and reckless profusion in money matters
should be universally reprobated. Never having earned their own
support, and being totally indifferent as to expenditures, they
corrupt the whole body of the people with their lavishness, and so
become a plague to all "who come this way after them."

As I reached the shore, a host of arms were extended to steady
me, or catch me in case I should fall. One broad-backed fellow
turned his shoulders to me, and loudly invited me to ride ashore on
nature's own saddle. But, not recognizing any Freemasons among
them, taking my overcoat on one arm, and slinging my little wallet
around my neck, I took a position on the bow of the boat, and

NOUREDDIN EFFENDI,
Governor of Joppa, 1868.

watching my opportunity, as the last wave receded, sprang ashore, and so *landed at the port of Joppa,* my heavier baggage being brought by an attendant.

Landed at Joppa. No ships here bound for Ethiopia. Those five large vessels yonder are British war-ships. Those ten little smacks are only used to skim the coast. There are no Mark Masters ready to assist me up the hill. So through the crowd of screaming, yelling, blaspheming boatmen, and hotel-runners, and beggars, and soldiers, and thieves, and idlers of Joppa, I force my way up, and follow my guide to the English hotel; past a row of kneeling camels; past a row of water-carriers, filling their goat-skins from the fountains near the shore; under the bewildering succession of arches which make Joppa, more than any town I have visited, the proper establishment for the *Royal Arch;* past a miserably deformed beggar, sitting by the roadside, and asking and getting alms, as his predecessors in all ages have done here, and so on to the *Locanda,* or hotel already named, kept by Messrs. Blatner.

As soon as I had taken refreshments, consisting of coffee and bread, which is all you get here till noon, I procured a guide, and went out to the American colony, about half a mile from the wall of the town, on the north side. Bro. Geo. W. Toombs, formerly of Illinois, had been lying quite low with Syrian fever, but was able to converse with me. I was much impressed with the honesty and sincerity of Bro. Floyd, who offered me, both in his own person and through his excellent wife, the hospitalities of his house, as he had done, several weeks before, to my associate. The Bishop, Bro. Adams, was likewise extremely kind to me, and labored to make my stay at Joppa agreeable. The manner of Bro. Toombs, though lying in his bed extremely ill, was most gentlemanly, friendly, and accommodating.

Next I called on the Governor, at his *Serai,* or court of justice, surrounded by a crowd of litigants. I found his Excellency to be a most gentlemanly and agreeable person, small, active, with keen eye and sharp features, voice loud and quick, and full of Masonic fire. In the Scotch Rite (Ancient and Accepted), he has advanced to the twenty-ninth degree, *Chevalier de Soleil,* or Knight of the Sun. His name, Noureddin, is pronounced with full stress upon the last syllable, *deene,* and his official title is that of *Kaimakam,* or Governor. In official parlance, he is addressed as *his Excellency the Effendi.*

Noureddin being a bachelor, lives in military style, his family consisting of his staff and male servants only. Besides the official language, which is Turkish, he speaks French fluently, and the Arabic. I was able to communicate with him only through an interpreter, M. Serapion Murad, Chancellor of the Prussian Consulate at Joppa, kindly doing the duties of interpreter for me, and a little French, which I mustered up for the occasion. I have had so much experience in this country, talking to the people of all nationalities, through interpreters, that the awkwardness of such intercourse has been mainly overcome, and I enjoyed this meeting with the Governor exceedingly. It was gratifying, too, to see that the object I had in view, in this conference, was one that had already occupied his Excellency's attention, viz., the establishment of a lodge at this place. The four American brethren of the colony are also warmly in favor of this project. I took my leave, having been invited to dine with his Excellency at seven o'clock, and promising to have the petition for the establishment of a lodge ready at that hour.

In drafting the petition to the Grand Orient of France, I labored under the difficulty of not possessing sufficient familiarity with the Constitution and Rules of Order of that body. I knew there was some difference between the forms of procedure in the Grand Orient of France and the various Grand Lodges with which I am acquainted. So I ventured on an original plan of my own. I wrote a letter as coming only from myself, setting forth the following facts, that there is only one lodge in this country (the one at Beirut working under the Grand Lodge of Scotland), although the number of Freemasons resident in various towns is large; that at this place (Joppa) there are five resident Masons—I specified their names—and testified that these brethren are ardently desirous of establishing a lodge here, believing that many initiates would promptly be secured, and those of the best quality, thus advancing the general interest of Freemasonry and the cause of universal benevolence and morality. Finally I suggested, on behalf of the seven brethren whose names I had given, that his Excellency Noureddin Effendi be nominated Deputy, or Provincial Grand Master of Syria, under the Constitution of the Grand Orient of France, with the amplest powers that such a patent embraces, with special authority to establish the *Lodge Jerusalem and Jaffa,* empowered to work at either place at its own convenience. This paper being carefully copied, was forwarded to the Grand Secretary at Paris, an answer being expected within a month. I may say here, however, that the proposal was declined, on the ground that the petitioners (except his Excellency) were not French Masons!

In this country you do not get breakfast till high 12. How I have
continued thus far to avoid a horrible death by starvation, I can
scarcely tell; but here at Joppa, you can *eat oranges,* for which
this vicinity is so famous. They are admittedly the largest and the
best in the world, some of the picked specimens more resembling
pumpkins than fruit. Usually they are seedless, particularly the
giants. They are of course very cheap; for half a piastre (two cents)
you can get as many as you can eat; for a whole piastre, as many
as you can carry away. They constitute a very large part of the
trade of this port, being sent as far as Constantinople, and in
every direction through the country. No one who has observed the
peculiar baskets used for transporting the Joppa orange will
forget them, the quantity carried by a donkey being simply, if the
donkey only knew it, preposterous. At this season, the orange-
gardens or orchards are at their prettiest, ripe fruit, green fruit,
immature fruit, blossoms, buds, and leaves, all growing good-
naturedly together upon the same tree and same bough. The
flowers exhale the most delicious perfume; the tree itself is a
model of beauty; while the sight of the large yellow fruit sets off
with equal grace the bright green of the leaves and the pure white
of the blossoms. Strange that the orange is not once named in the
Bible. Is it not most probable that by the term "apple" in
Scripture the *orange* is meant? I like to believe it, and to imagine
that, just as the boys and other orange-venders here hand you the
tempting fruit all day, and urge you to purchase and eat, so they
did to the swarthy Phœnicians who were drawing the heavy
cedar-trees up this hill, and across yonder sandy plain, and to the
top of those heights that loom up so grandly in the eastward; and
that those faithful craftsmen had their thirst assuaged by oranges,
and rested their limbs at night under the dense foliage of the
orange-orchards. If so, they were well accustomed to the fruit
before they came to Joppa; for I believe the oranges that I saw
near Sidon, two weeks ago, are only second in size and value to
these at Joppa.

As I said, breakfast at high 12 is an attempt upon the life of a
human being, and I attribute my escape from starvation only to the
sustenance afforded by the Joppa oranges. When at last the
breakfast has come—but let me describe it. First, two of the fish from
this harbor, sweet and delicious specimens of the finny tribe whose
forefathers did so much to strengthen our Masonic forefathers, as
they came floating down this way on rafts from the Masonic Bay, a
hundred and fifty miles above here. I ate them both. Next, a

stewed thicken, stewed to *rags,* as is the custom of the country; but by judicious use of sweet olive oil in place of butter, well flavored and toothsome, I ate it all. Then a plate of cold mutton, cut in slices. My eyes being indifferent, I mount my glasses now to give it a name, and easily recognizing it, I ate it all. Next some fried mutton, rather stringy and hard; however, I ate it also. Now comes a plate of oranges, and a cup of coffee; a woman's thimble is gigantic in size compared with it. This is my breakfast. Picking my teeth, I looked out at that fine palm-tree yonder, my favorite tree of all the trees in the world. They tell me the palm bears its fruit (the date) abundantly in the southern section of Palestine, which is more than it does about Beirut. There are a considerable number of palm-trees in this vicinity, while the pomegranate, so famous in Masonic symbology, is even more so. I secured ample specimens of the wood of both these trees.

Having spent the afternoon in a manner suitable to my mission, I sallied forth at the proper hour to fill my appointment with his Excellency Brother Noureddin Effendi, between whom and myself Freemasonry has already established an equality which no other society can accomplish. Brother Adams joined us in the party, and there were present Monsieur Serapion Murad, already named, together with half a dozen clerks and secretaries of the Governor. I showed his Excellency my diploma of the thirty-second grade, Scottish Rite. I had also my diploma from my lodge, *Fortitude* No. 47, La Grange, Ky., prepared expressly for this journey, and my firman from the Sultan. Upon his own part, the Kaimakam showed me written evidence of his membership in various lodges, and we passed esoterical evidences satisfactory to both. Two hours passed by before dinner was announced, which time was spent in conversation of a varied and pleasing character. His Excellency is one of the best of companions, and Brother Adams has the *art agréable* in perfection. Monsieur Serapion Murad is one of a thousand in making his friends happy, while I found myself both in the mood conversational and musical. Cigarettes and narghilehs were offered abundantly. The latter is the celebrated water-pipe, through which, when the fumes of this mild Turkish tobacco have passed, you cannot tell that you are smoking anything. It is this which, according to tradition, King Solomon used while inducting the Queen of Sheba into the art of using tobacco. The only drawback connected with its use is the vast expenditure of muscular energy requisite in drawing smoke through it. The first time you attempt to use one you become black in the face from the tremendous effort, and present an alarming appearance. I dislike the roar of water which it makes, for I always imagine it is raining torrents outside when I hear it. But I digress.

My mind is exercised at Joppa in observing the queer points of contrast between the people of the East and the West. Of these I note eleven, viz.:

1. *We* write and read from left to right; *they* from right to left.

2. *We* uncover the head at worship, and keep our feet covered; *they* cover the head and bare the feet.

3. *We* shave the face but not the head; *they* shave the head but not the face.

4. *We* draw the razor *towards* us; *they* push the razor *from* them.

5. *We* push the saw *from* us in sawing; *they* draw the saw *towards* them.

6. *We* chew and snuff tobacco as well as smoke; *they* use it only in fumigation.

7. *We* stand at reaping, preaching, etc.; *they* sit at all such labors.

8. *We* distinguish carefully the clothing of the two sexes, and the law (and the Bible) forbid similarity; *they* make little or no distinction.

9. *We* sleep in the house-rooms; *they* on the house-tops.

10. *We* drink alcoholic liquors; *they* religiously abstain from such.

11. *We* rejoice in active life; *they* are strictly sedentary. A maxim is found among them like this: "Never walk when you can ride; never stand when you can sit; never sit when you can lie!"

A seashore ramble of several hours was a charming episode in my visit to Joppa. The beach is lined with shells, especially the escalop, already named. Ever since I was made a Knight Templar, in 1850, I have desired to see the real *escalop* (*scalop, eschalop*) *shell* of the Crusaders. Here they are in millions. To wear them around the hat, as Scott described the Templar in *Ivanhoe,* implied that the wearer had made a long voyage by sea, particularly in attendance on holy wars. This shell, for some reason, was the emblem of St. James, the brother of Jesus, who is always drawn in the guise of a pilgrim; and it is largely seen in the churches dedicated to him. This shell is of the family *Ostrœadœ,* another name for *Pectinidœ.* The regular "pilgrim's shell" now in my hand is *Pectin Jacobœus* or that of St.

or that of St. James. Sometimes it grows four or five inches broad, but they are rarely much over one inch.

The steady movement of the tides upon this beach, along which I have wandered already so often, never ceases to attract my attention. Homer describes it just as I should today, only so much better:

> As when the ocean-billows, wave on wave,
> Are pushed along to the resounding shore
> Before the westward wind, and first the surge
> Uplifts itself, and then against the land
> Dashes and roars, and round the headland peak
> Tosses on high and spouts its foam afar.—*Iliad.*

The telegraph poles, extending in a receding line southward as far as the eye can reach, give me a homesick throb or two. Of telegraph lines in 1871, there were 684,000 miles in use throughout the world, 30,000 of which are of submarine cable. The lines are extending at the rate of 100,000 miles per annum. But for the dreadful expense (nearly $100), I would send a message of twenty words to the dear one who keeps the household lamp trimmed and burning, awaiting my return.

I visited the site of Bonaparte's daring and successful assault upon the city. Of the thousands who fell here, it may be said there is

> Not a time-wasted cross, not a moldering stone
>   To mark the lone scene of their shame or their pride;
> Not a grass-covered mound tells the traveler lone
>   Where thousands lay down in their anguish and died.

In the groves and orchards surrounding the city I noted the broad flagging leaf of the plantain, the first I had ever seen. Afterwards I found them in Egypt much larger. The fruit is shaped like cucumbers in clusters. According to Mohammed's theory, this was the forbidden fruit of Adam and Eve, and the large, peculiarly shaped leaves were those of which our first parents constructed their aprons. Who knows? They are big enough to cover the whole body.

But what are these objects slowly approaching me, dressed in the habiliments of the grave, enveloped in the white sheet, and recalling ghostly images of youthful terror? The women of Joppa, returning from their daily visit to the cemetery.

Observing an exchange of salutes between two war-ships, I am reminded of the piece of naval etiquette, that the ship answering returns fewer guns than the one that gives the hailing sign.

In the bazaars of Joppa, the women do most of the "truck" business,

ness, selling charcoal, parsley, snails, eggs, fruits, vegetables, milk, etc. These are women of the Fellahin Arabs—the *village* Arabs, as distinguished from Bedouin or wandering Arabs. They go unveiled, which the *Turkish* women never do. In the morning, the women bring their truck in baskets borne on heads and shoulders, while the man rides his donkey pleasantly, and smokes. Poor as Job's turkey though such a woman may be, she has glass rings, bracelets, and strings of beads in killing abundance, equal to Mother Rebecca herself, only of cheaper material. So too, with her child. Living in a mud-hut, on bread and water, in a chronic state of starvation, the child's head is decorated with gold and silver coins which the law of debt may not impound or the law of usage sell. The mother's dress is a blue cotton gown, open at the breast, but the sleeves hang to the ground, and she has the Oriental girdle round her waist. When she moves you know it by the tinkling of that lot of glass trumpery which hangs around her.

The Oriental method of carrying water, as I see it here, is perpetuated in heraldry. The yoke, with two leather water-pouches depending upon it, is particularly the device of the family De Ros, of England,— "gules, three water-budgets argent" as it is technically termed, referring to the method adopted by the Crusaders for carrying water through the desert. An English Baron somebody or other has also *trois bouts d'eau* in his heraldic device.

In the manufacture of soap, of which, to their credit, the people of Joppa make a great deal and make it *good* (no *auction-soap* here), they use ashes, lime, gall-nuts, olive-oil, and salt. It is always *made hard,* cast in blocks, and, when prepared for shipment, sewed in sacks. The vast olive product of this country affords considerable commerce in soap. The enormous heaps of bleached ashes near Joppa and Jerusalem have attracted the eyes of travelers for centuries.

Laughing, through the open door of a barber's shop, at the sight of a man bending over a basin in an attitude of seasickness, and having his head shaved. A Moslem only nourishes a lock of hair on the crown of his head, like a Sioux Indian's scalp lock. It is strictly for religious (traditional) purposes.

I saw an old man, in a church here, kneeling and devoutly praying before the altar. His beard was long, flowing, and white as that of old Brother Stillman Blanchard, of happy memory. His countenance was pale and meagre, his skin was withered, his eyes sunk deep in his head.

I studied a party of desert Bedouins here, just up from beyond Gaza on some business with the government. They were evidently unaccustomed to civilized scenes. Their eyes rolled over me like those of wild beasts in a cage. They were indeed wild and ferocious in appearance as so many beasts. Their visages were dark red—almost copper-colored. The one who answered my questions had a voice like that of a bird of evil omen. Talking to one another, they sent out volleys of Arabic gutturals rattling like hailstones.

The large yellow snails sold in the bazaars form a favorite article of diet through a considerable part of France as well as Palestine. They are said to be very palatable. I did not try them.

Of the lepers, whom I saw for the first time in Joppa, I will speak under another head. They are numerous here, and appeal to your charity both by the eye and ear—yes, and by a third sense equally urgent.

The sycamore-tree, so called in Scripture, is quite a conspicuous object around Joppa. But it is not at all the tree Cowper describes when he says:

> "The sycamore, capricious in attire,
> Now green, now tawdry, and, ere autumn yet
> Have changed the woods, in scarlet honor brought."

In memory of the vine-traditions of the hills of Judah, I took, at dinner today, a glass of the wine of Hebron, and ate heartily of its raisins and *olives*. In Christ's day, wine abounded in Palestine, and was the drink of the people, as it is now in Europe. Hebron wine is a bright wine, resembling the amber Muscat. It has a slightly astringent taste, and is said to be a remedy in bilious complaints. The raisins are not so large and thin-skinned as the Malaga box-raisins, and the seeds are larger; yet the flavor is good. The *dibs,* or syrup made from the raisins, often from the carob-pods, is equal to the finest sugarhouse syrups of our country. Some writers think this the syrup referred to in many passages of Holy Scripture, in which the term *honey* is employed.

It will be expected that I say something more in detail of the *American Colony,* whose setting-out in 1866 and misfortunes in 1867 filled the papers of this country, and drove many of us to our pockets deeper than we could well afford. About the time I started for the Holy Land (February, 1868), the dailies were publishing this morceau of news:

"The Maine Colony in Joppa has again been heard from. They now number twenty-five, and are in a state of bliss, in consequence of the departure of their leader, Adams."

At Beirut and vicinity, during March and April, the stories told about Adams and his people were incredibly harsh; and this naturally created a reaction in my own mind, so far, at least, that I wrote to Adams, assuring him that when I came to Joppa, he should have a fair showing as a fellow-countryman and a Masonic brother.

Rev. G. J. Adams visited Palestine on a prospecting expedition in 1865. His letter of August 10 of that year was written from Joppa, that of August 14 from the "Land of Ephraim," that of August 20 from Jerusalem, that of August 23 from Bethel. In the latter, he made these characteristic explanations: "One hour before sunset I began the ascent of the Hill of Hope (!) at Bethel, on which I had built an altar of twelve stones for the whole house of Israel. There, with the Lord's host above me, I prayed: Oh Lord God of Israel, thou great Jehovah; God of Abraham, and Isaac, and Jacob; God of the Prophets; thou great I AM. Have mercy upon these thy servants who have come this long journey to prepare this work, and forgive our sins and purify our hearts. In thy presence, in the presence of angels, in the presence of the hosts who surround us, we pour this oil upon this altar of twelve stones, to be a witness forever that we have done as thou directed us. I then filled a bottle of water from a well from which the prophets and patriarchs had refreshed themselves."

On my return home, I summed up all I knew of him and his operations in an article, of which the following is the substance:

On both my visits to Joppa (in May and June, 1868), I went out to the *Adams Colony* near that ancient city, about ten minutes' walk, and made myself inquisitive in regard to the history of the singular economic-religious movement which led to its establishment. As four of the colonists to whom I was introduced are members of the Masonic fraternity, viz., Mr. G. J. Adams, (the founder and Bishop), Mr. Rolla Floyd, Mr. Toombs, and Mr. Walker, there is a propriety in ventilating the subject with considerable detail in a Masonic journal, and I doubt not your readers will think so.

The Joppa Colony was founded under the sole auspices of the eccentric Rev. G. J. Adams, long publisher and editor of religious papers in New England; a preacher of the Primitive Gospel; a singularly erratic man, social to a degree, versatile in gifts, fond of pleasure, and possessing quite a histrionic genius. Indeed, it is averred that he was formerly a *play-actor,* but I did not ask him about that. I remember, however, that the day. I left Joppa for Jerusalem he was announced to play Hamlet and some other part upon the stage which he had erected *in the church edifice* connected with his colony, and he told me that day that he had $800 worth of theatrical costumes in his wardrobe, at Joppa.

Mr. Adams must have possessed a good deal of eloquence as a preacher, for he went amongst the educated, moral, hard-fisted people of Maine, and secured their pledges (and their money too) to unite in the establishment of a colony in Palestine under his presidency. Fortified with these he made a preliminary visit to that country about the year 1865; went to Jerusalem; went to Bethel (where he *set up an altar of stone,* and performed various mystical evolutions in connection with it), and returned to New England full of confidence in the feasibility of the scheme. The Turkish government was favorable to it (the Governor of Joppa, Noureddin Effendi, particularly so); the land was productive, and could be had upon the longest leases at a nominal price; *three crops* a year could be made; the climate was salubrious; fortunes could be made in a few years, etc., etc., etc. It was the California fever of 1850 over again.

Nearly *two hundred* persons, men and women, embarked for Palestine upon the basis of his statements alone; what a man to establish such confidence! As I talked with him in May, 1868, I endeavored in vain to detect the secret of his strength.

They brought with them to Joppa all the outfit for domestic life and for agricultural operations. Lumber from the hills of Maine was brought in abundance, for Adams had correctly told them there was no timber in Palestine. Furniture had been provided, for he had informed them that the Moslems used neither chair nor table. Food for several months and clothing for an indefinite period were not forgotten. By the favor of Noureddin Effendi, the custom-duties were all remitted by a device of his own, peculiarly Turkish.* The government afforded the colonists every favor they desired. The enterprise began under the most favorable auspices. Why then did it fail?

For several reasons. *First.* The climate. These people from the rocks, cold climate, and resin-trees of Maine all got the *chills and fever* in Palestine, just as they would have got it had they removed to Newark, New Jersey; or to the banks of Skunk River, Iowa. I should have had an attack myself, had I stayed on that coast two weeks longer. No one can be acclimated in Syria without it any more than he can in Mississippi or Louisiana. *Second.* The colonists persisted in working through the heat of the day, wearing black bats, eating big Maine dinners, and doing things generally exactly

---

* It was this: the Customhouse of Joppa is not under Noureddin's control, there fore he gave them a permit to land their effects *on the beach,* but a mile from the city he told me this himself.

the opposite of the customs of the natives, who have found out in four thousand years how to live healthfully and happily on the Plain of Sharon. *Third.* The government, of the ecclesiastical form, with a man for Pope (Adams) who could not "rule his own spirit." He was vain, conceited, intemperate, a *very poor* business man, ignorant of every principle of political economy, and an inveterate warrior (socially). He quarreled with everybody; quarreled with those whose bread he was eating; quarreled with the American Consuls, by whose favor alone he was kept from Oriental jails; quarreled with the Turkish authorities, who were willing to stretch every principle of law to favor him; quarreled with his own appointed Elders of his own appointed church. He was extravagant, yet does not seem to have got anything for his money. His sermons were vulgar and abusive. His theology was contradictory, execrable, and absurd. Without charging him with any positive crime, I must say that I never saw a man less fitted to *rule* than G. J. Adams.

So the colony crumbled and went to pieces. A few died; the rest returned as they could to the United States. When I went there, in May, there were seven or eight left; when I was there in June there were *only two,* viz., Brother and Mrs. Rolla Floyd, a most estimable couple.

Adams wrote, October 22, 1867, that "the natives are anxious to hire us. Our teams are all engaged. Our carpenters have employment at wages that allow each to save $5 per week, in gold. All our mechanics and laborers have steady work and good pay. Our wagons and carriages are engaged by the Pasha in building a fine macadamized road from Joppa to Jerusalem, one hundred feet wide; three thousand men are employed upon it. We are at peace with all the natives, the local officers, and the foreign Consuls; yet as a colony, we stand free from every government on earth, and, like Abraham, are strangers upon earth. We number now forty-five, and never since we landed have we been so happy and contented as we are now." The colony experienced the fate of similar undertakings. Some who went out were not fitted for the toils and privations of a pioneer effort, and all had mistaken views as to a *speedy* realization of their hopes. Poverty and disappointment, joined to mismanagement, disheartened many, and they sought relief from citizens of the United States that they might return home. More money was spent in getting them back than would have saved the success of the colony.

Adams is in England (1868), but what he is doing there, or how he expects to be supported, I do not know. He intimated to me that he expected to secure a new body of colonists in the west of England! This, however, is impossible, because he has alienated his title to the lands in the colony, and could not get further favors from any one.

Securing a guide from the proprietor of *The English Hotel,* where I was stopping, I went out by the east gate of the city, through the orange bazaars, then heaped to overflowing with the ripe and luscious fruit, nowhere in all the world so large and good as at Joppa;

through the Mohammedan graveyards (nowhere in all the world are graveyards such dismal places as in Turkish countries), through groves of prickly-pear trees, many of whose stems were ten and twelve inches in diameter; through caravans of kneeling camels, patiently waiting for their loads of oranges, to convey them to unknown distances eastward and southward over the deserts; through groves of pomegranates and orange-trees and lemon-trees, bending under the weight of fruit, or fragrant and beautiful with flowers red and white; and so on for a ten minutes' walk, whose variety of Oriental types would of itself repay a person for coming all the way to Joppa from America.

I said ten minutes; but in good truth it took me an hour. The sandy path was loaded with shells, over which I walked at first gingerly, as disliking to crush these beautiful forms, once the emblem of pilgrimage (see Byron's "sandal-shoon and scalop-shell"). The banks under the broad cactus were red with the flowers of the anemone, and blue with another floral type, and yellow with a third. Strange birds wooed me to pause and observe them; but at this rate I should never reach the colony, and so thought my staid dragoman, who looked back upon me occasionally with a smile of pity, not untinged with contempt at my simpleness in observing objects so commonplace.

The colony consisted of a dozen or twenty wooden houses, built of the lumber brought from Maine. The first I approached was Brother Floyd's. I found that good man preparing, with his wagon and team (the only wagon and team, be it observed, in all the realms of King Solomon), to load a British vessel with the bones that for unnumbered centuries had whitened and resisted the tooth of dog, jackal, and hyena, on the plains of Joppa. Waiting at the house, Mr. Adams joined me here; a heavy, shambling, good-natured, loquacious, self-conceited man, about fifty-five years of age. While I was sitting there the American Consul-General of Egypt (Mr. Charles Hale), who had come up on the same steamer with me the night before, called, and we all walked to Mr. Adams' house together. Mr. Adams raised the American flag in *our honor,* and this afforded me the opportunity of observing from his housetops that he had one of the finest views of sea and country that the place afforded. Mr. Toombs was lying ill with Syrian fever, and had been dangerously low. Mrs. Adams and her little son made up the family.

I conclude my article by saying that at the dinner given in my honor that evening by the Kaimakam or Governor, Noureddin Effendi and Mr. Adams were present; and during several hours that we sat together at that hospitable board he fully confirmed the impression I had previously formed of him, that of all men living he was one of the last to undertake to manage a colony upon the Syrian coast.

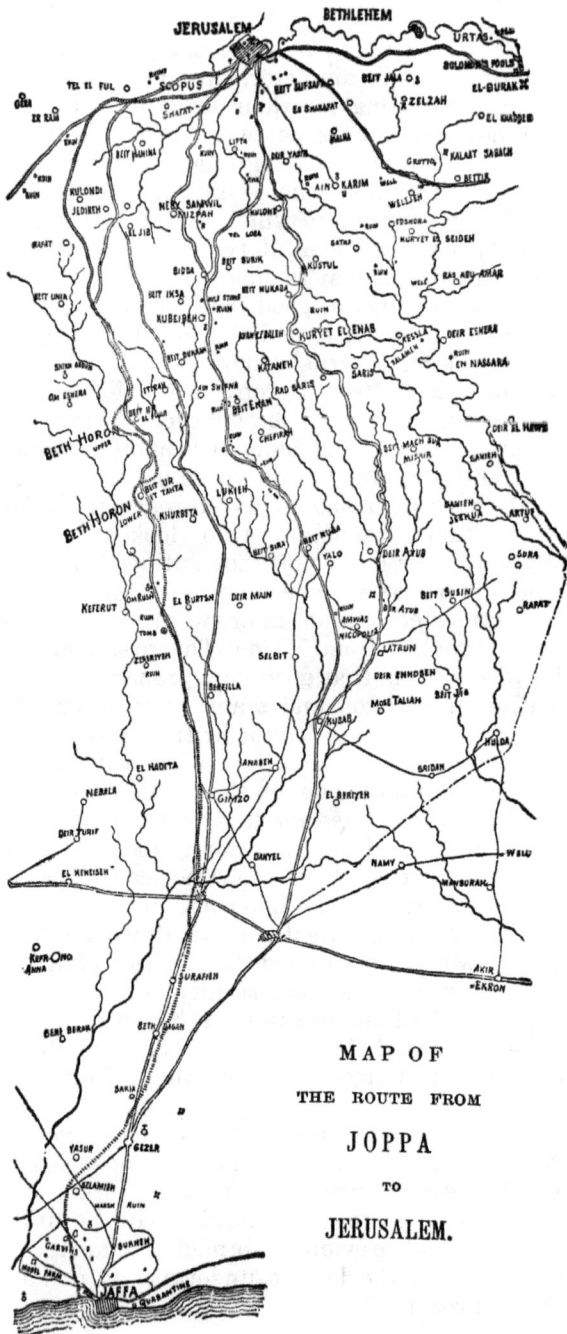

MAP OF

THE ROUTE FROM

JOPPA

TO

JERUSALEM.

CHAPTER XVIII.

GOING UP TO JERUSALEM.

FTER completing my examinations of the city of Joppa, I started, May 2, 1868, to follow "the Burden-Bearers," who bore the heavy beams of cedar and other ponderous materials up the precipitous cliffs to Jerusalem. I left Joppa at 3 P.M. to go by way of Ramleh and Kolonieh, on the new turnpike-road.

Passing through the *Jerusalem Gate,* the only gate on the landside, I note a few of the *noises* that struck my ear: they are the snarls and yelps of crowds of dogs; the wild, sweet notes of birds; the cry of the muezzin high in the minaret; the "poll-parrotings" of the natives—inveterate gabblers they are; the shrieks of the camels protesting against their loads, and the jingle of their bells; the snort, tramp, and squeal of horses; the swearing of a party of British sailors, "on leave" for Jerusalem, but unable to pass the alcoholic vender or dram-seller of *arrack*—a detestable compound made of dates, and likely to use up all their "leave" right here at Joppa; the awful Plutonian bray of the nine donkeys, all in the same key; and, finally, the laugh and frolic of mobs of boys idling away the hours of youth under the orange-trees. A Judge (Kadi) was holding court in the gateway, and had just ordered a fellow flogged for stealing a sailor's knife. Quick and condign the trial and judgment; from the moment the Kadi began to question him to the moment he was kicked out of the gate, lacerated and bleeding, was less than *five minutes,* and this included indictment, answer, summing-up, and flogging,—thirteen strokes, well laid on his bare soles. The fellow bawled manfully, but we all laughed. It was rich. I really felt good over it. *Fiat justitia,* etc. I think of the incident even now with satisfaction. My nine donkeys fairly roared with joy (in minors) at the transaction.

The ride in this weather and at this season is delightful. It only needs good companionship to make it perfectly delicious; but my companion, alas! is a negro *cavalier* (as the gentleman is styled in the grandiloquent dragoman-language). He is assisted by a muleteer of the lowest and most sinister class conceivable. There was a grievance of some kind that possessed that muleteer's mind from the start. He swore (in Arabic) all the way to Ramleh. His "allahs" were curiously intermingled with "mejeedy" and "howadjee," and "backsheesh," and he would not be comforted, nor would he keep up with me on the road, despite all that my cavalier and myself could do to instigate him. Once he threw my carpetbag on the ground, bursting it open and injuring it. I have it yet, with that muleteer's defacement stamped upon it. Altogether, he was an infamous specimen of a muleteer—and, by the way, he had no mule either, but rode a wretched horse.

But oh, that delightful ride over the Plain of Sharon! How the memory thereof stirs me to grateful tears as I write. They intermingle with the thoughts of that dead boy of whose decease I have just heard (February 2, 1872). The first hour was chiefly under orange-groves, yellow with heavy fruit, the largest and sweetest in the world. In them happy songsters made melody for the American *howadjee* as he rode along. The fences were of the immense *cactus,* or prickly-pear, whose trunks are often twelve inches in diameter, and leaves eighteen inches in length—large as elephants' ears—and thorns keen as cambric needles make good barriers, wherever used. I think if fences of these were set up among the "amazing trials" to be encountered in a Masonic lodge, but few candidates would get through! At this season, the owners are trimming off the dead leaves, the women and children bearing them away in baskets for fuel. Interspersed with the orange-trees are the lemon, fig, pomegranate, pear, carob, cherry, and others, of whose very names I am innocent. A large tree with thick blue blossoms is called by the English-speaking residents here *the lilac-tree.*

The only drawbacks to the scene are the lepers and other beggars, disgusting from physical mutilations, who pierce my ears with wailings. That they are miserable is plain to see, for death alone can terminate their anguish, and I do not try to resist the impulse to "give them an alms." Two elegant fountains stand by the roadside, showing by their inscriptions that they were placed here under promptings of philanthropy alone. Built into them are fragments of large and splendid columns of marble and granite, that speak loudly of Egypt; and the water-trough of one of them, like that which I saw three weeks ago outside of the old gate of Tyre, is a splendidly carved marble sarcophagus or stone-coffin, from which the original tenant had long since been expelled with ignominy and contempt.

I observed here an object, worn by the females, different from anything that had previously met my eye, viz., a black cloth tied over the face just below the eyes, in such a manner that the nose, mouth, and chin are hidden. This cloth is ornamented with embroidery and jewels, and is altogether the most ridiculous ornament ever imposed by fashion upon the fair sex. I imagine Madame Demorest enforcing it, and my daughters wearing it. Laughing at the conceit, I pass on.

The variety of characters met upon this road is endless. Amongst them is an Arab mounted on a beautiful horse, magnificently accoutered, who gave me the most graceful of salaams. I must say, when these fellows *are* polite, they outvie Monsieur Le —— —— himself.

A Fellah (a very low *feller* indeed) plowing with a cow and an ass yoked together—a palpable violation of the Law of Moses. He left his strangely assorted team to ask a *backsheesh.* I gave him a *para,* which is about the value of the *quadrin* or mite of olden time, worth one-tenth of a cent. The coin is but little used at present, but I had purchased a lot to carry home with me, and rather unwillingly spared him one. I fear he was not sufficiently thankful for the boon. The patent plow with which he was turning up the soil (loose with seashells) is the one lettered *a* in my cut.

Such a plow weighs about eight pounds, and there is money in it at $1 apiece.

It is pleasant to watch the numerous picnic parties coming out of Joppa to spend the

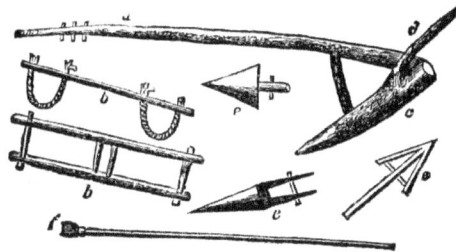

a, plow. b, yoke. f, goad, etc. e. petuts.

afternoon on this flowery carpet of Sharon. Each party consists of a single family only. They never come nearer than a hundred paces of me, then stop, the slaves and pipe-bearers spread rugs and mats on the ground, the party seat themselves, coffee is made and handed round in a minute, pipes are lit, and the enjoyment begins.

Sloth is their greatest curse; quiet (or, as they call it, *keef*) is their idea of enjoyment. Although I would not violate their laws of etiquette by approaching them, yet I could plainly enough hear their *phantageia,* their sharp, quavering notes of joy. They suddenly raise their voices from the lowest monotone to the highest pitch, then turn it into a real *war-whoop* by clapping the hand upon the mouth.

Passed the Fountain of Abraham (Ain Ibraheem). These *ains* or fountains were formerly much used for oratories or praying-houses, and it would be convenient to sit here by this cool water-pool if I had to listen again to the long, heavy prayer of Dr. —— when he opened the Grand Lodge of —— in my hearing.

At twenty minutes to four, the Plain of Sharon opens before me in all its flowery luxuriance, presenting, at one view, the variety of travelers and the pastoral and farming scenes identified with this ancient country from its earliest history.

I cannot name a tithe of the wild flowers that delight me as I ride along. The myrtle is certainly here; the lavender, broom, hyssop, sage, rue, and wild thyme abundantly. The winding valley rolls in waves of wheat and barley, the hillsides are mantled with groves of olives. It is a vast *mosaic* of green and brown, jasper and verdantique. The little hills laugh with plenty. The whole landscape bears marks of gladness. How beautiful the Plain of Sharon must have been in the days when it was cultivated by Hebrew skill and assiduity, irrigated and made gentle by rotation of crops. An experienced writer says: "No country in the world is blessed with a more beautiful and varied *flora* than the United States, and there are few portions of its flowery soil I have not trodden, from Florida to Minnesota. My eye is familiar with a very great variety of wild-flowers, but on the Plain of Sharon I entered upon a new experience of botanical wealth and glory."

As a fair specimen of the class of travelers met here, I append a cut. Upon this road were footmen, donkeys, mules, horses, and camels. Women borne along upon the backs of these different animals, in contrivances resembling large boxes, balanced with some skill. Others rode astride, like the "sterner" sex. A picnic party enjoyed themselves upon the soft grass. On every side, the plowmen were at their labors with their miserable plows, and their poor little heifers to drag them. Great birds (storks) stood upright around the marshy places, patiently waiting for frogs, which they love with a Frenchman's admiration. An eagle was skimming the plain in the distance, and hawks nearer at hand. Great fields of wheat and barley nearly ripe encroached upon the road, usually without fence or protection. Joppa is hidden behind me by the intervening groves. Far on the right, interminable sand ridges, crowned with telegraph poles, show where the coastline tends southward towards Egypt. This road is the one upon which at least one thousand workmen are engaged making a highway to connect Joppa with Jerusalem. It is well engineered, ditched at the sides, and with good bridges where needful. Upon a hill far ahead is an Arab village, appearing quite pretty in the distance, and opposite to it a wely or Mohammedan tomb. The natural features of Sharon resemble in almost every particular the prairies of the West, exhibited at their prettiest. It has not such a *matting* of flowers as our Western prairies, though the varieties are more numerous. The largest of the poppies, a conspicuous object here, grows about two miles from Tyre, near a fountain. Here are the ordinary "white weed" of our country, a small, yellow flower, like the dandelion, and many others.

BEDOUIN.

The mountains of Dan rise gloriously before me, while the mellow evening sun and the delightful sea breeze upon my back give the last grace to my journey that nature is capable of. Such are my first impressions of the *Plain of Sharon*. The long trains of sheep and goats feeding over the prairie, presenting the vivid contrast of black with white, are led (not driven) by their shepherds, who call them at intervals, according to the Scriptural allusion. May I be as ready to follow my Divine Leader to "green pastures" as these poor creatures are to follow theirs'.

Soon I overtake a line of camels laden with dragomans' goods, beds, bedsteads, tents, working materials, etc., etc., intended for some party of travelers coming on behind me. Before night, they will pitch those tents upon the soft, green prairie-grass, and enjoy their first night of "Tent-Life in the Holy Land," as Prime jauntily terms it.

And now there opens out upon my eyes a large olive orchard, always an attractive object to me. Under the trees is a blind man following his conductor, by holding out the end of a cane, and touching his back. A little further, and the village, which seemed so romantic in the distance, proves to be a mere collection of mud-huts, where cattle, sheep, human beings, and vermin of the liveliest quality herd indiscriminately together. A large watershed, in a grove of trees, points to the manner in which the precious fluid is brought to the surface from the wells of this plain. A grove of palm-trees next appears, by many degrees the most beautiful tree in the world. In two hours from Joppa, the tall tower of Ramleh comes in sight, the only object of the sort, I believe, in Palestine. Another hour brings me to the town itself, much larger and better built than I had expected to see it, and there I was welcomed by a universal cry of "backsheesh, backsheesh, howadjee," which I had heard before. I always take these words to imply the warmest sentiments of respect and bowing courteously in response, I pass on.

ARIMATHEA. RAMLEH.

What particular sin I had been guilty of, for which the penalty was to be sent to the *Locanda* or hotel of Ramleh, instead of the convent, I shall never know; but whatever it was, I feel that the penance was ample, if miserable fare, and a hard bed, only soft with fleas and only musical with mosquitoes, and noisy, drunken guests, deserve the term.

My fancies on this lively mattress kept pace with the skipping of the fleas. I thought of everything, from the way Brother O. G. S. canted his Senior Deacon's rod, and broke a chandelier over my head one night, to the circumstance of 600 men leaving here, on a certain occasion (Judges 18), and going a hundred miles north, plundering and insulting the people as they went, assaulting an unarmed town, and butchering everybody in it. My muleteer demanded, on arrival, five francs. As I had paid his employer everything in advance, I refused, and the fellow actually *howled* around the entrance to that *Locanda* all night. He ate nothing, gave his horse nothing, but simply swore and yelled until daybreak. He out-screamed the hyenas and jackals who made the noise in the graveyards out of town. In the morning my cavalier gave him a thrashing, took my carpetbag upon his own saddle, and drove the scamp back to Joppa, where I trust he lives to repent of his sins. Whereupon we "looked to the east," and pursued our journey in peace and harmony.

Riding out of Ramleh, it was striking to mark the quick transition from the gabble of the town to the stillness of the country. There is no such thing as country life here in Palestine, every dwelling, without exception, being in a town or village.

Early on Sunday morning, May 3d (as early as five o'clock), I started for a ramble to Jerusalem, and arrived at 1 P.M. A road was being rapidly completed by the Pasha of Jerusalem. All the rocky passes had been opened. The steeper hills were ascended by serpentine ways. The streams were substantially bridged, and at the rate of progress thus going on, there would be a carriageway from Joppa to Jerusalem within a few weeks. Around the town of Ramleh, the olive-trees grow by thousands. The land is rich and black in excess. A neat fragment of arches remains to show what was formerly a grand structure. An immense wheat-field was on my right, with the ripening grain rank and luxuriant upon it. A party of thirteen sailors, from the English ships at Joppa, were ahead of me, as merry as a ten days' leave and a bottle of arrack apiece could make them.

My cavalier looms up grandly this morning. He is a negro, but of a fine type, small head, keen, expressive eyes, sits erect upon his saddle, his carbine lying before him and short-sword at his side. His splendid stallion curveting under him, he looks the very picture of an armed guard. Yet for all that, I would rather depend on myself in a difficulty, than half a dozen of him. These native cavaliers are considered arrant cowards at best, strong as they look to the unsophisticated howadjee.

Advancing eastward, the mountains of Dan present their graceful outlines quite distinctly. Directly before me is a cliff in the heights, through which the turnpike passes. I have now an ascent to make of nearly 2,600 feet, "going up to Jerusalem." The soil is about eighteen inches deep, resting upon a foundation of gravel. The plants and flowers are as yesterday, except that the common American "dog fennel" which I learned to hate so bitterly in Mississippi (1841-'50), begins to abound, and a miserable interloper it is, wherever found. The solemn roar of the donkey is heard from the villages on the hillsides. Mellowed by the distance, even that Plutonian bray (in the most minor of keys) sounds tuneful. The camels browsing on the plains look like immense ostriches, as their long necks reach hither and thither in search of food. The wind makes mournful refrain through the insulators on the telegraph poles, just as it does along our wires at home. The swallows dart swiftly under my horse's feet, to catch the insects as we start them up.

At 6.30 A.M. I reach the town of Kahob, on the left, only a cluster of dirty mud-huts. Thus far, I have never seen a dwelling-place in all Palestine, outside of a town or village. Here now is a patch of tobacco, the plants being six or eight inches high, and looking dwarfish to the eye of a Kentuckian. An elegant chapter from some costly marble column lies on the ground and another one of the same class a little further on. A well of water, with a heavy stone resting on it, recalls many Scriptural allusions. The fig trees are uncommonly large and luxuriant. Three little backsheesh-seekers are standing by the roadside, with the totality of one shirt to the three, and that a dilapidated one.

At 7.45 A.M. I reach Latroon, the traditional home of the penitent thief, referred to in *Dies Iræ,* thus:

> "Et Latronum ex audisti,
> Mihi quoque spem dedisti,"

—As thou didst listen to the thief on the cross, so also give me nope.

I fear, however, that the *thieves* who live hereabouts so numerously at the present day are anything but "penitent." Here I overtake nine British sailors, who started yesterday to *walk* from Joppa to Jerusalem. These brave mariners are *stranded* here, high and dry, on a lee-shore. Their only money is *half-sovereigns,* and the whole nine of them cannot muster half an Arabic word. So I lend them a lot of small change to buy coffee with, instruct them graciously in the secrets of Turkish currency, and pass on. Two days afterwards, I met them in the streets of Jerusalem, and they paid me back my loan with thanks and British honor. Rising the hill east of Latroon, a romantic valley opens before me; well watered and, in its way, excelling anything I have seen in the country. What a paradise this *Vale of Avoca* would make under American cultivation! At its eastern extremity is a large and welcome spring of water, called in this country an *ain,* or *eye.* At 9 A.M., stopped for refreshments at a native khan. This Arabic style of "eating-house" is simple but effective. The chap who keeps this hotel (I call it *Khan Caroob*) found a natural cave to begin with. At right angles with that, he built of the abundant native stone a room twelve feet square. From the boughs of an ancient carob-tree, he laid poles across to his wall, covered them with bushes, and behold *Khan Caroob* complete—as complete as the St. Nicholas itself. Here all day he retails coffee, hardboiled eggs, and arrack, to passers-by. His terms are more liberal than at the first-class American hotels; for I only paid him three piastres (twelve cents) for several cups of coffee, and an assortment of "sundries" for self and cavalier. His eggs, I would remark, are boiled harder than I thought hens'-eggs capable of.

The vile drink which turns pale (white) when you pour water into it, is called *arrack,* from the word *arraga,* "to sweat." It is the whiskey of the Holy Land—well named *sweat-whiskey!* I can testify to perspiration following the drinking of the glass-full. It makes me sweat now to recall the miserable sensations produced by *arrack.*

As I sat on the cushions of Khan Caroob, I could hear, at the distance perhaps of several miles, the sorrowful cry of the females in some funeral ceremony. They keep the breath at the top of the voice as long as they can stand it without suffocation, and then and the shriek with a low sob. Here, too, I saw a native asleep, his head on a pillow made by heaping up small stones and laying his arba over them, like Jacob at Bethel.

Passing into the hill-country, the numerous little villages on the low swells of ground, with their whitewashed walls and white, flat roofs, look like a parcel of ivory dice scattered here and there over the country. And now the road begins in good earnest to ascend the hills of Dan. For four hours I ride along the really good way which the Pasha is macadamizing, until the crest is reached, near Jerusalem. At 11.05 A.M. I am opposite the romantic and well-known town of Abou Ghosh, formerly a celebrated robber upon these hills, of whose Masonic qualities I shall speak in another chapter. He was a sort of king in Syria, a customhouse extortioner of the "general order" system, who made levies upon all persons passing by his *Grape-town,* old Kirjath-Jearim. He was the Great Sheikh of the children of Beni Hassan, and they owned no other lord. In these still and sterile mountains, he struck more than a gold mine in "sitting at the receipt of custom." I have always had a high appreciation of his character.

At 11.35 a large vineyard, the only one I have seen, where the trunks of vines are so large that, like trees, they *hold up their own boughs and foliage.* At 12.30, a charming valley. I observe here a structure of massive stones, presenting the far-famed Hebraico-Phœnician bevel, so attractive to a Freemason's eye. At 1.10 P.M. (it being about 5 A.M. at my Kentucky home), I reach the crest of the hill, and shortly afterwards sight "the Holy City."

At *Khan Caroob* I fell in with Captain Edward Gladstone, attached to the British ship *Lord Clyde,* now at Joppa, and a member of Phœnix Lodge, Portsmouth, England. His companionship over these weary hills of Dan and Benjamin made the way agreeable. Afterwards we frequently consorted together under the mystical level.

It is impossible for a person of feeling to look over the desolate hills that surround Jerusalem without sorrowful emotions. Every other sentiment merges into pity and sympathy as the traveler approaches the Holy City. A stillness like that of the grave pervades the land. You meet and pass the wayfarer, native and foreigner, without the exchange of a syllable, and enter the gate of the city with a sensation of awe, as though you were about to visit a resting-place of the dead.

After my return home, an intelligent lady asked me, in the hearing of a congregation, "How does a person feel upon the first view of Jerusalem?" Others may propound the same inquiry. A sentiment almost feverish is aroused in the minds of some in anticipation of this. Crossing the broad Atlantic,—dashing over the iron-way (*chemin de fer,* as the French style the railroad, the *iron-road*),— plowing the blue waters of the Mediterranean,— climbing the hills of Benjamin,—all the time drawing nearer, the excitement increases, and I have known women, yes, and strong men, to pause, to calm themselves ere they surmount the last tumulus that hides from them the long-desired view. Others, as if anxious to have it over, gallop up that eminence, and so hasten the fulfillment of their joy. The reader will not fail to recall the story of the much-overrated Richard of England. When he had left his camp at Ajalon and reached Mizpeh, six miles northwest of Zion, his guide informed him the city was in sight. At this, the king covered his face with his mailed hands and cried out in French, "Ah, Lord God, let me never see Jerusalem unless I am also to enter it!" I may as well remark here that he never *did* enter it.

My first view was more prosaic. I was extremely weary with my ride from Ramleh. It was past noon of May 3, 1868, an extremely sultry day. Excessive fatigue is a sad destroyer of romance. Besides this, I had been already more than two months in Palestine and Syria, and the keen edge of novelty was blunted. Certainly, I felt a solemn impression,—a gratitude to God that, after forty years of earnest desire, I was so near the goal of my search; but it was mingled with a strange sentiment of doubt and mistrust as to whether I should really set foot within the courts of the city.

Afterwards I spent an hour among my books, gathering in the records of those travelers who have more feelingly described their sentiments as they stood where, on that auspicious day, I was privileged to stand, and I copy some for my readers. Enough will be found to show the character of the impressions made upon susceptible minds, on approaching a place above all others famed in the records of history—human and divine.

Bunyan, in his inimitable parable, gives the keynote to these sentiments. While his pilgrims were yet upon the Delectable Mountains, the shepherds said to one another, "Let us now show them the gates of the Celestial City, if they have skill to look through our perspective-glass!" The pilgrims lovingly accepted the invitation. So "they led them to a hill called Clear, and gave them their glass to look. Then they essayed to look, but the remembrance of that last thing the shepherds had showed them (that is, the By-way to Hell) made their hands shake, by means of which impediment they *could not look steadily* through the glass. Yet they thought they saw something like the Gate, and also some of the glory of the place." Is not this exceedingly good reading? Suppose Bunyan had really visited Jerusalem and the Jordan,—what descriptions he could have given us!

And again: When the pilgrims were got over the Enchanted Ground, and, entering into the country of Beulah, were within sight of the city they were aspiring to, there met them here some of the inhabitants thereof; "for in this land the Shining Ones commonly walked, because it was on the borders of Heaven!"

But to quote from some of our more literal travelers:

"Jerusalem, the central palatial city, bursts out from the mountains that encircle it, apparently but a few rods off. But the rods are miles. The first view is sublime, and your memory is taxed with peopling it again. As I near the gate of Solomon, contemplation quickens the reverential awe with which I gaze upon the birthplace of our Savior and of his religion."—*Train.*

"The guides pointed out a succession of bluish-gray hills, and a long, low line of wall, surmounted by a dome which stood out against the sky. *Behold Jerusalem!* Instinctively every one drew his bridle-rein and paused. The country around was arid, silent, solitary. In face of Calvary, nature itself stood still. Mournful, yet beautiful to the Christian heart must Jerusalem ever be."—*Herbert.*

"A sudden view of swelling domes and towering minarets rising dimly in the distance, causes us to check our horses and raise our hearts and voices gratefully to God. While we gaze upon Jerusalem, as she sits aloft begirt with battlements, some of the party falls in the dust silently breathing their fullness of joy. It is an era in our lives never to be forgotten."—*Miss Barclay.*

"A few moments brought us to the west of the hill Scopus. In the first sight of Jerusalem there is a thrill of interest that is scarce weakened by repetition, and we can only pity the man who is not, for the moment, at least, imbued with the pilgrim spirit, and does not feel the sight to be one of the privileges of his life. Enshrined in the depths of a Christian's affections, linked with every feeling of faith and hope, if I forget thee, O Jerusalem, let my right hand forget her cunning!"—*Tristam.*

"Our muleteer called out with a loud voice, *'Jerusalem, Jerusalem!'*

This was repeated by each of us with great joy. We halted for some time and gazed upon the memorable city. These lines occurred to memory:

> 'The Holy City lifted high her towers,
> And higher yet the glorious Temple reared;
> The pile far off appearing like a mount
> Of alabaster, topped with golden spires.'

"So excited were we with the gaze that it was long before we were sufficiently composed to resume our journey."—*Ward.*

"A glimpse of a hill whose slopes are dotted with olive-trees, whose summit is crowned with a cluster of buildings. *'The Mount of Olives!'* we exclaimed, and so it was. A moment after, advancing, we saw domes and minarets, and then the massive walls and gates of the city. Oh, sacred hour! oh, moment never to be forgotten! oh, blessed memorial day that our eyes actually rested upon Jerusalem! What wonderful associations are awakened! what powerful and tearful emotions thrilled my heart! Such a moment! such soul-thoughts and feelings cannot be described. I dismounted, and seating myself on an old wall, with the sacred objects before me, read portions of the Psalms and the New Testament that refer so beautifully, tenderly, and gloriously to the city of Mount Zion and of God."—*Phelps.*

"From the mountain-pass above the plain beyond Bireh we rode out on a wide waste of whitish rocks, and beheld in the distance a walled city, dim in the shades of the coming night."—*Browne.*

"I forgot my fatigue, quickened my pace, and was soon on the hill-top. Pausing to look round me, I required no guide to point out the long, low line of battlemented wall, with a few domes and minarets rising above it, crowning the table-land,—a hill which stood in the midst of hills. I knew I was looking upon Jerusalem, built as a city, and the mountains round about her. Though I have seen Jerusalem under more beautiful aspects and from more favorable points of view, the first sight had its particular charm."—*Miss Rogers.*

"Jerusalem was before our view. We stood still in solemn silence; again went forward, again stood still and gazed. Our feelings were so overpowering that we could neither understand them nor give them expression. 'I am strangely disappointed,' said my companion, yet there is something in the sight strangely affecting."—*John Wilson.*

"*El Khuds,* said Mahmoud, spurring his horse forward. *Gerusalemma,* murmured an old Italian, folding his hands in prayer, *Hegiopolis,* said a lusty Greek beggar by my side. As for me, I gazed upon the bright city, that sprung like magic from the bosom of the hills, as one in a dream, and before I followed on, I placed a stone upon the mounds to mark the hour when first my eyes gazed on the city of our Lord. Men in every tongue babbled some favorite scrap, treasured up for years to be sung or spoken, as a beloved song that dying men request to hear at their bedsides in the last supreme moments of life. This to us here, beneath the brilliant and uncheckered sunshine, the pale, distorted rocky wastes beneath, the bald and desolate plain in front, in sight of Olivet and Zion,—this was as natural as prayer."—*N. N. Leech.*

"The point gained, the Holy City lay fair and peaceful before our enraptured eyes. Not in the wild forests of the western world, not among the huge works of Egyptian art, not on the snow-clad peaks of romantic Switzerland, had any scene so riveted our gaze. Heaven threw its shekinah upon the scene, and clothed the hill of Zion with a robe of glory. The sweetest memories hovered, like fairest angels, over the towers of Salem; past, present, and future all concentrated in the oracle of God. Zion, Moriah, Olivet, rise as beacons to the wearied soul, and all are bathed in the radiance of the Cross. The scene was unspeakably grand. Our overflowing hearts sent forth their swollen streams of feeling in vocal rejoicing."—*El Mukattem.*

"That place! it is Jerusalem. What a thrill went through the heart! And have we seen Jerusalem at last! We ceased to speak, smitten dumb by a feeling of which I had never experienced the like, nor ever expect to know again. Wonder, solemnity, joy, sadness, all were mingled together. Yet above these, or at least with these, rose up *affection:* affection as tender and profound as that with which one regards the city of his birth, his father's resting-place, his children's home. Nationality seemed for a moment lost in something greater than itself. Jerusalem has a thousand objects of interest, and it was the sudden uprising of these in one glorious cloud that so fixed the eye and absorbed the mind. The city seemed to possess magnetic power. We felt drawn toward it, eager to stand within its gates."—*Bonar.*

Scores of such extracts, swelling into a volume, might be made. For my own part, I simply sung three or four *Jerusalem* songs, read a dozen Jerusalem chapters, and heartily praised God.

If there was any romance in my own associations with Jerusalem, it was connected with the solemn moment when, looking back from Mount Scopus, as the sun began to descend down the passes of Beth-boron, I took my *farewell view* of its battlements and towers, two

weeks afterwards. These thoughts, in due time, ran out into verse,
as follows:

> Farewell, Jerusalem;—thy sun bends low,
> And warns me with his parting beams to go:
> *One more fond look;*—never again to me
> On Moab's summit shall his *rising* be;
> Never on flowery Sharon's westward plain
> His *sunset*-visage greet my eyes again;
> Though other suns may lighten up my shore,
> Zion, *thy sun* shall gladden me no more!
>
> Farewell, blest city;—all thy sacred hills,
> Thy winding valleys, thy historic rills,
> Thy sepulchers that pierce the mountain's side,
> Thy fragrant gardens 'neath Siloam's side,
> With me I bear, by loving fancy's aid,
> Inscribed in images that cannot fade:
> Memory may forfeit many a precious gem,
> But never *thee*, thou best Jerusalem.
>
> Farewell, thou Mount beloved; can it be
> The gracious KING in wrath abandoned thee?
> There was no remedy: such clouds of sin
> Polluted all thy courts, without, within,
> That the fierce fire of vengeance long withheld
> Kindled at last; His loving heart was steeled:
> Then up those hills there surged such floods of flam
> They left thee but "a by-word and a name."
>
> Farewell! above the skies eternal wait
> Glories transcending far thy best estate;
> There gates and walls with precious jewels dressed
> And streets of gold allure the happy guest;
> There flows the river and there grows the tree—
> Water of life and endless fruits for me;
> And God hath given to the place *thy name,*
> The Holy City,—NEW JERUSALEM!

THE CLAY GROUND BETWEEN SUCCOTH AND ZARTHAN.

DIVISION SEVENTH.—THE CLAY-GROUND.

"I will go; peradventure the LORD will come to meet me: and whatsoever He sheweth me I will tell thee. And he went.'—Numbers 23:3

That hour of deep abasement and of shame
To Him the brightest of His life became
The tears of penitence His heart had spent,
The deep confession which to heaven He sent,
The vow of restitution, humbly given,
Brought to His soul a rich reward from heaven—
Not to approve the fraud His hand did trace,
But to exalt the gift of goodness and of grace.

Howe'er unworthy and how much forlorn,
From home an alien and from comforts shorn,
Oppressed with grief and chastened by the rod,
Abandoned, as he feared, of hope and God,
In vision bright before His inner eye
A glorious vista opens in the sky—
Troops of angelic forms now fill the air,
They bend from heaven to earth in grace divinely fair

Between two distant worlds a medium stands,
The space is crowded by angelic bands;
Rank above rank the glorious forms are seen,
Each face now lit by heaven's resplendent sheen;
And from the farthest point of that long line
Jehovah's face in rays benignant shine;
Descending gently and ascending, they
Bear messages of peace until the break of day.

CHAPTER XIX.

BETWEEN SUCCOTH AND ZARTHAN.

T HE sixth of the seven Grand Masonic Localities recognized in the present volume, is the Clay-Ground between Succoth and Zarthan (or Zeredathah). The allusions to these in the Masonic lectures are positive, though brief. In describing the brazen pillars and sacred vessels of the Temple, the following is the text: "In the plain of Jordan did the king cast them, in the clay-ground between Succoth and Zarthan" (1 Kings 7:46). "In the plain of Jordan did the king cast them, in the clay-ground between Succoth and Zeredathah" (2 Chronicles 4:17). The site of Succoth, now termed Seikoot, is, in a direct line, about forty-five miles northeast of Jerusalem, and "in the plain of Jordan," as described.

It was not in my power to visit the locality now under description. The extreme heat of the Jordan valley in the middle of May, the want even of a horse-track to that unfrequented quarter of Palestine, and, above all, the fearful thickets of thorns that covered the whole valley, which made it almost as impassable to a horseman, without a party to clear the way, as a Mississippi canebrake—these formed a body of reasons for my failure in this direction. But I journeyed that way as far as any passable road was found opened, and the present chapter shall give an account of what lies along the path.

A singular fact came to light under the investigations of my assistant at Jerusalem. He discovered that the jewelers of that city, at the present day, use a particular species of *brown, arenaceous clay* in making moulds for casting small pieces in brass, etc. Inquiring whence this clay comes, they reply, "From *Seikoot,* about two days' journey northeast of Jerusalem." Here then is a satisfactory reply to the question, Where was the "clay-ground" of Hiram's foundries? It is the best matrix-clay existing within reach of Hiram Abif, and it is found only in "the clay-ground between Succoth and Zeredathah;" and considerable as was the distance, and extremely inconvenient as was the locality, so important did that master-workman deem it, to secure a sharp and perfect mould for his castings, that, as the Biblical record informs us, he established his furnaces there. I secured two hundred weight of this clay of Seikoot for my patrons, and in addition caused 500 cigarette holders to be made of it for further distribution.

I left the city of Jerusalem by the Damascus gate, at 2 P.M., May 14, 1868, after exchanging valedictories with my acquaintances there. These were but a *few*, for I had come to Jerusalem with a far different purpose from that of forming the acquaintance of men and women. My desire was to shake hands with *David;* to greet *Solomon* face to face; to exchange grips with *Zerubbabel* and *Nehemiah;* to bow reverently under the words of *Jesus;* to walk with *Titus* and *Josephus* around the Roman lines of circumvallation; to share in the last great assault of Godfrey and Tancred; in short, to identify myself as much as possible with *the past.* Men and women in Jerusalem are no better than men and women in Pumpkinville; and the traveler who consumes his precious morning hours or evenings in social conference, is casting away, lightly, what thousands of the pious and zealous of his countrymen would give largely to enjoy.

So I had made but few acquaintances in Jerusalem, and after shaking hands with the good old Brother Peterman (Prussian Consul, made a Mason in 1828), and Brother Charles Warren, R.E., and Mr. Johnson, the American Vice-Consul (a most estimable young gentleman), and my landlord of the Prussian Hotel, I had few others to say "good-bye" to, but rode with a light heart down the *Via Dolorosa* (so called, but no more the *Via Dolorosa* of Christ's day than the *top* of a tree is its *root*), and up the Tyropœan or Damascus street to the old Damascus gate, in whose quaint "winding stairs" I had a few days before cut the *Square and Compass* so deeply that the city may be captured another seventeen times before it fades out So I went out into the open country. My last impressions of Jerusalem were like my first, viz., that the city is horribly *misgoverned;* for my servant Hassan, lingering twenty steps behind me, was incontinently seized by the Turkish soldiers who guard the gate, and by the time I got back to his rescue, one red-legged Zouave was holding his horse by the bridle, and another was unstrapping my pack of blankets, while a third was abusing the terrified Arab in the foulest

19

vernacular. At my approach they released him, and at my orders he rode on, while I handed one of the soldiers a *backsheesh* or fee, It was such a small sum (about half a piastre, or two cents), that I presume the whole party united in cursing me by *Allah* for my meanness; but, as my knowledge of the Arabic tongue does not extend to its *profanity,* and I had no call to give the rascals anything at all, I rode briskly after my party, and so shook the dust of Jerusalem from my feet.

Taking the lead, as I did in all pilgrimage through the Holy Land, I passed through the piles of rubbish that barricade the northern side of Jerusalem; the enormous quarries which have turned one-half the hill *Bezetha* into building materials; under the great olives that tell their Masonic story of "the oil of joy" there, from generation to generation; past the old building with an architectural ornament in the south wall (which ornament I intend some day to procure for my own museum); past the hill on the right, wherein is excavated the wonderful "Tomb of the Kings," and so through the suburbs of Jerusalem.

On the hill of Scopus, I pause to catch the last and best view of Jerusalem. It *is* by all odds the best view. From this, David, Shishak, Pompey, Titus, the Crusaders, had gazed on the devoted city. A day or two before, I had ridden around this hill, and scanned the modern city from the best points. The only drawback to the pleasure afforded in my parting glance, is the vile *congeries* of buildings stuck up on the rising ground northwest of the city, and called the *Russian Convent*. I could not help wishing, "Oh, for one hour of Omar, of Titus, of Nebuchadnezzar, of *any* devastator of Jerusalem, to earn immortal praise by blowing that miserable structure to the winds!" This was my *first* thought as I approached Jerusalem from Joppa; it was also my *last* as I left Jerusalem for Bethel.

No, *not the last*. One more long, comprehensive gaze from the heights of Scopus. See, all around me, on every protuberance of rock, those little piles of pebbles—three, five, seven, nine, eleven, or more—built up by the hands of pilgrims, who, like me, had come from distant lands to view "the City of the Great King," and from the hill-top caught their first or last view of Jerusalem. These are *mnemonics* of Jerusalem. They are like the altar which Jacob built at Bethel, memorials of gratitude to God in view of the accomplishment of a pious design. Standing among them, while my horse stamps, impatient to pursue his way, I look down upon that Jerusalem which I may never see again. It is all there; *Moriah,* with its classical Dome of the Rock and other edifices; the *Damascus Gate,* one of the few architectural remains of the time of Solomon; the hypothetical *Church of the Holy Sepulcher;* the *Tower of Hippicus* on Mount Sion, also the Armenian Convent and the Tomb of David beyond; the encircling hills of *Olivet,* of *Corruption,* of *Evil Counsel,* of *Mizpeh,* and the noted places, *Gethsemane, Siloam, En-rogel,* etc., nestling at their feet; the plain of *Rephaim* in the south; the mountains of *Moab* in the extreme southeast, with the sea of *Sodom* gleaming at their base; more to the left, the long range of *Gilead* and *Bashan* terminated, I know (although I cannot see it from here), by *Hermon,* noblest of sacred hills—is there in all the world such a historical *tout ensemble* as this? "If I forget thee, O Jerusalem, let my right hand forget her cunning; if I do not remember thee, let my tongue cleave to the roof of my mouth!"

In after-years, amid the views, pleasant or painful, that meet my aged eyes, will this vision of Jerusalem ever fade away? Eighteen centuries ago, there was a man of nearly fivescore years, an exile upon the Island of Patmos, banished forever from his loved Galilee and Jerusalem, who sat "in the spirit on the Lord's day," and recalled *his* memories of Jerusalem. Oh, but they were enshrined with a halo of glory! I shall read them:

"I, John, saw the Holy City, New Jerusalem coming down from God out of heaven, prepared as a bride adorned for her husband.

"And he (one of the seven angels which had the seven vials full of the seven last plagues) carried me away in the spirit to a great and high mountain (it might have been this hill of Scopus, which, relatively to the city below, is both *great* and *high;* or possibly Olivet, half a mile south of this, and which is but a continuation of Scopus), and showed me that great city, the Holy Jerusalem, descending out of heaven from God,

"Having the glory of God; and her light was like unto a stone most precious, even like a jasper stone, clear as crystal.

"And I saw no temple therein; for the Lord God Almighty and the Lamb are the temple of it."—Revelation 21.

Envy me, dear reader, the privilege of perusing this sublime and inspired description of Jerusalem while I pause upon the hill of Scopus. Our ancient Grand Master, St. John, could not have made a greater distinction in his Masonic lectures between operative and speculative Masonry, than he has done in his apocalyptic book between Jerusalem *real,* and Jerusalem *figurative.*

Forward now, the North Star for my guide for twelve days. For ward to Bethel, and Shechem, and Nazareth, and Tiberias, and Lebanon, and—home. Push on, my bounding steed, and seek with me "fresh fields and pastures new." But who is this sad specimen of humanity that, like myself, is taking his last view of Jerusalem on Mount Scopus? It is a Hebrew, a Sephardine Jew, an exile in the land of his fathers. Is it fancy, or do I hear him murmuring in the liturgy of his sect, "Oh may our Father in his infinite mercy compassionate his orphans and gather his dispersed to the pure land! For He is high and exalted; He bringeth down and raiseth up. He woundeth and He healeth, killeth and restoreth to life. Oh Lord return to thy city; build up thine holy oracle; dwell in thine house, and gather thy scattered flock! Oh Thou, who renewest the months, collect the saints, both men and women, to the erected city! Oh, may this month be renewed for good! and may it please God, who is mighty in works, thus to command!" It would be indeed a hard heart that could refuse to whisper *Amen: So mote it be.*

Forward again. Here are memorials of the world's "road-builders," *the Romans,* in this long stretch of ground, laid down with squared stones so firmly that, although the drift of sixteen centuries has worn their surfaces into ridges, they lie as firmly in their beds as when the subjugated peoples laid them here under the edge of the Roman steel. I have learned to distinguish these Roman roads. Around the Bay of Junia, near Gebal; between Beirut and Sidon; at the Nahr-el-Kelb; between Sidon and Tyre, and elsewhere, their solid masonry has spoken of "the eternity of Rome," and the magnificence of thought that caused all the highways of earth to concentrate in the seven-hilled city of Romulus.

And here I must be very near "the Stone Ezel," so named in 1 Samuel 20:19, and embodied in the degree of *Secret Monitor.* Among the good brothers and fellows of the last generation, much attention was given to the degree of *Secret Monitor,* or David and Jonathan.* It is easy to prove that side degrees of that nature were more highly valued then, than they are now. Perhaps the reason is, our old brethren were not so rich in "regular degrees;" (the 33 of the Scotch Rite; the 96 of the Memphis Rite; the 155 of the Sidonian Rite; the 299 of the Children of Hatipha; and the various other congeries of "ancient and adopted," "ancient and primitive,"

---

* A feeling of old-time friendship prompts me to record that my first acquaintance with that true man and Mason, Elisha D. Cook, was made through this degree.

"ancient and honorable," and "antique and desirable" systems)—I say they were not so rich in these as we of this blessed generation.

And the *Secret Monitor* is really worthy the praise formerly awarded it. Before the Odd-Fellows borrowed it ("the wise call it *convey*"), and when it was conferred with dignity, eloquence, and Masonic zeal, the impressions made by its communication were novel, sound, and good. I have listened to its lectures as they fell from the venerable patriarchs of the craft, and should find it difficult to suggest anything better in the rituals of the Masonic institution.

Passing north ward from Jerusalem to Bethel, the locality of "the Stone Ezel," which is connected with the history of the *Secret Monitor,* comes under my observation. Shall I describe the locality and its surroundings? It is a short distance south of "Gibeah of Saul," as the writer of 1 Samuel 11:4, terms it, and not more than five miles north of Jerusalem. Gibeah is now called in the native parlance "the Hill of Beans" (*Tell-el-Ful*). It is a beautiful rise, cone-shaped, and commands a most interesting view. Three miles to the southeast is Anathoth (Anata), the birthplace of lugubrious Jeremiah. At the same distance northwest the tower representing "Geba of Benjamin" is visible, near which is the pass of Michmash, the place of Jonathan's greatest exploit (1 Samuel 14.). The rocks Bozez and Seneh, it is thought, may still be traced out in this pass, although I turned too much to the right to see them. Mizpeh, now called Neby Samuel, towers in the west some six hundred feet above the surrounding plain, marking one of the oldest *watchtowers* in Palestine. For a long period Mizpeh was the national rendezvous, where the tribes met to worship, to declare war and peace, and to choose their king, It must not be confused with the Mizpah in Mount Gilead, east of the Jordan, so memorable in the history of Jephthah.

Few places fill so large a space in Bible history as this Gibeah, or Hill of Beans, on which I stand while contemplating the Masonic and Biblical account of the *Secret Monitor,* but I can only refer the reader to the proper portions of Scripture for a full explication. Our Rock *Ezel* stands at the foot of the hill between Gibeah and Jerusalem, and we will turn our attention chiefly to that. It calls up memories of two of the heroes of the first kingdom of Israel, Jonathan and David.

Jonathan first appears on the scene of action some time after his father's accession to the throne. He was then about thirty years of age, and was regarded as the heir to the kingdom. Like his father, he was a man of great strength and activity—"strong as a lion and swift as an eagle"—and excelled in those war-like arts which made his tribe, *the Benjamites,* so famous, viz., archery and slinging; his bow, particularly, was never laid aside. As his father's heir, he was always present at the royal meals, and his constant companion and confidant. During the king's frenzy, he was usually pacified by Jonathan's voice, and the attachment between father and son was close. But the character of Jonathan was peculiarly amiable and susceptible of warm friendship. This is seen in the fight at Michmash (1 Samuel 14.), when his armor-bearer says to him in fraternal words: "Behold I am with thee: as *thy* heart is *my* heart."

David first appears upon the scene of action when Samuel visited Bethlehem under the divine impulse, to anoint one of the sons of Jesse as king in the place of Saul, whom God had rejected. He was fair of sight, comely, goodly, short of stature, well made, and of immense strength and agility. In swiftness and activity, he was like a wild gazelle, and his arms were strong enough to break a bow of steel. In his genius for music and poetry, he was never excelled by Jew or Gentile. In the battle of the valley of Elah, David again appears, this time as the destroyer of the giant Goliath. Saul now commanded his attendance at court, and the acquaintance between him and Jonathan began; a romantic friendship which bound the two youths to the end of their lives. It is the first Biblical instance of a romantic friendship such as was afterwards common in Greece and has been since in Christendom; such as the ties of Freemasonry inculcate. This friendship was confirmed, after the manner of the time, by a solemn compact, often repeated. Jonathan, the heir to the Jewish kingdom, gave David as a pledge his royal mantle, his sword, his girdle, and his famous bow (1 Samuel 18:4). He twice interceded with the king for David's life, and the first time with success. Were not our Masonic brethren of the last generation justified, then, in their adoption of this friendship between David and Jonathan as the finest Biblical type of Masonic attachment? "The soul of Jonathan was knit with the soul of David, and David loved him as his own soul;" "Jonathan delighted much in David." These sentiments have never been surpassed in pathos by the best works of fiction.

David's life, as remarked above, was twice in great peril through the insane hatred of Saul, who had spoken to Jonathan and to all his servants "that they should kill David." On the first occasion

David was advised by his friend "to take heed to himself until the morning; to abide in a secret place; and to hide himself." This was "the whispering good counsel in the ear of a brother," of which the Masonic lectures speak. Furthermore, Jonathan proffered to go with his father to the field south of Gibeah, in which "the stone Ezel" lay, and commune with him there as to his intentions concerning David. This conference terminated favorably. Jonathan's plea of David's innocence and military services was effectual, and the king swore, "As the Lord liveth, David shall not be slain," where-upon David returned to court, and all was well again.

Upon the second occasion Saul endeavored to kill David with a javelin, whereupon he fled to Samuel at Naioth, and from thence, being personally pursued by the king, he again sought the protection of Jonathan, saying, "Truly as the Lord liveth, and as thy soul liveth, there is but a step between me and death." At this point the circumstances forming the degree of *Secret Monitor* more particularly come in. Let the reader look up the inspired narrative in 1 Samuel 20.

With passionate embraces and tears they parted. The two friends met again, and for the third time renewed their covenant. This was some time afterwards, when Saul was hunting David in the far-distant forest of Ziph.

They met no more. David went into exile with his family and friends, among the Philistines. Saul strove against the flood of evils that came over him in his latter days, the death of Samuel, the loss of the divine favor, and the growing power of the Philistines, emboldened by the exile of David. At last a national crisis occurred. The Philistines came and pitched in the plains around Shunem, where I passed the night of May 16. Saul gathered all Israel together, and pitched in Mount Gilboa, about six miles eastward. The next day the battle was joined on the slopes of Israel, and all Israel was smitten. Jonathan and two of his brothers were slain. Saul, being "sore wounded of the archers," committed suicide. The third day afterwards, tidings of this severe reverse were brought to David then at Ziklag, who uttered the Threnody, wherein he says:

"How are the mighty fallen in the midst of the battle! Oh Jonathan, you were slain in thine high places.

"I am distressed for thee, my brother Jonathan; very pleasant hast thou been unto me; thy love to me was wonderful, passing the love of woman.

"How are the mighty fallen and the weapons of war perished!"

The story of the *Secret Monitor* will not be complete if we omit that of Mephibosheth, only son of Jonathan. At the time of the death of his father and grandfather on Mount Gilboa, he was an infant of five years. In the hurry of flight, he was dropped by his nurse and lamed in his feet. He was carried into the mountains of Gilead, where he grew up to manhood. King David, being by this time firmly settled upon the throne, sent for him in pursuance of his early covenant with Jonathan, made him a daily guest at the royal table, and settled upon him all the property of his grandfather, King Saul. Thus, the brotherly covenant was maintained, and the sentiments of gratitude and honor firmly established. This, then, is "the Stone Ezel," and here the degree of *Secret Monitor* belongs. By special request, I conferred this degree upon two occasions on the craft at Jerusalem, and afterwards in Beirut, each time with marked effect. The degree is so highly valued in America that *Ezel Lodge,* No. 175, is seen on the Alabama register, and other allusions to it are found in our lodge nomenclature.

Forward again; and here is the fork of the way, the left hand going by Gibeon through the passes of Beth-horon, down toward Joppa; the right going northward. Yonder is the site of ancient Gibeon Let me at this point read the inspired story from the tenth chapter of Joshua:

"And the men of Gibeon sent unto Joshua to the camp at Gilgal.' That was down yonder on my right, about twenty miles, as the road runs. The message was:

"Slack not thy hands from thy servants. Come up to us quickly, and save us and help us." For the king of Jerusalem had joined forces with four other kings, and had besieged Gibeon, whose people were the allies of Joshua, and had threatened their total destruction. Around these green slopes, where the ripening barley shows so yellow this afternoon, was their encampment, and this was about the season of the year.

"So Joshua ascended from Gilgal, he and all the people of war with him, and all the mighty men of valor. He came up suddenly, and went up from Gilgal all night." It was probably at the hour before sunrise, that hour when deep sleep is deepest, and a panic is the most contagious, and the sword hangs heavily in man's hand, that the "sons of the Lion" came suddenly up this hollow to the right (this *Wady Suweinat,* as the natives term it, which opens out near Jericho at Gilgal), and fell, with a great shout, upon the allied kings and their hosts. What a discomfiture! The soldiers of Adonizedec were cut off from returning to Jerusalem, and driven, with the rest of their comrades, northward and westward by the upper pass of Beth-horon. Followed by the shouting and invincible Israelites, their headlong flight was precipitated down the terrible steeps of Lower Beth-horon, and so into the plains of Philistia. And as they ran, "the Lord cast down great stones from heaven upon them; and there were more which died with hailstones than they whom the children of Israel slew with the sword."

I reached the village of Beeroth in three hours. The road runs along the flat watershed of the country, the valleys descending from it toward the Jordan on the *east,* and the Plains of Sharon on the *west.* The way is paved with sacred memories. The history of the wanderer who sought a night's shelter at Gibeah (Judges 19) embodies much of the geography of this region. Samuel and Saul, David and Jonathan, have stamped their names upon these great stones as with an "iron pen and lead, in the rock forever."

At Beeroth, I took a cool draught out of my gum-elastic cup, from the time-honored fountain, with its cupola roof, at which, according to a rational tradition, the parents of Jesus first missed their little boy. Let me read from a record more reliable than tradition:

"Supposing him to have been in the company, they went a day's journey; and they sought him among their kinsfolk and acquaintance.

"And when they found him not, they turned back again to Jerusalem, seeking him.

"And it came to pass, that after three days they found him in the temple, sitting in the midst of the doctors, both hearing them and asking them questions" (Luke 2:44-46).

Though merely an Arab village, with houses built of the fragments of former massive edifices, yet Beeroth, or *Bireh,* as the natives term it, has the ruins of a once noble church of St. John, whose property the whole village was. The eastern apsis, with the north and south walls of enormous thickness, is quite perfect, and the architecture exhibits a curious transition from the Norman to the Early Pointed, or rather, perhaps, an attempt to engraft the Byzantine on

the latter. I did not explore particularly this relic, but derive from
Mr. Tristam these facts, and that the capitals of each pilaster are
distinct in their moldings, no two being alike. Mr. Newman
describes it more elaborately as a beautiful ruin, reminding him
of the ruined abbeys of Southern Scotland. The walls, the sacristy,
and the apsis are yet standing, and enclose an area one hundred
feet by sixty-three. The material is native limestone, like the
great wall around Moriah, and is well dressed. The finish of the
architecture is exquisite. The apses are crowned with beautiful
domed roofs, the partition walls ornamented with pilasters, the
capitals of which are well preserved. The sidewalls are divided
into sections by pilasters, and decorated with a rich cornice.

How poorly these Fellahin or Arab villagers compare with the
Bible picture—these miserable descendants of a noble race, with
their dirty shirts, brown faces, keen eyes, white teeth, bare legs,
and big slippers, who have descended the hill-paths to see if the
Howadjee has any *backsheesh* for them! But this Howadjee has no
backsheesh for such as they, and so he turns to the left and leads
his party again to the rising ground. On a peaked hill to the right,
a village upon its summit, I recognize the Orphah, or Ephraim, to
which Jesus returned after raising Lazarus (John 11: 54), and as
I couple the two places together, Beeroth and Ephraim, I
endeavor to unite in one train of thought all the incidents of that
adorable life that came between.

And here an altercation arises between my servant Hassan and
a native. The latter is certain I can find no place for the night's
lodging at Bethel, and advises, with all the gesticulation of a
pantomimist, that I go to *Ram Allah,* about a quarter of an hour
to the west, where the Latins have a convent in which strangers
are comfortably provided for. This being interpreted to me, I point
to the northeast and declare that *Bayteen* (as the word *Bethel* is
pronounced here) is the place of my destination that night, and
to *Bayteen* I shall go. To cut short debate, I start for Bayteen by
the only path I can discover trending in that direction, and my
party follow me. A pleasant hour is now spent, in which crowds
of Jews, returning from their annual visit to Safed and Tiberias
to Jerusalem, and herds of sheep and goats being led to their
evening repose, and rich fountains furnished with sculptured
drinking troughs, and crypts in the hillsides, once, doubtless,
costly and elaborate tombs, now filthy with all manner of
abominations—pleasantly   mingle   with   the   incidents

of great fields of wheat, barley, and beans, an occasional glimpse of Neby Samuel on the left, and the vast, unbroken range of Moab and Gilead on the east, and the pleasing uncertainty of where I am to sleep to-night. And so I approach Bethel.

If the historians are not at fault, it is now 3,629 years since the fugitive Jacob, the petted son of Isaac and Rebekah, came flying down this same pathway—for here pathways are never changed in their locality, they are *landmarks,* and therefore irremovable—flying as for his life. A long day's flight that erring man had! From Beersheba, past Hebron, past Bethlehem, past Jerusalem, and now to Bethel, was a summer-day's journey of fifty-three miles. An active Arab can make the distance today, if "the man of blood" be after him thirsting for his life; nevertheless, it is a long way over hills like these. Yet the "heir of the divine promise" accomplished it, and as I ride into this miserable village which represents ancient Bethel, let me read the inspired record:

"And Jacob went out from Beersheba, and went toward Haran.

"And he lighted upon a certain place and tarried there all night, because the sun was set; and he took of the stones of that place and put them for his pillows, and lay down in that place to sleep."— Genesis 28:10-11.

All this is in my mind; so as soon as arrangements have been made for my accommodation, with one of the village sheikhs (Bayteen has two, as miserable as the place is, the other one at present being at Jerusalem), I walk out to a rugged hill on the north side of the town, where the sight of some extremely large, rounded stones has attracted my attention. They were truly "stones of confusion and emptiness," huge limestone blocks, bleached white by the suns and rains of centuries, and leaving no traces, that I can see, of human handiwork. Between two of these I lie down, gathering some of the smaller stones for my pillow, and there endeavor to recall the dream of weary Jacob. Let me read it:

"And he dreamed, and behold, a ladder set up on the earth, and the top of it reached to heaven; and behold, the angels of God ascending and descending on it.

"And behold, the Lord stood above it, and said, I am the Lord God of Abraham thy father, and the God of Isaac; the land where on thou liest, to thee will I give it, and to thy seed.

"And thy seed shall be as the dust of the earth, and thou shalt spread abroad to the west, and to the east, and to the north, and to the south; and in thee and in thy seed shall all the families of the earth be blessed.

"And behold, I am with thee, and will help thee, in all places whither thou goest, and will bring thee again into this land; for I will not leave thee until I have done that which I have spoken to thee of."—Genesis 28:12-15.

How strange! the seed of Jacob *has* covered the earth. In the distant West, from whence I come, a number equal to one of the original tribes of Israel is nationalized, many of whom are directly interested in my errand here; and I am now looking upon the place of that memorable vision afforded to Jacob which has been realized by the union of earth and heaven, man and angels, in the person of the Son of Man and the Son of God!

It is a great contrast with the subject; but I cannot forget that here, too, that strange and eccentric mortal, G. J. Adams (a brother of the Masonic tie), came, when, on his first visit of exploration in the Holy Land, he stood on the site of Jacob's Bethel. Here he devoutly passed a watch-night, and in the morning raised an altar of unhewn stone (I tried to find it), upon which he poured his elements of consecration as a Freemason should. It needs not that I should excuse all the subsequent follies of the President of the American Colony at Jaffa, to pay this tribute of admiration to his self-consecration at Bethel. Perhaps, after all the abuse that has been heaped upon him, it was the *head* in Brother Adams that erred rather than the *heart*.

Having one hour of daylight, I walked around the high grounds to the eastward of Bethel, and inspected many a heap of stones that had been removed from the track of the plowshare, but to my disappointment, found not a chisel-mark upon any. Beyond me, to the east, however, and not more than a mile or two distant, is the mountain where Abraham pitched his tent and built an altar to the Lord; and there, three years later, he stood with his nephew, Lot, and afforded to sacred history that evidence of magnanimity and brotherly kindness which make him the model of Masonic nobility to the present day. I review the record here:

"The land was not able to bear them (Abraham and Lot), that they might dwell together; for their substance was great, so that they could not dwell together.

"And there was a strife between the herdsmen of Abraham's cattle and the herdsmen of Lot's cattle.

"And Abraham said unto Lot, Let there be no strife, I pray thee, between me and thee, and between my herdsmen and thy herdsmen, for we be *brethren*.

"Is not the whole land before thee? Separate thyself, I pray thee, from me; if thou wilt take the *left* hand, then I will go to the *right;* or if thou depart to the *right* hand, then I will go to the *left*."— Genesis 8:6-9.

Crossing the valley, I re-enter the dirty Arab village that represents ancient Bethel, and visit the remains of a church built, apparently, out of the fragments of some more classical edifice, of which the sculptured capitals and cornices occasionally peep out. Below these ruins, and around a plenteous spring, are the remains of an enormous cistern that remind me of the Lower Pool of Gihon, at the foot of Mount Sion. It is 317 feet by 214 in area, and its south wall is entire. The women of Bethel are bringing from that fountain their evening supplies of water in great jars, bearing them upon their heads, and stepping as easily under their burdens as a Broadway belle does under her microscopic bonnet. One of these, a veritable hag, old and ragged and poor, stops, holds out her disengaged hand and solicits *backsheesh*. This is the only instance I can recall in Palestine in which a *woman* addressed a word to me. I am sorry I did not give her some money.

And now it was getting dark, and I turned to find my quarters. This was no easy matter. All the dogs in Bethel clamored to confuse me in my quest. Repulsive in their gauntness and sores, these curs of low degree flocked around me, only keeping beyond the sweep of my stick. They climbed the stone-heaps, the walls, the very housetops, and threw down their maledictions upon me as I passed. At a place where four paths met, a group of villagers were sitting, apparently in council. But, surly and repulsive as their very dogs, the Bethelites scarcely answered my greetings, not one of them rising to his feet or expressing the least sign of welcome or interest.

The condition of the village that evening was at its worst. The narrow lanes, none of them more than six feet broad, festered in filth and garbage. The night was very warm, and the low cabins reeked with humanity and insects. The house which had been apportioned to my party consisted of a single apartment, about twenty by twelve feet, a cellar being excavated under the floor at one end, in which beasts were stalled. My portion of the room was, in fact, a *shelf* directly over the stable. There my blankets and traps were placed, and while Hassan attended to feeding his three horses, I

lighted some candles, which I had been provident enough to bring
with me, and prepared my frugal supper, consisting of coffee,
sardines, and English crackers. The only thing in the way of
edibles furnished by my host was milk to accompany the coffee.
While eating I could see, through the open door, the whole
population of Bethel watching my proceedings. Supper being over,
I told Hassan to inquire if any of the people had *antiques* for sale,
meaning coins, engraved gems, pieces of carving, funeral lamps,
etc., which in the Orient pass under that generic term. Nothing
was produced, however, except a few bronze coins of the Roman
period, and these, with a good quantity of the stone from the old
church, and one handsome petrified star-fish, are all the
specimens of old Bethel that I brought away.

Expressing the wish to *retire,* my bed was made up in the
following manner, viz.: First a cloth of camels' hair was made to
cover the entire shelf on which I was to sleep; over that was
spread a dirty mattress, suggestive of fleas and *other* insects; over
all these came my three pairs of blankets, carpet-bags doing
service as pillows. Stretching myself on these, with a row of
curiously-constructed vessels for wheat and barley at my feet; the
donkeys of the proprietor munching their grain vigorously in their
stalls below; the olive-oil lamp, which never goes out at night in
an Arab hut, burning in a little niche above my head; a crying
child and its mother in the furthest corner; and, finally, that
indigestible supper pressing upon my conscience like a mountain,
is it strange that my dreams, whatever they were, bore no
analogy to the one Jacob had? So far from it, that, when 2 o'clock
came, tortured by the insects, choked with the stench, and
parched with the heat, I resolved to leave Bethel forthwith. Never
was proposition more heartily met; and in half an hour my party,
consisting of two Americans, three Arab servants, and one of the
villagers to show me the way, were tramping through the narrow
lanes northward, and so passing into the open country.

I had discovered before bedtime, through my servant Hassan,
that the character of these villagers of Bayteen was
particularly bad. When I had paid my host the customary five-
franc piece at parting, he let me know, by indisputable tokens,
that he considered himself underpaid. The fellow who
accompanied me out of town claimed also a *backsheesh,* which,
the truth of history compels me to say, he did *not* get; and by
the time I was fairly out of the village, I was impressed with
the apprehension that my little party might be made

the subject of an attack by some of those scamps. Luckily the moon had risen and was about one hour high. This showed me the way between the great white rocks where Jacob dreamed of the Invisible, and awoke, exclaiming, "How dreadful is this place!" He who had calmed the troubled spirit of the sleeper by the promise of protection, cheered me likewise by the remembrance of many a gracious promise. So, arranging my little cavalcade in the best manner for defense in case of attack, I pushed my horse forward, nor ever slackened rein until the dawn, one hour later, showed me that we had passed *Ain-el-Hamareeyeh,* "the fountain of robbers," and were deep in the glens of Ephraim.

This name of *Bethel,* signifying the House of God (Beth-El!) is embodied in the nomenclature of American lodges to a very large extent. And nothing could be more appropriate; for a Masonic lodge is so far the House of God as to have the *Word* of God wide open upon its altar, and the *Name* of God high advanced in its East; and it cannot be opened until the *Favor* of God has been supplicated; nor can a man take the first step in it until he has openly declared his *faith* in God! So the following lodges, among others, are proud to be called *Bethel* Lodge, viz., No. 194, Tennessee; 134, Texas; 20, Oregon; 24, New Hampshire; 311, Pennsylvania; 62, Massachusetts, etc.

To establish the holy identity still more closely, I write here the names of the ten following "servants of God," and locate them at Bethel, thirteen miles north of Jerusalem, viz., J. K. Wheeler, Rev. J. Hyatt Smith, B. Rush Campbell, Ira Berry, Wm. Tracy Gould, A. A. Stevenson, John Dove, Wm. H. Wood, Thomas M. Reed, and J. S. Reeves, M.D.

My cut of Bethel conveys an excellent idea of its general appearance, viewed from the southwest.

As I remarked above, I visited the site of the old town formerly lying "on the east of Bethel, having Bethel on the west and Hai on the east" (Genesis 7:8), where Abram "pitched his tent, and built an altar unto the LORD, and called upon the name of the LORD;" but the place now is barren and dry; strewn with minute fragments of rubbish, as if literally ground to powder. Yet here occurred the incident in the life of Abraham, already referred to, which is held *memoria in œterna*—in perpetual memory. Seeing at Bethel a man fearfully emaciated with a disease hopelessly fastened in his vitals, the words of Job came forcibly to my mind: "His bone cleaveth to his bone and to his flesh" (19:20). The ladder which Jacob in his vision saw at this place, ascending from earth to heaven, is made

BETHEL, FROM THE NORTH.

use of, in the lectures of the Entered Apprentice, to inculcate one of the most hopeful lessons that the Masonic system affords. As an *emblem,* it has a prominent place on all our tracing-boards, and admits of only one interpretation.

The finest tracts of pasturage I have seen in this country lie east of Bethel, famous even in the days of Abraham. The clear sky of Palestine still gives an insight into the starry system that wheels over the hills surrounding Bethel, such as can be had in no other country I have ever visited. The cool waters gush from many fountains in the vicinity. The vine, olive, and fig tree give their welcome shelter in the noonday, and supply the simple wants of the inhabitants; but all the works of man lie in ruins. A few mud-huts shelter the people of Bethel, a population at the most of an hundred woe-be-gone, poverty-stricken creatures. The little children pursued me with clamor, and begged. Sitting at my meal, the whole village seemed gathered before the door, to watch me and count the morsels I ate. My night's stay at Bethel will ever be associated with memories of filthiness, squalor, insects, moral and physical degradation, and wretchedness.

My readers will doubtless recall the beautiful references made by Milton to Jacob's ladder at Bethel.

> "Far distant, he discerns,
> Ascending by degrees, magnificent,
> Up to the wall of heaven, a structure high,
> At top whereof, but far more rich, appeared
> The work as of a king by palace gate.
> The stairs were such as whereon Jacob saw
> Angels ascending and descending."

Meeting an armed courier galloping over the hills to Jerusalem, recalls a vivid description I have seen in some writer, of one of these men, who was riding express from Es-Salt to Jerusalem: "He sat erect and firm as a statue on its pedestal; his countenance was fixed and steady, every muscle and joint screwed tightly down. With firm grasp he held his cocked musket at arm's length horizontally, and dashing his heavy stirrup-irons into the bleeding sides of his swift Arabian, he flew over the ground like an eagle hastening to the prey." I also met here a sheikh on horseback, who was got up, really, regardless of expense. He wore a red silk gown, scarlet cloak, red tarboush with silk shawl tied round it, long red boots and sash, pistols, sword, spear with handle which seemed more than twenty feet long, pointed at both ends with steel. I should say he is the best *red* man I ever saw in Canaan! It is here near Bethel that I first enter the territories of "little Benjamin" (Ps. 58:27).

And now comes the morning of May 15th, 1868. I had left my filthy abode at Bethel, and while the stars yet hung their matchless lamps from the azure of the Syrian sky, undimmed by the approach of Phœbus, I had conducted my little company through the great white rocks north of the village, and so on in the direction of *Cynosure,* whose well-remembered light pointed my way *northward.* Daylight revealed the most highly cultivated and abounding valleys I had yet seen in Palestine. The flowers were yet abundant, although these lengthening days are almost too much for their delicate organs. The scarlet anemone, cyclamen, pink lychnis, blue pimpernel, veronica, yellow ranunculus, and other gems of God's own setting, afford a rich field for the collector, and made me wish that I had my old tin box this morning, and a holiday to fill it, instead of being here on horseback, at the head of a party bent upon reaching Nablous before night. They recall the lines of Keble:

> Sweet nurslings of the vernal skies,
>   Bathed in soft airs and fed with dew,
> What more than magic in you lies
>   To fill the heart's fond view?
> Relics ye are of Eden's bowers;
>   As pure, as fragrant, and as fair
> As when ye crowned the sunshine hours
>   Of happy wanderers there.

About sunrise, the deep valley begins to open into a plain. An old khan, that for many generations has sheltered wearied travelers, is now in ruins hard by, close to a cool and cheerful spring. Here once stood the ancient Lebonah. The hilltops, as I can plainly see, have each their village perched on the highest peak, as a better security against invaders. On the right hand, just beyond that rude cliff of limestone, lies, I know, the ancient Sanctuary of Shiloh. It is but a mass of shapeless ruins, scarcely distinguishable from the rugged rocks around them, with large hewn stones occasionally marking the site of ancient walls. There is one square ruin, as an English brother (Tristam) informs me, probably a mediæval fortress-church, with a few broken Corinthian columns, the relics of previous grandeur. This place for hundreds of years was the central rallying point of all Israel, equidistant from north to south to the tribes, and accessible from "beyond the Jordan." Here the Ark with its holy furniture was deposited, from about B.C. 1450 until they were captured by the Philistines, and, although regained, never restored to Shiloh. As I looked up these barren hillsides, once marked with highways from every quarter, and thought of the many generations who celebrated their feasts and fasts here in the spirit of the Sinaitic Code, I compared the history of Shiloh with that of the Sanctuary of Adonis, near Gebal, which I had examined a few weeks before. In the facts of their long holiness and present utter abandonment, there is great analogy. In the next chapter, I will refer to Shiloh more at length.

Passing a mile or two further, I find a congenial place to gratify a crying appetite, and dismount my company to prepare coffee and breakfast. It is on the edge of a luxuriant field of barley. The thorns for firewood are abundant. Good water is not far off. A melancholy owl cries lamentably upon a rock hard by. An old Arab is cutting down an old and useless olive. Very old indeed it must be if it is useless; for, as a general thing, the older the olive the more abundant and delicious the fruit. He uses a primitive weapon, compounded of hoe and axe. From the moderation of his strokes, and the extremely *andante* movement of his arms, he will be operating at the root of that aged olive more than this day. My breakfast is not a gluttonous repast; sardines, crackers, and strong coffee make up the bill of fare.

Remounting and passing northward, I enter the broad and fertile valley of Mokhna, passing down a hill terrifically steep, where another ruined khan and village attract the eye. Here a native has taken advantage of the abundance of water to irrigate his onion-beds, by draining a number of small trenches and passing the life-giving fluid from one row of onions to another. Certainly I never saw finer specimens of the *Allium* than that gardener is raising; and if the soldiers and robbers of the country will give him three months to work and wait, he will have enough to supply at least one Arab village with an edible of which above all others these people are fond. The Syrian onion is mild-flavored, compared with ours, and wholesome and delicious.

Yesterday afternoon I met quite a number of Jews, single and in companies, but today their numbers are greatly increased. They have just been making their annual visits to the sacred cities of Tiberias and Safed, and to the holy places, of which Joseph's Well, near Nablous, is one. I am told that they do this every year. They are very civil to me, returning my salutations politely, and seeming pleased with my respectful manner of greeting. However, they look jaded, especially the women and children. No wonder. The sun is threatening already one of his fiercest days, and they are going south, with his broad, hot face to stare them in *their* faces until his going down. I am too much of a traveler to let him stare me in the face. It was to avoid this that I sent my horses down from Beirut to Jerusalem, that I might turn my back upon the Great Luminary, as I go thus meandering through the heart of the land.

What a lovely valley this of Mokhna is! No wonder Abraham settled here on his first coming to Canaan. No wonder Jacob settled here when he came down with his wives and children, flocks and herds, men-servants and maid-servants, from Padan-aram. Although the ground has been cultivated for nearly forty centuries without manure, it yields all the products for which this country was ever famous. Indian corn, barley, wheat, beans, vegetables in variety etc., etc. Although the plowing is but child's-play compared to ours, being a mere *scratch,* three or four inches deep, more like *has rowing* than plowing, yet that barley yonder would not discredit the prairies of the West. The earth is red or reddish brown, and very friable. Not a tree nor hedge appears in the valley; but a little way up the hillsides, the olive, fig, pomegranate, etc., are abundant.

By noon I turn from this broad and beautiful valley, square to the left hand, and looking up a narrower vale, I know that I am passing ancient Sychar, Jacob's Well and Joseph's Tomb, while yonder town, a mile or two in advance, is Nablous. But now my want of sleep and rest the preceding night tell too hard upon me, and I can only escape a threatened attack of fever by hurrying to cover. In the hospitable mansion of Rev. Mr. Falshire, a German missionary, who is here in charge of a school of native children, I find the needed repose, and toward night, having had a few hours' sleep and a good dinner, I am able to accept the kind offer of that gentleman, and visit the Well of Jacob and the Tomb of Joseph. As we pass down the valley for that purpose, Mount Ebal, the place of *cursings*, is on my left, Mount Gerizim, the place of *benedictions*, on my right. When Jesus chose a hill near the Sea of Galilee for a mount of Beatitudes, was he thinking of the great scene where all the beatitudes and cursings of the Mosaic dispensation were read aloud in the hearing of the people? What a locality! I read the appropriate passages as I walked slowly along, and estimating the distance between these parallel ranges, satisfied myself that in this clear atmosphere, with the trained voices of men accustomed to the vocation of shepherds, every sentence could have been distinctly heard from one summit to the other. Still more readily if the respective spokesmen took their positions lower down, as it may be supposed they most naturally would. The popular notion that Ebal is a barren mountain, while Gerizim is fruitful, is not sustained by anything that I could detect. Yet there may be something in it, in the fact that the southern sun has a full face at the former, scorching his vegetation with the intolerable summer heat, while the latter has his northern slopes lying in the shade during the most heated period of the day. This, in process of ages, might make a distinction, although, as said before, I could not detect it. Certainly, the slope of Ebal is more gradual, and it therefore bears more olive and fig trees than the bold cliff of Gerizim, which is pierced with caves and moist with springs.

I must not forget to note that *Mount Gerizim* is adopted in Masonic nomenclature by *Gerizim Lodge,* No. 54, Louisiana; and

Mount Ebal by Mount Ebal Lodge, No. 169, Georgia. In view of this, and because the Divine Law was promulgated here, with a solemnity scarcely inferior to its first delivery on Sinai, I adopt it among the Masonic localities, and join to it the good names of John H. Anthon, D. W. Thomson, George W. Bartlett, Robert A. Lamberton, Thomas Haywood, W. J. Bates, Amos E. Cobb, Clinton F. Paige. Joseph D. Evans, J. M. Gilbert. It would be a rich experience for two of these men to visit here together, and, standing upon opposite slopes, half a mile apart, to "read all the words of the law, the blessings and cursings, according to all that is written in the book of the law" (Joshua 8:34).

The Well of Jacob, as a piece of human labor, is interesting in itself, irrespective of historical associations. It is nine feet in diameter, and was originally cut one hundred feet or more in depth through the limestone. Its present depth, as Tristam estimates it, is seventy-five feet, the Arabs having thrown in much stone and earth. The upper portion of the casing is composed of stones squared and neatly dressed. I do not recollect that there was water in it at the time of my visit. To find this well, I was conducted to a low mound, formed of ruins, surmounted by a broken wall inclosing granite columns, erect and prostrate. At the eastern end of this, the remains of a square, vaulted chamber point to the old "Well-house." To climb through this, down to the opening of the Well, demands considerable agility in the explorer. Sitting by the opening, I read from the fourth chapter of John the memorable incidents which have given to this Well such a reputation in history, as no other water-source can ever have. And here only can the full force of those touching lines be appreciated:

> Querens me sedisti lassus:
> Redemisti crucem passus;
> Tantus labor non sit casus—

"Wearied in search of me, Thou didst sit down (by this well-side). Having suffered the pangs of the Cross, Thou didst redeem me. Oh, that such sacrifice may not be in vain!" It is said the good moralist, Samuel Johnson, never could read those affecting words without tears. How would they have impressed him to have read them here, on the spot to which they allude, as I do now.

The sun was going down as I visited the Tomb of Joseph, a hundred yards or so northwest of the Well, and at the southeastern corner, so to speak, of Mount Ebal. It is a room about twelve feet square, containing a tomb three feet high, said to hold the bones of Joseph. The room, or chapel, is well preserved beneath a roof; and forming one of the sacred shrines of the Jews, its whitewashed walls are covered with pencil-marks, doubtless the names, in Hebrew, of the visitors. A luxuriant grapevine covers one of the walls, and forces its way into the open window. I secured one of its leaves for my collection.

Returned back to my kind missionary, I enjoyed several hours of the conversation of Mr. and Mrs. Falshire, whose pious self-devotion alone keeps them here. Their success in the Master's service runs chiefly in the direction of *education*. This is the experience of all the missionaries that I meet. The natives do not care much to hear them preach or exhort; but they are glad to have their children *educated*, both boys and girls, and so, every generation removes more and more the barriers separating Christians and Mohammedans. In many of the larger towns, there are good physicians connected with the missions, whose skill and philanthropy give them deserved eminence among the mercenary quacks who arrogate the title of *Hakeems,* or doctors, here. In this place, Nablous, where, a few years since, Christians were openly stoned and maltreated, a much milder spirit now prevails, and this is largely due to the efforts of the missionaries, Mr. and Mrs. Falshire.

In the evening I called on Mohammed Said, Pasha of Nablous, who had been vouched for to me as a brother Mason; but was disappointed to find he was absent from the city. I had anticipated a pleasant hour with this distinguished gentleman. It was from Mr. Falshire that I learned of the recent publication, in Arabic, of a tract against Freemasonry. The Catholic priests, everywhere the opponents of our system, finding that the spread of the order was enlarging the spirit of freedom and inquiry among this people in Syria, and hearing of my visit, have fulminated in this distant land the same tremendous threats against the institution, "thrice-cursed of the Pope," that we are accustomed to hear and despise in our free lands of the West. I endeavored to procure a copy of this tract, but in vain. It is easy, however, to conjecture the contents.

My cut gives an excellent view of the two mountains, Ebal (on the right) and Gerizim (on the left), as seen from the entrance of the alley, near Jacob's Well, looking west.

The route from Nablous to Zarthan, as the map will show, is northeast.

The places are about twenty miles apart. The best point to leave the Jerusalem road is, probably, Shiloh. It was always a problem

EBAL AND GERIZIM.

in my mind, why the astute Solomon should have sent the practical-minded Hiram a distance of forty-five miles from the site of the Temple, to do the hard and heavy work of casting the molten sea, the oxen, the lavers, pots, shovels, and basins, so minutely described in 1 Kings 7. Seeing that Succoth is not only at so considerable a distance from Jerusalem, but that it stands in an almost inaccessible district, a heavy descent of nearly 3,500 feet, perpendicular height, from the surface of Mount Moriah, and demanding the construction of a road through terrific defiles and along giddy acclivities— seeing, I say, that such is the case, as every one will testify who has traveled the road from Jerusalem to Jericho, why was this place selected? Forty-five miles, in a direct line, is equivalent to sixty in a broken country like this; and the difference in levels between Succoth and Jerusalem, up which the Temple furniture and the enormous shafts I. and B. must be lifted by manual efforts alone, being 3,500 feet, it would have been easier, some may say, for Hiram Abif

to cast the pillars, etc., at his own city of Tyre, and transport them
to Jerusalem, by way of Joppa, or to cast them at Jerusalem itself,
than to open foundries in this desolate plain between Succoth and
Zarthan, grown up as it is with thistles and thorns, the abode of
the wild beasts of the Jordan valley, at the foot of precipitous spurs
of the mountains of Judea, and at so great a distance from
Jerusalem. Such were my queries and imaginings when I began
the investigation of this question. Before I concluded them, the
explanation was clear. For here, near Succoth, is an abounding
water-course (the Jordan), furnishing its life-giving fluid, both to
the workmen to drink and as a *power* to drive the great blasts
necessary for smelting such enormous amounts of metal as were
required here. Here, too, abounded the fuel (wood), of which great
quantities were needed, and the arenaceous clay necessary for the
architectural moulds. This place was accessible by a level country
to the city of Achor (Acre), which was only twenty-five miles by sea
from Tyre; therefore easily reached by the laborers. The smooth
road made it practicable to transport the ores of copper and tin and
the machinery of the furnaces. The only drawback was the one
already named, the necessity of lifting the finished carvings up
those precipitous ranges to Jerusalem. But this was only of a piece
with the labor going on at the same time on the other side of those
precipitous ranges, in lifting beams of cedar and fir, granite and
porphyry, and marble columns and other ponderous masses, up the
heights between Joppa and Jerusalem.

On the other hand, to have established the foundries
immediately at Jerusalem was practically an impossibility, owing
to the scarcity of water, the scarcity of wood, and the want of the
needed clay. Between the various plans, then, Hiram naturally
chose the former On "the clay-ground in the plain of Jordan" he
erected his furnaces (of which, doubtless, traces of foundations and
the refuse slag will yet be discovered by diligent explorers), and
established a colony of skilled draughtsmen, moulders, and
foundrymen. These he often visited in person, furnishing the most
exquisite drawings for his own *stylus,* and correcting their work as
it progressed. He supplied the mechanical skill for forwarding the
mighty shafts up the ranges, past Shiloh and Bethel, to Jerusalem.
Even the paved way, which must necessarily have been made
through the gorges of these stupendous hills, was engineered
under his practiced eye.

A friend gives me, from his private journal, this passage, viz.: "The
thistles actually overtop the head of a person riding on horseback

through the valley by Seikoot. No such place as Zarthan or Zeredathah can now be recognized; but from the different passages in the Bible where the word occurs, it may be located not far above *Succoth,* near the old city of Bethshean. The clay-ground was, of course, situated between the two."

Dr. Robinson, in *Biblical Researches,* describes the village of Seikoot thus: "Here is seen merely the ruin of a common village, a few foundations of unhewn stones. The eastern bank of the lower Jordan valley opposite to us was precipitous, apparently nearly a hundred and fifty or two hundred feet high. The river was running close under it, about a mile distant from us. The water of the river was not in sight, because of the bushes and trees, but we afterwards saw it from a point a little further north. Mount Hermon is visible from Seikoot, and so are Little Hermon and Mount Tabor. Near the foot of a low bluff, east of the village, there breaks out a beautiful fountain of pure and sparkling water, under the shade of a thicket of fig trees. From this, the founders of Hiram must often have refreshed themselves. The region below is full of grass, wild oats, and thistles, with bushes of the *Spina Christi."*

Captain Wilson, in charge at that time of the researches of the *London Palestine Fund,* in a letter of March 17, 1866, describes a visit to *Sukkoot.* The name, he thinks, is applied to the *district* as well as to a small *tell* (hill), on which are some inconsiderable ruins. He observed no very marked features, such as would answer to the expression, *valley of Succoth,* in the Book of Psalms. The district is rich and well watered. When he visited Succoth, it was occupied by over two hundred tents of the *Sukhr Bedouins,* then at war with the Adwars. The River Jordan being unfordable at the time, the fighting was confined to an exchange of Arab abuse, and a few long shots across the stream, in which only some four or five men had been killed. This incident illustrates the story of the tremendous slaughter which occurred here, under Jephthah, three thousand years ago.

One of the worst blunders in the Blue Lodge rituals of Massachusetts is connected with this vicinity (Succoth), in the allusion to "the quarries of Zeredathah." There never were quarries at Zeredathah; and if there had been, it was the last place in Palestine to open them, considering the difficulty of removing heavy ashlars thence to Jerusalem. Another blunder of some manual-maker is to represent sleeping Jacob at Bethel, reposing by a *water-course;* whereas Bethel is thirty miles in a direct course from the sea, and twenty from the River Jordan, the nearest watercourse.

When Palestine founders shall come hither again to look for the best earth for moldings, and master-builders shall lay the foundations for furnaces, and Jordan again be made to drive the blasts of furnaces, as in the days of Hiram; then, "instead of the thorn shall come up the fir-tree, and instead of the brier shall come up the myrtle-tree" (Isaiah 55:13); for after all, traffic is king.

From Lynch's exploration (1848), I derive the following fact. At the close of the fifth day after leaving the Sea of Galilee (April 14, 1848), he says the surface of the hill behind him was thickly covered with boulders of quartz and conglomerate. Dr. Anderson found the remains of walls at the summit, and one large stone, dressed to a face, and marked thus:

STONE MARKS.

It was probably not far from "the clay-ground" that the celebrated "passages" (or fords) of Jordan were situated. Let us examine the Biblical account of Jephthah in this connection. He resided at Mizpah, on yonder hill, east of the Jordan. The Ephraimites, who occupied the territory immediately west, had conceived a bitter jealousy against him for his great success over the common enemy, "the children of Ammon," and had crossed the river to put him to death. Jephthah defeated them, as he did the Ammonites before them, and drove them back in disgrace. "And the Gileadites took the passages of Jordan before the Ephraimites; and it was so, that when those Ephraimites, which were escaped, said, Let me go over; that the men of Gilead said unto him: Art thou an Ephraimite? If he said Nay; then said they unto him: Say now *Shibboleth!* and he said *Cibbolet;* for he could not frame to pronounce it right. Then they took him and slew him at the passages of Jordan; and there fell at that time of the Ephraimites forty and two thousand" (Judges 7:5-6). It is a curious commentary upon these paragraphs, that there is not an Arab now living upon those hills, on either side of the Jordan, who can pronounce the word shibboleth in any other manner than as the Ephraimites did. If, therefore, the ghost of old Jephthah were to take his stand by this ford today, he would be tempted to destroy the entire Ishmaelitish population.

From an essay upon this subject that I wrote for one of our Masonic journals, I give this incident, with some repetition, a little more in detail.

THE FORDS OF THE JORDAN.

The whole story of the destruction of the Ephraimites, as associated with those important emblems, the Water-ford, the Ear of Corn, and the word *Shibboleth,* is rich in historical and topographical details. To do the amplest justice to the subject, the reader should have a map of Palestine before him, and familiarize himself especially with the situation of Mizpah, the fords of the Jordan nearest to that place, and the tribe of Ephraim in relation to its central city, *Shechem.* He should observe, also, where the principal valleys (*wadys*) are; because all military movements to and from the Jordan, both on the east and west sides, were necessarily made *along those valleys,* as highways from the hills where the towns were, and still are situated, in the interior of the country.

In the first place, then, let us see who and what was *Jephthah,* the name so intimately associated with this fearful slaughter of "forty and two thousand Ephraimites." The account given in the *Dictionary of Freemasonry* is so succinct and yet clear, that it might be transferred here with a little compression. Among the Judges of Israel, Jephthah flourished about B.C. 1183-1187. In his youth, he had been driven by his half-brothers from Gilead, the land of his birth, to Nod, a place on the frontiers, east of Gilead. There, gathering around him a company of lawless men, he became known as a mighty man of valor, maintaining a constant strife with the Ammonites, the traditional enemies of his people, and acquiring fame and wealth thereby.

At a serious invasion of the country by the Ammonites, Jephthah was called upon by the popular voice to be their captain, and lead them against the threatening foe. To this he consented. He brought his own tried band; and summoning all the people of Gilead and Manasseh, those tribes that particularly acknowledged his authority, because they resided east of the Jordan, he advanced against the Ammonites with irresistible resolution, and overthrew them with immense loss. He retook twenty cities from their hands, gathered a great accumulation of spoils, and inflicted upon them such a defeat that several generations passed away before the Ammonites could again make head against Israel.

This was *the first act* in the Biblical drama of Jephthah's life, and proved him a man possessing force of mind for great undertakings, bodily strength, and deep piety, which took the only direction that a man in his age and with his training could conceive; for he began his labors for Israel by a solemn dedication, "vowing a vow unto the Lord." Having accomplished his earnest desire, by returning in peace from the children of Ammon, he submitted like a brave man to the penalty, though it left him childless and broken-hearted. Short time had he to mourn. The powerful tribe of Ephraim, west of the river, challenging his right to go to war without their co-operation, crossed the Jordan at its "passages," and advancing up the defiles towards Mizpah, threatened "to burn his house upon him with fire."

The bold mountaineer accepted the challenge, and a terrible conflict ensued between those alienated sons of Jacob. Each party was embittered to desperation; each fought bravely. But the *Gileadites* were in a country with which they were familiar, and with them was the victory. The defeated Ephraimites hurried down the valleys to the river in a total rout, casting away sword and buckler in their panic; only intent upon enjoying a draught from the cool stream, and placing it as a defense in their rear. But this was far from Jephthah's intention. Accustomed, in his mountain style of warfare, to the tactics of flanking, as General Sherman practiced it, 3,000 years afterwards, in a similar country, he sent his reserves, by ways well known to him, around the flanks of the Ephraimites, and possessed himself of all the crossing-places ("passages") before his enemy could reach them. Then occurred one of the most horrible scenes of slaughter recorded in the annals of civil warfare. Forty-two thousand men were deliberately put to death by the Gileadites, not a man, so far as we can understand the record, having been spared!

The *exact* locality of these fords (or "passages," as the Bible terms them) cannot now be designated, but most likely they were those nearly due east of *Seikoot,* and opposite Mizpah. At these fords, in summertime, the water is not more than three or four feet deep, the bottom being composed of a hard limestone rock. If, as some think, the fords thirty miles higher up are those referred to, the same description will apply. At either place, the Jordan is about eighty feet wide, its banks encumbered by a dense growth of tamarisks, cane, willows, thorn-bushes, and other low vegetation of the shrubby and thorny sorts, which make it difficult even to approach the margin of the stream. The Arabs cross the river at the present day, at stages of low water, at a number of fords, from the one near the point where the Jordan leaves the Sea of Galilee, down to the Pilgrims' Ford, six miles above the Dead Sea.

A word here in relation to *Shibboleth,* so intimately associated with the fords of the Jordan. This word, in Hebrew, primarily implies a *flood* or *stream.* It was, hence, naturally suggested to the followers of Jephthah, when, having established themselves in the rear of the enemy, they sought to distinguish the foe through their known inability to utter the aspirated sound *sh.* The fugitives, instead of *sh,* gave the unaspirated sound *s,* wherefore they were slain without mercy. The certainty which the Gileadites felt that the Ephraimites *could not give that sound correctly* is very remarkable, and strongly illustrates the variety of dialects which had already risen in Israel. If what is here mentioned as the characteristic would not have been sufficiently discriminating as a test, Jephthah certainly would not have selected it. It was a curious subject of reflection that occurred to me, as I passed along towards Shechem (Nablous), not far from these fords, that among all the tribes of the natives who inhabit the country now, there is not on either side of the Jordan a person who pronounces the word as Jephthah did! All would say *Sibboleth,* or rather *Sibboleen,* just as they say *Bayteen* instead of Bethel, and *Seiloon* instead of Shiloh. If the different tribes had in reality acquired such differences in dialect in only three hundred years from the days of Moses and Joshua, it illustrates what the traveler will see every day in that country, viz., that the Jews now speak as many languages as there are countries in which they are spread abroad. The word *Shibboleth* also means *an ear of corn,* and (symbolically) *plenty;* and one tradition has it that an object of that sort was suspended from a branch near the river, and that the test of the Ephraimite was *to point to that* and ask him what it was. The reply, of course, led to the tribal detection. Any other word commencing with *sh,* however, would have served the same purpose, the reason for adopting this being that it meant *food, drink,* and *security* all in one, those three things for which the panting fugitives were striving at the close of that awful battle-day.

Almost every portion of this celebrated river of antiquity, the Jordan, is associated with some one or more of the Masonic legends. In the Order of High-Priests, by a pleasing coincidence, we have a narration which connects the head of the stream with its mouth. Is its rituals, commencing at Sodom, on the southern verge of the Jordan valley, we accompany the Father of the Faithful in his chivalrous essay to the town of Dan, hard by the fountainhead of the stream. The degree of Fellow-Craft leads us to "the clay-ground between Succoth and Zarthan;" also to the fords, at which the slaughter of the cruel and presumptuous Ephraimites was accomplished. Subsequent degrees refer to other portions of the streams, and thus the whole river is comprised within Masonic geography. In fact, according to the theory of Dr. Oliver, one of the earliest emblems in the Entered Apprentice's degree suggests the crossing of the Jordan by Joshua and his host, near the mouth of the river.

It is useless to add, that in all Christian systems the Jordan plays a prominent part. The baptism of Jesus occurred there. In his mission of mercy and divine favor, he frequently crossed this river. Some of his most striking miracles were performed near by its banks. It would be impossible, therefore, to separate this remarkable stream from our ideas of Christ, even though the hymnologists of the Christian system had not so often used it as their most fitting emblem of *the Stream of Death,* that separates our barren and desolate *Moab* from the fruitful and cheerful *Canaan* which we seek. How gloriously good old Isaac Watts of our youth has done this, it needs but a stanza to prove:

> "Sweet fields, beyond the swelling flood,
>   Stand, dressed in living green;
> So, to the Jews, old Canaan stood,
>   While Jordan rolled between!"

Or this one more verse, from another author:

> "Could we but stand where Moses stood,
>   And view the landscape o'er,
> Not Jordan's stream, nor death's dark flood,
>   Should fright us from the shore!"

I cannot resist the temptation to give place here to John Bunyan, and then I will conclude. Was ever symbol so clothed with verity? "Now I further saw that betwixt them and the gate was a river, but there was no bridge to go over. The river was very deep. At the sight, therefore, of this river, the pilgrims were much stunned, but the men that went with them said, You must go through or you cannot come at the gate. They then addressed themselves to the water. "The whole passage is equally affecting. As I rode down from Jerusalem to the Jordan, one hot morning in May, 1868, I asked my servant by what name the stream is known to the natives. He replied Esh-Shereeyah, meaning the *Place of Watering.* Some of the Arabs add the word Great (*El-Kebir*) to that, to denote its relative importance in the scale of streams.

The place of the clay-ground is marked in Masonic nomenclature by *Zeredathah Lodge,* No. 83, Georgia; No. 483, New York, etc. The name of the river is given in *Jordan Lodge,* No. 184, North Carolina; No. 386, New York; No. 47, Massachusetts; No. 237, England, etc. To establish the identity even more closely, I write upon the place of the foundries ten Masonic names, viz., Philip C. Tucker, J. B. Bradwell, George H. Raymond, L. Bradford Prince, William R. Clapp, Alfred Creigh, S. B. Olney, M.D., E. H. Hamilton, J. P. Sanford, William C. Preble. And for the locality of the "passages," or fords of the Ephraimites, I give the ten following, viz., A. G. Goodall, Charles Griswold, Charles D. Greene, Sylvester Stevens, Reeves E. Selmes, Robert Morris, Jr., John Thompson, Charles Eginton, Henry R. Cannon, G. B. Cooley.

PTOLEMY PHILADELPHUS: ARSINOE-BERENICE.

CHAPTER XX.

SHILOH is a place memorable on the rolls of American lodges, as witness, *Shiloh Lodge,* No. 131, Louisiana; No 202, Tennessee; No. 105, Alabama, and others. In that portion of Masonic history which relates to the Ark of Moses, its construction and various "resting-places," Shiloh assumes a prominent place; for here, and not at Jerusalem, was the Tabernacle set up, about B.C. 1550, and the Ark of the Covenant placed, and the Sacred Garments preserved. Here, and not at Jerusalem, was established the Colony of Priests, with the High Priest at their head; and here, for several centuries, was, in fact, the center of the Jewish worship. It was at Shiloh that Eli died and Samuel prophesied through his whole life.

But that which most practically unites Shiloh with the Masonic history, is the fact that here the subject of *jurisdiction,* which plays so important a part in the American system of *jurisprudence,* was established, its laws laid down, and all the details organized. The manner of doing this, and dividing out the land of Canaan among the tribes, was so curious that I devote a chapter to the subject.

The names of places in the Holy Land have been wonderfully preserved, some of them for four thousand years. I was often startled when, pointing to a place and asking its name, my guide would answer in the same word that Paul might have used, or David, or Jacob. The principal change in the words is that of *pronunciation* only, which is no greater than may be noticed when a foreigner endeavors to pronounce the name of a place in a strange country. Thus, for instance, they call Bethel, Bayteen; Bethlehem, Batelame; Jericho, Reha; Joppa, Jaffa; Nazareth, Nazaret Shiloh, Seiloon; Shunem, Solan; Sidon, Saida; Sodom, Usdom; Succoth, Seikoot Tiberias, Tiberceyah; Tyre, Tsur. etc.

On the other hand, there are many names pronounced exactly as we have them in our English Bible, such as Carmel, Gaza, Hebron, Kana, Nain, and the like. To look for Shiloh, then, you

THE RUINS OF ANCIENT GERASA.

must inquire for *Seiloon;* where, when God had presented the land to his people, they divided it, and afterwards conquered it at the edge of the sword. But this once great and armed city is now but a dry pasture, barely supporting a few flocks that lie down, and none to make them afraid. My cut gives a positive idea of its present appearance.

And now, let us together visit Shiloh, if but in fancy, and witness the great land-distribution, the grand and famous lottery of the early ages. While camping upon those bleak hills, let us recall what befell the people of Jehovah on that day when they put to *the lot* the important question of a division of the land among the twelve tribes Viewing this transaction by modern light, it seems almost blasphemous.

21

But not so did the chosen of the Almighty view it. Not so the happy apostles on their return from Olivet and the Ascension,

SHILOH, IN THE TIME OF SAMUEL.

when they *cast lots* to fill the vacancy made by the terebinth-tree and the cord. The use of lots among the Hebrews was general. It was used by them as an appeal to God, free from passion and selfishness. The very word used for *lot (sors)* implies an oracular response. So, too, the wisest of the heathen considered it. In the combat, *the lot* decided priority in attack, position, etc., as now among duelists. The appointment of magistrates and jurymen was settled in the same way. Also the division of conquered land, etc., as here.

Among the Jews, the *method* of casting lots is not given in the Scriptures; but the Rabbinical writings profess to describe it thus: Two inscribed tablets of boxwood, or gold, were put into an urn, which was shaken, and the lots drawn out The affecting account of the discovery of Achan will occur to the reader, as given in Joshua, seventh chapter.

And now for our *Famous Lottery at Shiloh.* First, let us examine and sketch the place itself. Rude and ruinous as it now is, it probably looks much as it did when the hosts of Israel first clambered up these steep *wadys* (valleys), and took possession of it in the strength of God. It stands just where the writer in Judges 21:19 locates it, "on the north side of Bethel, on the east side of the highway that goeth up from Bethel to Shechem, and on the south of Lebonah." All three of those places are now perfectly identified, and, consequently, Shiloh. If the sacred geographer had located *all* Hebrew towns with the same precision, no country in the world would have presented fewer obscurities in topographical details. Here it is, about six miles northeast of Bethel, exactly as we should expect after reading the book of Judges.

A small hill rises from an uneven plain, surrounded, much like Jerusalem itself, by other small hills, except on the south, where there is a narrow valley. The Tabernacle once occupied the crown of this modest eminence; and there, too, is the modern village, if indeed, so small a collection of huts deserves the name of village. A noble oak overshadows a Mohammedan church, and close by here is a ruined edifice, either a church that has served as a fort, or a fort that has served as a church—it is difficult to say which. About a mile from this, eastward, is a copious fountain, whose waters are collected into a large reservoir, watering flocks and herds. The hills overhanging the fountain are pierced with sepulchers, which tradition has attributed to Eli and his priestly sons.

When the land was subjugated, when the great contest at the waters of Merom had placed all Canaan in the possession of the conqueror, here to this little hill the Tabernacle was brought from Gilgal, near Jericho, and here it was set up, its elaborate furniture in place, its curtains drawn around. Upon the surrounding eminences, doubtless, the various tribes pitched their tents, and awaited the decision of Jehovah as to their future allotments. Sitting under this fine oak, today, let us spread out our map of Palestine upon this carved fragment of marble, once a portion of a Corinthian capital, and contemplate the strange event.

Reuben had received his share already. In the long pilgrimage through the desert, his place had been on the south side of the Tabernacle. His tribal standard, *the Deer,* had been set up in the mountains of Moab, as the great caravan passed through;

and when the moment for entering the Promised Land arrived, this tribe had asked that possession should be given to it, even in those mountains, and where they had sojourned. This was done; "The border of the children of Reuben was Jordan. . . . Their coast was from Aroer that is on the bank of the River Arnon."

Gad had likewise chosen his own possession east of the river. In the great wilderness-march he had gone side by side with Reuben, and together they had settled in the rich pasturage of the Mishor. So, too, with Manasseh. Marching with Ephraim and Benjamin in the west of the great procession, he had become fascinated with conquest, and "because he was a man of war" he concluded to retain the "sixty great cities" east of the Sea of Galilee, captured by his sons. Judah, also, had been awarded a possession west of the Dead Sea, and Ephraim in the central parts of Canaan.

Seven of the tribes were yet to receive an inheritance; and here in this long, narrow, spiral range of mountains, extending from Dan to Beersheba, we see the prizes for which the Great Lottery was opened at Shiloh: "By lot was their inheritance, as the Lord commanded by the hand of Moses." In the fifteenth to the seventeenth chapters of Joshua, the momentous work is recorded. From this place, Shiloh, where "the whole congregation of the children of Israel had assembled together," Joshua first sent out a practical committee of surveyors, "three for each tribe," with the charge, "Go and walk through the land and describe it, and come again to me that I may here cast lots for you before the Lord in Shiloh." And "the men went and passed through the land, and described it by cities into seven parts, in a book, and came again to Joshua, to the hosts at Shiloh." Doubtless, the general imparted to these surveyors his own recollections of forty-five years previous, when he, as one of the committee of twelve, was sent by Moses "to spy out the land of Canaan." So, too, the aged Caleb made himself useful in counseling these "prospectors" in their forty days' work.

And "the men went and passed through the land, and described it by cities into seven parts, in a book, and came again to Joshua, to the hosts at Shiloh." These parts were for Benjamin, Simeon, Zebulun, Issachar, Asher, Naphtali, and Dan. Probably the names of these seven tribes were inscribed upon tesseræ and placed in an urn; while the numbers one to seven, inscribed in the same manner, were placed in another urn. Then Joshua himself, as the immediate representative of the nation, drew them out one by one, and called the names. It is easy to conceive that high religious solemnities accompanied the act—prayers, incense, sacrifices. The chiefs of the nine tribes, as guardians of the personal interests of their respective divisions, stood near, all but "Nahshon the son of Aminadab," who was over the host of Judah, and "Elishama the son of Ammihud," who was over the host of Ephraim. These two tribes, having already secured their portions, were less interested.

As we sit here earnestly poring over the map (Rawson's is the best for our purpose), the whole business seems plain. The six heathen nations, with their thirty-one kings, lay with bleaching bones upon the hillsides and plains of the land which they had seized when Jacob and his family followed Joseph into Egypt, 261 years before. Small detachments of their armies, however, still wandered in deserts and inaccessible places; a few of the stronger fortresses, we know, were still held by them. Possibly from yonder eminence of Rimmon, twelve miles in the southeast, one of these bands may have been gazing with despairing hearts upon their great enemy, engaged in the very act of confiscating houses, fields, cities, plains, and graveyards. It is very probable that upon the mountainsides, thirty miles eastward, detachments, hidden in caves and among the thick oak forests, witnessed the scene that day, and cursed the hosts of Jehovah in the name of their God, Baal.

And now, amidst the blast of trumpets, comes forth *the first lot*. It is that small but beautiful tract, a parallelogram of twelve by twenty six miles, that lies immediately north of Judah, and embracing Jerusalem, Bethel, and Beth-horon. "Jordan was the border of it on the east side." "The stone of Bohan, the son of Reuben," was one of the landmarks on the line of it next to Judah. "The well En-Rogel," "The wilderness of Beth-horon," "The well of waters of Nephtoah," and other noted places, were marks along its boundaries. Its situation was highly favorable. The smallness of the territory, as Josephus affirmed, 1,500 years afterwards, was compensated by the excellence of the land.

To whom is this lot? Silently the majestic warrior who had lifted up his spear over Ai, and again, in the sight of all Israel, at Gibeon, turned to the second urn and drew forth the name of—Benjamin. To Elidad, the son of Chislon, the matter was entrusted; for he was the chosen one of Benjamin, named to Moses by the Lord Jehovah himself as one of those who should "divide the land." Thus Benja

min, whose place in the wilderness had been on the west of the
Tabernacle with Ephraim and Manasseh, was established in
Canaan, next south of Ephraim. There his tribal standard, *the
Wolf*, was set up. Yonder eminence of Mizpah was his; yonder
conic hill, Rimmon, was his. As we sit here, all that line of
summits to the south formed a portion of the first lot, which fell to
Benjamin.

And lo, the blast of trumpets announces the bringing forth of
the second lot. It is a district on the southwest of Judah,
containing at the time about twenty cities, with their villages,
spread around the venerable well of Beersheba. It was the
ancestral seat. Here Abraham lived nearly a century. Here Isaac
was born, and Jacob. It was the last place inhabited by Israel,
before going down to Egypt.

To whom is this lot? Simeon. In the desert-pilgrimage, he had
encamped with Reuben and Gad on the south of the sacred tent.
Now, far separated from them, he was to set up his tribal banner,
the Sword, in the extreme southwest of Canaan, and there wage a
steady warfare with Philistines, Amalekites, and all the uneasy
sons of the desert. To his representative, Shemuel, son of
Ammihud, the second lot was given, and then Joshua prepared
for the next.

The *third lot*. This is what was afterwards known as the far-
famed Land of Galilee, the home of Jesus, stretching from Mount
Carmel on the west, to the Sea of Galilee on the east. It embraced
Tabor, Cana, Tiberias, and Nazareth within its limits. It fell to
Zebulun. During the journey from Egypt to Canaan, he had
camped with Judah and Issachar on the east of the Tabernacle.
Now his tribal standard, *a Ship*, was to be fixed in the far north.
Joshua gave the matter into the hands of Elizaphan, the son of
Parnach, and proceeded with the great drawing.

The *fourth lot* comprised the territory immediately south of the
last. It embraced the fertile plain of Esdraelon, called "the seed-
plot of God," together with Beth-shean, Endor, Megiddo, and
many others. Next to Jerusalem, this region was to become the
most famous in Jewish history. It fell to Issachar.

The *fifth lot* fell to Asher. It lay northwest of Zebulun and
Issachar, on the Mediterranean shore, and contained some of the
richest soil in Palestine.

The *sixth lot* fell to Naphtali. It is the extreme north of ancient
Canaan, including the splendid valley of Cœlesyria, and the
mountainous country inclosing it, with a soil, as Joseph us wrote,
rich and productive, at the very apex of the country.

The *seventh lot* fell to Dan. It was the smallest of the twelve, but possessed eminent natural advantages. With Ephraim on the north, and Benjamin on the east, the city of Joppa as a seaport, and the rich plain of Sharon for his corn-land, it was one of the most fertile allotments found in the urn.

*   *   *   *   *   *   *   *   *   *   *

But the shades of evening are falling, and the lines upon our map have become indistinct. All the villagers of modern Shiloh are gathered around us, each with a right hand extended, not so much in token of unity, still less of hospitality, as in urgent demand for *backsheesh*. Our tents and company are a mile or more east, and these people have none of the best reputation. Theft, wounds, even murder, are attributed to them. So we will fold up our map; and taking a last look at the little eminence on which the Tabernacle stood and the surrounding hills, where the tribal banners served for rallying points to the children of Jacob, we will hasten down the incline eastward, happy at the privilege we have enjoyed of contemplating, here upon the very spot, the Great Lottery at Shiloh.

And as we lie down to rest, surrounded by this wild population, but feeling that "more are they who are *for* us than against us," we will recall lines written by one who many a year since attained to the heavenly Canaan, and walked the eternal hills:

> "Look up, my soul; pant toward the eternal hills,
>   Those heavens are fairer than they seem;
> There pleasures all sincere glide on in crystal rills,
>   There not a dreg of guilt defiles;
> No grief disturbs the stream.
>
> *That* Canaan knows no noxious thing,
> No cursed soil, no tainted spring;
> No roses grow on thorns, nor honey wears a sting."
>   —*Advance Herald.*

The boundaries, then, for many centuries, suggested the *jurisdiction* of the several tribes, just as the lines of circumvallation established by the Grand Lodge, in the establishment of a subordinate lodge, suggest the jurisdiction, allot the territory, and limit the work of each subordinate. But the tribal laws were far more rigid than the Masonic. No member of a tribe could hold land outside of his own jurisdiction, or marry a wife except of his own tribe, or acquire any legal rights except those of a stranger. Women were restricted in marriage to men of their own tribe, as is forcibly shown in the case of "the daughters of Zelophehad," described in the lectures of the adoptive degree of that name. It appears from the sacred record (Numbers 27) that Zelophehad, a most faithful man, had died in the wilderness before the great caravan reached Canaan. His five daughters, therefore, approached Moses, and asked that in the distribution of conquered territory they might have their father's share. The request was granted, and the record so made up. After the conquest (Joshua 17:1-6) Joshua "gave them an inheritance among the brethren of their father," in the tribe of Manasseh, east of the Jordan. In answer to the query concerning the marriage of these women, Moses had ordained: "Let them marry to whom they think best, only to the family of the tribe of their father (Zelophehad of

BANNERS OF THE TRIBES.

Manasseh) shall they marry. So shall not the inheritance of

the children of Israel remove from tribe to tribe; for every one of the children of Israel shall keep himself to the inheritance of the tribe of his fathers. And every daughter that possesseth an inheritance in any tribe of the children of Israel, shall be wife unto one of the family of the tribe of her father, that the children of Israel may enjoy every man the inheritance of his fathers. Neither shall the inheritance remove from one tribe to another tribe; but every one of the tribes of the children of Israel shall keep himself to his own inheritance. Even as the Lord commanded Moses, so did the daughters of Zelophehad; for Mahlah, Tirzah, and Hoglah, and Milcah, and Noah, the daughters of Zelophehad, were married unto their father's brothers' sons; and they were married into the families of the sons of Manasseh the son of Joseph, and their inheritance remained in the tribe of the family of their father." (Numbers 36.)

It is a fitting close to this chapter to present at one view the tribal badges worn upon the standards of Israel through the deserts, in the forty years' wanderings, in the campaigns that resulted in the conquest of Canaan, and in the national career for nearly five centuries, or until the division, B.C. 975.

PTOTEMY III, EVERGETES.

THE ROUGH AND RUGGED WAY TO JERICHO.

CHAPTER XXI.

JORDAN AND ITS SEA.

N Friday, May 8, 1868, at ½ A.M., I left my boarding-house at Jerusalem, the Prussian House of St. John, and with two servants and their horses, together with a guard, furnished me for the consideration of twenty francs by the Sheikh of Bethphage, took my way to the Dead Sea. This Sheikh of Bethphage, Mustapha by name, *farms* from the Pasha of Jerusalem *the privilege* of conducting and guarding travelers to the valley of Jordan and the Dead Sea. He has a good thing of it, out of the thousands who annually make this pilgrimage, and accumulates much wealth. His prices vary with the purse and in experience of travelers. I paid him a Napoleon ($4.00), because I went alone. Had there been a party of us, the expense would have been about five francs each. But I cheerfully admit that my social qualities are not expansive enough to endure a traveling party in the Holy Land I have never seen any two men, in such a combination, who wanted to go the same way, or stop at the same hours of the day, or eat at the same time, or do the same thing generally. There is always a dyspeptic preacher with each half dozen travelers here, and every thing gives way to his whims. No; I will sooner travel "on foot and alone" than "to make one" in a party to the Dead Sea.

Going down the *Via Dolorosa,* on the side of which our hotel is situated, our horses' iron shoes making an unholy rattling upon the stones of the sacred street, I passed the valley of Tyropœon, through which Damascus street runs, and began to ascend towards St. Stephen's Gate, observing the various "Sacred Stations," so called, along the way. At each of these, Catholic devotees pause and worship. Soon the arch of the *Ecce Homo* is before me, suggestive, but in name only, of the most solemn incident that this world affords. On the left of the arch I see a cluster of the scarlet poppy, growing upon a housetop; on the right the various entrances to the Temple area, or great platform of Mount Moriah, which seems green and inviting in this morning light. Little children are playing there in great numbers, and making the *Haram,* or Sacred Enclosure (as the Mohammedans term it), vocal with shouts. Women, closely wrapped in ghostly-white vestments, walk leisurely to and fro. But, tempting as the place appears through these open gates, I know very well that 'twere as much as my life were worth to enter without an order from Nazif Pasha, the Governor.

So, passing forward, I meet a large company of negroes, men, women, and children, who look shiny, and contented enough in this bright sunshine. Their cheerful laugh and chatter remind me of many a scene in my own country, so far in the West that it is only 1 o'clock in the morning there now. Next is the opening to the Governor's palace, the steps lined with red-legged Zouaves. Out of this building comes every afternoon, just before sunset, the wild Saracenic music so dear to Oriental ears, but suggesting to mine only the Plutonian bray of a cavoyard of donkeys. In the distance, it sounds well enough; but at short quarters, a good deal less *drum* and a good deal more *time* would be acceptable to me. Now I pass out at St. Stephen's Gate, the Mount of Olives rising in its gray and solemn majesty before me. On my left hand, in front, is the little enclosure of a half acre, *Gethsemane,* prominent now chiefly for its grove of eight aged olive-trees that peer over the high stonewall surrounding it. I pass close by the low entrance, suggestive of that humility so forcibly taught me, a quarter of a century since, in the degree of Royal Arch. But the blasphemy of inclosing that sacred spot in a high, whitewashed wall, and making a man pay a dollar to go in, destroys its best associations. On the right from St. Stephen's Gate is the vast wall, 1,500 feet long, which supports the Temple area on the east. At the further corner, this wall is eighty feet high; at the nearest, about fifty. The immense stones of which the lower strata are composed, show most significantly in this morning sunlight Under the wall, for a great part of the way, is a cemetery for Moslems, filled with whitewashed monuments, and crowded this Friday morning with Moslem company.

Passing across the brook Kedron, over a little bridge, I rise the first slope of the Mount of Olives. Here is another cemetery, whose gravestones show, in language and form, that a different race awaits the resurrection under them. They are *Jews*. Many of the stones are of great antiquity. The two races, always inimical to each other, lie face to face in death, unfriendly to the last, while the valley of the Kedron stands placidly between, suggesting better thoughts. My guard bursts forth here in a long, monotonous song, or howl, which the Arabs ignorantly conceive to be *music*. Music! It is worse than a hand organ; worse than the Fellow-Crafts Song as I used to hear Brother Y— sing it. I have heard a great deal of this Arab music, but it is always unpleasant. Scanning the appearance of the guard, I find his head covered with a cotton handkerchief, tied on with a rope; his feet enshrouded in large red gaiters, turned up at the toes, stockingless; his legs bare to the knees. His name, as nearly as I can speak it, is Hhhmdbh. He has the usual Arab cloak, with a hood; is girded with a sword like that which "the corpora; of the guard" used to wear, of a wet night, in "Company B, Sixth Regiment, Home Guards," and carries before him a double-barreled shotgun, I hope not loaded. If my life is to rest upon *his* pluck, I shall never return to Jerusalem again; and the Equitable Life Assurance may as well get ready to pay my widow that $4,000.

I passed successively a fanatic, wearing a sheepskin dress, traveling to Bethany in the fulfillment of a vow. His mode of locomotion was really peculiar. I have seen men, at home, so befuddled with drink as to use *both sides* of a road at the same time; but this poor chap is literally making tracks by *lying down and measuring his length* in the road! He looks for all the world like a huge measuring worm. Judging from the marks he made, I should say he was about five feet eight inches, and would reach Bethany, at present rate, by midnight. Great luck to him. I gave him an orange, and it seemed to do him good. The next person I encounter is a woman, driving a donkey before her, loaded with stone; she herself at the same time carrying a heavy load on her back, and *knitting a stocking* as she walks. I will say for her, however, that she is the only really industrious woman of her race I have met for a week. If I knew her name, I would embalm it here; but were I to speak to her the fellahs around would mob me.

Beyond the Garden of Gethsemane, and a little way on my left hand, is the path up which King David walked, weeping, and with naked feet and covered head, when submitting his sorrows to God (2 Sam. 15:30). This path runs up a series of little terraces abundantly productive in olives and figs.

Rising to the crest of Olivet, I take a survey, over my left
shoulder, of the splendid panorama of the City of the Great King,
on which I never weary with gazing. There is but one better
locality for seeing Jerusalem than this; that is Mount Scopas,
about a mile north of Mount Olivet. From Mount Olivet, however,
the eye ranges over the buildings and around the walls of
Jerusalem, as leisurely and accurately as though studying a
model of the city upon a table. Its bulwarks, towers, and regal
buildings, from this summit, must have appeared, in the days of
its prosperity, transcendently glorious. Perhaps Croly had this
point in view when, in his *Salathiel,* he describes the Temple of
Herod in words of great power.

And now the noble expanse of water, the Dead Sea, fifty by nine
miles in extent, which I am today to visit, breaks before my eyes,
fifteen miles distant. It looks from here like a *silver sea.* Pushing
on, past the beggar as naked as the law allows; past the long files
of native women, tattooed hideously with blue upon the lower lip
and chin, with their breasts indecently exposed, and each having
pendent upon the neck one or more heavy silver coins, I now
round the last point, and see the village before me, *Bethany,*
memorable as the locality where Lazarus was raised to a second
mortality by an enlivening voice (John 11), and where, on the
Wednesday of the Passion Week, two days before his crucifixion,
Jesus received the costly offering which a generous woman made
him in anointing his body for burial, eliciting the hypocrisy of
Judas, his covetous defense of the poor, and the overwhelming
rebuke of the Master. Here the brightness of his divinity shone
forth, and here, too, his condemning word fell upon the fruitless
tree, which then to the very root withered away. The loose stones
on this hillside, rattling under my horse's feet, recall the many
instances of stoning to death practiced in this vicinity. How those
old Jews did believe in "the virtue of stones." (Vide Noah
Webster's old Spelling Book). Lucky, the old man in the fable was
not so hasty in their use. Amongst the absurd, often ludicrous
stories told here of Jesus, it is a wonder that no one describes him
as fastening his cruel tormentors *on the stoop,* as they bowed over
to pick up stones for their hateful employment! Perhaps there
may be some such story, though I never heard of it. I give here an
accurate view of Bethany in its present degraded state.

Going over the path that Jesus so often trod, on his way to the
home of Martha and Mary, I wind through the miserable buts of

Bethany, running the gauntlet of its entire population, who stand by the roadside crying "*backsheesh,* howadji," and so on; out at the farther end, looking wistfully upon the house and garden in which,

BETHANY, LOOKING WESTWARD.

tradition says, Lazarus and his sisters lived. Upon a sultry day like this the traveler will prefer to *pass around* this village, rather than encounter the filth and vermin of Bethany.

On a hill, half a mile on the right, is the town of Bethphage, where my sheikh lives. It looks much prettier and larger than its sister town of Bethany. But probably, "'tis distance lends enchantment to the view," in this, as in many other instances. Here the road from the northern side of Mount Olivet joins my own; the way David is said to have come when he fled from before his rebellious son, as intimated above. Down this valley must often have walked the MAN, elegantly described as "one who displayed courage without rashness; humility without meanness; dignity without arrogance; perseverance without obstinacy, and affection without weakness."

We are now half an hour's ride from Bethany, at a gushing fountain, enclosed in a stone framework designed to collect the water for travelers' use. It is close by the roadside, and very convenient for wayfarers. As my guard informs me that we shall find no more water for several hours, my Arab servants drink their fill here, while I ride on, secure in a quart-bottle full of good coffee stowed away in my wallet. In Holy Land travel, a man should *lean* on his coffee-bottle. The road now rapidly descends, and I begin to realize that from Jerusalem to the Dead Sea I have a descent to make of nearly four thousand feet. The air, fortunately, what there is of it, blows *up* the valley; but, in spite of that, the heat already begins to be oppressive. The deep blue haze from the mountains of Moab, that rise up before me, suggests a fearfully hot day, and so does the dark leaden mist that hangs over the Dead Sea yonder, which I am approaching. I wonder if *Bahr Loot* (the Sea of Lot, as the natives call it) presented this appearance to Moses when he stood on that tall peak yonder, and looked over this way with such a longing gaze. It is quite likely; for it was this time of year, only four or five weeks earlier, that Moses died, and Joshua led the people across the Jordan at the place I am to visit before night.

Half an hour further, and the season is two weeks advanced from what it was on the hills about Jerusalem. Here the natives are gathering their crop of beans (lentils, the pottage-bean of Jacob and Esau), and cutting down their harvest of barley. Men *sit on their haunches,* and reach out with the left hand to grasp the barley. They cut it with a poor, dull sickle, about as big as a case knife, held in the right hand. After the reaper has cut all within reach, he rises up, hitches a step forward, and squats again. As fast as cut, the barley is tied up and taken away by the women and children. A flock of goats and sheep follow immediately behind the reapers, and glean all that is left for them; no very abundant leavings, I am sure. In the distance, a flight of vultures are hovering over some object, probably a wounded goat, for whose death they are anxiously waiting. The flies bred in this hot valley begin to distress our poor brutes; and I feel relieved when, two hours further, the road brings me upon open ground. Here are considerable ruins of what was once a large place. Bleached land-shells abound. Upon one of the squared stones, I trace an emblem similar to the *crux ansata,* so frequent in Egyptian hieroglyphics; upon another a handsome molding made upon its three sides. As nearly as I can draw them, the figures will be found on the next page.

Somewhere on my left here must have stood Bahurim, connected with various incidents in Holy Writ; and near it I see a curious specimen of curved stratification, which, had I the time to spare, I would examine more minutely. Now there passes me a sheikh, grave and patriarchal in appearance, with stately figure, calm, composed countenance, and long white beard. I know he looks just as Abraham did when *he* was here.

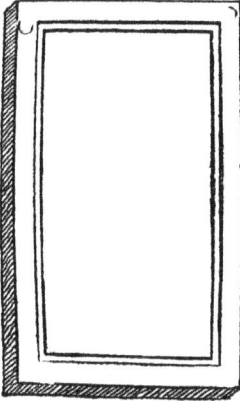

STONE MARKS.

The confused character of these hills, the contorted strata and general want of geological and topographical order that pervades the twelve miles of country I was passing over, throws some light, perhaps, upon the difficulty experienced in following the account in Joshua of the boundary lines, which ran somewhere here between the tribes of Judah and Benjamin. It is literally a "terrible, uninhabited wilderness."

In four hours' ride from Jerusalem, I catch a glimpse of the northwestern bay of (*Bahr Loot*) the Dead Sea. It is useless to endeavor to portray my feelings at this consummation of forty years' desire. Up to this moment I had always felt that to gaze upon the Dead Sea must be the highest privilege of a traveler. But everything around me now is as desolation. The barrenness of the hills approaching the sea is awful beyond description. A livid color hangs upon the rocks and clays. The scanty vegetation seems as stiff and dead as coral. Not a bird, not an insect is visible near the surface of the earth. The great precipices in the mountains beyond the sea actually seem to frown above me, as if warning me to proceed no further. I am conscious of a gloomy superstition oppressing my soul, and already can almost behold phantoms in the air. In such scenes as these dwelt the stern, high-minded teacher, John the Baptist, and here was the place of the temptation of Jesus.

A long descent to a valley gives some variety to the scene, and shuts the horrible vision from my eyes. Now I approach a Mohammedan mosque connected with a large but deserted khan. A well of water, but warm and sulphurous, invites me to alight from my horse and enter. The guide says this is *Neby Mousa,* the tomb of Moses, and that at certain seasons of the year it is much visited by the

22

natives for purposes of worship. The door is covered, not barricaded, by a chain ingeniously hung in front, like one that I saw in Gebal a few weeks since. The windows of the mosque are strongly protected by iron bars, upon which are tied innumerable rags of cotton, silk, and woolen, the tokens of Moslem devotion. Within I can see a tomb covered with a ragged cloth, once richly embroidered with Arabic inscriptions worked in silver, and a canopy hung over that. An elegant silver dish, chased in Saracenic ornamentation, stands on the window ledge, shaped somewhat like a bell. The khan or tavern is very large, and contains many stables for brutes, and apartments for men. The well or cistern is about ten feet deep. Inside of the inclosing wall of the whole, are seen, at intervals of ten feet, large stone rings for fastening horses, placed about two feet from the ground. The dome of the mosque is surmounted by the usual crescent, inclosing a star.

One writer informs us: "This tomb is held in great veneration by all native Mohammedans. The structure over the grave (whose grave cannot now be ascertained) is covered with elegant carpeting and painted calico, extending on all sides to the ground. This canopy is adorned with many long strings of wooden beads hung around it." The Greek Christians affirm that this building was simply erected by a Christian saint named Moses; but this, of course, the Moslems disavow. I am told, in Jerusalem, that some years men and women in great numbers come to Neby Mousa, all the way from Damascus and other places, to worship. An old traveler says "the name of its founder is unknown;" nor, as an author remarks, "is he much wronged by being forgotten, since so mean a building can give no fame to the founder." Another one describes a procession he met on the way to this place, having a live goat in company, which they were about to sacrifice, in the fulfillment of some vow; reminding us of the scapegoat of the Levitical worship, which was led into these hills by an appointed servant of the Temple, and here turned loose to the jackal and wolf of the wilderness.

The surroundings of Neby Mousa are extremely desolate; not a shrub or blade of grass being visible on the naked sides of the hills, scarred with fissures and gaps, where the old hermits used to dwell in the cliffs of the valleys, in the curves of the earth, and in the rocks, among the bushes (Job 30:6). If I could only look south from this scene of barrenness and desolation to the little white dome that covers *Neby Haroun* (the tomb of Aaron), on Mount Hor, two hundred miles distant! But the resting-place of the first High Priest of Israel is too distant for my eye.

Before descending lower, I look across the valley to detect, if it may be, the *Abel-shittim,* the last encampment of Israel ere entering the Promised Land, and read the appropriate passages. It was hard to read, and harder to gaze. Even the sight of the printed paper was lost, at times, in the hot and tremulous haze of the Oriental noon. At one place I caught sight of the road leading from Mar Saba to Jericho, passing through an apparently impassable gorge in whose depths the company of camels looked no larger than the head of the Senior Warden's gavel, in the West.

Resting at the khan of *Neby Mousa,* I again go forward, climbing the last range of hills that separate me from the object of my visit; then descending by a long and unpleasant way to the "plains of Jordan." About a mile below *Neby Mousa,* is the best spot for viewing the sea. It is now high noon, the most sultry hour of a fearfully hot day. Sand clouds are flying along the distant reaches of the valley, pushing last year's stubble over the plain. Flights of pigeons relieve, in a slight degree, the terrible monotony of the scene. Moving forward, another hour brings me to the canebrakes that skirt the sea. These canebrakes, when set on fire, burn like pine-shingles. Brother H. B. Tristam, at Ain Jidy, twenty-five miles south of here, put a brand to such a thicket, and it devoured the briers and thorns, kindled in the thickets of the forest, and mounted up like the lifting up of smoke (Isaiah 9:18). In one of these small canebrakes, my guide points out a small pool of water, from which he and the Arab servants greedily drink, but one mouthful suffices me. It is mawkish and sulphurous stuff. Strange to say, the water abounds in a small black shellfish, of which I preserved a few specimens in my vest pocket. The proper name is, I believe, *melania.*

A traveler fancies that the bark of these shrubs has the scent and taste of smoke. If true, I should attribute this, not so much to the allusion in Genesis as to the incessant puffing of cigarettes that goes on here, from the mouth of every visitor. The same writer, (Chateaubriand) elegantly testifies to Scripture images thus: "This burning sun, this impetuous eagle, this barren fig tree;—all the poetry, all the imagery of Scripture are here. This wild, barren, desolate scenery is a fitting accompaniment of the mysterious sea which rolls its waves over the guilty cities."

Passing the canebrake, only a short interval separates me now from the seashore. To my astonishment, a flock of large and elegant ducks were floating calmly near the water's edge, suggesting thoughts of a duck-supper. But, although I seized the shotgun from my guide and ran towards them, they were too fast for me, and scattered off to the further side of the sea. However, as I discovered afterwards that the gun was not loaded, or capable of it, it makes the less difference. This brief run, by the way, came near ending my mortal career then and there. The torrid heat reflected from the sand, the fact of my having fasted since early breakfast, and the fatigue of the ride, conspired to give me a vertigo which was own cousin to a sunstroke. I sat down upon the drifts of petrified wood that line the shore, drank my strong coffee, hastened to disencumber myself of clothing, ate heartily of my lunch, and in half an hour felt revived.

THE DEAD SEA! How sweetly and placidly it rippled that day at my feet, along its smooth, clean sand and pebbles; how cool its waters to my hands and feet. I could not resist the temptation, hot as the day was, and dangerous as the experiment was, under the dreadful sun, *to take a bath in it.* Carefully holding my umbrella over me, I waded into the sea until the water was up to my chin; then tested, what has been so often affirmed of this singular sea, that *a man cannot sink in its waters;* for I had only to draw my feet under me from the bottom, taking care to keep them perpendicular, and I *floated upright* under my umbrella, like a graceful merman. The only difficulty in the case is to prevent your feet from rising to the surface. I could have floated in this way to the other end of the sea. Inadvertently wetting my head, however, I got some water in my eyes, from which I suffered severely for half an hour afterwards. It took, in fact, several days to bring my eyes to their normal state. The pain is like that produced by getting diluted vitriol under your eyelids, a favorite experiment with boys. Coming out, I was covered, almost in a moment, by an inflorescence of salt and sulphur. My head and ears were stiff with the bitter mixture, which kept me licking my chops for an hour. A few drops of the Dead Sea water falling upon my clothes instantly evaporated, leaving the salt, which remained there until I washed it out a week afterwards.

It would take pages to collect all the absurd accounts on record concerning this *basin of chemicals.* One old fellow heard a dismal sound proceed from its waters, like the stifled clamors of the wretched Sodomites engulfed in its waters! He had probably taken a dose of *arrack* in this hot place, and it got into his head. It served me that way. The desolate but magnificent features of the locality have reminded some fervid fancies of the celestial dream embodied in Paradise Lost. Its rugged and pathless rocks; the native dignity of its scenery; its barrenness, so inhospitable to botanist and bee; the black fetid limestone which underlies it, and starts occasionally into view to suggest the horrors in its bed; the waste land that smoketh; its plants bearing fruits that never come to ripeness; a standing pillar of salt, a monument of unbelievers' souls (Wisdom 9:7)—all these have been described time and again in books. Poets have written:

> "The Dead Sea fruits that tempt the eye,
> But turn to ashes on the lips."
> "The Dead Sea air,
> And nothing lives that enters there;"

and many other words to that effect. Josephus, with his usual gross inaccuracy of detail, avers that "no one was ever drowned in the Dead Sea!" Lucky for the great historian, this test was not tried on him! A story is told down here about a Frenchman who brought a ship to the Dead Sea, a few years since, for exploration. But instead of getting bright copper-boats, as Lieut. Lynch did in 1848, this genius brought an iron one, so heavy it broke down the camels that "toted" the pieces from Joppa. Finally, it was got to the Dead Sea, with immense labor and expense, put together and launched. Then the heat in this awful hollow collapsed the sides and made it leak. The Arabs naturally stole the bolts and loose rigging, and bolted away with 'em. Nobody could navigate it. So the Frenchman gave it to the French Consul; the French Consul gave it to the Turkish Pasha of Jerusalem; and the Pasha of Jerusalem gave it (profanely) to the devil; and finally it was sunk at the bottom, to get rid of it, and now lies, I suppose, not far from the ruins of Sodom and Gomorrah, wherever they may be. But I have not told the hundredth part of the stories I heard about the Dead Sea. In 1322 a traveler declared that *iron* would float in this water, but *feathers* would sink! Some have called it the Lake of Asafœtida; some the Stream of Hell. Nothing but a dog ever had so many hard names as the Dead Sea. But the fellow who wrote that metal would not sink here, would have changed his mind had he seen how quickly my thirteen-bladed knife went under, and how rapidly I snatched it out again. The queer composition reminds me that it has every ingredient, except, perhaps, *antimony,* for making the celebrated *bengal lights.* Some day a Yankee chemist may become a millionaire out of this water!

Josephus says of the bituminous rock that floats from the bottom, "God set this stone on fire by a thunderbolt" (Ant. I., xi. 10). But my "literature of the Dead Sea" is so exuberant, I must throw in a page or two solid:

The people have traditions of cities whose walls and houses are built of slabs of native salt; a nice shelter for a rainy season! "A land of brimstone and salt, that is not sown, nor beareth; nor doth any grass grow thereon;" this is from the Apocrypha.

> "Where now the Dead Sea rolls its sluggish tide,
> And mournful solitude and death reside."

The ingredient bromide, dissolved in potash, as it is here, makes bromide of potassium and bromate of potash. It blackens vegetable colors. Its specific gravity is 2.97, much heavier than water. In ordinary seawater and seaweeds, it is associated with chlorine and iodine; also in some brine springs belonging to rock-salt deposits. This bromide of potassium is used medicinally, chiefly in *scrofulosis,* both internally and externally; dose, four to eight grains daily; the tribe around Jericho evidently do not use it for *their* disease. This exhausts my chemical knowledge. This scene of indescribable barrenness and desolation, of horrid dreariness and marshy despair, the *Valley of Salt,* is finely described in Bonar's work, page 326. I wish somebody would republish it in this country. Standing on the shore, in this seething, fervent heat, and reading with solemn awe the narrative of the destruction of the guilty cities of the plain, as in Genesis 19, a strange connection runs through my mind between the office of Senior Deacon in Fortitude Lodge, No. 47, Kentucky, and the history of Sodom. It takes a hundred times longer to write it than to think it out; yet here is the chain of thought: Lot was a model of hospitality (see Genesis 19); the Senior Deacon, in his admitted duty of "welcoming and accommodating visiting brethren," is the medium of lodge hospitality, so pleasant and so good to its recipient. Jesus declared (in Mark 6:11) that the punishment of inhospitality to his apostles should be greater than that inflicted on the Sodomites. (Q.E.D.) Seeing a flock of wild ducks swimming in these waters, I recall the fact that the American traveler, Stevens, when he was here, March 31, 1836, saw a flock of gulls (probably mallard-ducks, like mine) floating quietly on the surface. Some writers have averred with innocence that no bird ever alights in this water! Recalling David's image of hell, "Raining a burning tempest, fire, and brimstone, and a horrible storm" (Psalm 11:6), and many other passages, I looked over the sea and shuddered. Recalling somebody's account of the groans of demons issuing from the Dead Sea, I will acknowledge that in my own dizziness I seemed to hear deep sighs come from the water. They have a saying down here, that a man who spends a noontime at Bahr Loc: will see ghosts! If he does not look out, he will make one of himself. Visitors should come earlier in the day than I did, and spend several hours in experiments. For instance, boil three ounces of the water dry in a tin cup, and the sediment will weigh one ounce; cover eggs in the hot sand at your feet, and in thirty minutes they will be roasted, *done,* and burst at that; build a fire of the dry brambles your servant can gather at the base of the hills, and lay bits of bitumen on it, and it will smell like a box of Richardson's Detroit matches; drop a fresh egg in the sea and it will float one-third out; put a drop of the water in your right eye and you will weep; a drop in your left and you will howl. The coldest water in which a person can swim easily is 44° Fahrenheit. The stinted, stunted shrubs; the numerous aspects of desolation; the terrible convulsions of nature; the burning sun and the heated air; the barren, salt-crusted terrene, have all been described by hundreds of travelers; and why should I repeat facts published in a hundred volumes? A light boat was conveyed across here from Joppa, in 1837, by Moore and Beck. Previously to that, however, Costigan, who lies buried at Jerusalem, had performed the exploit of navigating the Dead Sea. Molyneaux came in 1847, and Lynch in 1848. There would be no difficulty in this matter, if people would only come here at the right season, say *December* or *January.* All the phenomena that excite so much amazement in the traveler result from the superabundance of salt in the water, and the tremendous heat of the sun. The deep parts of the great Swedish *fresh-water* lakes are *still salt,* owing to the *weight* of that mineral. A thought suggested to me when I spread forth my hands in the midst of the Dead Sea, as he that swimmeth spreadeth forth his hands to swim (Isaiah 25:11). In this relation, we have an abundance of analogies in the United States. Nevada, for instance, is capable of supplying the world with salt. It abounds in salt springs, salt marshes, salt mountains, and great plains, where the evaporation of ages has left deposits of salt almost illimitable in extent. For mining purposes, the salt of these deposits requires only to be shoveled into sacks and transported to the place of use. For table and dairy purposes, it is not quite equal to Eastern salt. It contains a slight percent of impurity, which would have to be removed by re-evaporation, or some refining process, to render it marketable for domestic use. This may not be the case with all deposits of this character within the State, but applies to such of them as have been worked. Within fifty miles of Reno, and not more than one mile from the railroad, are some of the finest salt springs in the world. One gallon of water will evaporate three pounds of the best quality of salt.

I found it profitable, hurried as I was, while sitting here under my white umbrella, to read every Biblical passage I could find in which the sea or its surroundings are named; and taking a piece of salt in my hand, which had been broken from the great salt-mountain (*Jebel*

Usdum), from the southwest corner of the sea yonder, to write this

STORY OF THE LUMP OF SALT.

"I saw the coming of righteous Lot into this circle (*ciccar*) of the Jordan, under the brotherly kindness of his uncle, the patriarch Abraham. I was present when Chedorlaomer invaded these regions from the east, and overthrew the kings of these cities, in a great battle, and captured Lot and his household. When, by the activity and prowess of Abraham and his 'trained servants, born in his own house, three hundred and eighteen,' Lot was rescued, I witnessed his return to Sodom. I recall with fidelity the days when all this region, now a howling wilderness, was 'well watered everywhere, even as the garden of the Lord,' and productive of all things fit for the use of man. I saw when 'there came two angels to Sodom at even; and Lot sat in the gate of Sodom, and made them a feast' (Genesis, 19); and when they warned him, saying, 'Up, get you out of this place, for the Lord will destroy this city," I saw the aged patriarch, with his two daughters, hasten from Sodom and enter into Zoar, his wife tarrying to be transformed into a pillar of salt. Finally, I saw when 'the Lord rained upon Sodom and upon Gomorrah brimstone and fire from the Lord out of heaven; and overthrew those cities, and the plain, and all the inhabitants of the cities, and that which grew upon the ground' (Genesis 19:25). Now, nearly forty centuries afterwards, broken from my native mountains, I am made to relate my *Story of the Lump of Salt!*"

As I could not find it in my heart to locate here the names of Freemasons, I concluded to dedicate it to that hearty opponent of "all secret societies," President Blanchard, empowering him to select nine other genial spirits like himself, and occupy the whole territory Much good may it do them!

Two hours in this tormented place sufficed me; and, having dressed and eaten a few oranges, I started for the Jordan, desiring to visit the traditional place of our Savior's baptism. This took me only forty-five minutes, for I rode fast, and the ground was level. At the first point of striking the riverbanks, they stand about twelve feet above the stream, and are caving in rapidly. At the *Pilgrim's Ford,* as it is called, I spent three hours taking a bath to wash the Dead Sea impurities from me. The water was cool and pleasant to the palate, though somewhat muddy. Here I sung the hymns, "On Jordan's Stormy Banks," "Shall we Gather at the River?" and others, and read accounts of our Savior's baptism, given in the four Evangelists. This is probably the very spot, or at least very near it, where this event occurred. A party of British naval officers was just leaving the place, with whom I exchanged a few words of greeting. I find this class of men always social, gentlemanly, ready to respond to a friendly salutation, and, as a friend suggests, "nothing stuck up about them." A kingfisher perched on the opposite side of the stream enlinked the historical Jordan with the streams and swims of my youth. A theological writer says "all orthodox Christians walk fondly together until they come to the bank of the Jordan; at the water's edge they draw the line."

I cannot record a tithe of the solemn reflections that moved me during my memorable hours under the shady banks of the Jordan. My Arab servants sat just above me, watching my movements, wondering why the howadji abode there so long, and hinting occasionally, "There is yet six miles to ride before we reach Jericho."

> I thought of Jesus in the rush
> Of Jordan's waters, cool and good;
>> How cheering was its noontide draught!
>> Never such healthful cup I'd quaffed;
>> So Christ, whose presence blest its wave,
>> Health and refreshing coolness gave;
> Then, as well-pleased, cheered, I stood,
>> This voice from Jordan's wave I heard:—
> "The stream is holy to our baptized Lord!"

The Jordan weaves itself into happy memories. A writer says: "This flowing, glittering type of swift death, sweeping humanity away in its current, is so interwoven in all our hymns and sacred poetry as the border of the promised land, the heavenly inheritance, that I wonder no poet has yet kindled, standing here, with the thought."

Lieutenant Lynch describes the baptizing scene at the Jordan thus: "In all the wild haste of a disorderly route, Copts and Russians, Poles, Armenians, Greeks, and Syrians, from all parts of Asia, from Europe, from Africa, and from far-distant America, on they came. Men, women, and children, of every age and hue, and in every variety of costume, talking, screaming, shouting in almost every known language under the sun. They dismounted eagerly, in haste, disrobed with precipitation, rushed down the bank, and threw themselves into the stream." I can appreciate the faith with which these ignorant people wash here, as if leaving every sin behind them It was the same that inspired Sigurd the Crusader, A.D. 1110, whose visit to the Jordan is told in these lines:

> "To Jerusalem he came,
> He who loves war's noble game;
> All sin and evil from him flings
> In Jordan's wave; for all his sins,
> Which all must praise, he pardon wins."

As I read the affecting passage—"the Holy Ghost descended in a bodily shape upon him" (Luke 3:22)—I found it pleasant to listen to the cooings of the numerous birds of that class that inhabit the shrubbery on each side of the river. The Arabian prophet Mohammed was accustomed to have a tame dove sit at his ear, claiming that the bird communicated divine precepts to him. Perhaps he borrowed the idea from the passage I have cited. I examined a nest of this bird near the baptizing place. It was shallow and mean, only a few sticks and straws thrown together to prevent the eggs from rolling out. I found a scrap of an English newspaper in it, strangely out of place. Probably some party of tourists dropped it. I can hardly conceive that the bird selected it for educational purposes And with this fragment of the leaden *Times,* I found a scrap of some work on the *Elements of Geometry,* which contained the following information, singularly out of place among these willow trees: "Therefore CD is equal to PQ. But PQ is given: therefore, the point D and the perpendicular DC are given, and, consequently, the point C is given." (But I could not *C* this!) But now appropriate it must have sounded to the doves

THE DOVE.

and nightingales to hear me sing "Shall we Gather at the

River?" and that favorite song of my dear Lottie, "Why have my Loved Ones Gone?"

On the preceding page is an excellent cut of the Syrian dove.

The familiar leaf of the willow caught my eye at once as an old friend, the *agnus castus* willow, and Isaiah's "willows by the watercourses" (44:4). How many a whistle I have made of willow-twigs in boyhood! Can I do less here than to carve a whistle from a willow-bush; called by Hassan *sassaf* (the Hebrew was *tsaphtsapha,* much the same), and cause the king-birds yonder to fly and scream at the unusual sound? But that terrific insect the hornet is here before me, busily engaged in collecting the *fuzz,* as we boys used to call it, for his paper-manufactory. No wonder Moses was afraid of the hornet, and used it (in Deuteronomy 7:20) as an object of divine threatenings against sin. I was once stung by a hornet on my neck, nearly to death.

But I must relate my experience with a nightingale. I was fully prepared to find nightingales here. Old Sandys (A.D. 1610) had said: "Here the nightingales sing more than elsewhere." The Arab poets, referring to

BULBUL. OR NIGHTINGALE.

this locality, had sung, in their fantastic way, of the *bulbul,* or nightingale: "She warbles her enchanting notes, and with her song rends the thin vests of the rosebuds and the rose." A modern poet has said, in the same spirit,

> "'Twas like the notes, half ecstasy, half pain,
> The *bulbul* utters ere her soul depart,
> When, vanquished by some minstrel's purer art,
> She dies upon the lute whose sweetness broke her heart."

Up to this time, however, I had never seen or heard a nightingale While sitting here, therefore, my feet laving in the swift current reading "These were the sons of Gad, captains of the host: one of the least was over an hundred, and the greatest over a thousand; these

were they that went over the Jordan in the first month (about
this time of year), when it had overflown all his banks" (1
Chronicles 12:14), and thinking of those valiant Gaddites, the
comrades of David in his time of trouble; and singing one of my
own old verses commencing, "From Moab's hills the stranger
comes," my ears were attracted by a bird-song of a note and
quality altogether novel and startling. Following it up, I found it
to emanate from a large bunch of the pink blossoms of the
oleander. When I stirred the bush, out flew the bird. *Voila!* here
he is! Not to say a handsome bird; but my own loved girls, Sarah,
Ruth, and Ella, do not touch my ears more delightfully with their
innocent songs and gayety than did the *bulbul* on the Jordan.

The acacia, to which I shall give a larger space in a subsequent
chapter, abounds here, the cut giving a most life-like idea of it.

Here, also, is the Christ's Thorn
(*Ramnus Spina Christi*), called by an
old writer "spring grass." Among the
numerous orders more or less directly
connected with Holy Land, I wonder
we have had none entitled *The
Knight of the Sacred Thorn*. What an
array of emblems and traditions
could be made to surround this
affecting object! Here also is the
castor-oil plant, a persistent shrub,
with wood as hard as poplar; not a
strange thing in this country, where,
as in Florida, the very blackberry has
a woody stock. Here once grew,
although, I think, not now to be
identified, the *Balsam of Jericho*,
esteemed precious beyond all other
tears wept by balmy trees. Incisions
in the bark were made, not with steel,
but with a stone instrument.

ACACIA.

As to the River Jordan itself, every Bible Dictionary gives
dimensions, etc., with elaborate care. Its way, from the Sea of
Galilee, sixty miles above, is made long and troublesome by the
steep descents and labyrinthine windings, falling more than 700
feet in sixty miles of latitude (200 miles as the channel goes).
The Ohio river at Louisville falls twenty-two feet in two

miles, eleven feet per mile—quite a difference. This swiftness of current was reckoned one of the greatest obstacles in building the noble railway bridge erected there in 1870. The Tigris is called by a name denoting *the Arrow,* on account of its swiftness, but it does not equal the Jordan.

It was a gallop across the plain of the Jordan to *Riha,* the relics of old *Jericho.* This is the *cicca* or circle of rich country which that extravagant gallant Marc Antony presented Cleopatra. The once populous city of Jericho has now but *one house,* independent of a cluster of mud-hovels, unworthy the name of human habitations. Look at Rawson's drawing of it.

VILLAGE OF JERICHO.

See the large two-story stone tower, whose owner, Mustapha, sheikh of the village, is brother to the sheikh at Bethphage, the enterprising contractor who supplies guards to travelers visiting this valley. On the housetop of that tower, I was accommodated with a high, rickety table, upon which to spread my blankets, and there I lay with the stars of Palestine looking down upon me all night. The Sheikh Mustapha is a man of courtesy and considerable dignity. He made coffee for me and served me with his own hands. When I expressed a wish to collect a sackful of the *Spina Christi* the next morning, he went out and out it for me with his own sword, really displaying a wish to make my stay at Jericho agreeable. In the tremendous row between him and his neighbors, which is a part of the Arab entertainment at every place I visit, Mustapha preserved his self-respect; and if he grumbled a little at the five-franc piece I paid him, that is only what custom requires him to do, and I think none the worse of him for it.

Lying awake upon my blankets, far above the fleas and lice of the dwelling, a crowd of thoughts occupied my mind. Just here, said I, was the house of Rahab, whose history I had so often recounted in the degree of Heroine of Jericho (Joshua 2). Above me, on the north, are the fords of Jordan that witnessed the extermination of the Ephraimites. The site of Mount Hermon, 100 miles in that direction, connects the source of the Jordan with its mouth. A little west is the Mount of Temptation. At the gates of Jericho, Jesus restored the blind to sight. Near by, Joshua met the captain of the Lord's host. The monster Herod died here, his foul light going out in great horror and agony, and was buried, with undeserved ceremonials, in that round hill to the southwest which I saw this morning from the top of Mount Olivet. A few miles below me is the Dead Sea. I am lying here in a chasm, a cleft in the earth's surface, 1,300 feet below the sea level, in the "City of Palm-trees," which now has not a palm-tree in it. So I meditate, while my blood, heated by the day's journey, cools slowly down; and at last, as the morning is breaking in the east, I sink to sleep, the choruses of the Jericho women sounding in my ears as they sing and dance in their lascivious sports for the entertainment of the naval officers, who fill the half-dozen tents pitched below the castle walls.

The next morning (May 9) I take a seat by the fountain, and all Jericho gather round me. They smoke and make themselves comfortable. I read and write, and make my stay profitable. The naval officers are gone to Jerusalem, and I am the only howadji left in all Jericho. The people watch with breathless interest my motions. My manner of pecking open eggs at the large end meets their hearty approbation. So does my way of peeling oranges, my style of coffee-drinking, teeth-picking, winking my eyes, and other personal peculiarities. My writing puzzles them; for their scribes write from right to left, holding the paper in the left hand, two things I would never do. But when I sing a verse or two of the "Level and the Square," the

Jerichoites express universal admiration of Ossian E. Dodge's music to the same. Oh, if Dodge was here to do it! The people are easily pleased. The women come to the fountain a dozen at a time, with water-skins; take a bold stare at the howadji (these Riha females are said to be shamefully immodest, and I more than half believe it); fill their vessels with water, and lingeringly depart. I take another look at the stone-tower, where I watched the glittering processions of stars all last night. It has no "flax under the roof," as in the days of Rahab, and I could discover no "scarlet cord" tied in the window. Yet there was a good pile of barley-sheaves upon it; strong battlements raised around the edge, according to the requirements of the Mosaic code, and the women of the house were sitting, a pair of them "grinding at the mill," as in Scriptural days. One of the wives of my landlord brought upon her head a "bundle of sticks" for fuel, like that mentioned in Elijah's visit to Sarepta (1 Kings 17:8-24).

In approaching the village last evening, I had been struck with the pastoral character of the scene. From every direction, the shepherd boys and girls were coming in, leading their flocks of sheep and goats, and securely housing them in the folds fenced by impenetrable piles of *Spina Christi* (Christ's Thorn), which forms the principal shrubbery here. Women were gleaning among the fields of barley just reaped, protected in large masses by the same kind of fences. Voices from all directions were calling to the cattle and to one another, answered by the plaintive cries of kids and lambs. The scanty fires, needful for cooking, were glaring up fiercely, as "the thorns under a pot" are said to do in the Bible. The ground underneath sparkles with salt. The ruins of that ancient landmark, Bethhoglah, rise in the south. Even now (March, 1872) the whole scene is indelibly inscribed upon my memory as I recall it.

But the noontime has come. It is high 12. The sun is hot over the sea of Sodom, and I must be off, or stay here until to-morrow. Receiving a *mah sallaharm,* or Moslem *good-bye,* from the Sheikh Mustapha, I mount my Arab steed and move to the great fountain (*Ain Sultan*), about a mile out of my way. My guide picks some fruit from the *Spina Christi,* a yellowish berry about as large as a hazelnut, and gives them to me, naming them *doom,* and claiming *backsheesh.* They taste dry and insipid, like the hawberry. On the way, I observe a thick umbrageous arbor, formed by trailing grapevines over poles. These remind me of the Scriptural expression, "under his own vine and fig tree." Looking back, I am struck with admiration at the beauty of the situation occupied by this ancient city, given up now to a few families of the vilest refuse of the earth.

The Great Fountain (*Ain Sultan*) is truly a magnificent outburst of the life-giving fluid, and I could have lingered there contentedly all the day. It is strange that the villagers of Riha do not move their miserable shanties up to this place, instead of depending for their water supply upon a filthy pool fourteen by six feet, into which the waste waters drip, whose surface is covered with sticks and straws, and having stables all around it, emitting nauseating flavors. The *Ain Sultan* might supply waters for a city. About ten yards below it is a grand old fig tree worthy the spot, and abundant remains exist to prove that once a fine edifice covered the spring, and that its waters were conducted off in various directions by regular aqueducts for irrigation and human use. It was not what we would call cool. Water never is cool in this country as in the springs of America; but it was "sparkling and bright in its liquid light," and truly delicious. A hard lot of women approached me there, sisters to the groups that perambulate Broadway at 10 P.M., and drove me away in disgust.

The largest fountain in the Holy Land is the one at the head of this River Jordan; and here, near its mouth, is another, copious and beautiful if not so large. It was a good time, under this magnificent fig tree, to write up some notes made last night by the light of my candles, on the housetop of Mustapha. If they seem desultory, what else could you expect of a man turning over every five minutes to make a pencil memorandum, every star in the heavens (metaphorically) cocking down its eye at him; as if to say, "Capital! go it, old fellow!"

I was welcomed at Jericho by the sheikh, with a grace that a king on his throne could not excel. (I have never seen a king on his throne.) He wore a large, loose frock, a striped handkerchief around his head (that needed washing; I should dislike to use that in conferring the Eastern Star Degree). His legs were bare (and barely decent at that). He had sandals on his feet (if I know what sandals are, and I am sure I do not). Finally, his beard was very scanty, and, like my own, elegantly twisted up in short knots. You need not pay him anything, unless you want to. But you had better *want to,* or Mustapha will follow you all the way back to Jerusalem, and haunt you in the Holy City until you do. What I mean is, he never *charges* anything for his accommodations. I shall pay him five francs in the morning, and I know he will curse me (in Arabic) the balance of this

Saturday because I do not give him ten. (If I gave him ten, he would curse me for twenty; if twenty, for thirty; if thirty, etc., etc. That's the way they do.) The value of sweet, cool water in this dry, hot atmosphere, that exhausts the powers of perspiration and causes great suffering from thirst, suggested many of the finest figures of the prophets, and even of the Divine Teacher himself. Amongst the females of this mud-made village, I have endeavored to recognize a descendant of the good and heroic Rahab. But, alas! the women of Jericho have nothing in common with heroism, or hospitality, of any other virtue that I know anything about. The town is notorious for being the most immoral place in all Palestine, every sin of ancient Sodom, it is said, being perpetrated here. Blear-eyed, haggard, prematurely old, brazen, and vile, the figures of the women more resemble the horrid phantoms of a nightmare than the pleasant romance of Rahab. Here, on my house-top, let me lie, face upwards (as some day I shall be laid under acacia-sprigs for a long, long slumber), and view these Oriental heavens, crowded with fantastic signs, crabs and fishes, scorpions, bulls, and rams, young ladies, and the locks of young ladies' hair. Herod, here, in his extreme death-pang, might have written, as another conqueror wrote, August 21, 1759, to his friend Dr. Argens: "The torments of Tantalus, the pains of Prometheus, the doom of Sisyphus, were nothing to the torments I suffer." Herod and Frederick were akin at more than one point. Here come Castor and Pollux in their turn, recalling the figurehead of the ship St. Paul sailed in from Malta (Acts 18:11). The elder wife of my landlord, the lady of the castle, who, in my own land, would be the pride, charm, and ornament of domestic life, is simply the household drudge. Ragged, haggard, faded, the word *hag* is the only name that suits her. (That word *hag,* by the way, pronouncing *g* soft, in Arabic, is a term for *holy;* not so in English.) Poor creature! How she jumps when the ungallant Mustapha talks to her. And how he does scold. I never address a dog so roughly. Jupiter, bright and beautiful, is shining just above the summit of the Mount of Temptation; the sky is clear and cloudless. A hawk, fastened by one foot to a basket, is my disconsolate companion on this housetop. Oh, the eager glances he casts at the mountains above! I ought, in common respect for bravery, to buy him and release him. I will tomorrow morning. The quick survey of his fellows as they screamed over him at sundown, and the despair that followed as he tugged in vain at his shackles! He does not sleep a wink to-night, but pulls and pulls at his fetters. Yonder are the telegraphic stations, by which the first observer of the new moon on Moab communicated the news by torches to the priests on Moriah, and so set the grand ceremonials of the Passover in motion. A fine star is just now coming up over them. The purity of the atmosphere brings every star out in its turn. Jupiter, in his brilliancy, suggests new comments upon the astral images of Holy Writ. On that page overhead are the figures of the arithmetic in which Abram was to compute the number of his posterity (Genesis

15:5). "Look now toward heaven," said God to Abram, "and tell the stars, if thou be able to number them; so shall thy seed be." I am canopied by all the gorgeous splendor of this Oriental sky; I am honored by being the reporter to this brilliant panorama moving over my head. There goes a brilliant meteor sailing across to the southward, full fifty degrees high; its luminous tail being visible for several seconds. Satan knew he had conquered the world when he deluded Eve. Had he overcome Jesus on the Mount of Temptation yonder, he would have kept the possession forever. My host is a respectable fellow enough, and endeavors to make my stay comfortable; but his friends and companions are so filthy and black that they might be "brothers to dragons, and companions to owls. Their skin is black upon them, and their bones burned with heat" (Job 30:29). The noble display of the castor-oil tree that I saw today is in itself a *moving* spectacle. I hasten to remember all I know about the bean, and pass on: in Persia it is used for lamp-oil; in Africa the virgins dress their hair with it; in America, naughty boys take it from a spoon. Looking upon Mount Nebo, only fifteen or twenty miles in the southeast, I hum to myself the lines I have so often sung at home, amidst the dear group of wife, sons and daughters.

> "Could we but climb where Moses stood,
>   And view the landscape o'er,
> Not Jordan's stream, nor death's dark flood,
>   Should fright us from that shore."

Mohammed, hearing me sing, climbed up on the roof to ask me if I was sick! So poor an appreciation have these Arabs of genuine music. Here are the Triones of Ursa Major, plowing their patient way round the North Pole, as oxen make their circuit in treading out corn.

> "In the bright even-time,
>   How the twinkling host rejoices;
> Every star in that chime
> Made a melody sublime,
>   Ere the birds tuned their voices."

The frowning cliffs above me, which in the evening sun had worn such a savage and forbidding aspect, look cheerful and habitable now. Vile as this place and its people and their history may be, the force of historical associations is sufficient to triumph over it all, and make Jericho a place of pilgrimage. I could contentedly stay a week here. Even Galen traveled through Syria, in the reign of the Antonines, in search of the opo-balsamum of Jericho, and of the Dead Sea bitumen. He was of opinion that "the watery wine of Palestine is good to cure fevers." How affecting to me the thought that, in a few brief years, the heavens will be a light over my *grave,* as now around my *path;* the stars, even the stars of God, enlightening my sepulcher (Isaiah 14:13). The Arab song goes on below me, a wild, barbarous, unearthly monotone, accompanied by regular clapping of hands, and motions of the body, for all the world like an Indian dance. Those naval officers must have vast powers of endurance. Here the great Joshua was made a witness to the people, and a commander of the people (Isaiah 55:4). That vile woman, Cleopatra, who justified the tremendous words of Isaiah (57:9), debasing herself even into hell, greatly coveted this little plain of Jericho, so rich and abounding. God has made of this city a heap; of this defensed city a ruin; of this palace of strangers no city (Isaiah 25:2). But now the seven clear stars of *Arthur's Round Table* are becoming dim.

> "The withered moon's
> Smote by the fresh beam of the reddening east."

Now, the Fellahin ladies having got their *backsheesh* and gone to rest, nothing interrupts the lonely solitude but the chirping of crickets and the cry of frogs. The reddening of the rosy light betokens a clear morning of pure air. The God of day is rising on Babylon, sending the lions of that ruined site to their repose; and if I expect to get any of the strength that cometh from sleep, it is time I began. So with a puff, out go my candles, and off into dreamland I embark.

Turning away from the Fountain of Elisha, I was accosted by a poor fellow who had been bitten the night before by a snake. The wound was in the junction of the fore and middle fingers of the right hand. In that hot atmosphere it was an alarming sight. His arm was swollen to enormous dimensions. He was pale. He vomited and hiccoughed. In fact, there was but one step between him and death. One of my servants mounted him upon his own horse, and took in exchange the little donkey the poor fellow had ridden, and so we all pushed forward to Jerusalem. I will remark here that, bad as such a wound must be in the Jordan Valley, as soon as I got him into the cooler atmosphere of Jerusalem he began to mend, and in a few days was quite recovered. The grateful creature then haunted me for *backsheesh* all the week.

At so noted a historical place as the *Circle of the Jordan,* including the Pilgrim's Ford, Jericho, the northern end of the Dead Sea, and the Fountain of Elisha, I write the names of ten worthy Masons. In the nomenclature of our lodges I find *Bezer Lodge,* No. 155, Iowa, the locality just east of Jericho, beyond the Jordan; *Bethany Lodge,* No. 176, Virginia, the village a few miles west; *Mount Nebo Lodge,* No. 76, Illinois, and No. 257, New York; *Pisgah Lodge,* No. 32, Indiana, and No. 200, North Carolina, the summit twenty miles in the southeast. Other names of lodges are suggested by this locality. As our distinguished Brother Richard Owen, of Indiana, has illuminated this wild region with a genial touch of geology, I place his name first at this locality, following it with that of his coadjutor, Rev. C. Nutt; then by Robert Ramsay, George B. Edwards, E. Warfield, Rev. F. C. Ewer, A. Coloveloni, Henry L. Palmer, Robert Rushing, Joseph Trimble.

Met a woman with a heavy water-skin on her head, and a heavier child mounted on her shoulder. Yet she stepped off jauntily, making her three miles an hour; and her little boy shook his fist pleasantly towards me, suggesting the cruel blow he would inflict upon my face were his muscles as strong as his will. As soon as I passed out of the valley, I began to see the caves in the cliffs of *Wady Kelt,* where the anchorites of the early centuries of our era scooped out prison homes in the rocky ramparts of these awful ravines. Walter Scott, in the *Talisman,* has given a good idea of one of these men, a man of sin, who in his old age repented and "past into the silent life of prayer."

It was well said of these fellows that they

> "Left human wrongs to right themselves,
> And cared but to pass into the silent life."

If ever I wanted power it was to drive all the idle, worthless race of monks, with which, even now, Holy Land is afflicted, to some useful employment.

Looking back from the acclivity, I observe the ruins of the old sugar-mills built here 800 years ago by the crusaders. The sugarcane stalk served those old pilgrims both for a staff and as a store of provision in emergencies. They had a sweet tooth, those old Simons, and Fellows, and Hatches, and R. N. Browns, and Fred Webbers, of the *Beauseant,* in the tenth century. What nowadays we get at Willard's on the half-shell, they sucked from the end of a sugar cane, viz., Masonic *nutriment.*

The sight of a wolf here brings to mind the tribal badge of Benjamin, to which this territory for so many centuries belonged. The dying father declared (Genesis 49:27), "Benjamin shall raven as a wolf; in the morning he shall devour the prey, and at night he shall divide the spoil." Far down in that valley, where Elijah hid, I see the trees I have just left, whose feet plunge into delightful water, the consolation of the traveler. An old pilgrim described the water as "bitter to drink and productive of sterility until Elisha salted it and blessed it, whereupon it became sweet." Just below it was a garden which, 600 years ago, was styled *the Garden of Abraham,* but no signs of that exist at present. As the water of St. Helena Island is famed for its purity, filtering through several hundred feet of rocks and gravel, so with this.

This country indeed is what the Hebrews styled *Shebarim,* "the rough and broken ground." If any Royal Arch Chapter will perform its work here, "the rough and rugged way" is already laid out for their use. In these crags our June-Saint, John the Baptist, was sequestered from the abodes of men, and fed on such wild nourishment as these uninhabited places afforded him.

Now I pass through valleys shut in by rocks and desolate mountains, and find the heat caused by the sun's rays to be very oppressive.

The next few pages are only to be read by those who have children and love children's stories. I have told the incident, always with "immense applause," in various Sunday-schools, and insert it here as my contribution to the Sunday-school literature of the day.

THE NEST OF YOUNG RAVENS.

When Jesus Christ tells us not to think of what we shall eat, or what we shall drink, or wherewithal we shall be clothed, He means that He will think of these things for us. He knows *what* we want, and *how much* we want, and *when* we want it. He made us, and He knows, even better than we do, what food and clothing and other things we need. So long as we trust in Him we may be sure He will abundantly supply us. In one of the Psalms, David says: "I have been young, and now I am old; yet have I never seen the righteous forsaken, nor his seed begging bread." I can say the same thing.

In coming up one day from Jericho to Jerusalem, I was very forcibly reminded of the fact that God feeds all his creatures with what they need. I will tell you the whole story. I was climbing the steep hill by the side of *Wady Kelt,* the same I believe that is called in the Bible *The Brook Cherith,* and if so, it is the place where Elijah was concealed when King Ahab sought his life, and where the ravens fed him from day to day, and preserved him from starving. As I got about half way up the hill I heard some loud screams far down in the ravine below me, and I knew that it was a nest of young ravens. Ravens are nearly the same as crows; their cry is the same, and you know how loud and harsh a noise a nest of young crows will make. Those that I heard were making the cry of hunger. It was noon. They had had, I suppose, no breakfast. The poor fledglings were lying in their nest, the old birds having gone away. The day was hot. The place was lonely. The little creatures could not get out to feed themselves; and even if they had they did not know what to eat, nor where to find food suitable for them.

As I stopped and looked down into their nest, five hundred feet below me, I thought of the Bible passage, "God hears the young ravens when they cry." Did God really hear those poor little screaming birds? Could it be that God was so near to that lonely, hot, disagreeable place as to hear cries of hunger from a nest of young birds? It was even so. Five hours before, God had sent their father and mother clear across the valley of the Jordan, and down by the riverside, to procure food for them. The black, wise creatures knew where to go to find it. God had taught them. They were God's messengers, God's providers, God's stewards for that nest of hungry, clamorous crows. They went in haste, flying over Elisha's fountain and over ruined Jericho, where I was sitting at that very time, writing my notes by a cistern of water, surrounded by fifty lazy Arabs; and over the thickets of thorn-bushes, and willows, and oleanders, and canebrakes; and so on down to the Jordan, where John baptized Christ. It is a journey of eight miles, "as the crow flies." And as I looked down into that screaming nest of crows, I knew what the little creatures did not know—that their Heavenly Parent was giving to their earthly parents wisdom, and wings, and strong bills, and loving hearts, to supply their necessities.

Still those loud, harsh cries were kept up. Would father and mother never come? It was time. The sun was so hot that all other birds had concealed themselves in shadowy places. Even the sneaking wolf that I had seen an hour before was only hurrying to some old, vacant tomb on the hillside, where he might lie and pant until dark. I began to be afraid, not that the parent ravens had forgotten their duty, but that somebody might have shot them down by the river. A party of English sailors were there this morning, popping their guns at everything they could see. As I thought of this, I felt sad; for I knew that nobody else would care for the little birds, and they would starve to death. I got off my horse; went down the hillside about a hundred steps; found the shadow of a great rock; lay down in it; took out my pocket-Bible, and determined to wait if need be an hour longer, or until those little creatures had had their breakfast.

And there I read verse after verse, proving that God is the great provider. He feeds the "fowls of the air," the "young lions," everything that He has made. Never a mouth but what there is food to put in it—"and shall He not much more feed you?"—Just as I got to that passage, a shadow passed before my eyes. I looked, and here were the old ravens coming with food for their little birds. The little birds had discovered them before I did, and were crying louder than ever. The old ones flew slowly; for they were carrying large pieces of some kind of food in their mouths, and the weather was very hot. But straight to the nest they flew, straight as an arrow. The noise of their hungry children ceased, and I knew their little mouths were filled. A few minutes passed in silence; then I heard the old one give a hoot of satisfied work, and all was still. God had "heard the young ravens as they cry," and had sent them plenty of food.

Climbing up the hill again, I wonder whether the great grandmothers of those noisy crows brought pieces of the tongue of the haughty Nicanor to feed their young ones. A raven lives, I believe, five hundred years, and Nicanor was killed only about two thousand years ago. His tongue, it is said, in 2 Maccabees 15:33, was given by pieces unto the fowls, while his "vile head and his hand, which with proud brags he had stretched out against the temple," were hung up before Jerusalem.

While I waited upon my young crows, my guard rode on ahead to a place I had resolved to visit, and lay down to sleep. This was his tabernacle of a shadow in the daytime of the heat (Isaiah 4:6); the khan or inn of the Good Samaritan, as in Luke 10. Near the ruins of this khan, there is a *ghudeer,* or pool of rainwater, warm, and so impregnated with the salts that abound in this soil as to be almost unpalatable. Not far from the old khan of the Good Samaritan stood the *stone Bohan ben-Reuben,* as in Joshua 6:6. It was on the boundary of the tribes of Judah and Benjamin. Here a party was attacked and plundered, in 1820, as every book on Holy Land since written has said.

Resting for an hour in this little cave hard by, the ancient "Inn" of the Good Samaritan, I occupied the time in investigating the uses made in Scripture history of clefts and caves, and the symbolical application of the same. In a future chapter the subject shall be renewed.

The name of this place, or at least the man who immortalized it, is found in the names of many American and English lodges, as for instance, *Good Samaritan Lodge,* No. 174, Kentucky; No. 104, Alabama; No. 479, England, etc. It accords with the plan of the present volume, therefore, to recognize and extend the sacred association by locating ten Masonic names here, viz., Ossian E. Dodge, David Vinton, George P. Morris, Rob. Morris, Henry Tucker, J. D. Webster, John C. Baker, Percival, Burns, Thomas L. Power—names associated with the poetry and music of Masonic literature.

Passing on to Jerusalem, I drew rein not again until I reached the water-fount below Bethany. Seated for an hour at this *Fountain of the Apostles,* as they called it, my privacy was, of course, invaded. First, by a lot of harvesters, who left their work and came across the valley, thinking to make *backsheesh* out of me. Secondly, by a blind beggar, who has been sitting here, I suppose, ever since yesterday morning, waiting for me to come back. His appeals I soon stopped by a bit of money and the balance of my oranges; and he is even good enough to go away out of my seeing, hearing, touching, tasting, and smelling. Shall I ever have a better time to summon up inspired memories, suggested by this poor blind fellow, who has so long "wandered in darkness," as certain incorrect rituals have it? Here they are, then; come out, pursy notebook; roll forth, facile pencil! Hassan throws up his hands in anguish, knowing that he is stuck for an hour here, and goes incontinently to sleep. (N. B. Note-taking and checker playing with me are vanities.) And here we are: "The blind man of Palestine walks in obscurity and darkness" (Isaiah 29:18), deprived of the pleasurable thrill and excitement which are the lot of others. He follows the traveler, groping, as once they followed Jesus at the base of this hill (Matthew 9:27). . . . . But here I am interrupted by the English sailors just up from Joppa. They need all this space, and more, to swig the last quart in their demijohn. Borne on an ass, the cork of that receptacle has been *out* ever since yesterday morning, and the poor fellows look it. If they do not need the ship's surgeon for a week or two, I miss a conjecture. Refusing to drink with them on the (false) plea that "I had some of my own," I hasten away and arrive at my hotel at about 4 o'clock. Have a difficulty with my guard upon the question of *backsheesh,* and then retire early to rest, thankful that my trip to the Dead Sea and the Jordan has terminated so well. Coming in sight of the city, from the lofty summit of Olivet, Pope's splendid couplets occurred to memory, and with them, I close the chapter.

> Rise, crowned with light, imperial Salem, rise;
> Exalt thy towering head, and lift thine eyes;
> See a new race thy spacious courts adorn,
> See future sons and daughters yet unborn,
> In thronging ranks, on every side, arise,
> Demanding life, impatient for the skies;
> See barbarous nations at thy gates attend,
> Walk in thy light, and in thy temple bend;
> See thy bright altars thronged with prostrate kings,
> And heaped with products of Sabæan springs.
> For thee, Idume's spicy forests grow,
> And seeds of gold in Ophir's mountains glow;
> See heaven its sparkling portals wide display,
> And break upon thee in a flood of day.
> No more the rising sun shall gild the morn,
> Nor evening Cynthia fills her silver horn;
> But lost, dissolved in thy superior rays,
> One tide of glory, one unclouded blaze,
> Pervades thy courts: the LIGHT himself shall shine
> Revealed, and God's eternal day be thine;
> The seas shall fail, the sky in smoke decay,
> Rocks fall to dust and mountains melt away;
> But fixed His word, His promise still remains,
> Thy realm forever lasts, thine own MESSIAH reigns.

JERUSALEM, LOOKING WEST FROM OLIVET.

DIVISION EIGHTH.—JERUSALEM.

The mind, bewildered with the mighty revolutions and desolations which the history of Jerusalem has revealed, delights, at last, to take in walls, churches, houses, and surrounding hills as tangible objects; at last Jerusalem is removed from the region of *fancy* to that of *fact*.

> Yes; if the intensities of hope and fear
> Attract us still, and passionate exercise
> Of lofty thought, the way before us lies
> *Distinct with signs.*

That shining bitter water that engulfs the guilty cities of the plain.

The city, once sacred and glorious, elected by God for his seat, and seated in the midst of the nations, like a diadem crowning the head of the mountains the place of mysteries and miracles.

> Why left a widow! oh, what scars disgrace
> Thy looks! who thus hath hacked thy sacred face?

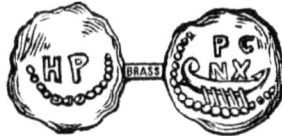

MITE OF HEROD ARCHELAUS. B. C. 4 TO A. D. 6.

CHAPTER XXII.

THE SURROUNDINGS OF JERUSALEM.

T HE literature of Palestine is in want of a good work on the various sieges and assaults to which Jerusalem was subjected, from its capture by Joshua, B.C. 1455, to that last and awful night of the assault, A.D. 70, so graphically described by Josephus, which recalls the prophetic words written eight

ALBERT J. HAWSON, ORIENTAL ARTIST.

centuries before: "Confused noise, and garments rolled in blood" (Isaiah 9:5). Such a work should include the several captures to the present time. Written in the light of military experience, this volume would give a better idea of the *surroundings* of Jerusalem, to which I devote the present chapter, than all the "memorandums" of tourists.

The seventh and last of the grand Masonic localities that these articles are designed to identify and describe, is *the City of Jerusalem,* upon which sacred place my longing eyes were first directed, as I have already written, on Sunday, May 3, 1868. My assistant had been detailed to this point of labor several weeks earlier, and had busied himself in collecting a large quantity of relics and specimens, designed for the cabinets of the zealous craft at home. This enabled me, after my arrival, to give almost undivided attention to sightseeing and note taking in the city and vicinity. The season of the year was highly favorable, the weather being a happy medium between cold and heat; days warm, nights cool; both pleasant. The throngs of pilgrims, who block up the narrow streets during the months of April and May, had departed. I had ordered my horses through to this place by land, so that I was not embarrassed for the means of locomotion. Altogether, my stay in Jerusalem and its surroundings was one of unmingled enjoyment and profit.

As my whole volume, thus far, has been only prefatory, so to speak, to the present division, because chiefly describing the materials (and the localities whence derived and through which transferred), of the Temple once erected at Jerusalem, I must now give large space and ample illustrations of the sacred metropolis itself, towards which, in the days of its gold and glory, all people brought their treasures on the bunches of camels, and the Lord of Hosts came down to fight for Mount Sion, and for the hill thereof (Isaiah 30 and 31). Even now, although Sion is a plowed field, and the foxes (jackals) walk upon it (Lamentations 5:18), there is enough to awaken all latent enthusiasm in the Masonic traveler; and by the aid of engravings, from the faithful hand of Professor A. L. Rawson, whose portrait heads this chapter, I hope to leave nothing that is important in darkness. But, as I said in my preface, though the holiest of holy ground is Jerusalem, yet the writer must use simple language if he would make the proper impression on the reader's mind. In 1840, when the English and French were having their own will in Palestine, the English engineers came up from Joppa, and made an accurate and most valuable plan of this city, to which I am indebted for many of my facts.

But, while acknowledging this, no American should forget how much we are all indebted to Dr. J. T. Barclay, the American missionary at Jerusalem. His close observations of facts, and conscientious adherence to truth, in his long and patient labors in exploring the city, give us, in his volume, *The City of the Great King,* all that can be desired on the subject. Captain Warren told me that the three best works in his possession, relative to Jerusalem and the Holy Land, are *American,* viz., Thomson's *Land and Book,* Robinson's *Biblical Researches,* and the work of Barclay, just referred to. It is a pity the work has been allowed to go out of print.

In giving the surroundings of this city, I have regard to the injunction of the Psalmist, "to walk around" Jerusalem, that I may "tell it" to those who come after me. Few places are so well situated for a reconnaissance as this, being circumscribed on three sides by hills higher than the place itself—a fact to which David makes a fine allusion in Psalm 125:2: "As the mountains are round about Jerusalem, so the Lord is round about his people." I commence this survey, for convenience sake, on the *north* side, from *Mount Scopus.* Here that vile collection of homely,

THE DAMSCUS GATE OF JERUSALEM.

massive structures, the Russian convent, conceals the view on the right. Directly before us is the knob, or swelling ground, to which a number of writers, with good judgment, have applied the name of Calvary, or Golgotha, conceiving it to be the spot where

> "The Lord of all things made himself
> Naked of glory."

Immediately below Golgotha is the traditional cave of Jeremiah, where, it is fabled, he wrote his *Lamentations,* from whence Burns derived *his* lamentable screed, "Man was made to mourn." A little to the left of this, the northeast corner of the city appears like a rambling agricultural village, the vacant places grown up with immense hedges of the prickly pear. The gate next to us is the Damascus Gate (*Bab-es-Shems*), of which I give a drawing.

On the left (east of this gate), there is an opening under the wall, which conducts us to the great quarry, to be described in a future chapter. Still further east is Herod's Gate, now permanently closed. Beyond the wall rises the lofty dome of the Mosque of Omar (improperly so called), the modern representative of Solomon's Temple. This point of view is probably the one taken by Titus for his first observation of Jerusalem, and for the establishment of his military camp, though some writers set the camp a quarter of a mile further west, and a little nearer the city.

DOOR OF A TOMB.

All around are small piles of memorial stones (three, five, seven, nine, eleven or more), set up by pilgrims as *mnemonics* to recall their first or last view of the Holy City. We will erect *our* monument likewise, and endeavor to imagine the reconnaissance made by Titus, so graphically described by Josephus

(*Wars,* II. 19:4, and 5:2-3). But, in speaking of Josephus in the presence of yonder group of Israelites, we will do it "with bated breath," for every Jew considers Josephus the Benedict Arnold of the Roman war.

All around us here are the ruins of the country-houses and happy homes of the ancient people. Even now, the malaria compels foreigners to reside outside the city through the summer months; and there is no better proof than the number and character of these antiquities, in the suburbs of Jerusalem, of the former existence of a wealthy, flourishing, and powerful people here. It must, indeed, have enjoyed an overflowing population, whose residences extended great distances around the central city. All the expressions of enthusiastic writers in the olden time confirm this belief. "Zion, ornament of a ruined world; bright star

INTERIOR OF A TOMB.

in the midst of a gloomy, stormy night, in the pathless, troubled ocean; until the sun of righteousness shall arise, and discover to our longing eyes the port of endless rest." So expatiates one of the most eloquent.

In this vicinity lies that celebrated

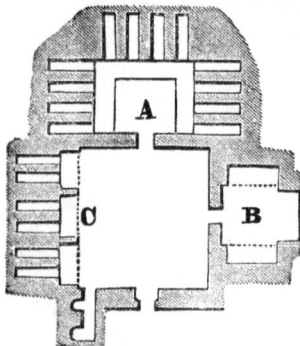

PLAN OF ANCIENT TOMB.

relic, *The Tombs of the Kings,* whose entrance, before De Saulcy cleared away the *débris,* a few years since, had an appearance as in the cut.

The sculpture over the entrance of this tomb, although now exceedingly mutilated, is very beautiful. It represents large clusters of grapes between garlands of flowers, interspersed with Corinthian capitals and other decorations, below which is a tracery of flowers and fruits extending quite across the portal, and hanging down along the sides. It is considered to be the finest specimen of sculpture around Jerusalem. In the walls, recesses are laboriously cut out for the reception of sarcophagi. I append a drawing of the interior of an ancient tomb, but will postpone the description to a future chapter.

SARCOPHAGUS.

When many people and strong nations shall come to seek the Lord of Hosts in Jerusalem, and to pray before the Lord (Zeph. 8:22) may we not expect that the Jews will clear out and reconstruct these sacred houses of the dead, and restore them to former uses? The following is an engraving, from a photograph, of a sarcophagus now in the Louvre, Paris, taken by De Saulcy from the tomb. I place it in contact with a celebrated sarcophagus, found about twenty years since, near Sidon, now also among the antiquities of the Louvre.

The manner in which the heavy stone-doors of these tombs were made to turn, will be seen in this cut of ancient stone-hinges.

SARCOPHAGUS AT SIDON.

24

We pass now along the neck of the ridge connecting Mount Scopus with Mount Olivet, and take our stand near the (improperly called) Church of Ascension. This is admittedly the best point of view from which to study Jerusalem. Here Mr. Church, whose paintings of Californian and Alpine views, and the Falls of Niagara, had placed him among the very first of living artists, took his sketch of Jerusalem, a few weeks before I was here, which has since developed into a $32,000 picture. I met this modest and diligent painter at Beirut, and watched with admiration the works of his life-giving pencil.

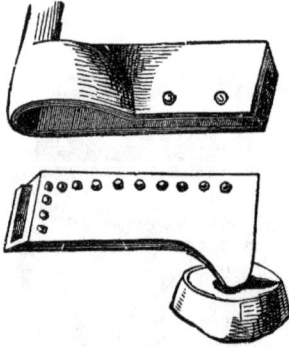

STONE HINGES.

Our view from this point comprehends a very large range of vision westward and northward; and we imagine the soldiers of the Roman Tenth Legion (a kind of crack New York *Seventh Regiment*), who were encamped here for a number of months during the memorable siege, recounting to hearers, in their old age, all the objects that met the eye from this observatory. Below us is an old square tower, used now, I believe, in summer-life, by a family of foreigners. The point of Absalom's Tomb peers slightly over the last ridge next the valley of Jehoshaphat. That enclosure of about one and a half acres, with its whitewashed walls, ten feet high, is the Garden of Gethsemane! It contains eight vast olive-trees, whose enormous roots stand high above the ground. Near it is the opening of the (apocryphal) Tomb of the Holy Virgin, adorned with lamps, flowers, pictures, etc., the ordinary furniture of a Latin chapel. And here I would remark that, in visiting what are considered as the Jewish tombs at Jerusalem, as distinguished from the Phœnician sepulchers, which I saw in such numbers along the cliffs at Gebal, opposite Sidon, Tyre, etc., I have been careful to bear in mind the radical differences between the funeral rites of the two peoples. Those of the Jews were marked with the same simplicity that characterized all their religious observances. The body was washed and anointed, wrapped in a clean linen cloth, and borne without any funeral pomp to the grave, where it was laid without any ceremonial or form of prayer. This severe simplicity was carried into the preparation of their sepulchers, which were always deep, and capable of being closed and sealed at the mouth. The Phœnicians seemed invariably to use the sarcophagus or stone coffin, which, being in itself hermetically sealed and containing an embalmed body, could be laid in a shallow cavity (called *loculus*), or even elevated, like the tomb of King Hiram, far above the surface of the ground, upon the very top of a sepulchral monument, without danger of giving out offensive odors. All purely Jewish rock-cut tombs may be recognized, it is thought, from this national difference of the deep *loculus* (or grave). To this is referred the passage in John 11:39, "take away the stone." Had Lazarus been laid in a Phœnician tomb, a heavy lid must have been removed to reach his body; not to say that the ceremony of embalming, which occupied many days, and occasioned the removal of most of the internal parts of the body, would have changed the entire nature of the miracle. But lying in the condition in which he died, in a tomb, on the level, or a little below the level, of the earth, the stone at the entrance of the *loculus* being removed, exposed the entire body to the eye of the observer. There are, perhaps, 1,000 of these rock-cut tombs around Jerusalem.

How I should like to hear the agreeable, tender, and elegant music of Beethoven's oratorio of "Mount Olivet" played here upon this historical summit, instead of yonder jingle of instruments on the steps of the Governor's *serai* (palace).

Among the most pleasing accounts I have read of the city, from this point of view, I reckon that in Bro. H. B. Tristam's *Land of Israel,* where he describes the birds of Jerusalem. Here he had the field all to himself, the rest of us, in the contemplation of stones and ruins, forgetting that such things as birds exist in the Holy City at all. But his notes under this head are full and charming. In the olive-trees, he says, the beautiful little palm turtledove dwells (*Tur-tur Senegalensis*), and remains here all winter. In the cypress-trees is the goldfinch (*Carduelis elegans*); also the great titmouse (*Parus major*). In the corner of a wall I marked the blue thrush (*Petrocincla Cyanea*); and running along the pavement, the white wagtail; and in the side and the dome of Kubbet es-Sakhrah, the kestrel (*Tinnunculus alaudarius*), and the little owl (*Athene meridionalis*). And much more to the same effect.

Studying here the history of the siege and assault by Titus, I cannot help wondering why for this he did not use the catapult. It was invented 450 years before, and was certainly capable of throwing huge stones much further than the distance from where we are standing, into the heart of yonder city.

One of the most remarkable pieces of *picture writing* in the world is that given in the cut of the siege of Jerusalem by the King of Nineveh, about B.C. 710. It was discovered by Layard, and is now in the British Museum. In it we see the olive-trees; the brook Kidron; the fortified city; Mount Olivet with a castle on the summit, and other characters.

SIEGE OF JERUSALEM.

Extending our vision westward, we have the deep gorge of the valley of Jehoshaphat, introduced (improperly) into Blue Lodge rituals. Through this valley ran the brook Kidron, now sunk fifty feet under loose earth, that chokes the ancient channel. I never could pass this brook Kidron without recalling the words which Ezekiel wrote concerning it. He makes it the connecting link between Jerusalem the *Holy* and the Dead Sea the *Impure*. In chapter 47 we read:

"Then said he unto me, These waters issue out toward the east country, and go down into the desert, and go into the sea; which being brought forth into the sea, *the waters shall be healed*. And it shall come to pass, that every thing that liveth, which moveth, whithersoever the river shall come, *shall live;* and there shall be a very great multitude of fish, because these waters shall come thither; for they shall be healed; and everything shall live, whither the river cometh." The two existing bridges here serve at least to keep us in mind of the prophecy, although there is no water here now to suggest them.

There is an elegant myth connected with the literature of Masonry, to the effect that, upon the arrival of Hiram Abif at Jerusalem, King Solomon conducted him to a point near the junction of the mountains now termed Olivet and Offence, and showed him the range entitled Moriah, which he had selected as the site of his projected temple. On one occasion I sought that spot, and endeavored to paint the scene in its natural colors. Moriah was a long, narrow ridge, deeply furrowed by ravines, divided primarily into three peaks by cross valleys, the top of the range rising nearly 400 feet above the bed of the valley of Jehoshaphat on the east, and that of Tyropœon on the west. Upon that most illy-fitted hill, the king had ordained the construction of his temple; the top to be cut off, the sides to be raised by immense walls, nearly 200 feet high, and the interstices filled in with stone. Such were the preliminary steps requisite to form even a platform for the temple. In point of fact, all this must be done before a stone of the building itself could be laid down.

Our story goes on to say that it was in that conference that Hiram initiated King Solomon into the mysteries of Adonis, as practiced for so many centuries in Phœnicia, and thus the two great men were drawn together by fraternal ties, only severed by death. The fate of Adonis, which forms the esotery of that system, was strangely paralleled, a few years afterwards, by the fate of Hiram himself. No spot in all the vicinity of Jerusalem is associated with matters of deeper Masonic interest than this.

And next we will take notice of the eastern wall of Jerusalem, in the center of which is St. Stephen's Gate, or Lady Mary Gate (Bab es-Sitti Miriam), of which I give a drawing

Nearly all the wall to the left (south) of this is the grand substructure of the Noble Enclosure, or Mount Moriah, marked out to us with distinctness by the great dome that we saw from Mount Scopus.

Long before reaching this city, I had resolved, at all hazards, to place *the Masonic mark* of the Square and Compass

ST. STEPHEN'S GATE.

conspicuously upon some one of the huge ashlars that make up the wall of the old Temple area on its eastern side. The task was by no means a pleasant one, nor altogether safe.

Across the valley of Jehoshaphat, in plain view, is the village of Silwan (Siloam), whose inhabitants are among the most fanatical people in the vicinity. Close by, on the north, is a large Moslem graveyard, often crowded with Mohammedan women, who would scarcely permit a Christian to walk so near their cherished tombs, much less commit the profanity of cutting into the Temple-wall with a chisel. Add to this, one of the principal roads around the city runs within thirty steps of the ashlar I had selected for my operations, so that I was liable to interruption at any moment— and the reader will appreciate the difficulties of the task. However, I was not easily deterred; and placing an assistant in the road below, with instructions to keep a vigilant lookout, I marked out my figure, and began. Perhaps the real danger of this attempt, after all, lay in the military lookouts upon the works one hundred feet above my head. Had they witnessed my operations, it was like them to pitch a donick or two over the wall, or even to fire their pieces down upon me; and this, according to the usages of that sanctuary, would have been justifiable in them. But I made my mark deep and bold, as future travelers will not fail to see. It is cut in the fifth stone of the second tier of blocks, counting from the southeast corner of the old Temple-wall to the north. The block is a large one, though not the largest in that part of the structure.

To a fragment of this vast wall which I brought home to America, I have attached this

STORY OF THE STONE.

"I lay darkly and silently in the quarries under Mount Moriah, when the first builders of Jerusalem, the ancient Jebusites, gathered their materials, and erected their walls of defense upon Mount Zion. I slumbered there at the time of the pious meeting between Abraham and Melchizedek; and when the patriarch brought his son Isaac here, forty-two years later, to an interrupted sacrifice upon the crown of the hill of Moriah; and when Jacob fled northward on his way to a divine vision, at Bethel; and when he returned, twenty years later, with his dying Rachel; and when Joseph passed here, ten years later, in the search of his brethren. I heard the shock of the onset when Joshua took Jerusalem, at the point of the sword, two hundred and seventy-eight years later, and burnt it with fire; and the shock of the onset when King David, at the head of all Israel, took it by assault, four hundred and four years later, and made it the seat of his kingdom.

I was taken, thirty-seven years afterwards, from the quarries, a great stone, hewed and squared, and laid up here in the east wall, one hundred feet from its base, facing the rising sun. Here I have remained for two thousand eight hundred and eighty years. I have witnessed great events. I saw the dedication of the Temple, seven and one-half years after its cornerstone was laid. I heard the shout of the assembled millions who bowed their faces to the pavement and cried, 'For He is good; for His mercy endureth forever.' The gleam of the fire from heaven and the shadow of the miraculous smoke alike passed over my polished face. I witnessed the coming of the great Chaldean, four hundred and sixteen years later; heard his battle cry; saw the irresistible assault of his armies; the city ruined, and the Temple burned. Fifty-two years afterwards, I saw the little company under Zerubbabel return from Babylon and begin the pious task of rebuilding. Three hundred and seventy-one years later, I saw the greater Maccabæus perform the same pious undertaking. One hundred and forty-seven years later, I saw a second re-edification of the Temple by the monster Herod. Fifty-one years later, I beheld the triumphant procession of the Son of Man, as he passed over the great bridge connecting Mount Olivet with Mount Moriah, when the people of Jerusalem shouted 'Hosanna to the Son of David.' A few days afterwards, the same people, fickle and untrustworthy, shouted, 'Crucify Him.' Then I saw the heavens darkened at mid-day, and felt a trembling of the solid earth, such as Jerusalem rarely experiences. Thirty-seven years later, I witnessed the armies of Titus fortifying the hill east of me, and drawing their lines around the doomed city; then heard those sounds of assault, resistance, and final despair, with which, by this time, I had become so familiar. These savage sights and sounds were often renewed afterwards. In A.D. 1099, I was shaken in my place by the onset of the crusaders, who put 7,000 men to the sword upon the platform just above me, until the blood flowed over our wall like the drenchings of a great rainstorm. Again and again I was an eye-witness of such scenes, until now, two thousand eight hundred and eighty years from my first establishment in this wall, I give to an inquiring Freemason from distant lands my strange story of the stone."

As an appropriate botanical emblem here, I note the plant of Solomonic fame, "the hyssop that springeth out of the wall," and give a cut of it. I have a specimen of it today (February 29, 1872), fresh and green, which I plucked nearly four years ago from Hiram's Tomb.

All intelligent visitors to Jerusalem have
united in praising the scenery from Mount
Olivet. It is mild and gentle, with soft
variations of light and shade. One elegant
writer calls the view "a solace of holy
reminiscences pure and native." Raised two
hundred and ninety-five feet above Mount
Moriah, which is the nearest part of
Jerusalem, the sketcher sees the city as a
continuous hill, standing out singly from
the surrounding mountains. Here David
stood, while contemplating with a soldier's
eye the strong fortress of Jebus on the
opposite cliffs, and preparing with his two
hundred and eighty thousand men, choice
warriors of Israel, to storm it. (1 Chron. 12)
Shishak stood here, and Nebuchadnezzar,
and Titus, and all the conquerors of
Jerusalem; for from this point the defenses
could best be viewed, and arrangements
made for the attack. From here, perhaps,
Josephus pointed out the various localities
to Titus, who, with his Tenth Legion, made
this his principal point of observation
during the long months of the siege. From
this commanding spot, all the imagery of
the Levitical worship was best seen; and
here the captain of Nebuchadnezzar
studied it day by day during the eighteen

HYSSOP.

months that *he* strove to capture Jerusalem. Observers also
stood here when the man born blind was led down to Siloam
yonder, and came back seeing (John 9:7); and when the
impotent man took up his bed and walked from the margin of
Bethesda yonder (John 2:2); and when the chief musician, on
Neginoth, with stringed instruments and high-sounding
cymbals, praised God according to His excellent greatness
(Psalm 150), on yonder platform; and when the great Antiochus,
swelling with anger, vowed proudly "that he would come to
Jerusalem and make it a common burying-place of the Jews" (2
Macc. 9:4); and when the early American missionary, Pliny Fisk,
entered the Damascus Gate yonder, in 1823, to "go about his
Master's business" at Jerusalem; and when Saul, "breathing out
threats and slaughter against the disciples of the Lord" (Acts

9), went out of that same gate to the persecution, and came back several years afterwards the humblest of the followers of the meek and lowly Jesus. Observers stood here when the Jews "stoned Stephen" on yonder hillside, "calling upon God and saying, Lord Jesus, receive my spirit" (Acts 7:59); and when the great procession passed westward along this very pathway by whose side I am sitting—passed over garments spread in the way, and over branches of trees, and went across the stupendous bridge, now destroyed, and through the portals of the Golden Gate, yonder, while "they that went before and they that followed said, Hosanna, blessed is he that cometh in the name of the Lord" (Mark 11); and when Jesus "beheld the city," probably at this very spot, and "wept over it" (Luke 19:41), just as he had wept over the sorrows of the disconsolate family at Bethany but a few days before (John 11); finally, on that dark, that doleful afternoon, when "the earth did quake and the rocks rent," and "darkness was over the whole land until the ninth hour," because Christ, on yonder ridge, scarcely a mile from this spot, had given up the ghost, first enduring the pangs of the cross,— but my sentence can never be completed. *All those scenes,* and a multitude of others, embracing incidents in the life of every Scriptural character from Abraham to Paul, occurred within sight of spectators upon this memorable slope of Olivet where I sit.

ABSALOM'S TOMB.

We pass now down the valley of Jehoshaphat, leaving successively on our left the old Hebrew burying-ground, the Tombs of Absalom.

Zechariah, etc., and reach first the Virgin's Fount, and then the pool of Siloam. My cut shows these monuments with distinctness.

A vivid fancy has drawn a parallel between this "bringing to light" of the blind man here and the symbolic representation familiar to every Mason. What a glorious sunlight kindled up his long sightless eyeballs, and brought the beautiful and cheering scenes of nature to his knowledge! How the heart of Judas must have clashed with his covetous nature every step of the way along this gloomy dale, as he went to the palace of the High Priest to receive the wages of his treason! On the left of us is the village of Siloam (Silwan), where the people live in the dark, damp tombs. My cut is of the upper spring, or Virgin's Fount.

VIRGIN'S FOUNT.

We cannot fail to observe, below the pool of Siloam, the extraordinary fertility of the soil, as displayed in the productions of the gardens here. These are the *King's Gardens* of Solomon's time. This is the valley of Shaveh, where the prince Melchizedek met the patriarch Abraham reclining as these lazy natives are reclining today, and gave him bread and wine in the name of the Most High God (Genesis 14:18). My cut, taken from a point further south, at Aceldama (the *Potter's Field* of Judas), shows us this extraordinary development, always apparent in this country when there is water enough for irrigation; also the village of Siloam, the church on the summit of Olivet on the right, and the dome of Omar on the left. This engraving exhibits the valley of Jehoshaphat in its best features.

VIEW NORTH FROM ACELDAMA.

Climbing again in a southwesterly direction, we find ourselves on the Hill of Evil Counsel, so called, honeycombed beneath with ancient tombs. The heavy, square edifice directly before us, near the south-western corner of the city, outside, is the Tomb of David, in which is the apartment traditionally styled *Cœnaculum* (supper-room), in which the Lord's Supper was instituted, and beneath which, with far more reason, we place the bodies of David and Solomon, and some fifteen of their royal successors. Here is a cut of the edifice so famed.

DAVID'S TOMB, MOUNT SION.

Between us and the tomb are the various Protestant cemeteries, American, English, and others. Included in the ten thousand tragedies surrounding this city, there is one that particularly touches an American heart. When W. M. Thomson came here in 1834, to open a missionary station, he left his wife in the city, and went back to Joppa for his furniture and clothing deposited there. In the meantime, a rebellion broke out, and for several months he was unable to return. The city, in this time, was cannonaded, decimated by cholera, and terribly shaken by earthquakes; so that, when at last he was enabled to return, his first view of Jerusalem caused horror and faintness to seize him, in the apprehension caused by seeing his house knocked to pieces by artillery. His wife died a few weeks afterward of the fright and exposure, and the afflicted man wrote, "The Lord hath put out the light in my dwelling, laid my earthly hopes in the dust, and rendered my dear little babe motherless in a strange land.' That child is now Prof. W. H. Thomson, of New York.

The visitor to this cemetery should also look up the grave of poor Costigan, and, before going down to the Dead Sea, read his melancholy history. Stevens (*Travels,* II. 235) records it with much feeling. Near the honored grave of Mrs. Thomson lies Dr. Asa Dodge, a zealous American missionary, who died here January 28, 1835.

Passing around the southwest angle of the city, leaving the vast "Lower Pool of Gihon" on the left, and striking out westward sufficiently far to secure a good view of the city from this quarter, our attention is first attracted to the massive Tower of David (so called) by the Joppa Gate. I place two cuts in juxtaposition.

THE DAVID TOWER.

Here, at the Joppa Gate, the Emperor Hadrian, about A.D. 120, set up the image of a *hog,* not an uncommon emblem on the Roman coins, but a most horrible insult to the nation that built Jerusalem.

This completes our circuit of the city, comprising a ride of about six miles, though the actual circuit of the walls themselves is but 4,326 yards, or two and a half miles. It is a curious subject of contemplation, that, in some far-distant day, a tourist from some

THE JOPPA GATE; OR GATE ON THE WEST SIDE OF JERUSALEM.

far-distant land may, in like manner, circumambulate the then desolate city of *New York,* stopping inquiringly at the corner of Fulton-street and Broadway, where the signs of old buildings have quite disappeared, and wondering how far in this direction, from the ruined stone piers at Castle Garden, the once magnificent metropolis extended! Like Mount Sion, Manhattan then may yield to the excavator its wealth of carved marbles, ancient coins, domestic objects, and human bones.

As I set out in this chapter regretting that we have no proper account of the sieges and captures, assaults and defenses of Jerusalem, I am glad to add that a history of Jerusalem from Herod to the present time will be published this year (1872) from the pens of Walter Besant and E. H. Palmer, giving special attention to the period 1099 to 1187, so interesting to Knights Templars.

The view of the stupendous ruins of Jerusalem one calm Sabbath morning called to my mind the beautiful Masonic allegory of "working in silence," founded as it is upon the following passages:

"And the house, when it was in building, was built of stone made ready before it was brought thither; so that there was neither hammer nor axe, nor any tool of iron heard in the house, while it was in building." (1 Kings 6:7.) This suggests one of the grandest purposes of the Masonic institution, viz., the promotion of peace and harmony. Mr. Beecher, in one of his inimitable prayers, has said, to the same effect: "Thy work, O Lord! in the structure of the human soul, and thy government that is established beyond and out of our sight, are wrought out here. Here thou art bringing forth the stones for thy building; here is the sound of the hammer and the chisel; here is all confusion, and here are all waste and noisome things; but here is but the ground where thou art *shaping.* Yonder is where thou art *building,* and there they that stand around thee behold the perfectness of all thy work, which thou hast had in hand since the beginning of the world!" These are grand, good words, and will touch a chord in every Masonic heart; for it is a Masonic precept, that "we are laborers together with God; we are God's husbandry we are God's building." That great man who, eighteen centuries ago, preached along these hills, teaching men everywhere to believe, repent, and be saved, was proud to make the claim: "According to the grace of God, which is given unto me, as a wise master-builder, I have laid the foundation." (1 Cor. 3:10.)

PTOLEMY I. SOTER. STRUCK AT TYRE.

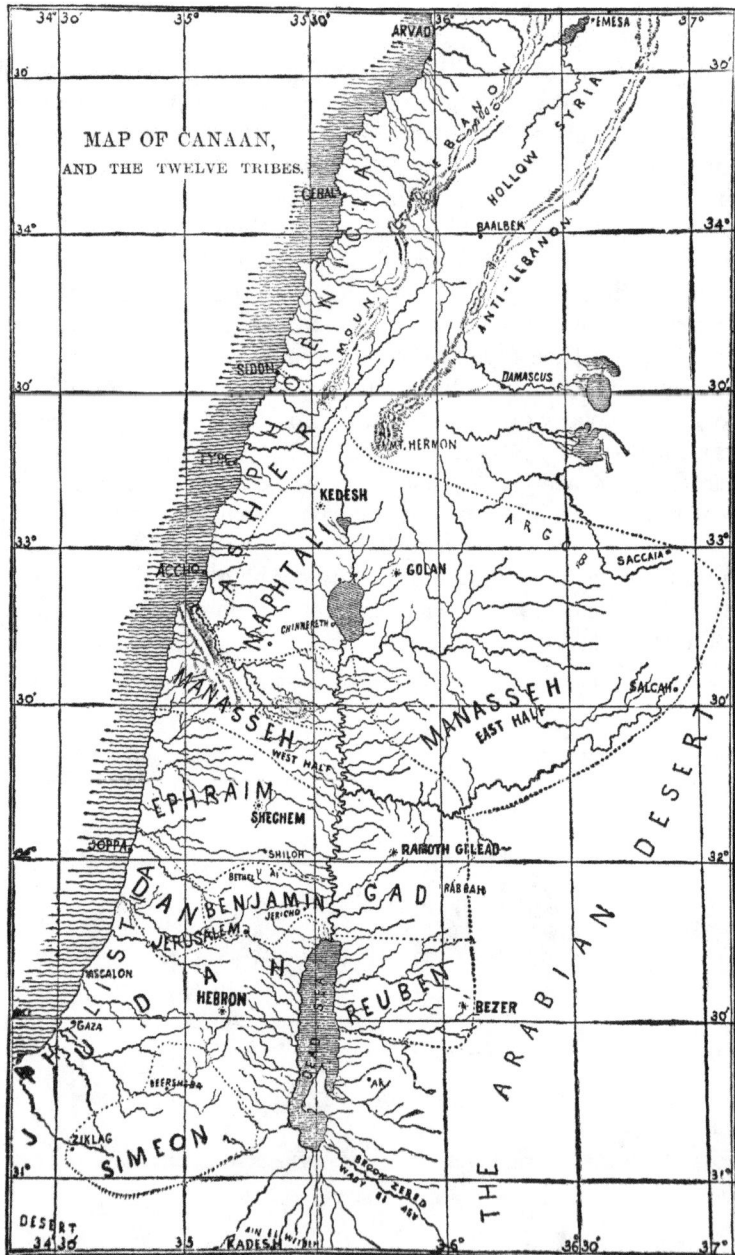

MAP OF CANAAN,
AND THE TWELVE TRIBES.

CHAPTER XXIII.

JERUSALEM IN 1868.

T HE incident of my sending a telegram, in 1868, from Beirut to a friend in Jerusalem, fitly illustrates the changes that have come over this ancient city since the days when, isolated by its vast precipices, wretched roads, and swarming enemies, the crusaders who held it in the eleventh century yearned for months and years to receive news from their distant homes, but yearned in vain. The recent setting-up of a steam-

REV. H. PETERMANN, D.D., LL.D.,
Resident, 1868, at Jerusalem; a Mason of 40 years' standing.

engine in Jerusalem for grinding grain is another illustration in the same direction; how had King Solomon's 183,300 workmen been diminished to the number of 10,000, could his architects have employed the power of steam instead of human labor, to saw, cut, remove, and lift in place the mighty ashlars now visible in the inclosing walls of Mount Moriah. The population is at present about 25,000, of whom nearly one half (10,000) are Jews. The city has two good hotels, and various boarding houses, in one of which, the *Prussian House,* under the patronage of the Prussian *Knights of St. John,* I made my abode. Missionaries of almost every Christian nation except America are engaged here in the education and conversion of the natives. Some of their establishments, such as the English Episcopal, the Roman Catholic, the Armenian, and the Greek churches, are imposing in magnitude. The American Vice-Consul at Jerusalem, Mr. L. M. Johnson (in 1872 a citizen of New Haven, Connecticut), is a gentleman of fine qualifications, and treated me with much courtesy and attention. The present incumbent of the office is Hon. R. Beardsley, a very ardent Mason, formerly of Elkhart, Indiana. At the Prussian House, where I boarded, all are welcome, up to the limits of the house; and only those who are able are expected to pay. My bill was only five francs ($1) per day, while the fare is abundant and good. The place is snug and comfortable; well described by a gentleman who was here some years since as "a singularly constructed concern. A high wall or foundation looks on the street, and on that the house is built. You climb from the street by a narrow wooden stairway, and enter a court about forty feet square, round which the rooms are huddled. From this court rises a second stairway, which leads to a row of rooms; another stairway takes you to another batch of chambers, and so you reach the housetop, flat, like all houses in this country." This affords, at a *coup d'œil,* a glimpse of Scopus, Olivet, the village of Siloam, Mosque of Omar, Sion, and many noted points besides. In the furniture of my boarding-house, scrupulously clean as it was, evidences could be seen of what I had observed more plainly in the English Hotel at Joppa, viz., the ravages of *the moth (Tinea tapetzella),* referred to in Bible passages, and which is very destructive in this climate. The general idea of my housetop, with its battlements, etc., will be gathered from the cut on the next page.

The streets of Jerusalem, like those of Oriental cities, towns, and villages generally, are extremely narrow. There are two reasons for this: *first,* that the population may be crowded, for defensive purposes, into as little space as possible—most towns being upon hilltops, where *space* is restricted; *second,* because the people believe they can *keep cooler* in this way. In the hot season, they

VIEW OF A HOUSETOP.

spread matting across from roof to roof, which throw the streets into a dense shade that certainly is cooler than our broad streets exposed to the full blaze of the sun. The streets of Jerusalem likewise are filthy. The reader will hardly conceive that so much carrion, so much manure, so much old vegetables, and the *débris* of humanity, can be packed into one alley six to ten feet wide. But they do it, and do it neatly. In regard to this nastiness, I am reminded that in the eighth century, annually, on the 15th September, immense processions used to traverse Jerusalem, and render them extremely offensive with dung; but they had no sooner left the city than heavy rains would fall, completely purifying it. It is not so now. One could wish that the builder of the *Cloaca Maxima* (B. C. 588) at Rome had an imitator in Jerusalem, to drain off the foul matters which have no outlet but the streets and a few shallow and restricted sewers. Is the view from these contracted streets an agreeable one? Not much. This passage from somebody's notebook describes it: "Bare stone walls; prison-like houses; very few latticed windows; the whole view wretchedly unsatisfactory to a civilized eye." The proud and stately Moslem, fingering his beads in abstracted mood, threads the bazaar with step as proud and stately as a Pharisee; and yet, if you look at his *feet,* you see a combination of every sort of excrement; and if you open your nostrils, you gather in, from the same, a variety of effluvias to which the celebrated "three-and-forty stinks of Cologne" were nothing. *Verbum sat sap.*

In coming to Jerusalem, I had certain well-defined objects of research, and confined myself mainly to them. This is prudent. To come simply "to see what is to be seen," as a traveler told me he did, is to see nothing coolly and deliberately. On the other hand, the visitor may waste his days seeking unattainable objects. A student once showed me a list of the things *he* intended to look up, should he ever visit Jerusalem. Among them were the mark of the Ass's feet that bore Jesus from Bethany over Mount Olivet, and into the Temple (Matthew 21) Sir John Maundeville said they were here when he came, A.D. 1322, visible at three places on the steps of the Golden Gate, which are of very hard stone. Also the pillar that Absalom in his lifetime had reared up in the king's dale, as in 2 Samuel 18. He had been told that everybody throws stones at it, as a mark of scorn at that cruel son, and he was determined to do it too. Likewise the pool of Siloam. The tradition is that the water of it will heal sore and inflamed eyes. He had resolved to carry a bottleful of it home and experiment upon it. Also a palm-tree standing on the side of Mount Olivet, from which the branches were taken to honor Christ. He assured me he would gather some of the leaves. (Matt. 21) And, finally, the stone column to which our Lord was bound when he was scourged. (Matt. 27:26.) Long afterwards, the marks of blood were to be seen on it, if the monks tell the truth, and I am sure they do not. I need not say that the traveler seeking for such things only wastes his time.

In reading accounts of such a monument of antiquity as Jerusalem, we want *to see it just as it is,* in its every-day, working dress. We would behold its dazzle and its dirt; its numerous classes of inhabitants grouped and herded together within the walls; the manners and customs of its motley populace; the character of the priests and monks; the remains of ancient civilization, and the prospects and possibilities of improvement. Such was my aim.

To get rid of a subject who is in everybody's mind, I commence with a sketch of the so-called Holy Sepulcher.

In my observations on this subject, I but express the feeling of all Protestants of my acquaintance who have weighed the

CHURCH OF THE HOLY SEPULCHRE.

arguments by which Papal and Greek writers endeavor to palm this place upon the Christian world as the veritable Calvary and Cemetery of Christ. For my part, I find no passage that so well expresses my views of these false traditions and unholy mummeries as one written by Brother Rev. Pliny Fisk, the missionary, who visited here in 1823, the same referred to in Chapter Thirteenth. After seeing the poor theatricals made up here of the crucifixion scene, he wrote: "I felt as though Jerusalem were a place accursed of God, and given over to iniquity and sin. The Jews hate the name of Christ, and gnash their teeth when it is spoken; the Turks exalt their false prophet above Christ's most glorious name, and are distinguished for their hypocrisy, tyranny, and deception; the Greeks and Armenians profane the Temple of the Lord. having little of the essential nature of Christianity."

Passing along by the so-called Holy Sepulcher, one morning, I looked in for a few minutes to witness some of its processions. The workmen had just completed the new dome, and were taking down the timbers. I had read all that can be said for and against accepting this place as the locality of our Savior's death and burial, and would not allow the gorgeousness of the scene to influence my mind. I believe it is all a *fiction,* got up by tradition-forgers for gain. The whole structure, every stone, arch, pillar, altar, statue, image, picture, and lamp, is a *falsehood,* a gorgeous imposture, an ecclesiastical hoax. The more the local traditions of Jerusalem are examined, the more I distrust them. Old writers tell us nothing else; modern writers must be fanatics if they venture to say anything about them except to deride them. They *coin legends* and frame an ecclesiastical topography without history or research. The business of travelers now is to collect *facts* one by one that will illustrate God's history, and these must explode the legends.

But even though this building should contain all the relics it claims, and ten thousand more, this would not countenance in the slightest degree the abominable idolatries practiced here. There is no idolatry on earth more offensive; no more unseemly and indecent behavior practiced in any heathen temple, than here, where the hopes and affections of the Eastern Church tend; where tens and hundreds of thousands come up to obtain pardon for their sins, and lull at the cross or the tomb their guilty consciences to sleep, never to be awakened until it is too late. The Holy Sepulcher is the Mecca of the corrupt Christianity of the East. From two minarets close by, the cry of "God is God; Mohammed is the prophet of God," floats over this broad roof, and announces to the four winds of heaven that the Moslem dominates the cradle of the Christian faith. In this building, by a monstrous stretch of faith, to which my boyhood's belief in Gulliver's Travels was mathematical accuracy, they have crowded seventy distinct "sacred localities" under one roof, and provided seventeen semi and demisemi sects of Christians to swear to their identity. The New Jersey brother who is said to believe in the "legends" of the *Scotch Rite,* is Solomon himself compared with this. The Wisconsin man who endorses the *Rite of Memphis* is Sir Isaac Newton personified compared with these. And after all, the building can scarcely be called a *church,* being more like a large *depot-building,* covering two score offices. Worthier than this, and really a larger church, because a *single edifice,* is the Armenian Church of St. James, on Mt. Sion. This, too, is unequalled in sacred vestments and rich decorations. Amongst its curiosities is the chair that St. James used to sit on. I forgot to ask for this, and cannot describe the pattern to my chair-making correspondents. The number of ostrich-eggs hanging from the roof of this church, however, suggests the prolific *lays* of that stately bird. The cry of an old pilgrim visiting the Holy Sepulcher, was, "Oh, who can behold without sorrow, without indignation, the enemies of Christ acting as the lords of his sepulcher!"

How analogous is this fine character to our memories of him who, not far from this same spot, was found

"Buried beneath the green sprigs,
Sleeping under the sod."

I thought of this when I found a large acacia-tree growing in an Englishman's garden, a short distance south of this spot.

I give four cuts of the ancient seals of Jerusalem.

SEAL OF THE KING OF JERUSALEM.
Amorium I. 1162–1137.

HOSPITALIS JERUSALEM.
Knights of St. John.

Having now said all that I have space for concerning this "thesaurus of lies," the Holy Sepulcher, I go on to record such thoughts as are naturally suggested by a walk through Jerusalem.

The tenements seem to be sinking into the earth. One story seems already sunk, and the others are so rapidly following, that in another generation the observer can lean from the street on to the flat roof.

The Jews here, although living in idleness and poverty, two things abhorrent to their nature, emulate the blessing pronounced in Nehemiah 11:2, "upon all the men that willingly offered themselves to dwell at Jerusalem." For they came to Jerusalem strictly for religions purposes, that living, they may pave the way for the future return of their nation to these holy hills, and dying, they may be buried in that ancient cemetery across

Jehoshaphat, where the slope of Olivet is already paved with their tombstones. How affectingly those memorial stones speak of the sleepers beneath, is seen in the two following epitaphs (translated from the Hebrew) from that place. There is a peculiar accent of touching grace in them; a humility; a certain hope of universal kindness; a sense of the happiness of reposing with the just; purity of morals and sweetness of family life; a mild acceptation of death, considered as *repose,* which have not had the attention of travelers they deserve. These two are the epitaphs of a lady and her husband:

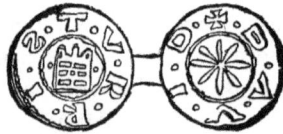

TURRIS DAVID.
Baldwin IV. 1174–1185 A.D

HOLY SEPULCHRE, 1150.

EPITAPH OF A WOMAN.

"Great in degree, and glorious; the heart of her husband trusted safely in her; praised as a woman that feareth the Lord. She was the king's daughter, all glorious within, who rose above all elevation, and was perfect in beauty, glory, and righteousness. She opened her mouth with wisdom, and in her tongue was the law of kindness; a stem of high descent and elevation. Was she not the Rabbiness (Mrs. Rabbi), the pleasant roe, and the widow of our master and teacher, the holy Rabbi, the holy, pious Chaim, the son of Ater, of blessed memory? She was daughter of the mighty and wise, the high prince, our honored teacher, Rabbi Moses, the son of Ater, of blessed memory."

EPITAPH OF A MAN.

"Here is a head of gold. Was he not beloved of the Almighty? A precious stone; to discourse of him, is easy. The Almighty meant it for good when he enlightened him from his glory, as they lighten the seven lamps; his shaft, and his branch, it kindled his people. And he called him by the name Hephzibah. He was a bringer to light of all that is kind; he was glory, he was brightness. Was he not the wonderful and honored Rabbi, the perfect theologian (cabalist) of the Almighty, the holy, the pious, our honored teacher and Lord Rabbi, Chaim, son of Ater? He grew old, seeking in the Upper Geshibah (place of study); on the fifteenth day of the month of Thamuz, in the year 5550 (*i.e.,* the year A. D. 1790), gaining the splendor of the Shecinah. He is the author of the book 'The Lord the King (Hammelech Hashene), and the book 'Taar' (Form), and the book 'Or Ha-haiiom' (Light of the Living), and the book 'Rishon le Zion' (Is. 51:27), (First to Zion)."

So great is the change in favor of the modern Jews, that, according to the New York *Independent* of June 1, 1871, the Sultan is inducing Jews to immigrate into Palestine, offering to sell them even the Mosque of Omar (but this is incredible). The same authority states that some of the hills around Jerusalem are already Jewish property.

The Armenians here are very strong in numbers, and wealthy. They have an immensely large convent (an enormous edifice) in the cool and quiet street that runs southward on Mount Sion, and I greatly enjoyed my visit to their library and printing press. I found the manager of the press a noble specimen of an Armenian gentleman, dressed in fur-robes, black hair and eyes, intelligent and affable. The librarian had an olive complexion, a face solid as marble, a calm, intelligent eye, and looked, as old Dr. Caswell used to, as if he knew what was inside of his books. My guide, Mr. Serapion Murad, is a fine young Syrian of striking appearance, set off by an elegant native dress. I had considerable intercourse with him in both Joppa and Jerusalem. The Armenian Patriarch is a gentleman of polished manners and sensible speech, quite well posted in American history and manners.

The spirit that moves these Latins, Armenians, and Greeks in their dealings with each other is quite Celtic, and of the Donnybrook Fair type. One side is perpetually dropping "the tail of me coat" on the ground, and the other side delights to tread on it. Once a year the Pope of Rome officially excommunicates the Greek Patriarch of Jerusalem for some of his shindigs; and in one of the churches in Rome a nail is driven into the ground with a hammer, as a mark of malediction. And still the Patriarch eats his allowance, and still it does him good. He is the handsomest man that I know of, and one of the best-tempered; and I can't help thinking, if Pius X. (or is it XX.?) had been with me the morning I called on him, and taken a spoonful of those preserves and a cup of that coffee, and shared in that genial chat, he would put his tenpennies hereafter to a better purpose. But what is the use of talking in that way?

The chapel near "Ecce Homo" Arch (as it is most improperly styled) is full of gaudy and ridiculous paintings and ornaments as suggestive of devotion to an educated Christian's mind as the Hindu idol that adorns my parlor at La Grange, Kentucky, is to an educated believer in Confucius; and this is the general impression made on a Protestant's mind in visiting these Oriental churches. They show the skull of one of their old monks, and boast that, although he lived here twenty years, he never visited the Dead Sea. I am

INTERIOR JERUSALEM HOUSE.

told the skull is a very thick one, and readily believe it. It is close by the traditional spot at which the Wandering Jew mocked Jesus, and received the sentence that drove him forth upon a ceaseless pilgrimage, and gave us such entertaining books as *Salathiel, Le Juif Errant,* etc. Close by this is a stone trough, out of which, they say, the beggar Lazarus took his stinted rations. I asked one of the monks if he knew that Josephus was born here A.D. 37? He replied that he had never heard of Josephus before. I believe him.

I found the Governor of Jerusalem, Nazeef Pasha, to be a short, stout man, handsomely dressed, a square-built, sailor-looking fellow. He was not over-courteous to me, not being a Freemason. In fact, he has the reputation of being an anti-Mason. They call him a religious fanatic, one who goes through his five series of prayers daily, and keeps all the feasts and fasts of the Mohammedan Church punctually, and hates Christians worse than anything else except Jews. One good thing stands to his credit, although he has been removed from the government since I was there; that is, he constructed the turnpike from Joppa to Jerusalem, to the delectation of all modern tourists. As to his ear for music, however, I cannot say so much, if the noises made by the brass band on his doorsteps, every evening about sunset, is done by his order.

The location of Jerusalem relatively to other places is thus tabulated:

Latitude, 31° 46' north.

Longitude, 35° 18' east of Greenwich.

From Joppa, 35 miles.
   "   the Jordan, 18 miles.
   "   Hebron, 19 miles.
   "   Bethel, 13 miles.
   "   Bethlehem, 5 miles.
   "   Samaria, 36 miles.
   "   Jericho, 13 miles.
   "   Nazareth, 45 miles.
   "   Acre, 75 miles.
   "   Baalbec, 165 miles.
   "   Capernaum, 82 miles.
   "   Damascus, 155 miles.
   "   Gaza, 48 miles.
   "   Palmyra, 160 miles.
   "   Tyre, 110 miles.
   "   Sidon, 132 miles.
   "   Beirut, 157 miles.

TABLE OF RELATIVE HEIGHTS.

I give two classes of heights; the first from the sea level, the second from the well En-rogel (Beer Eyub), at the outlet of the valley of Jehoshaphat.

Russian Convent	2,610	614
Mount Olivet	2,724	728
Mosque of Omar	2,429	433
David's Tomb	2,537	441
Pool of Siloam	2,114	118
Bridge over Kedron	2,281	285

CIRCUIT OF THE CITY,

commencing at the northwest corner.

To the Joppa Gate	300	steps.
" southwest corner	468	"
" Sion Gate	195	"
" bend in south wall	295	"
" Mograbbin Gate	244	"
" southeast corner	415	"
" Golden Gate	353	"
" St. Stephen's Gate	230	"

To the northeast corner	360	steps.
" Herod's Gate	359	"
" the bend	250	"
" Damascus Gate	150	"
" northwest corner	660	"

Total steps...................... 4,279 or about 2-2/3 miles.

TOPOGRAPHY OF JERUSALEM.

So many works have been issued on this subject within ten years that almost every reader has the information at hand, and I will not repeat at much length merely second-hand knowledge.

Jerusalem is a mountain-city. It was pre-eminently so to the Jew; for, with the exception of Samaria and Hebron, the other great cities within his ken, those of Egypt and Mesopotamia, Damascus, Tyre, Gaza, Jezreel, Jericho, were emphatically cities of the plain. The Bible teems with allusions to this local peculiarity of its site as a mountain-city. The plateau on which the city stands is of tertiary limestone; the strata nearly horizontal, the landscape showing generally a succession of plateau and flat-topped hills, broken here and there by deep narrow gullies.

At the point where the city stands, a tongue of land is enclosed between two of these ravines, and on this the modern, like the ancient, city, is built. The easternmost of these ravines, the valley of Jehoshaphat or of the Kedron, has a course nearly north and south; the westernmost, the valley of Hinnom, after running a short distance to the southward, makes a bold sweep to the east, and, forming the southern limit to the tongue of land above mentioned, joins the valley of Kedron, not far from the Beer Eyub, or Well of Joab. Both ravines commence as a mere depression of the ground, but their floors sink rapidly, and their sides, encumbered as they are now with the accumulated *débris* of centuries, and the ruins of buildings thrown down by successive invaders or domestic factions, are still steep and difficult of access. In ancient times, the bare rock must have shown itself in many places, and the natural difficulties of the ground were artificially increased in ancient times by the scarping of the rock-surface. Hence, we find Jerusalem to have been at all times, before the invention of gunpowder, looked upon as a fortress of great strength. On three sides, the east, the south, and the west, the encircling ravines formed an impregnable obstacle to an assailant;

the attack, therefore, could only be directed against *the northern face* of the city, where, as we are informed by Josephus, the absence of natural defenses was, at the time of the famous siege by Titus, supplied by three distinct lines of wall. To determine the actual course of these walls is, notwithstanding the detailed description of them in Josephus, one of the most difficult problems before us.

Besides these two principal ravines, a third ravine of less importance splits the tongue of land into two unequal portions. This is the Tyropœon valley, the valley of cheese makers, or, as some would have it, the Tyrian merchants. A marked depression of the ground runs from north to south through the midst of the modern city, from the Damascus gate to a point in the Kedron valley, somewhat north of its junction with the valley of Hinnom, forming in its course the boundary between the Mohammedan, and the Christian and Jewish quarters of the modern city. At one part of its course, it forms the western boundary of Mount Moriah. This depression has generally been identified in its whole course with the Tyropœon valley of Josephus, and all are agreed in identifying the lower portion, which runs under the west wall of the Haram, and thence to the Kedron, with the Tyropœon. In ancient times, this valley was much deeper than at present, and its ancient course was to the eastward of its present course. It is filled up with *débris* thirty feet, fifty feet, and even eighty-five feet in depth.

The city being thus split in the midst into two ridges by this valley, it may be observed, by a reference to the map of Jerusalem, that the western ridge is the most elevated and most important. Most authorities are agreed in placing on some portion of this ridge the original city of Jebus, captured by King David, and the Upper City of Josephus. All again are agreed in fixing Ophel on the end of the tongue of land called Moriah, and in making the site of the Temples of Solomon, Zerubbabel, and Herod, and of the castle of Antonia, either coincide with or occupy some portion of the Haram itself.

But here all agreement may be said to stop. There are differences of opinion whether we should fix the Mount Zion of the Bible and the Mount Zion of the writers of Christian times on the same or on opposite hills; whether the name is to be identified with the eastern or the western ridge. The exact position of the Temple is matter of controversy; the site of the Acra of Josephus, and the Acra of the book of Maccabees; of Bezetha, the fourth quarter and last added suburb of the city; the position of the Towers Hippicus, Phasaelus, and Mariamme, and of the Tower Pheshinus, which, if determined would go far to settle the disputed question of the course of the second and third walls of Josephus; the exact extent of the city in the time of our Savior; are matters of keen dispute, which can only be settled by patient and systematic burrowing into the *débris* produced by many successive demolitions of the city at those points where the absence of inhabited houses renders it possible to excavate at

It was always a matter of interest to me, and especially in the days of that vilified order, "the Conservators," to follow Nehemiah understandingly in his remarkable nocturnal survey of Jerusalem. It is quite a proper thing to compare Nehemiah, the Tirshatha of the Jews, the renowned wall-builder of the Jewish restoration, the philanthropic Peabody of his day, whose large wealth was profusely expended in the strengthening of Jerusalem and the care of its poor, to a Freemason, jealous of his honor, zealous in his work, feeling his responsibility to the Grand Architect of the Universe for the manner in which he spends his days. Such a comparison is just in all its parts. The history of this perfect model of a just and generous man is contained in the interesting book which bears his name: that he was "the son of Hachaliah" and apparently of the tribe of Judah; that he was born during the Babylonish captivity, about B.C. **500**, and that, at the opening of his biography, he was "the cup-bearer" of King Artaxerxes Longimanus, residing during the winter season at Shushan, are the principal data from which we must set out. In the twentieth year of that king's reign, viz., B.C. 445, in the month of Chisleu, or December, a near kinsman of his, one Hanani, brought him intelligence from Jerusalem that affected him deeply.

It will be remembered that in the year B.C. **536** (ninety-one years prior to the period of which we are writing) Zerubbabel had led a caravan of his people back from Babylonia to Jerusalem. These had rebuilt the temple and portions of the city. Seventy-nine years after that Ezra led a second caravan back to Jerusalem. But the united efforts of these bands and their posterity had done but little to restore Israel to its former glory. Marauders made property and life insecure; murder and robbery were rife even within the streets of Jerusalem; the people had largely abandoned the religion of their fathers, and the whole nation was in a state of abject affliction and reproach. This was the intelligence which had reached the ears of Nehemiah through his kinsman Hanani.

A prudent man, he gave himself until the following April to consider how best he could heal the wounds of his people. A pious man, he offered the prayer which his own pen had recorded, styling God "the great and terrible God that keepeth covenant and mercy," confessing that his people "had not kept his commandments, statutes, nor judgments," and asking that God would prosper his purposes in behalf of Jerusalem, and "give him mercy in the sight of the king." This being done, he laid before the king the doleful case of Israel; and, upon the monarch's asking him, "For what dost thou make request?" plead that "he might be sent to Judah to rebuild it." The favor was granted in the largest measure. Nehemiah was made the governor of Judah, with the power of life and death; a mounted guard was furnished him; letters to the governors of the intervening districts were given him by the king; special orders were issued that he should be supplied with timber from the king's forests; and so he set forth, amply furnished and endorsed.

His worst anticipations as to the condition of Jerusalem and the Jewish nation were realized upon his arrival. A late writer says: "It is impossible to overestimate the importance to the future political and ecclesiastical prosperity of the Jewish nation" of the coming of this patriotic governor. He spent but three days in preparations, for he was bound by promise to return to the king at a set time; and then began, but at first secretly, the most important work (that of building the city walls). Arising "in the night," he and "some few men" with him, telling no man "what his God had put in his heart to do at Jerusalem," the little company—all save himself being on foot—made the circumambulation of the ruins of Jerusalem, with a view to the speedy rebuilding of the walls.

This nocturnal reconnaissance has been until recently a blind track to Bible-readers. The labors of Dr. J. T. Barclay, for many years a missionary at Jerusalem, and a most diligent explorer of the ancient city, at length set up so many of the fallen "metes and bounds" as to enable me to nearly follow the steps of the great Tirshatha around its area. Dr. Barclay's solution of this zigzag problem is contained in the parentheses. Nehemiah says: "I went out by the gate of the valley (the Joppa Gate), even before the dragon well (the pool in the valley on the west), and (turning to the left) to the dung port (500 yards south), and viewed the walls of Jerusalem on the west side. Then (having gone round the point of Mount Zion to the south) I went on to the gate of the fountain (by the pool of Siloam), and (turning round the point of Mount Ophel to the south and east) to the King's Pool (the Fount of the Virgin); but there was no place for the beast that was under me to pass (owing to the accumulation of water and rubbish there). Then I went up in the night by the brook (Kedron), and viewed the wall (on the east side of the city), and turned back and entered (again) by the gate of the valley (the Joppa Gate), and so returned." To sum up this reconnaissance, the reader has only to take a map of Jerusalem, observe that the zealous governor went out at the Joppa Gate, turned to the left, circumambulated Mount Zion to Siloam, then round the point of Ophel to the valley east of the Temple. He then turned back, and retraced his journey to the Joppa Gate.

Having, like a skillful engineer, estimated the amount of labor necessary to be done, he now called together "the priests, the nobles, and the rulers," and in nervous language exhorted them to duty. He reminded them of the prevalent distress, Jerusalem waste, and her gates burned with fire, and said, "Come, *let us* build up the wall of Jerusalem, that we be no more a reproach." He told them of God's answer to his prayer in the distant land of exile, and of the kindness and liberality of the king; and so wrought upon them by his appeals that they cried out, *"let us rise up and build,"* and set themselves with decision to the work. Only one exception is noted in the popular response; the Tekoite nobles "put not their necks to the work of the Lord; all the rest had a mind to the work." With such energy did the people labor, that in a wonderfully short time the walls emerged from the heaps of rubbish and encircled the city as in days of old. Dividing the wall into ten parts, corresponding with the quarters of the city nearest which they dwelt respectively, the princes and leaders vied with each other in self-sacrifice and industry, and so in fifty-two days the work was accomplished.

Agreeably to his promise to the king, Nehemiah then returned to Babylon. He paid a second visit to Jerusalem, perhaps a third, at one of which he performed the splendid and triumphant ceremonial of dedicating the walls. This festival occasion is minutely described in the Book of Nehemiah.

In summing up the character of this man, we endorse the views of a late writer, that we are unable to find a single fault to counterbalance his many and great virtues. For pure and disinterested patriotism, he stands unrivalled. He firmly repressed the exactions of the nobles and the rich, and rescued the poor Jews from spoliation and slavery. He refused to receive his lawful allowance as governor from the people, in consideration of their poverty, during the whole twelve years that he was in office, but kept at his own charge a table for 150 Jews, at which any who returned from captivity were welcome.

I know of nothing to excite the interest of a Freemason in this building so much as the thought that here repose the ashes of knighthood's noblest exponent, *Godfrey de Boulion.* Here I read his inscription, which expresses a volume: *Hic jacet inclytus Dux Godefridus de Bulion, qui totam istam terram acquisivit cultui Christiano: cujus anima regnet cum Christo. Amen.* Let all who can admire dignity, virtue, generosity, and humanity combined in one noble soul, answer, *Amen, so mote it be!*

It has been said of the inimitable Godfrey, that in him the gentlest manners were united to the firmest spirit; the amiableness of virtue to its commanding gravity. He was alike distinguished for political courage and for personal bravery. His lofty mind was capable of the grandest enterprises. His deportment was moral. His piety was fervent. He regretted the stern necessity that drew him from the immediate service of God; but when in arms he was a hero. And his martial zeal in the cause of heaven was always directed by prudence and tempered by philanthropy. Faithful to his first simple wish of becoming the defender and advocate of the Holy Sepulcher, and pressed as he was by the voice of all the chiefs of the Crusade, he nevertheless refused to wear a diadem in the city where his Savior had worn a crown of thorns. His tomb, by which I stood, was watered not alone by the tears of friends, but honored by the commendations of many of the Moslems, whose affections his natural virtues had conciliated.

Godfrey was elected by the army, A.D. 1099, first king of the Latin monarchy of Jerusalem, but declined, accepting only the title of *Defender of the Tomb of Christ.* He granted a donation to the St. John's Hospital, which had been established at Jerusalem in 1048 (fifty-one years before), in which act he was followed by the other princes. This, in fact, originated the order of St. John of Jerusalem, with which many of the Crusader knights became affiliated, adding to the usual vows of poverty, chastity, and obedience, those of caring for the sick and warring against Mohammedanism. Godfrey died the following year, five days preceding the first anniversary of his government. His spurs are preserved here; also that formidable sword with which, A.D. 1098, on the bridge of Antioch, he clove in twain a gigantic Saracen.

So transcendent were the virtues of Godfrey, that Tasso closes
his immortal poem of *Jerusalem Delivered* by describing his
passage, armed as he was and in his sanguine vest, to the Temple,
where he

"Hung up his arms, his bannered spoils displayed,
And at the Sacred Tomb his vowed devotion paid!"

My own lines upon the immortal Godfrey are here given:

THE CHOICE OF GODFREY.

Not where the Savior bore
    Thorns on his brow;
Not where my king upon
    Cross-tree did bow;
Not where the Prince of Life
    Sorrowed and groaned,
Godfrey shall ever be
    Homaged and crowned.

Mine be the humbler name,
    Fitter by far,
"Warder of Tomb Divine,
    Christ's Sepulcher!"
Mine at its portal
    In armor to lie!
Mine in death's ministry
    When I shall die.

Knight of Christ's Sepulcher,
    Christ's Chevalier,
Good Sword of Jesus,
    Oh, live grandly here!
Ashes of Godfrey, there's
    No place like this,
Crowned in Christ's glory
    And reigning in bliss!

It would be easy to fill this book with the notes and
memorandums made relative to the street-scenes of Jerusalem. If
I am not mistaken, such things constitute a class of facts perused
with avidity by all, and whatever real originality a man can throw
around so worn and trite a theme as Jerusalem, must be looked
for in this direction. Therefore, I will be somewhat diffuse upon
this subject, and copy the notes from my diary as made.

STREET-SCENES IN JERUSALEM.

A little girl about six years old, another little girl about twelve, playing camel, and the big girl is the camel. She kneels down as camels do. Then the little one climbs her back, clasps hands over her forehead, kicks her in the side and makes a noise as cameliers do. The big girl screams and gets up awkwardly, as a camel does, turns her head back, grinds her teeth, spits and shrieks, then away they both go, laughing just as such a merry pair of sisters ought to. All the dress the two girls have on would not cover a candle-stand decently. Their clothes are made of blue cotton of the thinnest, cheapest, and raggedest character. But, oh, what a merry game of camel they do play!

A chicken-peddler with strings of poultry swung all over him. The man is covered with hens. A rooster's head is sticking out where *his* head ought to be. An enormous pair of wings flaps over his shoulders, reminding me of the ridiculous old angel that I saw painted in a Greek church yesterday.

Three laboring men sitting on the sidewalk near me, eating their breakfast. Their only victuals are *libbarn,* or curdled milk, in a small wooden dish, and *bread* that looks like such black sawdust as mahogany-wood makes. I gave them some boiled eggs. Nobody ever saw eggs boiled so hard as they boil them in Jerusalem. They must keep them on hand ready boiled. They boil them over night. Never was a lot of boiled eggs swallowed so fast before. Then the grateful fellows came up to thank me. Each one put his right hand under my right hand so as just to touch it, and raised it up to his lips and kissed it. This is the way they do here. They went off without even asking me for *backsheesh*. Probably they forgot it.

A dog, lying under the window, suckles her four pups, young things whose eyes are not yet opened. The sidewalk is only twenty inches wide. Thousands of people pass along this sidewalk every hour. Yet the creature gave birth to them there, and she will bring them up there; for nobody will disturb her on that narrow sidewalk. At first she snarled at me, for she does not like the style of my clothes; but after I bought her a string of *kabobs* and some bread, she changed her mind. She saw that, after all, these outlandish clothes may cover a human heart. And now, while I am writing up her family, she wags her tail, and turns her one motherly eye upon me with a grateful expression.

A furious dogfight surging down the street nearly carries me off my feet. Hassan, who was smoking outside a café near me, came up with his *koorbash,* and went in for them. Anything like humanity seems foolishness to these people. They used to sew up their prisoners in asses' skins, and then burn them alive; to cut their feet and hands off; burn out their eyes with hot irons; tear out their tongues by the roots. Hassan says he would love to treat his enemies that way; and I believe him. He told me of a family of four brothers, living on Mount Lebanon, whose feet, hands, tongues, and eyes were destroyed by a cruel tyrant more than thirty years ago. All the time this dogfight was going on, the mother lay perfectly unconcerned, suckling her little dogs. The heroes of the two factions had agreed that *she,* at least, should not be meddled with; though, to look at them, you would not think there was so much gallantry in them.

I enjoyed the joke of an English sailor measuring the width of the streets by *lying down* across them. He had been to Jerusalem before, and had made a bet with another sailor that he was *as long* as the street is *wide.* So he tried it in a dozen places, and won the bet every time, for his head touched one side and his feet the other. I am afraid he was drunk; at last a donkey tipped a load of oak roots on him.

The quantity of sugar cane that is sold in the bazaars of Jerusalem surprises me. I used to notice the little negroes, in Louisiana, all day long, chewing sugar cane. The custom is almost as common among the children here. It reminds me how surprised the Crusaders were when they found at Tripoli, sweet, honeyed reeds, called *zookra,* which they sucked, and liked so much that they could not be satisfied.

The musses made sometimes in these narrow streets make the very Turks laugh. The Turks hardly ever laugh. I watched a muss. A camel, loaded with vegetables, was coming down the narrow street. On each side of him great sacks-full bulged out. Piles of cauliflowers that grew around here, most as large as a bushel-basket, were heaped mountain high, on his hump. He loomed up like Vesuvius, as he came stalking along, his head level, his monstrous under-jaw swinging round the upper one like a barn door on its hinges, his wide, spongy feet flattening out on the stone pavement, in tracks like a mammoth's. As he came along, his rider roared *Ruak, ruak,* that is, Get out of the way. And everybody *did* get out of the way. One woman, who was carrying a bread-tray on her head, dove down

below the camel's stomach, and so got out. I jumped into one of
the little shops where they sell cakes. The merchant was fumbling
over his rosary and praying. But he stopped praying and tried to
sell me some eggs—a piastre a dozen. The rest of the crowd
jumped into the stores right and left as I had done. But just as
the camel had passed me, he met a procession of six donkeys, all
loaded down with oak-roots, the drivers on top. Here *was* a muss.
The camel screamed. The camel-driver yelled, *Ruak, ruak,* Get
out of the way. The donkeys raised their tails and brayed. The
donkey-drivers swore. I wondered how the thing would be settled,
for the donkeys could not turn round for their lives, as their roots
just filled up the width of the streets. The camel could not turn
round without pulling down the buildings on both sides of him.
Never was such an uproar. A soldier poked the camel's legs with
his bayonet to make him bite. At last, the men shouldered the
donkeys, roots and all, and carried them backwards into the side
streets, and so let the camel pass. Such scenes must be common
here, in the business parts of the city, especially at this time,
when there are more than five thousand strangers here.

Right behind this camel walked a ferocious bull, who had each
of his horns tied up with a wisp of hay, recalling the Latin maxim,
fœnum in cornu habet—he has hay on his horns.

How the people of this country do detest and despise dogs!
They seem afraid to touch them. They suffer the poor, cowardly
wretches that look more like wolf than dog, to lie right across
the sidewalk and block it up. Instead of driving a mangy cur out
of the way, they actually walk around him, lest their clothes
should touch him. I used up a beautiful olivewood cane today,
that I had just bought, by striking it over the back of a
monstrous brute that would not get out of the way when I
hallooed to him. The cane flew into slivers like glass. They bark
at me incessantly, seeming to hate new-fashioned dresses. I
suppose if I would wear the native dress they would not bark at me.
Maybe that is the reason the people wear the same fashions that
Abraham did; it pleases the dogs. The people here will not even
talk about dogs. They will not answer questions about dogs. If they
say anything in reply to such questions it is *Mar arrif,* that is, *I do
not know.* The Jews hate dogs as bad as the Mohammedans; yet
they lived in Egypt more than two hundred years, and the
Egyptians loved the dog enough to make an idol of him. So they
lived for many centuries under the Roman rule; and the

Romans honored and respected the dog. But this makes no difference with *them*. Jews never learn anything from other nations. What *they* do not know is not worth knowing. Jerusalem dogs are all of one breed. And such a breed! You never see here the bluff, surly, sturdy, intelligent mastiff; nor the slight-built greyhound; nor the sharp, shrewd terrier; nor the silent, courageous bulldog; nor the tawny, deep-voiced bloodhound; nor the noble Newfoundland. Instead of that, these are all gaunt, half-starved curs, mere scavengers of garbage, street-cleaners, who need cleaning themselves worse than the streets.

The dogs here seem to have a regular constitution and set of by-laws, not written out or printed, but nonetheless enforced. While sitting one day in a cool cavern, I jotted down what I suppose to be their regulations:

Rule 1. The City of Jerusalem is divided into ten dog-districts.

Rule 2. No dog shall ever go outside of the district in which he is born. Penalty, death.

Rule 3. The strongest dog in his district shall be the dog-sheikh in that district until some stronger dog whips him. Then, the stronger dog shall take his place.

Rule 4. When the dog-sheikh barks, all the dogs in his district shall bark too.

Rule 5. When the dogs in one district bark, all the dogs in all the other districts shall bark too.

Rule 6. No dog shall move out of a man's way.

I was surprised to see all the houses of Jerusalem numbered on the doors. Hassan says they tax people here not according to the number of persons in the family, but according to the number of houses! So the governor has had them all numbered. Of course, they use the Arabic figures. Miyah thalata aasher, means 113 Thamarneen arbaah, is 84. Alf sittah, is 1006.

I watched a poor fellah—that is what they call a farmer— coming in through the Joppa Gate with a load of oak-roots from near Hebron. The ground in that direction is full of oak-roots, although only a stray oak here and there has been seen up that way for hundreds of years. These oak-roots, when dried, burn first-rate; and the people of Jerusalem buy them for fuel.

How they will tax that poor farmer before he gets home to-night! His load of roots is worth in Jerusalem about a dollar, but not much good of that dollar will *he* get; for, first, the soldiers of Joppa Gate will charge him eight cents for permission to pass the customhouse with a load of fuel. The gate-duties on tobacco and silk are forty cents a pound; on all other articles eight per cent. At the bazaars, they will charge him ten cents more for market-duties and permission to sell his fuel. Then when he goes back through the gate they will charge him ten cents more for duties on the tobacco and cloth he has bought. And finally, when he gets home to-night, the sheikh of his village will make him pay at least ten cents more for *his* share of stealage. So there is fifty per cent., or one-half the value of his property, that will be paid today to this extortionate, iniquitous government.

I spend a good deal of time today at the Damascus Gate. They call it here *Bab-es-Sham.* This is the one that Dr. Barclay thinks was called in the Bible *The Old Gate.* (Nehemiah 3:6.) Very considerable and interesting remains of the ancient structure are yet to be seen in the towers on each side of this gate. An old Jewish tower and stairway are perfectly preserved there. He thinks that this is the same kind of stairway named in 1 Kings 6:8: "They went up with winding stairs into the middle chamber and out of the middle into the third."

I copied from this gate some ornaments of the modern style. I see a great deal of this sort of figuring on the houses at Joppa and Jerusalem. It looks very pretty when well cut.

As I passed a convent, of which there are many here at Jerusalem, a lot of priests peeped out through the grated windows at me. One of them was a jolly red-nosed fellow. He said to me, *Min aine ja yee.* That means, Where do you come from? I told him the United States of America and State of Kentucky. Then he said, *Charteerah,* that is, Good-bye. These priests looked like rows of convicts squinting through grated windows. They seem unhappy and unhealthy, and of course they are.

What a lot of village sheikhs there are, hanging round Jerusalem! They come in every day, from five to ten miles around, and loaf here. I think I have met a hundred this week. Most all of them want *backsheesh.* If I ask them any questions, the first one is, Do you know the name of the Sultan of Turkey? Only about one in five can tell me. And yet his name, *Abd-el-Asiz,* is stamped on every piece of money! It is little they read what is stamped on money. Every village has at least one sheikh. Bethel, with only thirty houses, has two. This reminds me of the passage, "For the transgressions of a land, many are the princes thereof." (Prov. 28:2.) These sheikhs are said to be very tyrannical, in their small, mean way, and the passage in Proverbs 28:3, just fits them: "The poor man that oppresseth the poor, is like a sweeping rain that leaveth no food."

I met a couple of musicians, one playing a sort of one-stringed fiddle, and singing like a good-fellow; the other collecting *backsheesh*. The singing was bad enough, but the one-stringed fiddle was fearful. The string was an inch wide. If it had been wider, I do not think I could have stood it at all. I asked Hassan what the song was about. He hesitated, and said it was a love-song, and meant that the sun beams from a lady's eyes; the seven stars shine from her mouth; the full moon rises from her breast— and a good deal more that he would not tell me. I was quite satisfied with that specimen.

I saw a man drinking water out of a little earthen cruse. He held it six inches over his mouth and poured the water down his throat. It did not strangle him a bit. I tried it; poured most of the water down my bosom, and choked myself with the rest.

A man was watering the streets from large skin bags under his arms. He has the knack of it, and does not waste a great deal of water.

A consular dragoman or *cawass* went by with solemn mien and silver stick, a long curved sword, long silver-headed staff, splendid uniform, and a strut equal to the drum major of the Forty-third New York. He reminds me of the saying here: "Buy a pipe and give a napoleon for it; let your dragoman buy it and give two." They are great cheats.

They are shoeing a horse close by. To keep him from biting, they fasten a hook-em-snivey in the upper lip, something like a clothespin. The blacksmith-shop measures seven by nine feet; so they have to shoe the horse out in the street. The blacksmith has a hole dug in the middle of his floor, so he can have the anvil on the level of his arm, and thus he need not *stoop* to his work.

At a corner is a place where three dog-districts meet—you can see delegates from all three of them. They will not cross the line. I tried them with a piece of bread. But they know the penalty too well, and are cautious. Such law-abiding dogs as they are!

There is a donkey-stand here; a blacksmith-shop; two coppersmiths, making a terrific din; three bakers' shops; another coppersmith; another donkey-stand; and a confectioner's, all within one hundred steps, on this side of the street.

A man with a board on his head, covered with cakes. He says they are *muldoon*. I bought some, and they are nothing but cornmeal cakes, dried, without baking, and then frosted over with sugar. Muldoon is a humbug. Yet he sold them fast, and everybody seemed to like them, except me.

A man with Joppa oranges. Then a camel loaded with green grass. Then some pilgrims from Russia, wearing sheepskin dresses, with the wool inside; full of *life* were those dresses. Then a group of soldiers, all wearing *tarboushes,* and a fine-looking negro for an officer. He stopped politely and talked with me; would not let his soldiers ask me for *backsheesh.* He had three medals hanging to his coat-lapel. Then a stately old man with cloak trimmed with fur. In this country, a common man's rank and position may be known by his dress just as much as an officer's. Then a party of men and women astride donkeys without stirrups; the saddles having an immense cushion in front to keep the rider from flying over his head when the donkey stumbles, which he is very fond of doing, and of lying down, too, right in the road. Every donkey has a boy to run behind and poke him up with a sharp stick. Then some Desert Arabs with large yellow handkerchiefs on their heads in place of the *tarboush,* tied on with a black rope made of camel's hair, all of them on foot; they walk as awkwardly as sailors. Then came a flock of sheep that a man was leading through the noisy, crowded streets of Jerusalem. In all that variety of sounds, the poor things only listened for the voice of their own shepherd, and *where he led they followed.* But I might write all day and not finish this paragraph.

I took another stand about two squares off, and counted a cook-shop, a tin-shop, a cook-shop, a blacksmith-shop, a cook-shop, and a tin-shop all in a row. Went into a number of carpenters' shops; their principal business is making, mending, and ornamenting pipes, pipe-holders, and pipe-handles. If there is any passage of Scripture they remind me of it is that one in which the Israelites are said to have "piped with pipes." (1 Kings 1:45.)

Going back to camp, I saw a crazy man. Among the Mohammedans, crazy men are worshiped. This one was nearly naked, very crazy, and very dirty. He went around among the shops taking bread and fruit, whatever he wanted to eat. Nobody interrupted him. The shopkeepers rather seemed to like it. I could not help thinking if he was in New York the star-police would have him locked up in ten minutes.

At the Joppa Gate of this great stone patchwork, I saw Arabic words on the wall. It is said they mean that the present walls of Jerusalem were built by order of the Sultan Suleyman in 948; that is, in our way of counting, A. D. 1542. The lizards were gliding in and out of the walls there as if they cared nothing for the mortar of Suleyman.

Today I have found mosquitoes in Jerusalem quite troublesome.

I notice that nobody I have talked to in this country knows the real name of our country, *The United States.* As they know we come from America they call us *Americans,* and they do not know any other name for us. The British, however, call us *Yankees.* I asked an Italian gentleman how he would like to be called a *European?* He did not understand me.

Humanity to brutes is a virtue unknown in the Holy Land. I wish our New Yorker, Mr. Bergh, could be pasha here for twelve months. The drivers shout at the poor, patient, willing mules. They twist their tails, overload them, curse them in that dreadful Arab slang, strike them over the head and face, and throw stones at them, oh, so cruelly!

The streets of Jerusalem today are full of pilgrims dressed in all sorts of costumes, and travelers who are not pilgrims, English, French, German, Americans, etc. A sea captain rolling along, full of arrack and sin, caught hold of my arm and stopped me, and said, "Can you tell me anything about the people of this country?" Says I, "Yes, I can." "Well then," said he, "tell it." Said I, "They never refuse *backsheesh!*" He let me go with a laugh that could be heard to the top of Mount Olivet, and said I was right. *There is* one class of people here, however, that never ask for *backsheesh,* and that is the *Jews.*

A big Arab was sitting by a pile of oranges. I do not know which was the dirtiest, the fruit or the fellow. As I knew that the oranges cost him in Joppa about ten for a cent, I priced some of them here at Jerusalem. They were five for a piastre, that is about a cent apiece. I told him that was a thousand percent profit. He answered, *Backsheesh,* and that ended the argument. His oranges, however, were not the fine large ones that I admired so at Joppa, but a much inferior stock.

When a boy, mother has checked me in faultfinding by saying that "the way that Jerusalem is kept clean is, everybody sweeps the pavement in front of his own house." She is mistaken. Nobody sweeps these streets. They are not swept at all. The city does not look as though it *ever had been* swept. A strange mistake for mother to make! I never saw a town that has so many disgusting sights and smells as this.

I got a friend to give me the names of such persons as he should get acquainted with today, so that I could write them down in my diary. They are a queer lot of words to call people by. About half the natives have *Mohammed* to their names, and the other half have *Hassan,* or *Hosseen,* or *Hosine.* As far as I can write the names he gave me, they are: Yahyah, Haroun, Yezid, Meslem, Hulakoo, Akeel, Mustarfer, Nasser, Guzzaway, Ibraheem, Awad, Karder, Abdallah, Sayid, Jussoof, Kosroo, Mosedden, Noureddeen, Solyman, Sajceb, Soofy, Marlek, Essedeen, Haymoor, Nomarn, Nisamee, Ferhard, Majnoon, Narmer, Mnedh-dhin, Yebrood, Abdellatti, Dayood, Goorundel, Howarrer. A Russian gentleman who saw what I was doing, took my notebook and politely wrote his name in it, *Kratismayoshajewsky,* or words to that effect.

After visiting Mount Scopus, I undertook to reconstruct in imagination the Camp of Titus built on that summit.

It was a Standing Camp (*campa stativa*), for the standards were never to be raised from their sockets, until yonder proud and doomed city should come once more under the Roman yoke. In form, it was square (*quadrata*). It was surrounded by a ditch (*fossa*) some nine feet deep, and twelve feet broad. A rampart (*vallum*) was composed of the earth which had been dug from the ditch. In this rampart, sharp stakes bristled, pointing outward from every side.

The camp had four gates, one on each side. That which was so long presented to the frowning eyes that watched it morning and evening, from the walls of Jerusalem, was the *porta prœtoria.* The one in the rear was the *porta decumana;* those on the east and west, *porta principalis dextra* and *p. p. sinistra.*

The camp was divided into two parts. The upper portion, next the enemy, contained the tents of Titus and his retinue, also the prætorium cohort. Near him were his lieutenant-generals, and the quæstor those of the tribunes, præfects of the allies, etc., etc. Mr. H. B. Tristam says: "There is one of the Roman camps still standing near Masada, at the southwest corner of the Dead Sea, about fifty miles southeast of here. Its lines, angles, ditch, and rampart are as plainly sketched there as in the pages of a classical dictionary. And yet the head that planned it, the arms that built it, and the war-like spirits that defended it, are but the dust of 1800 years."

Here in this camp of Titus, on Mount Scopus, every evening, when the general had dismissed his chief officers and friends, after giving them his commands and distributing the watchword of the night upon *tesseræ*,—all the trumpets of the legion were sounded:

Tuba mirum spargens sonum.

This scornful challenge to the enemy was promptly taken up by Jewish soldiers, and then the hills around Jerusalem echoed with the sonorous wind instruments used at that period. Those martial sounds, through the clear evening air, reached to an amazing distance on all sides. Flowing over the range of Olivet, they were heard by the Christian refugees at Pella, far across the Jordan in the northeast. Flowing over the range of Mizpah, the bold and thrilling peals were heard by the Jewish refugees along the Plain of Sharon. At Hebron, at Masada, at Bethel, these war-signals were recognized as tokens that the enemy was not yet in possession of Jerusalem, and great was the joy they inspired.

The *post-restante,* or post-office at Jerusalem, is a queer affair. It is only open once or twice a week. It is a hard place to find, and still harder to get the postmaster to understand your wishes. The custom in this country is *to deliver* all postal matter, as our carriers do in New York. Therefore, if you want your letter to lie in the post-office, you must mark it "post-restante." But the best way is to have all correspondence directed to the care of the American Consulate. Letters are dispatched by the French post from Jerusalem for England, on the 2d, 12th, and 22d of each month; for Beirut and Constantinople on the 8th, 18th, and 28th. Rate of postage, fifteen cents per one-quarter of an ounce. Letters arrive from England on the 10th, 20th, and 30th; from Beirut and Constantinople on the 4th, 14th, and 24th. Letters from Europe and Beirut are only prepaid as far as Joppa. Eight cents extra is charged for each letter from Joppa to Jerusalem, about thirty-five miles. The package containing our diaries for the past week, drawn off upon thin French paper, weighed ten ounces. The prepaid postage on it was six dollars, that is, sixty cents per ounce.

I visited the counting-room of Messrs. Bergheim & Co., bankers here, who also do a general dry goods and miscellaneous business. These gentlemen are highly respected by both natives and foreigners. They have been very useful in missionary operations in Jerusalem and vicinity. The manner in which I arranged my money matters for our journey was to deposit with Messrs. Brown, Brothers & Co.,

Wall Street, New York, the amount necessary for the journey. For this, they gave me *letters of credit,* upon which I can raise money in any part of the world where there is a banking-house.

I was surprised to find a first-class photographic gallery here.

At the Lower Pool of Gihon, I was struck with the immense preparations of that wonderful monarch, King Solomon, for the water supply of his royal city. Massive magnificence is the grand characteristic in all the remains of Solomon's work extant. This reservoir, now empty, and its bed green with barley, was a miniature lake in itself. Perhaps a miniature fleet may once have been moored here, a company of tiny vessels for the recreation of the young princes of David's house. Doubtless, the Wise King himself often promenaded along its margin at the base of his own Mount Zion, while the royal minstrels made the echoes of the hills resound with their music. But now, nor minstrel's nor shepherd's pipe nor plowman's song moves these echoes. Sadness inexpressible broods here. Stillness and sluggishness reign in joint dominion over Jerusalem.

My pleasantest association with that immense reservoir, that "broken cistern that holds no water," is with a blooming patch of *cyclamen,* presenting many large and handsome specimens. Its circle was brilliant, its leaf delicate and soft. Here, in this dry bed of King Solomon's Croton Lake, it sparkles, shooting forth among its prickly neighbors.

It was in the mighty amphitheatre formed by this valley of Gihon, between the Upper and Lower Pools, that the coronation of Solomon was performed, B.C. 1015, and his brilliant reign of forty years began. No place more fitting could be desired. These hills, now so bald and covered as to their shoulders in sackcloth, were then crowded with the ten thousands of Jerusalem. The royal palaces upon Mount Zion, overlooking the scene—palaces whose tesselated pavements lie now in disjointed *tesserœ* through these heaps of rubbish—were thronged with women and children, elate with an event that promised so much for Israel. The city itself, upon its throne of rock, walled all around, enclosed in deep valleys and marked out as the site of a stronghold, was spectator of that memorable coronation.

I read the sacred story upon the very spot: "They caused Solomon to ride on King David's mule. And Zadok, the priest, took a horn of oil out of the tabernacle and anointed Solomon. And they blew the trumpet, and all the people said, God save King Solomon. And all the people piped with pipes, and rejoiced with great joy, so that the earth rent with the sound of them" (1 Kings 1). No wonder the band of conspirators that had assembled on the other side of the hill, by the well En-Rogel, stood aghast at the danger they had incurred, for the people had unanimously accepted the choice of Solomon, and for the rejected prince there was but one escape.

At Hezekiah's Pool, I was delighted to see many hundreds of the Jerusalem sparrows, drinking, bathing, and twittering to each other in their happiest strains. This was a little world within a world. *Without,* the bustling city of many nations, intent upon cares of business, ceremonials of religion, sightseeing—*within,* the merry family of birds congregated at their gathering-place, all heedless of the distraction of humanity. Truly "the sparrow hath found a place," "and one of them shall not fall on the ground without your Father," said He who knew all the intensity of the Father's love (Luke 10:29). In view of this daily assemblage of birds here, this Pool better deserves the name of Struthion (sparrow) Pool than the one now dry, north of the Tower of Antonio, to which Josephus attached that name. These sparrows are the same species that were introduced a few years since from England into New York, where they have increased so fast as to be familiar to every one who visits Union Park. Mr. Beecher thinks their pleasant chirp is destined to go with the English language around the world. If it does, it will increase the world's cheerfulness, and lessen the number of the world's insects.

Nor do I think it trifling to write here, that while upon the housetop, adjacent to Hezekiah's Pool, I observed a little Jerusalem girl of five or six, rocking and singing to her doll, with an intensity of interest and absorption of thought deeply affecting to me.

From there I went through the Jews' quarter, composed of streets closed in by hovels abounding in disgusting sights and pestilential smells. The Jews were idly sauntering about, their long ringlets hanging down over their ears. Large handbills printed in Hebrew were posted up on the walls.

Next, by the Mograbbins Gate, to the Pool of Siloam. Seated upon one of its rude steps, in the southwest corner, the cool water flowing just under my feet, I read from John 9 the story of the man born blind, who came here to receive his sight. "Jesus said unto him, Go, wash in the Pool of Siloam. He went his way, therefore, and washed, and came seeing." Even to the present day, there is belief here that the water of Siloam will heal sore and inflamed eyes. Mr. Prime, in his "Tent-life,' writes that he "laved his eyes in

Siloam, whose waters go softly." Josephus often remarks that these waters are sweet and abundant. But of course, all this is as nothing to the stupendous gift by which the MASTER, standing in the Temple on yonder eminence, communicated to it the miraculous energy of imparting light to one born blind. I, too, bathed my eyes here, and, as I did so, the soft and gentle stream perfectly justified my conception of Siloam. And here, too, in the olden time, came the Levite, with his golden pitcher, on the last and great day of the Feast of Tabernacles, to fill it with Siloam's water, to be poured over the sacrifice in commemoration of the miraculous water supply at Rephidim. To this golden pitcher the Lord pointed, when He cried in the Temple, "If any man thirsts, let him come unto me and drink." It is at Siloam that tradition locates the death of Zacharias (Matthew 23:35), and even so late as the fifth century after Christ the stones here were fabled to be red with his blood. (*Rubra saxa.*) Our enthusiastic countrymen, Robinson, Smith, and Barclay, entered the channel of the pool, and followed it under the lofty hill, through a crooked and narrow rock-hewn passage, sometimes walking, sometimes stooping, sometimes kneeling, sometimes creeping, about one thousand seven hundred feet to the Virgin's Fountain, at the upper entrance. Recently, Lieutenant Warren performed the same feat.

Around the Pool of Siloam I observed the beautiful maiden's-hair fern that grows profusely here; also the hyssop "that springeth out of the wall" (1 Kings 4:33), and others. The hyssop, I find, grows in green tufts in every ancient wall in this country.

From the Virgin's Fountain, I went through the King's Gardens, anciently so called, to the Beer Eyub, or Well En-Rogel. The King's Gardens, or "royal Paradise," as a writer terms them, were probably the ancient Valley of Shaveh or the King's Dale, in which occurred the affecting scene wherein participated Melchizedek, "King of Salem and Priest of the Most High," and Abraham, "the Father of the Faithful." From yonder rocky eminence of Zion on the west came the venerable Shem, or Melchizedek, with bread and wine. Here he saluted the victorious hero. "Blessed be Abram of the Most High God, possessor of heaven and earth" (Genesis 14). It is the greenest and loveliest nook around the whole city, and I could scarcely tear myself away from the contemplation of it, in association with events so pathetic; although the women and children from the neighboring village of Sylwan (Siloam) had crowded around me, filling the air alike with clamorous demands for *backsheesh* and an aroma not at all derived from the sweet gardens covering the King's Dale.

These gardens, I must not neglect to write, are watered by "cool Siloam's shady rill." "The waters of Shiloah that go softly," as the prophet Isaiah describes them, flow here, and make the valley the greenest spot in the vicinity, reclaimed from sterility into an oasis of fig trees, olives, pomegranates, and vines by means of this tiny rill, which fertilizes and beautifies all the region through which it passes Here, too, are the kitchen-gardens which, with those of Etham, near Bethlehem, supply Jerusalem with its vegetables.

I am forgetting a pleasant fact connected with the Pool of Siloam; that is, the great number of *bees* I observed watering there. I had noticed on the west side of the city a collection of beehives, long earthenware jars, piled horizontally one upon another to the depth of six or eight courses, upon the roof a small out-house, the same style of beehives observed all the way from Joppa; and several honey peddlers already have visited our tents, offering to supply us with the delectable food so often named in the sacred narrative. It is the experience of all travelers, as well as our own, that the honey of Canaan possesses a finer flavor than any we have at home.

The Well En-Rogel, or Beer Eyub, is of special interest in an historical point of view. It lies just below the Akeldama, or Potter's Field, that gloomy investment of a traitor's ill-gotten gain. Such a traitor! Such a treason! As I sat for an hour in the shade of the buildings surrounding Beer Eyub, memory was faithful to recall the story of that dreadful "Field of Blood" that covers the slope of the rocky hill just above.

The enclosure, termed by the Roman Catholics the *Garden of Gethsemane,* is a plot of ground a little more than half an acre in area, surrounded by a high stone wall, having but one entrance, and that through a low gate. As the janitor justly said, "all must bow who enter here." This hollow in the hills, a half-mile of garden-ground, is termed *Jesmoniya* by the natives, and somewhere in it, no doubt, the garden stood. It is quite likely that this is the very spot. It is neatly kept, and stocked with olives, cypresses, and flowers. The olive-trees are eight in number, each boarded up and protected from the pilfering propensities of visitors. Such noble and venerable trees! Rough in their trunks, so aged that their cavities are built up with stone for strength, but fruitful as only such patriarchal trees can be. Each has three, four, or five stems springing from a single root, and these roots the same, doubtless, that supported the trees under whose shade Jesus walked, turned aside, prayed, knelt, and agonized his soul even unto death. The thought is overwhelming. My mind, while here, was chiefly occupied in the thought that the resurrection of Christ is the guarantee of the resurrection of all mankind. A young lady went past me as I sat and read of the agony, the tears, and the sweat. She was making the circuit of Gethsemane upon her knees,—her costly garments already soiled and ragged by her morning's work,—sobs and tears shaking her whole frame,—her hands wildly thrown above her head. I had never seen such a sight before. It recalled the long trains of Irish Catholics that I have observed on snowy winter mornings *on their knees,* outside one of their churches, each patiently waiting his turn to enter. It recalled the poet's words:

> "With knees of adoration wore the stone
> A holy maid;"

though whether this was religion or fanaticism must be left to the Great Searcher of Hearts to say.

FOUNTAIN, DAMASCUS.

CHAPTER XXIV.

THE EXPLORATIONS OF JERUSALEM.

S O much notice has been taken through the press, pulpit, and lecture-stand of the work of exhuming the Sacred City, that my readers will expect to see a summary of the results accomplished by the *London Palestine Fund,* which has had the lead in the investigation. There were thousands of Masons who shared in the satisfaction felt by English

R. BEARDSLEY,
U. S. Consul at Jerusalem, 1872.

scholars at the formation, six years since, of a society for the accurate and systematic investigation of the Archæology, Topography, Geology and Physical Geography, Natural History and Manners and

Customs of the Holy Land, for biblical illustration. The rather inexpressive name of this association is *The Palestine Exploration Fund,* of which the well-known biblical expositor, George Grove, writer of so many first-class articles in Smith's Dictionary of the Bible, etc., is Secretary. I had some opportunities, through the eminent Dr. J. T. Barclay, of our own country, and Captain Charles Warren, last in charge of the surveys and explorations at Jerusalem, to look into the management of this society, and will combine my notes into one article. I wrote it just before leaving Jerusalem, while the dust of my last visit to the excavations made by Captain Warren was still clinging to me, and the voice of this modest but thoroughly educated and indefatigable man ringing in my cars. Some degree of haste, therefore, may be observed in the preparation of this article, but I will vouch for the accuracy of the statements.

It is superfluous to say to a newspaper reader in the United States, that John Bull, *plebeian,* can do nothing except under the shadow of the throne and in the path of the nobility. Therefore it was deemed a good and happy thing to secure the Queen of England as "Patron" of the *Palestine Exploration Fund;* and such names as the Dukes of Argyle and Devonshire, the Earls of Carnarvon, Derby, Russell, Zetland (the latter the then Grand Master of Masons), and Shaftesbury; the Bishops of London, Oxford, Ely and Ripon; the Deans of St. Paul's, Westminster, Christ's Church and Canterbury, and a host of minor functionaries, seventy-eight in all, to constitute the committee. I think no such combination of great lights, historical and scientific, was ever formed before in behalf of an enterprise purely historical. I need only instance Dr. William Smith, Sir Henry Rawlinson, A. H. Layard, Rev. E. H. Plumptre, Rev. H. B. Tristam, Rev. Norman McLeod, Cyril C. Graham, John Murray, and many others of the very first class of explorers in the field of Oriental investigation.

It is reasonable to expect that such men set forth upon a good work in a proper manner. One of the staunchest English societies reporting on the subject, said: "We believe this work to be one of the greatest pith and moment, and worthy of the warmest and most liberal support. The undying interest of the land explored, the sound and scientific basis upon which the explorations are conducted the vast importance of the results obtained, and the still greater value of the discoveries which are on the eve of being made, commend this great work to the general sympathy of all." This was the keynote of every public expression referring to this subject.

Outside of Palestine, all was expectation, and hopeful for great results.

This society gave its exertions for the first two years to surveying, exploring, and photographing Capernaum, Nablous, Damascus, and other places; settling disputed questions of latitude and longitude, of levels and distances, and laying out a program for a thorough topographical survey of Palestine. Latterly, however, they restricted their operations to Jerusalem.

One peculiarity concerning the present city of Jerusalem is the fact that it stands, as it were, *upon a heap of dust and rubbish,* under which is *the Jerusalem* of the Bible. And this singular position is not attributable merely to the fact that ancient Jerusalem was seventeen times captured, and more than once leveled to the ground, thus converting its splendid edifices into piles of dust and ruins. This, although it goes very far to explain the phenomena, is not sufficient altogether to account for it. It is rather the fact that the stone of which the houses and walks of Jerusalem are built is very friable, and exfoliates rapidly; so rapidly that a few centuries are sufficient to reduce a square block to a shapeless mass. This, of course, produces *pulverized earth;* the earth which has buried fifty, seventy-five, and even a hundred feet deep, the Jerusalem of our Savior's period. I have upon the table before me as I write a piece of the so-called "Jerusalem marble," taken from the immense quarry (the Cotton Megara) which underlies so much of the northeastern quarter of the city, and which has been excavated during the last three thousand years expressly for building materials. This stone, as it first comes from the quarry, is so soft that it may almost be crushed between the fingers. It is but little firmer than a well-crystallized loaf of sugar. True, it hardens upon exposure, and in time becomes a fair material for building purposes; but if any one is surprised to find the city of Jerusalem standing upon a pile of disintegrated limestone, fifty feet thick, as it surely does, he has only to explore that enormous quarry, a quarter of a mile deep, to discover where the rubbish originally came from.

This explanation will enable the reader to understand what is meant by *exploring Jerusalem.* It is simply *to go to the bottom* of that enormous mound of dust and ashes, and let in the light upon streets and foundations upon which it shone two thousand years ago. In this respect, there is a most exact analogy between the exploration of Jerusalem and of Pompeii. Over the latter city, the superincumbent mass is scoriæ, lava, and volcanic ashes; in the former, the accumulations are of pulverized limestone, added of course to the garbage of the city, shreds of pottery, bones, etc., etc., the accumulations of that extended period. It is no romance to say that the present Jerusalem overlies *many Jerusalems* that have gone to dust, in the centuries since the Jebusites established their citadel upon Mount Zion, before the time of Abraham; and that the explorer's spade must pass these graves of cities one by one, to find the remnants which he seeks. These remarks are likewise applicable to the old sites of Tyre, Sidon, Gebal, etc.

With these explanatory remarks we can see what Captain Warren, in charge of the works undertaken by the Palestine Exploration Fund, undertook. The historians of the Temple of Herod (the only temple with which the Christian or Jew is particularly interested) go much into detail relative to "the Courts of the Temple," "the Beautiful Gate," "the vast Causeway" connecting Mount Moriah with Mount Zion, and many other things. In describing the walls built up by Solomon, and renewed by Herod, to enlarge the area upon which the Temple was built, Josephus speaks of their height as bewildering, and the blocks that entered into their construction as enormously great. Now to verify such details as these was the aim of Captain Warren's party, and their labors were productive of much that corroborates the testimony of Josephus, and of Scriptural writers. He found the great Causeway, or Stone Bridge, that once connected the Mount Moriah with Zion, lying where it was cast, probably, at the destruction of Jerusalem by Titus, but lying under fifty feet of earth. Each of the stone blocks that composed it bears a proper relation to adjacent rocks, to show that they once formed a whole that was the admiration of all beholders. He found the whole area representing Mount Moriah to be banked in with mounds of earth, to the enormous depth, at one corner, of one hundred feet; the great wall extending to that enormous depth before its foundation, *the native rock,* is exposed to view. He found near the southeast corner of this great Temple area (Mount Moriah) a series of arches and abutments supporting the solid structures on which the pavement of the area at that corner rests. He found evidences of immense works built far beneath the present surface, for the supply of ancient Jerusalem with water. And yet these discoveries are but just begun. While no one will venture to name the result that may be achieved by explorers, surely no one can place any bounds to them.

There is one thought that grows out of this subject that may be of use to those who are just beginning to study the topography of Jerusalem. It is, that all those so-called traditional places connected with the *Via Dolorosa* must necessarily be fabulous, because the *Via Dolorosa* of our Savior's time—that is, the road or street along which he passed, in his sad journey from Pilate's house to Golgotha—lies many score feet (part of it fifty or seventy-five feet) *below the present surface*. The ground upon which Christ trod lies so far beneath the present ground, that to go to the bottom of the excavation made to show the former pathway, makes even a clear head swim. The person walking along Water-street, New York, cannot say that he is walking where the fish once swam; he is walking fifty or one hundred feet *above* their former haunts. And so it is with the *Via Dolorosa*.

Among the subjects that will, in due time, demand the attention of explorers in the vicinity of Jerusalem, is the search for ancient tombs among the surrounding hills. No sensible person can for a moment suppose that the few rock tombs already opened (amongst which "the tomb of Kings," "the tomb of Prophets," and "the tomb of the Virgin Mary" are the chief), represent more than a small part of the tombs with which those hills were formerly honeycombed. Great discoveries in that direction a wait the zealous excavator; discoveries more important perhaps in a historical point of view, if not so brilliant, as those which Egyptian soil has yielded. Too much cannot be projected concerning this "city of hallowed memories and entrancing recollections. Its very name is music and magic; the theatre of the most memorable and stupendous events; a place of hallowed associations, endearing reminiscences, and glorious contemplations."

So much under this head was written just as I was leaving Jerusalem, May, 1868. I continue the subject, aided by much subsequent correspondence with Oriental friends, and the publication of works by other writers upon the subject. The following is a succinct history of the society that has pursued these explorations.

Early in the year 1864, the sanitary state of Jerusalem attracted considerable attention; that city—which the Psalmist had described as beautiful for situation, the joy of the whole earth—had become one of the most unhealthy places in the world; and the chief reasons assigned for this melancholy change were the inferior quality of the water, and the presence of an enormous mass of rubbish which had been accumulating for centuries. With the rubbish it was hardly possible to deal, but the water-supply seemed an easier matter, and several schemes were proposed for improving it, either by repairing the ancient system, or by making new pools, cisterns, and aqueducts. Before, however, any scheme could be carried out, it was necessary to obtain an accurate plan of the city; and with this view, Miss Burdett Coutts, a lady ever ready to promote good works, placed a sum of £500 in the hands of a committee of gentlemen interested in Jerusalem. The committee requested Lord de Grey, then Secretary of State for War, to allow a survey to be made by a party of Royal Engineers from the Ordnance Survey, under the direction of Sir Henry James, and obtained a favorable answer.

Captain Wilson, R. E., was in command of this party, and performed with thoroughness and skill the particular task assigned to him. The opposition of the Turkish authorities frustrated his plan for improving the water supply of Jerusalem; but the discoveries of ancient ruins which he incidentally made while tracing out the aqueducts and cisterns of the times of Solomon and Hezekiah, awakened new zeal for the exploration of the old city, with a view to the settlement of disputed points of topography. Accordingly, a society was formed in England, under the name of "The Palestine Exploration Fund, for the accurate and systematic investigation of the Archæology, Topography, Geology and Physical Geography, Natural History, Manners, and Customs of the Holy Land, for Biblical Illustration." In 1867, a party was sent out, under command of Captain Warren, R. E., which remained in Palestine for three years, chiefly occupied in and around Jerusalem. The reports and journals of Captain Warren, and other matters relating to the expedition, were published in a series of Quarterly Statements, which are of great interest and value; and the general results of the three years have been embodied in an illustrated volume, called "The Recovery of Jerusalem."

How far progress has been made, and what is yet contemplated, may be gathered from the following accounts:

"Master, see! what manner of stones and what buildings are here!" Surely it is not unworthy of Christian study to find out, if it be still possible, what those stones and buildings were. We are able to do it to a greater degree than has been supposed, as the discoveries of the "Palestine Exploration Fund" show. These discoveries have been made at great cost of money and labor, and no little danger, by sinking shafts a hundred feet deep, and running galleries at right angles to these shafts, the explorers feeling their way under ground, burning magnesian wire, and so throwing light upon stones and pavements which have been buried 2,000 and 3,000 years from human sight. The results have been invaluable, because the least information upon such subjects is precious. Of these results, we will mention some of the more prominent.

Let it be borne in mind at the outset that no city in the world has presented so difficult a problem as Jerusalem. The reason is, no city has been so often and so thoroughly destroyed. It has been captured, burned, overthrown, more than twenty times. Names and memories have perished, so that scarcely a feature of the natural landscape has been recognized beyond dispute. Mount Moriah within the walls, and the Mount of Olives outside, we are sure of. We thought we had certain knowledge of Mount Zion also, but the most recent and successful explorers have cast doubt even on this, and deny that the modern "Zion" corresponds with the ancient.

Mount Moriah has been found to be originally a sharp crag or ridge, with so little space on the top as scarcely to afford room for a temple of small dimensions. On all sides it fell off rapidly and very steeply, except from northwest to southeast, the direction in which the ridge ran. The area on the summit was enlarged by walls built along the declivities, the outside wall deep down the valleys, from 100 to 150 feet below the area on which the Temple buildings stood. One hundred feet again below this lay the original bed of the brook Kedron. The foundations of the Temple, therefore, were 250 feet above the deep defiles around. This area, originally built by Solomon and enlarged by Herod, still exists, running on the south along the valley of Hinnom 1,000 feet, and along the Kedron 1,500.

This enclosure was originally covered with splendid edifices. First were the porticoes, or covered walks, built along the outer walls, and overlooking the Kedron and Hinnom. They were magnificent structures, resembling the nave and aisles of Gothic cathedrals. The middle walk, or nave, was 45 feet broad, and the two aisles 30 feet. The aisles were 50 feet high, and the nave, rising like a clear story between the two, was more than 100 feet high. Add now terrace-walls to the height of the porticoes, and we have a solid and continuous wall of masonry 250 feet high. But these were only the outer buildings of the Temple area. The porticoes opened inwardly upon a court paved with marble, and open to the sky. Steps led up to a second court. Beyond this, again, through beautiful gateways, was a third, and rising above them all was a fourth, in which stood the Temple proper, ascending story above story, and said to have been 100 or even 150 feet high.

These horizontal measurements have been verified. Of course, we cannot vouch for the correctness of the reputed height of these immense structures. We have the less reason, however, to doubt the last, as we have established the first. If one looked upon Mount Moriah from the Mount of Olives opposite, coming round the brow of Olivet on the way from Bethany, as our Lord did when beholding the city, it must have been a sight which, for architectural beauty and grandeur, perhaps, has never been equaled, certainly not surpassed. It was an artificial mountain from the deep ravines below, wall, column, roof, pinnacle, culminating in the Temple within and above all and probably measuring between 500 and 600 feet.

The palace of Solomon, too, added to the impressiveness of the sight. It is settled by recent discoveries that this pile of buildings was on the southeast corner of the area, joining on the House of the Lord above, and extending below to the King's Gardens, where the two valleys met and "the waters of Siloah go softly."

James Fergusson, Esq., the distinguished architect, writes: "The triple Temple of Jerusalem, the lower court standing on its magnificent terraces, the inner court raised on its platform in the center, and the temple itself rising out of the group and crowning the whole, must have formed, when combined with the beauty of the situation, one of the most splendid architectural combinations of the ancient world."

Josephus wrote: "If any one looked down from the top of the battlements he would be giddy, while his sight could not reach to such an immense depth." This passed for foolish exaggeration until recent explorations vindicated the statement.

All these buildings, porticoes, columns, pinnacles, altar, and Temple have perished. "Not one stone remains upon another which has not been thrown down." The area alone remains, and the massive substructures that for 3,000 years have been sleeping in their courses. The preservation has been due to the ruin. Buildings so vast have been toppled down the slopes of the Moriah, that the original defiles and valleys have been almost obliterated. What has been regarded as the original surface has been found to be *débris* from 70 to 90 feet deep.

With pickaxe and shovel British explorers have been down to the original foundations. Fallen columns have been met with, and avoided, or a way blasted through them. The cinders of burnt Jerusalem have been cut through, and turned up to the light— rich moulds deposited by the treasures of Jewish pride. The seal of Haggai, in ancient Hebrew characters, was picked up out of the siftings of this deposit. The first courses of stones deposited by Phœnician builders have been reached, lying on the living rock. Quarry-marks, put on in vermilion, have been copied—known to be quarry-marks by the trickling drops of paint, still visible—only they are above the letters, showing that when they were written the stones lay with the underside uppermost.

In the southwest corner of the area, *débris* has accumulated to a depth of not less than 125 feet—the accumulation of ages, made up of the ruins of successive Jerusalems; and here some of the most interesting discoveries have been made. Here is the famous Arch of Robinson, shown now to be an arch, as he conjectured, by the discovery of the pier upon which the first span rested. It is the remains of a bridge which crossed the valley on arches, and connected Mount Moriah with the mountain opposite—the modern Zion. It is the skewback, or abutment that slopes to receive the end of the arch. Three courses remain. The stones are 5 or 6 feet thick and 20 or 25 feet long. The valley here is 350 feet wide, and this must have been the length of the bridge, connecting the Temple with the Royal Palace on the other side. At a depth of 30 feet a worn pavement was found, worn by feet that passed over it in our Lord's time. Lying on this pavement were the voussoirs, or wedge-like stones, belonging to the arch. Breaking through this pavement, and through 24 feet of *débris* beneath, they found a still more ancient roadway, and resting upon this, the keystones of a still more ancient bridge.

The explanation is probably reached: Robinson's Arch is the remains of the bridge that was standing at the siege of Jerusalem, upon which, at the eastern end of it, stood the Roman General Titus, holding a parley with the Jews, occupying the other end of the bridge. The older bridge, the remains of which were found beneath the pavement, belonged to the palmy days of Solomon; may have been standing at the time of the Queen of Sheba's visit; and possibly was part of the "ascent" by which Solomon went up into the House of the Lord, which when the queen saw, there was "no more spirit left in her."

The whole of Mount Moriah has been found to be fairly honeycombed with cisterns and passages. One of the cisterns, known as the Great Sea, would contain two millions of gallons, and all together not less than ten millions. The wall of Ophel has been exposed— at the present time 70 feet high—though buried in *débris;* and the remains of towers and houses have been lighted upon, belonging to the age of the kings of Judah. The Pool of Bethesda has been, in all probability, identified; an intermitting fountain, which explains the popular legend of the troubling of the water by an angel.

The first impulse toward the exploration of Palestine, in recent times, was given by Dr. Edward Robinson in 1838, who went through not as a mere traveler making notes of passing observations, but as a student of Biblical History and Antiquities making researches upon a well-defined method, with the scientific motive of preparing a work on Biblical Geography. He had fitted himself for the journey by the special studies of fifteen years, had mastered the whole literature of his subject, and had mapped out distinctly the points of inquiry which previous travelers had left undetermined. But he had also qualifications for his task such as are seldom combined in any one man—a discriminating judgment, a retentive memory, comprehensive and well-digested knowledge, accurate powers of observation, the habit of patient and cautious investigation, and a rare faculty of common sense in sifting facts and weighing evidence. The most eminent geographers of Europe at once recognized the great value of Dr. Robinson's researches in a geographical point of view; but controversy was awakened by his opinion touching the Church of the Holy Sepulcher and other places of reputed sanctity, and by his broad canon of historical research—"that all ecclesiastical tradition respecting the sacred places in and around Jerusalem and throughout Palestine is of no value, except so far as it is supported by circumstances known to us from the Scriptures, or from other contemporary history." Next to the testimony of the Scriptures and of Josephus, Dr. Robinson gave importance to the preservation of the ancient names of places among the common people. In this branch of inquiry he had the invaluable aid of Dr. Eli Smith, a master of the language and the character of the Arabs, and an acute and careful observer.

But Dr. Robinson was not equipped for a thoroughly scientific exploration of the Holy Land. He went at his own charges, having but a single companion, with few instruments, and no trained assistants for a proper survey. He opened the way to a scientific exploration, provided sound instructions and positive data for others; but he himself reported that "there yet remained much land to be possessed."

In 1848, Lieutenant Lynch and his party made a scientific examination of the Dead Sea, so careful, thorough, and complete, that the official report of the United States Expedition under his command has become the standard authority upon that anomalous feature of Palestine.

The publication of "The Land and the Book," by Dr. W. M. Thomson, in 1859, while it added much to our knowledge of biblical localities in Palestine, popularized the illustration of the Bible from the natural scenery and history of the Holy Land, and from the manners and customs of its inhabitants.

Dr. Barclay's "City of the Great King," published in 1858, made some substantial additions to our knowledge of the topography of Jerusalem; Mr. Osborn's "Palestine, Past and Present," 1859, was a contribution to the natural history and the cartography of the Holy Land; Professor Hackett's "Illustrations of Scripture," published in 1860, gave a life-like tone to many passages of the word of God from the natural phenomena and the social customs of Palestine; and other Americans, travelers and missionaries, have enriched our literature with journals, reports, and monographs, upon the same fruitful theme.

Of photographs, the society has published 349, many of them being of places never before taken. They include views of the ruins of Tel Hum (Capernaum), Kerazeh (Chorazin), and Jerash (Gerasa). Kedes (Kedesh), and Sebastiyeh (Samaria); many points in and around Jerusalem, Hebron, Damascus, etc.; the district of Nablus, Gennesareth, etc.; and the cities east of Jordan.

From the various reports made to the Home Office, and addresses delivered at the London meetings in encouragement of the movement, I make extracts at the risk of some repetition. Dr. Porter, author of "Giant Cities of Bashan," and other works, said of the enormous substructure of the Temple that it is doubtless to these substructions the sacred writer refers, when he says, "And the foundations were of costly stones, even of great stones, stones of ten cubits, and stones of eight cubits." On the southwest and southeast, the foundations of colossal walls were laid nearly at the bottom of the Tyropœan and Kedron. Josephus' account of it is almost startling. They surrounded Moriah, from the base, with a triple wall, and accomplished a work which surpassed all conception. The sustaining wall of the lower court was built up from a depth of 300 cubits (450 feet), and in some places more. There were stones used in this building which measured forty cubits. Perhaps some may be inclined to smile incredulously on hearing such measurements as these: if so, just wait a little until I describe the wonderful discoveries made by recent excavations.

We go first to the southeast angle. Here is a magnificent fragment of the Temple, and one of the finest specimens of mural architecture in the world. The stones are colossal, ranging from ten feet to thirty feet in length, by five feet in height—all noble "cornerstones," polished after the similitude of a palace. The elevation of the wall above the present surface is seventy-three feet. The Royal Engineers sank a shaft to the foundation, which they discovered at the depth of sixty feet. This angle must, when perfect, have been 140 feet high. And this is not all. It stands on the rocky side of Moriah, which sinks, almost perpendicularly, 200 feet to the bottom of the Kedron. And, besides, on the top of the wall stood the royal porch, 100 feet in height. Consequently, the summit of the porch was 240 feet above the foundation of the wall, and 440 feet above the Kedron! This was that "Pinnacle of the Temple" which was the scene of one part of our Lord's Temptation. We now go over to inspect the still more extraordinary discoveries at the southwest angle. We pass on our way two ancient gates, which opened from the low suburb of Ophel, where the priests dwelt, two long subterranean avenues leading up to the Temple. The masonry of the southwest angle is even finer than that of the southeast. At present, the angle rises ninety feet above the ground. Captain Warren, with great labor and at no little risk, sank a shaft, and discovered the foundation laid upon the rock, at the enormous depth of 100 feet. The grandeur of this angle almost surpasses conception. The cornerstones are colossal, measuring from twenty to forty feet in length, by about six feet in height. One stone, which I myself measured, and which is placed 110 feet above the foundation, is thirty-four feet long, and weighs about 100 tons! I believe that I may say to raise a stone of such dimensions to such a position would try the skill of modern engineers. It was near this angle the bridge stood which spanned the Tyropœon, connecting the Temple with the palace. The remains have been discovered.

The following measurements will give some idea of its stupendous size and grandeur: The spring-stones of one of its arches are twenty-four

feet long by six feet thick. The breadth of the roadway was fifty
feet, corresponding exactly to the central avenue of the Royal
Porch. The span of each arch was forty-six feet. The height above
the bottom of the Tyropœon was 225 feet. This stupendous bridge
would bear favorable comparison with some of the noblest works
of the present century. Can we wonder that, when the Queen of
Sheba saw it, "there was no more spirit left in her"?

At a meeting held under the presidency of the Archbishop of
York in support of the Palestine Exploration Fund, which has for
its purpose the accurate and systematic investigation of the
archæology, topography, geology, and physical geography of the
Holy Land, the Secretary stated that the committee had confined
their attention mainly to explorations in or near the city of
Jerusalem. In spite of many difficulties, Lieut. and Bro. Warren
had succeeded in carrying on extensive excavations, with little
interruption, and had made discoveries of the utmost importance,
which not only tended to throw new light upon the original
features of the Temple Hill, but led to the hope that before long
sufficient data would be obtained for forming a tolerably accurate
opinion upon the various sites in the Holy City which had been so
long matters of dispute. For the first time, the actual streets of
the ancient city have been reached, underground passages which
have been hidden for centuries by the mass of superincumbent
ruins have been brought to light, and by degrees a complicated
network of drains and reservoirs is being laid bare, which, when
fully explored, will no doubt aid very considerably in settling
many difficult points connected with the level of different portions
of Jerusalem. In the valleys of the Kedron and Tyropœon, by a
succession of shafts, many of them sunk to enormous depths,
discoveries of intense interest have been made, with regard to the
original course and character of those valleys. The limits of the
hill and position of the wall of Ophel have been in a great
measure ascertained, and shafts sunk on the south of the wall of
the Haram area have shown that the account given by Josephus,
of the giddy height of the battlements of the ancient city at this
point, is not, after all, the gross exaggeration that up to this time
it has always been believed to have been. The report went on to
speak of the difficulties to be met with in carrying out such an
exploration as this among a population like that of Jerusalem,
difficulties which had been increased by the treacherous
character of the soil and the imperfect nature of the apparatus
which had to be employed. The zeal and perseverance

of Lieut. Warren in overcoming these difficulties, were warmly commended; through his ability the field for excavation at Jerusalem had never appeared so open, while, at the same time, the discoveries of last year gave the surest promise of future excavations being attended with still more interesting results; and if, as Lieut. Warren hoped, we should be able to dig in the Haram area itself, it was impossible to overrate the interest of the discoveries that were in store. The researches of Jerusalem had caused other operations to be suspended, but several surveying expeditions had been made, and Lieut. Warren had thoroughly surveyed the Philistine Plain as far north as Gaza, together with a large tract of country to the southwest of Jerusalem. He had also surveyed portions of the Jordan and its valleys. The report, after stating other general facts as to the operations carried on by Lieut. Warren, went on to say that the work had been supported by subscriptions from many classes, and, among others, by the large and influential body of Freemasons, who had encouraged the attempts being made to search out the sites of the works erected by the famous operative craftsmen of that ancient order.

Lieut. Warren was then called upon to speak, and on rising to do so, he was cordially cheered. He proceeded to read a very interesting report of considerable length, and he explained the works being carried out by means of a small map of Jerusalem, of which every visitor had a copy. He said there were at present engaged on the works, two corporals of engineers, and about seventy Muslims of different races, and though the latter required great supervision, yet, what with the jealousies of race and religion, the dragoman being Greek, and the overseers Jews, anything going wrong soon "cropped out." Very few articles found in the works had come to hand, and what had been found consisted mostly of pottery, bronze nails, and glass (the former of many different dates, and the glass of the third and fourth centuries of the Christian era); but a few Hebrew coins had been turned up. Among the findings was a seal with characters showing it to be that of "Haggai, the son of Shebaniah," and it was supposed in Jerusalem to be of the time of Ezra. However, the main object of the work was with regard to nether Jerusalem in its topography, and it was desired particularly to find out where the Temple stood. In studying the Holy Land it was most disappointing to find a dearth of evidence as to sites of places, and the more the matter was looked into, the more difficult it became

There were points which were known beyond contradiction, such as Jaffa, Jerusalem, and others; but when details were sought, there was the most conflicting evidence.

All parties agree that the Temple stood somewhere in a rectangular spot, called by the names of Haram and Moriah, and that the Mount of Olives was on the whole or part of a hill indicated on the map. It was probable, too, that the valley of the Kedron could be traced; but about all other points there were controversies; and if he made use of Biblical names in speaking of places, he did so because they were generally received names, and not because they were established as such. The explorers must be content, he feared, to be baffled and perplexed for a long time to come before they could bring out Jerusalem as it was; for, startling as it might appear, they had not yet a single fixed point from which to commence. For instance, though the Temple was known to be on a particular space (the Moriah area), yet there was space there for three such sites; and Mount Sion was put to the north of Moriah by some, and to the west by others of authority. It was only by patient investigation that hopes could be entertained of a satisfactory conclusion. He then proceeded to describe the Haram area, in which he said there was no doubt a mine of information. The Moriah area was scooped out into large tanks, and one would hold one million gallons of water; another was found capable of holding seven hundred thousand; and altogether about five million gallons could be stowed away. Near here was a place called the Well of the Leaf, of which the legend was told that a man wandered down it, and coming to a door, opened it. He found himself in a beautiful garden, and plucking a leaf he returned. On telling his tale, he was greeted as of little sense for leaving a garden which his listeners believed to be Paradise, which he would never have another chance of seeing again. The gallant officer continued at some length, and explained that the stables of Solomon had been discovered, as well as streams of water which led to the opinion that the source of King Hezekiah's hidden spring of water would be discovered. He concluded, amid warm cheers, by expressing the interest taken in the works by those who are called the Anglo-Saxon race, from both Britain and America.

Mr. Layard, M.P., said that few persons could understand how arduous were the labors Lieutenant Warren had carried out, not only as respected the heat and the other influences, but from the fact that the exploration party were working amid a hostile people, who saw places given over to strangers which they regarded as sacred. As to the "findings," he reminded those present that he warned them they were not to expect any monuments like those found at Nineveh, for the Jews did not make such things, for religious reasons, and for another—they had no material. He spoke about monuments in the Louvre at Paris, at one time stated to be Jewish, and threw grave doubts upon the character of those monuments.

Among the loose objects found here by the English explorers, and taken to England, are a number of *stone* balls, missiles of war. These may have been used by the Crusaders possibly earlier. In 1418, the English had 7,000 stone balls made for such a purpose in the quarries at Maidstone, and there are many cannonballs of stone, enormously large, lying on the banks of the river near Constantinople.

Among the specimens recently brought to Jerusalem, found in the vicinity, is a stone bearing the figure of a god sitting on a throne, with priests on both sides, and a Hunyaritish inscription two lines in length, which had been brought from Yemen, and was offered for sale. Dr. Oscar Meyer, the Chancellor of the North German Confederate Consulate since Dr. Peterman resigned, succeeded in obtaining an impression, which is now in the hands of the Confederate Consul, Dr. Blau, who is residing for a time at Berlin. The inscription is said to contain the name of Athtar (*Astarte*). Doubtless, Jerusalem will become a great center now for the distribution of Oriental antiquities.

THE MOABITE STONE.

In connection with these explorations of Jerusalem, I call attention here to the discovery of the Moabite Stone, because the search and the finding of this relic grew out of the excitement awakened by the *London Palestine Fund* in its varied labors. My engraving is the large one prepared for *Scribner's Monthly,* and my description that of the (American) "Palestine Exploration Society," to whose courtesy I am greatly indebted for the use of this and several other engravings used in the present volume. The territory selected by this young and vigorous society is that in which this stone was found, viz., the land of Moab. Every member of the Executive Committee of this (American) has visited the Holy Land, and has therefore, a personal enthusiasm in the work; and the wishes of all true Masons must go with them in their labors.

The most exciting incident of recent explorations in Palestine was the discovery among the ruins of the ancient Dibon, east of the Dead Sea, of a stone in a perfect state of preservation, containing an inscription of thirty-four lines by Mesha, a king of Moab, a little after the time of Omri, king of Israel. In a quarrel of the Arabs over the possession of the stone, it was broken into fragments, and the inscription seriously impaired. The translation given is that of Christian D. Ginsburg, LL.D., according to his text.

The Moabite Stone was a neatly cut block of black basalt, 3 feet 8½ inches high, 2 feet 3½ inches wide, and 1 foot 1 78/100 inch thick, rounded at both ends, and inscribed with thirty-four straight lines of alphabetic writing.

It was found by Rev. F. A. Klein, August 19th, 1868, at the entrance of the ruined Moabitish town of Dibon, once a capital city of Moab (although built by the children of Gad, Num. 32:34), and records the successful rebellion of Mesha, king of Moab, against the Israelitish yoke (see 2 Kings, 3:4), after a forty years' oppression by the house of Omri.

Although broken to pieces through Arabic jealousy, its inscription has been preserved, with the exception of about one-seventh; and two-thirds of the stone itself is now in the possession of M. Ganneau and the Palestine Exploration Society. This inscription is the oldest alphabetic inscription extant, dating about the year B.C. 890.

It shows us—

1. That Moab must have been independent between Solomon's reign and that of Omri. Under David and Solomon we know it was subject to Israel.

2. That Dibon was its capital.

3. That the Semitic alphabet was the Phœnician, which is our alphabet in its earlier forms. The letters A, N, K, M, O, U, D, T, L, H, R, are almost identical with the Roman and Greek characters.

4. That punctuation was carefully observed in old writings, so far as to separate by marks both words and sentences.

5. That the plural in N is not a late form.

6. That Moab was called by the Moabites, Mab or Meab.

7. That the name of Jehovah was openly spoken and known by nations around as the name of Israel's God, and that the pious horror of the Tetragrammaton did not exist nine centuries before Christ.

8. That Pliny's and Aristotle's views that only sixteen or eighteen letters were brought by Cadmus from the East into Greece, and that

the Greeks invented the rest, are false, the whole twenty-two being here found. Hence the 119th Psalm, and the other alphabetic Psalms, and the Book of Lamentations (having an alphabetic division), are not to be deemed modern, as some would have them to be for this reason.

TRANSLATION OF THE INSCRIPTION ON THE MOABITE STONE.

1 I Mesha am son of Chemoshgad King of Moab, the
2 Dibonite. My father reigned over Moab thirty years, and I reigned
3 after my father. And I erected this Stone to Chemosh at Karcha [a Stone of]
4 [Sa]lvation, for he saved me from all despoilers and let me see my desire upon all my enemies,
5 and Om[r]i, King of Israel, who oppressed Moab many days, for Chemosh was angry with his
6 [la]nd. His son succeeded him, and he also said, I will oppress Moab. In my days he said, [Let us go]
7 and I will see my desire on him and his house, and Israel said, I shall destroy it forever. Now Omri took the land
8 Medeba and occupied it [he and his son and his son's] son, forty years. And Chemosh [had mercy]
9 on it in my days; and I built Baal Meon, and made therein the ditch and I [built]
10 Kirjathaim. For the men of Gad dwelled in the land [Ataro]th from of old, and the K[ing of I]srael fortified
11 A[t]aroth, and I assaulted the wall and captured it, and killed all the wa[rriors of]
12 the wall, for the well-pleasing of Chemosh and Moab; and I removed from it all the spoil, and [of-
13 fered] it before Chemosh in Kirjath; and I placed therein the men of Siran and the me[n of Zereth]
14 Shachar. And Chemosh said to me Go take Nebo against Israel. [And I]
15 went in the night, and I fought against it from the break of dawn till noon, and I took
16 it and slew in all seven thousand [men, but I did not kill the women
17 and maidens,] for [I] devoted [them] to Ashtar-Chemosh; and I took from it

MOABITE STONE.

18 [the ves]sels of Jehovah and cast them down before
     Chemosh And the King of Israel fortif[ied]

19 Jahaz, and occupied it, when he made war against me;
     and Chemosh drove him out before [me and]

20 I took from Moab two hundred men, all chiefs, and
     fought against Jahaz and took it,

21 in addition to Dibon. I built Karcha, the wall of the
     forest, and the wall

22 of the city, and I built the gates thereof, and I built the
     towers thereof, and I

23 built the palace, and I made the prisons for the men
     of . . . . with [in the]

24 wall. And there was no cistern within the wall in
     Karcha, and, I said to all the people, Make for
     yourselves

25 every man a cistern in his house. And I dug the ditch
     for Karcha with the [chosen] men of

26 [I]srael. I built Aroer and I made the road across the
     Arnon.

27 I built Beth-Bamoth, for it was destroyed; I built
     Bezer, for it was cu[t down]

28 by the fifty m[en] of Dibon, for all Dibon was now loyal;
     and I sav[ed]

29 [from my enemies] Bikran, which I added to my land,
     and I bui[lt]

30 [Beth-Gamul], and Beth-Diblathaim, and Beth-Baal-
     Meon, and I placed there the Mo[abites]

31 [to take possession of] the land. And Horonaim . dwelt
     therein . . . .

32 And Chemosh said to me, Go down, make war against
     Horonaim, and ta[ke it] . . . .

33   Chemosh in my days

34   year and I . . . .

In immediate connection with this great discovery, I give an engraving and description of some interesting and important inscriptions found by Mr. J. Aug. Johnson, United States Consul-General in Syria (now a resident of New York), showing what a great field awaits exploration in the valleys and plains of Northern Syria. For this engraving, I am indebted to the society already named. Mr. Johnson's account of this discovery is as follows:

"Hamath, on the northern border of the 'Promised Land,' was

the capital of a kingdom at the Exodus; its king, Toi, yielded allegiance to King David (2 Sam. 8:9); it was called "great" by Amos (6:2), and was spoken of by an Assyrian monarch as among the most celebrated of his conquests (2 Kings 18:34). It was originally the residence of Canaanites (Gen. 10:18), and is frequently mentioned as the extreme limit of the Holy Land towards the north. Hamath, as it is now called, has at present a population of about 30,000 inhabitants.

"While looking through the bazaar of this old town, in 1870, with Rev. S. Jessup, of the Syria Mission, we came upon a stone in the corner of a house which contained an inscription in unknown characters. We did not succeed in getting squeeze-impressions, for fanatical Moslems crowded upon us when we began to work upon the stone, and we were obliged to be content with such copies of this and other inscriptions subsequently found on stones over and near the city gate, and in the ancient bridge which spans the Orontes, as could be obtained by the aid of a native painter. In this we were greatly aided by Mr. Jessup, and by Mr. F. Bambino, of the French Consulate, who pronounced the copies to be accurate. Mr. Jessup endeavored to purchase a blue stone containing two lines of these strange characters, but failed to obtain it because of the tradition connected with, and the income derived from it. Deformed persons were willing to pay for the privilege of lying upon it in the hope of a speedy cure, as it was believed to be efficacious in spinal diseases.

"We should naturally expect to find in this vicinity some trace of the Assyrian and Egyptian conquerors who have ravaged the valley of the Orontes, and of their struggles with the Hittites on this ancient battlefield, and of Solomon, who built stone cities in Hamath (2 Chron. 8:4), of which Palmyra was one. But we find nothing of the Palmyrene on these stones. The arrow-headed characters are suggestive of Assournasirpal. In the inscription on the monolith of Nimroud, preserved in the British Museum, in relating his exploits 915 B.C., he says: 'In this time I took the environs of Mount Lebanon. I went towards the great sea of Phœnicia. . . . I received tributes from . . . Tyre, Sidon, etc. . . . They humbled themselves before me.' And a little later, 870-8 B.C., Salmanazar V. says: 'In my twenty-first campaign I crossed the Euphrates for the twenty-first time; I marched towards the cities of Hazael, of Damascus. I received the tributes of Tyre, Sidon, and Gebal.'

"Until the interpretation of these mysterious characters shall be given, a wide field is open to conjecture. Alphabetic writing was in use 1500 B.C., but the germs of the alphabetic system were found in the hieroglyphic and hieratic writing of the Egyptians, upwards of 2000 B.C. Some of the attempts at picture writing on these Hamath stones suggest the Egyptian system, which consists of a certain number of figures to express letters or syllables, and a vast number of ideographic or symbolic forms to represent words. Other characters represent Phœnician letters and numerals not unlike the Phœnician writing on the foundation stones of the Temple at Jerusalem, recently deciphered by Dr. Deutsch, of the British Museum.

"In framing their alphabet the Phœnicians adopted the same process previously employed in the Egyptian phonetic system, by taking the first letter of the name of the object chosen to represent each sound; as, A, for aleph (a bull); B, for beth (a house); G, for ghimel (a camel); in the same manner as the Egyptians represented A, by an eagle, *akhem;* M, by an owl, *moulag,* etc.

"Some scholars have designated Babylonia as the true mother of the characters employed in very ancient times in Syria and Mesopotamia. And it appears that besides the cuniform writing found on Assyrian and Babylonian monuments, a cursive character was also employed identical with the Phœnician, and therefore possibly borrowed by the latter. Kenrick, however, remarks on this theory, that the occurrence of these characters only proves the intercourse between the two people, and not that the cuniform was the parent of the Phœnician. We have in these inscriptions of Hemath a melange of all three, and perhaps a connecting link between the earliest systems. To suppose them to be bi-lingual or tri-lingual only increases the difficulty of interpretation in this case, for there is not enough of either to furnish a clue to the rest.

"The 'Carpentras Stone' contains an analogous inscription; it comes near to the Phœnician, and has been thought to present the most ancient specimen of the Aramean series. This and the Palmyrene writing form the links between the coin characters and the square characters, and are supposed to represent a language in a state of transition. That the Hebrews borrowed the use of writing from Mesopotamia or Phœnicia has been universally admitted; and, according to Gesenius, the old form of their writing was derived from the Phœnician, and retained by the Samaritans after the Jews had adopted another character of Aramaic origin.

DEFACED.

DEFACED.

INSCRIPTION DISCOVERED AT HAMATH IN NORTHERN SYRIA.

"Now may it not be that in these Hamath inscriptions we have fallen upon a transition period, when the Phœnicians, or their predecessors in the land, were using the elements of writing then in existence, and before the regular and simple Phœnician alphabet had been perfected?

"The 'Carpentras Stone' has been considered by Gesenius to have been executed by a Syrian of the Seleucidian period. The 'Rosetta Stone' dates back to 193 B.C. The characters on these stones have much in common with those of Hamath. 'Champollion's Key to the Hieroglyphics' will be of aid, perhaps, in solving the present mystery. But we shall be surprised if the inscriptions of Hamath do not prove to be older and of greater interest than any recent discovery of Egypto-Aramean or hieroglyphic characters.

"Mr. E. H. Palmer, of the British Syrian Exploration Fund, saw our copies at Beirut, while on his way from an exploring tour in the Desert of Tîh. He was so persuaded of their archæological importance, that he induced the British Society to send a learned Orientalist, Mr. Drake, to Syria, to obtain squeeze-impressions and photographs of all these and any other similar inscriptions. His report will be looked for with great interest. In the last number of the *Journal of the American Oriental Society,* it is stated that Mr. Palmer has already found in a Syrian MS. lying in the University of Cambridge, other copies of these Hamath inscriptions. They are said to be imperfect. We do not learn, however, that the Syrian MS. has been translated, or that any theory of interpretation has been advanced. Dr. Eisenlohr, Professor of Egyptology at the University of Heidelberg, in a letter asking permission to publish these inscriptions in Germany, says: 'Though I believe we are at present not able to give a translation of these inscriptions, I am still persuaded they will be of the highest interest for the scientific world, because they are a specimen of the first manner of writing of the people of that country.'

"These inscriptions and the bas-reliefs on the monument called Kamua Hurmûl, in Cœlo Syria, near the source of the Orontes, and possibly of the same period, are an enigma, as yet, to the most learned Orientalists. It is to be hoped, however, now that attention is again called to the subject, that the clue may be found that shall unlock their meaning, and that Northern Syria will be no longer overlooked by the explorer"

SEARCHING FOR THE FOUNDATIONS OF MOUNT MORIAH.

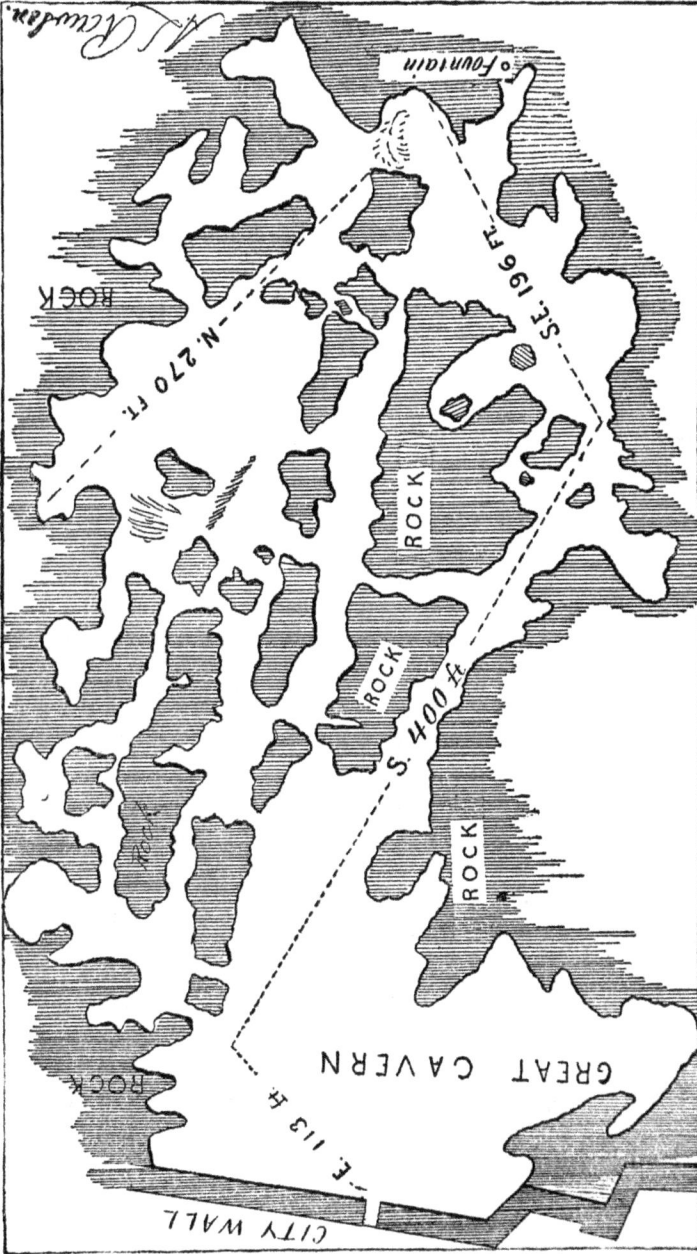

PLAN OF THE GREAT QUARRY UNDER JERUSALEM.

CHAPTER XXV.

MOUNT MORIAH.

I N my lectures since 1868, I have found no subject connected with the Holy Land so difficult to elucidate as the platform or foundation walls on which the Temple of Solomon was built, where stood in cedar and gold and marble that grandest expression of national power and magnificence the world has ever seen. The ordinary newspaper notices concerning "the foundation of the Temple," only mislead the reader, as he conceives nothing but

PLAN OF MOUNT MORIAH.

the ordinary appearance presented when a building has been destroyed by fire or violence, leaving nothing but the heavy work partly in and partly out of the ground.

THE FOUNDATION OF THE TEMPLE.

It is difficult for the superficial reader to comprehend that although the Temple of Solomon is *absolutely gone*—effaced from the earth, so that not a crumb or fragment can be recognized—yet its *foundation* remains. By this term is not meant the *walls* upon which the Temple was built (comparing it with an ordinary edifice), but the *platform,* the hill, the mound artificially erected to serve as a basis for the sublime structure. In the present chapter, I commence by clearing up this matter, so essential to a proper understanding of Solomon's Temple, and show what was the foundation that has so well withstood the changes of twenty-nine centuries.

The hill, styled in the Old Testament Moriah, and more recently *Mount* Moriah, was, by nature, a narrow, knobby, crooked ridge (of the class familiarly known as "hog's back"), deeply channeled by ravines and gulleys, honeycombed with caves, and in no proper sense fit to be used as the basis of a great temple. With radical reconstruction to transform this unsightly and circumscribed ridge into a solid, broad, high, and durable platform, was a problem of stupendous magnitude; as great a one, perhaps even greater, than would have been that of making a platform entirely artificial.

In my illustration of this subject in my public lectures, I have sometimes used the following figure as conveying a partial idea of the task that devolved upon Hiram and his builders: Go out upon a level plain; measure off an oblong square 1,600 feet by 1,000, equal to thirty-six and a half acres; build a wall around it of great stones, eight, ten, twenty, and even forty feet long, and of proportionate breadth and thickness; bind the foundation-stones of this wall firmly together with clamps of iron and lead, and in the same manner fasten them into the native rock that lies below; raise that wall to an average height of one hundred and fifty feet of solid masonwork; *fill up solid* the whole area of thirty-six and a half acres to that great height of one hundred and fifty feet! This being done, you will have such a platform as was erected by Solomon's craftsmen, upon which to build the Temple.

The figure is not absolutely correct; for there was a *central core* to the platform, viz., the original Mount Moriah; and in the masonwork *many large vaults* and subterranean chambers were left. But the figure is sufficiently exact for an ordinary lecture.

Now, when we describe the foundations of King Solomon's Temple as still remaining, we allude to this stupendous base, the platform of thirty-six and a half acres, constructed in so substantial a manner that neither time nor the devastations of barbarian force, nor the mighty bruit of earthquakes, has had power to break it up So large are the stones of which the outer walls are built, so artistically are they laid together in relation to each other, and so firmly mortised at their interior edges, and at their points of junction with the native rock, that it is safe to say that no power that human hands can apply will ever remove them, nor will any volcanic force affect them, less than that which would elevate the bed of the sea and sink the mountains into the depths.

It is mythically related that when the architect Hiram was brought to Jerusalem, and conducted by King Solomon to the summit of Mount Olivet, from which he was shown the general contour of the hill of Moriah, that skilled artist pointed to Scopus, the broad and beautiful elevation less than a mile to the north of the city, and suggested *that* as a much more appropriate basis for the Temple. Such an idea will occur to the observer even at the present day; still more when he considers that all this elevation before him, enclosed in thirty-six acres and a half, and containing so many buildings, is of *artificial construction,* and originally presented nothing but a rugged, unsightly succession of knobs. The elevation on the north of the city had everything of beauty and magnitude to recommend it, while all that could be alleged in favor of Moriah was the historical facts connected with the offering of Isaac by Abraham, and the Destroying Angel who stood there in the days of David.

Fortunately for my subject, there is a platform or artificial basis analogous to this foundation of Solomon's Temple near a place called Alma, about fifteen miles southeast of Tyre. To reach it you go from Alma in a southerly direction, down a ravine called Ain Hor, for about three miles, and enter Wady Benna near the village of the same name, which lies under mighty cliffs full of caverns. Passing down this wady (or valley) a little way, you turn up a branch wady to the southeast, and reach, through a woody and almost trackless region, the Wady el Kurn, directly opposite the castle. Here the wady is 600 feet deep, the sides being almost perpendicular, and covered with bushes and briers.

Now, the ridge upon which the castle of Kurein stands was, like Mount Moriah, originally extremely narrow. Even now it is only a few feet wide (from south to north) at the point beyond the castle, and has ragged cliffs descending on each side to a great depth. The castle, top of this ridge was widened by walls built up from below, as was done by Solomon on Mount Moriah, to enlarge the platform of the Temple. This basement-work is very solid, and exhibits very fine specimens of the old Jewish or Phoenician bevel. On this platform stood a noble tower of extremely well cut and very large stones, but not beveled. They are all three feet thick, and of various lengths up to ten feet. It must have been quite impregnable before the invention of cannon. The ridge falls down rapidly toward the river, in a direction nearly west, having the sides almost perpendicular. There are three other towers or departments, each lower than the one above, and also wider, for the hill bulges out as it descends, and the lowest of all encloses a considerable area.

These various departments were so connected as to form one castle, and yet so separated that each would have to be taken by itself. The second from the top has in it a beautiful octagonal pedestal of finely polished stone about eight feet high, with a cornice, and over it stood eight demi-columns, united inwardly, a column for each face of the pedestal; it probably supported an image or statue. Above all spread a lofty canopy of clustered arches, like those in the building at the river. The entire castle and its hill are now clothed with magnificent forests of oak, terebinth bay, and other trees, whose ranks ascend shade above shade, and underneath is a tangled network of briers and bushes, which make it difficult to explore the ruins. The hill of Castle Kurein is inexpressibly beautiful and imposing; a swelling pyramid of green hung up in mid-heaven, with the gray old tower peering out here and there.

This must present much the appearance that Mount Moriah did in the days of the Maccabees, about 165 B.C. The Temple-worship had ceased several years before, and the hill had grown up in forest trees, amid which the great Temple and its surrounding courts, cloisters, etc., rose up as a series of ruins, stately and imposing.

The sketch I have given of the great platform, will still convey an imperfect idea, unless the reader recalls the fact that around it, at the base, is an embankment of loose earth from fifty to one hundred feet deep. This earth represents all the *débris* of rubbish, relics of architecture, relics of domestic vessels, and the disintegrated stone used in the buildings above and around it for 1800 years. Solomon's Temple itself (reserving the woody portions that were burnt, and the metallic portions that were carried away) lies in that huge bank of earth! I found there, in a few minutes' search, specimens of various kinds of building materials that may once have shone in the rays which were reflected back on the day of the great dedication, when Solomon prayed: "Have respect to the prayer of thy servant, and to his supplications, O Lord, my God, to hearken unto the cry and the prayer which thy servant prayeth before thee, that thine eyes may be open upon this house day and night, upon the place whereof thou hast said that thou wouldst put thy name there, to hearken unto the prayer which thy servant prayeth toward this place." (2 Chronicles 6:19.)

Were that great dust-heap around Mount Moriah sifted, and its contents observed and preserved, it is not extravagant to say that a mass of remnants would be collected of Parian marble, Egyptian black marble, Verd-antique, Syenite, and Gray Granites, Porphyry, and other valuable building materials, which would come near to representing the bulk of the Temple and its subsidiary buildings.

The cubic contents of the great platform exceed ten million cubic yards! The magnitude of the structure (supposing it all artificial) is three times that of the great Pyramid of Cheops, which is about three and a half million cubic yards. Admitting that one-half of the Temple-platform is comprised in the native hill (Mount Moriah), and it is still three-tenths in excess of the pyramid. This fact is the more noteworthy because we have persistently been assured that the Pyramid of Cheops is the largest artificial structure in the world. According to historians, it took one hundred years to complete it, although no less than one hundred thousand workmen were engaged upon it; while the Temple-platform, with its one hundred and fifty thousand builders, was less than eight years in course of erection True, the latter had the immense advantage of procuring their stone within half a mile of the spot on which it was to be laid, and from a quarry so much higher, in relation to the platform, as to afford an inclined plane of just the convenient descent for their purpose.

Estimating other great accumulations of materials by this, we see that in the Plymouth (England) Breakwater, begun in 1812, the amount of granite blocks used was 3,666,000 tons, at a cost of about $7,000,000, reaching to more than half the material used here.

The seven successive objects that have occupied this sacred ridge, to which a Mason's attention is directed, are—

1. The Altar of Abraham.

2. The Threshing-floor of Ornan.
3. The Altar of David.
4. The Temple of Solomon.
5. The Temple of Zerubbabel.
6. The Temple of Herod.
7. The Mosque of Omar, believed to be the work of the Knights Templars. This Omar was an ascetic, living on barley-bread and dates, making a vaunt of poverty and humility, preaching in a ragged cloak. In the fourteenth century, his building was described as a very fair house, lofty and circular, covered with lead, well paved with white marble. At that time, it was said no such foul, impure men as Christians and Jews were allowed in such holy places.

I visited the place on which the Temple of King Solomon stood; explored the subterranean passages so far as allowable; inspected the present buildings, mostly of modern structure, and mourned, in common with all Masonic visitors, for the desolations visible nowhere more than here. It is a broad court, only sparsely covered with trees and buildings, and paved with marble, about 1,500 feet in length from north to south, and 1,000 in breadth, presenting the immense block (or rough ashlar) over which the Mosque of Omar is built, a rude stone nearly sixty feet long, that beyond doubt represents the original surface of the mountain. Why it was left here when all the rest of the combing of the ridge was cut away, is a question upon which antiquarians have long been at war.

INTERIOR OF THE DOME OF THE ROCK.

29

The great stone stands inside the railing. One of the love-songs of the Arab poets has the name of this celebrated rock as a figure of comparison:

> "Great is my love: if my love were in the Sakhrah,
> That great and wonderful rock the Sakhrah,
> It would be broken into a thousand pieces."

In stepping around and over this "Noble Enclosure," and reckoning up the measurements, my thoughts take their flight to the mighty structure near Cairo, the great Pyramid of Cheops, from which the primeval standard of measurement was deduced. The unit of the Pyramid was the *one five-hundred-millionth* part of the earth's axis of rotation, and twenty-five of these units formed the sacred cubit by which all this ground and the splendid erections thereon were measured. The progress of antiquarian research may yet connect the Patriarch Shem, who, under the name of Melchizedek, occupied yonder hill of Sion, with that wonder of Egypt.

The round protuberances seen on the largest ashlars, were, I think, left for the convenience of fastening the grappling hooks, in raising the heavy ashlars to their respective places. In the great Pyramid Cheops, holes are found in the sides of the larger stones, made undoubtedly for the same purpose. Had Solomon's builders been able to procure syenite, as those of Cheops did, we should have seen these walls made of granite slabs finished off with the skill and polish of a jeweler.

The importance that King Solomon gave to this idea of having his Temple due east and west may be seen in this, that the range of the hill on which it stands is almost exactly with the meridian, and therefore the more natural situation for the Temple was north and south. In contrast with its present ruined and desolate condition, compare the magnificent word painting of Croley (in *Salathiel*), describing the mountain and its glorious occupant, the year of its destruction, A.D. 70:

"I see the Court of the Gentiles circling the whole, a fortress of the purest marble, with its wall rising six hundred feet from the valley; its kingly entrance, worthy of the fame of Solomon; its innumerable and stately buildings for the priests and officers of the Temple, and above them, glittering like a succession of diadems, those alabaster porticoes and colonnades in which the chiefs and sages of Jerusalem sat teaching the people, or walked, breathing the air, and gazing on the grandeur of a landscape which swept the whole amphitheatre of the mountains. I see, rising above this stupendous boundary, the court of the Jewish women, separated by its porphyry pillars and richly-sculptured wall; above this, the separated court of the men; still higher, the court of the priests; and highest, the crowning splendor of all *the central Temple,* the place of the Sanctuary, and of the Holy of Holies, covered with plates of gold, its roof planted with lofty spear-heads of gold, the most precious marbles and metals everywhere flashing back the day, till Mount Moriah stood forth to the eye of the stranger approaching Jerusalem, what it had been so often described by its bards and people, *a mountain of snow studded with jewels."*

"The grandeur of the worship was worthy of this glory of architecture. Four-and-twenty thousand Levites ministered by turns, a thousand at a time. Four thousand more performed the lower offices. Four thousand singers and minstrels, with the harp, the trumpet, and all the richest instruments of a land whose native genius was music, and whose climate and landscape led men instinctively to delight in the charm of sound, chanted the inspired songs of our Warrior-King, and filled up the pauses of prayer with harmonies that transported the spirit beyond the cares and passions of a troubled world."

What a fine comment upon Croley's beautiful thought is this passage from the Fellow-Craft's lecture:

"Even the Temple of Solomon, so spacious and magnificent, and constructed by so many celebrated artists, escaped not the unsparing ravages of barbarous force."

But where are those alabaster columns, those porphyry pilasters, of which these authors speak? Who can tell? Many of them, doubtless, lying in fragments in this stupendous mass of *débris* of earth and stones, surrounding the mountain a hundred feet thick; some of them, if tradition speaks truly, in the ancient Church of the Nativity, at Bethlehem, five miles south of this place; some of them, perhaps, Nebuchadnezzar compelled his captives to carry away with them into Babylon, as they carried away so many other things, trophies of the Temple of Solomon.

Seeing a piece of fine marble loose in the pavement as I walked along by the old Temple site, I feed a soldier to lift it with his bayonet. It proved to be a fragment sawed from the side of a pillar, the convexity on that side remaining perfect. This specimen I still

have at my house in 1872. It illustrates the shocking destruction
of the finest works of art that has been going on here for many
centuries. Sueborda, in his "Seven Churches of Asia," describes
similar instances of beautiful columns being sawed up into slabs
for gravestones, pavements, tablets, etc. To one who enjoys the
privilege of personal inspection of that thrice-sacred area in which
the Temple of Solomon once stood, every portion of *the Great
Platform* is full of interest. Not a block of the original foundation-
wall, however weather-stained and weather-worn, but is a feature
in the grand old physiognomy upon which we love to dwell. The
same class of interest, though in less degree, is felt by all
Freemasons when contemplating the local peculiarities of the
sacred work. Let me describe *the southeast corner.*

Above ground, there is nothing that particularly attracts the
observer's attention in the southeast corner. The splendid Mosque
of Omar, nearly a quarter of a mile to the northwest, would most
probably fill his eye and occupy his thoughts for the brief period
that he is permitted to remain in this part of the sacred enclosure.
Looking over the battlement of the wall, he would see that he is
seventy-seven feet from its base, and if his head does not become
giddy —as Josephus says it will—he may note the great size of
the blocks of which it is constructed. These are truly cyclopean,
and stand, range upon range, sixteen courses high of the original
ashlars, each stone beveled clear around the exposed surface.
Near him, and immediately in the corner of the enclosure, he will
observe a small building covered with a dome, called by the
Moslems *Sidna Issa* ("of our Lord Jesus"), in the lower room of
which is an irregularly shaped trough, made of Jerusalem marble,
quarried in the great excavation on the northern side of the city,
to which we shall call attention in a future chapter.

But it is *below ground* that the chief interest of the Masonic
explorer of this immense Platform will extend. Here are
substructures worthy, in magnitude and the architectural skill
necessary for their construction, of the genius of Hiram himself, the
Sir Christopher Wren of his day. As he stood upon yonder spur of
Mount Olivet, a quarter-mile east, and looked across the valley to
Moriah, then a narrow, sharp-backed ridge, and computed the amount
of material necessary to bring up the Platform seventy-seven feet to its
present level, he might well ask himself from whence should come the
supply of earth and stone? The country around presents, and

ever did present, a rocky surface hard to loosen and break up; and it were a design worthy of the prince of architects to devise a method *to save earth and stones* where earth was so scarce. This was done by the substitution of arches for solid filling. This entire southeast corner inside of the foundation walls is hollow, being made up of arches. Of this great under-ground work, Bonar (*Land of Promise*) says it forms the foundation for the platform of the Temple area. The arches are singularly massive and strong; *strength* alone, not beauty or grace, has been consulted here. Not that there is anything *out of taste* in that interminable vista of arches, but it is *its solidity* that impresses the mind from first to last. There is nowhere anything like it. As we moved slowly down the slope of the hill, and felt the arches increasing in height and massiveness as we advanced, we seemed to be wandering through the rock-cut crypt of some vast Egyptian temple. It looked more as if the hill had been excavated into these cells, than that these cells had been built upon the hill. The cost and labor must have been great, and the engineering skill which they indicate is much beyond what modern ideas are inclined to allow to ancient science. The level platform which they produced above forms a large addition to the ancient hill, whose summit, as it stood originally, must have been narrow and quite unsuited for any building beyond that of a tomb. As you first enter by a kind of trap-door from the platform above and go southward, you think you might touch the roof with your hand, for the supporting pillars cannot be more than nine or ten feet high; but as you move down the long slope, you seem to be receding from the roof till at the extremity you find that it must be about thirty feet above you. Wherever we looked, we saw the same massiveness in wall, or arch, or pillar. There appeared to be no small stones in any part; these would have been inadmissible in such a structure. We measured some of the stones, and found them to average fifteen by eight feet. Concerning these great works, Dr. J. T. Barclay writes: "They are doubtless those alluded to by Josephus in his description of the construction of the Temple-wall. The declination of the hill at the southeast corner being greater than at any other part, it was found more advantageous to bring it to a general level by erecting vaults upon lofty columns than by filling up either with solid masonry or by earth, as in the case of the narrow ravines. The length of these rock galleries, measured westward from the wall on the east, is 319 feet; from the wall on the south, measuring northward, the different measures vary considerably; the one from the Triple Gate (277 feet from the east wall) being 247 feet in length; the third row from the eastern wall and the seven next rows to the west of it are each 188 1/2 feet in length. To sum up, then, the space occupied by these substructures, and which otherwise must have been filled up by solid masonry or earth, is represented by a mass 319×247×30 feet—less the space occupied by the rough spurs or projections of the ancient hill.

The stones in the wall near the southeast corner, though not quite so large as those in the northeast and southwest respectively, are yet cyclopean in magnitude, as has been shown before.

No description can do justice to these subterranean vaults without an engraving.

Considerable resemblance can be traced in the style of work done on these crypts of Mount Moriah and the ancient Roman aqueduct made to supply the city of Smyrna with water.

The importance of a full supply of water for the ceremonial observances always going on in and about the Temple, and for the beverage of the armies of priests and multitudes of visitors, is seen in the illustration of the Royal Sea, an immense cistern that is found about 500 feet south of the old Temple site. The cut conveys a good impression of it.

PIERS UNDER S. E. CORNER OF THE TEMPLE-PLATFORM.

I found the opening to this great reservoir as I was looking for the place where lie the assassins of that tempestuous firebrand of Rome, Thomas á Becket, who were buried here. The dimensions are given on another page. Its water supply was derived from Solomon's Pools, eight miles southwest, the line of aqueduct being distinctly marked all the way.

To show the steepness of this slope from Mount Moriah to the valley of Jehoshaphat, I rolled a good-sized stone from near the base of the wall, and it continued its flight without a pause until it reached the original bed of the brook Kedron.

Oh, that a nation would do for these masses of *débris* what the French Army in Egypt did in 1799 to the greater accumulations of

ROMAN AQUEDUCT AT SMYRNA.

sand and broken stones at the base of the Great Pyramid, removing it all, and bringing the foundation-stones of the Eternal Monument to the clear light of day! May not the great Mason-fraternity yet be induced to undertake it?

CISTERN ON MOUNT MORIAH.

In comparing the size of the tremendous blocks in these walls with those of the Great Pyramids, it will be seen how far Hiram's builders excelled those of Cheops in this respect. In a future chapter, I will give measurements of many pyramid-stones. The two marble casing-stones discovered by Vyse were twelve feet long, eight feet three inches broad, four feet three inches high. These were worked with such exquisite skill that the edges were not thicker, he said, than silver-paper.

Earthquakes have affected this great eastern wall, breaking many of the large blocks, and in places destroying notably the alignment of the wall; but the strong internal iron bands of which Josephus wrote have held block to block as the ligaments hold the bones, and the whole to the stony core on which it rests. It is worth one's while, standing here at the base of the wall, to read the words, "there was a great earthquake" at the Resurrection (Matt. 28:2); "the earth did quake and the rocks rent," at the Crucifixion (Matt. 27:51); "the place was shaken where they were assembled," while the disciples were praying together (Acts 4:21); "the year of the earthquake" Am. I., 1; "the hills did tremble" (Isaiah 5:25); and similar expressions. All these phenomena affected this great wall to a considerable extent, breaking the huge stones, etc.; but the construction thus far has defied the utmost efforts of internal fires to overthrow it.

It was quite a pleasant coincidence, in recalling one of David's expressions in the Psalms, to see, as I stood on the wall south of the Golden Gate, a nest of the sparrow (*passer cisalpina*) in a nook of one of the grand ashlars far below me.

The construction-marks of the Phoenician masons who built the Temple are unquestionably of great antiquity, and, I think, the actual *memorandums* of the stone-squarers of Gebal who took Solomon's contract to build the Temple. However rude these were, they were sufficient to check the workmen—to place responsibility in its proper quarter—to make the correct tally of wages, and, if necessary, of penalties, and secure the placing of each stone in its proper place. They are quite as distinct as those to be seen on the marble stones of which the public buildings at Washington are now being constructed. Those in the Pyramid as well as in this wall are sometimes *upside down*.

While I was observing the remains of this *gabbatha* (pavement) my foot slipped, and I nearly got a fall on a glassy bit of Parian marble remaining *in situ*, about the size of my hand. It was a pleasant coincidence that near the same spot slipped and fell in Titus' time "one Julian, a centurion, that came from Bithynia, a man of great reputation," as Josephus, who knew him well, describes him. (*Wars*, 6:1-8.) "Pursued by fate, which it was not possible he should escape," says the historian, he fell backwards on this smooth pavement, "having his shoes all filled with thick and sharp nails," and was stabbed to death and his throat cut by the Jews, who thronged around him with spears and swords. The whole incident is vividly described by Josephus, and fits in to my little tumble very neatly.

The muezzin, or man who does the call from the top of the minaret near by the Mosque of Omar, is a *blind man,* necessarily so, to prevent him from seeing the faces of the women, who would otherwise pass under his observation. The poor fellow cannot even "go a single eye on them," as the story says. Rambling through the extensive and beautiful grounds; inspecting the green and red satin canopy over the sacred rock (*Es-sakhara*), which is the gift of the Sultan; recalling the Mohammedan traditions of the builders of the first Temple here, and

> "The magic powers
> Of him, who in the twinkling of a star,
> Built those high-pillared halls,"

I felt that the true poet of Masonry might derive from this hallowed locality all the store of images and inspiration that it has given for thirty centuries to Jewish, Christian, and Mohammedan poets.

So frequently does Jerusalem and its particular mountains and fountains appear in the nomenclature of American lodges, that I have room for only a small part: *Mount Moriah Lodge* No. 106, Ky., and some fifty more; *Mount Sion Lodge* No. 147, Ky., and many others; *Mount Olivet Lodge* No. 29, Ky., and very many others; *Bethesda Lodge* (referring to the Pool here of that name) No. 201, Tenn., and others; *Siloam Lodge* No. 99, Georgia, etc.; *Mount Calvary Lodge* No. 95, Iowa; *Temple Lodge* No. 9, Del., and numerous others; *Solomon Lodge* No. 5, Ky., with a long list of others; finally, the city itself, *Jerusalem Lodge* No. 9, Ky., and a host of like names. *King David* is used for No. 139, Geo.; 62, Maine; 68, Md., etc. *Zabud* is honored in No. 175, Geo.; *Widow's Son Lodge* is No. 60 and 150, Va.; 75, N.C.; 335, N. Y.; 66, Ct.; 72, Ala.; etc. *Zerubbabel* is recognized in No. 199, Ky.; 15, Geo.; 329, N. Y., etc. Other places connected with this locality are used in like manner in our rather jejune lodge naming.

As at other places, I make the Masonic identifications complete, by writing here the names of zealous and worthy Masons whose labors in their sphere "keep light and warm" the lodges in which they work. At the site of the ancient Temple: Capt. Lemaitre, Thomas J. Jolley, Ralph Applewhite, Charles Craig, Lyndon A. Smith, John Beach, Rev. Colley A. Foster, A. W. Blakesley, Samuel Catherwood, J. H. Barlow.

At the southeast corner of the Great Wall: Christopher G. fox,

Israel Baldwin, John Christie, James P. Tucker, Thomas J. Pickett, J. D. Stockton, Lewis I. Coulter, Lewis S. Williams, Peter Thatcher, Jr., Robert Dott.

At the Joppa Gate: James A. Hawley, Ferd. Basler, C. K. Peck, Michel Pinner, E. S. Ross, W.W. Austin, W. H. Fogg, Vincent L. Hurlbut, Wm. M. Howsley, Christian Fetta.

At the Damascus Gate: E. Richardson, M.D., W. T. Woodruff, W. F. Coombs, M.D., W. P. Allen, M. O. Waggoner, Hiram W. Hubbard, E. H. M. Berry, E. H. English, J. C. Luckey.

At St. Stephen's Gate: James M. Austin, M.D., W. C. Munger, Rev. Stephen H. Tyng, Sr., Wm. S. Whitehead, A. H. Drummond, Samuel Wilson, Wm. T. Walter, Albert P. Moriarty, A. M. Black, Joseph Robbins.

In my account of the Clay-ground in a preceding chapter, I referred to the immense work performed there, of casting the brazen (bronze?) columns for the use of the Temple on Mount Moriah. I did not fail, while walking over this area, to make up my judgment as to the spot where those ponderous shafts were set up, and to kindle the imagination with the splendid view they must have presented to the traveler from any direction, and particularly from the east Turning the southwestern point of Mount Olivet, where the view is the finest, the sight of those mighty and mysterious pillars must have absorbed the attention of the traveler beyond anything else that the Temple of Solomon presented.

While writing up this paragraph (Feb. 1872), I fell in by good luck with some articles from the skilled and elegant pen of Prof. Herbert Bright, of New York, in "The Industrial Monthly," entitled "Observations on Columns." Speaking generally of this greatest of all architectural features, he says of certain ancient columns, "the incomparable excellence of their designs and proportions has defied the scrutiny of generations to detect a fault or add an embellishment." Making no special reference to the brazen columns of Solomon, he yet reprehends the erection of isolated columns like that of Pompey's Pillar, etc., and suggests that some of those monuments which we have been in the habit of supposing merely *solitary pieces,* did in fact *support entablatures.* It is the opinion of some of the best writers on Solomon's Temple, that such was the case with J. and B., and that *in fact* they were *not* disengaged columns at all. I am very much of that opinion, too. His description of a wrought-iron column of great antiquity, some fifty or sixty feet high, connected with a celebrated temple in

India, is a commentary upon Hiram's work, which old Dr. Adam Clarke describes as being "beyond the ability of any workmen of the present day to equal."

The Mohammedan Mosques on Mount Moriah being considered by those religionists the most holy of their churches, except the ones at Mecca, I introduce here a brief account of their mosque-worship. The best time to observe the ceremonies is on Friday, which is the Mohammedan Sabbath, but every day in the week will answer, for, like the Catholic churches in our large cities, they are always open to worshippers. I entered one about ten minutes before noon, and was much interested in their manner of worship. To avoid giving offence, I occupied an obscure corner near the door, and took my seat cross-legged, according to the native custom. I had been careful to remove my shoes, which I wore for the purpose, and slipped them unperceived into my coat-pocket.

As the company came in, they took their places side by side, in straight lines, all facing toward the south, which is the direction of Mecca, denoted by the *kiblah* in the southern wall of the mosque. These lines were about five feet apart, to leave a convenient space for prostration during the prayers. Perfect silence and decorum were observed. The muezzin or crier was all the time calling out, in the steeple (minaret) high above us, in long, harsh tones that could be heard to a very great distance, the following Arabic sentences:

> Allah hoo achbar;
> Allah hoo achbar;
> Oo ishod la illah il Allah;
> Oo ishod la illah il Allah;
> Oo inne Mohammed el Resool Allah.

This in plain English is:

> God is greater;
> God is greater,
> And bear testimony to one God;
> And bear testimony to one God;
> And testify that Mohammed is the Prophet of God.

This cry is made five times a day, viz., at daybreak, noon, middle of afternoon, at sunset, and at bedtime. In the daybreak call, these words are added:

> Es salat ophdel min en-noom;
> Es sullah koom wa kheddin es salat.

Prayer is better than sleep;
Rise up and offer prayers.

In making these calls, he goes to the four cardinal points, walking around his little balcony near the top of the minaret for that purpose.

As the worshippers came in, and while the muezzin was still making his circuit and invitations, every one began to move his lips; then to bow and kneel, and place his forehead on the floor between his hands, which were spread open and lying flat on the floor, about six inches apart.

As the muezzin stopped, the Imams, or priests, who were in the gallery, gave the word of command, and the performance commenced. The evolutions were performed with military precision and promptness, all rising, bowing, kneeling, and prostrating with the system of the far-famed New York Forty-third Regiment on a field day. An aged man near me, evidently stiff and agonized with rheumatism, still kept up with the rest, though the sweat stood in great beads on his forehead, and an occasional groan of anguish escaped from him. When the exercises were finished, he had to be lifted to his feet and led off by two men, apparently his sons. But the veteran had accomplished his task, and he left the place smiling.

The services occupied about an hour, the same words being repeated and the same evolutions performed without the least change. When they all fell on their knees in unison, the great stone building was jarred with the shock. The voices of the Imams were affected and unnatural, but their command over the worshippers in producing uniformity of ceremony was equal to that of a general over the most thoroughly disciplined troops. No one seemed to pay any attention to my presence. The silence, decorum, and absorbed devotion of these people, with the absence of pictures, relics, and idols, made a pleasing contrast with the scenes of noise, confusion, crosses, images, emblems, and auxiliaries of worship that fill the corrupt Christian churches here. But, on the other hand, the fact that *not a female* was present, or would have been allowed *to be* present, contrasted unfavorably even with the worst forms of corrupt Christianity.

CHAPTER XXVI.

HILE in Jerusalem, I held two Masonic meetings in a room at the Mediterranean Hotel, near the Damascus Gate, in which assemblies several officers of the British war-ships lying at Joppa were present; also the venerable Brother Petermann, Prussian Consul, and Captain Charles Warren, R.E., who is in charge of the explorations, as named before.

E. T. ROGERS,
W. M. of Palestine Lodge 415, at Beirut, 1868.

These conferences were delightful to me. Nothing can exceed the zeal of our English brethren upon such occasions; and we exchanged genial sentiments and formed and cemented friendships which I think will be permanent.

The names of these brethren are here given:

Lindesay Goodrich, Zetland Lodge 515, Malta.

John Oxland, R.N., St. Auburn Lodge 954, Davenport, England; also Zetland Lodge 515, etc.

Edward Gladstone, Phoenix Lodge, Portsmouth, England.

Rev. J. Every, Fidelity Lodge 1042, England, P. P. Grand Chaplain, Eastern Archipelago, Singapore.

All the above were connected with H. M. S. *Lord Clyde,* now lying in the port of Joppa.

Charles Warren, Past Master of Lodge of Friendship 278, Gibraltar.

Henry Petermann, Royal York of Berlin, Prussia, initiated in 1826, Member of the Fourth Degree (*Ober Meister*).

One of the most agreeable episodes in my visit here was an assemblage of Freemasons in the vast quarries that underlie the northeastern quarter of the city of Jerusalem, and the opening of a *Moot Lodge* there: this event occurred on the afternoon of Wednesday, May 13.

A description of these enormous caverns seems necessary as a preface to the subject. The entrance is under the city walls on the north, a short distance east of the Damascus Gate. This opening was first discovered about ten years ago, by Dr. J. T. Barclay, author of the celebrated work *The City of the Great King,* to which I have more than once referred. At that time, the entrance was extremely difficult of access; but when the Prince of Wales was here, a few years since, it was made easier. In fact, the matter of entering and traversing the entire quarries is now one of the lightest and pleasantest parts of a traveler's business in Jerusalem.

A city that has been seventeen times captured, and often partially (and several times totally) destroyed, has, of course, drawn immensely upon the building material of the vicinity. Add to this the fact that the native stone around Jerusalem is friable, and dissolves rapidly in the open air, and the reader will understand that somewhere in the vicinity *great quarries* must exist. These, as I said, are on the north side, and *under* the northeast quarter of the city. Outside of the walls a space of several hundred feet in width and a quarter of a mile in horizontal depth has been quarried to the depth of twenty-five to fifty feet; while adjoining those excavations on the south, and immediately under the city, there is a cavern, as already intimated, of equal extent. This is termed by the natives the *Cotton Megara,* by us the great *Jerusalem Quarry,* and it is here that we opened our Moot Lodge.

Entering with a good supply of candles, we pushed southward as far into the quarry as we could penetrate, and found a chamber happily adapted to a Masonic purpose. It was a pit in the ancient cuttings, about eighteen feet square. On the east and west, convenient shelves had been left by the original workmen, which answered for seats. An upright stone in the center, long used by guides to set their candles upon, served us for an Altar. About ten feet above the master's station there was an immense opening in the wall, which led, for aught I know, to the original site of the Temple of Solomon. We were perfectly tyled by silence, secrecy, and darkness, and in the awful depths of that quarry, nearly a quarter of a mile from its opening, we felt, as we never had before, how impressive is a place which none but the All-seeing Eye can penetrate.

Laying my pocket Bible open on the central stone, three burning candles throwing their luster upon it, and the trowel, square, etc., resting near by, a few opening remarks were made by myself, to the effect that never, so far as I knew, had a Freemasons' lodge been formed in Jerusalem since the departure of the Crusading hosts more than seven hundred years ago; that an effort was now making to introduce Freemasonry into this, the mother-country of its birth; that a few of us, brethren, providentially thrown together, desired to seal our friendship by the associations peculiar to a Masonic lodge; that for this purpose, and to break the long stillness of these ancient quarries by Masonic utterances, we had now assembled, and would proceed to open a Moot Lodge, under the title of Reclamation Lodge of Jerusalem. This we now proceeded to do, in a systematic manner. A prayer was offered, echoing strangely from that stony rock that had heard no such sounds for centuries, and the other ceremonies proceeded.

Remarks were offered, very feeling and appropriate, by the venerable Henry Petermann, Prussian Consul at Jerusalem, a member of Royal York Lodge at Berlin, a Freemason of many years' experience. Brother Peterman is the deputy of his Grand Lodge to the lodges of Palestine. He is a gentleman of great learning and the highest social standing, speaking eight languages with fluency. He expressed his opinion, in the plainest terms, that the times were propitious for reinstating the Masonic institutions in the Holy Land.

Brother Petermann was followed by Brother Captain Charles Warren, R.E., a member of Friendship Lodge No. 278, at Gibraltar, the learned and zealous officer who has charge of the excavations going.

JOHN P. BROWN,
District Grand Master at Constantinople, 1872.

Suddenly, without warning, the spirit of their genial and wise Brother Brown, to whom I allude on page 599, was summoned "by the God who gave it." He died of heart disease, at Constantinople, Sunday, April 28, 1872. I had received a communication from him the day before, and was preparing a reply when, by telegraph, the afflicting intelligence reached me. Freemasonry in the Turkish Empire has no *Elisha* worthy to wear the mantle of this *Elisha*. "Alas, the chariot of Israel and the horsemen thereof!"

R. M.

on here under patronage of the Palestine Exploration Fund. This gentleman, in some extremely happy observations, expressed his pleasure at this meeting, called together under such singular circumstances, and was equally impressed with the importance of introducing Freemasonry, though cautiously and judiciously, into the Holy Land.

He was followed by my assistant, who excelled himself in clear and forcible expressions of the importance of Freemasonry, just now, in a land of jarring nationalities and religions such as this is. He professed a willingness to do any part in the introduction and reestablishment of the society here, and showed how much of the misery to which this country has been subjected might have been spared, had Freemasonry existed here during the different crises of its history.

We separated; and endeavoring to return to the entrance through the devious and interminable passages of that enormous cavern, lost our way, and came nigh being compelled to remain there until our friends would search for us, the next day.

Then, when we deemed ourselves lost and booked for a long night in the Great Quarry, we groped for the wall like the blind; we groped as if we had no eyes; we stumbled (Isaiah 59:10). However, by good fortune, this evil was spared us, and we reached the City Gate before it was closed at sunset. The vast quarry thus consecrated by Masonic forms, shows at every point the marks of the chisel as well defined as the day the workmen left it. Slabs of stone partially dressed are lying upon the floor; others, partly cut out of the wall stand where a few more blows would detach them. Many emblems of crosses, Hebrew characters, etc., remain, and the next visitor will see amongst them the Square and Compass, as cut by our hand.

Associating the names of worthy Masons with this truly Masonic locality, I unite Henry Petermann, Nazif Mesharka, John Oxland, Edward Gladstone, Rev. J. Every, Lindesay Goodrich, Abdel Kader, Samuel Hallock, E. G. Storer, Noureddin Effendi.

My engraving presents a correct view of the interior of these excavations.

The following drawing of the Great Stone at Baalbec, whose dimensions I gave in a preceding chapter, having been mislaid at the proper time, comes in appropriately here.

Further notes relative to researches in this great quarry will be interesting to the general reader.

30

This enormous excavation, after lying for many ages sealed from the knowledge of man, was accidentally discovered by Dr. J. T. Barclay, about the year 1855. His dog was scenting in a hole under

GREAT STONE AT BAALBEC.

the city wall, and suddenly disappeared. This led Dr. Barclay to imagine that there might be a quarry or cave worth exploring there. By enlarging the opening with a spade, he found his conjectures verified. A few years ago, quite an opening was made for the accommodation of an English party, and now it is an every-day matter for visitors to enter and inspect the quarry.

In my drawing of it, the *light* portions show where the stone has been removed, the *dark* portions where it was left in great natural columns to support the roof. But in spite of these large and frequent supports, this white limestone is so soft before it has been exposed to the air and light, that large pieces are constantly falling from the roof and accumulating in great heaps upon the floor. In entering the quarry, we first went east one hundred and thirteen feet, as marked upon the map, then directly south four hundred feet, then southeast one hundred and ninety-six feet. Here is the deep circular pit in which Dr. Barclay discovered a human skeleton—some poor wretch, no doubt, who became bewildered in the windings of the

INTERIOR OF THE GREAT QUARRY.

STONE-MARKS AT JERUSALEM.

EXQUISITE GEM-CARVING.

great cave, and fell in unawares. With an abundant supply of candles, however, we turned northward around the pit, and went two hundred and seventy feet, where the excavation seemed to end abruptly. Near the circular pit is a small basin chiseled in the rock, about five feet in diameter, and two and a half feet deep, into which the water was anciently collected for the use of the workmen. We found it full and running over; but the water is bitter and disagreeable to the taste.

That this great cavity is a *quarry,* and not a natural cave, is plain enough, both from the general appearance of it and from the marks of the chisel on every side. The floor is piled deep with clippings made by working implements. Along the sides of the quarry, deep, narrow grooves were cut lengthwise between the blocks, some of which were unusually large, and these were then burst off by long levers or some other mechanical contrivances. Magnificent halls were formed in this manner, while innumerable chambers and recesses stretch away to the right and left, showing that the rock was worked wherever it was found best in quality.

Dr. R. W. Stewart (in the "Tent and Khan") considers this quarry one of the most interesting discoveries yet made in Jerusalem. It proves that the great blocks seen in the walls of Mount Moriah were not brought from the very great distance formerly supposed, but from a place upon the continuation of the same mountain. This quarry being higher than the top of the platform on which the Temple stood, it was easy to roll the heavy stones down the inclined plane to their places. It proves, too, from its vast capacity, how much stone was used in the various structures connected with Solomon's architecture.

Great numbers of bats were clinging to the roof of the quarry, which in places is forty feet high. Bones of various kinds, brought in here probably by jackals, prove the use to which the great cavern has been turned. Numerous crosses are traced upon the wall, indicating that Christians, probably Crusaders, had been here; and a few Hebrew and Arabic inscriptions, too much effaced to be readable, may be seen.

The history of Dr. Petermann is full of interest. He has been in the Prussian diplomatic service for more than two score years at Baghdad, in Egypt, in Asia Minor, and other quarters of the globe. I found the good old man very complimentary in his appreciation of America and its literature. He assured me, as Brother Warren had done, that American authorities on Holy Land explorations (Robinson's, Barclay's, Thomson's) are reckoned the best on the catalogue, and said that Motley's *History of the Netherlands* is highly popular in Holland and Germany.

This venerable Mason and Christian gentleman was born in Glauchan, Saxony, in the year 1801. In 1815, he went to the gymnasium of Schulpforte, near Naumburg, and in 1821 to the University of Leipzig. Here he studied theology four years. In 1825, he went to Berlin, and engaged in the study of philosophy (especially Oriental languages) for four years. In 1829, he took the degree of Doctor in philosophy. In 1830, he entered upon the vocation of an academic instructor. In 1833, he received the grade of Professor Extraordinary in the Philosophical Faculty. In 1849, he became a member of the Academy of Science in Berlin, and in 1857 was nominated Doctor in Divinity by the Theological Faculty of Greiswalde.

During the years 1832-33, he was in Venice studying the Armenian tongue. In 1852-53, he traveled in the East, remaining for a considerable period in Damascus, Jerusalem, Nablous, Cyprus, Baghdad; then four months in Persia, and a short period in Egypt. In 1868, he received his appointment at Jerusalem, which, however, is only temporary, as he shortly returns to Berlin, to spend the remainder of his days in quiet. The object of his stay in Jerusalem was that he might study the Armenian manuscripts belonging to the monastery of the Armenian Patriachate there, a collection of rare interest and value.

As a Freemason, Brother Petermann was initiated in 1825, in the Lodge Frederick William, belonging to the Royal York Grand Lodge of Friendship; received the degree of Fellow Craft the same year, and that of Master Mason the following year. About the year 1840 he was advanced to the fourth Degree, what is styled in that system the *Degree of Knowledge;* similar, probably, to our Past Master. In his own Lodge he held the offices first of "Surveyor," finally of Honorary Master.

In the Fourth Degree (Knowledge), called also that of St. Andrew, he was appointed Surveyor, then Chief Master of the Lodge, and in the "Innermost Orient" he was made Substitute Chief Master. In his mother Grand Lodge he is Representative of the Grand Lodge of Germany to the Orient.

In this age of Masonic skepticism it is refreshing to have this testimony

over the signature of so venerable and learned a man as Dr
Petermann:

"If you will have a confession of my opinion upon the scope of
Masonry, I think we are obliged to consider it as a mission for
promoting true Christianity. Among our Christian brethren, we
must promote the inner mission in order to make true Christians.
Among the Jews, Mohammedans, and Heathens, we are obliged
to prepare the work for the Missionaries, because the true and
genuine Mason, in my opinion, must be a true and genuine
Christian."

In the course of a social evening passed with that learned and
experienced Jerusalem Missionary, Dr. J. T. Barclay, prior to
leaving the United States, he advised me to give special attention
to an object of rare Masonic interest, found near the Damascus
Gate in Jerusalem. This is a true pattern of the *Winding Stairs,*
so minutely wrought out in the lectures of the Fellow Craft. Upon
my arrival here, I made two visits to this singular structure, and
examined it minutely. It is situated on the right-hand or eastern
room of the Damascus Gate, and, as Dr. Barclay says, "is
connected with the best specimens of ancient Jewish mural
structures that the battering-ram and tooth of time have spared
to us." This winding stairway commences on the left and leads to
the top of the tower. It is not contained in a *circular* tube, as in
modern buildings and the ordinary Masonic pictures, but is
square-shaped, each step being about seven feet long and three
broad, and built *in the body of the structure.* After passing
through it, I am quite of the opinion expressed by Dr. Barclay
that this was the kind of ascent by which, as the inspired
historian says, "they went up with winding stairs into the middle
chamber, and out of the middle into the third," situated in the
southern wing of the Temple porch (1 Kings 6:8).

Without drawings, it is difficult to make this ingenious device
clear to the reader; but I can assure him I saw but few remains of
ancient architecture about Jerusalem, or anywhere else, so well
worthy of study as this. Upon a plain surface near the top, I
chiseled the Square and Compass.

All attempts made by me to increase the number of Lodges in
Palestine and Syria, under English authority, failed. The Grand
Lodge of England does not, masonically *know* any Mason not
enrolled upon her own Grand Lodge Register; and no matter how
numerous the petitioners or how respectable the petitions we
prepared and forwarded, from Damascus and elsewhere, they were

thrown out in London "for want of jurisdiction." The Grand Orient of France issued a warrant for a second Lodge at Beirut, and that, up to 1872, was the only result of my labors in this direction. At the issuance of the present volume, however (April, 1872), a measure is on foot with the best prospects of success to organize *The Solomon's Lodge at Jerusalem* under American auspices.

Brother R. Beardsley, United States Consul in Jerusalem, and a member of the Order at Elkhart, Indiana, is at work, with great energy, backed up by a strong feeling here and in America, to accomplish an end desirable in itself and particularly so at the present time—the establishment of the Masonic Order, on a legal and permanent basis, in the city of its origin. The points presented to the Masonic authorities of America and Europe, in justification of this movement, are these:

The Turkish Empire, masonically considered, is *neutral ground:* to prove this we show that the Grand Lodges of England, Scotland, France, and Italy (perhaps others), have exercised the right to establish Lodges there.

The General Grand Chapter of the United States has entered that field in establishing St. John's R. A. Chapter in Smyrna, Asia Minor.

Our Consul at Jerusalem, who will be the W. M., is an American, and so will be at least one other petitioner. They wish to work the American Constitution and Rituals.

The petitioners will be personally vouched for by a resident Mason in Kentucky, as to standing and proficiency.

No Lodge will be asked for a recommendation, because the nearest Lodges are at Beirut, 150 miles, and the two Lodges there, at the present time, are inert. But we can get the recommendation of American Lodge, if the technicality is insisted on.

The rituals to be worked are the "Webb Rituals," translated into Arabic.

As a pleasant summary of Jerusalem notes, I conclude the chapter with a letter written shortly after my return from the East, and while my mind was warm with Oriental life and reflections. Some repetition of facts already introduced will not be considered a blemish in the epistolary style.

The guidebooks with which I have already advised you to provide yourself are so full and explicit in relation to "Jerusalem the Golden," that it would be excessive for me to offer to pilot you around the city. If you can possibly procure a copy of Barclay's

"City of the Great King," and study it before you leave "the land of the free," do so; it is incomparably the best book upon the subject. However, you will have to go to a public library for it, as the book is out of print and excessively scarce. Dr. Robinson's "Biblical Researches" will never be obsolete in relation to Jerusalem, and you must not fail to peruse that portion. Thomson's "Land and Book" is reliable in *every part*. Other works are full of this subject; it can never become stale. Be sure to post yourself up before you go there.

And here let me warn you against putting any faith whatever in the lamentable mummery with which the convents at Jerusalem and elsewhere abound. The so-called "holy places" about Jerusalem Bethlehem, and Nazareth have not a particle of foundation to stand upon. Their history is mostly modern, and where it claims anything of antiquity, it is so mixed up with fable that the safest belief is *unbelief*. The best guide through the lands of the Bible *is* the Bible; and as an old writer said, "The delight afforded by the internal evidences of truth will surpass all that can be anticipated." Such extraordinary instances of coincidence even with the customs of the country as they are now exhibited, and so many wonderful examples of illustration afforded by contrasting the simple narrative with the appearances presented, will fill your notebook and confirm your faith in the accuracy of the narrative itself. The Scriptures, for instance, guide us to Bethlehem, but *not* to the Cave of the Nativity; to Gethsemane, but *not* to the place where Jesus knelt in agony; to Olivet, but not to the spot from which Christ ascended; to Jerusalem, but *not* to Golgotha. Here is where pious men materially err, viz., in trying *to localize too minutely*. The priests encourage them in this, because it brings gold and fame to their shrines. They pick out a place, label it with a legend, build an altar and a chapel over it, and henceforth it is knelt to and kissed and worshipped *ad nauseum,* A disgusting specimen of this is seen in the so-called *Via Dolorosa,* or road by which Jesus bore his cross to Calvary. Now, if there is any one thing better established than another, it is that the *Via Dolorosa* does *not* represent the road that Jesus traversed; for, even if it follows *the same course,* the road stands from twenty to fifty feet at a *higher* level than it did 1,800 years ago, in consequence of the enormous accumulations of *debris* that have filled up the Tyropœon. Yet the priests profess to show every station along the *Via Dolorosa* at which Jesus fell, arose, fell again, was presented with a handkerchief, was relieved by Simon of Cyrene, etc., etc.; and the stone wall opposite each of those "Sacred Stations" is annually kissed by thousands of pilgrims until great holes are actually worn in them by the pressure of pious, well-meaning, but grossly-deluded lips.

'My counsel is, prepare an *agenda* before you reach Jerusalem of what you will visit, and *adhere to it* rigidly, turning from it neither to the right nor to the left. This *agenda* includes, among other objects, the following:

1. Visit the Ancient Tower near Jaffa Gate.

2. Walk on top of the wall from Jaffa Gate to St. Stephen's Gate, around the north side of the city.

3. Carefully examine the ancient constructions, the winding stairway, etc., at Damascus Gate. See whether the *Square and Compass* remains where I cut it in the wall at the top of the winding stairs.

4. Take a whole day to visiting the old Temple platform. No matter if the guide wants you to leave in an hour; you pay for a *whole day,* and every hour you lose will cause you subsequent regret. Descend into the Great Cistern at the southern side of the platform. Take a candle and wade clear through it.

5. Take enough leisure to scan closely the whole vast wall forming the eastern supports of the platform. Do not hurry. Have a small chisel and mallet, and when you see a stone of peculiar value, quietly *chip off* a few preservation crumbs (but do not let the soldiers who are overhead see you, or you may never *leave* Jerusalem!) See if my *Square and Compass* is chiseled plainly near the southeast corner, where I indented it at the peril of my life.

6. Visit Olivet. Best begin at Scopus early in the morning, and take a day on foot to the journey round Olivet, across the Kedron at Ain Joab, climb the Mount of Evil Counsel at Aceldama, and so on, clear round by the hilltops to the Damascus Gate, where you went out. Such a day's memory will abide forever.

7. Visit, with a guide, the great quarry under the city. If possible, get Captain Warren, of the Royal Engineers, to accompany you and show you where a few of us "good fellows" opened a Freemason's Lodge in that midnight stillness and darkness. Perhaps Dr. Petermann, the Prussian Consul, will also go with you—a noble old man, and a true and faithful brother.

8. At a convenient day, secure Captain Warren's company to guide you through the excavations made under his guidance by the London Palestine Exploration Fund. He will doubtless furnish you with

printed descriptions. Although he will say nothing to you about
the matter, yet the enterprise needs funds, and you ought to
contribute a sovereign at least to the work. You will be astonished
at the amount of excavation done, at the evidences presented of
the gigantic plans of former ages now being exhumed. As one of
the London members said: "Discoveries have been made of the
utmost importance, leading to the hope that before long sufficient
data will be obtained for forming a tolerably accurate opinion
upon the various sites in the Holy City which had been so long
matters of dispute. The actual streets of the ancient city have
been reached, underground passages have been brought to light,
and a complicated network of drains and reservoirs laid bare."
You will find Captain Warren to be as thoroughly posted and
energetic as he is modest and diffident.

9. In going round the city by way of "the rim of the basin" of the
hills that overlook Jerusalem, look carefully for the place
masonically known as "Hiram's Pulpit." The tradition is that
when King Solomon held his first conference with that celebrated
artist, Hiram, the Widow's Son, he took him to a place near the
conjunction of the two eminences, now known as the Mount of
Offence and Mount Olivet, situated nearly upon the prolongation
of Mount Moriah, and pointed out the spot where he designed to
erect the Temple. You will recognize the place by a large flat rock
with a cave under it, and an old olive-tree just below. "Hiram's
Pulpit," in connection with the myth that embodies it, is one of
the sacred places of Freemasons' travels.

Looking inquiringly from "Hiram's Pulpit" up the slope of
Mount Moriah, as if in search of the vast Temple described by
Josephus, we may reflect that the one part, the marble, was earth,
and went to the earth; the other part, the cedar, was of the
atmosphere, and went to vapor under the torches of Titus' legions.
The former lies there yet in the great piles that conceal one-half
the face of the old platform wall, and contain countless relics of
the coins, the marbles, the weapons, and the bones of those who
gave their lives to their country on that fearful night of the
capture. The latter returned, perhaps, to Lebanon, to enter
through the foliage of the cedars into the great trees that shall
glorify those historic shrines. Such thoughts as these not only
serve to identify important localities, but to surround them with a
halo of glorious associations that will survive all ordinary
memories of the Holy Land.

10 Visit the Tomb of the Kings on the north side of Jerusalem,

also other of the vast tombs with which "the hills round about Jerusalem" are so honeycombed.

Listening at sunset to the solemn cry of the muezzin from the minaret in "the Sacred Enclosure" of Mount Moriah, you will be interested in reading a copy of the first sermon preached on Mount Moriah, by a Mohammedan priest, on the Friday after the capture of Jerusalem by Saladin, in 1187. The priest ascended the pulpit, read all those passages from the Koran which contain aspirations of praise to God, and then delivered the following Klothbek or Sermon:

"Praise to God, who by his aid hath glorified Islamism; by his power hath debased polytheism; by his will rules the affairs of the world; prolongs divine blessings according as we show gratitude for them; by his wisdom defeats infidels; gives power to dynasties accustomed to his justice; by his goodness reserves future life to those who fear him; extends his shadow over his servants; causes his religion to triumph over all others; gains an irresistible victory over his servants; triumphs in his caliph without any one being able to stay him; orders what he wills against all objectors; judges according to his own pleasure, and no one is able to avert the execution of his decrees.

"I praise this God for having, by his assistance, rendered his elect victorious; for the glory he has given them; for the end he has granted to his defenders. I praise him for having purified the polluted house from the impieties of polytheism. I praise him with soul and body. I give testimony that this God is the only God; that he has no associate; the only one; the eternal one, who begets—is not begotten, and has no equal. I give testimony that Mohammed is his servant and his messenger; this prophet who has removed doubts; confounded polytheism; extinguished falsehood; who traveled by night from Medina to Jerusalem; who ascended into the heavens, and reached even the cedar *Almontchy*. May the eternal felicity of God be with him and with Abon Bekr, Alsadic, etc.

"O men! publish the extraordinary blessing by which God has made easy to you the recapture and deliverance of this city which we had lost; and has made it again the center of Islamism, after having been, during one hundred years, in the hands of the infidels.

"This house was built and its foundations laid for the glory of God and in the fear of Heaven. For this house is the dwelling of Abraham; the ladder of your prophet (peace be with him); the Kiblah to which you prayed at the commandment of Islamism; the

abode of prophets; the aim of saints; the place of revelation; the
habitation of order and defense. It is situated in the land of the
gathering; the arena of the meeting. It is of this blessed land that
God speaks in his precious book. It was in this mosque that
Mohammed prayed with the angels who stand in the presence of
God. It was this city to which God sent his servant, his messenger,
the word which he sent to Mary. The prophet he honored with his
mission did not stray from the words of his servant. For God said,
"The Messiah will not deny that he is the servant of God. God has
no son, and has no other God with him. Certainly they are
impious, who say that Messiah, the son of Mary, was God."

It is unfortunate, in one respect that nearly all published
communications concerning the Holy Land are from the pens of
the clergy. These gentlemen, unaccustomed to physical hardships,
give pictures colored with hues drawn from their own fancies,
rather than the facts In comparing my own experiences with
those of the Reverend this and the Reverend that, whose books
fill my shelves, I marvel to see how different they have been. The
enormous "fatigues" of which they speak so lamentably as the
harder incidents of travel, were simply those of men who probably
never mounted a horse before. The "dangers of travel" are simply
bosh. The "noisy contests" of the natives are only clamors in their
own unmusical tongue for *backsheesh,* clamors which it only
needs a sharp and stern denial to stop, and to rid one's self of the
pack at a word.

It chanced to me just now to open a letter published in the
Cincinnati *Gazette,* July, 1867, a copy of which I happened to
have with me, and this tendency to describe Oriental travel from
an *effeminate* point of view, is so manifest in it and in all his
series, that I am prompted to say a word upon the other side of
the question. The writer's opinion was that of a man accustomed
to a quiet, studious life, dyspeptic in his internal arrangements,
to whom a prancing horse is a terror, and the cry of a jackal at
midnight as a voice from the dead. Now look at the other side.
Take a person who knows how to mount a horse from the left side,
and to load and fire a pistol, one who is in the habit of sleeping
soundly after a hearty supper, and every "adventure" described by
the reverend gentleman in his twenty-seventh letter is but the
commonest frolic.

And the most erroneous impression conveyed by such writers is in
regard to the expense of travel. They have no idea that a man can see
any thing in the Holy Land unless he has a dragoman, with tents, an

army of horses, a *cuisine* or kitchen apparatus, and all the appliances of civilized life. No wonder these things are expensive. No wonder that "eight dollars a day in gold" (equal to twelve dollars in currency) scarcely covers the bill. And no wonder that the tourist hears the jackal scream at midnight, and sees "blood and thunder" upon the countenance of every Arab he meets. Why, look at it! the first proposition made you by one of these *first-class dragomen,* when bargaining with you, is that he will give you "five courses for dinner." I say, look at it! A dyspeptic little clergyman gets on his horse at Beirut, almost the first time he ever straddled one, and rides eight hours, to the vicinity of Sidon. The unwonted motion has stimulated his appetite to absolute voracity, but without increasing the amount of his gastric juice or his power of digestion. Arrived at his camping-ground, he waits almost crazed with hunger until eight or even nine o'clock at night for his dinner, for "five courses" cannot be prepared in a minute. When it comes, the poor fellow, half-witted by starvation, eats a meal of soup, fish, meats, and dessert, that a healthy ploughman could scarcely digest, and immediately afterward, worn out by fatigue and the intolerable delay, goes to bed, to contend, through a long night, with nightmare and apoplexy. Does not he get his eight dollars' worth? No wonder he hears the jackals!

Read the works of ninety-nine travelers out of a hundred who "do the Holy Land," and would not the reader suppose that there is only one way to visit the Holy Land?—that you *must pay a dragoman* to kill you with dyspepsia—to drag you hither and thither at his pleasure—to lie to you from hour to hour, and pass off his impudence for bravery? I vow that when I have heard and seen the things to which travelers submit in this country from their hired servants, I have felt that in emancipating American slaves, public opinion stopped only half-way: the slavery to dragomen is worse.

Do you ask how, then, the tourist should proceed to get the proper information and see the country? I reply, very much the same as he would at home. The only differences are that if he cannot speak the language, he must have an interpreter; as there are no public conveyances, he must hire his own horses; and as there are some places where accommodations are scanty, he should take his own blankets and a moderate supply of provisions. He needs no expensive dragoman, or tents, or *cuisine,* or any nonsense of the sort. If he travels alone, which is perfectly safe and pleasant, he wants an intelligent fellow who knows enough English to give him the names of places, etc., and is willing to be *his servant*. Two horses carry him and the servant, while a pack-mule carries his two pair of blankets and supply of provisions, say for a week ahead. With a good fowling piece for game, a good reference Bible in his pocket, an easy conscience and digestion, a man may thus see the Holy Land upon three dollars a day, and fare like a (Syrian) lord. If three such travelers go together, it need not cost them more than two dollars a day for each.

And the great advantage of this plan is, *you can go where you please*. Now, a dragoman will not permit that. Either by the broadest lying or by sheer bullying, he takes you where *he* pleases. You start when he bids you, go just so long as he directs you, and halt for night-quarters wherever he decides that you should. For instance, I left Jerusalem May 14, about 3 P.M., designing to pass through Bethel. There was not a dragoman in Jerusalem who could (or would) tell me where Bethel is. *They* only know Rameleh, a few miles west of it, and the secret of their ignorance is that there is a convent at Rameleh where they always stop. But I found Bethel by the map, and spent the night at Bethel. And I do not know of a prettier route for a few days than to stroll through the country between Bethel and the Jordan valley, tracing out the ancient localities of Ai, Rimmon, Shiloh, and others, that in the imagination of a dragoman are but fabulous places.

There is no difficulty in contriving a route from one end of the Holy Land to the other, so as to secure accommodations at convents and respectable native houses nine nights out of ten.

A stout man could make a pleasant *walking* excursion through Palestine at the most trifling expense. Were I twenty years younger, there is nothing I would sooner undertake than to make up a party of good legs and sound stomachs, and shoulder a knapsack with them for a six week excursion among the sacred hills and valleys. There was a man at Jerusalem this Spring who was doing this very thing—doing it alone—and doing it with an ease and safety that put to blush the colored fancies of those writers who are bent upon convincing the world that the days of Marco Paulo have returned again, because they heard a jackal scream, or saw an Arab with a twelve-foot spear-handle that could be used offensively about as easy as an old-fashioned arquebuse.

More than six hundred years have passed since the Holy City was visited by an Emperor, the difference between the two visits being very remarkable: in the one instance, Frederick II of Germany took the city from the Moslems by force of arms about the year 1230; and in the other case (1869), Francis Joseph comes, welcomed and fêted by the followers of Mohammed, every attention which real feeling alone can show being by no means stinted, and this, coming from a people whose religion teaches them that to murder Christians is a sure road to heaven, marks the progress of civilization in the East. The Governor-General of Syria, Raschid Pasha, came overland all the way from Damascus to Jaffa, to meet the Austrian Emperor, and, considering the poor resources of the country, entertained his Majesty in a most princely manner. Roads were made, hills were leveled, bazaars and streets thoroughly cleared of ages of lumber, regardless of expense, and everything was done to show that the honor of the Emperor's visit was truly appreciated.

The Emperor's fleet remained off Jaffa nearly the whole of the night of the 7th of November, so as to be ready to land early on the morning of the 8th. After the usual salvos of cannon, the Emperor's boat was seen approaching, bearing the Austro-Hungarian flag in its stern, and the flag of the House of Hapsburg in its bow, the Governor-General awaiting the arrival on a jetty improvised for the occasion, and which consisted of a covered passage and a saloon of reception, decorated with oranges, sugar-canes, and the numerous products of the country, the whole being covered tent-fashion with striped red-and-white silk, the production of the looms of Damascus. The streets being very narrow and inconvenient near the landing-place, all ceremony was dispensed with till the party arrived at a camp which had been erected by the Governor-General among the orange-groves for which Jaffa is famous, and through which for nearly two miles the royal party had to be conducted. Here the various consuls and Turkish officials were presented to the Emperor, after which a troupe of some six hundred Bedouins performed the various exercises for which these Desert savages are so renowned. Charging one another with their spears, firing their muskets, shouting and yelling, their horses twisting and turning in every direction, combined with the flashing of the gay colors in which they were dressed, they presented a sight to be seen nowhere but in the East.

The Emperor, dressed in a gray shooting-coat, and well mounted on a splendid Arab belonging to the Governor, commenced his journey with fine weather and a sun robbed of its fierceness by light, fleecy clouds; the suite, some in carriages and some mounted, following in every description of mufti and on every description of horse and saddle, from the well-made pigskin to the unmade sheepskin. On reaching Rameleh, luncheon was provided by the staff of servants sent expressly by the Sultan from Constantinople, all of whom were particularly chosen because they spoke German. The service was entirely of silver and gold, and of a completeness which defies description, every possible item, even to carpets and bedding, being sent from Constantinople for the use of the visitors. After refreshment the journey was resumed, and, as evening drew on, lighted beacons of wood and bitumen were borne by men in front of the procession. About 9 P.M. the royal party arrived at their resting-place for the night—a splendid camp, which was placed near the village of Aboo Ghosh.

A repast of every delicacy was here provided, not only for the Emperor's and Pasha's suites, but for all the troops and followers, which numbered nearly two thousand, and, the night being dark, bonfires ranged in every direction, making the scene quite a gay one.

After a good night's rest, the Emperor started for the Holy City at 8 A.M., and, after a two-hours' ride, Koloniah was reached, where the royal party dismounted and changed their mufti for uniforms, which are not only simple, but exceedingly becoming, especially the Hungarian one, in which many of the suite were dressed.

Koloniah shows many ruins of Roman architecture, and is believed to have been a Roman station of the time of Adrian; the traditions of the present day, however, point it out as the place where David slew the giant.

The procession, preceded by three standard-bearers, then proceeded on their pilgrimage, winding up the last steep hill which hides the Holy City from sight, and every eye was strained as the summit was being neared, to catch the first glimpse of Jerusalem. The Emperor dismounted and kissed the holy soil of Palestine the moment the city came in sight, and in every action showed that deep emotion stirred his soul. Triumphal arches of every kind, and priests and laity of every known religion of Europe and Asia, thronged the road, from time to time cheering as lustily as Orientals, unused to the "hurrah!" could do, and thus the city was reached. At the Jaffa gate the horses were dismissed, and the Latin Bishop of Jerusalem, accompanied by a crowd of priests, read an oration in Latin, and presented a crucifix purposely reserved for kings, for the Emperor to kiss; the guns thundered, and the Turkish bands added to the uproar, as the procession of priests and military filed slowly away down the streets leading to the Church of the Holy Sepulcher, where the Emperor attended high mass, and visited the tomb of our Savior.

Two facts of note may here be appropriately noted: firstly, by order of the Emperor, who, though religious, is liberal, all the Protestant clergy were specially invited; and also another fact, that the Governor-General of Syria and other Turks were present during the saying of mass in the Church of St. Sepulcher.

The city was splendidly illuminated in the evening, the Holy Sepulcher and the Austrian Consul's being the most remarkable Rockets, Bengal lights, and muskets were fired the greater part of the night.

The next day, Bethlehem and other places of interest were visited, and on the 11th, the royal party left for the Dead Sea.

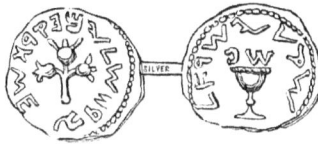

HALF SHEKEL OF SIMON. MACCABAEUS B. C. 143

31

A GROUP OF FLOWERS

In this group of flowers, collected and arranged for me by a Prussian family at Jerusalem, there are ten specimens gathered, at ten different localities, viz.: 1. The Shepherds' Plain, near Bethlehem. 2. Rachel's Tomb, between Bethlehem and Jerusalem. 3. Bethany. 4. Mount Zion. 5. Mount Moriah. 6. The Valley of Jehoshaphat. 7. Mount Olivet. 8. The Valley of Hinnom. 9. The Land of the Kings. 10. The Garden of Gethsemane.

The group has been chromolithographed by Mr. A. L. Murdoch, of Boston, Mass., in a style absolutely incomparable.

DIVISION NINTH.—GALILEE AND DAMASCUS.

"Tis long ago, yet faith in our souls
Is kindled just by that fire of coals
  That streamed o'er the mists of the sea:
While Peter, girding his fisher's coat,
Went over the nets and out of the boat
  To answer, Lov'st thou me?
  Thrice over, Lov'st thou me?

  Stabat mater dolorosa,
  Juxta crucem lacrymosa,
    Dum pendebat filius;
  Cujus animam gementem,
  Contristatem et dolentem,
    Per transivit gladius.

  O quam tristis et afflicta,
  Fuit illa benedicta
    Mater unigeniti!
  Quæ mœrebat, et dolebat,
  Pia mater dum videbat,
    Nati pœnas inclyte.

  Quis est homo qui non fleret,
  Christi matrem si videret,
    In tanto supplicio?
  Quis posset non contristari;
  Piam matrem contemplari,
    Dolentem cum filio?

  Pro peccatis suæ gentis,
  Vidit Jesuin in tormentis
    Et flagellis subditum
  Vidit suum dulcem natum,
  Morientum, desolatum,
    Dum emisit spiritum.

CHAPTER XXVII.

N a preceding chapter I conducted my readers as far as to Jacob's Well. Spending a night in Nablous, as there explained, I went on Saturday, a very hard day's journey, to Shunem, near Nazareth. It was my purpose to reach the latter place the same night, but the distance was too great, considering the terrific mountain-paths to be traversed during the first part of the journey.

The notes of the day are numerous, but will be used chiefly to embellish special chapters. Going around the western slope of Mount Ebal, I was afforded a fine view of Shechem and its valley from Jacob's Well to Samaria. No monument on earth is better identified than Jacob's Well; no vale is more fertile than Shechem.

Nothing puzzles the hearers of my lectures more than to tell them that "everything in this country is *buried up*." All the modern towns here are standing *above,* many of them high above, *the old towns*. Jerusalem in places is a hundred feet *above* old Jerusalem. The Tyre of Solomon's days is twenty to fifty feet *under* the Tyre of the Metarvelies. So it happens that to reach the *curb* of Jacob's Well, that portion on which the wearied MAN "sat (John 4:6) about the sixth hour," you have got to jump *down* some six feet. Just so in visiting Nôtre Dame, at Paris; the threshold which, A.D. 1163, was eight steps *above* the street, is now level with the street! At this rate, A.D. 3469, it will be seven steps below the street. The Forum of Rome, formerly considerably elevated at the threshold, is now twelve feet below the pavement.

The explanation as to Jacob's Well is simple enough: the stone of this country, unlike the imperishable granite of Egypt, is extremely friable. The walls of edifices crumble to earth, at the most, in a few centuries, and the dust (earth) thus formed accumulates and buries in massive layers the works of successive generations. Let the observer compute the amount of mud in the streets of New York at the end of the winter months, and imagine it unmoved for centuries; the piles would almost overtop the houses.

Jacob's Well is only referred to in that Gospel (John) whose simplicity, naturalness, and vividness in the entire narrative give it to many readers preference over the whole four. No wonder Free Masons have *desired to believe* that St. John was a Mason, a patron of Masons, a *Grand Master Mason,* as the Scotch would call him. In mind, spirit, affection, circumstances, and character, he was *sui generis.*

A friend, at Joseph's Tomb, describes a group under his eye—a white-bearded Jew kneeling by the side of this tomb, and telling his three little grandsons, kneeling by his side, the affecting story of Joseph.

The valley of Shechem, over which I was looking, is truly "a watered garden, a spring of water that faileth not" (Isaiah 58:11). The soil, as a writer remarks, is "apt for vines, and not destitute of corn."

"What a lovely valley!" says another. "Well did the wise Mohammed say: 'The land of Syria is, above all lands, beloved of God; that district he loves the best is the portion in which Jerusalem lies; the best of that portion is the valley of Nablous,'" at whose entrance are the Tomb of Joseph and the Well of Jacob. The profits of the cotton crop for three years, owing to the American war, had turned all heads in the Orient. In some parts, they went wild over their prosperity, making *silver* plowshares and cartwheels. The general result after all is favorable, as it has set the people to improving their houses, clothing, and habits. Never was so much parlor furniture and kitchen furniture (the same thing) used in Nablous as now; and those who got up the Civil War are really the benefactors of Nablous!

"A fair and fruitful vale," says an old pilgrim; "a fair and good city is Nablous."

A lady is reported as having collected nearly one hundred distinct specimens of flowers in a morning's walk in the suburbs of Jerusalem. On Carmel, a traveler procured forty-seven varieties of flowers in a short time. Around Nablous, the armies of plants seem innumerable, its olive-trees and almonds appear like patriarchs among the younger groves of figs, pomegranates, mulberries and other trees;

its tall cypresses shoot up their somber cones as if anxious to peep over Ebal or over Gerizim. It is a vale of the woods as well as the gardens. This is the only place, in Palestine, in which I remarked my old American acquaintance the mistletoe (*Phoradendron flavescens*), the plant of Druidical fame, which always suggests the tune of *Casta Diva* to my mind. Probably I am the only man who ever attempted to sing that song in the valley of Shechem since Jacob's time, and I am sure I failed egregiously.

Here was born, about A.D. 110, that eminent divine, Justin Flavius Martyr, who was endowed with an intense longing for knowledge in divine things, even from early youth. He was martyred at Rome, A.D. 167.

To pass away from Nablous without referring to the lepers would scarcely be rational. The mutilated and dreadful appearance of these creatures is mournful to contemplate. I am told that a person may live a lingering death, with this disease, for fifty years! One writer calls it *Lepra Abrahami*. A lady writer describes it as a sickening sight to look at these loathsome creatures, their fingerless hands, their handless arms, many without noses, lips, or eyes, every possible proof of the ravages of this disease. Among my last views was that of the halt and maimed and blind; some of them crawling through the streets like nondescript monsters, aided by elbows and hands; very many of them blind, and sitting by the wayside begging, or calling, ragged, filthy, pitiable, from door to door.

And oh, how magnificently does the anemone paint these hillsides of Ephraim with scarlet!—the coy anemone, that never uncloses "her lips until they are blown on by the wind."

The Greeks fancied the anemone originally a nymph beloved by Zephyrus, and therefore transformed into a flower by the jealous Flora. If so, Flora, for once in her life, did a good thing, in turning a loose-minded damsel into an exquisite flower! Writers attest that the plains of Asia Minor abound in the scarlet, purple, and lilac varieties of anemone. I saw numbers of them around the railway station at Brindisi, Italy, in June, 1868. A noted Persian writer called his book *The Garden of Anemones*. In the superstitious days of England, the earliest specimens of this flower were religiously gathered and preserved as charms against pestilence, being wrapped in scarlet silk and worn about the person. Galilee, for the abundance of these beautiful flowers, might well be entitled *Phaselida,* or the place of lilies; and my childhood's favorite poet, Mrs. Hemans, ought to have been here when she wrote—

"Lilies, when the Savior's calm, benignant eye
    Fell on your gentle beauty; when from you
    That heavenly lesson for all hearts He drew,
Eternal, universal as the sky;
Then in the bosom of your purity
    A voice He set as in a temple-shrine,
That life's quiet traveler ne'er might pass you by,
    Unwarned of that sweet oracle divine;
And though too oft its low, celestial sound
By the harsh notes of workday care is drowned,
    And the loud steps of vain, unlistening haste,
Yet the great lesson hath no tone of power
Mightier to heart and soul, in thought's hushed hour,
    Than young, meek *lilies* chosen thus and crowned!"

An old, hoary-bearded resident, squatted on his housetop, was looking over the beautiful valley, a proper figure in such a scene; and then, as I passed around the point of the mountain, the valley was shut from my sight. Samaria, five miles to the west, appeared shrunk like a shriveled gourd, dismantled and dismembered. How thickly all this country was once settled and what a population it supported may be inferred from the statement that Joshua captured 600 towns, in one of which, Ai, 12,000 persons were slain, and that "Gibeon was greater that Ai."

A few miles of mountain travel, and I observed the sun beating with meridian splendor upon the valleys, driving the people to seek shelter from its scorching rays in their miserable huts. Among the associations of these mountains not the least are those connected with the Prophet Elijah, always an object of interest to the Biblical writer. It was a joy to read here what an English writer says of the wonderful man: "His rare, sudden, and brief appearances; his undaunted courage and fiery zeal; the brilliancy of his triumph and pathos of his despondency; the glory of his departure, and the calm beauty of his reappearance on the Mount of Transfiguration, throw such a halo of brightness around him as is equaled by none of his compeers in the sacred story."

About two o'clock, I stopped for an hour at a charming spring of water near a village whose name I have not preserved. Surely there breathes not a people more savage and nasty, crusted with dirt, and smelling of smoke, by reason of the manure used for fuel in the houses that have no chimneys. While thus enjoying my noonday lunch, the whole village stood around me: whenever I raised my elbow or opened my mouth they sympathetically did the same, seeming, in imagination, to devour every morsel that I did. I found here in the filth an elegant petrifaction of the starfish, similar to the one I had discovered at Bethel. This is averred by competent authority to be the most regular and geometric in form of all created things; it is certainly the only handsome object I saw in Bethel. "The Divine Geometer who conceived it," says a vigorous author, "never realized a creature more regularly formed in shape, more perfectly harmonious in symmetry."

Coming near the Plain of Esdraelon, Joseph's Pit at Dothan suggested itself to my mind. What a history lay between the boy in the pit at Dothan, and the patriarch in the tomb at Shechem! The French word for well, is *puits,* much like our word pit. In the Scriptures the word stands for what we call in Kentucky *sinkholes,* as in Jeremiah 2:6, "a land of deserts and of pits," signifying, no doubt, dry openings washed through the soil and rocks by rains.

The great Plain of Esdraelon, on which I entered about 4 P.M., has been a thousand times described. Some lines recently published in an Alabama paper, embody my views of its capacity, were such a people to possess it as its beauty, national importance, and extraordinary fertility demand:

> "My valleys shall whiten all over
>   With snows never born of the cold;
> And grain, like a Midas, shall cover
>   Every slope that it touches with gold.

> "The clink of the artisan's hammer
>   Shall scare from the forest its glooms;
> In the brake shall the water-fowl's clamor
>   Be drowned by the clash of the looms.

> "Then up from your torpor, ye sleepers!
>   The dream ye are dreaming deceives;
> Go forth to the fields with the reapers,
>   And garner the prodigal sheaves.

> "With flocks gladden meadow and mountain,
>   With tinkling herds speckle each hill,
> And blend with the plash of the fountain
>   The rumble and roar of the mill."

Passing along in sight of the fatal battlefield of Megiddo, the place of Josiah's death, was a good time to review the life of this last of Judah's worthy kings, and I did so. How faithful to his God. Such a man could not but be faithful to his trust, and he was as much "a martyr to his fidelity" as the man who died at Jerusalem 390 years before. The grief of Josiah for the sins of his nation, as old Fuller quaintly records it, "was no low-flood of present passion, but a constant channel of continued sorrow streaming from an annual fountain."

The day was hot, no breezes stirred, and I began to appreciate such tremendous passages as that in Deut. 28:23; the clouds seemed like molten mirrors, the heaven overhead was brass. On this plain, I met parties in all the quaint costumes of the land. A Turkish gentleman, neatly dressed, white-beard, countenance ruddy, and, like David's, "fair to look upon," his eye kind and expressive, particularly attracted my attention. The grace of his *salaam* was extraordinary.

A number of the beautiful light-footed antelopes of these plains, the *gazelle,* trod before me as on the air, flying like passing shadows. Ossian E. Dodge must needs be fleet if he can do what his "Serenade" promises: "I'll chase the antelope over the plain!" However, they are easily *chased,* but with difficulty caught. Farther east from Palestine, they use the *cheetah,* or hunting-tiger, upon them, with success. The animal is brought hoodwinked in a cart as near to the game as possible. A herd being discovered, the cart is carefully driven up to the leeward of them, advantage being taken of any ground which may favor the approach of the cheetah. They are accustomed to see the oxen and carts of the cultivators in the fields, and, unless something unusual strikes their eye, will allow the party to approach within sixty or eighty yards. The leather hood is then slipped off, and the cheetah's head turned in the direction of the herd.

The glare of the sun, after the enforced darkness of the hood, makes the animal blink and stare for a moment, and then, the gazelle catching his eye, he drops from the cart, and, according as the ground favors him or not, lollops or creeps toward them. Arriving within what he considers fair starting distance—that is to say, as near the herd as possible—he singles out the largest buck, and, to use a slang but expressive phrase, "lays on to him." The buck strains every nerve for dear life, but, however fleet he may be, if the grim enemy behind has a fair start, it is a hopeless struggle from the first. At such a time the cheetah's rush is most astonishing. The buck, although going at his best pace, appears to be scarcely moving, giving the idea often carried away by spectators, that he is paralyzed with fear. The buck in his agony makes a spurt, the cheetah responds, the buck again, then the cheetah—a blow of the latter's paw, a cloud of dust, a confusion of legs, and the buck is on his back, the cheetah holding the game by the throat.

Approaching the beautiful tower of Jenin (En-gannim) at the embouchure of the valley, I observed the palm-trees shooting far above the houses into the blue sky. As I enter the place, a woman, whose eyes are artificially colored black and look frightful, frowns upon me as though I had said something naughty, whereas I can testify that I was not even thinking of her.

At Zerin (ancient Jezreel, where Jezebel lived) a company of Arabs had pitched their tents, making in the wilderness a lodging-place of wayfaring men (Jeremiah 9:2). Their girdles and bosoms were profusely stuffed with the weapons of murder. They looked, though intending to be benignant, yet full of wildness, blending the fierceness of the tiger with the boldness of the lion. As to the town itself, I had intended, as a wayfaring man, to turn aside here and tarry for a night (Jeremiah 14:8); for, as Southey says:

> "'Twas a late hour to travel o'er these plains,
> No house for miles around us, and the way
> Dreary and wild; the evening wind already
> Made one's teeth chatter."

But the fact of the houses being filled with dirt and nastiness, inhabited promiscuously by the people and their cattle, as I had seen at Bethel two nights before, and the difficulty my servants experienced in purchasing grain for their horses, caused me to go on to Shunem, two miles farther, by starlight. I particularly remember one of the Zerinites, a hag, who had

> "A pair of large dead eyes sunk in her head,
> Just like a corpse, and pursed with wrinkles round."

Truly a frightful creature. She recalls the incident I was about to forget of meeting a deranged man in the valley a few hours before —one of those poor creatures in whom dwell madness, melancholy, the frenzy of the brain, coming nearest to my idea of the Scriptural demoniac. These people, like the two who were healed by Jesus, live amidst the sepulchers of the dead. They go naked. They are ungovernable, often cry out, beat themselves, and sometimes attack travelers to their great injury.

Thistles, the largest I ever saw, abound on the plain of Esdraelon Some of these thistles, having milk-white spots on the glossy green surface of their leaves, recall the name *milk thistle* by which they are commonly known, and which originated in the legend that as Nôtre Dame (or Lady Mary) suckled her infant while passing along the way from Bethlehem to Egypt, a few drops of mother's milk fell on the thistles, and perpetuated the tender fact forever! A more serious reflection, however, grows out of the fact that one of them struck me a most painful dab in the eye, and so recalled the threat of Joshua that his people should be afflicted with "thorns in their eyes" (23:13) if they should presume to break God's commandments!

To the left of me here was Acre, so warm a residence in summer that all who can, "fly to the mountains" (Lebanon or Carmel) for coolness. The very name Accho, by which the Hebrews knew the city, signifies *hot.*

Going to Shunem, the last two miles was one vast wheatfield, without a fence, a path, or any boundary between owners, except upright stones ranged at proper intervals. The heads of wheat struck my feet as I rode through it, heavy and hard, promising a good crop. Approaching the village, a gang of rough-looking Arabs was leaning on the gateposts, moodily smoking and gazing toward me. At the public spring was a group of muleteers and cameleers bearing sacks of wheat to the seaport, Acre—hideous fellows, strong of scent, but respectful. One of them offered me a cigarette. The others petitioned in proper form for *backsheesh.*

The sheikh of the village, after some grumbling and delay, furnished me a room, "a chamber on the wall," exactly like that which was built for the Prophet Elisha at this very town 2,700 years ago, But all the horrors of my night at Bethel were repeated and intensified. No wonder the Philistines worshipped Beelzebub, the lord of *lice,* flies, *fleas,* and other entomologia with which their country was (and is) afflicted. If they believed their particular Baal served the purpose of a good corrosive sublimate, or Costar's "roach remedy," it was a good-enough worship for pagans. I will not attempt to describe my sufferings, but I know I got up early, and left just as

> "The trembling pulses of the dawn
>   Fill with faint gold the violet skies,
> And on the moist day-smitten lawn
>   The peace of morning lies."

As soon as I got into the edge of the village, however, I divested
myself of pants, etc., without the least romance, and, regardless of
police regulations, stood so until I had removed thronging
millions of the tormenting creatures from my scarified, tortured,
and speckled person.

Passing around the slope of "Little Hermon," as David calls it, I
approached the village of Nain, where Jesus raised from the dead
"the only son of his mother, and she was a widow," and where was
exhibited that tender, penitent love that bathed Christ's feet with
tears. At this place the old pilgrims used to complain that they
were "derided and spurted at by divers of the baser people;" and
in good truth the people *do* look a shade nastier and a trifle more
inhospitable than the majority I have met. But it will not always
be so. In the regeneration to which this country ere long will be
subjected, Nain, the place of holy, happy remembrances, shall
have its share.

Near this place I note one of those fellows styled Cawass, from
Nazareth. He is dressed in stunning red (redder than Solomon's
robes, said to have been the reddest thing ever known in this
country), with a scimitar of state slung by a broad sash across his
shoulders, a huge silver-mounted staff of office in his right hand,
with which he clashes the pavement as he walks. Another
description of one of these officers is that of a man in picturesque
costume of embroidered blue, with rich turban, scarlet saddle,
and long scimitar.

About 9 A. M., after climbing the most tremendous hill I ever
saw a horse go up, I came in sight of the place where was reared
from early infancy the child of the star and the song, Nazareth. A
dove was approaching me from the direction of Mount Hermon,
and a pelican from that of Mount Carmel, recalling Hosea 11:11,
"as a bird out of Egypt, and as a dove out of the land of Assyria."
Crowds of people, travelers, traders, natives, covered the hills in
all directions. The cry of the muezzin floated on the morning air,
Allah il Allah, wa Mohammed resoul Allah, There is but one God,
and Mohammed is his Prophet. I passed the Fountain of the
Virgin, noticing particularly the Nazareth women who throng
there; their complexion darker than our American ladies, "a rich,
clear olive, through which the blood seems to glow like light
through an alabaster shade, their lips delicately chiseled and
ripe-red." (I borrow all that.) But, exhausted by the want of sleep,
I hurry to the convent, where, on a clean, white bed, in fresh
garments   unpolluted   by   the   vermin   of   Shunem,

I lie down, and in an instant Nazareth and the Holy Land and every other sublimary scene were to me as nothing. I was awaked about 3 P.M. by the usual chorus of an Oriental town, in which the ringing of the chapel bell, barking dogs, braying asses, howling natives, and squalling children, are some of the ingredients. Doves were cooing at my windows, reminding me that the sacred doves of Mecca like these are blue, and that none dare to kill one under penalty of death. My experience in this place is given in an article composed for a religious journal, entitled

A SUNDAY AT NAZARETH.

It was unfortunate for my visit to Nazareth that I had been kept awake the night before by the myriads of insects that swarmed the house in which I had my abode at Salem (Shunem). Arriving there after dark, and being allotted an empty room, apparently clean, I had spread my blankets and sought repose, under pleasing expectations and necessity based upon a twelve-hour ride from Nablous (Shechem). But how egregiously was I disappointed! The fleas apparently regarded me as sent for their especial accommodation, and actually devoured me.

The next morning, May 15, I got away from Shunem, came around the spur of Little Hermon to the west, starting up immense flights of storks and at least one jackal, traversed eastward to the edge of Nain, welcomed old Tabor for an hour, passed through Iksal, and climbed the mountain above it toward Nazareth. No wonder that an ignorant priesthood has appropriated this mountain as the *Mount of Precipitation,* although no person of common sense can agree with them; for it is the steepest ascent I ever undertook with horses. Several times it seemed as if my nimble beast, which had never before hesitated to go up anything that I could ascend, from the heights near Jebail to the heights near Jericho, paused, and seemed disposed to expostulate with his rider. However, I persuaded him to push to the top, and then rode two or three miles farther to Nazareth. So much for the pseudo Mount of Precipitation.

The town of Nazareth, as I approached it from the east, presents the most graceful appearance of any town in Palestine. Lying not quite in the valley on the left, and not quite upon the mountain on the right it hangs gracefully upon the slope, as if hesitating between the two. The fountain at the eastern opening of the valley is properly the boundary of the town.

A great crowd of women was congregated there, and groups were coming and going with the great Nazareth water-jars upon their heads, and the strange Nazareth coin-rolls around their faces. So the mother of Jesus, during a period of not less than twenty years, brought her water-jar morning and evening, and wore perhaps the same curious ornament upon her face. Occasionally, among the groups, I could see the figures of little boys and girls running by mothers' sides, clinging trustfully to mothers' hands. So, during the years of childhood, must the little form of Jesus have been seen, as he ran by his mother's side, and held as firmly to his mother's hand.

To the east of the spring there is a Christian church—I do not remember of what denomination; and still further eastward, among the groups of olive-trees, a few tents, over which the British flag was waving. Passing the fountain, and moving toward the town, my attention was called to an object painfully incongruous with the holy day and the holy place. It was a company of Turkish soldiers engaged in drill, their instruments sounding, and words of command reverberating from the lofty ridge behind them. Discordant as it was, however, I could not help thinking that but for the protection afforded me by these and such as these, my journey through so many of the most dangerous localities of Palestine could never have been accomplished. Justice requires the traveler's praise to Governor-General Raschid Pasha at Damascus, and his admirable supporters at all the large towns, for making these roads as free to their feet as in the days of King David himself.

I was a guest at the Latin Convent during my stay in Nazareth. This is a clean, cool, stone edifice of two stories in height, containing about fifty rooms, in which all travelers are welcomed "without money and without price." The term of each one's stay, however, is limited to three days, and each guest is expected (although no public intimation is given him to that effect) to contribute something on his departure toward the expenses of the house. The usual donation is five francs per day, and I can testify that when I tendered that sum, it was accepted with a smile of approval which led me to believe that it was deemed sufficient. The fare is abundant, and as well cooked as is ever done in this country. Good wine, coffee, oranges, and dried fruits form the dessert. The bread, as usual in this part of Palestine, is execrable.

Toward the close of the day I climbed the hill on the north of the city, the veritable Mount of Precipitation, and enjoyed an enlarged view of the surrounding country. No writer has done justice to this glorious panorama, the finest in all Palestine. Did not Jesus stand here? This was the thought that gave a coloring to this sublime outlook as I gathered it in. On the west the Great Sea opened before me, apparently so near that I could throw a stone into it; on its shores, Caiffa and Acre; a little more to the left the Plain of Esdraelon, terminated by Mount Carmel, redolent of glorious memories. The River Kishon, "that ancient river," could be traced out as a green ribbon through the plain. Turning more to the left were the ranges of Samaria, ending in Ebal and Gerizim; then little Hermon, Gilboa, and Tabor. Then I could trace out the spot where, in its deep basin, lies the Sea of Genesareth, which I am to visit to-morrow. Next is old Jebel-es-Sheikh, Hermon, its snows gleaming in the sunset. Next the spurs of Anti-Lebanon; and so on round to the Mediterranean again. Did not Jesus often stand here? Let me solemnly retire from a place more sacred than Pisgah, more sacred than Sinai, and fill my soul with such memories of this hour as will arouse the Christian love of many in the distant land over which that sinking sun is at this moment shining with noonday splendor.

> "I thought of Jesus in the vale
>   Of Nazareth, sweet Nazareth;
> HIS name was murmured in its fount,
> HIS praises swept along its mount,
>   His youthful feet had trodden here,
>   His earliest thoughts had moved in prayer."

Then, as I bowed in faith,

> "This voice from Nazareth, I heard,
>   'The Vale is holy to our youthful LORD!'"

Reclining here under a fig tree, while the natives yonder smoke their poor tobacco, and the great sun yonder lowers his head and slants his rays to the eastward, let me give the season to a comment upon this overshadowing tree, which is my present creditor for coolness and use. The names *fig* and *fig tree* are spotted here and there all over the Bible; referring in all cases to the *Ficus carica,* which is now under observation. The country of the Jews ever abound in it (Deut. 8:8), as Moses said; and Chaplain Drake justly says (in Smith's Dictionary) "the character of the tree, with its wide-spreading branches, accords well with the derivation of the Hebrew name, *teenah, to stretch out.*" People here still call the fig *teen,*

which shows how the old names *stick*. In fact, a name is as much
a landmark, when applied to a *tree,* as to a Masonic *grip.*

Come forth, then, old companion, my pocket Bible, and yield the
testimony of thy many voices to the symbolical value of the fig
tree.

Not to enlarge upon the prudery of our first parents, who,
finding themselves naked, "sewed fig-leaves together and made
themselves aprons" (Genesis, 3:7), I summon first the Prophet
Zechariah (B.C. 522), who so forcibly delineates the branch-type of
Jesus, to say what use his sacred reed makes of our Ficus?

Zechariah. When I wrote, Judah had but just returned, few and
feeble, from Babylon, but buoyed up both by temporal and
spiritual hopes. To increase this spirit of expectancy in them, I
promised that, although now the trees were just planted and the
foundation just laid, yet in the good time coming "they should call
every man his neighbor under the vine and under the fig tree"
(3:10).

Micah. I was more than two centuries earlier than Zechariah
(B.C. 740), but I was favored to witness the same vision, and
predicted that they should sit "every man under his vine and
under his fig tree, and none should make him afraid" (4:4).

Ezra. When I wrote of the peaceful days of Solomon (his very
name denotes *peace*), I could find no better image of safety and
repose than those you have just recorded; and I said, "Judah and
Israel dwelt safely, every man under his vine and under his fig
tree, from Dan even unto Beersheba, all the days of Solomon" (1
Kings 4:25). Yonder, some forty miles northeast, is Dan; one
hundred miles to the southward is Beersheba. (As my interlocutor
quoted his old words he seemed to sigh, as if to imply, "But that
was more than four centuries before my day (B.C. 536). Alas for
the bitter change!")

Jeremiah. In my jeremiads (B.C. 628), I symbolized the coming
fury of the avenging God in the fruit of this useful tree, and said,
"The Lord will surely consume them; there shall be no figs on the fig
tree, and the leaf (this broad-lobed, thick, succulent leaf) shall fade"
(8:13). But when, thirty years later, the breaking up of my nation
began, and the best of us had been deported captives to Babylon, the
Lord showed me, in a vision, two baskets of figs set before the
temple (at Jerusalem); one having very *good* figs, even like the figs
that are first ripe; the other very *naughty* figs, which could not be
eaten for badness. By the good figs I taught that portion of Judah
who were captives, that in their foreign homes they should find
hearts to know God, and should again become His people, and

be brought back with prosperity to their old land. But by the naughty figs I warned the residue of Jerusalem, who remained, that for their sins they should yet be driven out and forever cut off from the favor of God (chapter xxiv).

Hosea. Yearning to awaken the gratitude of my people toward "Him who giveth, upbraiding not," I compared Israel in the wilderness, downtrodden and servile as she had been, but rich and happy in my love, to the goodly fruits of this tree: "I saw your fathers as the first ripe in the fig tree at the first time" (9:10). But, alas, their first fruits were deceitful.

Solomon. Looking over "the fat valleys" of my dominions for figures that should entice the spirit of my love, I said, "The fig tree putteth forth her green figs. Arise, my love, my fair one, come away" (Canticles 2:13).

Other witnesses abundantly testify to this fruit.

The next day (Monday, May 16) I received a note from Rev. Mr. Zelner, English Protestant Missionary here, with a membership of some five hundred, warning me against going, in that hot weather, to the Sea of Galilee. His apprehensions of danger, from fever and sunstroke, were by no means unfounded; yet I could not forego my settled purpose to visit places so consecrated to Jewish and Christian history, and about noon I started.

The name Nazareth is often found in the catalogue of Masonic Lodges. Mount Tabor, close by, is used by Lodge No. 65, Massachusetts. To make the association more intimate, I locate here the names of ten well-known Masons, viz: Charles Vaill, M.D.; Thomas A. Carnahan; H. G. Hazelrigg; John F. Sandford, M.D.; Henry C. Banks; Lewis A. Rousseau; Ambrose W. Wilson; James M. Fuller; Horace Chase; William T. Anderson.

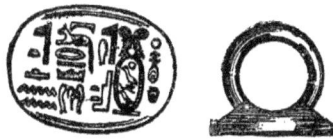

RING OF SUPHIS, PHARAOH OF EGYPT.

32

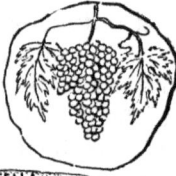

CHAPTER XXVIII.

A T such a convent as this of Nazareth you are sure of finding clean beds, good, wholesome, and abundant food, marks of courteous attention, and no questions asked in relation to your religious faith. At breakfast I had fish, mutton, eggs, vegetables, bread, fruit, wine *with* the food, and coffee *after* it. Had I time to spare, I should like to spend a week with that monk who wears his curiously-knotted cable-tow four times around his body, and does his own cooking.

I left Nazareth, as described in the last chapter, about noon on Monday, and reached Tiberias at 3 P.M. The ride is a pleasant one, having the companionship of Cana of Galilee, Mount Tabor, the battlefield of Hattin, and above all, *Mount Hermon,* who has rarely been out of sight for more than thirty minutes at a time since I rounded Mount Ebal two days ago. If that calm, solemn, hoary head of Hermon has good eyes, at his age, what secrets of history he ferrets out, looking out from his great height of 10,000 feet clear over this country, watching every company of travelers, every change of seasons, every stormy cloud—watching the approach of all invading armies, and the spires of smoke sent up from their campfires and the torches they put to habitations, and their battlefields, and their retreats—as he watched Abram with his followers coming around his foot, 4,000 years ago, and Jacob, who fled eastward in the succeeding century, and the deportation of the Jewish exiles twelve centuries later, and their happy return—as he watched Alexander and Titus and the Crusaders, and is now watching *me.* With all his vigilance and careful storing up of historical facts, awaiting the first "interviewer," the old mountain (Jebel-es-Sheikh they call him here, the *Mount of the Chief*), busies himself every night at this season, in cooling and sending down "the dew of Hermon" (Ps. 133), as welcome to this country as its counterpart is figuratively to a Freemasons' Lodge.

The frequent and copious dews and fogs of Palestine—much more abundant than one would suppose in such an arid climate— have furnished the inspired writers with many of their beautiful and expressive figures. Our readers will of course recall the beautiful extract from Psalm 133, introduced into our ceremony of Entered Apprentice: "As the dew of Hermon, and as the dew that descended upon the mountains of Zion," etc. In the summer, the dew of Palestine is so copious as to supply to a considerable extent the absence of rain, and becomes important to the farmer. In proof of this, the well-known sign of Gideon may be adduced (Judges 6:37, etc.). In the divine blessing (Genesis 27:28) it is coupled with rain or mentioned as a prime source of fertility. Its withdrawal is attributed to the divine curse. In prophetic imagery it becomes a leading object, by reason of its penetrating moisture with the apparent effect of rain, while its speedy evanescence typifies the transient goodness of the hypocrite. In several places, it is named as a token of exposure in the night.

Every traveler remarks upon this subject of dew. Coming to Shunem on Saturday night, my coat was nearly wet through with dew. Like the person in Canticles 5:2, "my head was filled with the dew, and my locks with the drops of the night." Some of the passages where the dews of this country are mentioned, are as follows: "Your goodness is as the early dew" (Hosea 6:4); "will be as the dew unto Israel" (Hosea 16:5); "His body (Nebuchadnezzar's) was wet with the dews of heaven" (Daniel 4:33); "Thou hast the dew of thy youth." (Ps. 110:3.) There are twenty-five more allusions in the Bible to the word *dew*. I observed at the mouth of Dog River how the dampness of the dew on the rocks brings out the remarkable figures and inscriptions delineated there. At Tiberias, I noticed the tents of a party encamped there, drenched with dew. They looked as if they had been exposed to a fall of rain during the night. This is the same affusion so often referred to in Scripture, that "descended upon the mountain of Zion," recalling the expressions in Psalm 133, and others.

At Cana of Galilee, a few miles east of Nazareth, I spent an hour under the shade of the immense cactus hedge, every leaf of which is a vast pincushion stuck full of needles, enjoying my noontide repast at the spring of water historically associated with the performance of the first miracle of Christ (John 2:1-11). Here was that "beginning of miracles which Jesus did, and manifested forth his glory, and his disciples believed on him." Every recovered limb, every spared eye, every purified leper, from the setting out upon the divine labor, proved that Jesus came "that they might have life, and that they might have it more abundantly."

The place itself comes very accurately under the poet's description:

> "Here is a vale, sequestered, green,
> From which a crystal fount is welling
> Its silvery tide, whose rippling sheen
> Over the tufted marge is swelling."

The rankness and greenness of the willows here recall the divine promise to his people, as in Isaiah 44:4: "And they shall spring up as among the grass, as willows by the watercourses." The oleander blossoms give out their delicate almond-like fragrance from such dense clusters as hide the foliage of the trees that bear them; and here again I recognize the song of the nightingale, that mingles so delightfully with all my memories of the Jordan. I can endorse most heartily the words of Jules Michelet when, speaking of this bird, he says: "His is the nocturnal melody, the deep poesy of the shadows, the hidden meaning of the grand effects of evening, the solemnity of midnight, the aspirations before dawn; in fact, that infinitely varied poem which translates and reveals to us, in all its changes, a heart brimful of tenderness."

The remains of aqueducts here, and in connection with all water-fountains in Palestine, recall what occurs to me in every large place I visit in the East, that Roman colonies seem always to have supplied themselves amply with water, brought often from great distances at vast expense, and on a scale far beyond anything attempted in modern times. The old Christians here were taught to believe that the hot springs a few miles beyond are the tears of angels. The town of Cana itself is a wasted city with but few inhabitants, houses without men, land utterly desolate, the men removed far away, a great forsaking in the midst of the land! (Isaiah 6:12.) As for the people, I must not slander my fellow men, but *will* affirm, using sound Scriptural expression too, that, though they had washed themselves with niter and taken to themselves much soap, they had not been clean (Jeremiah 2:22). As on the banks of the Jordan where Christ laid his clothes, a church

was erected a thousand years afterward, the river here being
called a *sling's-throw* across, so here at Cana, to which place he
came from his baptism, a three-day journey, the people profess to
identify every locality on which he sat, stood, or worked in his
divine mission.

The pomegranates here seem to me larger and finer than any
groves of the class that I have seen in Palestine. I must not
entirely overlook the fact of Bonaparte's remarkable defeat of the
Arab troops close by here, at the foot of Mount Tabor, in 1799; but
will summon Mr. Headley to recall some of its incidents: "The
whole plain was filled with marching columns and charging
squadrons of wildly-galloping steeds, while the thunder of cannon
and the fierce fire of musketry, amidst which was now and then
heard the blast of thousands of trumpets and strains of martial
music, filled the air." With all the horrors of these engagements
around the Plain of Esdraelon, they were spared the cold,
distressing rains that always follow the great battles of modern
times, and so dreadfully aggravate the sufferings of the wounded.
In their three-days fight there was no explosion of artillery to
shake water from the clouds. In fact, the Crusaders, A.D. 1099,
would have been glad of a little of it to ameliorate the horrors of
their July siege of Jerusalem.

Passing eastward, the next place of special interest demanding
my pencil is the battlefield of Hattin, that fatal field of chivalry.
Peter the Hermit, who, a century before, stirred the heart of
Europe to go crusading hopelessly against the Paynim could have
had no premonition of this great day of slaughter, when every
hollow on these slopes became a Golgotha, a place of skulls, whose
bodies were dragged from their graves by beasts as an
abominable branch (Isaiah 14:19). In my chapter upon Knight-
Templary more will be found upon this society, which in theory
was an embodiment of perfect truth, justice, mercy, and purity,
drawn upon the only model that history affords, Jesus of
Nazareth. My notes during a brief tarry in the battlefield bring
together Ramleh, Joppa, Masada, Acre, Jerusalem, and a score of
other localities sacred to their memory. The warcries of the
Templars were *Deus vult* (God wills it) and similar expressions.
The names of distinguished leaders were used as warcries, as
Scott has well expressed in his various historical novels. Yet it is
not to be credited that the expression "Hip, hip, hurrah," was a
Templar cry, derived from the initials of the phrase *Hierosolyma
est perdita,* "Jerusalem is lost," although I find the fact stated in
the papers, and, as a rule, what the newspapers say is true! To get

a good account of the exploits of the Knights Templar and other crusading orders, we must go to French authors rather than English. The reason is a national one: all the leaders of the Crusades were French; the architecture introduced into the Holy Land is strictly French (Norman); the language spoken by the Crusaders was French; and in fact the English part of the work from 1099 to 1187 was quite insignificant. Today there are no such thoroughly scientific and readable books on the Holy Land as those of Chateaubriand, De Saulcy, Renan, De Vogüé, Lamartine, and a host of French authors, of whom scarcely a tithe has been translated into our own tongue.

A nervous writer of the seventeenth century sums up the story of Knight-Templary in a dissertation upon their troublous reign, their high valor, their alternate changes of toil and fight, foes always at hand, but succor afar off; finally overthrown through homebred treason. The tombs of the later heroes of this Order in its legitimate succession are best seen, I am told, in the splendid church of St. John at Valetta, Malta, where four hundred of them lie buried in such close embrace that the slabs of beautiful parti-colored marbles, profusely sculptured with heraldic devices, form the floor of that edifice, as those of the ancient Hebrews line the western slopes of Olivet near its base. It is in explanation of theory on which these warriors fought and lived that the following privileges, among others, were secured to them by law:

1. They could not be sued for debt.

2. They were exempted from interest on borrowed money.

3. They were exempted from taxes.

4. They could sell their lands without asking permission from their feudal lord.

5. The church was under pledges to anathematize all who should dare to molest them.

6. They could plead spiritual jurisdiction alone.

7. All their sins had plenary forgiveness without proof of penitence. In an age of carnal rule such privileges as these must have prompted many "to go to the wars."

No member of the Masonic Order of Knights Templars should think of visiting London without taking a day or two to examine the old Temple church, whose foundations were laid A.D. 1185. A few years since, this venerable edifice underwent a restoration at the cost of $250,000, and is now as nearly as possible in the condition it presented at its erection, nearly seven centuries ago. It is known that when the Order of Knights Templars was destroyed in the fifteenth century, the possession of this building fell into the hands of a company of lawyers, who have held it with their successors ever since.

Quaint ancient customs are maintained there, recalling old practices and forgotten causes. The lawyers dine together, two by two, and the fragments are given to the servants, who are styled *paniers,* as in the Crusades. Quarrelling, murmuring, and insubordination are forbidden, and in many ways the influence of the old Masonic system which lay at the basis of Knight-Templary is exhibited.

The harmony of the proportions of this old building and its fairylike beauty and gracefulness of form delight every beholder; but nothing will attract the eye of a Knight Templar so much as the sight of a row of famous monumental effigies of secular warriors, with their legs crossed, in token that they had assumed the cross, and taken the vow to march to the defense of the Christian faith in Palestine. These have been so perfectly restored as to show few signs of age or misuse.

Almost the entire history of this heroic band is local to the Holy Land. Its origin is referred to the necessity of affording to pilgrims from Europe protection in coming from the seacoast to Jerusalem, in going from Jerusalem to the Jordan, and generally in passing to and from the holy places of Palestine. Many of the pilgrims had been plundered and subjected to various outrages, when, in the year 1118, nineteen years after the capture of Jerusalem by the Crusaders, it was proposed to organize a society under the distinctive title of the "Poor Soldiers of Jesus," whose one duty it should be to clear the read of marauders, by constituting themselves an escort for all such. So small was the beginning of an Order which in 200 years became the wealthiest, most powerful, and, unless history belies them, the most licentious organization of monks the world has ever seen.

The name *Knights Templars* was derived from the circumstance that the buildings allotted to the valiant and magnanimous Order were contiguous to the Temple and in the same enclosure; while those occupied by the Knights of St. John were a quarter of a mile west, upon the adjacent hill. These buildings, it is claimed, are the same now styled *Mosk-el-Aksa,* on the southern verge of the great platform, and about 500 feet from the site of King Solomon's Temple.

The fortified places attributed to the architectural energy and skill of the Crusaders are seen in many parts of the country, and at least a portion of these are accredited to the Knights Templars. The churches at Lydda and Gibon, the Castles of Safed and Tibnin, the ruined forts at Masada and Kerak, the great edifices on the sea near Cæsarea, and very many other constructions, are referable to these working and fighting Knights.

The almost entire destruction of the Order occurred in July 1187, on Mount Hattin, near the western shore of the Sea of Galilee. In a great battle with the Saracens commanded by Saladin in person, the Christian hosts were defeated, nearly all of them slain upon the field, and the remainder inhumanly butchered by the Sultan himself or in his immediate presence. The description of this battle, one of the most desperate on record, has occupied the pen of Michau, Prof. Robinson, and other writers of eminence, but the story in all its heroic details is yet to be written. Though treachery had paralyzed the hearts of the Christian warriors, excessive heat unnerved them, and the want of water parched their vitals and glazed their eyes with despair, yet the innate valor of the Knights and the chivalric lessons instilled by their Order, held them up; they clung to the sacred relic which was their banner, to the very last, and fell one by one around it, until scarcely a man was left. The mountain-top which twelve centuries before had been the pulpit from which were heard those divinest utterances, "Blessed are they that mourn, the pure in heart, the peace-makers, the meek, the merciful," was covered by the bodies of those who died for *the Cross*.

I have written a summary of their history in an article entitled

SALADIN, THE ARAB CONQUEROR.

The Sultan Saladin sprung from a mountain stock beyond the Tigris. His father was a soldier of fortune, of high rank in the service of the Sultan of Baghdad. Being obliged to flee from Baghdad, in consequence of a personal altercation with an officer of justice, he joined Noureddin, Sultan of the Attabeks of Syria, against the Christians. Here the young Saladin began his career, which at first promised but little, as he was addicted to dissipation, and seemed averse to employment. His first military fame was acquired during the defense of Alexandria, in Egypt, and this led to his appointment to the post of vizier. This position called forth the best traits of his character; his gravity, liberality, and austerity of devotion marked him at once as the genius of the age.

At the death of the Sultan Noureddin, Saladin was made his successor.

At the death of King Amaury, of Jerusalem, he was succeeded by Baldwin IV., a leper in person, and an obstinate, intractable man, quite unfit for the station. Becoming blind from his disease, he resigned the crown to Guy, of Lusignan, whose only traits of character were haughtiness and most disgusting pride. Thus, at the very time when the Christian empire in Palestine demanded its best defender, seeing that no such foe as Saladin had ever before opposed it, the crown was held by the most incompetent king of the entire series. A truce, however, was entered into with Saladin, which, had not the folly of one of the Crusaders broken it, might have been maintained long enough to strengthen all their defenses, and even perpetuate the Christian power.

The circumstances which led to the renewal of the war and the destruction of the Christian kingdom were these: Renaud, Count de Chatillon, was lord of Kerak and other castles in that vicinity, where he had associated with him a great number of Templar Knights. Refusing to acknowledge the truce with Saladin, he plundered the Mohammedan caravans on their way to Mecca, imprisoned women and children, and massacred unarmed men. The complaints of Saladin were disregarded, nor could the commands of King Guy himself put a stop to these outrages. Then Saladin declared war in bitter earnest, ravaged Galilee, besieged Beirut, and advancing toward the castle of Kerak, had nearly taken the place. Failing in this, he burned Nablous and Samaria.

The Christian lords at this time were in a most frightful state of anarchy among themselves. The kingdom was covered with strong castles, the commanders of which scarcely recognized the authority of the king himself. The barons made war and peace at their own pleasure. The Knights Templars, the Knights Hospitallers, and the other military Orders were divided among themselves, and sometimes shed their blood in quarrels fatal to the cause of the Christians. Discipline had degenerated in the camp, the warriors still displaying their natural bravery. None knew whom to obey or to command.

Amidst all these calamitous circumstances, King Baldwin IV., who had taken away the authority conferred upon Guy, died. His son, Baldwin V., followed him speedily to the grave. Again Guy, of Lusignan, assumed the crown, his haughtiness and severity being increased by the vicissitudes of his career. He made war with Baldwin,

Count of Tiberias, and the disorder and agitation of the kingdom became greater than ever.

All this was made available to the revenge of Saladin. He gained a victory in Galilee, May 1, 1167, and destroyed five hundred Knights of the two Orders. The terror, which this sanguinary defeat created, appeased for a while the discords of the country. The King became reconciled to Baldwin, and the two swore in the presence of all the people at Jerusalem, to fight in unison for the heritage of Christ. Saladin had crossed the Jordan at the head of eighty thousand horsemen, and was advancing around the northern shores of the Sea of Galilee.

At a council of war held at Jerusalem, it was agreed that the Christian forces should rendezvous on the plain of Sepphoris, a few miles north of Nazareth. Here they came from every direction, and soon an army of fifty thousand, embracing the Knights of the three Orders, the troops of the King and the nobles, the garrisons of the cities, and all Christians able to bear arms, was assembled. The wood of the true cross, which had so often animated the Christians, was brought from Jerusalem, and entrusted to the keeping of the army.

A council of war was held at Sepphoris, July 3, 1187, and it was resolved, only the Grand Master of the Templars dissenting, to remain in camp and await the attack of Saladin there. Had this plan been maintained, doubtless the result would have been favorable to the Christians; but the fickle King Guy, changing his mind a few hours afterward, caused the advance to be signaled at midnight and the camp to be broken up. A few hours brought the army in sight of the enemy, strongly posted on the hills between them and the Sea of Galilee. It was too late to retreat, and the daring resolution was formed of cutting a passage through them to the waters in their rear. A desperate contest ensued, in which Saladin had the advantage, when night put an end to the conflict.

The hours of darkness were full of hope to the Saracens; but sad and sinister presentiments deprived the Christians of their courage. Though their camps resounded with the noise of drums and trumpets, it was only to increase their alarm. Daylight was the signal for their utter destruction. Surrounded upon all sides, they could only sell their lives dearly. In their despair, they endeavored to pierce through the battalions of the enemy, but everywhere were met with an invincible resistance. Consumed with thirst, faint with hunger, they saw nothing

around them but burning rocks and the sparkling swords of their
enemies. At the close of the day, only the Knights of St. John and
the Temple were left of all that mighty host. These had performed
prodigies of valor from the break of day. Their standard-bearer,
the Bishop of Ptolemais, was killed. He was succeeded by the
Bishop of Lydda, who was taken prisoner and the cross captured.
Not until then did these good swords become paralyzed. Then the
King was taken, with Geoffrey, Grand Master of the Templars,
the Count of Chatillon, whose crimes had brought this sure ruin
upon the land, and others of the most illustrious Knights of
Palestine. Only Count Raymond, Prince Bohemond of Antioch,
Renaud of Sidon, the young Count of Tiberias, and a small
number of soldiers, escaped. The prisoners were kept in custody
until next day, when the larger number of them were massacred
by the command of Saladin and in his own presence.

The cities of Palestine soon fell into his hands. Tiberias,
Ptolemais, Nablous, Jericho, Ramleh, Cæsarea, Joppa, Arsuf, and
Beirut, soon flaunted the yellow standards of Saladin upon their
walls. Asculon and Gaza followed; Emmaus surrendered without
a struggle, and in October, scarcely three months from that
dreadful day at Hattin, Jerusalem capitulated to his power.

To establish a just relationship between the worthy men of "the
Trowel and Sword" of the present day, I place here the names of
ten Freemasons, equally worthy and not less celebrated: James
Penn, Giles M. Hillyer, Henry Wingate, Thomas Ware, Thomas
Todd, J. H. Davis, H. B. Parsons, William N. Howe, J. A.
Dougherty, F. S. Carrington.

Pushing still eastward, I await with warmest anticipations
my first view of the Sea of Galilee. My advice to a Christian
traveler, whose stay in Palestine is limited to *a week* (and this
is the *maximum* of time allotted by nineteen-twentieths of
American tourists to the Lands of the Bible; *three months* to
Europe, but *seven days* to Palestine!)—my advice to such is to
land at Caiffa, at the foot of Mount Carmel, hasten thence to
Nazareth and the Sea of Galilee, and give all attention *to this
region.* Of Jerusalem and the Dead Sea, you can *read* all that is
to be said; but the Sea of Galilee you must *see for yourself,* to
form a true idea of its beauty. Comparatively few visit this
region of Syria, and the field for exploration is, therefore, fresh
and inviting. It is the place of our Savior's life and principal
labors, and is, therefore, full of historical interest. It is the most
fruitful field of the botanist, mineralogist, and ichthyologist

that Palestine affords, and will, therefore, abundantly stock the album, the box, and the notebook of the scientific traveler. Being remote from the customary routes and haunts of travelers, its people are less sophisticated, have suffered fewer changes in costume and manners, and are less greedy than those around Jerusalem, Damascus, etc. In the annoyances of beggars, nowhere so pertinacious and numerous as about Jerusalem, you will suffer but little in Galilee.

Glorious old Hermon lifted his cheerful forehead above the clouds and threw the full light of his snowy front upon me, on the left hand, as I rode forward; hill after hill that rose upon my path was surmounted, but still no Sea. I should have feared that we had taken the wrong pathway, only that I knew too well the points of the compass. I found two cisterns that travelers describe "covered with large perforated stones much worn by the friction of the ropes." Stones were now piled thickly around me—black basalt, suggestive of millstones, and the Hauran, and metamorphic geology, and currents of melted lava, and all that sort of thing. My servant Hassan now imparted to me a fact which he had acquired from a *fellah* upon the way, viz: that amongst these basaltic rocks *snakes abound.* (He calls them in Arabic by some guttural word.) It may be so. Perhaps the rich disintegrated basaltic soil produces plants whose seeds attract mice, moles, and other vermin; and the mice attract the snakes. Such is the chain of connection woven by nature. This idea seemed original with myself, but since Darwin's last book is issued I find a similar thought. Darwin says that the more cats we have, the fewer will be the mice; the fewer the mice, the more bumblebees; the more bumblebees, the more clover; the more clover, the more honey. *Ergo,* the more cats, the more honey! Q.E.D. Dr. Robinson says he started a wild hog here; but the only specimens of the hog family that I saw in Palestine were some wild pigs amongst the thick rock-heaps near Gebal, six weeks ago.

At last, and suddenly, the calm blue basin slumbering in placid sweetness beneath its surrounding wall of hills burst upon me, and I found myself looking down upon the hallowed scenes of the Lord's ministry. I was on the brow of a very steep hill, across which the wind from the heights on the opposite sides of the Sea blew fresh and cool. Below me was a narrow plain sloping to the Sea, whose beach I could trace to its northern extremity. At my feet lay the town of Tiberias, the only remaining town on its shores, enclosed by crumbling fortifications, with shattered but once massive round bastions; the only remaining town of nine large cities and nearly twenty flourishing villages that once fringed this beautiful Lake of Gennesaret.

At that first grand and resplendent view of what will ever be to me the most memorable portion of the earth's surface, I burst forth, involuntarily, with the song I had learned three months before, while lying sick in my berth upon the Atlantic steamer, entitled "Jesus by the Sea;" nor am I ashamed to acknowledge that until I finally lost sight of the Sea of Galilee, three days later, on the heights north of Safed, that melody and those words occupied my mind as no words and melody had ever done before.

The breeze blew so freshly upon the summit of that hill above Tiberias, and indeed imparted so grateful a coolness to my blood, that I quite forgot the warning of Mr. Zellner, the English Missionary at Nazareth, who had kindly taken the trouble that morning of writing me a note before breakfast, counseling me not to go to Tiberias on account of the excessive heats and the consequent danger of fevers. Looking down upon the sparkling sea, it was hard to conceive any thought but that of *coolness*. But I soon found the truth of Mr. Zellner's prediction. For, descending by the zigzag pathway, I had scarcely reached the walls of Tiberias when my lungs were so oppressed with the heat that I could scarcely breathe, and I was forcibly reminded of what I had experienced at the Dead Sea, ten days before. I am not prepared to say what is the hottest place on the surface of the earth, but my own observations would dictate that if not *Tiberias,* it is *Jericho!* No wonder the Arabs call the place Tibereeah: I should soon call it so too, were my lot cast there!

The city of Tiberias was almost totally destroyed by an earthquake, January 1, 1837. The walls then thrown down have never been rebuilt; and the northern quarter of the city, occupied chiefly by Mohammedans, still lies in ruins, illustrating that pleasant feature of Turkish character, "they build, but never rebuild." As I entered the city, crossing a prostrated marble column, once the subject of artistic skill in the distant quarries of Paros, I observed a large open space, where this portion of the Tiberians had lived.

My search for quarters was at first a failure. I was taken to the Latin convent, a cool but not over-cleanly place, and regaled with lemonade (never lemonade like *that* lemonade) by the one monk who kept it, but for some reason (imparted, no doubt, to Hassan, but never comprehended by *me*), his reverence declined to accommodate me further. In vain, I expostulated at being ejected from that apartment, whose stonewalls, six feet thick, had reduced the thermometer to sixty degrees, into the burning, fiery furnace of the street of Tiberias, where Fahrenheit unmistakably rose to 115, with "an upward tendency." In vain, I protested. The gentleman with the cable-tow four times around his body had a heart more indurated than granite, and politely but firmly insisted on my leaving him. Could it have been that his supply of lemonade was threatened?

But, after all, my departure from that one-horse convent was for the better, for Hassan secured for me the house of Mr. Wiseman, a Hebrew gentleman, whose name is given by travelers. It is a large, substantial room, about twenty-five feet square, with stone floors, and walls immensely thick, with the additional advantage of having extracts from the Hebrew Bible nailed on the doorposts. For ten francs a day, I secured the whole house, three meals a day for two of us, and the Hebrew inscriptions thrown in. Wiseman and his wise woman and his three (married) wise daughters, besides the rest of his Solomonic offspring, slept outside in the court of the house, and never disturbed me during my stay. The meals were regularly served (and they were ample and good), and all things were agreeable.

And now, being comfortably located by the Sea of Galilee, let us attempt a description. The names scripturally applied to this beautiful sheet of water are—*Sea of Gennesaret* (Luke 5:1, 1 *Maccabees* 11:67); *Sea of Chinnereth* and *Cinneroth* (Numbers 34:11, Joshua 12:3); *Sea of Galilee* (Matthew 4:18, Mark 7:31, John 6:1); and the *Sea of Tiberias* (John 6:1). The native name at present is *Bahr Tubariyeh,* or *Sea of Tiberias.* It is of an oval shape, about thirteen miles long, and six broad. The River Jordan runs in near the northeast corner, and passes out near the southwest corner. In its relation to that river, it is a mere expansion of its bed, just such a sheet of water as the Jordan would form at any other part of its long course, did the hills recede sufficiently from each other to make such an expansion. Its area is about sixty square miles.

The excessive heat of Tiberias and the whole locality is accounted for by the fact that the Sea of Galilee is 700 feet below the level of the Mediterranean. In other words, were a canal opened to connect the two bodies of water, this Sea would be filled to the depth of 700 feet, covering the sites of Tiberias, Medjel, and all the little plains around the northwestern corner of the Sea. A person going from this place to the Dead Sea is actually traveling toward the center of the earth, and at pretty rapid rate too!

On the east of the Sea the mountains rise about 2,000 feet, without trees or grass, and are deeply furrowed by ravines. All the cliffs and rocks around the Sea are mostly a hard, porous basalt, giving a volcanic appearance to the whole basin. The water is sweet, cool, and transparent. The beach is everywhere pebbly, and has a beautiful sparkling look under the bright sun. Fish of fourteen species greatly abound, but the fishery is sadly neglected. A few men, stripped naked, stand on the points of rocks, as I had seen them doing along the Mediterranean coast, and throw hand-nets over the fish as they approach. Writers, also, describe a method of catching the fish by poisoning with bichloride of mercury, but of this I saw nothing.

Toward evening, I walked down the beach south of the town of Tiberias, and saw with pleasure that the peculiar shell of the Sea of Galilee can be gathered there in abundance. It is a small purple shell that adheres to the pebbles in shallow water. All the dead shells are perforated by a borer which has unceremoniously intruded in the *sanctum sanctorum* of their mysteries and destroyed them. The water shelves off so gradually from the shore that a man can wade, in places, for a hundred yards before going out of his depth. In passing along this side of the town, I observed the many traces of ruins described by Dr. Robinson and others, which evidently belonged to the ancient city, and proved that it extended much farther south than at present. These ruins consist mostly of foundations, with traces of walls, heaps of stones, and a thick wall for some distance along the Sea. Near the middle lie several scattered columns of gray granite, twelve or fifteen feet long, and at some distance a single solitary column is still standing. Among the threshing-floors on the west side of the town are two blocks of a column of polished red Syenite granite, about three feet in diameter.

The next morning I rode down the beach nearly to the point where the Jordan emerges from the Sea, and took a bath in the sweet, transparent water. Here the shore presents a hedge of *oleanders* (called by the natives *Difleh*), now in their fullest bloom. This shrub grows in the torrid climate of the Sea of Galilee to the height of fifteen or twenty feet, and is crowded with blossoms of a massiveness and size that I had no conception of. It is worth going all the way to Galilee to view the oleander hedges in the month of May.

In this morning's ramble, the Hot Baths constitute a prominent object. They are the first I had ever seen. They flow out, some four of them, from black and brittle sulphurous rocks, and elevate the mercury in the thermometer to 144° Fahrenheit. I could not bear to dip my hand in it, except with a hasty withdrawal; and an elaborate attempt to immerse my naked foot in one of the springs, nearly cost me my toenails. The taste is excessively salty and bitter, quite as much so, I think, as the water of the Dead Sea, and there is a strong smell of sulphur about it. Crawfish, which some one had thrown in the springs, lie at the bottom, red as boiled lobsters. The water deposits sediment as it runs down to the sea. Evidently, the springs contain different chemical constituents, for the sediment from one spring is white, from another greenish, from another reddish yellow, etc.

Over the most northern of the springs is a building, now wretchedly dilapidated, which was erected by Ibrahim Pasha, about the year 1834. The birds have built their nests in the ornamental work of the cornices. The roof leaks in every part. The tessellated pavement is but a trap, the loose *tesseræ* flying up and catching the feet. A miserable rascal controls the concern. He gave me the stingiest cup of coffee that I found in Syria, and grumbled the loudest when I paid him twice as much as it was worth. Thirty-one years ago (1838), Dr. Robinson described this bathhouse thus: "The principal bath occupies the center of the building, consisting of a large circular apartment, with a marble pavement all around the circular reservoir in the middle, to which several steps lead down. The roof is supported by columns. In the same building are private rooms for wealthier guests, furnished in an uncommonly good Oriental style. In one was a large and beautiful bath of white marble." I copy this sentence to enable me to point to what changes thirty years produce in Syria. *Now* all is dilapidated, tumbling to pieces. About a hundred yards farther south, some one is erecting a really handsome stone house, just at the base of the hill. If designed for a winter retreat for invalids, I can heartily recommend it.

I was forbidden to enter the innermost bath room by the warning word *Hareem,* implying that women were bathing that morning. A German gentleman had pitched his tent upon a rise of ground a few steps northwest of the bath-room, and although he had no language in which I could converse, yet his evident pleasure at meeting me, and the sympathy expressed in my face at the sight of his swollen and fevered wrists, made the call mutually profitable. Surely, if there is anything in hot medicated baths for rheumatic diseases, that poor, lonely foreigner has long ere this gone home cured. The baths are regarded as efficacious in rheumatic complaints and cases of debility, and are visited principally in July, says Dr. Robinson, by people from all parts of Syria. They are mentioned by Josephus (*Antiquities* 18:2-3), who says, "there are warm-baths at a little distance from Tiberias, in a village named Emmaus;" in other places he speaks of them more definitely. The Arabic name for them is *Hammam,* much like the Hebrew word; both words signify *warmbaths.*

What a speculation it would be for a few really energetic, well educated physicians, with a moderate capital, to build here good bathhouses and a hotel, and let the traveling world know it. I venture to predict that their wildest anticipations would be realized by a rush of patients; and if the waters are in reality as efficacious as they have been deemed for nineteen centuries, the fame of all other hot springs in the world would be eclipsed by them. For only sit with me here for an hour, upon this spur of the hills, that gives so commanding a view of the lake and its surroundings; open the Bible by my side, and let us read together all the wonderful events associated with these placid waters before us. It is enough to make a sick man well to enjoy the scenery and the history together. Shall I point them out to you?

Off there to the right (as we sit facing the east), where that little boat has gone across the lake for its matutinal load of wood, is the scene of that memorable event, the restoration of the two demoniacs who lived in the tombs. Then from that precipice, the herd of swine ran violently down into the sea and were drowned. Turning more to the left, we discover the hallowed spots consecrated by the presence of Him who went there at night, alone, and "continued all night in prayer." Heaven has been drawn very near to earth on the summits of those black, furrowed, basaltic knobs.

> "Its stars on heaven's broad pages write
> How Jesus prayed beneath their light."

Turn a little farther, and there opens before us, near the shore, at the northeastern corner of the Sea, a meadow-place, tolerably level. This is the traditional spot of the feeding of the five thousand men with a few loaves and fishes. We gaze long and earnestly upon that meadow, where "there was much grass." There is a clump of palm trees, appearing very picturesque in the distance, and a group of Arab tents.

Still more to the left, the entrance of the Jordan from the north is distinctly visible, bearing northeast by north, with the plain just described extending from it eastward. We know that only a mile or two up that river, and lying upon both sides of it, was the ancient city of Bethsaida (the "fish-town") of Peter, James, and John. There Jesus healed a blind man. To-morrow I will visit a site so hallowed.

Still more to the left, and the projecting point of Tell Hum is seen. I shall find it to-morrow, strewn with fragments of capitols, friezes, and sarcophagi, and shall accept the theory with but little hesitation that this is *ancient Capernaum.*

Turning yet more to the left (the westward), and the *Plain of Gennesaret* opens before us, a green, marshy plain, called by the natives *El-Ghuweir,* whose eastern extremity is marked by the building styled *Khan Minyeh,* supposed by Dr. Robinson to be *Capernaum,* and over whose northwestern corner hangs the "city that is set upon a hill," *Safed.* Beyond this fertile prairie, and high above it, towers the long face of snowy Hermon, in beautiful relief, against the deep blue sky. Although forty miles distant from us, it seems scarcely *four.* This plain is exceedingly well watered and productive, the soil being a rich, black mould. Josephus describes it as a paradise.

Still more to the left, and the little village of *El-Medjel* is all that remains to represent ancient Magdala, the house of *Mary Magdalene;* that name familiar and loved throughout Christendom. It is truly but a squalid and filthy collection of hovels, with one watchtower to remind us of former greatness.

Still more to the left, and turning so far that the town of Tiberias itself will be on our right, we recall the Hill of Hattin, famous not only for the disastrous battle of July 5th, 1187, alluded to on a preceding page, but still more as being the traditional site of the delivery of the *Sermon on the Mount,* from which, indeed, it is styled the *Mount of Beatitudes.*

Is not such a panorama worth of a visit? For my own part, I could have spent weeks, and even months, here—hot as it was—lying by in the fierceness of noon, and giving my morning and evening hours to the contemplation of scenes so dear to the souls of faithful Christians. It is enough to know that of all the thirty-five miracles of Jesus, the following are associated with this place and its immediate vicinity:

No. 3. Miraculous draught of fishes. Luke 5th.

No. 4. Curing the demoniac. Mark 1st.

No. 5. Curing the fevered woman. Matt. 8th.

No. 6. Curing the leper. (In the vicinity.) Luke 5th.

No. 7. Curing the paralytic. Matt. 9.

No. 9. Curing the withered hand. Luke 6th.

No. 10. Curing the centurion's servant. Luke 7th.

No. 12. Curing the blind and dumb demoniac. Luke 11th.

No. 13. *Stilling the tempest.* Mark 4th.

No. 14. Curing the demoniacs. (In the vicinity.) Matt. 8th.

No. 15. Curing the woman twelve years afflicted. Luke 8th.

No. 16. Raising the damsel from the dead. Luke 8th

No. 17. Restoring to sight two blind men. Matt. 9th.

No. 18. Curing a dumb demoniac. Matt. 9th.

No. 19. Feeding the five thousand. John 6th.

No. 20. Walking upon the sea. John 6th.

No. 22. Curing the deaf stammerer. (Vicinity.) Mark 7th.

No. 23. Feeding the four thousand. (Vicinity.) Mark 8th.

No. 24. Curing the blind man. Luke 8th.

No. 25. Curing the lunatic child. (In the vicinity.) Mark 9th.

No. 26. Securing the tax-money. Matt. 17th.

No. 35. Miraculous draught of fishes. John 21st.

Thus we see that twenty-two out of the thirty-five miracles (distinctly defined) of our Lord, were done at or near the Sea of Galilee.

Some travelers seem to regret the great changes time has produced here. That this mean little town of Tiberias, and that horrid mass of filth yonder, styled *El-Medjel,* should represent the twenty-seven flourishing towns and villages of the days of Josephus, is certainly suggestive of mournful reflections. That these four little skiffs should represent the great fleets of Roman times, and the few poor naked fishermen the whole fraternity of fishers out of whom so many of the disciples were chosen, gives us a startling contrast, to be sure. But to my mind, there is a fitness in all this, and I should be sorry to see it changed—in my day, at least. That great pelican yonder, whose young ones are waiting in their nest upon Mount Carmel, forty miles away, for the load of fish that God will give her in reward for her maternal toil—that solitary and industrious bird is to *me* the best emblem of the Sea of Galilee, a better representative than the new generation bustling with life and activity, which is promised us by enthusiastic writers, in the days when "Israel shall return," and the Land of *Promise* become once more the Land of *Fulfillment*.

To give an idea of the extreme swiftness of the Jordan, which runs out of the Sea of Galilee, I refer to a book which was very celebrated in its day, *Eothen*, by Kingslake. This river is so narrow, and, to an American's eye, accustomed to look across great streams, so insignificant, that the real force of the passage commemorated in the Fellow-Crafts degree concerning the destruction of the Ephraimites, is apt to be lost in the mind of the traveler when he views it. The inquirer may ask, as I have been asked many times, How could a mere brook of sixty or eighty feet in width stop the despairing fugitives who had *home* before them and *destruction* behind? Why not spring into the river, and swim it at every hazard?

The reply is, on account of the *tremendous current,* the extreme swiftness of the Jordan. Falling at a descent of more than ten feet to the mile, this deep and rapid river is a very river of death to an ordinary swimmer. To swim a stream is a rare thing in warfare, and causes heavy loss. In the History of the Crusades, nearly the whole Christian army perished before Damietta, in an attempt to swim a narrow canal, not swift nor deep. In fact, it is admitted by all military writers that crossing a stream in the face of an enemy is one of the gravest of problems. But to our quotations:

The author of the work referred to visited Palestine about 1840, and made some highly original and interesting notes of his journey. He came down from the Sea of Galilee with a company of servants, on *the east* of the Jordan, and crossed about five miles from its mouth. Here, he says, a body of water about equal to the Thames at Eton, but confined within a narrower channel, poured down in a current so swift and heavy that the idea of passing with laden baggage-horses was utterly forbidden. He thinks he could have swum across himself, and probably might have swum his horse over, but it would have been madness to attempt the powerful stream at that place. Meeting a camp of Arabs, however, he succeeded by their aid in crossing; and here is his story:

"The Arabs now went to work in right earnest to affect the passage of the river. They had brought with them a great number of the skins which they use for carrying water in the desert; these they filled with air, and fastened several of them to small boughs which they cut from the banks of the river. In this way they constructed

a raft not more than about four feet square, but rendered buoyant
by the inflated skins which supported it. On this a portion of my
baggage was placed, and was firmly tied to it by the cords used on
my pack-saddles. The little raft, with its weighty cargo, was then
gently lifted into the water, and I had the satisfaction to see that
it floated well.

"Twelve of the Arabs now stripped, and tied inflated skins to
their loins; six of the men went down into the river, got in front of
the little raft, and pulled it off a few feet from the bank. The other
six then dashed into the stream with loud shouts, and swam
along after the raft, pushing it from behind. Off went the craft in
capital style at first, for the stream was easy on the eastern side;
but I saw that the tug was to come, for the main torrent swept
round in a bend near the western bank of the river.

"The old men, with their long gray grisly beards, stood shouting
and cheering, praying and commanding. At length the raft
entered upon the difficult part of its course; the whirling stream
seized and twisted it about, and then bore it rapidly downward;
the swimmers flagged, and seemed to be beat in the struggle. But
now the old men on the bank, with their rigid arms uplifted
straight, sent forth a cry and a shout that tore the wide air into
tatters. The swimmers, one moment before so blown and so weary,
found lungs to answer the cry, and shouting back the name of
their great destroyer, they dashed on through the torrent, and
bore the raft in safety to the western bank.

Afterward the swimmers returned with the raft, and attached
to it the rest of my baggage. I took my seat upon the top of the
cargo, and the raft, thus laden, passed the river in the same way
and with the same struggle as before. The skins, however, not
being perfectly airtight, had lost a great part of their buoyancy, so
that I, as well as the luggage that passed on this last voyage, got
wet in the waters of Jordan. The raft could not be trusted for
another trip, and the rest of my party passed the river in a
different and (for them) much safer way. Inflated skins were
fastened to their loins, and, thus supported, they were tugged
across by Arabs swimming on either side of them. The horses and
mules were thrown into the water, and forced to swim over; the
poor beasts had a hard struggle for their lives in that swift
stream, and I thought that one of the horses would have been
frowned, for he was too weak to gain a footing on the western
bank, and the stream bore him down. At last, however, he swam

back to the side from which he had come. Before dark all had passed the river."

I have never seen anything that gives so good an idea of this remarkable river as the passage cited.

If, as is believed, the national peculiarities of the Swiss, Irish, and other airs are somehow associated with the natural scenery in which they originated, and amidst which, for many ages, they have been played and sung, it would be a question of no small interest—What was the character of the melodies that once vibrated along the shores of Galilee?

This thought possessed my soul that calm, bright morning in May 1868, when I left the village of Tiberias, passed through its broken walls, and rode south, along the pebbly beach of the charming Sea of Galilee. On my right, the basaltic mountains lifted themselves a thousand feet or more showing in their mighty escarpments numberless tombs, wherein once reposed the ashes of princes and rulers. On the left was that most beautiful of all lakes, so intimately connected with the life of the Redeemer of man, and styled the Sea of Galilee. The season was the most propitious. The oleanders, which line the shore and lift their dense foliage to the height of fifteen or twenty feet, were full of blossoms, fragrant with odors and melodious with song. The waters abound with fishes, representing many different classes in ichthyology, one sort of which lay thickly, almost touching each other, at the margin of the shore, and could not be persuaded, so tame were they, that man was their natural enemy. The small purplish shell, so abundant in those waters, adhered to every pebble along the beach, rendering it an easy matter for the collector to fill his pouch without wetting his feet. The morning sun, that had just mounted the hills of Bashan, began to throw his rays upon the glassy surface of the lake, making it glow like a furnace, and startling the many birds, pelicans, didappers, etc., that had been solemnly enjoying their matutinal meal out of the abundance below. The shepherd boys were calling to each other from the summit of one ledge to another, and arousing my never-satiated astonishment at the distance at which sounds can be heard in that clear atmosphere.

Amidst the profusion of novel and interesting sights and sounds, the question occurred to my mind that I have stated in the paragraph above, viz: What was the character of the melodies that vibrated along these hallowed shores in the days of the ancients?

Is there anything in the music of our time analogous to it? While considering these topics of inquiry, my voice involuntarily attuned itself to the well-known Sunday-school air written by Prof. Root, and known as "Jesus by the Sea."

I had committed to memory the words and melody of this pretty song while lying in my berth on the ocean steamer four weeks before, during a storm at sea. The stately measures had attuned themselves to the swash of the ocean billows, to the songs of the sailors, to the rush of steam, to the rattling of cordage, to the majestic movements of the ship itself. It had become indelibly associated in my mind with all the sights and sounds familiar to those who "go down to the sea in ships," who "do business in the great waters." The day of my arrival at Tiberias, as my longing eyes first caught sight of that most beautiful of lakes (the Sea of Galilee), I had formed the determination, so far as in me lay, to associate Jesus Christ *with every locality around its shore* in which he had done any wonderful works. Sitting now above the oleanders, on that charming May morning, I sang the first verse:

> "Oh! I love to think of Jesus as He sat beside the Sea,
> Where the waves were only murmuring on the strand;
> > When He sat within the boat,
> > On the silver wave afloat,
> While He taught the waiting people on the land.
>
> "Oh! I love to think of Jesus by the Sea,
> Oh! I love to think of Jesus by the Sea;
> > And I love the precious word
> > Which He spake to them that heard,
> While He taught the waiting people by the Sea!"

The location of this passage is at or near the ancient city of Capernaum. In the 13th chapter of Matthew, we learn that the incident occurred "the same day" in which He performed sundry miracles at Capernaum. Writers have differed as to the exact locality of Capernaum; but late explorers have set it, as my own conclusions do, at yonder point of land, two miles west of Jordan. The place is heaped up with masses of buildings in marble, elegantly carved, and proving that this was once the emporium of the Sea. The Scriptural words upon which the lines are founded are: "Great multitudes were gathered together with Him, so that He went into a ship, and sat; and the whole multitude stood still on the shore" (Matthew 8:2).

And now I will sing the second verse:

"Oh! I love to think of Jesus as He walked upon the Sea,
When the waves were rolling fearfully and grand;
    How the winds and waves were still,
    At the bidding of His will,
While He brought His loved disciples safe to land.

"Oh! I love to think of Jesus by the Sea,
Oh! I love to think of Jesus by the Sea;
    How He walked upon the wave,
    His beloved ones to save,
While He brought them safely o'er the stormy sea.

To locate the scene of this stupendous miracle we have only to turn the eye upon that meadow place, lying around the mouth of the Jordan, at the east side, now the location of an Arab encampment, whose tents we can see at this distance. There is the hallowed table where the Lord fed five thousand men with five loaves and two fishes. The multitude being all filled, He directed His disciples to get into their boat, and cross over to the plain at the northeast corner of the Sea, called "the land of Gennesaret," now yellow with its crops of wheat and barley, and musical with the harvest songs of the reapers, as I shall hear when I cross it to-morrow. Upon that indentation there where the sea washes the land, occurred the miracle of stilling the tempest, although not at the same period of time. The placid little bay presents none of the agitations of that fearful hour; but we know, from the experience of travelers, that the gusts which rush down through the ravines in the East do distract the waters precisely as in Scriptural days, rendering them very unsafe for the small craft that still sail upon the Sea of Galilee.

The third verse will now have my attention:

"Oh! I love to think of Jesus as He walked beside the Sea,
Where the fishers spread their nets upon the shore;
    How He bade them follow Him,
    And forsake the paths of sin,
And to be His true disciples evermore.

"Oh! I love to think of Jesus by the Sea,
Oh! I love to think of Jesus by the Sea;
    And I long to leave my all,
    At the dear Redeemer's call,
And His true disciple evermore to be."

Yonder is the point where the Jordan runs into the Sea. Here 'Jesus, walking by the Sea of Galilee, saw two brethren, Simon, called Peter, and Andrew, his brother, casting a net into the sea; for they were fishers. And He said unto them, 'Follow me, and I will make you fishers of men.' And they straightway left their nets, and followed Him. And going from thence, He saw two brethren, James, the son of Zebedee, and John, his brother, in a ship with Zebedee their father, mending their nets; and He called them. And they immediately left the ship and their father, and followed Him" (Matthew 4:18-22). The same record is given in Mark 1:16-20, and Luke 5:1-11. In John 1:44, we learn that "Philip was of Bethsaida, the city of Andrew and Peter." This Bethsaida lay, as we know, upon both sides of the Jordan, and from where I am sitting my eye falls upon the spot where

"He bade them follow Him,
And forsake the paths of sin,
And to be His true disciples evermore."

And so the entire of this affecting hymn is associated with the far-famed Sea of Galilee. The person who wrote it *must have viewed the localities,* or at least familiarized himself with them from the description of others. So long as I live, I shall never hear it without recalling the circumstance named. The day after, I went around on the north side, as far as to the Jordan; and as I rode through fields of barley, or crushed the shells on the beach under my horse's feet, or climbed the sharp rocky ridges over which the path passes, or wondered at the magnificence of the marble ruins of Capernaum, I sang over and over those beautiful lines. They attuned themselves to every sound that stirred the breezes or echoed from the cliffs that day; to the harvest song of the Arab reapers, and the responses of the Arab gleaners; to the dull crooning of the pedestrian met in the stony paths traversed; in the sweet melody of the bulbul among the oleanders; in the chattering of the sparrows as they thronged their sociable nests among the Spinal Christi; in the cooing of the pigeons in Wady Hammam; in the hoarse shriek of the fish-hawks, swooping down upon their abundant prey. Let the Sea of Galilee henceforth be consecrated by a new glory, that of *Jesus by the Sea!*

"I thought of Jesus by the Sea
    Of Galilee, blue Galilee:
His Sermon blessed its peaceful shore,
He stilled its tempests by His power;
    His mightiest deeds He wrought, and drew
    From fishers here His chosen few:
Then, as I bowed the knee,
    This voice from Galilee I heard,
    'The Sea is holy to our laboring Lord!'"

TIBERIAS AND GALILEE.

CHAPTER XXIX.

HE day of my departure from Tiberias was hot and unpleasant. Wednesday, May 20, 1868, will be associated in my memory as one of the most sultry days I ever experienced. In my last chapter, I gave the incidents of the ride around the northern shore of Lake Gennesaret. At the mouth of the Jordan, the stone is basaltic, black under the weather, and unsightly. Such material has more than once given its name to the towns of which it is composed. Thus, in Sapor's time (A.D. 359), one city was termed *Kara Amid* from this circumstance.

About noon I returned to the northwest corner of the lake, and there, on the bank of a cool, sweet stream of water, embowered in thickets of oleander that were melodious with the song of the bulbul, I had my frugal dinner, moistened with strong coffee, delicious water, and a few drops of *arrakia,* a fiery article distilled from dates, and which serves the place, in this *anti-bourbon* country, of whiskey. Just above me, a gang of laborers were at work draining off the water from the spring-brooks, in dirt channels, dug along the hillsides, so as to make it available for irrigation. It will be but a few weeks now, and all this fertile plain of Gennesaret below me will be, under this terrific sun of summer, baked to clods of iron. Then the sweet waters will be *the life of the soil,* and cucumbers, melons, and other garden stuff will reward the work of these native engineers. As I muse over my scanty diet, how fondly do such passages as these recur to my mind: "Drought and heat consume the snow waters;" "The waters are dried up, they are gone away from men;" "As the waters fail from the sea and the flood decayeth and drieth up;" "The stream of brooks may pass away; what time they wax warm they vanish; when it is hot they are consumed out of their place;" and many other expressions from Job, who probably lived in the country a day's ride east of this, where water is the *life of the earth.*

And now I begin to climb the acclivity for Safed, that "city which is set upon a hill," so far above me in the north. Many a halt and "last, fond look" do I bestow upon the sweet lake below me, which I may never see again. The whole upper margin of it is visible here in a semicircle; and as I mount higher and higher, it opens before me even to its southern extremity. Only a little portion, that in which the Jordan leaves the lake, is concealed from the eye by the projecting point of hills just below Tiberias. What a place this would have been to occupy (or, no doubt, it *was* occupied that day by a crowd of terrified refugees) during the terrific sea-fight at the southern end, when Vespasian destroyed the last power of the people of this region! As Josephus describes it, the country must have been one of surpassing beauty. He says its soil was so fruitful that all sorts of trees could grow upon it, and names walnuts, palm-trees, fig trees, and olives as representing the various kinds of trees. He uses the term *ambition of nature,* as suggesting the happy combination of such diverse fruits and plants in one locality. And all this had been subjected to fire and sword by the Romans. Every town and village of these happy valleys had been taken and destroyed. Of all the twenty-seven that had encircled this beautiful inland sea, the last place to surrender was Tarichæa, at the southwestern corner. Many of the inhabitants of this devoted place got on board their boats and sailed to the opposite shore. The Romans instantly fitted up a number of vessels, and set sail in pursuit of them. The seafight was but one unmitigated slaughter, until, as the historian says, "the lake was all bloody and full of dead bodies; not one of the Jews escaped." The sword and the flood consumed that day more than 6,000 of the unhappy people.

Such sights as these give interest to that steep ascent toward Safed. The ridge of Hermon on the north, sprinkled with snow, was now a grand object, and in his quiet, majestic manner, he gazed upon the American pilgrim that day. A deep serenity and calm pervaded the scene. No wonder the rabbins used to teach, "God loved the Sea of Galilee beyond all other seas."

The road begins now to be full of sharp projections, which hurt the horses' feet, and one of them, that has been complaining all day, goes almost dead lame. It must be a bad road, indeed, that can daunt one of those Lebanon horses, almost as much accustomed to climbing as a chimney sweep.

And now we descend again to a long, broad valley that once formed a part of the possessions of Naphtali. What splendid land; what crops an American farmer could make here; "how beautiful upon the mountains" must have appeared this noble tribe of Naphtali; how proudly must the array "of a thousand captains, and with them, with shield and spear, thirty and seven thousand," have borne themselves in the presence of Zebulun, Issachar, Manasseh, Ephraim, Benjamin, as they marched southward, through the territories of those tribes, and "came to David to Hebron," "ready armed to the war," "to turn the kingdom of Saul to him, according to the word of the Lord"! (1 Chronicles 12) Under their own banner of "the bounding hart," the warriors of this noble but remote district displayed their grandest characteristics under their own great hero, Barak, when "he went up with ten thousand men at his feet" to Mount Tabor (Judges 4), and met the hosts of Sisera on the banks of the Kishon, with his nine hundred chariots of iron, destroying them utterly, until "there was not a man left."

What a rich and productive soil! Well may Josephus describe it as "full of plantations of trees of all sorts, so fertile as to invite the most slothful to cultivate it." But although *the most slothful* are here in abundance, yet they do *not* cultivate it, and Naphtali is almost a wilderness. "Every city is forsaken, and not a man dwells therein" (Jeremiah 4:29). The wild bee is the only living object that suggests the good emblem of the beehive; except it may be a *hornet* (of which the Jewish legend affirms that *five will kill a man*), who is gathering materials for his paper-mill from the flocky leaves of the thistle that grows rank in this fat soil.

Rising again from this deep valley, in which the oak or terebinth shows here and there (though mostly destroyed by the charcoal-makers from the coast), and suggests the expression of Deborah's hymn, "Naphtali in the high places of the field," better translated "Naphtali is a towering oak; he hath a goodly crest" (Judges 5:18), —rising from this valley, I gain another view of the Sea of Galilee, and yet another, never seeming any more distant from me, although a steady movement northward of hours increases the interval to many miles. Old Hermon before, and the Sea of Galilee behind, appear like the fixed points in a dream, which, struggle as I may, I can neither approach nor recede from.

Going down a long and sharp descent, I now observe a remarkable range of high and precipitous rocks, composed of reddish sandstone, on the right. The openings to many caverns in its steep walls are plainly to be seen. These are said formerly to have been occupied by robbers; but as I passed by, the only rogues that looked after me were the eagles hovering around the summit of the cliff, intent, I presumed, upon the care of their young, or perhaps looking after the rabbits that might naturally be expected to burrow in that immense range of caves. Great masses of stone have been detached from these cliffs at no distant period, probably by earthquakes, and the old roadway is changed. This is the only instance that I saw in Palestine of *the removal of an ancient landmark*. The ancient road of Naphtali, which ran up the right-hand side of the valley, now goes up the left. In this valley is a fresh stream of running water, springing from a copious well, the oleander blossoming all around. On the banks of this delicious water couch, a party of Jews, on their way from their holy city Safed to their holy city Tiberias, was temporarily encamped, and a merry set they were. Beating little tambourines, smoking, merrily conversing, and refreshing themselves with fruits, and possibly something stronger, surely this cheerful little band is the happiest party that all Naphtali can now produce.

But no; a few miles farther, and off on the left hand, is a veritable picnic, *a wedding party* of the Hebrews, enjoying themselves in the most uproarious manner, firing muskets, beating drums, and singing all sorts of *epithalamiums*. The young men, as we approach Safed, make quite a display of themselves, wearing the short, close jacket which Dr. Robinson describes, "with embroidered sleeves hanging loose from the shoulders, the back of the coat being at the same time ornamented with strips of cloth of another color." This, with a certain peculiar twist of their white turbans, gives them quite a jaunty air. The women, in their jewelry, etc., abundantly proved that a maid cannot forget her ornaments nor a bride her attire (Jeremiah 2:32).

At last, I raise the hill on which Safed is situated, and begin to enter the suburbs of another one of the Holy Places of the Jews. (Hebron, Jerusalem, and Tiberias are the other three.) It is believed by the Jews to be the place where Jeremiah hid the ark at the national destruction under Nebuchadnezzar, and whence the Messiah will come first at his appearing. The Scotch Presbyterians once proposed to make Safed the headquarters of Missionary operations in these parts, as its climate is very delightful, even in the heat of summer. I feel this very sensibly, having come out of that heated atmosphere

surrounding the Sea of Galilee below me. By contrast, the breezes
are cool and bracing. Even in July, the thermometer at noon
indicates but 76° in the shade.

At first, I feared that I was to have some difficulty in the way of
accommodations at Safed. My host at Tiberias (Mr. Wiseman) had
directed Hassan, my head-servant, to take me to the quarters of
the Austrian Vice-Consul; but that gentleman declined to receive
me. He, however, designated another person, who very cheerfully
took me in, giving up his whole house to my use, according to the
custom of these Jewish householders, and sleeping with his own
family upon the pavement in the courtyard outside. The room was
small, but cool and pleasant, and soon a bountiful repast of coffee,
eggs, bread, and excellent wine was spread.

Having eaten, I took advantage of the declining hour of day to
roam through the Jewish quarter of Safed, in which my lot for the
night had been cast. Truly a romantic spot is Safed! It occupies
the northern extremity of a steep ridge, having deep valleys on
the east and west. My quarters were just below the ruined castle
at the northern part of the city. So wearied was I with the days'
peregrination, that I avoided the steep climb necessary to reach
them. A little outside the town on the north, the view is truly
magnificent. Olive-orchards, vineyards, and innumerable fig trees
everywhere clothe the slopes of the mountains with verdure, and
suggest abounding promises of oil and wine. Villages named Ain
Zeitoun, Kadyta, Saccas, and Marona, lie off to the westward. The
situation is singularly beautiful. The eye lingers over it. The noble
mountain of Naphtali, behind which the sun is hidden, is a mass
of foliage. The country people can be seen through the whole
length of the intervening valley, returning home from their day's
labors. Off to the southward may be traced my five-hour ascent
from the sea. How solemn, calm, and silent seems that sheet of
water now, and so near it scarcely looks two miles distant! The
three ridges that I have come over this afternoon seem only so
many furrows in a plowed field. That noblest of summits, Mount
Hermon, never shows so well to me as at this hour. The last rays
of the sun glancing up from the Mediterranean Sea are reflected
dazzlingly back from the huge banks of snow which tell
unmistakably of his great elevation, and so disappear. It is long
before I can withdraw my eyes from his hoary crown.

Returning slowly through the filthy lanes of Safed, the sound of chanting and the appearance of a public gathering draw me into an apartment, where I am deeply interested to see the Jews at their evening devotions. The room is neat and clean, and lighted with lamps of olive oil. Upon a shelf are several folio volumes, doubtless copies of the Talmud in Hebrew. Several venerable-looking men came promptly forward to welcome me with the right hand of fellowship and invite me to a seat. These are Polish Jews, who wear the fur cap, etc., that I have seen among the Ashkenazim at Jerusalem and Tiberias, as badges of the sect. Many of the worshippers had long white beards and flowing hair of the same color. In their devotions, they are very earnest and vehement. They read with all their might. Some clap their hands. Some clasp both hands together, and use them as the "mourning women" do at their funerals, while frequent cries of *Ah-min, Ah-min,* form the *so mote it be* of the responses. Leaving this place of worship, I enter another, in which the exercises are of the same character, and where my welcome by the elders is of the same sort. Here I remarked that all the worshippers, upon entering, hold their hands under the spout of a water-cooler, from which a few drops trickle upon them. This formed the ceremonial ablution previous to the service.

I was not so unfavorably struck with all this, however, as Sandys, who observed it nearly 300 years ago. He says "their fanatical gestures exceed all barbarism, continuously waving their bodies, and often jumping upright. They esteem action and zeal marks of spiritual elevation."

Early the next morning I said *salaam* to my host, and struck again northward, resolved to reach Tibnin. This would be an easy march for the day, only one of my horses had given out and had to be driven. The first half-hour was down into the deep valley to the northwest, past the finest vineyards and orchards of Syria.

Rising again, I observed heaps of black stone and lava surrounding an oval basin, now full of water that is reckoned as the crater of an extinct volcano. Its depth is about 40 feet; length from north to south, about 400 feet; breadth, 120. It is called Birket-el-Jish. The village of the same name was just before me. This village was totally destroyed by the earthquake of January 1, 1837, at the time Safed, Tiberias, and other Galilean towns were so sorely shattered. The Christians were at their prayers when the church fell in upon them and crushed them to death, to the number of one hundred and thirty

Passing El-Jish, I went down a long valley finely cultivated. Going

34

out of this, I bore a little too much to the westward, and took my
noonday luncheon at a village called Kefr Birini, which has ruins
of some fine old structures. Over what was formerly a gateway is
a long Hebrew inscription, of which the first word implies *peace*.
But the principal ruin is the front of a large building with two
rows of limestone columns before it, once belonging to a portico. I
hope some day to see good photographs of these.

Here, say the old writers, the Jews of Safed used to make their
annual pilgrimage at the festival of Queen Esther *(Purim),* and
here they did "eat, drink, and rejoice," as I saw them doing
yesterday, a few miles farther south.

Passing on a few miles northward, I was interested to see by
the roadside a very large sarcophagus, or stone coffin. The lid was
very heavy, as much as two feet thick, stout, and cut off each way
so as to look like the roof of a house. It is now thrown aside; the
coffin itself has been dug out, and turned partly over, as if to
search for treasures beneath it. This tomb almost exactly
resembles one I have seen pictured near Delphi, Greece. Dr.
Robinson thinks, from the fragments of column near by, that this
might once have formed a solitary tomb upon a heavy pedestal,
like that of King Hiram *(Kebr Hairan)* near Tyre. It did not strike
me in that way, however. Observing some very large rocks about
a quarter of a mile westward, I went among them in pursuit of
adventures, and was rewarded by discovering the most
remarkable receptacle for the dead that my whole explorations
had developed. In preparing it, the stonecutters had simply
smoothed off the top of a knobbed fragment of stone, without
removing it from its place, and thus chiseled a coffin in the rock,
leaving the sides ragged as nature had made them. The lid was
gone.

Passing on, I reached Bint Jebail about noon, and remained
there several hours. It was, by good chance, the day of the
weekly fair (Thursday), and I was thus afforded an opportunity
of seeing the commercial transactions of these people right at
home. The business done was decidedly of a peddling
character—one merchant having a few pounds of figs, another
some candy, another a handful of notions, the next a little
tobacco, while one venerable old dame presented the commercial
attractions of *three small squashes* as her stock in trade. Yet
there were a few Syrian traders with cotton and silk goods,
whose value must have been several hundred dollars each. All
were extremely polite, and I purchased soap of one, candy of
another, figs of a third, and so on, until I had invested quite a handful

of the greasy and corrupted coins current in Bint Jebail. As one of the horses had cast his shoe, it was a treat to witness the primitive operations of our blacksmith—how he pared the hoof with a jackknife very old and very dull—how he put just four nails and no more into the foot, and clinched them by holding the foot down upon a rock and pounding well at the points. The shoe of this country is uniformly made to cover the whole foot. From the loose manner of the Vulcan of Bint Jebail, I should think he was preparing work for the blacksmiths on ahead of me.

Observing a noble fig tree on a hill north of the town, I directed my party there, and we spent some cool and refreshing hours until the sun warned us off toward Tibnin. The country, like that for the last few hours, is undulating, cultivated, wooded, and beautiful, a succession of hill and dale, with more distant hills still higher and more thickly wooded. Presently we came into a region of great beauty, with the Castle of Tibnin upon an isolated hill in the midst. As we are slowly approaching it, charmed with these enchanting landscapes, each of which is more beautiful than the last, a few historical notes from Robinson, that prince of *notists,* will be useful. The Castle of Tibnin was built by St. Omer, Lord of Tiberias, A.D. 1107, only eight years after the capture of Jerusalem by the Crusaders, and seventeen years before Tyre itself came into their possession. St. Omer selected it as a kind of security against Saracenic incursion from the coast, choosing a secure hill in a most fruitful country, and named it Toron, but the natives called it Tibnin. Immediately after the battle of Hattin (July 5, 1187), Saladin captured it by assault. It came afterward into the possession of the Crusaders, and in 1286 was again captured by the Saracens, under Sattan Bibars. The still more celebrated and romantic Castle of Belfort lies a few miles northeast of Tibnin, but this I did not visit.

Avoiding the castle, whose Pasha would readily have acknowledged my credentials had I called upon him, I engaged lodgings in one of the houses of the village below, a cleanly and respectable apartment compared with the general range of native houses. During the night, the soldiers came down from the castle, and conscripted the head of the family next door. When I arose, I was surprised to find a group of women around my courtyard. They had heard that I was in favor with the Pasha-General, and hoped I would use my influence to have the man released. It was certainly a painful sight, the tears of the women, the wife thus suddenly deprived of her protector wailing and wringing her hands. But all that I could do was to advise them to make up a sum of money and hire the Cadi to go up to the castle and *buy off their neighbor*. It was probably nothing, after all, but an attempt of the soldiers (who are extremely tyrannical to the natives) to extort money from the villagers.

The next day's ride to Tyre was, like the last, full of interest. The disabled horse was left behind, his owner, Hassan, remaining with him, and so depriving me of the only one of my three servants who knew a word of English. But as I was to stay in the family at Tyre where I had previously spent several days, this was of less consequence. A short distance west of Tibnin and I gained a splendid view of the Mediterranean Sea, which I had last looked upon at Nazareth. Tyre was the only town in sight along the coast. Then a long descent took me into the most gloomy and romantic valley I had ever seen. Its name, *Valley of the Wolf (Wady Deeb),* is quite in keeping with its appearance. At the place where I left it, the hills must be quite **600** feet in height, and so nearly perpendicular that no four-footed beast save goat or gazelle, or Lebanon horse, would venture the ascent. Writers say that wolves and bears abound in *Wady Deeb,* and there is a pond, near which we passed, at which the mountain leopards slake their thirst at night. But I will say for them, in the language of the poet—

> "The very leopards of the dells
> Looked down and let me pass."

This valley is a long, narrow, winding, magnificent chasm, scooped out by the creative energy on a scale of savage and magnificent grandeur. I cannot leave this romantic valley without repeating that nothing can exceed its wild appearance; yet many kinds of trees and shrubs adorn it—the beech-tree and velonea oak, the wild rose, the broom, etc.; while the white flowers of woodbine and clematis load the air with fragrance. The pleasant memories of this deep dale will haunt me through life.

About noon, I reached the fountain at Kanah, a Christian village about seven miles east of Tyre. Some time before, when I made my first visit to Tyre, I had contributed something, by special request, to the purchase of a bell for the Christian church here, and felt, therefore, that I had an interest in Kanah. But whatever it was, I took it out in spending a noontide hour at the fountain, watching the women as they came after the household supply of water, and observing the ancient and primitive method of watering the flocks by the shepherds and shepherd boys. Every flock of sheep and goats as it came down from the hills *followed* its leader, confirming a host of Scriptural readings, many of them of the most tender and affecting nature. The water-troughs, as usual, were stone coffins (sarcophagi), pilfered, doubtless, long ago, from the tombs in the rocky sides of these old hills, and made to do duty to the living generations who will soon be as the great men who occupied these receptacles—dust and ashes. The coffee made from the sweet fountain of Kanah, and heated by the crackling thorns that lay around, was all the sweeter, as I knew that these people, who watched my movements with such gentleness and respect, were believers in the Son of God.

Half an hour more toward the west (through a slight shower, the first I had encountered since March) brought me to Hiram's Tomb (Kabr Hairan), which has been described in a former article. I took the present occasion to verify and correct my measurement of this remarkable monument, said by the most experienced of all American travelers to be the most extraordinary monument of antiquity yet remaining in the Holy Land, an immense sarcophagus of stone, resting upon a lofty pedestal of large hewn stones, a conspicuous ancient tomb, bearing among the common people the name of Kabr Hairan, or Sepulcher of Hiram. A traveler from Scotland (Bonar, 1839) says that in two hours from Tyre, his attention was attracted by a singular monument or tomb, resting upon immense hewn stones. The upper stone was very large, and it was not easy for him to see how it had been lifted on to its fellows. A better idea of the magnitude of Hiram's Tomb will be gained by estimating that the sarcophagus weighs fifty tons, calculating the stone at 160 pounds to the cubic foot. The lid, six feet thick, is of nearly the same weight, and fits with the cavity in the top of the sarcophagus (where the body was deposited) by a shoulder about four inches deep. I crowded, with difficulty, into the coffin, by the opening left by those who deposited it perhaps 2,900 years ago, and, stretching myself at full length upon the spot where the corpse had once lain, found that I could touch one extremity of the cavity with my toes, while my head pressed against the other.

Having finished up with care and accuracy all the measurements, I went on to *Ras-el-Ain* (or head of the fountain), the remarkable water-works that once supplied all Tyre with the necessary fluid The place is about three miles from the city, and close to the ??

into which the vast supplies are now emptied, with but little other practical use save the turning of one or two shackling gristmills. These are the most interesting water-works in Syria. There must originally have been some very strong springs bubbling out here, with great walls, immensely thick, built around these springs as high as the water would rise, viz., about twenty feet, and thus the supply could be passed along aqueducts to a great distance. There are substantial steps made to ascend these walls, and a broad walk emborders the basins. A piece of the ancient aqueduct, consisting of three arches, is seen about two miles from Ras-el-Ain, and a good deal of the work that lay near the ground. So much lime exists in this water that its drippings have produced masses of stone of the nature of stalactites. The whole structure is grand and imposing, and it is no wonder that the Mohammedans, who attribute so much to the wisdom and generosity of King Solomon, affirm that these noble fountains were erected at his expense, and presented by him to his friend and companion, King Hiram, after the latter had, through his skilled craftsmen, completed the Temple at Jerusalem. Other fountains and reservoirs lie along this plain, but none comparable, either in their natural or artificial features, to these at Ras-el-Ain.

About six o'clock I turned down to the beach and followed it on to Tyre. Shells, the spines of cuttlefish, live sand-crabs in abundance, and other objects living and dead, added variety to the way, and it was in quite a refreshed condition that I entered the decayed gate of Tyre and claimed lodging at the hands of my old host, whose *el fuddel* (welcome) it was pleasant once more to hear.

The amount of notes taken upon these two days' journey, to be incorporated into other chapters, will prove how industriously my time was spent. I work in a few here which, "being neither oblong nor square," do not so readily fit elsewhere. At the place where the Jordan and sea meet, the river flowing clear, cool, swift, and shaded with oleanders, I recalled the Apostle Peter, born near this place, who, though slower than John to *recognize,* was the first to *hasten* to the Master. The character of Simon Peter is one that always possessed a strange fascination for me. If I have *sinned* as Peter, may my *pardon* be as speedy, tender, and sure. In referring to the beautiful valley near the northwest corner of the sea, which Josephus praises so highly, I must use the words of an old writer, who affirms that it is the most pregnant and pleasant valley that ever eye beheld, full of flowery "beauties."

In relation to the celebrated Christ's Thorn, very abundant here, I write: The various names are Christ's Thorn, and by the Greeks, Judas' Thorn, or *Judenborn. Paliurus aculeatus* is one of the botanical terms. The same species, it is said, is used in Italy for fences, its sharp spines and pliant branches adapting it for that. The fruit has a singular contrivance, being flat and thin, attached by the middle to the footstalk, the middle raised like the crown of a hat, while the expansion resembles the brim. The seeds are used in the East medicinally. It is said the plant is common in English shrubberies, but the fruit does not ripen there. A years' study of nature around the delightful sheet of water called the Sea of Galilee would afford a rare volume. The members of the Scotch rite could study their favorite emblem, *the pelican,* who displays all his wise oddities here. Catching a fish crosswise, he adjusts it for swallowing by tossing it in the air, and catching it as it comes head downward with the expertness of a juggler. Nine times out of ten the finny fellow gets into the bird's gullet; the tenth one drops back into the water to relate his terrific experience to the rest. When the fowl's pouch is loaded, he returns to his nest, often twenty-five or thirty miles from the fishing-grounds, and disgorges the finny spoil to his young. I notice in watching a flock of pelicans, that when one yawns, all yawn. Is this analogous to the Scotch rite practice? I have heard it said so!

It would take a volume to embody my recollections of Capernaum, and the parallels presented by the place. Sitting upon these desolate rocks, every one of which bears marks of the mason's chisel, one has but to close his eyes and recall the spirit of humanity that once made this place a home of men. Children, fountains, schools, gardens, shady bowers, synagogues, places of custom, hospitals, singing birds —where are they now? Where stood the rich city, the port of entry and customs for all Galilee, is now utter desolation; "gladness is taken away, and joy out of the pleasant fields; in the vineyard there is no singing, neither shouting; the treaders tread out no wine in the press, their vintage shouting has ceased" (Isaiah 16:10). It is well styled by another "a waste of ruins, dwellings, palaces, temples, and triumphal arches, all piled in indiscriminate confusion." With Solomon's signet as an emblem to settle the question of proprietorship, and the Jewish sacred candlestick to give the hope of returning light, these ruins are of the profoundest interest to a Mason—a heap of pillars, cornices, entablatures, jambs, altars, mullions, sculptured

tablets, and other things that exhaust my range of architectural
nomenclature. Here, where was the ruin of a great city, naught
remains but heaviness and sorrow (Isaiah 29:2); the line of
confusion has been stretched out upon it, the stones of emptiness
have been heaped upon it (34:11). The material is bastard marble,
procured, probably, from the quarry near Kedesh, twenty miles
northwest.

Galilee is a sea tempestuous and unfaithful, at an instant
incensed with sudden gusts; and there is

> "No one now
> Hath power to walk these waters like our Lord."

As I went out of Tiberias,

> "Under the opening eyelids of the morn,"

I was accompanied by the shepherds of the place, who, like all
their craft in this vicinity, lead their flocks into the houses of the
town, where they can be under their watch-care all night. In this
part of the country, I do not see them

> "Battening their flocks with the fresh dews of night;"

nor do they exemplify the words which Milton sang:

> "The shepherds on the lawn,
> Or ere the point of dawn,
>   Sat simply chatting in a rustic row;
> Perhaps their loves, or else their sheep,
> Were all that did their silly thoughts so busy keep."

At the mouth of Wady Hammam (Pigeon Ravine), I recalled
the celebrated exploit of Herod, who exterminated the band of
robbers that infested these caves, by letting down his soldiers in
strong boxes hung by chains. The plan was imitated, with equal
success, by Sigurd, the Crusader, A.D. 1109. He let down two
boats, filled with his sailors, from the top of a precipice, and
these grappled the thieves at their caves' doors, and destroyed
them with but little loss. The ruins in this neighborhood are of
squared stones, of hard, black, and spongy basalt. A story is told
here characteristic of Herod's cruelty, as manifested in the
slaughter of the children of Bethlehem, and of his own wives and
children. In putting one of the robbers to death, captured in
these caves, he tied 400 live pigeons to his body to break the fall!
The historian fails to state whether the *fall* was broken, or only
the robber. But they have no end of traditions here. One is that
Joshua ordered this lake opened as a fishing-place to *all comers*.

No Cape Cod exclusiveness about him! It always was a sort of Lake Minnetonka for fish, and I hope the time will come when fishing of the right sort will be practiced there. It is really insulting to see how impudent the fish have become for want of masters. The pelicans and didappers absolutely have it all to themselves.

Those wise creatures of music, the birds, always know where are the best quarters! The dove of Noah returned to the ark for shelter and food, and, no doubt, gave the patriarch a solo of cooing, soft and gentle as the one I hear in the oleander. The little Egyptian fantail *(Drymœca gracilis),* runs up the sides of the reeds, as described by Prof. Tristam, with its loud, clear note, and long, white-tipped tail. Among the flowers that crowd this rich meadowland, may be seen a large bunch of aggregated white flowers, like wild parsley, whose name I cannot give. Thorns and thistles abound here with a profusion and vastness wonderful to contemplate. Thus the first curse pronounced upon the earth for the sins of men, that of "thorns and thistles" (Genesis 3:18), was literally applied to Christ. To Him, it might be said, with Isaiah (5:6), "there came up briers and thorns." Amongst them are "the rivers, the floods, the brooks of honey and butter," of which the Patriarch Job, who lived but a few miles to the southeast, wrote (20:19).

Thoughtfully climbing the slopes into the purer air of the hills, my eyes can scarcely withdraw themselves from Hermon soaring on my right hand. The expression in Isaiah 5:26 occurs to me with added meaning. The Great Illumer describes Jehovah seated yonder on that lookout, from which all Palestine is clearly spread before the eye, and viewing the sensuality and falsehood of the people. He had named his Chosen, He "hisses" for the destroying nations to come, as a man hisses or calls in a sibilant breath to his flocks; He "hisses" for the Assyrian 1,000 miles eastward; and for the Egyptian 500 miles southwestward; and for the Greek 2,500 miles northwestward. How sublime the figure! Turn, O reader, and read it. These instruments of God's wrath were but too ready for the spoil. *Maher-shalal-hashbaz* was their watchword. They came with speed swiftly, their girdles bound up, their shoe-latchets strongly tied, as the prophet predicted. Their bows were bent, their arrows sharp, they roared like lions, yelling to do the irresistible will of Jehovah. Then Capernaum yonder felt the woe; then Shechem; then Bethel; then Jerusalem. The Assyrian, "the rod of His anger, the stuff of indignation in His hand," swept over all, absorbing all, consuming all.

The noble Jove-bird, the eagle, sailing over the high mountain-passes, shared with Hermon my admiration. The eagle and the mountain—how appropriate the conjunction! I thought so one day, a few weeks since, when, reclining under a vast cedar on Lebanon, I saw the regal fowl soaring far in the blue heavens above me.

The view northeastward, as I mounted the hills, embraced the country around Lake Huleh, of which Dr. Thomson says the lake is alive with fish, the trees with birds, the flowers with bees. In that direction, the mountains rise high, broken and rugged. The towns give evidences in their materials of extreme old age. A Californian will recognize in the dry and dusty appearance of this country a parallel to his own State. The early explorers there thought nothing could grow in that dry country; but California proves to us one of the most productive States in the Union. Directly east of me, and about seven miles distant, is the Jordan, and Jacob's Bridge is in sight. There are numerous fords between the place where the stream enters the Sea of Galilee and Jacob's Bridge. Looking back from time to time, the sea gets apparently no farther off, only a little lower down. The present name of this sea, which is 165 feet deep and 653 feet below the Mediterranean, Galilee, Lake of Tiberias, Lake Chinneroth, etc., is *Bahr Tibereeah*. While on this subject, I will put all the *bahrs* I have found together:

Dead Sea	is	Bahr Loot.
Galilee	"	" Tibereeah.
Lake Meron	"	" Hoolah.
Mediterranean	"	" (I forget the rest).

It is in Lake Huleh that the best reeds, used for ordinary writing purposes in this country, are collected. The Latin adage, *Currente calamo,* with a swift-running reed, is therefore sacred to this spot. And this naturally reminds me of the comforting thought expressed in the Arabic proverb: "Paradise is for him who rightly uses the *pen* (reed), as well as for him who died under the stroke of the *sword."* Probably that swaggering soldier yonder would dispute the maxim; but personally I have no doubt of it, and my fellow-writers on Masonry (Mackey, Simons, Macoy, Wheeler, Moore, Ransom, *et id genus omne),* will doubtless agree with me.

The bulrush, too, attains to great dimensions here, suggesting the passage, "bowing down their head like bulrushes" (Isaiah 58:5). Here too we find fragrant specimens of the pond lily, nowhere more delicious, as I have seen, than in the Minnesota lakes. This is not,

however, the lotus of history; the correct name of that is
nelumbium, and it abounds in the Mississippi river-bottom. It
resembles a wasp's nest, as was noticed long ago by writers.
These lilies of Huleh remind me of the old painting that haunted
my youthful memory, a head of Christ surmounted by three white
lilies; also, of a line in the Battle-Hymn of the Republic to the
same effect. The natives here prepare a cooling drink of the stem
of the yellow water lily *(Nuphar luteum).* The sweet-scented and
magnificent "white pond-lily," which I never saw anywhere so
well represented as when on a boat excursion in Minnesota, in the
summer of 1871, in company with Mr. O. E. Dodge, Jr., also
abounds here, as I have said. It is the *Nymphœa odorata;* while
the Nile lotus, the most historical of all, is the *Nymphœa* lotus.
All these lilies are common to the Orient. Waterfowl abound in
Lake Huleh, which, in this sense, is

> "A lake where water-fowl of many tribes,
> Geese, crane, and long-necked swans, disport themselves."

And here, to make the circle complete, grows the *papyrus,* of
which paper was so long made.

In the depressions of the hills, the country is extremely fertile,
justifying the account of a traveler, who entered a goodly forest
full of tall and delightful trees, intermixed with fruitful and
flowery lawns. Perhaps the earth affordeth not the like; it cannot
be more pleasant —a wooded, fertile succession of slopes and
valleys, watered by good streams, having internal sources of
riches in abundance. But passing out of these delightful spots, the
white, parched soil dazzles the eye and scorches the face with
reflected heat. One locality was especially impressive, a hill-
chasm rent of wrinkled, water-worn rocks. Mounting still higher,
I am almost in sight of the three affluents of the Jordan, which
come down from the north to form the sacred river; viz., the *Large*
(Leddam), the *Long* (Hasbahny), and the *Beautiful* (Baniasy). The
old story perpetuated in editions of Jesper Harding's Bibles, of
"two rivers, the *Jor* and the *Dan,*" is unmitigated nonsense, the
conceit of some commentator who never saw the river or the
country. Occasionally I see the shining face of Lake Huleh,
where were "the waters of Merom," the scene of Joshua's
mighty battle and victory. As soon as I became able to recognize
the locality, I turned to Joshua 11, and perused the magnificent
description. What an exploit! It was worthy of the best days of

Napoleon, whose battlefield near Mount Tabor, only twenty miles south of here, I had inspected two days before. Other thoughts are suggested by Lake Huleh. It affords an enormous supply of leeches (bloodsuckers), which some day, like the salt of Jebel Usdum and the chemicals of Bahr Loot, may prove of economic value to the nation. At present, Australia chiefly supplies the European market with leeches, to the number of ten millions annually, and the principal use of bloodsuckers here, in Palestine, is to suggest fruitful images to the tax collectors.

In the house of my Hebrew host I observed, as I had in Mr. Wiseman's at Tiberias, a small package of parchment nailed to the doorposts. This scroll, which by unchangeable law must be written in Hebrew, is termed the *Mezuza*. In other cases, they are covered with glass and fastened to the doorjambs. They are written by the rabbins, and signed with the name of God. These are never printed, but written on parchment, prepared expressly for the purpose, with ink of a prescribed composition, not with a quill, but reed. One Jew I saw here struck me with so much interest that I apply to him the description of another writer, slightly altered: "A grand old Abrahamic face, with bold outline, nose curved like a bird's beak, firm full lips, massive jaw, from which, like floss-silk, flowed a massy beard even down to his chest; a man of full height, with an eye like an eagle's undimmed by age, possessed of evident strength and will, quickness of intellect and pertinacity of purpose."

This place was one of the centers of disturbance in the dreadful earthquake commencing New Year's Day, 1837, and continuing for several weeks. The ancients were taught by Anaxagoras, about B.C. 435, that these phenomena were produced by subterranean clouds bursting forth into lightning. One of the most terrible earthquakes this country has ever experienced was A.D. 742, when more than 500 towns were destroyed, and the loss of life surpassed all calculation. In 1754, half the city of Cana was overwhelmed, and 40,000 people perished there. In 1759, the Holy Land was again shaken to its center, and Baalbec destroyed. These stone houses, having no braces, tumble in under an earthquake like broken eggshells. The piles of stone and earth come down in heaps, with no resistance. A man who had come to see the governor, was mounted on a fine Arab mare, beautifully caparisoned; the rider was wearing a political decoration.

In 1833, there were three Jewish printing presses at Safed. Purchasing a coin of a Jew here, I afterward wrote the following article and give it in illustration of the subject before me.

WHAT AN ANCIENT COIN TEACHES.

This coin is of the period of Alexander Balas, whose reign of seven years covers the period of B.C. 152-146, or 2020 years ago. It is about the size and weight of an American twenty-five cent piece, but handsomer than any of our American coins are made. The mintmarks are nearly as sharp and clear-cut upon it as on the day of its issue. On the obverse is the portrait of Alexander Balas, king of the country in which I find his coin. He sports a handsome but rather inexpressive countenance, indulges in short whiskers, and ties his hair, which is bushy and abundant, with a fillet. On the reverse of the coin is the eagle, appropriated, I believe, by all the Alexanders, successors of the Great Alexander, or of his lieutenants. Its head is turned to the left. The inscription is *Alexandrore Basileus,* etc.

And now for the lesson taught by this coin. About the year B.C. 154, Demetrius Soter, King of Syria, found his claims opposed and his throne disputed by a young man of obscure birth, named Balas, who was acknowledged and his cause espoused by the powerful King of Egypt, Ptolemy Philometor, who even gave him his daughter Cleopatra in marriage. The Roman Senate likewise favored young Balas, and authorized him to raise forces to possess himself of the kingdom. He therefore assumed the name of Alexander Balas, as upon the coin that lies before me, together with the title "King of Syria." Jonathan, governor of the Jewish nation, also espoused his cause. The contending monarchs came to arms twice in the year B.C. 152, the latter contest resulting in the death of Demetrius and the elevation of Balas.

Alexander Balas had manifested considerable ability during the short war for the succession, but no sooner was he firmly settled upon the throne, than he fell into the vices of luxury and idleness. This created so much dissatisfaction, that in B.C. 148, a son of the deposed monarch, named Demetrius Nicator, excited a rebellion against Alexander, being encouraged in it by Alexander's own father-in-law, Ptolemy Philometor, who took his daughter Cleopatra away from her husband and gave her to his rival. The contest was short. Alexander Balas was defeated, and fled to Arabia, where he was treacherously murdered in the year B.C. 146.

Two years afterward, the son of Alexander Balas assumed the title of Antiochus VI., and recovered the kingdom of Syria from Demetrius Nicator, which he held, however, for only a few months, when he too was murdered. This led (by processes which the present article does not require me to record) to the absolute independence of the Jewish nation, for the first time in six hundred years They struck coins in B.C. 143, a thing they had never done before, and made an epoch of that year from which to compute their future chronology. This epoch is used by Josephus and the author of the first book of Maccabees.

But this coin of mine possesses much more of valuable history than this. As one of a series of the coins of Syrian kings, it refers us back to the dynasties that successively rose and fell, from the death of the Great Alexander, B.C. 324, to the period of Alexander Balas. Unhappy Palestine! placed between Egypt and Syria, she could never extricate herself from the wars incessantly waged between those rival powers. As Josephus finely observes, "She resembled a ship tossed by a hurricane, and buffeted on both sides by the waves, while she lay in the midst of contending seas." Ptolemy Lagus assumed the throne of Egypt, and conquered Palestine; B.C. 315, Antigonus made himself king of Syria and the East, and conquered Palestine; while, in B.C. 312, the Egyptian king reconquered Palestine, and Seleucus Nicator became king of Syria. Again, Antigonus became the conqueror, and placed his son Demetrius Poliorcetes upon the throne; B.C. 301, another change was made, and Palestine again returned to the Egyptian yoke, under Ptolemy Lagus; and, upon his death, B.C. 283, under his son Ptolemy Philadelphus. It was this man whose enlightened zeal caused the translation of the Hebrew Scriptures in the form now styled the *Septuagint*. Upon his death, in the year B.C. 247, Ptolemy Euergetes assumed the crown.

He was murdered, B.C. 222, by his own son, who came to the throne as Ptolemy Philopator. At this time, Palestine and the most of Syria had for about sixty years enjoyed uninterrupted tranquility under the government of Egypt. The Eastern kings, Antiochus Soter, Antiochus Theos, Seleucus Callinicus, Seleucus Keraunos, and Antiochus the Great, made their reigns more or less troublesome to the Jewish nation, who were their neighbors on the south; but upon the whole this period may be called one of their happiest.

Antiochus the Great conquered all Syria and Palestine from the Egyptians, B.C. 218, but lost it a few months afterward, when it reverted to Ptolemy Philopator, who died B.C. 205, leaving his crown to his son, Ptolemy Epiphanes. The war was renewed by Antiochus, the Great, who speedily reconquered Syria and Palestine. Again he lost it, B.C. 204, and again recovered it B.C. 198; B.C. 190, he came into contact with the Roman power, by which he was terribly defeated, and two years afterward was murdered.

Seleucus Philopator, his oldest son, succeeded to the throne, but was himself murdered, B.C. 176, his brother, Antiochus Epiphanes, succeeding him to the throne; B.C. 171, this king defeated the Egyptians at Pelusium, and again B.C. 170. This monarch so greatly oppressed the Jewish nation that, B.C. 167, the daily sacrifices ceased in the Temple, and the city of Jerusalem was almost deserted. Never before were they exposed to so furious a persecution as by Antiochus Epiphanes. Then arose the great family of the Maccabees, in the persons of Mattathias and his five sons, who organized a religious war, which was heroically maintained for twenty-six years against the Syrians, under five successive kings, viz.: Antiochus Epiphanes (who died, B.C. 164), Antiochus Eupator (who was murdered, B.C. 162), Demetrius Soter (who was killed in battle, B.C. 152), Alexander Balas, whose coin lying before me has suggested this series of historical facts (and who was treacherously murdered, B.C. 146), and Antiochus Theos, who was murdered, B.C. 144.

All these and numerous other matters of history, essential to the perfect understanding of Biblical history, belong to the study of the coins of the Syrian and Egyptian kings, and to this one of Alexander Balas, as a member of the series.

My stay at Bint-Jebail afforded me an uncommon insight into local customs, and were I to visit the Holy Land again I would make it a point to visit these weekly fairs frequently, as the best places to study the natives when unbent. The professional Scribe is here in all his glory; an unarmed man, for his pursuits are peaceful ("the pen mightier than the sword," you know!), an immensely large turban answering almost in place of a parasol, long robes, a large brass inkhorn by his side bristling with reeds from Lake Huleh, a few miles yonder in the northeast. I regret that I did not give one of them a job. The beeswax sold in this bazaar is of a dirty yellow color, mixed with many impurities; twenty per cent of it would have to be strained out: it put me in mind of the maple-sugar I saw brought into Detroit, Michigan, by Indians, in 1836, nearly one-fourth of it filth. I enjoyed my laugh at the local jests, so far as Hassan could interpret them to my feeble understanding. They are well characterized by the poet as local jests," those:

"Mirthful sayings, children of the place,
That have no meaning half a league away."

The better class of the men are in turbans and long robes, the
better class of the women in figured silks and headdresses of
golden-coins. Passing from the fairgrounds to a nooning under the
fig tree, my mind was aroused into uncommon activity, and I read
and wrote abundantly. Every traveler in this country seeks such a
noble fig tree to escape what Isaiah (49:10) calls *sharab*, "the heat
and sun" so oppressive here. I found it wholesome to review
various Scriptural expressions while reclining here. "As the trees
of the wood are moved with the wind" (Isaiah 7:2) is brought to
vivid recollection by a pleasant whiff that moves the fig leaves.
"Too young to have knowledge to say, My father, and my mother,"
(Isaiah 8:4), is suggested by a poor little wailing creature, scarcely
a week old, whose pale and feeble mother wins a little backsheesh
from me, encouraged thereto by my pitying look at the infant.
"The bur den taken away from off the shoulder, and the yoke from
off the neck" (Isaiah 10:21), occurs through the circumstance of a
fellah bringing a yoke of oxen into the fair for sale, removing their
yoke and the heavy packs with which he had loaded them.
"Judging the poor with righteousness, reproving with equity for
the meek of the earth" (Isaiah 11:4), comes from observing a cadi
or local magistrate, a mild, honest fellow, if ever I saw one,
walking among the people and summarily settling their disputes.
And this suggests other passages: "The firstborn of the poor shall
feed, and the needy shall lie down in safety" (Isaiah 14:30). "As a
ruinous heap" (Isaiah 17:1) is referable to the hilltop yonder,
where was once a flourishing town, but now nothing but a pile of
ruins. "A cloud of dust in the heat of harvest" (Isaiah 18:4) is
suggested by yonder Hermon, whose snowy crown dominates all
this land, and will an hour after sundown overflow all these
hillsides and valleys with his cooling dews. But I might go this
way all day. Repeating the close of Habakkuk's prayer here,
suggests that this combination of the fig, olive, and vine, being
the meat of the *field,* the *fold,* and the *vineyard,* embraces the
victualling of the land. The celebrated figs of Chios are ripened,
according to travelers' accounts, by hanging one unsavory fig among
the ripening ones. Out of the decaying fruit issue worms which,
entering the others, hasten maturity. This is a story, however, as a
conscientious   fig-eater,   I   prefer   not   to   believe;

and I turn my attention therefore to the green or dust-colored grasshopper, that has found a bit of wasted confectionery among the horses' feet, and recalls the passage in Isaiah 40:22, where God is represented sitting upon the circle of the earth, whose inhabitants are as grasshoppers. But now the day goeth away, the shadows of evening are stretched out (Jeremiah 6:4), and it is time to move forward to my intended place of rest. My last thought in this chapter shall refer to him whose name connects in such close associations the seven Masonic localities I have now described, viz.; Hiram Abif. Brother Albert Pike, in his *Morals and Dogmas of Masonry,* defines this name thus: The word Khairūm or Khūrūm is a compound one. Gesenius renders khūrūm by the word *noble* or *freeborn;* khūr meaning *white, noble.* It also means the opening of a window, the socket of the eye. Khri also means *white* or an *opening;* and khris, the orb of the sun, in Job 8:13, and 10:7. Krishna is the Hindu sun-god. Khur, the Parsee word, is the literal name of the sun.

PALESTINE LILY.
35

MOHAMMED RASCHID,
Pasha General of Syria.

In correcting the plates for the second edition, June 1, 1872 I am under the painful necessity of announcing the death of our distinguished Brother, whose portrait is given above, and to whom this volume, by permission, was dedicated.

His courtesies had afforded me so much satisfaction and solid advantage while traveling through his Jurisdiction, that I feel to mourn him as an old friend and benefactor.

His decease occurred about March 1, 1872, but I cannot secure the exact date. He had been recalled to Constantinople a short time before, under charges of maladministration, that sword of Damocles' under which every Turkish ruler continually sits. Being in ill health, and foreseeing his early death, he had united with one of the strictest sects of the Dervishes, and died soon after. It is by no means unlikely that his taking-off was hastened by the poison or bowstring of the government.

ABD-EL-KADER.

CHAPTER XXX.

DAMASCUS.

I T is a fact, and a most suggestive one to the reader of a well-filled book, that an experienced *traveler* gets impressions of a country with a freshness and vividness of form and color unknown to an *inhabitant*. What is but commonplace to *them* is uncommon to *him;* the languor of habit has not repressed its novelty and truth. He sees with unworn feelings. In Chapter X., I gave a minute account of my interesting journey from Beirut to Damascus. Nearly four thousand years ago, an old man named Abram (afterward Abraham) came down this way, accompanied by his wife and nephew (Genesis xii). They had large possessions of bondmen and cattle, but no children. His steward, or general manager, was one Eleazar, of this city of Damascus, which then, as now, was the gem of the East, a wealthy and beautiful emporium. Doubtless he pitched his tents outside the gates, as all caravans do, for at least one night, and, walking out alone in the solitude of the night, consulted the Divine Guide who had led him thus far upon his future course. Upon the determination of that night rested the future history of the Land of Canaan, then almost totally unoccupied by human beings. Had Abram pursued a *southern* or *western* course, instead of taking the way of the Jordan valley southwestward, the country called Palestine might never have been named in sacred writ. How much easier to understand these things looking upon the very places where Scriptural events occurred! Yonder is the path that Abram took: the historical consequences were that the Chosen Race possessed themselves of that region beyond the Jordan; returned to it again and again for 1,500 years; made of it the most renowned nation on earth; and, scattered as they are in every division of the earth, to this day they yet look for one more triumphant and permanent occupancy of Palestine. All this is due to Abram's choice that night; and to the same fact may be ascribed the comparatively insignificant fact of *my coming here* to "look over the land" granted to Abram and his seed. More than that: it is to the circumstance that occurred here, near this gate of Damascus, almost 4,000 years ago, that we owe the country of Palestine as our *Masonic country*. But for that, Joppa and Jerusalem, and Bethel and Bethlehem, and Succoth, and the passage of the Jordan, had had no names in Masonic tradition; Phœnicia had borne no relationship to our rites; the story of the Widow's Son of Tyre would have been lost to us. There might have existed a system of speculative Masonry, but how different from the sublime institution that now encircles and brightens the world!

These were the thoughts with which I entered Damascus. Having letters to his Excellency Mohammed Raschid Pasha, the Governor-General of Syria and Palestine, I secured an early opportunity, through Brother E. T. Rogers, H. B. M.'s Consul here, of an introduction, and found him indeed an affable gentleman, thirty-eight years of age, a Turkish officer of fine education and long experience, and possessing a high appreciation of Free-Masonry, into which he had been initiated several years before, while living in Smyrna. As I came in on the stage, I met his Excellency riding in the suburbs with his staff, and was struck by his fine horsemanship, which really is worth describing. He rode a horse of the best blood of Arabia, sitting him as though he were a part of the noble animal, and, as we passed, bowed with a nobility and dignity of manner known only in the East. I could see that he was fair and fat in flesh, like the Hebrew prophet (Daniel 1:15). He jerked the bit of his horse until he was mad with pain, and snorted, reared up, and bounded into the air, endeavoring to throw his rider; but the *Vali* sat him firmly— surely as he sits in the chair of government of this country, recalling a poetical thought of the days when

> "The chieftains of Damas* were proud to see
> The flashing of their swords' rich marquetry."

The Pasha wore stirrups so short as to bring his knees on the level of the pommel of his saddle. This is the invariable custom of the East, a mode of wearing the stirrups theoretically preferable, both

---

* The name here is never pronounced Damascus, but *Dames,* or Es-Shems.

to man and horse, to our own. It gives greater firmness to the seat, and causes the rider to depend for his safety on the clamp of the thighs rather than the balance of the body. As his heels touch the horse's flanks, he can use his spurs rapidly without changing the position of his legs. All equestrian nations that use saddles at all, ride with short stirrups—Arabs, Turks, Tartars, Persians, Magjars, Cossacks, English foxhunters, Circassians, Egyptians. The Mamelukes, acknowledged to be most excellent horsemen, had the stirrup so high as to form a letter V with each leg, the lower part being horizontal. This threw the muscles of the leg and thigh into the greatest possible prominence, developing the utmost adhesive power of the limb. It is claimed that a weak man, wearing short stirrups, can draw a strong man from the saddle who rides with his legs extended.

In my call upon this eminent man and Mason, he listened with marked interest to a narration of my plans, and promised me all the assistance I should require. At that time, he was chiefly absorbed in a contemplated movement to Palmyra (Tadmor); and as I was extremely anxious to visit that ancient relic of King Solomon's day, he placed me upon his staff, and tendered me the advantages of a position in his own military family. This was more than I could have anticipated, even from so generous a man. As the detachment was to embrace some three thousand men of all arms, he assured me of whatever help I needed in measuring the ruins of Tadmor and excavating the tombs. It was therefore a disappointment of no light magnitude that, for political reasons, the expedition was afterward postponed to a period so late that it was not in my power to join it. In fact, it was nearly twelve months before it was accomplished.

Before parting with this excellent brother, he presented me with an official paper directed to all Pashas, Governors, Sheiks, etc., under his authority, ordering them to see me accommodated with lodgings for myself and party, wherever I went, and provided with guards to pass over all dangerous places. My obligations for this courtesy are very great. The following is a translation of this important document, as made for me by Brother Nazif Meshaka, of Damascus, to whose kindness in many ways I was then and have been since greatly indebted:

A Buyuruldi to all whom it may concern: To the officers and chiefs of villages within the Pashalic of Syria. The bearer of our Buyuruldi, the American Emir, General Morris, is traveling to certain famous places. You, both small and great, must show him the greatest respect, and designate for him places of abode for himself and servants wherever he may go, and supply his wants at just prices. And in his going from one place to another, furnish him ample horsemen for his safety on the way, so that he may reach the localities he desires to visit. And pay him honor wherever he may go. And therefore, we have furnished you this Buyuruldi that you may act accordingly.

Dated 16th Zilhadjeh, 1284 (that is, March 26, 1868).

From a sketch of this distinguished ruler, written after my return I copy these extracts: The Pasha-General of Syria and Palestine resides at Damascus, eighty miles east of Beirut. I made haste to pay my respects to him, and to ask for his powerful protection. He examined my credentials, and appointed an evening to meet me at the office of the British Consul, Mr. Rogers, Master of the Lodge at Beirut. That meeting was to me a most interesting occasion; an humble individual from the far West, brought by the *influence of Freemasonry* alone, into the most cordial, and I may add, *confidential* intimacy with the immediate representative of the Ottoman Empire.

The Pasha gave me several hours of his time, nor was it until the mystical low 12 that we separated. I often met him afterward at his own palace.

The Pasha-General (or Vali), *Mohammed Raschid* by name, is a gentleman of pleasant and polished manners, short and compact in build, quick in comprehension, and thoroughly educated in the military and diplomatic service of his country. In personal intercourse, I found him philosophical, humorous, argumentative, and critical, by turns. He possesses a fine taste for poetry, and the *belles-lettres,* and recited for my gratification various passages from the poets of Turkey and Persia. His sense of the humorous is more *French* than Mohammedan; it was displayed in the relation of witty anecdotes of an Oriental type. Altogether, he had not one trait of my traditional idea of a Turkish Pasha.

Mohammed Raschid Pasha, the successor of "Cyrenius, governor of Syria" (Luke 2:2), has given proofs of uncommon vigor during the four years he has wielded this government, having made travel entirely safe by placing garrisons in the principal towns, and inflicting the sternest chastisement upon offenders. He was deeply interested in my errand. In common with all the craft of this country, he was profoundly astonished that a brother from the Western Hemisphere should traverse a quarter of the globe on a Masonic errand; but expressed his admiration and approval, giving me valuable information concerning the existence of an ancient form of Masonry and the chiefs (Sheiks) of the Desert tribes, of whom he related various anecdotes.

His name is the same as Haroun-al-Raschid, dear to every schoolboy's memory. This is also the familiar name for *Rosetta* in Egypt. I reminded him of this in our conversation, and referred to the warm friendship that existed between his great namesake and Charlemagne of France.

In his position, with the reputation he has acquired, such a man is more precious than fine gold, than the golden wedge of Ophir (Isaiah 13:12). God, who weighs the path of the just (26), has so weighed his.

In answer to his queries as to the purposes of the Masonic institution in the United States, I find from my existing notes that I told him the institution was introduced into our country prior to 1733. That in its membership many of the statesmen and soldiers of our country are affiliated, particularly naming Benjamin Franklin and George Washington. That in 1826, an unfortunate affair connected with the abduction of one William Morgan brought a storm of popular wrath upon the Order, which checked its spread for ten years. That the society has entirely recovered from this, and stands today one-third of a million strong, working in more than eight thousand lodges. That the charities of the Masons are large, and blest of the Most High God. That its principles of conciliation were strongly felt during all our late unhappy civil war, and are doing some part in restoring the era of national brotherhood and good feeling for which all good men pray. And finally, that our theory does not permit us to receive into our communion any but men of good morals, true and trusty. All of this agreed well with his own conception of the great fraternity.

My efforts to organize a Lodge at Damascus are recorded in the following article, written for an English paper:

THE FIRST MASONIC MEETING IN DAMASCUS.

Somebody has said, and very truthfully, that "Damascus is rightly named the oldest city of the world." It dates back, certainly, anterior to the days of Abraham (B.C. 1920, or thereabout), having been founded, according to the best records, by Uz, the son of Aram, the son of Shem, the son of Noah (Genesis 10:21-23). If we omit the first eleven chapters of Genesis, there has no recorded event occurred in the world's history but Damascus was in existence to receive it. Had the good hebdomadal now issued at Damascus under the auspices of H. E. Raschid Pasha, Governor-General, entitled *La Syria,* been commenced a few thousand years earlier, its files would certainly be a *thesaurus* of historical facts unequalled for value, because containing nothing less than that "universal history" which Sir Walter Raleigh and other aspiring composers meditated. Go back as far as you will in the past, and there was *always a Damascus.* In the writings of every century, for more than four thousand years, its name has been mentioned and its praises sung. To this old place, years are only minutes, decades only flitting trifles of time. She saw the foundation of Baalbec and Thebes and Ephesus laid; saw them grow into mighty cities, and amaze the world with their grandeur; saw them desolate, deserted, and given over to the owls and bats. She saw the Israelitish empire exalted, and she saw it annihilated. She saw Greece rise and flourish her twenty centuries—then die. *In her old age* she saw Rome founded, built, overshadow the earth with greatness—then perish. All that has ever occurred upon the earth Damascus has seen, and *yet she lives.* She has looked upon the dry bones of a thousand empires, and will probably see the tombs of a thousand more before she passes from the stage. Far more truthfully than the "seven-hilled" city of Rome does Damascus deserve the name of the *Eternal City.*

Perhaps all this is not much to the purpose in indicting an article upon "The First Masonic Meeting in Damascus," yet it is this which makes all the difference between one place and another. The new town of Pumpkinville, in the new State of Nebraska, is a more sightly object by far than this old city on the banks of the Baraba, as its river is far larger and more noble than this; but who can arouse any mental or spiritual glow in Pumpkinville? Every drop in the flow of the Baraba is historical. The very mud of which these walls of Damascus are constructed contains the dust of a thousand generations. Those overhanging hills yonder have witnessed in their grand reticence such sights as, could we rend their secrets from them, would fill volumes of history! And it is the consideration of these things that made my entry upon the top of the diligence, through that mountain-cleft and down by that singing stream, "a joy forever."

I had been in Damascus but a day when I paid my respects to H.

B. M. Consul, Bro. E. T. Rogers. This gentleman is acting in the absence of the Consul-General of Syria, Bro. Eldridge; but his own official position is here. He is the Worshipful Master elect of the Lodge at Beirut, Palestine (No. 415, Scotch Registry), while Bro. Eldridge is Deputy Grand Master of the district. The fame of Bro. Rogers as an exemplar of gentlemanly courtesy, benevolence, and the largest cosmopolitan friendship, has gone out, long years ago, and all that I can say in regard to it is just so much more. His knowledge of Arabic is remarkable; even here, where so many foreigners learned in that rich and abounding language are found. His French is that of a native. Standing as the representative of so great a nation, foremost among Syrian consuls, his own urbanity, shrewdness, knowledge of the people and their peculiarities of government, religion, and habits, place him far higher than any mere office could do.

My call upon "Bro. Rogers" (for so in unbent hours he delights to be styled) was at an opportune moment. We had "spiritual affinities" (whatever that expression means). An hour was sufficient to lay the foundation of a friendship that *mors non separabit*. I may forget a good many things that have occurred in my life (and hope I shall), but I never expect to forget this and subsequent conferences with the good Consul Rogers at Damascus.

Amongst my first requests (and goodness knows I made enough) was a personal introduction to our distinguished brother, the Governor-General of Syria, Raschid Pasha. This was readily had, and "we three" passed an evening together in Bro. Rogers' parlor, much to my gratification. At that time it was proposed that the Masonic brethren of Damascus should be invited ere long to come together in the same apartments, to become acquainted with each other, to take the preliminary steps, should prudence dictate, for the organization of a lodge in that city, and to hear some remarks of a Masonic nature from myself. This meeting was accomplished a few days later, and it is this that forms the basis of the present article, to which, I must confess, there has been a most unconscionable preface tacked on.

It was Tuesday, April 7, 1868, that this "first Masonic meeting in Damasens" was held. There were present ten out of the fifteen Masons residents of that city, viz: E. T. Rogers, Worshipful Master elect of Palestine Lodge (No. 415, Scotch Registry), Beirut, Syria; Joseph Pilastre, Lodge La Verité, Marseilles, France; Christophe

Delenda, Lodge Stella Ionia, Smyrna, Asia Minor; Nazif Meshaka, Palestine Lodge (No. 415), Beirut, Syria; Asari Messedié, ibid.; Mohee-ed-Deen, son of the Emir Abd-el-Kader, ibid.; Mohammed, son of the same, ibid.; Ali Ibn Khalil Mohassini, ibid.; Mustafa Sebace, ibid.; Saleh Izdachir Azm, ibid.; Robert Morris, Fortitude Lodge (No. 47), La Grange, Kentucky, United States, and Past Grand Master.

After the proper introductions and tea drinking—the latter being among the landmarks of Oriental life—and the preparation and ignition of a suitable number of cigarettes, your correspondent was called upon for his remarks. These I had written out in English. Bro. Rogers translated them into French, and a portion of them from that tongue into Arabic, for there was but one of the native brethren present (Bro. Meshaka) who knew any English. What I said would not be worth detailing here, except as it forms a part of the history of this transaction. It was designed to be a sketch of the practical influence of Freemasonry, particularly in the country from which I came, and in which, as my hearers had already been informed, I had played some part as a Masonic writer and oral instructor. I told them that "in the United States we had more than eight thousand lodges, two-thirds of all the lodges in the world; that these are divided into forty-five Grand Lodges; that there is very much zeal manifested amongst the members therein affiliated, who love one another and venerate the ancient Order; and that they had sent me to this distant land that I might see with my own eyes how many Masons are here, what kind of persons they are, and what is their condition, and tell them the facts when I return home."

I informed them that, amongst American travelers to Damascus, there are very many Freemasons; but they cannot find their brethren here for want of a lodge. When I notify them that in this city there are not less than fifteen of the brotherhood, they would be equally surprised and delighted. I assured them that, should they visit the United States, they would find lodges in every town and village. Our largest city, New York, not one-half so large as Constantinople, has alone more than one hundred Freemasons' lodges, and in every American lodge they would be greeted with welcome, and their acquaintance hailed with undissembled joy. Then I informed them that the grand objects of Freemasonry are the honor of God, the increase of brotherly love among men, and the relief of the poor and distressed. The world in which we live is afflicted with sorrow and cursed with selfishness.

Strangers are usually unkind to each other, or, at the best, indifferent; while those professing opposite creeds hate and worry each other. But in this ancient and worldwide institution we have a common religion—the worship of God—and a common language—that of sign, the hand-grasp, and the word; so that we both recognize and fraternize with each other through it. In its rites we are assimilated by solemn obligations, and thus, by duty as well as love, we become brothers. The world, it is true, cannot understand this; nor do we care that they should. Those who have not penetrated our charmed circle are slow to believe this; nor are we careful for that. We know it to be true. I, who for more than twenty years have traveled from lodge to lodge, studying and instructing—bearing the light of Freemasonry as upon a torch from heart to heart—I know that this claim is well founded. Ever since I left home, I have secured additional proofs of this. The steamer upon which I crossed the Atlantic had among its officers and passengers ten Freemasons. We recognized each other, and exchanged the undying proofs of sympathy and fraternal esteem. The steamer which brought me from Marseilles to Beirut was not wanting in the "good men and true" who bore their Masonic covenants gracefully. At Smyrna, where I remained for a few hours, the craft conducted me to their halls; heard my message gladly; entertained me with the largest courtesy; nor suffered me to depart until they had loaded me with their grateful burdens of sympathy, loving wishes, and prayers. At Beirut I found more than sixty Masonic brethren.

Then I said: "I came to this city (Damascus) a total stranger. Our kind host, Bro. Rogers, took me by the hand. His Excellency Raschid Pasha took me by the hand, welcomed me as a brother, offered me every facility in my mission that his exalted station permits, and has attached me to his staff as an honorary member during his proposed journey to Tadmor, the renowned city of King Solomon. The distinguished Emir Abd-el-Kader took me by the grip fraternal. In like manner, I have now been greeted by you. So that, only one week a resident of Damascus, I am no longer a stranger here, but an acquaintance, neighbor, brother—yea, a brother of the same Father—the Father in Heaven. Nor do I believe that ever we shall become strangers to each other again. There is a Lodge in which all good men hope to meet—a Master at whose feet all good men hope to worship and adore through the cycles of eternity."

I then informed them of the difference (of rituals merely) between American Freemasonry and that in which they had been instructed. I did this not to produce confusion, but to prevent it. Being nearly all young and inexpert in the practice of the Art—only one or two of them ever having visited lodges other than their own, I knew they would desire some light upon this subject, and indeed they were greatly entertained by the sketch of the *esotery* of Masonry which I communicated to them. This I followed by the poem "Our Vows." Speaking of the funeral practices of American Masonry, I sang for them the opening stanza of the ode which all our American brethren expect will some day be sung around our graves:

> "Solemn strikes the funeral chime
> Notes of our departed time;
> As we journey here below,
> Through a pilgrimage of woe."

I also sang a verse or two of "The Gavel Song," quite popular at present in American lodges, in which the peculiar concussion of that implement is introduced as the chorus. Following this, I exhibited my "Mark Master's mark," explaining my chosen device, "the Broken Column;" also my ring connected with the Lodge of Perfection, A∴and A∴R∴ and my token, in marble, of the Order of H—m. These things were absolute novelties to my hearers, not one of whom has a degree above the third.

But I might spin out the particulars of this pleasant meeting to a half ream. We adjourned "in peace and harmony" at a suitable hour; and as I assumed my couch at "Demetry's," I endeavored to conjure up the spirits of the departed visitors to Damascus, who could have shared in congenial mood all the events of the occasion —Abraham, Eliezer, Jacob, Elisha, Paul, the great Saladin; perhaps Mahommed himself, who, I suspect, was a very much better man than our Christian historians paint him. I called this group around me and mentally repeated before them the sentiments I bad just expressed. Every one, without exception, *endorsed my views.*

A few days subsequently to this meeting, a petition was drafted to the Grand Lodge of England, soliciting authority to organize and work King Solomon Lodge, at Damascus, Syria. This was signed by the following brethren: Bros. E. T. Rogers, H. B. M. Consul; Dr. P. Nataley, Nazif Meshaka, Secretary to American Vice-Consulate; A. Joseph Pilastre, LL.D; Caisar Messedie, Abbas Kulli Khan,

Persian Consul in Damascus; Mustapha Effendi Sabax, Inspector of Entailed Property of the Greek Mosques; Mohammed Ali Effendi Mohasin, Secretary of the Grand Court of Justice in Damascus; Mohammed Effendi, son of His Highness the Emir Abd-el-Kader. Several other brethren, native and foreign, who were temporarily absent, afterward attached their signatures to the petition. Several of the Beirut Masons did so. The following American Masons asked leave, upon an additional slip, to be attached, viz: Bros. Robert Morris, LL.D.; Samuel Hallock, of Lodge No. 9, Philadelphia, Pa., U.S.A.; and David W. Thompson, of Fulton City Lodge (No. 147), U.S.A.

In the petition which we sent forward from Beirut in the mail of April 22nd, the following facts are set forth: "There is but one Masonic lodge in this large and populous Pashalic of Syria, viz., Palestine Lodge (No. 415), working under warrant from the Grand Lodge of Scotland. This is at Beirut, seventy-five miles northwest from Damascus, a point always difficult of access, often inaccessible. Besides this, the nearest lodges are those of Alexandria, in Egypt, and Smyrna, in Asia Minor. The petitioners, although in good strength as to numbers and social position, and second to none in zeal and veneration for the Order, are thus practically debarred from all enjoyment and advantage as Masons; although united together by the most solemn and enduring covenants, they are almost strangers to each other; although amongst the crowds of tourists who annually throng Damascus are many competent to instruct them in their Masonic duties and obligations, yet, for want of organization, that privilege is lost; that Masonic charities languish from the same cause; and that there is no city over which the jurisdiction of the Grand Lodge of England extends in which the establishment of a lodge is so imperatively demanded, or where a respectable circle of members could so soon be found as at Damascus." All this I can heartily affirm, and would add that I never saw a company of Masons in which such large social, commercial, and political interests were represented as the fifteen at Damascus. I could not but hope that these facts would have due weight at headquarters, and that ere the hot season came on to put an end to the Masonic labor, a warrant would reach these shores and the organization be effected. In the garden of Bro. Rogers, there is an ancient mosque that seems to have been erected on purpose for a lodge-room; and in this I trusted to see King Solomon Lodge at work before my own fiftieth birthday came round. But in all this I was disappointed, the Grand Lodge of England refusing the petition on the ground that the petitioners were all members of lodges under other Grand Lodge jurisdictions.

My opinion of the religious condition of affairs at Damascus will appear from the following paper, written for a religious journal in the United States:

A SABBATH IN DAMASCUS.

It is on a pleasant morning, this of March 29, that I set out to spend a Sabbath in the ancient and beautiful city of Damascus. The western breezes mingle just enough of the flavor of Lebanon's frost and snow with the flavor of apricot blossoms that whiten the thousands of groves environing the city upon that same side, to soften the hot sunbeams that even in March tell of a torrid June and make all foreigners turn their backs upon Damascus before July. I had my matutinal meal at 7 A.M., composed of Damascus bread with the grit of cornmeal and the millstone in it, and honey that no bees of Hymettus could ever match, and fruit, jellies, appetizing and delicious, a boiled egg or two, good coffee, and butter, which every one, however, must salt to his own taste, for Damascus cooks will not salt it for you.

I had learned from one of the Protestant ministers here, that Sabbath services are divided into three parts, viz: Religious services in the Arabic language at 9 A.M.; the Sunday school immediately following it, also in Arabic; and services in the English language at 2 P.M. I am resolved, if possible, today to attend all three.

I hire a person who professes to know the way to the Protestant church, and give him five piastres (about thirty cents) for his trouble. It is a good half hour's walk (about a mile and a half) to the Christian quarters; and as neither of us can in the least understand the other's language, I am practically alone, having only to follow my guide and attend uninterruptedly to the objects around me. So we go past the crowd of donkeys, ready for hire, saddled and bridled, in the public square, each with his half-nude but bright-eyed, good-natured boy, who will run along contentedly all day, urging his beast upon a trot, if you will only give him a little *backsheesh* in the evening; past the groups of horse-traders, who buy and sell here every morning with loud words and gestures, and doubtless any amount of lying and swindling; right into the heart of the bazaars, all open and

driving their respective trades on this Sunday morning, as a
hundred generations have done in their places before them;
through all manner of crooked, narrow, filthy lanes, offensive to
sight and sound, thronged with miserable curs, one half too lazy
to get out of your way, the other half too surly; past hundreds of
donkeys, mules, horses, and camels, the latter swinging along
their way solemnly, and regarding nothing on the right hand or
on the left; past the mosques, at the gates of which are beggars
sitting with outstretched hands, clamoring for alms of Christians
as well as Moslems; past a group of dervishes with their conical
and most comical felt hats, and looking not at all the fanatics they
are said to be; and now we come into the Christian quarter; where
the shops are mostly closed, and where a vast ruin of many acres
in extent points to the scene of the horrid massacre of July 9-11,
1860. My guide, mistaking his way, takes me to the house of Rev.
Mr. Robson, who by good fortune is to preach the first sermon
today. He invites me into his house with Christian cordiality, and
gives me the opportunity, while preparing for church, to glance
over his library of excellent editions of good books. He is evidently
from Great Britain, for all the volumes bear London imprints.

We walk together to the church, he showing me more in detail
the ruined houses to which I have already referred. Happily, he
was out of the city the week of the fearful massacre, and so
escaped. The church is a handsome stone edifice, the walls nearly
thirty inches thick, capable of seating 200 or 300 persons. It is
divided longitudinally by a green curtain separating the males
from the females, and there is a separate door for each sex to
enter and depart. Twelve windows lighten the church. At each
door hangs a heavily quilted curtain, the corner of which is to be
lifted when you enter.

This is the Protestant Church of Damascus. About fifty persons
are present, mostly natives, in their own costumes. Among them,
I was introduced to the venerable, pious, and influential Dr.
Meshaka, American Vice-Consul here, and truly a pillar of the
church. He has since deceased. His two sons are likewise active
members of this congregation. There were also present Rev. Mr.
Crawford, formerly of Washington County, N. Y., and Rev. Mr.
Wright, of Ireland, two ministers associated with Mr. Robson in
this missionary work.

The service began by a song in Arabic to the tune of *Ortonville,* a
prayer by Dr. Robson, to which the deep gutturals of that language
gave great solemnity, and the reading of a chapter in Genesis. Then

two infants were baptized, one the grandchild of Dr. Meshaka, the other a child of Rev. Mr. Crawford. The sermon was short, and, as I could not understand it, I gave more especial attention to the surroundings. Behind the pulpit was painted, in Arabic characters, the Lord's Prayer, and upon tablets on each side the Ten Commandments.

All the natives wear slippers, which they can readily shuffle off and on, as occasion requires. One elderly person I noticed, getting tired of our method of sitting, dropped his slippers, drew his feet up under him in the snuggest manner, and so seemed to enjoy himself. Almost every male person, particularly the boys, wear the red cap *(tarboush),* which they never take off in church, in the house, or, I presume, even in bed. The women had bright-colored handkerchiefs round the back of the head and neck, and large white sheets wrapped round them, as is universal in this country. It seems corpse-like until you get accustomed to it. Children ran about and were noisy during all the service. This church has a genuine American stove and pipe, really homelike.

The Arab language does not sound agreeable to me in a sermon. It is dry and hard, like the basaltic rocks with which so much building is done here. Yet as a written language, it is one of the most fruitful and perfect in the world.

This church was only finished last year, at an expense of about $6,000. The floor is of white and red marble, tessellated in handsome style, but the main body of the church has little or no ornamentation.

At the close of the services came Sunday school. In these exercises I took an interested part, telling the young people of the joys we Christians anticipate

"In those everlasting gardens
Where angels walk and seraphs are the wardens;
Where every flower brought safe through death's dark portal
Becomes immortal."

And I sang for them, in English, such songs as "Jesus by the Sea," and "Shall we gather at the River?"

The Sunday-school exercises were followed by services in the English language, conducted by Rev. Mr. Crawford. Only eight or ten persons were present, nearly all English and American. As one

of the ministers accompanied me to the hotel, he pointed out the
reputed house of Ananias, described in the ninth chapter of Acts
as "a certain disciple at Damascus," whom the Lord commanded
in a vision "to go into the street which is called Straight, and
inquire in the house of Judas for one called Saul of Tarsus, for
behold he prayeth." The house of Judas is also shown, and the
place where Paul was let down from the wall in a basket, and
anything else you choose to ask for.

I was also further shown the ruins of the Christian quarter, laid
waste in 1860 by the fierce fanaticism of the natives. All was
destroyed, burnt, or plundered, save such houses as stood
abutting upon Moslem houses, and which could not be destroyed
without endangering the latter. Mr. Crawford computes the
number of persons murdered in this city at 2,500. There is a
feeling of satisfaction in reflecting that the Pasha, the Governor-
General of that period, was put to death by his Government for
his participation in the crime, together with one hundred and fifty
of his assistants.

Returning to my hotel, I met a few of the low-wheeled wagons
beginning very recently to be used in Damascus for the
conveyance of heavy goods through the city. It is curious that I
should stop and look with so much interest upon them. Listening
to the conversation of American and English friends long resident
here, and who are proficient in the spoken Arabic, I conclude that
the use of that language imparts a deep guttural tone to the voice,
which grates harshly upon the unaccustomed ear. As the Italian
is the sweetest, so the Arabic and the Turkish are the least
musical of tongues. Yet the poetry of either, when properly recited,
is not unpleasant.

Thus passed my Sabbath in Damascus. A little before night I
took another stroll, following the telegraph wires for my own
security, and observed the Pasha's palace and gardens, the
castle, and the other sights. The great Tree of Damascus, forty
feet in circumference, I often visit. What an enormous age it
must have attained to! I like to stand near the doors of the
mosques and observe the worshippers. First, they wash their
head, feet, and hands. Then, standing erect with their faces
toward the south (toward Mecca), they go through the
traditional gymnastics and repetitions of their faith. They show
no displeasure at my watching them, nor, if I will leave my boots
at the door, do they object to my entering. But I have too much
respect for my boots, lest they should walk off by themselves

before I return! This religion of theirs, sincerely as it may be believed and published, does not prevent one of the faithful from robbing a Christian—at least, this is their own confession.

I was here two weeks, intensely busy making observations and taking notes, which I will insert, as usual, somewhat at random.

Watching the operations of that excellent institution the Sunday school with prayerful interest, I experienced a natural pride in the reflection that to my own country must be accredited the origin of Sunday schools. Ludwig Hacker founded the earliest one on record, viz: in 1740, at Ephrata, Pennsylvania, and continued it regularly until, in 1777, the battle of Brandywine broke it up. That opened by Robert Raikes, so often referred to, was not commenced until 1782.

In one of my rambles, I took considerable time in visiting a Turkish mosque. I was of course obliged to uncover my feet before entering. As this custom is so thoroughly Oriental, it will be well to quote some thoughts from Dr. Oliver, exhaustive of the subject. In the early ages of the world, one important indication of pure worship consisted in *taking off the shoes* when about to enter a temple dedicated to God. This was a very ancient observance, as we may infer from the interview with which Moses was favored, at the Burning Bush. The heathen nations used the same method of expressing the humility of their devotion. Not only did the wise and judicious Pythagoras command his disciples to worship *with bare feet,* as an expressive symbol of humility and contrition of the heart, but even the grosser worship of the Greeks and Romans enjoined the same practice. In public religious processions, the priests walked barefooted; the highborn ladies of Rome did not dare to enter the Temple of Vesta with covered feet; and in Greece, the female votaries walked barefooted in the procession of Ceres. The same usage prevailed equally in India and the islands to the west of Europe; and even the American savages thought that uncovering the feet while in the act of devotion was a sublime method of paying honor to the Deity. Going barefoot was a sign of much sorrow, assumed by David to express his woeful expulsion from his own country by his rebellious son; and distressed captives used it in their bondage in another country. In entering the Turkish mosque at Beirut, therefore, I was performing an ancient Masonic and devotional exercise in *removing my boots.* I left them outside, however, in charge of the person employed to guide me through the city. No other ceremony was required of me but this. I removed the thick curtain that separated the inner apartment from the outer, reminding me of the inner veil of the sanctuary, and, with hat on head, stepped in and noticed as long as I chose the ceremonies of Turkish worship. Every worshipper had carefully washed his face and his feet at a copious fountain near the door of entrance, and the whole ceremony of worship was pursued with gravity, decorum, and silence, more resembling the work of a Freemason's lodge than anything I can compare it with. The forms being the same as all Mohammedans use in public worship, I will describe them again. First, the worshipper opens his hands and raises them until the thumb of each is directly under the corresponding ear, the fingers being erect. This is the only comical part of the proceeding. It does indeed remind me of an asinine movement in that most absurd and ludicrous of travesties, *The Sons of Malta.* As the worshipper makes this initial movement, he says to himself, not very loudly, *Allah hu akbar* (God is great). Then whispering to himself some prayers from the Koran, he brings his hands down and folds them together over the girdle which constitutes as essential a part of his dress as a soldier's sword-belt does of his uniform. While the hands are thus folded, he recites the first chapter of the Koran, and other sentences from the same. Then he bends gravely forward to a horizontal attitude, places his hands upon his knees, and repeats three times an ascription of praise to the Great God. Then rising, again he cries, *Allah hu akbar.* Now he falls on his knees, and bends forward to the floor, laying his open hands thereon, and his face on the floor between them. This movement brings his feet perpendicular, resting upon his toes; in other words, the soles of his feet are turned backward and entirely exposed. With his body bent forward in that manner, the worshipper repeats three formulas of petition and praise. He now rises to his knees, settling back upon his heels, and repeats further prayers. He has now completed one round of the ceremonies, called a *Rekah,* occupying about one minute. Rising up to the same spot where he began, he then commences a second *Rekah,* exactly as before, and, if devotionally inclined, will even complete a third or more before he retires.

As I stood "within the veil" of that Turkish mosque and observed a hundred or more of the Mohammedan worshippers, representing so many countries under the rule of the Crescent—Levanters, Syrians, Persians, Nubians, Egyptians, Circassians, Arabs—I asked myself, in a spirit of unprejudiced inquiry, whether these grave and impressive solemnities have any soul in them! Every one turned himself in the direction of Mecca, where it is believed by them Mohammed has for twelve centuries lain buried. Every one seemed wholly absorbed in devotion, manifesting a power of isolation and abstraction quite surprising. These ceremonies are the traditional exercises of 1,200 years, and practiced by more than two hundred millions of worshippers. I cannot look on them otherwise, therefore, than with respect as representing, poor and heartless as they may be, the devotions of nearly one-fourth the human race. To a Freemason, to whom all ancient national usages have (or had in their origin) important symbolical references, these Mohammedan services of prayer are worthy of the closest attention.

Divested of their references to the arch-impostor of the Orient, Mohammed, how beautifully appropriate would be these entire forms of worship in the Freemason's lodge! One thing remarkable in the Oriental usages is, when in my remarks on the Masonic lodge at Smyrna I had occasion to name the name of God, every one rose, without any call from the Master's gavel! This is solemn and grand, being precisely the lesson inculcated on the Fellow Craft in the important part of his degree.

> "That NAME! I saw it o'er the Master's chair,
>   That hieroglyphic bright; and, bending low,
> Paid solemn homage at the emblem there,
>   Which speaks of God, before whom all should bow."

As evidence of the fidelity of the Moslems to their forms of worship, I instance the case of a Turkish family we had on board our Mediterranean steamer. The head of the family, at certain hours of the day (one of them, I particularly noticed is "high twelve"), spreads his carpet upon the deck (having first, I suppose, washed his face and feet), casts off his overshoes, and performs the entire ceremony, just as I have described it, regardless of the jostling of the sailors and the observations of by-standers. I suppose he found out the direction of Mecca (southeast from there) by the ship's compass, as the Jews discover the location of Jerusalem when they prepare to pray.

Some of my readers will understand the esoterical application of my remarks if I say that, however Freemasonry may again spread throughout the Eastern world, as I hope and believe it will, and whatever influences it may exercise in removing national prejudices and restoring ancient brotherhoods, and I sincerely believe in its efficiency for this, yet *Adoptive Masonry* can never be introduced into Turkish families, so long as the present system of isolation and veiling is practiced. The wife of the Turk who was a passenger with us, sat all day behind a screen, formed on one side of the ship's deck (they are deck passengers), and when she came out, her whole form was closely veiled. Observing her on one occasion sitting with her back toward me, and apparently unveiled, I quietly slipped round to the front. But not so quietly but that she heard me. By the time I was in a position to *take an observation,* the thick cotton cloth was drawn over her face and entire form, and I have no doubt she was laughing to herself at the failure of my attempt. The veil of Jephthah's daughter will, therefore, not be raised while Mohammedan customs prevail. In Shoberl's *Persia,* illustrations are given of this custom of veiling. He says: "There are Armenians who would not know their own wives were they to find them in the arms of another man. Every night before they unveil, they extinguish the light, and most of them never uncover their faces in the daytime. An Armenian returning from a long journey is not sure to find the same wife. He cannot tell whether she may not be dead, and whether some other woman may not have stepped into the place of the deceased." This is very bad.

The books say that in the Great Mosque of Damascus is preserved the copy of the Koran that Othman had in his hand when he was assassinated; but I could learn nothing of it here. From the top of the minaret of this mosque, I could see what Æschylus describes as

> "The wandering Arabs, mounted on their camels,
> Along the tufted plain outstretching wide."

I look eastward from this minaret, over the boundless Desert from whence Abraham and Jacob and Zerubbabel came, where a human cry falls flat and echoless on the wild waste, muffled and dull, like my voice three months afterward in the sacred chamber of Cheops. The west side of Lebanon, being terraced, presents varieties of infinite forms. The summits often appear toothed like a saw, the sides torn and creased; sometimes a hill is in the strangest form of a cone; the walls of the cliffs are often perpendicular to a great height. I should like to see a good painting made from this point.

They tell fearful stories here of the locust. About the year B.C. 128, no less than 800,000 persons perished in Egypt and Libya from diseases generated by the putrefaction of locusts, which had infested the land that year in unparalleled numbers. About A.D. 406, Palestine was visited with such swarms of locusts that they darkened the sun. After eating every green thing, they perished in countless hosts, and produced pestilence by their death. The Arabic name of this "Scourge of God" is *Sarsar*. In Hebrew it was *Tslatsal,* as in Dent. 28:42. There is a sparrow called by himself *Smurmur* (and his own pronunciation is adopted by the people), that uses up the locust as thoroughly as the English sparrow did the measuring worm in the New York parks.

Walking the bazaars recalls my experience of four weeks ago at Smyrna. Here are representatives of all nations. The Aleppines and Northern Syrians, with their fur-lined jackets, brush against the Arab with his scanty garb of Desert life. The Armenian in blue, sober costume jostles the Jew in black. The Persian, with dangling sleeves and high, bell-shaped, conical (and comical) cap of black wool, exchanges curses with the ubiquitous dervish; while the American *ego* laughs at all, while eating an inimitable apricot tart, and is doubtless laughed *at* by all. The sheik's *abah* or cloak recalls St. Paul's garment of that name, which he unfortunately left at Troas (2 Timothy 4:13) when he needed it at Rome; also his figure, "the cloak of covetousness" (1 Thess. 2:5), which I am afraid fits these Desert Arabs as close as a cloak worn by a street operator in Wall Street. The manner of trading suggests the term "uttermost farthing" (Matt. 5:26) used by Jesus, for these merchants *do* cut their prices down to the ultimate *para* in making your change. If the Missionaries are not prejudiced in their opinions of the natives before conversion, their character is low and degraded as that expressed by Isaiah so long ago (9:17): "Every one is a hypocrite and an evil-doer, and every mouth speaketh folly;" "a people of unclean lips; very vulgar; their hearts fat; their ears heavy; their eyes shut" (6).

I observed the rich men's houses, with their single door "duly tyled" on the inside by the *bowa* (porter), who sits and dozes and smokes on his stone bench there day and night. Also the poor men's houses, a single story of rough stones, their mud roofs green with grass, the owners ragged and filthy, sitting and dozing, and smoking *their* poor lives out; in one instance, kneeling and praying on the housetop, "right before folks," facing the south toward Mecca, as all good Moslems should.

The position of Damascus being in a military point of view absolutely indefensible, the city has often changed masters. At the present

day, any company of soldiers who will plant a few cannon or
mortars on yonder heights, is master of Damascus. Our
accomplished brother Lamartine says: "Damascus is stamped on
the world's map by the finger of Providence as the site of a great
city."

The streets of Damascus are pleasant combinations of
slaughterhouse and privy. Some poet gives me a few lines
appropriate to this description:

"Many a grim and loathsome lane
Swarming with the outcast children of disease and want and pain,
Where the foulness of pollution on the pavements, on the walls,
Reeks and fumes like witch-sweat poison that in hidden cavern
    falls."

To walk here at night, it used to be said, four dangers await you:
either you will touch a leper, or you will be kicked by a camel, or
bitten by a dog, or fall into a pit. You *might* suffer from all four.
The profanity of the people is wonderful. As much ingenuity is
used in the invention of new oaths in Arabic, as in the discovery
of Howe's sewing machine. I should, like to see the notice set up
here that a good boy of mine has posted up in the railroad office
at Memphis junction, Kentucky: "No swearing allowed here!" It
would be a stunner. I boarded at Demetry's Hotel, in Damascus,
for two weeks. Like all Damascus houses, it has its fountain in
full play, throwing up jets of silvery spray into the air, bubbling
and murmuring with soothing sound, and really very nice. There
I used to sit looking out of my second-story window, which was so
low that the camels would stick their snaky heads into my
bedroom and disturb my morning repose. Here is a page of notes
made from that locality:

The costume of that group is simple, and reduced almost to first
principles: a blue cotton shirt descending below the knees and tied
with a girdle, the legs and feet being exposed; a cloak *(abah)* of
coarse, heavy camel's-hair cloth, usually striped black and white
vertically, with holes for the arms, the whole cloak simply a square
piece of cloth. Sometimes the foot is covered with the buskin, which
is nearly the ancient *cothurnus,* as the Classical Dictionary shows.
Here comes a Brahmin, whose fair complexion, regular features, and
high forehead mark the purity of his Aryan origin. He needs the
O. B. of a Past Master concerning "haughtiness." Here comes a
Barbary Jew in a long, loose wrapper of dark silk, a red morocco
belt around the waist, and an undershirt of striped silk with silver

buttons. He has an aquiline nose, curved like an eagle's beak, a broad thoughtful brow, large inimitable eyes, a face perfectly oval, with an olive tint and movable lips. Here comes an opium-eater, recognizable by the dull, dead appearance of his eyes. Now I am watching a regular gang of Arabs, whom a traveler in North Africa thus describes: "Their notions of *meum* and *tuum* are somewhat vague, their moral code discouragingly shaky. As highway robbers, they are a success; and their achievements in grand and petty larcenies are of the most eminent. To lie when the truth will serve them as well; to move crookedly from sheer love of double dealing; to play the knave systematically; to practice pious frauds; to covet a neighbor's goods, and seduce a neighbor's wife, are the cardinal principles of their creed. A most unchristian hatred of Christian dogs is best manifested in blood." Here comes an alarmed horse, unaccustomed to the noise of cities; but his owner pats his neck and speaks to him in language of the Desert, and the creature turns his head and gazes into his master's face with a look quite as human as the master wears. Now I notice the deep grunting bass of the camels, the resonant bray of the donkey, the hoarse guttural oaths of the Arabs, the shrill treble of the donkey-boys, the sight of the hideous sepulchral-looking camels with their shapeless splay-feet like huge sponges, their long crooked necks, and serpent-like heads—a queer *tout ensemble*. Here comes a hermit, over his breast and shoulders a miserable covering of rags. His skin dry, horny, and blotched with large scales, which on his knees look like ancient mail. Somebody has said this is the only country in the world where romance enters into the daily life of the people, and the dreams of the poet ripen into realities. And now I observe one of the noblest-looking Arabs I have yet seen. He is tall, thin, his beard of uncommon whiteness and length, his face dried, scarred, wrinkled, costume clean, turban white, red jacket and sash, white trousers, red slippers. The ancient Ionian tunic was made of linen, having short, loose sleeves. The Jews here dress better than in Egypt, where the costume of the lower class is a yellow cap and gabardine, distinctive of his race. His misery and squalid poverty there are stamped upon him. Now comes a group of women who have hired a lot of donkeys to ride to the cemetery. An experienced lady observer describes the dress of a woman at Acre which resembles one of these. She wore a tight-fitting, crimson jacket, richly worked in gold, over a white satin chemisette heavily embroidered, a row of small gold buttons up the front, which was cut very low, displaying the neck and bosom. Over this were full Turkish trousers (shintians) of rich silk and, falling loosely over this, a straight skirt or petticoat of the same stuff, terminating in a train behind. A golden girdle was around her waist, and she wore dainty little slippers and a little round cap. In short, her make-up is fearfully elaborate. A group of Bedouins, with their long guns slung on their shoulders, their black cloaks fluttering in the wind, riding quaint, ungainly camels that jerk themselves along by moving both feet on a side at once, like pacing (racking) horses. Now comes along a dervish, who, seeing me angry at an insult from a fellow in the street, kindly suggested that whenever he was mad, he always repeated the alphabet to himself before he spoke! Now we have a merchant, dressed in this style: a long, red, silk gown; black cloak of camel's hair over the gown; red tarboush, with a handkerchief rolled over it, of green and yellow, in the form of a turban; white trousers; large red shoes with yellow slippers over them; blue sash; belt containing sword and large, showy pistols. And now a group of tourists. This page would be incomplete did I not refer to the costume adopted by tourists fearful and wonderful indeed. One of these (British, I suppose, from his speech) wore a most exaggerated dress of coarse tweed stuff of the loudest pattern, having a short shooting-jacket, full of pockets, the tightest of pantaloons, the most complicated straps of leather crossing his breast, a small Scotch cap with silver thistle, and above all wearing an enormous nose, ruddy, colored with pale ale and exposure to the sun—his voice, as he hails me sitting in my window, "like the clarion's blast" (whatever a *clarion* is; I'm sure I do not know). An Arab sheikh, introduced to me in my bedroom, seems extremely anxious for me to adopt the nomadic life, offering, if I would accompany him into the Desert, to be my father, mother, brother, sister, and all my relatives. I could not quite swallow his protestations, although I had heard of one of these sheikhs whose name was Abd-el-Hag, *the slave of Truth.* In the parlors of houses here, they have large mirrors set in the walls on all four sides, with divans covered with embroidered damask for seats. They run more to looking glasses than any other people in the world. And here comes a large iron-gray horse, strong and splendidly built, a noble specimen from the Shurmur stock. No price is set on such an animal here; the owner laughs in your face when you ask him for it, and is only mollified by *backsheesh,* or a handful of cigarettes, which amounts to the same thing. Looking north from my window, I gaze in the direction of Baalbec, where are the great stones alluded to in former pages. If some thoroughly instructed architect of our country would simply follow up traces of all the beveled (rabbeted) stones remaining *in situ* in Syria and Palestine, it might be a clue to the whole subject of ancient architecture. In this same direction, too, I have an outlook toward Riblah, and a vision of the great Nebuchadnezzar attaching itself to the place. Here he waited, immersed in his mighty projects, while one of his armies was besieging Tyre and one Jerusalem. The sacred city being captured after a seven-month siege, the spared captives were led here bound and heart-broken, to be dealt with in despotic judgment (Jeremiah 40). There that Napoleon of the sixth century B.C. sat, "the stretching of his wings filling the breadth of the land" (Isaiah 8:8), so that he could at the same time, by *aides-de-camp* and couriers, direct the siege of Tyre and the siege of Jerusalem, and yet watch and countermine the plotting of conspirators at home. The plane tree yonder is the largest tree of these regions. Readers of Pliny will remember his description of one in Lycia, measuring thirty feet in diameter, in which the Roman Governor, Licinius Mercianus, gave a dinner to eighteen guests. De Candolle, in *Physiologie Végétale,* refers to one in the valley of Bussekdere, three leagues from Constantinople—a plane-tree one hundred feet high and twenty-three in diameter, its shadow extending over 500 square feet. Here comes an Arab with a long red dress streaming on the wind, his spear poised in the air, dashing at full gallop down the basalt-paved road. And next is the professional oilman, saturated with grease. He sweats oil, literally "larding the lean earth;" with alkali he would make 150 pounds of honest soap.

It will naturally interest the reader to know how an American Mason, a stranger in the East, whose knowledge of the Arabic language is exceedingly limited, can give and receive such evidences of a Masonic nature as will render it safe for him to exchange the secrets of Freemasonry. I cannot make this matter entirely clear in a printed volume, but will say that much of the recognition is connected with the exhibition of a *certificate,* called among us a *diploma,* furnished us by our Grand Lodges preparatory to going abroad. As every lodge visited in the Old World endorses the fact and date of that visit upon the certificate, great facility is thereby given to the Masonic traveler in moving from place to place; and, upon the whole, the visit to a strange □ is easier in those countries than in our own.

Among the foreign consuls throughout the Holy Land, much the larger number are Freemasons, and it was plain to see that even their diplomatic functions were made easier by this key to a Mohammedan's heart.

Among the lower classes, however, there exists an intense prejudice against Freemasonry, amounting to bigotry. This is seen in various things. When two Arabs quarrel, it shows the most bitter feeling for one to call the other a *Jew* (Yahoodi); but if the other retaliates by calling his opponent Fermâson (that is, a *Freemason*), there is nothing for it but a fight!

This city embalms the name of the Mason brother, soldier, and statesman, Fuad Pasha, who died Grand Vizier of Turkey. Sent here in 1860 by the Turkish Government to repress disorders and punish the guilty murderers of the Christians, he displayed the highest qualities of a stern yet humane ruler.

This man would have been deemed a remarkable one in any age and any nation. So able, enlightened, and progressive a statesman s not today to be found in Europe. He was a good linguist, was

forward in science, a poet, and a writer. His political career was
active and brilliant. The terrible massacres at Damascus in 1860,
described in this volume in connection with the name of Abd-el-
Kader, were put down and punished under his stern
superintendence; shortly after which he was appointed Grand
Vizier. In 1863, he resigned that post and became War Minister,
then Minister of Foreign Affairs. He was born in the year 1814.
To such men the maxim of the *Zendavesta* fitly applies: "We
praise all good thoughts, all good words, all good deeds, which are
and will be, and we likewise keep clean and pure all that is good."

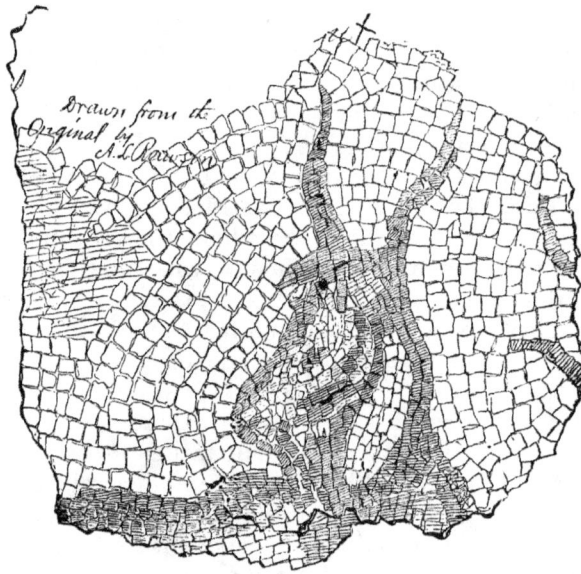

MOSAIC GOAT'S-HEAD.

CHAPTER XXXI.

URING my stay in Damascus an interview was arranged for me, through the courtesy of Brother Nazif Meshaka, with the thrice-celebrated Ex-Sultan of the Arabs, His Highness Abd-el-Kader.

This illustrious Arab, whose chivalrous defense of the persecuted and distressed at Damascus, in 1860, has ennobled Freemasonry and human nature itself, was born in May 1807, near Oran, in Algeria, North Africa. His father was a celebrated Marabout, a class of Muslims who profess extraordinary devotion to the religion of Mohammed. At the age of five, the lad could read and write; at twelve, he was proficient in the Koran and religious works, and traditions of his creed; at fourteen he was enrolled as a Hafiz, or person who had committed the entire Koran to memory. He is a man who, even at the age of sixty-one, exhibits fine symmetry and compactness of figure, being about five feet six inches high, and having a frame formed for untiring activity. As a horseman and swordsman, he is unexcelled.

The countenance of Abd-el-Kader, in his prime, was of the purest classic mould, and singularly attractive from its expressive and almost feminine beauty. His nose, middling-sized and delicately shaped, was a pleasing mean between the Grecian and Roman types. His lips, finely chiseled and slightly compressed, bespoke dignified reserve and firmness of purpose; while large, lustrous, hazel eyes beamed from beneath a massive forehead of marble whiteness, subdued and melancholy softness, or flushed with the rays of genius and intelligence.

This splendid specimen of the Arab race of North Africa, married at the age of fifteen, agreeably to the injunction of the Koran, "Marry young;" but, contrary to the practice of Muslims generally, he was content with one wife. At the age of sixteen, he made the pilgrimage to Mecca in company with his father.

In 1830, the capture of Algiers by the French opened the way for the exercise of his patriotic impulses. At the age of twenty-three, he began to move the hearts of his people by an eloquence which ranked him at once as one of the masters of human speech. He formed a league of the Arab tribes against the invaders, and on the 21st of November 1832, was elected by acclamation their *Sultan* His speech of acknowledgment was an effort perhaps never paralleled. Not for minutes, but for hours did the soldier-orator pour forth one continued stream of burning and impassioned eloquence. He expatiated, in heart-rending tones, on the sins, the iniquities, the crimes, the horrors, which polluted the land. In vivid terms, he depicted Heaven's judgments overtaking a godless and abandoned people; and now again he conjured up before the minds of his audience, in characters of flame, the appalling picture of their country ravaged by the infidel, their domestic homes violated, their temples desecrated.

For years he conducted this war, with varied success, against the French, when a temporary peace was concluded, and Abd-el-Kader began to establish his government on the principles of peace. A mint was opened and various coins struck, rising in value from four cents to one dollar, each having upon one side the words, in Arabic, "It is the will of God." Cannon foundries and manufactories of muskets were established. He even designed to form schools and colleges, but the exigencies of his active life never permitted him the opportunity. For three years he devoted his immense energies to the arts of civilization and national improvement; and could he have continued unmolested this pacific career, it is impossible to over-estimate his influence as one of the great men of his age.

Being a man of large possessions, he imitated the conduct of Washington in refusing all personal compensation from the national treasury. Noted for his liberality, he spent his own surplus of income year by year, in assisting the poor, the traveler especially, and those who had been disabled in the war. His military code has this paragraph concerning himself: "Il Hadgi Abd-el-Kader cares not for this world, and withdraws from it as much as his avocations will permit. He despises wealth and riches. He lives with the greatest plainness and sobriety. He is always simply clad. He rises in the middle of the night to recommend his own soul and the souls of his followers to

God. His chief pleasure is in praying to God, with fasting, that his sins may be forgiven."

On the 18th of November 1838, war was recommenced between Abd-el-Kader and the French, and continued until the 23d of December 1847, when he finally surrendered himself to that great power, and was taken to France. In his surrender, he had stipulated to be removed to either Egypt or Syria; but the French Revolution of 1848, and the establishment of the new order of affairs in France, nullified the bond, and he was detained in various fortresses until 1853. While there, he composed two remarkable volumes, one on "The Unity of the Godhead," the other called "Hints for the Wise, Instruction for the Ignorant." The first is an exposition of Mohammedanism as against Paganism.

In 1853, a pension from the French Government of $20,000 per annum was settled upon Abd-el-Kader for life. Having given his parole not again to engage against the French, he settled first at Broussa, in Turkey, then, in 1855, at Damascus, in Syria, where on his arrival the entire population turned out to meet and greet this distinguished chief. More than one thousand of his old chiefs and soldiers gathered round him here, and constituted themselves his suite and bodyguard. Of these, I saw many while in Damascus. He opened a theological school in Mohammedan doctrines, with about sixty scholars, and twice a day taught them the dogmas of his faith.

We now come to that epoch in the life of Abd-el-Kader which gives him, in the sight of Freemasons and of all lovers of justice and mercy, so distinguished a place. Heretofore, we have chiefly viewed him as a brave and accomplished warrior and indomitable patriot, first in the attack, last in the retreat, neither sparing himself or others while there was a hope of accomplishing good in his invaded country. Then we viewed him patiently submitting to adverse fortune, going cheerfully into exile, and devoting his splendid gifts of mind and soul to the spiritual improvement of his race. But Providence had reserved him to be the protector of Christians. Strange and unparalleled destiny; he, an Arab, was to throw his guardian ægis over the outraged majesty of Europe; a descendant of the Prophet was to shelter and protect the spouse of Christ.

The Christians of Syria, who form already a great and constantly increasing proportion of the population, have ever been viewed by the Turks with gloomy jealousy. Their increasing numbers, wealth, and prosperity are to the Turks a perpetual source of exasperation exciting in their breasts feelings of hatred and revenge. Of all the parties who most exhibit these sentiments, the Druses, who inhabit Mount Lebanon, are the most vindictive. In May 1860, a civil war between them and the Christians, which had long been fostered and encouraged by the Turks, broke out, and in a few weeks made the Lebanon district a scene of fire and blood. The Christians, dispersed and unprotected, were hypocritically inveigled into the Turkish garrisons, where, as soon as collected in sufficient numbers, they were massacred by thousands.

Abd-el-Kader, hearing of the storm that was about to burst over the Christians, wrote to the Druse chiefs, warning them of the consequences to themselves of such an outbreak, and characterizing their plundering propensities as unworthy of men of good sense and wise policy. Three times he called upon the Governor of Damascus, and stated his apprehensions of an outbreak, before he could secure a distribution of arms to his followers. On Monday, July 6, 1860, in the afternoon, the slaughter began. The town had risen. Abd-el-Kader hastened to meet and restrain the rioters. He harangued them; threatened them; expostulated with them; but in vain. In three hours, the Christian quarter of Damascus was in flames.

The hot blast, fraught with the moans of the tortured and the shrieks of the defiled, rolled over the city like a gust from hell. Our hero, with one thousand of his Algerians, hurried from place to place, rescued and collected such as he could, and hurried with them to his own house. This being soon filled, he induced his neighbors to evacuate their dwellings and fill *them* likewise with refugees. Then he conducted a great multitude to the castle. For ten days he labored in this work, by day and night.

Once the mob approached his house, and with frantic yells demanded that he should deliver up the Christians to them. He drew his sword, and, accompanied by a strong band of his followers, at once went out to confront the yelling crowd.

"Wretches," he exclaimed, "is this the way you honor the Prophet? May his curse be upon you! Shame on you, shame! You will yet live to repent. You think you may do as you like with the Christians, but the day of retribution will come. The Franks will yet turn your mosques into churches, my brothers! Stand back or I will give my men the order to fire."

The mob withdrew. All the European consuls flew to Abd-el-Kader for protection, and remained his guests for more than a month.

At fast, the whole body of refugees were forwarded to Beirut under protection of his men.

He was at length enabled to repose. He had rescued twelve thousand souls belonging to the Christians from death, and worse than death, by his fearless courage, his unwearied activity, and his catholic-minded zeal. All the representatives of the Christian powers then residing in Damascus had owed their lives to him.

Thus was the most chivalrous act of the nineteenth century consummated. The civilized world acknowledged the grandeur of the deed, and sent him marks of gratitude. From France, he received the Grand Cordon of the Legion of Honor; Russia honored him with the Grand Cross of the White Eagle; Prussia, with the Grand Cross of the Black Eagle; Greece, the Grand Cross of the Savior, etc. From America, he received a brace of pistols inlaid with gold. The Masonic Order in France presented him, though not at that time a Freemason, with a magnificent star.

In June 1864, this illustrious man, then in his fifty-seventh year, was made a Freemason in the Lodge of the Pyramids (*Loge des Pyramides*), at Alexandria, in Egypt. It may readily be conceived that the time-honored principles of this Order found a worthy lodgment in his heart. He has more than once expressed his opinion as to the high character of Freemasonry, and may be looked to at all times to bear a similar testimony. Three of his sons are also Freemasons.

The last years of Abd-el-Kader are being spent in a round of daily life marked with charity and humanity.

The simplicity, the scrupulous regularity, the exact and unvarying conscientiousness which guide and influence his actions operate upon the thread of his existence with all the harmony of fixed laws. He rises two hours before daybreak, and is engaged in prayer and religious meditation until sunrise, when he goes to the mosque. After spending half an hour there in public devotions, he returns to his house, snatches a hurried meal, and then studies in his library until midday. The muezzin's call now summons him again to the mosque, where his class is already assembled awaiting his arrival. He takes his seat, opens the book fixed upon for discussion, and reads aloud, constantly interrupted by demands for those explanations which unlock the varied and accumulated stores of his troubled years of laborious study, investigation, and research. The sitting lasts for three hours. Afternoon prayer finished, he returns home, and spends an hour with his children, especially his ten sons, examining the progress they are making in their studies, etc. Then he dines. At sunset he is again in the mosque, and instructs his class for one hour and a half. His professor's duties for the day are now over. A couple of hours are still on hand, which are spent in his library. He then retires to rest.

This ancient and honorable man is punctual in his charities. Every Friday, the street leading to his house may be seen filled with the poor, gathered together for the appointed distribution of bread. The poor who die, if utterly without means, not merely in his own quarter, but throughout Damascus, are buried at his expense.

My reception by this distinguished brother was cordial in the extreme. He kissed me, according to the Oriental manner, led me to the "highest seat," or the seat of honor, in his private apartment, and entered into the most confidential communications with me. He is a melancholy man in temperament, feeling, as he told me, that *his mortal work is done;* yet when I assured him of the world-wide respect entertained for him, and invited him, in behalf of the Freemasons of the United States, "to come and make his abode in our free land," his eye flashed, and his voice rolled in his throat as I can imagine it might have done in the days when he had fifty thousand men at his back. I secured an excellent photographic likeness, taken by one of the first artists in Paris.

The full name of our heroic brother is Abd-el-Kader-Ulid-Mahiddin. He is a great admirer of George Washington, of whom he said to me, in effect, that he was magnanimous in sentiments, sublimely raised above sublunary and selfish considerations, depressed by the malevolent accusations of his enemies, but serene, because sustained by his conscience, the type of the unselfish, whole-souled enthusiast. He described to me the ferocity of mountain warfare. A Druse chief sat quietly smoking amidst a pile of thirty Christian heads, slain in battle as expiatory sacrifice for the death of his son in battle. The British Consul, meeting him under those circumstances, was greeted with the extraordinary expression, "May God bless you for your thoughts of peace!" His salutations were fervid and extravagant as those of his race. "This day will be as white as milk," said he on my introduction. He took my hand, and pressing it tenderly to his forehead and lips, invoked upon me the richest blessings of Allah. I could not help recalling my images of Abraham. He does not wear the *tarboush* or the clipped costume coming into use among the Turks of these degenerate days; but has his fine head overshadowed by a turban of prodigious amplitude, long majestic beard, and robe descending to his heels. A friend, who visited the old Chateau of Pau, the prison of Abd-el-Kader, described the plain chamber still shown to visitors, where he passed seven weary years looking out upon the Spanish hills; and the graves of five of his children, in full view, give point to the sad story. I reminded him of it, and his eyes filled with tears.

The Emir is accounted one of the finest horsemen and swordsmen of the East. They say of him: *Eques ipso melior Bellerophonte;* a better rider than he who mounted Pegasus. Shakespeare's estimate of true manhood elegantly applies to Abd-el-Kader:

> "His words are bonds, his oaths are oracles,
> His love sincere, his thoughts immaculate,
> His tears pure messengers sent from his heart,
> His heart as far from fraud as heaven from earth."

In relation to his Masonic initiation, I translate freely from a pamphlet published at the time under the title of *A Solemn Assemblage of the Lodge Henry IV. (Paris, France), on the* 1st *September,* 1864: *The Initiation of Abd-el-Kader.*

Preliminary Notice.—All Europe, nay, all the civilized world shuddered with indignation and grief at the recital of the events of 1860, which bathed Syria in blood, when the ignorant and benighted masses, animated with fury, rushed, under the influence of fanaticism, upon the unfortunate Christians. Humanity, dumb with horror at the sight of such atrocities, experienced, however, one consolation at the sight of a person who, although a Moslem, long ago an enemy to us (the French), made his own gallant and generous breast a buckler to our brethren. The Emir Abd-el-Kader saved, at the peril of his own life, 12,500 persons devoted to the sword; thus performing through them one of those splendid deeds which history will render imperishable. Upon it our admiration beams without a cloud. All who feel in themselves hearts susceptible to noble emotions and to the love of humanity render praise to him who came to give such a shining example of tolerance and devotion.

Freemasonry, also, is aroused by the performance of acts so conformable to the aims of her institution. The Lodge "Henri IV.," amongst others, decided that a letter of congratulations should be addressed to the Emir, accompanied by a jewel of honor.

This letter, recorded in the minutes of the session which adopted it, closes with the following words:

"By this title (the friend of humanity) we offer you the accompanying jewel; and should you consent to receive it, whenever you chance to look upon it, let it express to you yonder, far away in the Eastern world, that it comes from hearts that beat in unison with yours; from men who hold your name in veneration; from a fraternity which loves you already like its own, and that is trusting, if its extremely close bands permit, to count you among the number of the adepts of the institution."

The Emir's reply was not long delayed. It contained, as will be seen further on, a formal request for Masonic initiation. The Lodge "Henri IV.," regarding the fact of such an initiation as a happy opportunity for Masonry in the Orient, received this request with eagerness, and immediately set about to discover means for its accomplishment. A second epistle was written to the Emir, laying before him the conditions of Masonic initiation, and the questions to which he should respond. He replied in the most frank and categorical manner. Satisfied with his responses, the Lodge instructed Brother Wannez, its Worshipful Master, to come to an understanding with the Grand Orient of France, as to the proper manner of procedure with regard to this initiation, which offered a serious obstacle in the absence of the recipient.* His Highness Prince Lucien Murat, desiring to bestow upon Freemasonry so glorious an acquisition, held himself in readiness with a good will to do his utmost to favor the same; and we had prepared ourselves to consummate this grand act, when the events which disturbed the good harmony in the bosom of the Order, caused an unfortunate delay in its execution (referring to one of the periodical schisms in the Grand Orient at Paris).

Upon the elevation of the illustrious Marshal Magnan to the Grand Mastership, the Lodge desired to advance the matter by virtue of the authority which had been granted to it by the preceding administration. The obstacles opposed to it were now overcome. It was known that a French Lodge was held at Alexandria, "Lodge of the Pyramids," and report affirmed that the Emir was upon a voyage to those countries. The Lodge "Henri IV.," considering that by means of this Lodge in Egypt it could attain the end so desired, decided to write to that respectable workshop† to assume the management of

---

* Abd-el-Kader, being a prisoner on parole at Damascus, could not then visit Paris save by consent of the French Government, nor then, without personal inconvenience and expense.

† A pleasant technicality in the French system; *atelier* denoting a workshop.

the whole affair, and proposed to it to perform, according to the circumstances of the case, the initiation of the Emir Abd-el-Kader in the name of the Lodge "Henri IV."

With a courtesy and good will altogether Masonic, Brother Custos, the Worshipful Master, let us know that Pyramid Lodge was willing to conform itself to our wishes, and that the movements of the Emir, then coming from Mecca and Medina, should be regarded, in order to profit by the occasion which would then be presented. All the necessary documents were expedited, and by the end of June, 1864, we were officially informed that the Emir had been initiated to the First Grade, "and that to complete the work, that Lodge had conferred upon the illustrious recipient the Second and Third Grades, in conformity with the interval of time fixed by the statutes. These tidings, which even exceed our dearest wishes, Brother Poullain, the Worshipful Master of the Lodge "Henri IV.," was requested to make known immediately to our Illustrious Grand Master. At the same time, he imparted to him our intention to convoke a solemn assembly, to give this event such publicity as it demanded, and to salute the new initiate, by laying before the eyes of our brothers of all rites the correspondence interchanged on the subject.

July 13, the Illustrious Brother Blanche, Grand Master Adjunct,* addressed us, in the name of the Illustrious Grand Master, the subjoined paper:

"GRAND ORIENT OF FRANCE: SUPREME COUNCIL OF FRANCE AND THE FRENCH POSSESSIONS.

"ORIENT OF PARIS, July 13, 1864.

"BROTHERS: It is with very lively pleasure that our Thrice Illustrious Grand Master has received the communication announcing to him that the Respectable *Lodge of the Pyramids* has initiated in the name of your Workshop, and by virtue of a delegation which you had given them, the Emir Abd-el-Kader.

"I am instructed to address you his felicitations upon this initiation, due to your conception and your perseverance; he has received with interest the minutes which you presented to him.

"All French Masonry will unite with eagerness in the sentiments of our Grand Master; and for my own part, I have the good fortune

---

* This officer is the acting Grand Master; the Grand Master elect being some nobleman or gentleman in high station, elevated on account of his rank.

to insert in the *Bulletin Official** the minutes which you have given us.

"Receive, brethren, the assurances of our affectionate sentiments.

"The Grand Master Adjunct, in Charge of the Administration.

"ALFRED BLANCHE."

The Solemn Assembly, set for the 1st of September, 1864, was held with great *éclat,* and we have deemed it for the best interests of Freemasonry to publish *in extenso* the minutes of that occasion, together with all the documents which had been previously interchanged. Such is the subject of the present publication.

TO THE GLORY OF THE GRAND ARCHITECT OF THE UNIVERSE. In the Name and by the Authority of the Grand Orient of France:

A SOLEMN ASSEMBLY.

September 1, 1864. Year of True Light, 5864.

The Respectable Lodge of St. John, under the distinctive title "Henri IV.," regularly convoked and fraternally assembled, opened upon the First Degree, under charge of Brother Acarry. The minutes of the meetings of August 4th and of the 18th were read, and adopted without alteration. Entrance to the Temple was then accorded to visiting Brothers, who promptly ranked themselves along the columns. Brother Senior Warden announced that various deputations were in attendance in the porch of the Temple. The Lodge arose and received in due order the visiting Lodges.† The Venerable Brothers (Lodge officers) of all the rites took their places in the East.

The Worshipful Master informed the Lodge, through an official communication from the Secretariat of the Grand Orient, that the Grand Master Adjunct, being absent from Paris, could not assist at our assembly today. He then announced the business of the meeting. He rehearsed the proceedings which had resulted in the initiation of the Emir Abd-el-Kader, by the *Lodge of the Pyramids,* in

---

* The Official Journal of the Grand Lodge, published monthly at Paris, is so styled.

† It is thought unnecessary to encumber our notes with mere lists of names Six lodges were represented on the occasion—from Paris, Boulogne, Argenteuil, Rueil, and Pontoise.

R. M.

the Orient of Alexandria, in the name of the Lodge "Henri IV.,"
and he announced that the new initiate had been solemnly
proclaimed and acclaimed an active member of the Lodge "Henri
IV."

The Brothers who in the present ceremony represented the
Emir and the Lodge at Alexandria, retired to the *Pas-Perdus*.*
They were immediately announced by the Senior Warden, and,
upon the invitation of the Worshipful Master, a deputation
retired to conduct them in. The Brethren, standing in due order,
sword in hand, the Worshipful Master commanded the door
opened, and the cortege entered, in the following order, viz:
Grand Expert, two Masters of Ceremonies, Banner of the Lodge,
Masters bearing Lights; the three delegates, the one in the center
bearing on a waiter the official documents; then, marshalling the
procession, the two Experts; finally, the younger members of the
Order.

In passing under "the arch of steel," the delegates, through their
spokesman, Brother Silberman, one of themselves, thus spoke:

"Worshipful Master, and you, my Brethren: We, the delegates of
the *Lodge of the Pyramids,* Orient of Alexandria, have the honor
to place in your hands the official minutes concerning the
initiation of Abd-el-Kader. This was done by our body upon the
invitation of the Lodge 'Henri IV.,' June 18, 1864. The Worshipful
Master, in the name of the Lodge, made the acknowledgments."

Then, the delegates having resumed their places, the Junior
Warden, Brother Arnoult, read the first letter addressed to the
Emir by the Lodge:

"Thrice Illustrious Emir: Wherever virtue moves with splendor,
wherever tolerance and humanity have been deemed safeguards
and honors, Freemasons hasten to acknowledge and proclaim him
who, at the price of great sacrifices, accomplishes the work of God
upon earth, and lends to the oppressed a tutelary and
disinterested support.

"It is because Freemasonry feels that *these men are her own,*
and that they march in the same path, she feels the need of them,
and cries out to them, *Thanks and courage,* in the name of the
unfortunate, in the name of the Society, in the name of the *grand*
principles upon which her Institution rests.

"On this account, thrice illustrious Emir, we, the members of
the Masonic Lodge Henri IV., of the Orient of Paris, following the
example of so many others, but with no less ardor and gratitude,

---

* A technical term for an adjacent apartment.

add this modest wreath to the crown of benedictions which the civilized world places today upon your noble and sacred head. We come to offer our tribute of admiration to him who, superior to all prejudices of caste and religion, has shown himself to be a man before all, and has only listened to the inspirations of his own heart in opposing an inexpugnable rampart to the furies of barbarity and fanaticism.

"Yes, you are a true representative, the veritable type of that vigorous Arab nationality to which Europe is indebted, in a great part, for its civilization and the sciences which enlighten it. You have proved by your acts and by the magnanimity of your character, that this race has not degenerated; and that if it appears to be inert, it can arouse itself for great works by the appeals of a genius as powerful as your own. After having wielded your sword with a glory and a grandeur that France, then your enemy, knows how to admire, you gained yet greater glory by the generosity and devotion of which you gave such proofs in favor of civilization. The Omars, the Averroes, the Alfarabi, you have resumed in yourself alone; the warriors, the wise men, the philosophers, of whom your nation is proud, by so just a title.

"To you, then, thrice illustrious Emir, to you be renewed glory and thanks! The God whom we all adore—the God who from his throne established all generous hearts—was able to achieve his work by your hands. Would it not truly appear that you have been brought, after so many vicissitudes and through the secret design of Providence, into the midst of those Oriental countries, to scatter the clouds of ignorance, extinguish the torches of brutal fanaticism, and to cause to remount to the grade of civilization the unhappy people misled by ignorance? We, too, share in pitying them so much as to expect that the result of your holy influence will advance our lights and our virtues.

"Freemasonry, which has for its principles the existence of a God and the immortality of the soul, and for the foundations of its doings the love of humanity, the practice of tolerance and of universal fraternity, cannot without emotion look upon the grand spectacle which you have presented to the world. She recognizes, she claims, as one of her own children (at least by a community of ideas), the man who, without ostentation, out of his first inspiration, put so perfectly into practice her sublime device, ONE FOR ALL!

"It is under this impression, thrice illustrious Emir, that the Lodge Henri IV., a little group of the great Masonic family, addresses you this weak but most sincere expression of their ardent sympathies, and offers you the homage of its symbolical jewel. This modest emblem has no value save by these devices, *the Square, Level, Compass,* teaching *Justice, Equality, Fraternity,* but it glitters upon the consecrated breasts of humanity and lives upon the love of one's fellows. By virtue of this we offer it to you; and should you deign to accept it, whenever your eye falls upon it, let it assure you in the distant East, that it comes from hearts beating in unison with yours, from men who already love you as their own, and who hope that if their exceedingly restricted rules may permit, they may count you among the number of the adepts of their Institution."

Brother Laverriere, representing the Emir Abd-el-Kader, made the following response:

"Praise to God alone!

"Honorable and Respectable Gentlemen, Chiefs, and Dignitaries of the Eminent Society of Freemasons, which may God the Most High protect!

"After you have caused me to obtain my wishes and my consideration, which prove the sincerity of my heart, it is proper that I should say to you that, pending the consideration of your noble sentiment and while I was reflecting that the Great Creator of the world has not accorded to his servants all these benefits at one time only, but little by little, by which they were able to relish constantly their savor, and have toward him a continuity of uninterrupted recognitions, I received the kind letter of your Excellencies, a letter which I owe to that good friendship of which I entertain no doubt, so that the beautiful flower, of which the allegorical excellence surpasses the odor of the precious and perfect rose, and which, by the indication of justice, the equality and the fraternity which the jewel represents, excels the wisdom of Aristotle, and comprehends the excellent qualities and the desire of possessing them. That is then the token of your fidelity and the summit of my unspeakable joy:

"1st. For the sake of the matter itself, since I consider myself to have discovered the true treasures of the world.

"2d. For the sake of the good chance of its arrival: may God be honored and exalted! because I consider that when you desire a community of my thoughts with yours, when one favor among the favors of God of whom I have been privy hitherto, a particular gift without which he gives me neither cost nor pain.

"Praise to God! and from me felicity and happiness concerning that of which you accord me this favor, because I corroborate and approve the thought that your intentions are good and your ideas just. There is no better testimony that your inclination agrees with mine, than your declaration that I have succored my brothers for humanity's sake, and that I was an aid to them in the time of barbarous animosity which threatened them. What excellence is there that surpasses the love of man! O philanthropy! if that love is not found in me, have I sincere religion? God forbid! Verily, love is the true foundation of religion. God is the God of all, and He loves us all.

"In reality, I address to your very excellent Society this letter for three reasons, conformable to my desire, viz:

"1st, To manifest my gratitude to your Highnesses for the beautiful tokens which you wish me to accept, and which have duly arrived, but of which I am not worthy. Yet that is not the cause of my great affection for you all, and for my particular propensity for your good association; although its value, in my eyes, is greater than that of the crown which adorned Alexander, son of Philip the Greek, and I receive it with joy and high veneration.

"2d. For this your Excellencies well know, that I have a very true desire to associate myself with your fraternity of love and to participate with your purposes, within the scope of your excellent rules, because I am disposed, in this way, to display my zeal. And when you shall make known to me the conditions and the obligations which will be imposed upon me, I will faithfully observe them as your Excellencies shall indicate to me. And I shall esteem myself extremely happy when I shall meet the members of your Society, so considerable and so distinguished, because of the advantageous opinion which you entertain toward me.

"3d. In order that, henceforth, a friendly correspondence may be established between us without interruption, because I have prayed to do this as you believe I ought to work, in performing with joy that which the statutes of your friendly Society exact of me, when I shall understand where I shall go to acquire my obligations.

"I conclude by renewing the expression of my acknowledgments to you all, at the present time and place, and by addressing the assurance of my respectful consideration for all the Society at the four cardinal points.

"May the Most High God render you satisfied and contented. Amen.   Your faithful friend,

"ABD-EL-KADER."

Brother Schneitz read the second letter addressed by the Lodge to the Emir, conceived in the following terms:

"Thrice Illustrious Emir: It is with an unspeakable sentiment of happiness and gratitude that we have received the very beautiful and excellent response by which you honored our fraternal felicitations; and it was quite impossible to have replied sooner to the desire which you manifested to unite with us in the place of the Masonic fraternity. We hasten to repair this painful but involuntary delay, and advance with no other preamble to the capital point of the question.

"In your venerated letter, thrice illustrious Emir, you said to us:

"'In fact, I address your Society my letter for three reasons, viz:

"'1st. To manifest my gratitude.

"'2d. For this your Excellencies well know, that I have a very true desire to associate myself with your loving confraternity, and to participate in your aims within the scope of your excellent rules, because I am disposed in this manner to exhibit my earnestness. And when you shall make known to me the conditions and the obligations that will be imposed upon me, I will faithfully observe them.'

"Nothing could be more agreeable to our hearts, and we have considered this declaration from so illustrious a representative of the Arab nationality as a glorious recompense which the Most High has deigned to accord to our labors, and glorious in its results to progress and civilization. We so judge because you will be called, by virtue of the initiation to be conferred upon you, the apostle of the great religion of humanity. It is upon this account that we proceed to give you a clear and precise account of the engagement which each one contracts in entering upon Freemasonry.

"One word upon the point of a general view of the institution greatly simplifies the question. We proceed, then, in the attempt to demonstrate to you our point of departure, our aim, our aspirations. For this reason, we are obliged to quote the first articles of our Constitution, articles which comprehend our entire profession of faith.

ARTICLE FIRST.

"The Order of Freemasons has for its object beneficence, the study of universal morality, and the practice of all the virtues.

"It has for its foundation-stone the existence of God, the immortality of the soul, and the love of humanity.

"It is composed of freemen, who, submissive to the laws, unite themselves into a Society governed by general and particular statutes.

ARTICLE SECOND.

"Freemasonry occupies not herself with the various religions spread throughout the world, nor the constitutions of different countries. Having her place in the sphere of ideas, she respects the religious faith and the political sympathies of all her members. And so at her meetings all discussion upon such subjects is formally interdicted.

ARTICLE THIRD.

"Freemasonry ever maintains her ancient device, liberty, equality, fraternity; but she reminds her members that, walking in the domain of ideas, one of their first duties as Masons and as citizens is to respect and to observe the laws of the country in which they live.

ARTICLE FOURTH.

"Freemasonry, considering the obligation to labor as one of the imperious laws of humanity, imposes it upon each one, according to his strength, and consequently proscribes voluntary idleness.

"This, then, is the essence of the Masonic code, and it is upon condition of practicing these principles that we share the radiation of Masonry with modern society, and the good which she calls forth and produces.

"We essay, then, to develop these principles according as we comprehend them, and as we have the agreeable conviction that you, yourself, thrice illustrious Emir, comprehend them.

"Our Society has for its object beneficence, the study of morality, and the practice of all the virtues. Upon this subject, we have no explanation to give you. Your acts have proved that this section concerns you, and that it was written concerning you. Upon this head, then, you have already performed an integral part of Freemasonry.

"She has for her foundation-stone the existence of God, the immortality of the soul, and the love of humanity. A scrupulous observer of the Koran, the first two points are likewise the basis of your religion. Here again you have a new communion of ideas with us. As to the love of humanity, you have given proofs of a sort that leave no room for doubt. As to the third article, it is here that all our Institution discloses herself and the very solid foundation upon which she rests.

"Freemasonry has no regard to the diversity of rites. She admits to her breast all those who have faith in the Creator of all things, under whatever name they may invoke Him. She inscribes on her banner the word "Tolerance," and look how she explains it! This tolerance is not a systematic indifference to all dogmas, but a very bright manifestation of respect for free will, for free examination, for the convictions based either upon the result of scientific researches, or, still more, upon the interior convictions of the conscience. As, therefore, in exacting so much of honor and integrity from her members, she respects the religious faith and political sympathies of each one, so therefore she forbids all discussion upon these matters at her meetings.

"For her device she maintains Liberty, Equality, Fraternity: *Liberty of thought* and of examination before all: *Liberty of action* according to the eternal laws of nature, subordinate to the laws of justice, primordial and social. *Equality,* as to the moral, for the progressive instruction and education of the masses; as to the physical, for the realization of a general, relative well-being, the fruit of common toil. *Fraternity,* the love of each one for the others—a sentiment by which all live in one alone—who make of all lives one single life, who mingle all efforts in one sole and supreme effort, have for their aim to attain to the distribution of one equal sum of happiness to each member of the human family.

"Freemasonry prescribes *labor.* But, far from considering it a *punishment,* she esteems it an honorable and sacred *obligation,* because, in her eyes, labor is the basis of society. It conduces to the physical development of everything. It gives to man the perfection of his physical force, the perfection of his mind. It conduces to the amelioration of the condition of humanity, since everything in this world is the fruit of individual labor, that, by a providential dispensation, forms the sum of social good.

"This is a summary exposition of our principles. A complete exposition, thrice illustrious Emir, must progress with the degrees which you will receive. It is sufficient to prove to you that Freemasonry is a work of edification, of law, and of justice, and that its means of action are love, beneficence, the study of the virtues, and of good. It is very natural, then, that knowing what you desire, knowing well how much you can do to co-operate with us in out aims, we have read with profound interest the request you have made to us. It seems to us—and our hope gives point to our understanding—it seems to us that through you the Orient may be summoned to a moral regeneration; that, through you, Freemasonry may be restored to the places where she had her cradle; the work of intellectual emancipation, already so gloriously commenced in these latter times, over the marches of the throne of Persia.

"One great obstacle, caused by your living so far from us, seemed, at first, to oppose itself to the realization of your desire, which is equally our own. Masonic initiation, symbolized by the ceremonies and emblems of a moral and philosophical signification, must necessarily be done in a manner *entirely personal,* in order that the initiate, by his replies to the queries propounded to him, may open his heart to those who are his *judges* before they become his *brothers,* and permit them to penetrate even to the lowest depths of his thought, even to the most secret recesses of his soul.

"This condition, essential, but impossible to perform at this moment, we have obtained authority, in your case, to dispense with, and in its place have sent you a request to furnish, in writing, your opinion upon the manner in which you understand and interpret these three fundamental questions, given to each neophyte of Freemasonry. The three questions are:

"1. What are the duties of a man toward God?

"2. What to his fellow-men?

"3. What to himself?

With your reply to these three questions, we wish that you give us, as corollary, your ideas

"4. As to the immortality of the soul;

"5. As to the equality of the human races in the eyes of God;

"6. As to the manner in which you understand the *tolerance* of our fraternity.

"Concerning these, thrice illustrious Emir, you are requested to give the result of your mature reflections, which will conform, we doubt not, to that which we expect of you.

"This formality being complied with, it will remain that you direct to us your TESTAMENT. This word will surprise you, and we hasten to explain to you the extent of its application. The candidate, consenting to submit to the proofs of his initiation, is at first introduced into a gloomy place, representing night, far away from the noise of men and from the light of day; where, written upon the walls, are inscriptions which recall the vanity of human greatness and the nothingness of life. In the presence of a *skeleton, alone,* he is reminded of his own death. Then he discovers, before him upon a table, *a paper,* where are written the first three questions which we propounded above, and to which he will reply, in writing. Below these questions he will find a gap, indicating the word TESTAMENT, which he must also fill up. By this word we would have him understand that his entry into Masonry is the death of worldly egotism, that world of "everybody for himself," and like the duties of the family, he ought, in this important moment, to remember the misfortunes which we alleviate at all times, and hasten to relieve them.

"To resume. We await a clear and categorical reply to the questions which we present you; and immediately upon the interval required by our rules, we will address you a collection of the different degrees, with the instructions allowed, and the rights conferred. As you have penetrated in this spirit, you will feel the necessity of propagating them for the good of humanity. You will call the nations again to light who have slept in the shadow of death. You will revive in them the sacred fire, and invite them to the grand work of universal fraternity.

"The blessing of God attend you, because you are his true apostle. We rejoice in this, because, through you, his work shall increase and multiply with the majesty of Lebanon's cedar, with the perfume of Sharon's rose; and, through your grace and glorious efforts, future generations shall relish in peace the fruits of the Tree of Life!

"That the Most High may deign to listen favorably to us in spreading all his benedictions over you, is, most illustrious Emir, the most ardent wish of your devoted Brothers,

"THE MASONS OF LODGE HENRY IV.

Brother Laverrière continued, by reading the reply of the Emir it the following letter:

"Praise to God alone.

"To the illustrious Seigniors and sagacious Directors, to all Freemasons both in general and particular, Chief of the Lodge Henri IV. Your letter has reached me, and your discourse has honored me. I cannot express my joy. I reply succinctly, according to the translator's version of your letter, without knowing whether this rendering is conformable to your intentions.

"*First Question.* What are a man's duties toward God? *Reply,* A

man ought to honor the Most High God, to love him, to hasten to
do that which is agreeable to him, to draw near to him, to model
himself upon the Divine attributes! Pity, pardon, protection,
generosity, science, justice, beneficence, etc., shall attend upon
these actions; to strive to do the Divine will; to resign himself to
his commandments; to delight himself in his decrees; to support
his trials with patience; and as no one can oppose that which he
has established, to be convinced that naught but good is
performed by this God, who is the Most High, the One God, and
who has no associate in the creation.

"*Second Question*. What are a man's duties toward his fellow
men? *Answer.* Whatever presents itself in the way of good
counsels and directions to the advantage of the world and each
other; whatever will avail them in this, in instructing the
ignorant, and warning the indifferent, in protecting them, in
respecting the great without envying them, in compassionating
the humble and providing for their wants; in holding before them
useful things, and withdrawing from them evil ones. All these
laws rest upon two foundations; the first is to glorify God, the
second to have compassion upon his creatures. A man should
consider that his soul and those of others are of the selfsame
origin; whatever diversity may appear is but the *envelope* and the
exterior; because the entire soul proceeds from an entire spirit,
which, as Eve proceeded from Adam, is the origin of all souls. The
soul is one, not many. The multiplicity is not as in the coverings
by which she arrays herself and in the forms by which she shines.
It is that the bodies are obscure houses, dark regions, which,
when the lights of the entire soul envelop them, shine and glitter
by the lights which overflow them. It is so also that the places
enveloped by the light of the sun glitter, although the light of that
star may be one and not many. The disk of the sun is single; it is
up there its essence. It follows that the light which emanates
clearly from many places, so multiply themselves for radiation.

"This multiplicity comes from the different sides of bright places,
and not from the side of the sun, which, in its essence, changes
not; it is the same sun. The light which is in Syria is no other than
the light of France. So the vestment of souls is one; it shines in the
exterior parts, and the multiplicity discovers itself in those parts,
and not in that which enlightens them. It is the same thing with
numbers; they multiply themselves by one of the units, the dozens,
the hundreds, the thousands. Each step in these classes of numbers
a as unity; because, for example, *two*—it is not one and one which

combined, form two; it is not *the repetition* of one and one. It is the same with all the degrees of numbers to infinity; they all reduce themselves from unity; they are *numbers;* but unity is always *one.*

"Another comparison. The entire soul is as *the center* of a circle; particular souls are *the circle.* The circle, when entire, is formed of lines and of points joined the one to the others. The central point is directed to all the points of the circle, and each point of the circle is in view of the central point, with relation to its isolation and from its opposition from this central point, which is also surrounded by all the points. Therefore, it is good for a man to love his own person (his essence) in others besides himself.*

"*Third Question.* What are a man's duties to himself? *Reply.* He ought to purify himself, to correct every vice, and to embellish and adorn himself with virtues and merits. Though these merits are numerous, they can be reduced to four principles, which, seized and harmonized, comprise them all. They are—science, courage, passion, and *justice,* which lies within the other three. The harmonization and goodness of *science* consists in that which comes through her to seize upon the difference between sincerity and *falsehood* in words, between verity and falsity in opinions, in the beauty and the homeliness of actions. As science is harmonized, balanced, her fruit is wisdom, and wisdom is the highest merit. The harmonization of *courage* is to refrain, and to abate within the limit traced by wisdom. It is passion placing itself under the command of wisdom, that is to say, of reason and the divine laws. Justice is the curbing of passion and of courage; the brave ought to harmonize this. On the one hand is temerity, on the other cowardice, feebleness. The two extremes are blamable.

"The harmonization of science is wisdom. It is in excess when its possessor uses it to deceive men. Then it is entitled cunning, deceit. As she is deficient, it is entitled ignorance. The two are blamable.

"As to justice, she is charged to direct passion and courage conformably to wisdom. Another duty man owes to himself is to observe the laws applicable to his physical system, because the body is a portion of the world of creation and of destruction. The body claims material attention, nourishment, drink, clothing, sexual union. It was created for a serious and useful purpose, and joined to the soul by the

---

* The French translator says in a note, that the philosophical nature of this letter makes its translation very difficult. So I have found it.

wisest direction. When the soul took this direction, the obscurity
of nature enwrapped her, and she required science and knowledge.
It is necessary, then, that it should strive to find and seize all
those things which God sends upon earth, as a means of giving
strength to body and mind. Entirely neglecting the body and
exposing it to death, is a great sin, as opposing the Creator, and
acting contrary to wisdom. This is the Most High.

"As to the immortality of the soul, reason and the divine laws
agree upon this subject, because death is corruption or separation;
and corruption is one of the attributes of the body. Quitting one
form, they assume another, as the water when it changes to vapor,
as the plant when it becomes earth, as the earth when it becomes
a plant. As to that which is not the body, and is not needed to
strengthen or perpetuate the body, we cannot conceive of its
corruption. The soul is not a body, nor a chance; she cannot be
divided, she cannot be diminished, she inheres not in one thing or
one place. Not one of the qualities of the body is assigned to her.
The soul is a spiritual essence without composition, and that
which is not composed neither dies nor ends. The spiritual is not
submissive to time, and that which is not submissive to time,
cannot change. Therefore, the soul is immortal.

"*Fourth Question.* Are all men equal before God? *Answer.* In
that which relates to the essence, which joins all men to the
human race, we have said *they are equal* and they are one,
although their investments, forms, and names are many. So is
one the quality white or whiteness in clothing, or a precious stone,
or paper, flour, or paint. Truly, the whiteness appears *one,* in the
paper as in the precious stone. It is the same of the ligneous
quality in a bit of wood, flesh, a coffin, a carriage, and other
material objects.

"As to the equality of men before God, under the relations of
contentment or discontentment, there may be such a thing. But
reason and the divine law prove that the traitor and the deceiver
are not equals in fidelity and sincerity. To him who possesses the
vices, to him who possesses the virtues, to him who seizes the
goods of the poor, the feeble, and the orphans, and destroys their
soul, and to him who gives them comfort in all good things, and
causes them to live;—no, souls are not equal in *remuneration*
before God.

"For there are four sorts of souls: 1st. Souls that by the researches
of reason and the desire of their heart succeed in understanding the
Creator and acquiring the possession of the truth of things, as much

as is given to man to know. 2d. Those that neither do nor struggle against these researches, but possess the truth by the grace of God. The state of these souls is one, blessedness. 3d. Those ignorant souls, which by habit follow the contrary, opposing themselves to all true researches. 4th. Those unblessed spirits, who prefer to oppose the true reason of things, and persevere continually in evil. The souls of this class are lost.

"*Fifth Question.* How do you understand the tolerance of the Masonic fraternity? *Answer.* We know that God did not create man in vain and without a design, because he is wise, and makes nothing uselessly; he creates not alone to eat, to drink, to rejoice, and to people the earth, but that his creatures, when removed from this earth, may live forever! The intention of God in creation was that his creatures should be cognizant of his attributes and his works."

I have copied more of this most interesting document than I really have space for; but it so perfectly opens the heart of this great philosopher, that I could not forbear to afford my readers the privilege I have enjoyed in its perusal.

POMEGRANATE

CHAPTER XXXII.

SUMMING UP.

O N pages 68 and 69, I gave my itinerary, showing that I left Beirut, June 12th, 1868; called and spent a few hours at Joppa on the 13th, treating Governor Noureddin to a farewell at Blattner's Hotel; spent Sunday, June 14th, at the mouth of the Suez Canal at Port Said; reached Alexandria, June 15th; went to Cairo on the 16th; spent the 17th at the Great Pyramid, of which I give an engraving on page 70; returned to Alexandria on the 18th; left on the 21st; reached Brindisi, Italy, the 25th; Paris, the 28th; London, the 2d July; left Southampton, July 7th; reached New York, the 18th, and Lagrange on the 21st, where I found my family in perfect health, waiting with joy to greet the wanderer, after his seven months' absence.

From September 1868, to March 1872, I was occupied closely in making up this volume, while traveling and lecturing before lyceums, churches, Sunday-schools, church conventions, colleges and seminaries, and Masonic lodges, earnestly striving to develop the thought that "the HOLY LAND is a permanent, satisfactory, and divine testimony to the truth of the HOLY BOOK." My specialty was the exhibition and description of Holy Land objects, a species of instruction extremely pleasant and satisfactory to old and young. In showing that the *Narrative of Jesus* is true, these object-lessons bear a powerful testimony; and the distribution of more than *one hundred thousand* such, through my personal labors, has done its part, I prayerfully hope, in counteracting the tendency to infidelity, which is the curse of the times. A society, entitled *The American Holy Land Exploration,* has been formed upon the basis of my labors, whose aims comprise the collection, description, and distribution of Holy Land specimens upon the largest scale.

In May 1869, a Masonic Expedition was projected, to embark from

New York, January 10, 1870, for the Holy Land and other Masonic jurisdictions of Western Asia, Africa, and Europe. It was to be composed exclusively of Master Masons; to rendezvous at London, January 25th; Paris, February 5th; Alexandria, Egypt, March 1st; Beirut, Syria, March 25th; and then make a journey of two months among sacred places, disbanding at Constantinople June 15th, and returning home. The specific aims of the expedition embraced, with other things, an "examination into the condition of Freemasonry in the countries visited, an inspection of their rituals and forms of work, an inquiry into their origin and history, and particular observations of those ancient societies in the Orient resembling Freemasonry." The proposition, however, was not accepted by a sufficient number of the craft to justify its adoption; but seeds were sown and ideas suggested which may yet lead up to it.

Such a project promises successful results. For the East is permeated with Masonic thought. All our emblems are there; our traditions are there; our covenants and penalties, our customs, our religious observances, our ceremonies glow with Oriental light; and there is no country in the world where Freemasonry promises such harvests of useful results as the Holy Land in particular and the Turkish Empire in general. In this chapter of summing up, I must briefly suggest the idea, regretting that my volume is too near the close for details.

MASONIC EMBLEMS.

The abundant diffusion throughout Palestine of Masonic emblems, and objects used by Freemasons as illustrations in their traditions and moral inculcations, is seen in my lines under this head:

THE EMBLEMS IN THE HOLY LAND.

North, South, East, West, and everywhere,
    O'er hill and dale, in holy earth,
The emblems of the Masons are,
    Where Masonry itself had birth.

    .   .   .   .   .

I met them on the stony hills,
    Where olives yield the "oil of joy;"
I marked them by the sunny rills
    Where lilies hang their petals coy;
I found them on swift Jordan's shore;
    Upon the verge of Galilee
I read their "quaint and curious lore,"
    Those ancient types of Masonry.

Where *vines* upon Judea's fields
   Pour forth their sweet, refreshing juice;
Where Ephraim's *cornland* bounteous yields
   Its nourishment to human use;
Where the tall *cedars* glad the sight
   On high and snowy Lebanon;
And Hiram's *palm-trees,* strong and bright,
   Hold forth their branches to the sun.

The *almond* taught me all its lore;
   On Joppa's beach the *scallop-shell*
Lit up the old historic shore
   With many a song remembered well;
By Junia's Bay, *the broken shaft*
   Recalled the fate of "him that died;"
And far and near the ancient craft
   Their *checkered pave* had scattered wide;
The fair *pomegranate's* scarlet flower
   Revived me in the noontide gleam,
Flaming through many a verdant bower
   That overhangs the murmuring stream

In every *cave* I saw the print
   Of gravel marks and working band;
On every *hill* the skilful dint
   Of chisel in the working hand;
Each mighty *ashlar* bears a trace
   Indelibly inscribed, to show
That till old time those marks efface
   Freemasons have their work to do.

The *Parian marble* meets the eye
   In ruined shrines and palaces—
And yields its sacred purple dye,
   The *murex* of Sidonian seas;
The *salt* presents on Sodom's shore
   Its test of hospitality,
As though the patriarch at his door
   Stood yet, the coming guest to spy.

The *funeral lamp,* within each tomb,
   Speaks grandly of the ancient faith,
And burns and lightens up the gloom
   With its own doctrine, "life in death;"
The *acacia* too, in bloom outside,
   Tells to the moldering form within—
"Not always shall the dead abide;
   "The morn will break, the sun will shine!"

All these I saw; and by the Sea
   Of Galilee, upon a stone
Of wondrous grace, appeared to me
   The *signet of King Solomon;*
The gentle *dews* that on me fell
   When midnight stars inspired the sky,
Told where the old historic hill
   Of Hermon soared in majesty.

'Twas like a vision thus to rove
   Amidst the emblems of the Art,
Which cheer the eye below, above,
   And with their wisdom fill the heart.
No wonder—'twas my frequent thought
   At noontide's stilly hour of ease—
No wonder Tyrian craftsmen wrought
   Inspired by emblems such as these!

THE DISTRICT GRAND LODGE OF TURKEY.

This organization, which comes nearest the American idea of a Grand Lodge of any thing in the East, is now under the efficient care of Hon. John P. Brown, long associated with the American Embassy at Constantinople, whose portrait I give on page 464. His patent is from the Earl of Zetland, Grand Master of England; his first exercise of Masonic power bears date Feb. 17th, 1870, when he was installed, and opened "the District Grand Lodge of Turkey," in due form. He drafted a set of by-laws for the government of that body, and expressed the belief, in his opening address, that "Freemasonry has a wide field of usefulness in the East." The lodges represented were Oriental No. 687, of Constantinople; Homer 806 of Smyrna; Deutscher Bund 819, of Constantinople; Bulwer No. 891, of Constantinople; La Victorie No 896, of Smyrna; Dekrau No. 1014, of Smyrna; Areti No. 1041, of Constantinople. Three other lodges belonging to the jurisdiction—viz: St. John's 952, Elensinian 987, and St. George 1015—sent no representatives. At the Annual Communication of the District Grand Lodge, March 17, 1871, the same seven lodges were represented, together with Sion Lodge, of Smyrna.

From the printed proceedings of these two sessions, now before me, I could find it in my heart, did space permit, to call largely from Brother Brown's most admirable addresses. They have been copied equally in English and American Masonic journals, and have excited the largest admiration wherever read. His views so broad and commanding, his brotherly charity so comprehensive in its grasp, and his acquaintance with the details of Masonic government so minute, point him out as the man of the times for Masonic extension and inculcation in the East. In 1850, he was initiated in Scioto Lodge, Chilicothe, Ohio, and by special dispensation received the second and third degrees the same evening. On his return to Turkey in 1851, the brethren of Constantinople made an effort to organize a lodge, of which he was one of the founders. Thus, the Oriental Lodge No. 687 came into existence. He was first Master of Bulwer Lodge No. 891. He received the Chapitral degrees in the Scotch Chapter "Thistle of the East," and was nominated in 1869 District Grand Master, as successor of Sir Henry Bulwer.

In the Turkish Empire there were at work in 1871 the following Lodges, viz: English, 17; French, 15; Italian, 8—40.

FREEMASONRY IN EUROPE.

I had no opportunities, going or coming, to inspect the lodge working in Europe. However, in the study of Masonry, I have never cared so much to visit *lodges* as *individuals*. An inquirer experienced in Masonic details, and knowing what questions to ask, can gather more information in an evening's cross-examination of a few bright Masons than in visiting a score of lodges and observing the work. So we learn the doctrines and usages of denominations more in the pastor's study or the deacon's workshop than in a host of public exercises. I enjoyed ample opportunities in Paris and London, during my few days' stay at each place, to get rehearsals of the work, and to listen to the peculiar views of Masonry entertained at those great Masonic centers.

ANCIENT MONEY.

In this volume, I have given a number of engravings of the coins found in excavations all through the cities and villages of the East. My space does not permit me to dwell at length upon a subject admittedly the most interesting of all to the student of history; but every reader of this book is informed that through the operations of the *American Holy Land Exploration,* of which the author of this volume is Secretary, all ancient coins, either single or in suits, can be secured from the abundant collections making for us throughout the Holy

Land. The cost of bronze coinage, ancient and reliable, with full printed descriptions, is brought by this society within the means of all.

ACACIA.

On page 348, I give a cut of the acacia-tree, growing in many portions of the Holy Land. The flowers of this tree have an excellent smell. Osborne (in *Palestine, Past and Present*), passing down from Beirut to Tyre in the summer of 1857, writes: "Over the plain comes, with the gentle evening breeze, a sudden fragrance of some blossoms which we have known before. It seems wild, yet, in the little round yellow furze blossoms on the long, delicate-leafed branch we recognize the beautiful and fragrant mimosa (*Mimosa farnesiana*), which grows to the height of seventeen or eighteen feet." This is not strictly the Masonic acacia, but the distinction between them is slight.

THE SPRIG OF ACACIA.

Lines written and attached to a framed sprig of the plant so sacred to Freemasonry, by the Author:

> It flourished in historic earth,
>   Land long and greatly sanctified;
> It had its proud and noble birth
>   Among the hills where Hiram died:
> It minds us of Masonic faith,
> That knows no counterpart but death.
>
> Though torn away from native dust,
>   And faded from its mother-tree,
> Its leaves still whisper "sacred trust,"
>   They still impart love's mystery:
> They blend in one all thoughts of them
> "Who last were at Jerusalem."
>
> How many graves these leaves embower!
>   How many forms they lie above!
> Mingled with tears, affection's shower,
>   And bursting sighs, and notes of love:
> But oh! *the comfort* they have given!
> A balmy zephyr, straight from Heaven:
>
> Telling of that not distant day
>   When parted love is joined again;
> Bidding the storms of sorrow stay,
>   Affording antidote to pain:
> Suggesting an all-powerful HAND
> Will raise the dead and bid him stand.

Soon will these leaves be showered on thee—
    Thy months are numbered, every one;
Soon the last solemn mystery
    Above thy coffin will be done:
Once more thy requiem will be said,
Though thou, in silence, will not heed.

So live, that when these cassia leaves
    Shall blend with thy forgotten dust,
Kind Mother-Earth, who all receives,
    Will yield, unchanged, her sacred trust,
While angels lead thee to the Throne,
And GOD, the MASTER, claims his own.

MASONIC DEDICATIONS.

The Masonic craft of America will fully justify me in locating their great names in the old *motherland* of Freemasonry as I have done with so many, when we recall the fact that out of 12,000 Masonic lodges in the world, we have over 8,000 in our Great Republic. Well did the secular prophet sing:

"Westward the star of empire takes its way;
    The four first acts already past,
The fifth shall close the drama of the day—
    Time's noblest offspring is the last."

In addition, therefore, to the large number already located in the pages of this volume, I connect with the glorious associations of Acre the names of ten American craftsmen, viz: L. V. Bierce, W.J. Law, M. J. Williams, J. C. Gilbert, W. M. Ellison, J. H. Fairchild, George Armstrong, H. H. Hemingway, Albert Pike, and Thomas Bradley. With the charming scenery and thrilling histories of the Sea of Galilee, I combine pleasant memories of J. K. Hall, Jacob L. Chase, S. B. Chase, C. B. Thurston, W. Bolivar Smith, R. Delos Pulford, Henry C. Nutt, Ray B. Griffin, John Sherer, Gabriel Bouck. With the great and romantic name of Abd-el-Kader I conjoin those of ten American Masons worthy of the relationship, viz: Dwight Phelps, Nathan Dikeman, Rev. B. Eastwood, E. S. Quintard, Geo. L. Lownds, E. H. Cushing, C. H. Titus, Enoch T. Carson, Rev. W. H. Jeffreys, C. G. Wintersmith.

THE GRATEFUL TESTIMONY.

"This was a testimony in Israel."—RUTH iv. 9.

FAREWELL LINES BY THE AUTHOR.

There is no guiding hand so sure as His,
    Who guided me, a weary pilgrim, home;
There is no utterance so true as this:
    "Go, trust in God, and you shall surely come,
Though broad your pilgrimage, across the ocean-foam."

In all my wanderings I met no harm;
    I could not go where God, OUR GOD, was not;
Though *weak,* I leaned on His Almighty arm;
    Though *ignorant,* on His Infinite thought,
Which both on nature's page and in His Word is taught.

You sent me, Craftsmen, to the Holy Land—
    It was my dream from youth to manly age—
Birthplace and cradle of our mystic Band,
    Whose charities adorn earth's brightest page,
Refuge of loving hearts, the Masons' heritage.

Receive now from that Orient-land the tale
    Gathered for you on Lebanon's snow hills,
From Tyre's granite reefs, from sad Gebale,
    From Joppa's crowded slope, from Zarthan's rills,
And from Jerusalem, the world's great heart that fills.

The spirit of our Craft is reigning yet
    Through every hill and dale of Palestine;
Strong hands, warm hearts, great sympathies I met,
    And interchanged around the ancient Shrine,
And brought my wages thence of corn and oil and wine.

I stood in silent awe beside the tomb
    Where Hiram, Prince of Masons, has his rest;
Its covering is the cerulean dome,
    So fitting one with Mason-burial blest;
His sepulcher o'erlooks his Tyre on the west.

I knelt beneath the cedars old and hoar
    That streak with verdure snowy Lebanon;
The mountain eagles o'er the patriarchs soar,
    The thunder-clouds of summer grimly frown,
Where large and strong they stand, those giants of renown.

I mused along the bay from whence the flotes
    Went Joppa-ward, in old Masonic days;
Its waters sing, as when the Craftsmen's notes
    Made the shores vocal with their hymns of praise;
And fervent notes and true my grateful heart did raise.

I plodded midst the heaps of sad Gebale;
    Of all her glories not a trace is found,
Save here and there a relic, left to tell
    The School of Mystic lore, the holy ground,
Where Hiram's matchless brows with laurel leaves were crowned.

I climbed the hill of Joppa, at whose foot
    The unceasing tide of stormy waters beats;
Though raftsmen's calls and gavel-sounds are mute,
    The generous Ruler of the port repeats
Our SACRED WORD in love, and all true Craftsmen greets.

From Shiloh's cap I overlooked the site
    Of Hiram's foundries, Zeredatha's plain;
Beyond, on Gilead's ranges swelled the fight
    When Jephthah drove the invading force amain,
And Jordan tinged her waves with unfraternal stain.

Upon Moriah's memorable hill,
    And in the Quarries 'neath the city's hum,
And midst the murmurs of Siloam's rill,
    And in Aceldama's retired tomb,
My Mason-songs I chanted, fraught with grief and gloom.

For oh, in sadness sits Jerusalem!
    Queen of the earth, in widow's weeds she lies;
Shade of historic glory, low and dim,
    Thy Day-star gleams upon our eager eyes;
Oh, that from her decay loved Salem may arise!

Now homeward come, my Mission I return
    To this warm Brotherhood, dear Sons of Light;
My Testimony stands—my work is done,
    Yours be the honor, as is just and right!
Be all your jewels bright, your aprons ever white.

Honor to those who bore this generous part,
    Writing their names upon the Holy Land!
Honor to every true and loving heart
    That makes Freemasonry such matchless Band,
And may the Great I AM amongst you ever stand!

ADDITIONAL NOTES.

JUNE 1, 1872.

I TAKE advantage of the space afforded me in this page, to add some facts that came in too late for insertion in the current pages. The lamented decease of John P. Brown I have recorded in a footnote to page 464, and that of Raschid Pasha, to page 546. The presence at Washington at this time of Richard Beardsley Esq., United States Consul at Jerusalem (whose portrait is seen on page 418), will delay the full organization of the Masonic Lodge there until his return.

NOUREDDIN EFFENDI,

The Governor of Joppa, whose portrait I give on page 256, is now (June 1872) Governor of Tripoli, a seaport fifty mites north of Beirut. The policy of the Muslim Government is to make very frequent changes in officials.

The portrait of Dr. Peterman appears on page 385; since my visit he has returned to Berlin. The Rev. Dr. Meshaka, American Vice-Consul at Damascus, named on page 560, has recently deceased, but his son Nazif, a Masonic brother, still resides there. J. Aug. Johnston, United States Consul-General of Syria, and his brother, the late Vice-Consul at Jerusalem, both named in this volume, have resigned their respective offices, and returned to America. They are both active members of the American Society for Oriental Exploration.

It was my purpose to have labels attached to the engravings of coins so elegantly and accurately cut on pages 362 and 498; but this was accidentally omitted. In the present edition, however, I have named them, under the head "Coin-notes," on pages 189 and 204. The general interest in coin-studies (numismatics) demands that every opportunity should be taken in a work like this to impart light on so important a branch of Masonic antiquities.

Rolla Floyd, Esq., of Joppa, to whom I have made several allusions in this volume, has been acting as dragoman and collector of the AMERICAN HOLY-LAND EXPLORATION for the last year. Travelers through Holy Land will find it immensely to their interest to secure his counsel and personal aid in their journeys.

INDEX.

TM
Stone Guild
Publishing
SGP

Look for these and other great titles at:
http://www.stoneguildpublishing.com

Book of Ancient and Accepted Scottish Rite Freemasonry by Charles T. McClenachan

The Book of the Holy Graal by A. E. Waite

The Book of the Lodge by George Oliver

The Builders by Joseph Fort Newton

The Chymical Marriage of Christian Rosencreutz translated by A. E. Waite

The Doctrine and Literature of the Kabalah by A. E. Waite

Fama Fraternitatis and Confession of the Rosicrucian Fraternity by A. E. Waite

Freemasonry in the Holy Land by Robert Morris

The Freemason's Manual by Jeremiah How

The Freemason's Monitor by Daniel Sickels

The History of Freemasonry and Concordant Orders

The History of Initiation by George Oliver

Illustrations of the Symbols of Freemasonry by Jacob Ernst

The Kybalion by The Three Initiates

Low Twelve by Edward S. Ellis

The New Masonic Trestleboard by Charles W. Moore

Opinions on Speculative Masonry by James C. Odiorne

The Perfect Ceremonies of Craft Masonry

The Poetry of Freemasonry by Rob Morris

Real History of the Rosicrucians by A. E. Waite

The Symbolism of Freemasonry by Albert G. Mackey

Symbolism of the Three Degrees by Oliver Day Street

Taylor's Monitor by William M. Taylor

Taylor-Hamilton Monitor of Symbolic Masonry by Sam R. Hamilton

Three Hundred Masonic Odes and Poems by Rob Morris

True Masonic Chart or Hieroglyphic Monitor by Jeremy Cross